IN THE COURTS OF THE
CONQUEROR

The 10 Worst Indian Law Cases Ever Decided

Walter R. Echo-Hawk

FULCRUM
GOLDEN, COLORADO

Library of Congress Cataloging-in-Publication Data
Echo-Hawk, Walter R.
  In the courts of the conqueror : the ten worst Indian law cases ever decided / Walter R. Echo-Hawk.
     p. cm.
  Includes bibliographical references and index.
  ISBN 978-1-936218-01-1 (hardcover)
  1. Indians of North America--Legal status, laws, etc.--Cases. 2. Indians of North America--Legal status, laws, etc.--History. I. Title.
  KF8204.5.E28 2010
  342.7308'72--dc22

                            2010009284

Printed in the United States on recycled paper by Malloy, Inc.
0 9 8 7 6 5 4 3 2

Design by Jack Lenzo

Fulcrum Publishing
4690 Table Mountain Drive, Suite 100
Golden, Colorado 80403
800-992-2908 • 303-277-1623
www.fulcrumbooks.com

Dedicated to the Native American Rights Fund for
*Standing firm for Justice.**

*www.narf.org

CONTENTS

ACKNOWLEDGMENTS

I am indebted to many who made this book possible. First and foremost, I thank three University of Colorado (CU) professors: Patricia N. Limerick and Charles F. Wilkinson, for their encouragement and outstanding contributions to this book, and the late Vine Deloria Jr., for his inspiration. I bow also to the scholars of federal Indian law whose writings are cited and relied upon in these pages. Three comrades-in-arms must be specially honored. Carl V. Ullman, Donald R. Wharton, and Amy Bowers spent endless hours providing insight for most chapters. Every social movement is anchored by an intelligentsia, including the tribal sovereignty movement.

Four organizations, the Native American Rights Fund, the National Indian Law Library, the Center of the American West, and the Cody Institute for Western American Studies (CIWAS), provided invaluable assistance. Historian Jason Hanson provided historical research and perspectives for the discussion of nineteenth-century cases. His work was supplemented by CU students Donna Bonetti, Jason Van Horn, Seth Schermerhorn, and Joanne Hays. Law students Jennifer Bear-Eagle, Merrill Yesslith, Martina Gauthier, Crista Maestas, Sylvia Curley, Claire Laura Evans, and Meghan Kelly contributed valuable legal research.

Along the way, I interviewed, traveled with, and enjoyed many outstanding folks who helped tell the stories in this book: Bertram E. Hirsch, Bryant Rogers, Tony Strong, John E. Echohawk, Roger Welsch, Rev. Walter Soboloff, Susan Johnson, Richard B. Williams, Taylor Keen, Suzan S. Harjo, Mark Van de Loht, Helaire Echo Hawk, Wallace Johnson, Robert Pickering, John T. Autrey, Myron Echo Hawk, Roger Echo-Hawk, Dr. James Riding In, James Botsford, Robert M. Peregoy, Sue Noe, Huston Smith, Phil Cousineau, Myrtle Driver, Monica Martins, Chris Peters, Rosita Worl, Chris McNeil, David Gover, Jack Trope, Steven C. Moore, D. Michael McBride III, Harvey D. Ellis, Betsy Richards, Joy Harjo, and Sam Scinta. Above all, I thank my beloved wife, Pauline, children, and grandchildren, and I appreciate all of the Echo Hawk family elders—including my mother, Jeanine—for instilling values that I hope are reflected in these pages. Finally, special thanks go to my son, Walter "Bunky" Echo-Hawk III, for the original artwork he created for this book.

This project was partially funded by a resident fellowship of CIWAS at the Buffalo Bill Historical Center in Cody, Wyoming.

A final note: the opinions expressed herein are my own, unless specifically attributed to someone else, and do not necessarily represent the views of the aforementioned organizations and persons.

Iri we turahe, cariks rakitu! (Thanks to everyone, it's all good!)

—Walter R. Echo-Hawk II

When it comes to dealing with misfortune and injustice, the most effective tool to use if we want to make sure that troubles will persist without relief is a simple sentence: *That's water under the bridge. No use crying over spilled milk. The past is over and done with. The goose is cooked. What's done is done.* We have marshaled a phalanx of platitudes to hold our hope in captivity.

Whenever people have their attention called to injuries that occurred in the past, it is almost certain that someone will pipe up with a demand that everyone cut short the desire to improve the world and, instead, defer to the water-under-the-bridge school of history.

There is a simple corrective to this widespread pattern of defeatism. The corrective is as simple as pointing out that the river of time has not stopped flowing. The river continues to flow toward the bridge and under it, and every moment presents a fresh opportunity to find a fresh, and better, way of living in that flow of time. When anyone responds to historical misfortune by saying, "That's water under the bridge," a resounding chorus should respond, "Maybe not."

The book you are holding is an effective challenge to the fatalistic school of history. Its author does not flinch from a full and honest confrontation with the troubles of the past, but he is equally intense and forthright in his proposals for how we can break from that pattern of sorrow.

A decade ago, a colleague and I had a prolonged opportunity to observe the water-under-the-bridge strategy for forcing history to validate defeatism. We held workshops to ask citizens around the American West to suggest answers to the question, "What should every westerner know?" In nearly every forum we held, from Bend, Oregon, to Sedona, Arizona, a non-Indian participant would say, "We must remember that the Indians were here first." Each time we heard it, this remark would push us to the edge of our chairs, wondering if *this time* any suggestion of action or change in conduct was going to follow. But, without exception, that was that. With an apparent conviction that any injury done to Indian people was an episode of sorrow long past any opportunity for corrective action, our participants moved quickly on to other subjects.

But what if someone in those groups had asked me, "Now that we have acknowledged that Indians were here first, and that our ancestors and predecessors displaced them, is there anything we can do?"

The publication of the wonderfully titled *In the Courts of the Conqueror* supplies the answer. Americans who read this book will find options far better than fatalism, resignation, and empty regret. This enhancement in understanding will arrive in their hands as a gift from a person endowed with extraordinary goodwill. Like the best of teachers, Walter Echo-Hawk does not waste time in lamenting or condemning the public's ignorance. On the contrary, he works hard to give that ignorance its chance to make a quick and beneficial departure.

When I started reading this book, I thought I already knew quite a bit about the major court decisions in Indian law. Very soon, it turned out that this flattering estimation of my knowledge needed a more modest recalculation. And so, from personal experience, I can offer this confident prediction to readers: 460 of pages from now, you will be noticeably, measurably smarter. The knowledge you are about to gain will not only carry intrinsic interest, it will allow you to become a more responsible, more valuable citizen of your nation. Your knowledge is about to become blessedly robust on some very important topics.

When you finish this book, you will know a great deal more about the real-life impacts on distinctive and recognizable human beings of unfortunate federal policies, and you will also know about the spirited efforts undertaken by many of those people to turn to the courts for remedy. And yet, when it turns out that the legal arena was often closed to these efforts, you will also gain a deeper understanding of the dynamic by which injustice piles on injustice when a group is systematically denied access to the courts.

You will be better informed (the technical term here is probably "sadder but wiser") about the pattern by which the decisions of the United States Supreme Court reflected the prevailing mind-set and assumptions, prejudices and blind spots of its times. And, as you confront the heritage of the cultural attitudes built into decisions of great consequence, you will sharpen your ability to distinguish between legal precedents that deserve respect, and legal precedents that deserve a definitive retirement. You will become much better acquainted with the contrast between the rejection of racism in jurisprudence involving African Americans and the lagging pace of this change in jurisprudence involving Indians. And, on every page of the book, your thinking will be expanded by an intense encounter with an author who has worked for decades, with extraordinary persistence and dedication, to make the case for the rights of Indian people.

The settlement of North America by Euro-Americans is a historical process that has often been portrayed in public discourse in terms of a triumphant national pride. Thus, some passages in this book may unsettle non-Indian readers. Reading the author's forceful critique of the justifications that tried to give legitimacy to a settler state's practices of invasion and conquest, or learning of his reasons for interpreting Indian history in terms of genocide, some readers may find themselves slipping into defensiveness, an emotion that may, actually, be a welcome sign of taking the book seriously. In a similar way, Echo-Hawk's commitment to placing the conduct of the United States in the planetary framework of the 2007 United Nations Declaration on the Rights of Indigenous People will provide strenuous intellectual and ethical exercise for readers who may or may not make full peace with this international framework.

And yet Echo-Hawk's thoroughness and clarity in showing how the ten worst Indian cases enshrined and preserved attitudes that have long lived past their time will wear down the resistance of even very prickly readers. When he quotes from the decision *United States v. Sandoval* (1913), in which the Court described Pueblo Indians as a people "governed chiefly according to crude customs inherited from their ancestors," every alert reader will note that this phrasing seems uncomfortably effective as a characterization of the Supreme Court's own deference to "inherited" and "crude customs," customs that Echo-Hawk now asks jurists—and Americans in general—to reconsider.

This book, unavoidably, contains stories about the "crude customs" of American Indian policy that are painful to read. To use one example, it is hard to read chapter nine, "*In re Adoption of John Doe v. Heim:* Taking the Kids," without wanting to evade, ignore, or step away from the lasting sorrow of the forcible separation of thousands of Indian children and parents. But when Echo-Hawk asks us to contemplate these ten worst Indian law cases ever decided, the goal is not to paralyze readers with sadness and regret. On the contrary, the goal, as he says at the very beginning of the book, is to "explore the need to rethink the doctrines" that created these unhappy judicial outcomes and to encourage the Supreme Court to "find some theory other than conquest, colonization, or racial superiority to justify its decisions" to seek an alternative theory that would lead to a "just resolution." The scale of Echo-Hawk's good nature and goodwill is breathtaking: "Americans are fundamentally fair," he says. "They can be relied upon to confront injustice and do the right thing, once educated about pressing indigenous needs."

People who become judges, as much as any other professional or occupational group, are people capable of self-examination and of change. In contrast to a well-established image of the Supreme Court as a remote and distant array of gray eminences, quarantined and separated from the emotions, drives, and passions of their times, this book recognizes their full humanity. The stories, arguments, and recommendations brought together in *In the Courts of the Conqueror* offer an enormously effective way to correct the image of judges as detached and sequestered from their social and cultural setting, and to recognize, instead, their actual power to moderate or even to defy the prejudices of the society in which they live.

In a well-designed joke, a father takes his young son to see the Supreme Court hear arguments in an important case. As the attorneys make their arguments and the justices deliberate, the boy watches them closely. A fly enters the room, buzzes around, and then lands on one head, causing the justice so selected to reach up to brush the fly away.

"Look!" whispers the little boy in amazement, tugging on his father's sleeve. "One of them is *alive!*"

The early twenty-first century, Echo-Hawk believes, offers a prime opportunity to put judicial vitality to work in facing up to the mistakes of the past and in widening the reach of justice. "*We,*" he writes, "have already made a good start in [the] stride toward a more just culture" (the italics are mine). That quiet, inclusive pronoun *we*—embracing both Native people and the descendants of the settlers—offers a great gift of inclusiveness. "The function of the law," Echo-Hawk tells us, "is to serve a changing society and uphold its values, not to hold it prisoner to an unjust past." "By peering into the dark side of the law in these pages," he declares, "I hope to point directions where the law should go."

Treat this book, then, as the guidebook in which Walter Echo-Hawk conducts us through the troubles of the past and then gives us our directions to a better future, encouraging *us* to travel there together.

—Patricia Nelson Limerick
Center of the American West
University of Colorado at Boulder

Inauguration

PART ONE

At the Courthouse Steps

CHAPTER ONE
The Courts of the Conqueror

IN THE VERY FIRST CASE to come before the United States Supreme Court involving a significant Native American issue, Chief Justice John Marshall ominously described the American judicial system as "the Courts of the conqueror." Thus clothed, the Supreme Court handed down a sweeping opinion that appropriated legal title to the United States, even though most of the continent was still owned and occupied at the time by Indian tribes. Since that fateful decision in *Johnson v. M'Intosh* (1823), American law has often worked against Native Americans, legitimizing the appropriation of their property and the decline of their political, human, and cultural rights as indigenous peoples at the hands of the government.[1] By 1950, American Indians had hit the lowest point and were living life in abject poverty at the bottom of a segregated society bent upon stamping out their culture, reneging on remaining government commitments, and assimilating them out of existence. This book examines the troubling fact that American law rendered this destruction perfectly legal, and it explores the need to rethink the doctrines that underpin this national embarrassment.

During the 1960s, the civil rights movement arrived in Indian Country. After years of heavy paternalistic rule by the Bureau of Indian Affairs, Indian tribes began to awaken to the possibility of emancipation from the dark side of federal guardianship and to the need to reclaim Native pride, culture, land, and sovereignty. I came of age in rural Oklahoma, and among Native youth then, our hero during the birth of the Red Power movement was the Ponca Indian activist Clyde Warrior. He rejected the stamp of inferiority impressed upon American Indians by the mass media and mainstream society by proclaiming, "the sewage of Europe does not run through these veins."[2] Though his life was cut short, the awakening in Indian Country was carried forward by his organization, the National Indian Youth Council, and a generation of tribal leaders, activists, and lawyers who recast the civil rights movement into a Native American tribal sovereignty movement that more closely reflects the aspirations of America's indigenous peoples. That movement led to the rise of modern Indian nations.[3]

At the inception of this sovereignty movement, only a handful of American Indians were lawyers, perhaps a dozen, even though the condition of Native Americans has always been highly dependent upon the courts. My folks urged me to go to law school in the late 1960s to help correct problems in our Pawnee tribal community.[4] Heeding their advice, I followed the moccasin tracks to law school made by visionaries such as F. Browning Pipestem (Otoe-Missouri/Osage), Urban Bear Don't Walk (Crow), John Echohawk (Pawnee), and others. Our goal was to learn the law and then use the white man's own rules to achieve justice in his courts. That strategy worked well in the courts of the conqueror. Significant legal battles were won by modern-day warriors during the early years of the sovereignty movement since even under the conqueror's own laws much of the oppression of Indian people was illegal. The successful use of law to solidify the presence of Native America is a great testament to the vitality of the American judiciary. However, those victories are not the subject of this book because they have been well documented by legal scholars and historians.[5]

This book explores the dark side of the law experienced by Native Americans and their efforts to overcome the hardships imposed upon them by American courts. For purposes of this discussion, I have selected the ten worst Indian law cases ever decided from among a very long list of worthy candidates clamoring for selection. Some were chosen because of their far-reaching legal impact and others because they illustrate larger problems in the law. By "worst," I refer to those cases that embody or expose the roots of injustice and highlight the use of nefarious legal doctrines.

Only rarely in US history has the law served as a shield to *protect* Native Americans from abuse and to further their aspirations as indigenous peoples. The law has more often been employed as a sword to *harm* Native peoples by stripping away their human rights, appropriating their property, stamping out their cultures, and, finally, to provide legal justification for federal policies that have, at times, resorted to genocide and ethnocide. These concerns about the role of law are not raised out of passing interest in a dimly lit past. For the most part, the cases discussed in this book remain the law today and have never been reversed. The Supreme Court continues to rely upon them as legal precedent for deciding Native American cases.* Indeed, these cases form in significant part the foundation of federal Indian law, which is the body of law pertaining to American Indians and Alaska Natives that defines their bundle of political and legal rights as indigenous peoples.

---

*The term **Native American** denominates American Indians, Alaska Natives, and Native Hawaiians, with the latter terms being used where appropriate. They are descendants of indigenous peoples who inhabited the land before Europeans arrived.

The ten worst cases I have selected have little to do with "justice." Each decision is based upon (1) unabridged racially derogatory stereotypes and (2) antiquated legal doctrines developed during the colonial era (circa 1492–1960), including ill-defined notions of conquest, for appropriating indigenous land and subjugating Native peoples. These concepts are turned into bedrock American legal principles by the cases discussed in this book.

Even though colonialism was rejected as repugnant by the international community shortly after World War II, the legal underpinnings of colonialism remain implanted in the domestic law of the United States. In addition, the Supreme Court continues to rely upon legal doctrines infected with bare race-based notions as it decides contemporary Indian cases, long after the ideology of race has been discarded by virtually every other governmental institution in the country. Thus, the legal system ironically remains one of the last to perpetuate a form of racism. These fundamental problems in federal Indian law have prompted a call for reform among a growing number of prominent legal scholars who present a powerful case for decolonizing federal Indian law and confronting the Supreme Court about its continued use of legal precedent tainted with racism.[6] As professor Robert Williams asks in *Like a Loaded Weapon*, how can legal advocates expect to win lawsuits by citing cases that call Native Americans "savages" and by relying upon legal principles founded on the racial inferiority of their clients?[7]

Today, the greatest challenge facing advocates and others concerned about the well-being of Native peoples is to root out these vestiges of racism and colonialism in the law and replace them with legal principles more in keeping with the postcolonial world. However, this task is not without its risks. Many scholars argue that the Supreme Court has already begun this departure, with disturbing results, and insist that fidelity to the foundational principles of federal Indian law, espoused during the 1800s, is a better alternative to current Supreme Court trends. There is no question that since the 1980s the Court has begun to stray from the bedrock Indian law principles toward trimming Native American rights even further, and the Court's guiding legal principles currently appear rudderless.[8] The ad hoc approach used by the Supreme Court since 1986 to batter the protective shield and foundational principles of federal Indian law smacks of common law during the age of colonialism.[9] The pivotal question becomes, toward what set of guiding principles should advocates attempt to steer the Court? Regardless of the outcome of this debate, most observers agree that in embracing and applying antiquated legal doctrines and notions of racism, the Supreme Court is confronted with the embarrassing situation described by law professor David Williams:

> [T]he ideology of conquest—with its attendant racism and cultural imperialism—is no longer widely shared. While a few Americans may believe that Indians are still emerging from savagery, that the conquest was just because it substituted a superior for an inferior civilization, and that the best course is the wholesale assimilation of the tribes, such views today have few public defenders.[10]

It is painfully apparent that the Court needs to find some theory other than conquest, colonization, or racial superiority to justify its decisions. That change would entail a paradigm shift in American legal thinking similar to that which prompted the Court to overturn the legal bases for segregating America. Such a sea change for Indians has not yet emerged. Until change is demanded by society at large, the Court will continue to apply outmoded rules to Indians that "the Courts of the conqueror cannot deny."[11]

I hope that a discussion of the ten worst cases will contribute to a just resolution of this dilemma. This is important because American courts have always played a powerful role in determining the fate of Native Americans, sometimes as a shield to protect their rights and aspirations as indigenous peoples, but most often as a sword to constrict and confine their rights and appropriate their property. David H. Getches, the dean of the University of Colorado Law School, observes that American Indians are impacted by the law and Supreme Court decisions more pervasively and gravely than most other Americans.[12]

Though American courts are concerned primarily with interpreting and enforcing the law, society has also charged the courts with the task of providing a bulwark against injustice. This latter function is critical for marginalized Native Americans. Indian tribes comprise a small minority group with vastly different cultures. Their interests go largely unnoticed, unprotected, or subordinated by society because there are no American Indians in Congress, the White House, or on the federal bench. In this vulnerable situation, tribal people are too often completely at the mercy of the federal or state judges. Such judges confront several problems. First, they must cross a cultural divide to consider Native American issues. This cross-cultural task is difficult, according to Williams, because most judges "are almost totally ignorant of the conditions of reservation life" and "[p]erhaps most find even the basic analytical categories of Indian law strange and anomalous."[13] The chore of applying the law under those circumstances can be difficult for even the most sensitive jurist. The bulwark function is further hampered when the legal principles to be applied are infected with notions of racism and doctrines of colonialism, as previously discussed. Finally, to avoid miscarriages of justice, there remain the fundamental problems of judicial courage and the ever-present need for the judges in our independent judiciary to rise above the prevailing politics and prejudices of the day when oppressed minorities are concerned. Given this set of problems, it is hardly a wonder that there exists a dark side to the law in the courts of the conqueror. Reform is needed until American courts no longer consider themselves to be "the Courts of the conqueror."

I hope that by the reform of federal Indian law, a more just culture can be achieved in the United States as our society matures some five hundred years after the arrival of Columbus into the New World. By a just culture, I mean a society with ingrained values and a legal system that fairly takes into account, addresses, and reflects the fundamental values, needs, and concerns of all segments of society, including those of the indigenous peoples. A just culture is not a melting pot where aboriginal cultures have become extinct through enforced assimilation, but a rainbow where different peoples and cultures coexist and enrich each other. Such a society in the postcolonial world means one that has taken significant steps to shed the harsh edges of settlerism that drove the conquest and colonization of the continent during the era of Manifest Destiny and has begun to adapt more closely to the land where we live in ways similar to that which the Native peoples have done—that is, to become more indigenous to place. The legal system, whose function it is to serve the society, should evolve along the way and support this quest for a just culture.

As a Native rights attorney since 1973, I am aware of the challenges that Native Americans face and have faced to protect their political, human, cultural, and property rights as indigenous peoples. While it is natural for American culture to evolve, hopefully toward the just culture, our legal system does reflect the culture that it is intended to serve, for better or worse, and it is limited by that cultural context. It is also limited by the judges who serve on the bench, who are products of their day and age, the manner in which they are appointed, and the doctrine of stare decisis (that is, the need to rely upon and apply court decisions as legal precedent so that there will be predictability in our legal relations), which, like the common law, ensures that cultural bias from earlier times is built into the system. Nonetheless, the law should not hold us hostage to an unjust past. Social change often comes slowly, but it is possible for me to look to the future based upon my perceptions of the past. By peering into the dark side of the law in these pages, I hope to point directions where the law should go, as we stride toward a just culture, one more protective of Native America, with a legal framework more accountable to its needs.

Like an anchor, history plays an important role in examining the dark side of federal Indian law and pointing the direction toward a more just culture. We must confront the forces of colonialism and conquest and understand how they have become imprinted upon the legal system. The history of conquest is the history of mankind; and the treatment of the conquered or the colonized tells the world much about the nature of the occupying victors. We are familiar with the removal of the Hebrew peoples from their fertile territories in the sixth century BC, and the Roman expansion is another example. They "went to stay," sending, then retiring, their army in place— so vestiges of Roman culture can be found throughout the territory of the Roman Empire today. The American experience is quite personal for me as a Pawnee Indian born in rural Oklahoma on the Pawnee Indian Reservation. The way our government addressed the Native American peoples affects me and my family directly, as I will describe, where appropriate, later in this book. The government attempted to exterminate the Native Americans in war, herd them upon reservations then thought to be worthless, and assimilate them through enforced acculturation. A protectorate was established, most often through treaties, that sets the stage for today's situation and makes this book a relevant means for all of us to learn more about who and what we, as a civilization, are and can be, as indigenous and nonindigenous peoples living in the same land.

The first written records of mankind address the manner in which one people lived with others as migration and exploration allowed civilizations to relocate and take their peoples into new lands and better circumstances. Archaeological and historical examination around the globe, including the New World, tells us how difficult the questions of expansion were for the new settlers. Should the laws of the preexisting indigenous peoples govern?

What came along with these settlers by way of cultural experience? Did the settlers, conquerors, and colonists desire anything more than the resources of the new territory? These questions have perplexed scholars for centuries and are the basis for much I address in this volume. All history must be considered contextually. Today's values were not yesterday's, and realizing that should not distort the lessons of history.

So what is the record of our American experience? I seek answers to this question by studying the actions of the American judiciary. How did our courts address conflict with the Native peoples? But the thesis of this book is bigger than that. My thesis here is how *should* the American courts address issues relating to the indigenous peoples? I hope to explain through an examination of legal history how future legal history must be written. And that is what I hope you learn from the study of the ten worst federal Indian law cases ever decided.

Our American experience is unique, but not without its parallels in world history. A study of the Babylonian exiles is fundamental to the development of Judeo-Christian religions. Pilgrims and Puritans came to American shores driven in part by the desire, which is expressed in their colonial charters, to advance the Christian religious experience. What lesson did these colonists learn from the study of their Bible? Nebeccanezer separated out the leadership of the Hebrew peoples and sought to assimilate them into Babylonian culture, leaving behind those who he believed would prove not disruptive. But then this strategy did not work and the Hebrew nation was restored some centuries later. But all that happened thirty-five hundred or so years ago. We are living today with our American experience and that history is yet to be written on how the American peoples will be judged.

This book will address these issues, concerns, and challenges in four parts. Part one provides a context for understanding these cases. Chapter two offers a perspective for better understanding contemporary indigenous issues in the United States by using an international frame of reference. Chapter three provides some preliminary observations about the nature of "justice" in American courts and the role of the courts in Indian affairs. Part two is predominately concerned with the mundane affairs of the living. It shows "how the West was won" in the courts of the conqueror. Marching roughly chronologically through time in the sweep of American history, chapters four through nine examine how the legal system pervasively affected indigenous peoples in the United States, starting with their ownership of land and the political status of Indian tribes, including the internal affairs of Indian tribes, down to individual Indian families and even to the souls of the children. Here we shall also contemplate the role of law in the use of outright violence when different lifestyles come into conflict. Part three takes a sharp detour into the spiritual world. Chapters ten through thirteen examine how the law affects the land of the dead, the spiritual side of Native American life, and the mystical relationships between Native people and the animals, plants, and waters that comprise their aboriginal habitats in this corner of Mother Earth. Finally, part four returns to the land of the living with concluding observations about the courts of the conquerors and recommendations for reforming the dark side of federal Indian law. Hopefully, you will close this book with a thirst for justice and an eagerness to confront the many challenges that lie ahead as we stride toward a more just society in the postcolonial world.

CHAPTER TWO
A Context for Understanding Native American Issues

EACH YEAR, THE US SUPREME COURT hears several Native American cases, and Congress passes numerous laws affecting vital Native American interests. Occasionally these struggles receive cursory attention in mainstream media, but more often they go largely unnoticed by the public and are not well understood. What are these issues about and how can they best be understood?

There is a serious information gap about Native Americans in the United States. Most Americans have never met or talked to an Indian, have never been on an Indian reservation, and know very little about Native Americans in general. Public schools teach us almost nothing about Native history and culture. Shortly after dining with the Pilgrims, the Indians often disappear from schoolbooks or become a sidebar when necessary to tell the story of popular American heroes, like Andrew Jackson or Lewis and Clark—a role not unlike that of the Lone Ranger's sidekick, Tonto. Most information reflects racial stereotypes and cultural myths about Native Americans that are depicted in Hollywood films and dime Western novels or impersonated by Indian mascots at sporting events. Consequently, the attributes of real Native life are usually seen as strange aberrations with little place in modern society. And many people are left to ask questions like, Treaties grant special privileges to Indians, don't they? Aren't tribal governments unfair, race-based institutions? Are Indians segregated since they live on reservations reminiscent of apartheid South Africa? Shouldn't Indians blend into the melting pot like other minorities, instead of stubbornly clinging to their outmoded cultures?

The aspects and aspirations of contemporary Native American communities can only be understood by a study of their history in the United States. Unfortunately, that history is not taught in school. It is often learned by government policy makers, lawmakers, and judges for the very first time, if at all, only after they begin addressing vital issues affecting Native Americans. This is a troubling state of affairs because, as is frequently seen in history, ignorance in human relations can spawn prejudice and other forms of discrimination and lead to human rights violations when it becomes embodied in the machinery of government. The widespread lack of reliable information about Native issues is the most pressing problem confronting Native Americans in the United States today. The following discussion, using an international frame of reference, will provide a context for better understanding indigenous issues in the United States.

As used here, the term *Native American* refers to members of the American Indian tribes, nations, and groups who inhabited North America before Europeans arrived. Contemporary Native American issues can be understood against the backdrop of colonialism and the closely related need to protect indigenous rights, because Native Americans share a common history, fate, and aspirations with indigenous peoples around the world. Anthropological distinctions aside, *indigenous peoples* are defined for purposes of this discussion as the non-European populations who resided in lands colonized by Europeans before the colonists arrived. In general, the human family can be divided into two groups: indigenous and non-indigenous. This division is a function of European colonialism, which is defined by law professor Robert Clinton as "the involuntary exploitation of or annexation of lands and resources previously belonging to another people, often of a different race or ethnicity, or the involuntary expansion of political hegemony over them, often displacing, partially or completely, their prior political organization."[1]

During the colonial era (1492–1960), the nations of Europe competed to conquer, colonize, and Christianize the rest of the world. The indigenous nations of Africa, the Western Hemisphere, Australia, the Circumpolar World, Oceania, India, and most of Asia were colonized. The non-European populations of those lands are variously called "indigenous," "tribal," "native," or "aboriginal" peoples.[2] In the United States, the indigenous peoples are called Native Americans. They consist of 2.5 million American Indians, Native Alaskans, and Native Hawaiians, according to the 2000 Census.

Today, the world's indigenous population is about 350 million people, or approximately 6.4 percent of the human family. They reside in seventy-two nations across the world as invisible nations within nations. Indigenous peoples are frequently minority groups in these nations, but are sometimes the dominant population in places like Guatemala, Bolivia, and New Guinea. Though not indicated on world maps, they live in diverse ancestral habitats ranging from the frozen tundra and seas of the Circumpolar World to tropical islands, from barren desert regions of Africa and the American Southwest to the lush rainforests and jungles of the world, and from the highest mountain regions in South America to the Great Plains of America and Russian steppes, and to the floor of the Grand Canyon. Their aboriginal homelands include some of the most sensitive natural places left on the planet. The cultures of indigenous peoples who continue to reside within their traditional aboriginal habitats are based upon close observations of the natural world, living among and talking to the animals and plants inhabiting what many westerners would call "wilderness." These special relationships have produced some of the most profound and remarkable religious beliefs and practices in the world.[3] A treasure of ancient wisdom and knowledge is stored in the world's estimated fifteen thousand remaining tribal cultures. This indigenous knowledge has become the subject of growing appreciation in recent years, as concern for the survival of indigenous cultures has mounted and the sustainability of modern nonindigenous societies appears dubious.[4] In short, indigenous peoples comprise a vast, worldwide presence; and they share a common historical experience of colonialism.

According to the late Vine Deloria Jr., the overarching question for Native peoples in the twenty-first century is: will we survive? The nineteenth and twentieth centuries were brutal. Ninety tribes completely disappeared in Brazil from 1900 to 1957. Most of the world's wars documented in 1987 were domestic wars conducted by modern nations against their own indigenous peoples. During the nineteenth and twentieth centuries, many colonies and former colonies, including the United States, went through periods of warfare and forcible assimilation against Native peoples. They engaged in the appropriation of Native land and the removal of indigenous populations from aboriginal areas, and they implemented policies to stamp out indigenous cultures, prohibit Native languages, and suppress the practice of indigenous religions. As a result, many cultures have vanished along with the tribal knowledge and wisdom painstakingly assembled over millennia.

Colonialism and the Law of the Conqueror

For indigenous peoples, colonialism was a harsh, life-altering experience because it invariably meant invasion of their country, appropriation of their land and natural resources, destruction of indigenous habitats and ways of life, and sometimes genocide and ethnocide. The early conquest stage of colonialism in the New World was filled with acts of Spanish genocide. More than twelve million Indians died during the first forty years after Columbus landed as Spaniards infected, killed, tortured, terrorized, and destroyed each Native civilization they encountered. The depopulation of the Americas during this period was witnessed by Bartolomé de Las Casas

(1474–1566), who arrived in Hispaniola in 1502 and spent more than forty years in Spanish colonies. He chronicled the death of millions and claimed that over forty million died at Spanish hands by 1560.[5] Estimates vary, but according to demographer Russell Thornton, more than seventy-two million indigenous people could have inhabited the Western Hemisphere circa 1492, and this population declined to about four million in a few centuries in one of the largest population collapses ever recorded.[6] In the North America of 1492, five million Indians inhabited the area now comprising the United States. By 1900, only 250,000 remained—a decline of over one million persons per century. Greed for gold and silver drove the brutal colonization efforts of the Spanish. In North America, it was all about *huraaru* (the Pawnee word for "land")—even though gold had a great deal to do with the demise of Indians in California, Georgia, Colorado, and South Dakota. These harsh aspects of colonialism have left deep marks on the colonized and colonizers who endure today in the social structures of many nations with colonial histories.

A popular justification for colonialism among the colonizing nations was the white man's burden. Originally coined by Rudyard Kipling, the term is a euphemism for imperialism based upon the presumed responsibility of white people to exercise hegemony over nonwhite people, to impart Christianity and European values, thereby uplifting the inferior and uncivilized peoples of the world. In this ethnocentric view, non-European cultures are seen as childlike, barbaric, or otherwise inferior and in need of European guidance for their own good. As thus viewed from European eyes, colonization became a noble undertaking done charitably for the benefit of peoples of color. As it turned out, however, the reverse was true: the white man became the burden of the black, brown, yellow, and red men and women.

In the United States, the alleged altruistic motives of the white man's burden took on spiritual clothing under the hubris of Manifest Destiny. This doctrine invoked divine sanction for settling the frontier and justified the stupefying impacts on Native people. Under this view, American expansion was inevitable and Indians would simply vanish before oncoming pioneers. Manifest Destiny was not confined to white settlement on Indian lands in the United States, but also justified American colonization of the Philippines, Guam, Puerto Rico, Hawaii, and other places.

Was the conquest and colonization of the New World legal? Colonialism was legalized by the law of nations developed by the Europeans during the colonial era. That body of law was developed largely to facilitate the conquest and colonization of the New World. A brief examination of Spanish and English thought that gave rise to the Law of Nations is instructive.[7]

The roots of colonial thought originate in medieval times, when the Catholic Church espoused principles for dealing with non-Christian societies. The church asserted jurisdiction and supremacy over all of humanity. This extraordinary claim was predicated on the notion that there is only one true god (the Christian god) and one true religion (the Roman Catholic Church). Therefore, the church's version of truth, religion, and reason are universal norms binding each society and culture across the world. This ethnocentric religious view accorded inferior legal status and rights to non-Christians, who were variously described as "pagans," "infidels," "barbarians," and "nonbelievers," and, eventually, to the indigenous peoples of the New World who were seen by Europeans as "uncivilized barbarians" and "heathen savages." This thinking—which is based upon the supposed religious and cultural superiority of Europe over nonwhite races and cultures—provided the intellectual foundation for the law of conquest and colonization.

At the dawn of the colonial era, European kingdoms began to build on that foundation. Early principles sprang from the pope when the Spanish Crown petitioned the church to grant Spain legal title to the lands discovered by Columbus. Under his papal authority, Pope Alexander VI issued two papal bulls, or decrees, in 1493 that conveyed legal title to the Western Hemisphere to Ferdinand and Isabella.[8] The first bull declared that Columbus discovered remote lands and peaceable people in the New World who could easily be made Catholic and proceeded to *give* the New World to Ferdinand and his wife, Isabella.

> [I]n order that you may enter upon so great an undertaking [to convert the American Indians to the Catholic Faith and place their countries under the sway of Spain]…we…by the authority of Almighty God… do…give, grant, and forever assign to you and your heirs and successors, kings of Castile and Leon, all and singular the aforesaid countries and islands thus unknown and hitherto discovered by your envoys and to be discovered hereafter.[9]

To clarify the boundaries of Alexander's gift, the second bull drew a line west of the Azores Islands "from the Artic pole…to the Antarctic pole" and conveyed all of the islands and mainlands west of the line to Spain, with a sliver going to Portugal.[10] Though Alexander's authority for the world's largest land transaction is implausible, his bull nonetheless gave birth to the doctrine of discovery. Under this doctrine, European explorers may claim title to Native land "discovered" in the name of the monarch who sponsored their journey—a title recognized by all of Europe. Pretty sweet, huh?

To legalize occupation of the New World, Spain enacted the Laws of Burgos in 1512. This legislation specified procedures and guidelines for invading the Americas by force of arms.

> Should the natives attempt to oppose the settlement [of a colony], they shall be given to understand that the intention in forming it, is to teach them to know God and his holy law, by which they are to be saved; to preserve friendship with them, and teach them to live in a civilized state...They shall be convinced of this by mild means, through the interference of religion and priests,...and if, notwithstanding, they do not withhold their consent, the settlers...shall proceed to make their settlement...without doing them any greater damage than shall be necessary.[11]

Force of arms, however, must begin with the *Requerimiento*—a formal declaration of war that must be read aloud in Spanish to uncomprehending Indians before hostilities could commence. It demanded that they accept Spanish missionaries and domination, or face war. This procedure turned invasion and slaughter into a just and legal war.

The idea of a "just war" originated in medieval church doctrines about the rights and status of infidels. Franciscus de Victoria (1480–1546) secularized that body of law and developed legal principles to justify Spanish domination of the Americas. His influential work became a primary source of Spanish and English colonial law and a cornerstone of the law of nations. According to Victoria, the "natural law" of Europe imposed certain servitudes upon the Indians of the Western Hemisphere. If Indians prevented Europeans from enjoying their right to travel, sojourn, trade, or "share" in communal property belonging to the Natives, the Europeans may engage in a "just war" to conquer and colonize the barbarian infidels as punishment for violating the rules of civilized society. A "just war" includes "all the rights of war, despoiling [the Indians] of their goods, reducing them to captivity, deposing their former lords and setting up new ones."[12]

Victoria also espoused a guardianship principle: a Christian nation's duty is to civilize and Christianize the backward people of the New World. Under the rubric of the "Spaniard's burden," the self-appointed guardians could travel, sojourn, and trade in barbarous lands under natural law and enjoy broad rights to preach the gospel and to conquer and colonize Indians who refused to hear the word of the Christian god. Victoria's guardianship principle, which granted enormous powers of intrusion, was based upon the assumption that the Indians had no laws or civilization and were incompetent beings. Spanish guardianship in the New World, then, *was supposed to be good for the Indians.*

> It might, therefore, be maintained that in their own interests the sovereigns of Spain might undertake the administration of their country, providing them with prefects and governors for their towns, and might even give them new lords, so long as this was clearly for their benefit.[13]

Thus, under Victoria's law of nations, religion and guardianship became potent instruments of colonialism, along with the cross, sword, and the law. As it turned out, the Spanish were the barbarians who were not qualified to be the guardians of anyone, according to most historical accounts. Victoria was wrong, but his guardianship principle remains alive and well in the United States, as will be seen in the ten worst Indian law cases ever decided.

Prior to the Pilgrim and Puritan incursions of North America, English legal thinkers developed a similar legal basis for colonization by England. Prominent theorists, like Sir Edward Coke and Oxford scholar Alberico Gentili, incorporated Victoria's law of nations into English colonial theory. Coke also incorporated the Catholic Church's medieval discourse on the rights and relationships with infidels in his work, including his famous decision in *Calvin's Case* (1608).[14] In that case, Coke argued that non-Christian infidels are "enemy aliens" of Christians with no rights in English courts, and Christian kings may wage war against infidels and upon conquest abrogate the laws of infidel nations. The Royal Charter for the Virginia Company (1606) transplanted Coke's principles to the shores of America with the arrival of the Jamestown colonists.[15] The charter grants the company the right to establish a colony in Virginia "not now actually possessed by any Christian Prince or people." The colony was assigned several tasks. It was supposed to propagate Christianity among the "Infidels and Savages" who "live in Darkness and miserable Ignorance of the true Knowledge and Worship of God"; to bring "human Civility" and a "settled and quiet Government" to America; and, oh yes, "dig, mine and search for all Manner of Mines of Gold, Silver, and Copper" and yield a cut to the king.[16]

With bible in hand, then, Pilgrim miners would be busy founding the colony and searching for gold, while bringing about religion, civilization, good manners, and sound government to Native North America. Much of this book recounts the Pilgrims' progress and their use of law to accomplish the tasks laid out by the king. But the underlying legal premise was that the Indians were infidels with no legal rights in Pilgrim courts, and it was perfectly legal under the law of England for the colonists to wage war to accomplish their goals.

The legal basis for just wars by England against the Indian infidels of North America was provided in Alberico Gentili's writings on the law of war before 1600.[17] Gentili's law of war made it plain that if North American savages violate English notions of natural law or are without a European-style religion, they are like animals in the eyes of the law of war and a just war may be waged against them.[18] Thus, religious intolerance and the Christian religion were placed into the service of England as legal bases for war, conquest, and colonization of America. Under these Eurocentric doctrines, Native lands can legally be invaded and colonized simply because Native Americans are different or enjoy the wrong religion. It's for the Indians' own good.

As you will see in the cases discussed in this book, the colonial doctrines of discovery, conquest, guardianship, and religious intolerance found their way into American law. These concepts, which are supported primarily by a set of foolish and unjust legal fictions, remain embedded as cornerstones of federal Indian law. Early on, the Supreme Court noted in *Johnson v. M'Intosh* (1823) that the "religion and character" of American Indians "afforded an apology for considering them as a people over which the superior genius of Europe might claim an ascendancy."[19] The white man's burden emerged in *Cherokee Nation v. Georgia* (1831) when the Court explained that, "[Indians] are in a state of pupilage. Their relation to the United States resembles that of a ward to his guardian."[20] This role is said to require federal hegemony over Indians, according to *United States v. Kagama* (1886), because "[t]he power of the general government over these remnants of a race once powerful, now weak and diminished in numbers, is necessary to their protection."[21] The white man's burden also provided the source for the plenary or absolute power of Congress over Indian people and their property. In confirming this absolute power over Indians, the court in *Lone Wolf v. Hitchcock* (1903) promised only that its exercise will be tempered "by such considerations of justice as would control a Christian people in their treatment of an ignorant and dependent race."[22] In short, whenever the Supreme Court wishes to expand state or federal power over Indians and their property or to trim the exercise of power by modern tribal governments, it need only resort to the legal mantra of colonialism. *Oliphant v. Suquamish Indian Tribe* (1978) is a good example. There, the Court refused to let tribal courts try whites for crimes committed on Indian reservations.[23] Even though tribal courts are as sophisticated as any other court, Justice Rehnquist's opinion severely restricted their reach. Tribal courts are *not really* a part of the American judicial system, because tribes lost their sovereignty and gave up "their power to try non-Indian citizens."[24] Under the colonial structure, only courts of the conqueror may judge a white man and tribal government tribunals cannot sit in judgment of white citizens.

As discussed previously, the Supreme Court's continuing practice of relying upon the old doctrines of colonialism has led legal scholars to call for the decolonization of federal Indian law. The time is long overdue for reforming the dark side of the law if appropriate doctrines can be found to protect indigenous rights and to strengthen the foundational principles that shield the Indian tribes from harm. With the collapse and repudiation of colonialism, we no longer need American law to support and enforce a domestic colonial system that few would openly admit to, much less defend. In the present circumstances, it becomes increasingly unseemly for courts to wield such an outmoded, inherently unjust, and oppressive set of legal doctrines against a tiny minority of indigenous Americans—unless it remains the United States' goal to subjugate Indian tribes and control Indians as colonial subjects with diminutive rights. Surely we can find a more appropriate legal basis to define indigenous relations than bald settler-state control.

Like racism in our society, the vestiges of colonialism in the law must go. They have become inconsistent with modern mainstream values and no longer enjoy a legitimate place in a land devoted to higher values. Now that we no longer consider Native Americans to be barbarians, infidels, or savages, or ourselves as colonial masters of an inferior and backward people, the legal doctrines built upon those classifications become legal fictions that are no longer tenable, logical, nor entitled to any effect. The same is true for legal principles built upon the discriminatory notion that Indians have the wrong, non-Christian religion. Such notions have no place in a nation that cherishes religious freedom and requires the separation of church and state. Religious discrimination against infidels is not even applicable to Christian Indians—they now have the "right" religion. Nor can principles of religious discrimination be applied to Indians with the "wrong" religion without running afoul of the First Amendment.

The time has come to bring domestic law more into line with international norms that reject colonialism and to find more appropriate legal principles for protecting the aspirations and survival of indigenous peoples in the United States. Because judges have not inherited a set of clear and viable theories of postcolonial power over Native Americans, we must develop a new analytical framework—a brand new set of rules. Can that be done in a nation with strong settler-state traditions?

The Fall of Colonialism and the Rise of the Settler State

The United States has the dubious distinction of being a settler state, along with several other former colonies. The modern settler state is a by-product of colonialism found in several present-day nations that are former colonies. Toward the close of the colonial era, during the twentieth century, most colonies achieved their independence from European nations. After independence, what happened to the settlers? Some simply left and returned to their homelands. In other former colonies, the settlers stayed and merged with the Native population or cast their lot with the Natives so that the newly independent nation reverted back to its aboriginal character. However, in still other instances the settlers stayed, but did not merge with the Natives. Instead, they retained the language, religion, and culture of their distant homelands and kept the preexisting colonial structure for dealing with the aboriginal peoples. Such former colonies can be described as *settler states*.

In settler states, the settlers achieved independence for themselves, but the lot of the Native people remained unchanged because the settlers simply replaced the colonial system of the motherland with their own, thus embedding colonial relations into the social structure of the newly independent nation. Those colonial relationships are often irreversible since the settlers now claim the land as their homeland. The American experience affords one example of a settler state and settlerism. Examples may be found in other countries, like Canada, Australia, New Zealand, apartheid South Africa, Rhodesia, Brazil, and other Latin American nations.

One challenge of settlers in settler states is to justify their dubious foundations of conquest and dispossession of indigenous peoples, which sometimes included genocide and enslavement. The glorification of that history is done through a set of justifying myths and rationalizations, which are reflected in the history books, mass media, institutions, legal doctrines, and laws of the nation. One collective story, popular among settlers in places like Australia and South Africa, goes something like, "We didn't *really* conquer and dispossess other nations. We merely moved into vacant, uninhabited, or at least sparsely settled territory." Other stories admit that we did conquer the natives, "but they either deserved it (as violent savages) or it was for their own good (since the backward infidels stand to benefit from our presence)." According to Theodore Roosevelt in 1900, "the settler and pioneer have at bottom had justice on their side; this great continent could not have been kept as nothing but a game preserve for squalid savages."[25] Of course, in no instance, however, does settler-state mythology concede that the state's dubious origins are illegitimate. History is invariably kind to the conquerors—after all, they wrote it.

Another interesting aspect of settlerism is the tendency of the settlers to retain a cultural identity with homelands far away. This tendency hampers their adaptation to the land in the way that the Native people have adapted. In that respect, the settlers frequently remain, in an odd way, strangers to the land or visitors in their outlook, even though they have become the stewards of the land. The phenomenon of retaining cultural identity with land thousands of miles away, while at the same time ignoring or marginalizing the local indigenous cultures, has engendered much of the human suffering and conflict found in settler states. That alienation was aptly noted by Dakota Chief Luther Standing Bear in 1933:

> The white man does not understand the Indian for the reason he does not understand America. He is too far removed from its formative processes. The roots of his tree of life have not yet grasped the rock and soil...The man from Europe is still a foreigner and an alien. And he still hates the man who questions his path across the continent. But in the Indian, the spirit of the land is still vested; and it will be until other men are able to divine and meet its rhythm. Men must be born and reborn to belong. Their bodies must be formed of the dust of their forefathers' bones.[26]

The features of the settler state are familiar. The basic political relationship between indigenous and nonindigenous peoples remains one of colonialism. Under this unmistakable colonial pattern, basic legal relationships are still built on the trusteeship doctrine under which the government owns and manages all Native property as a "trustee" for the benefit of the Natives. In exchange, the government is obliged to look out for the best interests of Native "wards." Under the trusteeship system, the Natives are usually the poorest of the poor, living life at the bottom of almost every socioeconomic indicator. The economic system features the familiar one-way transfer of property from indigenous to nonindigenous hands. Natural-resource extraction from Native lands and intrusive development of indigenous habitats primarily benefit non-Natives. Social relationships within the colonial structures are often harsh. The Native peoples are typically marginalized politically, legally, and socially. This treatment renders them strangers in the lands where they live, aliens in their homelands, and invisible nations. Finally, the ever-present problem of racism is often manifested in stereotypes, assimilation, and sometimes genocide.

The dual concepts of the settler state and settlerism provide tools for understanding indigenous issues. One can look both abroad and here at home to see where the pattern fits. Furthermore, contemporary Native American issues can be understood against the backdrop of colonialism and settlerism, which brings into focus the need to strengthen laws to protect indigenous rights. Cultural conflicts can be understood in this light. Colonists invariably retained close cultural ties to homelands across the sea and rarely assimilated indigenous values or ways of looking at Mother Earth. Instead, they imposed their European cultures, languages, and religions upon tribal people. Missionaries, schools, soldiers, and governments tried to assimilate Native Americans into the settlers' culture. Today, Native Americans depend on domestic law to protect their remaining cultural integrity, but often that law is weak and ill-suited for the task, and sometimes it is nonexistent.

Struggles to protect indigenous property can also be understood against the backdrop of colonialism and settlerism. The central purpose of colonialism was to provide riches and land for European elites. To that end, a massive one-way transfer of property occurred in most colonies. In the United States, this included land, natural resources, and personal properties (some of which are called "artifacts" by anthropologists and art collectors). Even dead bodies (called "specimens" or "archaeological resources" by anthropologists) were dug up and carried away. The appropriation extended to intellectual property, such as animal and plant knowledge patented by corporations; tribal names, art, and symbols converted into trademarks; and religious beliefs borrowed by New Agers. Even tribal identities have been taken by wannabes masquerading as Native Americans for personal, professional, or commercial gain. In beleaguered Native eyes, little else is left to take and Native legal efforts attempt to stem and reverse that one-way transfer of property and cultural wealth and to protect what little remains. The challenge for settler states is to find a just balance of indigenous rights and relationships so that distinct Native cultures and their nations within nations can coexist and flourish—and not be doomed to extinction.

Examining the Social and Legal Challenges of Settler States

Can a settler state be made legitimate? This is not an easy task, but as settler states mature, they become subject to other influences and might ultimately replace tainted concepts of settlerism with a nonsettler culture that is more native to place. After all, there will come a time in each settler state when the descendants of settlers no longer wish to be culturally estranged from their adopted homeland. The threshold task in this transformation is one of critical self-evaluation by those with settler backgrounds to come to grips with the legacy of conquest and to discard the myths and justifications of settlerism. Some western families who have been on the land for several generations have already begun that process. In nations like Canada, this has been described as a healing process. If attempted on a superficial level, however, the process of adaptation can be socially challenging, even amusing. This is demonstrated by pilgrims in muumuus and flowered shirts who say "aloha" at Hawaiian-resort luaus, or by New Age "shamans" who chant while awkwardly dressed in "authentic" Indian attire. (Miss Manners should develop socially appropriate rules of etiquette so these good-hearted folks can avoid becoming objects of amusement.)

What will be the place of indigenous peoples in new nonsettler states? The paramount human rights question facing each nation that contains indigenous peoples, including the United States, is: to what extent should indigenous peoples be secure in their land, cultural integrity, human rights, and political rights as Native people? How this question is answered by each nation tells the world much about the national character, values, and principles of that nation. In fact, the actual domestic treatment of indigenous peoples tells the world far more about that nation than its announced policies and principles on the international stage. For that reason, Felix S. Cohen, the father of modern federal Indian law, observed in 1953 that America's treatment of its Native peoples is a barometer of the United States' commitment to fundamental liberties:

> Like the Miner's canary, the Indian marks the shift from fresh air to poison gas in our political atmosphere and our treatment of Indians, even more than our treatment of other minorities, marks the rise and fall of our democratic faith.[27]

There is an obvious lack of adequate legal protections in the nations that allow abuses against indigenous people. This can be attributed to many factors, such as the wardship or other second-class legal status of Native peoples, the lack of meaningful access to the courts, inadequate or nonexistent laws protective of indigenous rights, outright discrimination, and the nearly complete absence of legal protection under international law.

Without adequate legal protections, it is hardly a wonder that the survival of Native peoples is at stake, as seen in the massive slide toward extinction, homogenization, and culture loss that occurred during the twentieth century. To reverse these trends in new nonsettler states, it is critical to educate nonindigenous peoples about the inherent worth of Native peoples and the need to protect their cultural integrity and human rights as indigenous peoples. Then it becomes the task of the law and the judicial system to protect these values. As in all modern societies, social change in new nonsettler states does not germinate from policy changes or goodwill alone. It requires a regime of law that, in turn, must be enforced. For example, the black civil rights leaders could not rely on bare policy to eradicate centuries of ingrained discrimination. Some of their most courageous work confronted oppressive laws and forced their repeal, amendment, or judicial neutralization. Where existing law was useful but not enforced, they embarrassed, harassed, or otherwise prevailed on law enforcement authorities and on the courts to enforce these laws evenhandedly. And they obtained new remedial laws in areas necessary to protect their human rights and to afford them with equal protection of American laws.

The broad challenge as the young century unfolds is to develop and enforce a set of statutes and legal principles in the United States that provides a just balance in protecting the rights and relationships of its Native peoples. Congress has already laid a strong foundation during the twentieth century's self-determination era.

Currently, the domestic law in many settler states fails to achieve that balance because the laws are weak, ineffectual, or nonexistent, and the courts in the postmodern era of federal Indian law (1985 to present) are not often up to the task of providing a bulwark against infringements of Native rights. In the land of Manifest Destiny, federal Indian law is the body of law designed to protect Native rights; and some grievous flaws in that body are revealed in the cases discussed in this book. The immediate challenge in the United States is to identify and root out vestiges of racism and colonialism. The courts that continue to rely upon legal principles infected with these doctrines have either forgotten, were never aware of, or accept their dark origins. Yet, dispossessed Native Americans have not forgotten. Does American law have sufficient vitality to protect and respect the totally different worldviews and aspirations of America's indigenous peoples? If it cannot, those worldviews are doomed to extinction.

On the international level, the challenge is to bring indigenous peoples within the ambit of international law so that it may provide meaningful legal protection. Until recent times, the law of nations was not only used as an instrument of colonialism, it also completely excluded indigenous peoples from enforceable legal protections. During the development of international law by the nations of Europe in the colonial era, the scope of international law was limited to external relations between "civilized" nations. The indigenous nations that had been conquered, colonized, and annexed did not, of course, meet this definition. Since they were no longer "nations" with external attributes of sovereignty, the fate of indigenous peoples was relegated to the exclusive domain of domestic law—that is, the very law used to dispossess and oppress them in the first place. Thus, international law allows the fox to guard the henhouse. We can no longer tolerate being relegated to purely domestic law under those circumstances. However, virtually every member state of the United Nations with indigenous peoples refuses to allow any external scrutiny of its treatment of its Native people.

By what yardstick should these domestic and international legal reforms be measured? They should be measured against the aspirations of the world's diverse indigenous peoples, ambitions that are remarkably similar around the world. Those aspirations are in large part embodied in the recent United Nations Declaration on the Rights of Indigenous Peoples, approved by the

UN General Assembly on September 13, 2007.[28] This historic international convention provides a benchmark. Though implementation of the declaration's standards is only in the beginning stage, the law of each nation in the postcolonial world should ideally comport with the minimum standards contained in the declaration. Article 43 provides: "The rights recognized herein constitute the minimum standards for the survival, dignity and well-being of the indigenous peoples of the world." Where the law of a particular nation, including the United States, does not pass muster under the UN's minimum standards, human-rights violations are often found. A brief summary of some of those standards and issues shows remarkable similarity to the aspirations long cherished by Native Americans in the United States:

1. The survival and equality of indigenous peoples are expressed as freedom from genocide, discrimination, and assimilation, and from the forcible removal from Native lands. (Art. 2, 7, 8, 10, 21, 30)

2. Political autonomy is sought through "self-determination," that is freedom of Native tribes, nations, and communities to choose their political status, and in the full participation in decisions affecting indigenous lives, property, and political status. (Art. 4, 5, 18–20, 32–34)

3. The right to exist as distinct peoples is a right to maintain and strengthen the distinct political, economical, social, and cultural characteristics of Native peoples, as well as their legal systems, while at the same time retaining their rights to participate fully if they so choose, in the political, economic, social, and cultural life of the nation state. (Art. 5, 9, 33)

4. "Cultural survival" is described as a freedom to (1) practice and revitalize cultural traditions and customs; (2) protect cultural, religious, and burial sites, as well as intellectual property; (3) perpetuate language, religion, and ceremonies; (4) provide education opportunity from the state through Native-controlled schools taught in the Native language with culturally appropriate teaching methods; and (5) reflect in public education, information, and the media Native cultures, traditions, histories, and aspirations. (Art. 11–16, 25, 31, 34)

5. Social standards seek improved social and economic conditions for indigenous peoples, including elders, women, youth, children, and the disabled. (Art. 21–22)

6. Health standards include access to and protection of traditional medicines and health practices and protection for medicinal plants, animals, and minerals. (Art. 23–24)

7. Environmental and subsistence standards would allow indigenous peoples to maintain and strengthen their distinctive spiritual and material relationship with the lands, territories, waters, coastal seas, and other resources that they have traditionally owned or otherwise occupied or used. (Art. 29)

8. Land-rights standards include legal rights to own, develop, control, and use the land and territory (including the total environment of the lands, air, waters, flora, and fauna) that Natives have traditionally owned, occupied, or used. (Art. 25–28)

From the times of Red Cloud, Seattle, Chief Joseph, and into the modern era of Vine Deloria Jr. and Clyde Warrior, Native American leaders have fought to achieve these freedoms for their people. These ideals, even today, motivate many Native Americans to wear the American uniform in distant places, like Iraq and Afghanistan, hoping that the principles fought for abroad will abide for relatives at home. US law should guarantee and safeguard the rights set forth in the UN declaration as minimal standards for protecting the human rights of Native Americans. As you will see, many of those standards contradict the holdings of American courts in the ten worst Indian law cases discussed in this book and call their legitimacy into question. It is not surprising that the United States opposed the declaration—the dark side of federal Indian law falls short of the UN benchmark and is exposed as rank law in need of reform.

As the United States matures, there is a need to discard worn-out attitudes of settlerism and to replace the outmoded settler state with a new, nonsettler society. This is part of the quest toward achieving a just culture. To achieve these goals, significant domestic law reforms will be required to decolonize federal Indian law, root out vestiges of racism, and eradicate unjust legal fictions embedded in that important body of law. After all, we are no longer an abject British colony. American courts should not be courts of the conqueror, harboring foolish and unjust legal fictions, and our legal system should no longer be used as an instrument of colonialism. The current and next generation should focus instead upon elevating federal Indian law to achieve all of the minimum standards of the United Nations Declaration on the Rights of Indigenous Peoples so that the survival, dignity, and well-being of Native America can be assured. We have already made a good start in that stride toward a more just culture.

CHAPTER THREE
Justice, Injustice, and the
Dark Side of Federal Indian Law

PEOPLE OFTEN EQUATE THE AMERICAN LEGAL SYSTEM with justice, but courts of law are not always concerned with dispensing justice. As I will show, they often fall short of the mark in important cases. At its best, the law does indeed embody that high ideal. This is readily seen in the landmark cases that stamp out injustice. *Brown v. Board of Education* (1954) is a famous example.[1] In that decision, the Supreme Court threw out as unconstitutional the deeply ingrained "separate but equal" doctrine, which had long furnished segregationists with a legal basis to separate the races in all aspects of American life. The court held that separate schools for black children are "inherently unequal" because segregation generates feelings of inferiority "that may affect their hearts and minds in a way unlikely ever to be undone."[2] In *Wisconsin v. Yoder* (1972), the Supreme Court extended First Amendment protection for the religious way of life of the Amish.[3] It struck down a state compulsory school-attendance law requiring all children to attend public schools until age sixteen on the grounds that it conflicted sharply with the way of life mandated by the Amish religion. This small, harmless minority objected to compulsory school attendance beyond the eighth grade because public schools exposed their children to mainstream values destructive to their way of life. As a bulwark against conformity, the decision safeguards the continued survival of this culturally distinct community in our largely secular nation as a matter of the free exercise of religion.

At its worst, however, the law can become a perversion of justice. The German judiciary during the Nazi era exemplifies this extreme. The widespread complicity of German judges, prosecutors, law professors, and attorneys in the destruction of many thousands of lives was established at the criminal trial of German judges in Nuremberg in *United States of America v. Alstoetter et al.* (1948).[4] Most German judges were sympathetic to Nazi goals and, with only a few courageous exceptions, became willing instruments in the Nazification of Germany.[5] An evil pattern of judicial and prosecutorial support for Nazi crimes against humanity was demonstrated in *Alstoetter*.[6] The independence of the judiciary had been thoroughly compromised by the Third Reich, and many judges identified with the regime, embraced its goals and brutal laws, including the notorious Nuremberg Laws (1935), and allowed the judicial system to become an instrument of terror.[7] Their complicity demonstrates that justice as an ideal disappears from the safeguards of civilized society when judges succumb to popular movements and prevailing prejudices that are injurious to minorities, or when judges place political loyalty above their role as a bulwark against government abuse.

American courts, on the other hand, comprise an independent branch of government that is designed to protect the integrity of judges and minimize the risk of prejudice. Because society has built numerous safeguards into the American legal system, we fully expect judges to be impartial decision makers, free from bias and prejudice, and able to apply the law and decide cases in keeping with basic considerations of truth and justice. The US Constitution guarantees life tenure to federal judges to insulate them from political influence and enable them to make courageous and correct decisions without fear of removal. When judges have conflicts of interests or cannot otherwise be impartial, judicial ethics require that they disqualify themselves to protect the integrity of the system. Modern courts are *designed* to provide a fair trial. The procedural rules, together with rules of evidence, are designed to seek truth through the adversarial process and at the same time minimize the risk of prejudice or unfairness. The doctrine of stare decisis (the need to rely upon and apply court decisions as legal precedent so that there will be predictability in our legal relations) bolsters these safeguards by requiring courts to follow established legal precedent. That requirement makes legal relations predictable and allows society to rely upon the rule of law. Where a court fails to follow the procedural or substantive rules, appellate review is usually available. In short, we reasonably expect fairness and justice from the judicial branch of government. The canons that govern judicial ethics in the United States list "justice in our society" as the paramount goal of the judiciary.[8]

Despite these safeguards, the courts sometimes produce what can only be described as manifestly unjust results. How, then, do we explain such outcomes?

The easiest explanation is to simply deny that injustice exists. This, at least, minimizes discomfort. Denial allows us to completely discount the possibility of injustice. That seems to be the approach favored by the late Chief Justice William Rehnquist in *United States v. Sioux Nation of Indians* (1980).[9] In that case, he simply could not countenance patent wrongdoing committed by the government against the Sioux Nation because this contradicted his views of history and Manifest Destiny.[10] In *Sioux Nation*, the Supreme Court examined at length the uncomfortable history surrounding the government's acquisition of the Black Hills from the Sioux after their military defeat and confinement to a reservation following the Great Sioux War of 1876–77. The evidence established that the Sioux, who were then living under starvation conditions, had been coerced by the government into "selling" the Black Hills in exchange for government food rations. The Court held that in such circumstances, rations alone (even *very good* rations) could not constitute adequate payment for the Black Hills and that the government was liable to provide fair compensation.

In so holding, the Court's majority could not ignore the obvious and central aspect of the case: the government had committed wrongs. After all, the lower court had declared that "[a] more ripe and rank case of dishonorable dealings will never, in all probability, be found in our history"; and the historical record in the case suggested that "[f]ew conquered people in the history of mankind have paid so dearly for the defense of their way of life." In his dissent, Rehnquist refused to see the elephant in the room. To admit wrongdoing would impugn his cowboy-and-Indian views of American history and Manifest Density and create an unwanted "stereotyped and one-sided impression both of the settlement regarding the Black Hills portion of the Great Sioux Reservation and of the gradual expansion of the National Government from the Proclamation Line of King George III to the Pacific Ocean."[11] Under his version of history, Indians were to blame for the problem (they "did not lack their share of villainy") and settlers were absolved ("Judge not, that ye not be judged.").[12] Rehnquist denied the hard evidence in the case and refused to discard popular myths—decrying instead the unfairness of judging facts "by the light of 'revisionist' historians or the mores of another era."[13] To be sure, historians must be sensitive to such concerns; however, some situations are manifestly unjust under any set of standards—whether they are contemporaneous, contemporary, contextual, or whether they embody universal truths or otherwise—and those situations cannot be so easily brushed aside.

A more concrete explanation for rank injustice in the American legal system can be seen in the closure of courthouse doors. No legal system is accountable or responsive to groups who lack access to the courts. Nor can excluded groups reasonably expect justice from a closed judicial system. In the Third Reich, for example, the law removed Jews and non-Aryans from the bench, lawyers were not allowed to represent Jews in the courts, and the judges were under heavy government pressure, including surveillance, to implement the racist policies of the state in cases involving Jews. Access to such courts by Jews was nonexistent for any practical purposes. The Final Solution could not be enjoined by the German courts of law. Jews could not reasonably expect even lesser forms of justice from courts that were effectively closed to them. Nor could slaves in the pre–Civil War United States reasonably expect justice in American courts because the courthouse door was closed to them. In the *Dred Scott* case (1856), the Supreme Court held that a slave may not sue for his freedom in federal courts because blacks are not, and could never be, citizens entitled to use the courts.[14] Thus, from behind courthouse doors closed to the slaves, American courts decided questions pertaining to slavery. That unjust body of law developed with no representation or other participation by the slaves at all. The *Dred Scott* decision had door-closing ramifications for American Indians, as well. Indians were not citizens until the Indian Citizenship Act of 1924. As Justice Horace Gray explained in *Elk v. Wilkins* (1884), Indians were not citizens with a right to vote under the Constitution; instead, they were considered wards of the government until Congress decides "that they should be let out of the state of pupilage and admitted to the privileges and responsibilities of citizenship."[15]

Indeed, the first time an Indian nation went to the Supreme Court to seek protection from state laws enacted to abolish, harass, and remove the Cherokee, the case was dismissed for lack of jurisdiction. The case was *Cherokee Nation v. Georgia* (1831), and the court closed the courthouse doors to the Cherokee Nation because it was not a "foreign nation" entitled to bring suit in the Supreme Court.[16] Native access to the courts began to emerge several decades later, through decisions like *Standing Bear* (1876), which allowed a Ponca chief to challenge his confinement by the army in federal court.[17] Not surprisingly, during the critical time in American Indian history when the tribes were confronted with removal, dispossession, and violence at the hands of the government, the courthouse doors were largely shut.

But how can we explain manifestly unjust decisions rendered by American courts after the courthouse was opened to blacks, Indians, and other minorities? One explanation is that justice is not the principal function of the courts. As Supreme Court Justice Oliver Wendell Holmes Jr. put it, "This is a court of law, young man, not a court of justice." It is troubling that courts often eschew any interest in, or duty to inquire into, questions of morality or justice; instead, the avowed task is simply to apply existing law, regardless of any harsh or unjust outcomes. Indeed, many of the cases discussed in this book begin their legal analysis with exactly that apology. We cannot accept this explanation as the principal cause of unjust decisions, at least in modern times, without undermining public confidence in a judicial system that operates under a set of judicial ethics that are specifically designed to achieve justice in our society.

The fundamental explanation, in my view, is that judges are simply not up to the task of articulating and applying enduring notions of truth or justice. Supreme Court justices are often frail creatures of their time, captive to prevailing prejudices and unable to rise above the politics of the day. We can hardly expect more since justices are *not* appointed to the bench because they are the most learned, wise, brave, or even just jurists, but mainly because they hold the same ideologies as the president who appoints them. That frailty is evident in the authoritative Supreme Court decisions eloquently written by learned justices in the most persuasive terms that uphold and rationalize manifest injustice. Some prominent examples follow.

Manifest Injustice in American Law

Chief Justice John Marshall is considered the greatest chief justice of all time. Like Elvis, he is widely considered the king. Nevertheless, he bowed on numerous occasions to the prejudices of his day. Marshall upheld human slavery in *Boyce v. Anderson* (1829) and *The Antelope* (1825), even though he knew the institution was morally wrong.[18]

The Antelope involved a dispute between Spain and Portugal over the ownership of 280 Africans. Marshall found that the slave trade was contrary to the law of nature and prohibited by the laws of most civilized nations. But so long as it was not prohibited by the law of the two nations who claimed ownership of the slaves, he upheld it.[19] In upholding the morally repugnant law of those nations, Marshall apologized, stating "this Court must not yield to feelings which might seduce it from the path of duty [to] obey the mandate of the law."[20] Morality and abstract notions of justice could play no role in the resolution of the property dispute:

> Whatever might be the answer of a moralist to this question, a jurist must search for its legal solution, in those principles of action which are sanctioned by the usages, the national acts, and the general assent, of

that portion of the world of which he considers himself a part, and to whose law the appeal is made. If we resort to this standard as the test of international law, the question, as has already been observed, is decided in favour of the legality of the [slave] trade. Both Europe and America embarked in it; and for nearly two centuries, it was carried on without opposition, and without censure. A jurist could not say, that a practice thus supported was illegal, and that those engaged in it might be punished, either personally, or by deprivation of property.[21]

The institution of slavery was thus confirmed, irrespective of the harsh outcome for the Africans. That reprehensible institution was never struck down by the Supreme Court, although it had several opportunities to do so. Tragically, slavery remained in effect until the close of the Civil War, when it was finally banned, not by the courts, but by the Thirteenth Amendment to the US Constitution.

The *Dred Scott* case (1856) furnishes another infamous example where the Supreme Court eschewed a just outcome.[22] In that case, Dred Scott, a slave, placed the legality of slavery squarely before the Court when he sued his master for his freedom and that of his family. Such a claim was unheard of in 1856, when the law permitted slavery in most states, but Scott nonetheless asked the courts to protect this most basic human right. However, the Supreme Court dismissed the case, disclaiming jurisdiction to hear the controversial action. The problem confounding the court was whether a slave has access to bring lawsuits in American courts:

The question is simply this: Can a negro, whose ancestors were imported into this country, and sold as slaves, become a member of the political community formed and brought into existence by the Constitution of the United States, and as such become entitled to all the rights, and privileges, and immunities, guaranteed by that instrument to the citizen? One of which rights is the privilege of suing in a court of the United States in the cases specified in the Constitution.[23]

Writing for the Court, Chief Justice Roger Taney held that neither slaves nor their descendants could sue in the federal courts because they are not, and could never become, *citizens*, even after emancipation, as that term is used in the Constitution. They were not intended to be citizens because the framers of the Constitution considered them "a subordinate and inferior class of beings, who had been subjugated by the dominant race."[24] Like Marshall, Taney disavowed any interest in ethics or justice. He focused only upon divining the intent of the long-dead framers:

> It is not the province of the court to decide upon the justice or injustice, the policy or impolicy, of these laws. The decision of that question belonged to the political or law-making power; to those who formed the sovereignty and framed the Constitution. The duty of the court is, to interpret the instrument they have framed, with the best lights we can obtain on the subject, and to administer it as we find it, according to its true intent and meaning when it was adopted.[25]

Since Dred Scott was not entitled to use the courts, Taney dutifully dismissed the case. This outcome safely ducked the controversial issue and comported with popular opinion about the inferior status of blacks in the American political system. Taney asserted that his unjust disposition rested not upon prevailing prejudice, but upon supposedly immutable legal principles:

> No one, we presume, supposes that any change in public opinion or feeling, in relation to this unfortunate race, in the civilized nations of Europe or in this country, should induce the court to give to the words of the Constitution a more liberal construction [than intended by the framers]. Any other rule of construction would abrogate the judicial character of this court, and make it the mere reflex of the popular opinion or passion of the day. This court was not created for such purposes. Higher and graver trusts have been confided to it, and it must not falter in the path of duty.[26]

Despite this sanctimonious attempt to clothe an unjust ruling with a legal principle, Taney's decision was repudiated by the Thirteenth Amendment to the US Constitution, adopted in the wake of the bloody Civil War. The infamous case is no longer cited by the Supreme Court as legal precedent.

The slave cases produced unjust outcomes that even Rehnquist cannot explain away, not only because the courts were closed to slaves, but also because leading jurists were captive to prevailing prejudice and unable to rise above the politics of the day. Even after the courts were opened to blacks by the Thirteenth and Fourteenth amendments, the judicial system continued to produce uniformly unjust outcomes in cases involving blacks until 1954, when *Brown* was decided. Most of the judges in those cases willingly reflected and implemented prevailing prejudices against blacks and other groups—and their decisions belie the widely held notion that the legal system equates with justice. Discussion of a few of the postslavery cases illustrates the frailty of the bench.

Plessy v. Ferguson (1896) announced the infamous separate-but-equal doctrine for segregating the races in all aspects of American life.[27] That case upheld a Louisiana law requiring separation of races. When Plessy, a black, attempted to sit in a train car designated for white people, the conductor removed him and placed him in a car set aside for blacks. The unfortunate traveler was later prosecuted for violating a law that prohibited persons of one race from riding in the same car with members of another race. In upholding the law, it was self-evident to Justice Henry Brown, who wrote the opinion, that similar laws segregating schools, theaters, and juries have "no tendency to destroy the legal equality of the two races" and do not "imply the inferiority of either race."[28] Based upon these legal fictions, which are assumptions of fact used by the courts to decide questions of law, the Court held that enforced separation "neither abridges the privileges or immunities of the colored man, deprives him of his property without due process of law, nor denies him the equal protection of the laws."[29] Bowing to prevailing prejudices, the Court allowed Louisiana "to act with reference to the established usages, customs and traditions of the people."[30] If Plessy felt enforced separation of the races "stamps the colored races with a badge of inferiority...it is not by reason of anything found in the act, but solely because the colored race chooses to put that construction on it."[31] After all, "[i]f one race be inferior to the other socially, the Constitution of the United States cannot put them upon the same plane."[32] Not all of the justices agreed with Brown's sophistry. Justice John Marshall Harlan's blistering dissent pointed out the apparent injustice of the law and the practical absurdities of segregating America. He rejected the "cunningly devised" doctrine to separate the races "under the pretense of recognizing equality of rights" and predicted that the decision would "in time, prove to be as pernicious as the decision made by this tribunal in the Dred Scott case."[33]

Justice Brown's long-lived separate-but-equal doctrine left an enduring brown stain on the country. It was applied to Chinese Americans in

Gong Lum v. Rice (1927).[34] It legalized white supremacy until repudiated by *Brown* in 1954.

Like blacks, Asian Americans have been subjected to miscarriages of justice by the courts when prejudice against these minorities was prevalent. In *Korematsu v. United States* (1945), the Supreme Court upheld a sweeping military order issued during World War II that removed the entire Japanese population from the West Coast for alleged security reasons and placed them in concentration camps, based solely on their ancestry.[35] Their removal was summarily executed without evidence, hearing, or any other inquiry into their loyalty or security threat. Justice Hugo Black acknowledged that "all legal restrictions which curtail the civil rights of a single racial group are immediately suspect," but nonetheless concluded that the removal program was legal. The sweeping program was upheld based upon the government's fear that some Japanese might engage in espionage, though no evidence of either allegation was ever presented. It must be remembered that racial animosity against "Japs" and undifferentiated fear of the "Yellow Peril" were intense following the attack on Pearl Harbor. Justice Felix Frankfurter readily concurred, stating that the removal program must be judged in the wartime context and not be "stigmatized as lawless, because like action in times of peace would be lawless."[36]

Three justices dissented. One bluntly noted that the "assembly center" was simply "a euphemism for prison" and the "relocation centers" were "a euphemism for concentration camps" and described the program as a "plan for forcible detention." Another justice felt the program "goes over the very brink of constitutional power and falls into the ugly abyss of racism."[37] He decried governmental decisions based upon the discriminatory attitudes toward Japanese Americans pervading the country and warned that judicial sanction of such decisions would encourage "discriminatory actions against other minority groups in the passions of tomorrow."[38] He dissented "from this legalization of racism." The third justice noted that court approval constitutes a greater threat to liberty than the removal program itself because the legal principles used to validate racial discrimination will become "like a loaded weapon ready for the hand of any authority that can bring forward a plausible claim of an urgent need."[39] He pointed to a recent example of that concern, the approval of a race-based curfew placed upon Japanese Americans in *Hirabayashi v. United States* (1943),[40] stating:

[I]n spite of our limiting words we did validate a discrimination on the basis of ancestry for mild and temporary deprivation of liberty. Now the principle of racial discrimination is pushed from support of mild measures to very harsh ones, and from temporary deprivations to indeterminate ones. And the precedent which it is said to require us to do this is *Hirabayashi*.[41]

This dissenter also argued that when a court approves an unconstitutional military order, it ceases to be a court of law and becomes an instrument of military policy. Despite these well-reasoned dissents, the popular prejudices prevailed.

Rather than provide a bulwark against racial animosity, the Supreme Court bowed to prevailing racial hostility. We cannot turn a blind eye to the miscarriages of justice in *Korematsu* and *Hirabayashi*. Those decisions destroyed the liberty of over 100,000 people. Recognizing this grave injustice, Congress later enacted a law in 1988 to apologize to the interred Japanese Americans, and it provided reparations of $20,000 to each victim.[42]

Does *Korematsu* provide legal precedent for removing and imprisoning Americans of Middle Eastern descent during the war on terrorism, as feared by the dissenters in that case? Absolutely. The legal system cannot always be relied upon to dispense justice nor can it always be equated with that ideal.

There are many reasons why the system sometimes fails to live up to our expectations and ideals in important cases affecting the most basic human rights of American minorities, despite safeguards built into the system. The primary responsibility lies with those jurists who cannot rise above prevailing prejudice and politics hostile to minority groups. In cases involving oppressed minorities, our safeguards and ideals do insist upon a heightened judicial *responsibility* to protect their human rights. That defining task of the courts requires judicial independence and the courage to row against the tide of popular opinion. The troubling reluctance of judges to act as a bulwark against injustice places them—and other officers of the court who accept or support a system that is oppressive of human rights—in the moral predicament aptly described by Martin Luther King Jr.: "To accept passively an unjust system is to cooperate with that system," or, even worse, to become a willing instrument of that unjust system.[43] Despite judicial disclaimers found in unjust court opinions, the American system has invested courts with the power to strike down unjust laws and acts of government. Alexis de Tocqueville correctly observed in 1835 that American judges enjoy the remarkable power "to found their decisions on the Constitution rather than on the laws" because the Constitution "left them at liberty not to apply such laws as may appear to them to be unconstitutional."[44]

There Is a Need to Root Out Vestiges of Racism in Federal Indian Law

Many cases affecting Native Americans have produced stark injustices like the ones described previously. Those cases usually describe Indians as "inferior," "ignorant," "savages," "heathens," or "uncivilized." In *Lone Wolf v. Hitchcock* (1903), for example, the Supreme Court upheld congressional authority to abrogate Indian treaties partly because Indians are "an ignorant and dependent race."[45] In *Montoya v. United States* (1901), "uncivilized Indians" did not possess ordinary nationhood, "[o]wing to the natural infirmities of the Indian character, their fiery tempers, impatience of restraint, their mutual jealousies and animosities, their nomadic habits, and lack of mental training."[46] *Johnson v. M'Intosh* (1823) approved the appropriation of title to all tribal land in the United States, because Indians are "heathens" and "fierce savages."[47] In *Johnson*, the Supreme Court referred to Indians as racially inferior people. Based upon the language employed by the Court for the next one hundred years, that perception never changed. Thus, in the important cases defining Native American rights, the decisions branded Indians as savages—that is, brutish people who lack attributes normal to civilized human beings—and treated them accordingly. This judicial attitude ushers us into the realm of racism, a dark place where prejudice and hatred preside. That realm will be investigated closely as we examine the ten worst cases.

Racism is defined in *Webster's* dictionary as the assumption of inherent racial superiority of certain races and the consequent discrimination against other races, and it includes any doctrine or program of discrimination based on such an assumption.[48] The pejorative racial descriptions and stereotypes of American Indians found in court opinions are hallmarks of prejudice that fall squarely within the definition of racism. They comport with widespread white animosity toward American Indians that prevailed during the expansion of the frontier and settlement of the West.[49] Racism has pervaded Indian-white relations since colonial times, and based upon the language found in court opinions, it is strongly evident in federal Indian law. The unique themes of racism against American Indians (i.e., savagery versus civilization, heathens versus Christians, and inferiors versus superiors) are the by-products of Manifest Destiny, which are familiar, according to Justice Stanley Reed in 1955, to "every American schoolboy."[50] Racial prejudice against Indians could provide comfort to settlers and others who dispossessed them; and open contempt for their culture affords justification for replacing it with a superior Christian society. In studying the dark side of federal Indian law, we shall examine racism in all its forms—from the old-fashioned, foot-stomping racism of the South, to more sophisticated institutional, scientific, and legal racism, as well as its nasty little brother, ethnocentrism; and we shall also confront religious discrimination and intolerance engrained in the dark side of the law.

This unfortunate line of thought was thoroughly embedded in the American psyche. Its origins date from medieval times, when European religious and legal thinkers developed legal doctrines for relating to non-Christian infidels of other lands and the newly discovered inhabitants of the New World. Those doctrines were transplanted to the Western Hemisphere after 1492 as the cornerstone for relations with Native peoples, ultimately finding their way into the American judicial system in cases like those illustrated earlier. By incorporating this cultural baggage, the courts have created a remarkable body of law, one that is derived from a racially discriminatory ideology. Through repeated use in Indian cases, racial prejudice has been turned into legal principles by the Supreme Court. While the Supreme Court no longer openly describes Native Americans in pejorative terms in modern opinions, it commonly relies upon and gives effect to older cases that turn on such descriptions.

Unlike the African, Japanese, and Chinese American cases, the tainted legal principles of federal Indian law have not been overturned or repudiated. No paradigm shift in legal thinking similar to that which motivated the Supreme Court to overturn principles of segregation in *Brown* has prompted the Court to abandon these oppressive legal principles. The nation has not seriously addressed the by-products of Manifest Destiny in the same way that it came to terms with the institution of slavery. Historian Patricia Nelson Limerick aptly observes:

> To most twentieth-century Americans, the legacy of slavery was serious
> business, the legacy of conquest was not…The subject of slavery was the
> domain of serious scholars and the occasion of sober national reflection;
> the subject of conquest was the domain of mass entertainment and the

occasion of light-hearted national escapism. An element of regret for "what we did to the Indians" had entered the picture, but the dominant feature of conquest remained "adventure." Children happily played "cowboys and Indians" but stopped short of "masters and slaves."[51]

The reasons for this disparate treatment are all around us. The depopulation of Native Americans has reduced the demands of this small minority group to a whisper; the popular cultural myth of the vanishing red man, along with America's preoccupation with maintaining a positive self-image, contribute to the inattention. Also, Americans often employ a sort of mental statute of limitations that provides, "if injustice occurred it must have been long ago in a dimly lit past, so it is no longer relevant."[52] Or, like Rehnquist, we can simply deny that injustice ever occurred. "Selective amnesia [has] its uses," Limerick points out, "even in a nation devoted to the memory of its frontier origins."[53]

However, until Native Americans are freed from unjust legal principles shaped by racism, they will not fare well in the courts of the conqueror and justice will remain elusive. What will it take to motivate the Supreme Court to rethink, reverse, and replace these tainted legal principles, and how long? Native Americans find it difficult to wait, for the same reasons expressed in Reverend King's "Letter from Birmingham Jail":

> For years now I have heard the word "Wait!" It rings in the ear of every Negro with a piercing familiarity. This "Wait" has almost always meant "Never." We must come to see with the distinguished jurist of yesterday that "justice too long delayed is justice denied."[54]

Judges and legal practitioners should not passively accept an inherited foundation of unjust legal principles. Courts can discard them as self-evident vestiges of racial discrimination in appropriate cases without waiting for congressional mandates or social upheaval. That is a task for the entire legal profession as we stride toward a just culture in the twenty-first century.

There Is a Need to Eradicate Unjust Legal Fictions in Federal Indian Law

The need for legal reform becomes painfully clear when we examine the unjust legal fictions found in federal Indian law. Many settler states foster unjust legal fictions in their domestic law pertaining to Native peoples. In settler states, it is amusing to see the lengths jurists go in fashioning legal fictions, theories, and doctrines to support the taking of Native land and the governance of Native peoples as colonized subjects. A legal fiction is an assumption of fact made by a court as a basis for deciding a legal question.[55] Apparently, the assumptions of fact need have little or no bearing to reality.

Some far-fetched legal fictions used to decide legal questions in the United States and other settler states are:

1. *Aboriginal land is vacant land.*[56] Of course, nothing could be further from the truth. Unless we also assume that Natives are invisible, this legal fiction cannot be taken seriously. Nevertheless, this assumption that Native land is vacant and thus owned by no one operates to transfer indigenous property to colonists in some cases and statutes, such as the South Australia Act of 1834. This fiction was enlarged into a larger fantasy in some colonies to equate settlement of inhabited land with settlement of uninhabited land.[57] This allowed Europeans to simply walk in and occupy inhabited land.[58]

2. *The Pope of the Catholic Church can give the Western Hemisphere to Spain.* The pope has no such legal power, even under the most tortured view of property law. Yet, Spain appropriated Central and South America under this legal fiction, destroying every civilization in its path and killing millions of innocent people during the conquest and colonization of those lands.[59] A similar view is found in British statutes, like the South Australia Act of 1834, that sell Native land in distant places to British subjects.

3. *Royal charters empower colonists to settle Native territory as if they were the first human beings in the area.*[60] This curious legal fiction ignores the presence of indigenous people and tortures the purposes of royal charters establishing British penal colonies in places like Georgia and Australia. Georgia's charter simply resettled English inmates in an American penal colony. That hardly grants prisoners "the soil, and [power over all Native American] inhabitants from sea to sea," as later espoused by Georgians.[61] Besides, how can royal charters have binding legal effect on foreign landowners? It is hard to imagine the jurisdictional basis for giving legal effect to British law in America. That idea contravenes fundamental jurisdictional principles since the domestic laws of any nation do not normally have effect in lands beyond national boundaries.

4. *The discovery of North America by European explorers transfers legal title to Indian land to the United States.*[62] This legal fiction is a fixture in America law, even though the Supreme Court describes it as "an extravagant and absurd idea."[63] I agree. If Europeans really possess such extraordinary legal power, every country would ban their presence to protect their soil and prohibit entry, even as visitors, lest the land be appropriated by itinerates with such immense extraterritorial powers of appropriation. Besides, this legal fiction is arbitrary. Why should only Europeans possess such immense legal powers that extend far beyond the borders of their own lands?

5. *The discovery of North America by Europeans can be equated with the conquest of that continent.*[64] This is another illogical and absurd assumption. American soil "was occupied by numerous and warlike nations, equally willing and able to defend their possessions."[65] The legal fiction espoused in *Johnson v. M'Intosh* (1823) grew into a judicial myth that all "the savage tribes of this continent were deprived of their ancestral ranges by force," when, as a matter of fact, most Native American lands were not acquired by force of arms.[66] While the ideology of conquest is no longer shared by the American public, it is still harbored by the courts.[67] Europeans may be powerful folks, but the mere sight of foreign lands by their sailors scarcely brings the inhabitants to their knees under any stretch of the imagination.

6. *The normal rules of international law requiring conquerors to respect property rights in the lands they occupy do not apply in America because Indian tribes are too savage and warlike.*[68] Under international law, the United States does not own Iraq or Afghanistan simply because it invaded those countries, even though the tribes and warlords of those lands might be described as warlike. Furthermore, this novel exception to international law created by Chief Justice John Marshall in *Johnson* would completely nullify international law if applied uniformly to most nations of the world, especially the warlike United States.[69]

7. *Native land is wasteland or a savage wilderness that no one owns, uses, or wants and is available for the taking by colonists—therefore any aboriginal interests in the land are extinguished as soon as British subjects settle the area.*[70] This fiction ignores the inherent value of land and the uses made by Native peoples in their aboriginal habitats. It is nothing more that a pretext for taking land

belonging to others; and it is the central premise of the South Australia Act, which declared all the land as "waste and unoccupied." If Native land was worthless, why did the colonists invest so much time, money, and bloodshed to wrest it away from the Native peoples? Why not give worthless wasteland back to the people who valued it? Furthermore, the same can be said for vast wastelands and savage places like the ghettos of New York City or the seamy side of Hollywood, California, but that does not mean foreigners can simply take those lands. Otherwise, Spaniards and British colonists would be streaming into many American cities, claiming them for pointy-headed potentates in Europe.

8. *Native peoples have no concept of property, do not claim any property rights, or are incapable of owning land.*[71] This fiction is bolstered by the false beliefs that indigenous peoples have no notion of property, that Natives are nomads who do not stay in one place long enough to own property, or that they are too low on the social scale to own land, and so forth. In Australia, the English immediately pronounced that Aboriginals were "landless" and "propertyless"—a fiction that continued until 1992, when the High Court belatedly admitted that Natives "are very tenacious of their ownership of the land" and capable of owning land.[72] Those fanciful ideas evaporated much sooner in American colonies, when settlers were confronted by powerful Indian tribes intent on defending their land and found preexisting property-rights systems everywhere they went.[73]

9. *Christians have a right to take land from non-Christians because heathens lack property rights.* Since colonization brings Christianity to heathens, so the argument goes, surely this benefit is payment enough for taking their land.[74] The supposed right to simply take non-Christian land (a notion found in royal charters) turned on the Eurocentric legal fiction that heathens lack property rights. At bottom, however, the religious justification for confiscating land was largely a pretext. British colonization had little to do with Christianity, and as time went along the pretext was largely abandoned.[75] Furthermore, if heathens (i.e., non-Christians) really do lack property rights, precious few landowners can be found in most places.

10. *Native lands are surplus lands.* Under this "there is room enough for everyone" argument, colonists can occupy "surplus" land since any unused portions of

Native territory should simply be available for the taking. (Gee, do the Indians really need all the land?) This theory sees entire continents as largely empty places—vacant wildernesses—abounding with idle land unused for farming or other pursuits, waiting for Europeans. Does this doctrine apply to the vast ranches and other landholdings of rich Americans, Canadians, and Australians—do they really need it all? Put in that light, the doctrine immediately becomes a far-fetched basis to simply take someone else's land.

11. *Native peoples cannot govern themselves—they need guardianship or tutelage for their own good.*[76] This assumption of fact, which is relied upon as the legal basis for imposing European hegemony over Native peoples, stems from Franciscus de Victoria's law of nations.[77] It is based upon the false idea that indigenous peoples had no forms of government and are inherently incapable of self-government. The legal fiction also contributed to popular ideas of the white man's burden and Manifest Destiny that elevated bare imperialism as a noble undertaking in the public mind. The justifications for guardianship over Native peoples rest on notions of racial supremacy and extreme cultural ethnocentricity in which indigenous peoples are viewed as inferior, backward, and uncivilized heathens, without the capacity of self-government. However, the barbaric conduct of the Spanish in the Western Hemisphere demonstrated they were not qualified to be the guardians of anyone.[78] Nonetheless, the rule of Native peoples by guardianship is a venerable instrument of colonialism. At its core, this institution simply means, "I own your property and can control your person any way I see fit." Premised on the presumed racial, religious, and cultural superiority of Europeans, guardianship has been used extensively by colonizing nations to manage Native peoples and control their property in colonies around the world while they shoplifted their resources and wealth.[79] The guardianship principle is also the source of the plenary power doctrine of *Lone Wolf v. Hitchcock* (1903), which unleashed absolute legislative power over Native peoples in the United States.[80] While the protectorate nature of the guardianship principle is critical to the well-being of Native peoples in settler states, the principle sometimes leads to abuse. The dark side of guardianship arises when the principle is relied upon to unilaterally increase federal hegemony over Indian tribes, supplant tribal authority over internal affairs, and even to peer into bedrooms on Indian reservations to ensure that the dress, religion, and marital customs of Native Americans comport with "civilized" standards imposed by the government. The enforced acculturation, including

the taking of children and stamping out of Native languages, religions, and ways of life that occurred in the United States amounted to ethnocide—it was justified by courts under the guardianship principle.[81]

12. *Native peoples are racially inferior.* American court opinions describe Native Americans as "inferior," "savages," "heathens," and "uncivilized."[82] The use of pejorative racial invectives and stereotypes amounts to racism, as commonly defined in dictionary books.[83] The continued reliance by the US Supreme Court on decisions that turn upon the legal fiction that Indians are racially inferior has led to a call among legal scholars to root out vestiges of racism from federal Indian law.[84] Most of those cases have never been reversed. One would expect courts to be the last places to harbor racial prejudice, which should have no place in any courtroom. With such attitudes, it is hardly surprising that "the coming of the whites was an unmitigated disaster for everyone with black skin" in Australia.[85] Early colonial reports in Australia noted that colonists felt Aborigines were "not members of the human family, but…inferior animals created for their own use."[86] If a group of people are racially inferior and backward, colonists can simply occupy their lands without bothering to conquer them under the law of the colonizers, since the benefits of Christianity and civilization will uplift the inferior races and provide justification for colonizing their land.[87]

13. *Europeans can engage in just war against Native people if they do not submit to colonization.*[88] Was the use of military and civilian force to colonize Native territories legal? In America and Australia, the indigenous peoples were hunted, shot, poisoned, and attacked by settlers and soldiers as part of the colonization process, and a one-hundred-year period of constant warfare took place between Indian nations, bands, and confederacies and the United States. Some of the violence may have been lawful acts of war and others pure murder. No comprehensive factual and legal analysis of the legality of that violence has been performed.

It is time to identify and retire the many foolish, unjust, and injurious legal fictions in the law pertaining to indigenous peoples. They simply have no place in any legal system and should be rejected, not perpetuated, by modern courts. There comes a time when every society rethinks its values and readjusts the law to root out unjust principles from bygone eras. Just like the legal fictions applied in *Plessy v. Ferguson* (1896)—that blacks are racially inferior and segregation is not harmful or denigrating—were finally rejected in *Brown v. Board of Education* (1954), similar legal fictions regarding indigenous peoples must go.

In *Brown*, the Supreme Court overturned the invidious separate-but-equal doctrine of *Plessy*—a foundational legal principle in American society that had been used by segregationists for over half a century to segregate the races in all walks of American life. It was a skeletal principle since the American economy and most social and educational institutions were built on it. However, the court rejected the legal fictions of that doctrine and found that segregation is harmful to black schoolchildren as a matter of fact:

> Whatever may have been the extent of psychological knowledge at the time of *Plessy v. Ferguson*, this finding is amply supported by modern authority. Any language in *Plessy v. Ferguson* contrary to this finding is rejected. We conclude that in the field of public education the doctrine of "separate but equal" has no place. Separate educational facilities are inherently unequal.[89]

Similarly, in the watershed, but belated case of *Mabo and Others v. Queensland (No. 2)* (1992), the High Court of Australia recognized that unjust legal fictions invite critical examination:

> Although this Court is free to depart from English precedent which was earlier followed as stating the common law of this country (59), it cannot do so where the departure would fracture what I have called the skeleton of principle...The peace and order of Australian society is built on the legal system. It can be modified to bring it into conformity with contemporary notions of justice and human rights, but it cannot be destroyed. It is not possible, a priori, to distinguish between cases that express a skeletal principle and those which do not, but no case can command unquestioning adherence if the rule it expresses seriously offends the values of justice and human rights (especially equality before the law) which are aspirations of the contemporary Australian legal system. If a postulated rule of the common law expressed in earlier cases seriously offends those contemporary values, the question arises whether the rule should be maintained and applied. Whenever such a question

arises, it is necessary to assess whether the particular rule is an essential doctrine of our legal system and whether, if the rule were to be overturned, the disturbance to be apprehended would be disproportionate to the benefit flowing from the overturning.[90]

The *Mabo* Court declared that when legal doctrines and fictions "depended on a discriminatory denigration of indigenous inhabitants, their social organization and customs," which are "false in fact and unacceptable in our society," the courts can overrule them.[91] Similar to *Brown,* the Australian High Court overruled cases that fail to recognize Native land title:

> To maintain the authority of those cases would destroy the equality of all Australian citizens before the law. The common law of this country would perpetuate injustice if it were to continue to embrace the enlarged notion of terra nullius and to persist in characterizing the indigenous inhabitants of the Australian colonies as people too low in the social scale of social organization to be acknowledged as possessing rights and interests in land.[92]

In sum, twenty-first-century scholars, jurists, and lawmakers should identify the unjust legal fictions pertaining to indigenous peoples and root them out to cleanse the law. I respectfully disagree with the suggestions in *Mabo* that the "law is a prisoner of its history" or "skeletal principles" are sacrosanct.[93] No unjust skeletal principle can command slavish adherence where it defeats the values of justice and human rights ideals sought in contemporary legal systems. The function of the law is to serve a changing society and uphold its values, not to hold it prisoner to an unjust past. The unjust notion that indigenous peoples are "so low in the scale of social organization" that they have no rights was rejected by the *Mabo* court as no longer untenable in contemporary society. The court explained:

> If it were permissible in past centuries to keep the common law in step with international law, it is imperative in today's world that the common law should neither be seen to be frozen in an age of racial discrimination…The fiction by which the rights and interests of indigenous inhabitants in land were treated as non-existence was justified by a policy which has no place in the contemporary law of this country…Whatever

the justification advanced in earlier days for refusing to recognize the rights and interests in land of the indigenous inhabitants of settled colonies, an unjust and discriminatory doctrine of that kind can no longer be accepted. The expectations of the international community accord in this respect with the contemporary values of the Australian people.[94]

The presence of manifest injustice in American law need not be tolerated. We can address the dark side of federal Indian law and make it more just. There is no longer any need for settler-state legal systems to treat Native people as racially inferior, colonized subjects. The peace and order of no civilized society depends on oppressing minorities. To the contrary, the United Nations Declaration on the Rights of Indigenous Peoples (2007) calls on each nation to uplift the legal rights of its Native peoples so that their survival, dignity, and well-being are assured. *Mabo* correctly states that contemporary international law "is a legitimate and important influence on the development of the common law, especially when international law declares the existence of universal human rights."[95] Therefore, just as early international law was relied upon by settler states to strip indigenous peoples of their legal rights, the declaration calls upon the legal systems of those nations to restore those rights. If the declaration is implemented with the same fervor that earlier international law doctrines were followed in the colonial era, a sea change in the way that the law views indigenous peoples will occur.

The Prosecution Rests

PART TWO

Affairs of the Living

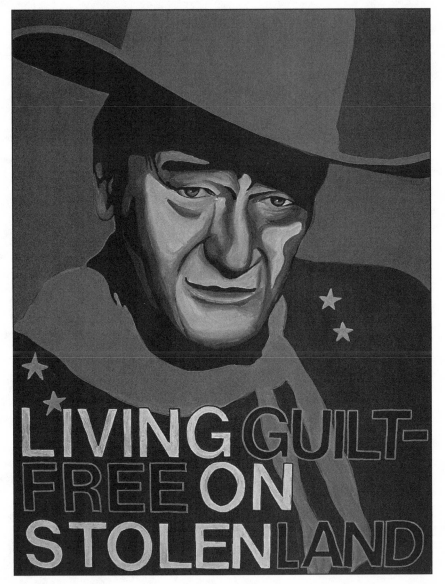

Your Hero

CHAPTER FOUR

Johnson v. M'Intosh: How the Indians Lost Legal Title to America

IN 1773, WILLIAM MURRAY bravely crossed the Allegheny Mountains carrying a forged British legal opinion into the forbidden zone set aside by the king for Indian tribes. The fraudulent document was altered to allow him to purchase Indian land, an act otherwise prohibited by the law of the redcoats. Once deep in the heart of Indian country, the sweaty-palmed agent handed the fake document to the local British commander, who fell for the trick. Thus, Murray was allowed to buy land, even though he and his wealthy backers knew it was illegal under British law. Thus begins the story of the spurious land claim in *Johnson v. M'Intosh*, one of the ten worst Indian law cases ever decided.[1]

Huraaru—from the beginning, it was all about land. To the American Indian tribes, Mother Earth is the wellspring of indigenous culture, religion, and economic life. It forms the identity of Native Americans as indigenous peoples. Unlike Central and South America, where Native American civilizations adorned with gold and mountains made of silver lay available for the taking, Mother Earth was the principal asset in North America. Even before the first British ships landed on Virginia shores, the colonists wondered, *Can we simply take the land, or do we have to buy it?* The astounding "discovery" of the New World was one of the most important events in the history of mankind, and an equally remarkable legal doctrine was needed by the Europeans to reduce the land to their ownership and possession. The problem, of course, was the Indian tribes. By 1600, the British knew the continent was already fully inhabited, but did the Indians *really* own the land? That question was of paramount importance in founding the colonies because "the dominant purpose of the whites in America," according to the United States Supreme Court, "was to occupy the land."[2]

Indeed, the *very* purpose of the colonists was to acquire the vast expanse of land that lay before them that was seemingly available for the taking; and the unrelenting greed for land—Indian land—became the driving engine for the expansion and settlement of the western frontiers by the American settlers after they won independence from Britain. In a remarkably short span, nearly the entire continent was transferred from indigenous to nonindigenous hands by various means. Was that massive, one-way transfer of land legal?

This chapter explores the legal foundation for land ownership in the United States. Plainly, a clear and very potent legal right was needed by the colonists to support their occupation of Indian territory and to obtain ownership of the land. Otherwise, their occupation must at its core be considered illegal and illegitimate.

To provide the setting for the *Johnson* case, we will first examine early legal theories for acquiring Indian land in British North America under the redcoats and then look at land speculation during colonial times and in the early days of the new republic until 1823, when *Johnson* was decided. Finally, I will tell the story of the *Johnson* case and its far-reaching impacts on American Indians.

It is amazing that over 750 law review articles and several books have been written about *Johnson v. M'Intosh* in recent times, yet it was not until 2005 that the first complete story of this case was told. In 1991, a law professor named Lindsay G. Robertson made a startling find: a trunk containing the complete corporate records of the plaintiff land companies in that case. The records reveal a truly sordid tale of collusion by many of the leading figures of the day, surrounding a fraudulent purchase of an enormous tract of Indian land by wealthy land speculators. They sought to validate their illegal purchase through a friendly lawsuit about a feigned controversy that was conceived and prosecuted by crafty lawyers—influence peddlers, really— and this case was decided by a chief justice of the Supreme Court who possessed an enormous stake in the outcome. The opinion thus produced contained far-reaching dicta that gravely compromised Indian land rights in the United States, even though no Indian tribes were parties to the case. This entire affair occurred within the context of speculation in land owned and occupied by Indian tribes.[3]

The serious irregularities in this litigation brought to light by Robertson gravely impugn the legitimacy of the *Johnson* decision and should leave many to wonder whether the decision is entitled to receive continuing effect by the courts. Yet at this writing, *Johnson* does remain a *landmark* decision in the United States and several other settler states that restrict indigenous land rights. It provides the foundation for modern land ownership in those nations.

Early Theories for Obtaining Land Occupied by Indian Tribes

In the beginning, the Pilgrims and Puritans debated several theories to justify occupation and acquisition of land inhabited by Indians. The most optimistic viewpoint was that the land was not owned by anyone and was simply available for the taking. After all, the British royal charters clearly empowered the newcomers to settle and occupy any non-Christian lands and establish colonies, didn't they? As law professor Stuart Banner observes, the charters granted property rights as if the colonists "were to be the first human beings in the area."[4] This fiction was bolstered by the false notions that the Indians themselves had no concept of property, did not claim any property rights, or were otherwise seen by the newcomers as incapable of owning land.[5] Indians did not have any laws, they argued, and were nomads who did not stay in one place long enough, it seemed, to acquire property rights in land. However, once the settlers were confronted by powerful Indian tribes, the belief that no one owned the land quickly evaporated and nagging doubts arose whether their settlement on Indian land was actually legal. Furthermore, any notion of unowned land was complete nonsense, according to Banner, since the "English found a pre-existing system of property rights everywhere they went."[6]

Even if Indian land ownership was conceded, some colonists and colonies took the land under other theories. Foremost among them was the "religious justification" argument—that Christians have a right to take land from non-Christians. Since colonization brings Christianity to heathens, so the argument went, surely this benefit is payment enough for taking Indian land. *After all, we cannot Christianize the Indians unless we can settle nearby on their lands.* This supposed right to simply take non-Christian land turned also upon the Eurocentric legal fiction that heathens lack property rights. At bottom, however, the religious justification of the English, like that of the Spanish, was largely a pretext. The colonization of the Americas had little to do with Christianity, and as time went along the pretext was abandoned. As the "English settled more of North America, the religious justification for acquiring land virtually disappeared," according to Banner, and the supposed right of Christians to take non-Christian land is scarcely found after the early seventeenth century.[7]

Yet other viable theories remained. Under the "there is room enough for everyone" argument, colonists could occupy surplus Indian land. After all, did the Indians really *need* all the land? Any unused portions of their territories should be available for the taking. This theory saw America as a largely empty continent—a vacant wilderness, really—abounding with idle land unused for farming or other civilized pursuits. *The greedy Indians were selfishly keeping all of the land to themselves!* Unfortunately, this theory also had its flaws.

First, even if American Indian tribes were being greedy, greed is not a legal basis for taking land. If it were, much land in the United States today would be available for the taking. *Do white people selfishly need all that land?* Second, the theory ignored the fact that many "vacant" lands were, in fact, places completely depopulated by the introduction of European diseases. Pilgrims could stroll through vacant villages and burial grounds looking for food because these places were already emptied by disease borne by newcomers from the Old World.[8] For example, most of the Inca were already dead before Francisco Pizarro entered their Peruvian empire, swept away by the advancing small pox introduced by the conquistadors.[9] Similar catastrophes rocked Native populations in North America. When Hernando de Soto entered the Mississippi Valley in the 1540s, he mapped numerous, heavily populated Native towns throughout the region. Yet one hundred years later, when the next Europeans entered the valley, the region had been completely depopulated by the apocalyptic diseases introduced by the de Soto expedition.[10] Finally, cultivation has never been a prerequisite to land ownership, even in England. The aboriginal use of land for hunting, fishing, and gathering is comparable to European-style farming since both uses provide subsistence and trade. Besides, Indians did farm their lands extensively, yielding indigenous crops (like corn, beans, squash, and pumpkins) for hungry Pilgrims and Natives alike.

In the end, the colonial authorities reluctantly concluded that the land *really did* belong to Indian occupants and the colonists would have to purchase it from them, despite wording to the contrary in Old World documents, such as the papal bulls and royal colonial charters, crafted by pointy-headed potentates of Europe. Consequently, the colonial practice of buying Indian land from Native owners over the next 150 years became widespread. This practice is documented by numerous Indian deeds recorded throughout the colonies, by statutes in every colony regulating purchases from Indian landowners, and in colonial court decisions recognizing Indians as landowners.[11] At bottom, the English were too weak to simply wrest the land from the more numerous and powerful tribes of the eastern seaboard, and they needed Indian allies against French competitors. Once the English began purchasing tribal land throughout the colonies, it became impossible to deny that Indians owned the land. But after the colonies achieved independence, the Supreme Court of the new republic was free to take a second look at the question of Indian land ownership in the United States. A strong legal foundation was needed for acquiring Indian land if the aspirations of the young nation were to be realized.

Land Speculation in the Colonies and the New American Republic

The *Johnson* case was decided in 1823 amidst a national economy that had been built over the past fifty years, in large measure, upon rampant speculation in Indian land, including land still owned and occupied by Indian tribes. The Supreme Court used that case as a vehicle to confirm American legal titles obtained under that system.

British law recognized Indians as owners of the land. In British America, the long-standing practice of individual colonists buying land directly from the Indians finally came to an end in 1763. To avert costly and unwanted Indian wars over increasingly shady private land sales, King George III issued the Royal Proclamation of 1763. This decree prohibited the settlement of any Indian land west of the Allegheny Mountains, ordered squatters to leave, and authorized only the Crown to acquire Indian lands. Thus, beginning in 1763, Indian land could only be purchased by colonial governments in the name of the Crown.

The proclamation transformed the booming market in Indian land, spawning a black market for those crafty colonists who could find ways around the British law. Some black marketers were simply land-hungry individuals who secretly bought small parcels from nearby Indian landowners for family farms or larger amounts for investments, despite the prohibition. For George Washington, black-market buying was simply a good investment opportunity. His writings indicate that he illicitly bought up as much Indian land west of the demarcation line as possible, as did many other prominent colonial figures, because

> notwithstanding the Proclamation that restrains it at present...I can never look upon the Proclamation in any other light (but this I say between ourselves) than as a temporary expedient to quiet the Minds of the Indians...Any person therefore who neglects the present opportunity of hunting out good Lands and in some measure marking and distinguishing them for their own (in order to keep others from settling them) will never regain it.[12]

Much speculation also was conducted by land companies funded by wealthy investors and formed to buy enormous tracts of land from Indians directly, even though it was illegal to do so, in the hopes of making immense profits by subdividing and reselling the land to Pilgrims in coonskin caps after the area was legally opened to settlement. One tactic was to acquire Indian land, then lobby colonial officials to buy it in the name of the Crown as the legal purchaser, using money provided by the speculator, and then grant the land back to the speculator. The well-capitalized companies greased the skids for this process by granting company shares to accommodating officials.[13] The only significant risk run by black-market speculators, like Washington, was that their illicit purchases might not be upheld or confirmed by the colonial authorities once the Crown actually acquired the land from the Indians. However, for those wealthy, well-placed speculators with influence over colonial and early American officials—who were often shareholders in the same enterprise—the risk was small and the potential returns were great.

In short, acquisition of Indian land was the preoccupation of many British colonists. The very purpose of the colonies was to occupy Native North America and generate wealth for colonists and kings.

After independence, the desire to own Indian land in the new American Republic continued unabated as the engine that drove the expansion and settlement of the nation. According to historian R. Kent Newmyer, land was the most abundant and ardently sought-after resource—a "magnet that attracted millions of immigrants."[14] George Washington observed that the "rage of speculation" in certain parts of the country was so intense "that scarce a valuable spot…is left without a claimant."[15]

The speculation increasingly extended to land still occupied by Indians. While the American government, like King George III, tried to limit and control private-land grabs, schemes for obtaining Indian land continued. Investment in land before it had been acquired from the Indians by the government was conducted by wealthy and prominent Americans through venture capital companies or purely private investment. Speculators lobbied the new government to take the necessary steps to confirm their title and possession of the land, no matter how it was acquired. It was hard for the government to keep pace with the land-hungry settlers.

In places like New York, Virginia, and Georgia, speculation was so intense that state legislatures—which were themselves composed largely of land speculators—not only recognized but granted legal, marketable interests in land *still owned and occupied* by Indian tribes, interests that took effect as soon as the tribal ownership interest could be retired by the federal government. These rights in Indian land were called "preemption rights." States commonly granted preemption rights to "deserving" citizens, such as Revolutionary War veterans. As investments, those rights soared in value as the machinery for displacing the tribes developed.

William Strickland, an English visitor to the early republic in the 1790s, was astonished at these practices. He observed that much speculation was in land still occupied by Indians. The market was trading in the prospect of owning Indian land once the government displaced the Indians. Accordingly, the traders cheered events like a "fortunate war" or "small pox."[16] By the time of Strickland's visit, virtually the entire eastern seaboard had been disposed of by the market. This placed immense pressure on the government to acquire Indian land and upon the courts to legitimize the process. More than thirty years later, Alexis de Tocqueville captured the land-hungry spirit of the new American nation in 1831 and 1832:

> It is difficult to describe the rapacity with which the American rushes forward to secure the immense booty which fortune proffers to him. In the pursuit he fearlessly braves the arrow of the Indian and the distempers of the forest; he is unimpressed by the silence of the woods; the approach of the beasts of prey does not disturb him; for he is goaded onwards by a passion more intense than the love of life. Before him lies a boundless continent, and he urges onward as if time pressed, and he was afraid of finding no room for his exertions...These men left their first country to improve their condition; they quit their resting-place to ameliorate it still more; fortune awaits them everywhere, but happiness they cannot attain. The desire of prosperity is become an ardent and restless passion in their minds which grows by what it gains.[17]

In sum, before stock markets were created in the United States, land was king and speculators drove the economy. Virtually every prominent leader during the Revolutionary War and first- and second-generation American politician was deeply involved in land speculation. Schoolbook fixtures like George Washington, John Marshall, Thomas Jefferson, Andrew Jackson, as well as most of the governors, judges, and legislators of the thirteen states were heavily involved in the buying, selling, investing in, or otherwise acquiring land or preemptive rights in Indian land. The market even extended to Indian land protected by treaties between the United States and Indian tribes. By 1823, when the *Johnson* case reached the Supreme Court, the US government was actively acquiring Indian land through treaty cessions throughout the nation—sometimes by arm's length negotiations, but often by coercion or the use of military force—and setting aside small parcels for the tribes. However, the pace of the government could not match the booming preemptive market because the states and private parties were busily granting warrants and investing in treaty-protected land set aside for the tribes before the ink on the treaties dried.

As might be expected, the frenzied circumstances surrounding the pervasive American land speculation were often intense and sometimes sleazy. On the seamy side of the market, things could be as crooked as a barrel of snakes. One such nefarious enterprise was William Murray's Illinois Land and Wabash Land companies, which in 1773 set about to secure 43,000 square miles of prime Indian land located in present-day Indiana and Illinois. The companies' determined efforts to legitimize their fraudulent and illegal purchases over the next fifty years led to the remarkable legal doctrine announced in *Johnson* for overcoming Indian title to America.

The Story of *Johnson v. M'Intosh*—
A Pattern of Shady Behavior

In 1773, the redcoats still ruled the American colonies. Our story begins during the tumultuous period leading to the Revolutionary War with an attempt by land speculators to buy Indian land in the forbidden zone beyond the Allegheny Mountains. Colonists hungered for land in the Northwest Territory, but it had been set aside from white settlement by the Royal Proclamation of 1763. This law created great anger among the colonists and became one of their complaints in the Declaration of Independence against the motherland, which led to the American Revolution. *How could the king allow Indians to live in a gated community where pioneering Pilgrims were not allowed?* No squatters of any kind were allowed in the Indians' territory and, worse yet, British law barred the purchase of Indian land in the forbidden zone by anyone but the Crown. Yet, someone in the black market had found a potential way around the law by altering an authoritative British legal opinion that originally pertained to the India Colony. By omitting and changing a word or two, the fake opinion was made to appear to authorize land purchases directly from Indians in North America, despite the prohibition of the proclamation.[18]

This forgery quickly prompted opportunistic investors to form the Illinois Land Company and send a buyer, William Murray, deep into Indian Country, to the very shores of the Mississippi River, which formed the western boundary of the British Empire. Murray presented the fake document to the local British military commander and was allowed to negotiate several large purchases on the basis of the fraudulent legal opinion. Murray first acquired 23,000 square miles of land in present-day Illinois, near St. Louis, for twelve horses, twelve cows, a quantity of flour, corn, and tobacco, some blankets and other articles of clothing, and miscellaneous implements, including twenty guns.[19] His second purchase was an enormous tract along the Wabash River north of the Ohio River in present-day Indiana and Illinois, which he bought from the Piankasaw Tribe for the Wabash Land Company. In all, Murray bought 43,000 square miles, an area about the size of New Jersey.

All of Murray's land lay within the boundaries of Virginia established by her royal charter. Today, Virginia is rather tiny, but it was once an enormous colony that extended from the Atlantic Ocean to the Mississippi River, near present-day St. Louis. In 1773, the Virginia Colony was bordered on the north by the Six Nations Confederacy and the Illinois Territory and on the south by the Cherokee, Chickasaw, and Choctaw nations. Over time, Virginia was split into numerous present-day states, including West Virginia, Kentucky, Tennessee, and parts of Indiana and Illinois. The Royal Proclamation of 1763 bisected Virginia, leaving most of its territory, west of the Allegheny Mountains, in the occupation and possession of the Indian tribes.

Over the next five decades, the speculators toiled unsuccessfully in high places to confirm the validity of their illicit purchase. The British authorities immediately declared the purchases illegal under British law. Virginia also refused to recognize the sale because the state claimed exclusive preemptive rights in Indian land and prohibited its unlicensed purchase, and after the Revolution, Virginia intended to cede the lands in question to the American Republic. Congress also refused to recognize the claims on several occasions. In the meantime, the investment began to slip away as the subject land found its way into federal ownership through a series of Indian treaties and Virginia land cessations to the new republic. By 1817, the speculators were desperate. As a last resort, they turned to the federal court system to obtain judicial approval of the illegal purchases. *Surely the courts would approve the sale—speculation is commonplace.* With a favorable Supreme Court decision in hand, the companies would gain leverage in pursuing their claims in Congress.

Attorney Robert Goodloe Harper, a son-in-law of one of the investors, was retained to guide the last ditch litigation effort. Harper was a leading Supreme Court advocate with a questionable ethical past. He bears a close physical resemblance to W. C. Fields in surviving portraits. Like the scallywag actor, Harper was considered "a pompous dandy" by fellow congressmen.[20] A Washington insider who served in the Senate and House of Representatives, Harper was hired for his success in *Fletcher v. Peck* (1810), a somewhat similar case involving the Yazoo scandal.[21] That infamous purchase of thirty-five million acres in Georgia outraged many in the nation because it was obtained by speculators who bribed nearly every state legislator to pass a law authorizing the illicit sale. Despite the shocking corruption surrounding the sale, Harper managed to obtain Supreme Court approval; but he was only able to accomplish this remarkable feat by highly questionable means, even by the standards of the good old boy network.

In *Fletcher*, Harper fabricated a deed between the parties in a friendly, collusive lawsuit. The fake deed allowed them to feign a breach of contract action needed for federal jurisdiction to hear the made-up case brought to validate the purchase.[22] The Yazooists had already bribed the Georgia legislature and they now turned their attention to bending the rules of the court system to secure their enormous prize. By comparison, a handful of black-robed judges might be far easier to influence. They confidently expected a favorable ruling from the Supreme Court because Chief Justice John Marshall was himself a well-known speculator in land for most of his adult life.[23] As expected, Marshall did uphold the Yazoo purchase despite the widespread legislative corruption that surrounded the deal. The Court was also well aware of Harper's shady tactics in bringing the feigned case, but the black robes gave the influential lawyer the benefit of the doubt. Several justices informally expressed their reluctance to decide the made-up case.[24] However, one justice did slap Harper on the wrist in the dissenting opinion, warning him not to play fast and loose with the Court again:

> I have been very unwilling to proceed to the decision in this cause at all. It appears to me to bear strong evidence, upon the face of it, of being a mere feigned case. It is our duty to decide on the rights, but not on the speculations of parties. My confidence, however, in the respectable gentlemen who have been engaged for the parties, has induced me to abandon my scruples, in the belief that they would never consent to impose a mere feigned case upon this court.[25]

As demonstrated in *Fletcher*, Harper was willing to bend the rules before the high court and cut ethical corners to gain advantage. The speculators must have thought, *Surely, this crafty lawyer can grease the skids to confirm our claims in the friendly Marshall Court.*

Harper resigned his senate seat in 1816 to guide the speculators' lawsuit through the court system, where he would use even shadier tactics than in *Fletcher*. He would contrive another feigned controversy in a friendly, collusive lawsuit to bring the validity of the sale to the Supreme Court, with a few added tricks. First, he selected *all* of the players in the lawsuit—not only the plaintiff, who Harper would represent, but he also hand-picked the defendant and hired the defendant's attorneys who were paid by the land companies and told what to do throughout the litigation.[26] Harper picked Thomas Johnson, a prominent Wabash shareholder, as the nominal plaintiff because of his close ties to people admired by Chief Justice Marshall, such as George Washington. The pretend defendant was William M'Intosh, who owned land within the Wabash purchase but derived his title from the United States rather than the Indians. M'Intosh was picked because of his willingness to collude and play ball with the law.[27]

Harper next went shopping for a suitable trial court judge. His first choice was Judge Benjamin Parke of the federal court in Illinois. Parke had formerly represented the two land companies in their efforts to secure recognition of the very land claims that would be presented in the lawsuit. However, Parke's scruples got the best of him. Rather than force a conflict of interest upon the reluctant judge, Harper opted to file the case with his second choice, Judge Nathaniel Pope, in the new federal court in Indiana. Pope had close family ties to the plaintiff, Johnson, but his judicial ethics apparently did not bar him from hearing a case involving his brother's family.[28]

Next, Harper began to mark the cards. He crafted an agreed statement of facts favorable to the plaintiff and detrimental to the defendant. This pleading solved various factual problems faced by Harper and limited the legal issues in the case to one which Harper thought he could win fairly: whether the pre–Revolutionary War purchases were barred by the proclamation—an unpopular law of England. M'Intosh, of course, agreed to this contrived pleading, which limited his defenses in this friendly lawsuit because his job was to take a fall. Finally, Harper decided M'Intosh should win in the district court. That might give him advantages as the appealing party before the Marshall court, where he would be allowed both an opening and a closing argument. However, in "losing," Harper did not want Judge Pope to issue a lengthy opinion as that might complicate the appeal. Harper wanted to present the Marshall court with the agreed statement of facts limiting the issues in the appeal solely to the validity of the proclamation.[29] Pope accommodated by issuing a short order.

Thus, as the collusive case came before the Supreme Court, it was in the best possible position for winning. Only a few more details remained. To add grease to the skids in the Marshall court, Harper selected the great Daniel Webster—the most eloquent and powerful orator of the day—as his cocounsel to assist in arguing the case on behalf of Johnson, and then he picked less-qualified attorneys to argue M'Intosh's case, paid them, and told them what to say.[30] *Now the deck was stacked and all the cards were marked in advance.* Despite the Court's admonition in *Fletcher*, the crafty lawyer was back once again with another collusive case.

With the stage thus set, Harper's team would argue the "Indian" side of the case: the sales were legal because Indian tribes owned the land and had the power to sell it, and any British prohibition was invalid. To throw the case, M'Intosh's attorneys would argue only that the sales were barred by British law. Marshall was expected to reject that unpopular argument and uphold the purchase, as in *Fletcher*, due to his well-known love of land speculation, even though the claims had already been rejected by the English, Virginia, and Congress. Marshall had already demonstrated high tolerance for corruption in *Fletcher*. For these reasons, he was considered tailor-made for upholding a speculator's claim.

But what about the Indians? It was *their* property rights and sovereignty at stake, yet they were not a party to *Johnson*. As the oral argument began, only white people were in the courtroom. They would fashion the rules affecting Indians, just like they developed the law of slavery without the input, representation, or presence of the slaves. No one thought to ascertain the views of the Indian tribes in *Johnson*. To Harper, they were simply "savage tribes."[31] To M'Intosh's attorneys, they were "an inferior race of people, without the privileges of citizens," with "no proprietary interest in the vast tracts of territory which they wandered over."[32] To Marshall, they were nothing more than "fierce savages, whose occupation was war, and whose subsistence was drawn chiefly from the forest."[33] *Were they going to fashion property rules based upon the color of one's skin?* We do not know how the Indian nations would have responded to the legal arguments or the racial stereotypes that filled the courtroom. They were not present. Everyone's use of racial invectives in *Johnson* leaves us to ponder the Court's ability to render an impartial decision concerning Indian land rights.[34] The avowed racist views expressed by the Court and the parties virtually assured that those rights would not be respected. Equally important, the absence of the affected tribes impaired their ability to protect the Indian interests.[35] Today, those tribes would be considered necessary or indispensable parties to the *Johnson* litigation since the proceeding affected their core interests; and the courts would have either had to join them so their interests could be fairly protected, or dismiss the case.[36] Yet their interests were advocated solely by the attorney for the land companies. But that's just the way it goes in the courts of the conqueror.

Harper bent the rules beyond recognition (at least in my thirty-six years of federal court litigation experience). The spurious claim in *Johnson* came to the Supreme Court as collusive litigation between pretend parties, fraught with conflicts of interest among the attorneys, and based upon a contrived record. The American Indian tribes who sold the land in controversy were indispensable to a just adjudication, but they were not before the court. *The case was a scam.* It had been presented to a trial judge with family ties to the nominal plaintiff. While many of Harper's methods are familiar to modern litigators, such as forum shopping and agreed statements of facts, these tools are misused when applied in collusive cases by attorneys and judges with conflicts of interest. Now the appeal came before a chief justice who, as we will see, owned property that could be affected by the case. These highly irregular aspects of the case combined to thoroughly compromise the integrity of the legal system. At minimum, that system is built on the adversarial process, where the actual disputes between real parties with opposing interests are resolved through counterarguments vigorously advanced by attorneys not employed by their client's adversaries. Furthermore, the public expects such controversies to be decided by impartial judges who are not relatives of any of the parties and own no property at stake in the outcome of the litigation. The attorneys and judges responsible for the deplorable ethical situation in *Johnson* would surely be subject to sanction under current legal ethics. The pattern of multiple ethical abuses of the legal system and inappropriate behavior evident in *Johnson* set the stage for a dangerous miscarriage of justice. This was almost certain to occur given the racial invectives hurled against American Indians by everyone concerned. And that's just the way it turned out for the American Indians in the courts of the conqueror. But not before Harper received his just desserts.

Did Marshall Have a Conflict of Interest in *Johnson v. M'Intosh?*

Unfortunately for Harper, the gods of litigation are fickle. Sometimes even the best-laid plans go astray, and fate has a way of giving cheaters exactly what they deserve. The Supreme Court ruled against Harper just eight days after the oral argument, ending, once and for all, the spurious claims of the Illinois Land and Wabash Land companies, which soon faded from history.

Three unexpected factors beyond Harper's control combined to doom his cause. First, five days before the oral argument, Congress denied another petition to recognize a land purchase made in violation of the Royal Proclamation of 1763, sending another signal that claims like those in *Johnson* were illegal. *Bad timing.* Second, on the last day of the windy, three-day oral argument, as Harper was making his closing argument, three cabinet officials exposed Harper's contrived statement of agreed facts as "collusive" and containing facts "that could not be proven."[37] *The jig was up!* Alas, these actions by the other branches of the federal government drove a stake into the heart of the claims—even before the pompous dandy and his silver-tongued sidekick packed their briefcases and left the courthouse. Third, and most importantly, Harper failed to recognize that Marshall's well-known interests in land speculation were not going to be helpful to his cause, as anticipated. To the contrary, those interests created conflicts that would strongly motivate the chief justice to rule against the claims in a sweeping opinion that went far beyond the single issue framed by Harper.

Marshall's opinion quickly rejected the spurious claims. That part was easy: the Court simply found that Murray fraudulently purchased the land under a fake legal opinion in 1773 in violation of British law.[38] Furthermore, Murray's purchase was also barred by state law, which granted Virginia exclusive preemptive rights over Indian lands within its borders and forbade the purchase of that land without a license.[39] Finally, Virginia had already disposed of Indian land in the state by granting most of it to Revolutionary War veterans and ceding the remainder to the United States.[40] These holdings completely disposed of the claims.

Yet, Marshall did not stop there. The bulk of his opinion went on to strip the legal title to land away from American Indian tribes in North America and to justify what amounted to judicial theft of Indian land. This portion of the opinion, which is called *obiter dicta* (literally, "something said in passing") because it is merely incidental to the central issues of the case, is what *Johnson* is famous for. Scholars have often wondered why his opinion went beyond the issues necessary to decide the case.

It appears that the chief justice had other fish to fry. First and foremost, he owned enormous amounts of land located near the Illinois and Wabash purchases. John Marshall and his father, Thomas, acquired over 240 square miles of land under Virginia's land grant system. This real estate empire lay immediately south and also due east of the land purchases in *Johnson*. Like M'Intosh, Marshall's title did not derive from Indian tribes. It came instead from the State of Virginia. Land grants in the region could be acquired under state law through military warrants issued to war veterans and by purchasing treasury warrants for land from Virginia.[41] Marshall acquired land in both ways. First, a 1782 military warrant allotted four thousand acres to him in Virginia's military district. Under his warrant, Marshall was granted two thousand acres in 1786. The district is located in present-day western Kentucky, south of the Wabash purchase.[42] Second, Marshall obtained treasury warrants for another 292,813 acres. Under those warrants, 152,229 acres were granted to Marshall and his father.[43] Much of the treasury warrant land lay in Fayette County, which in the 1780s was situated due east of the *Johnson* case area. In all, the Marshall family owned 240 square miles of land, an area six times larger than the District of Columbia, nearly the size of a small state—quite a chunk of land by any standard. Title to that land could be affected by the outcome of *Johnson*.

We do not know the extent of Marshall's personal land holdings by 1823, when he wrote the *Johnson* decision. Pertinent land records were reportedly destroyed by fire.[44] However, under any conceivable set of circumstances, he or his immediate family likely retained an enormous personal and financial stake in the outcome of the case. By 1823, the Marshall family either owned all, more, or portions of that land empire, or they had sold it altogether for a fortune. In either case, a judicial conflict of interest arguably comes into play that should have disqualified Marshall from participating in the *Johnson* case. The first scenario seems probable, since Marshall's speculation in land lasted well into his tenure on the high court, sometimes causing conflict of interest problems when legal disputes over his personal land interests came before the Supreme Court.[45] Even if all family members were completely landless by 1823, the chief justice still held significant interests in protecting the good title to those 240 square miles of land obtained under Virginia's land grant system, because the family fortune made from its sale could be jeopardized if legal title to the land was defective. *Innocent purchasers could demand their money back!* Thus, under either scenerio, the chief justice had seemingly enormous property or financial interests at stake in the outcome of *Johnson* that compelled him to side with M'Intosh; and that is precisely what he did.

This situation easily leads reasonable minds to wonder whether Marshall's personal property and financial interests preordained the outcome of *Johnson*. Under current federal law and judicial ethics, those self-interests would almost certainly require his disqualification from hearing the *Johnson* case. Though formal judicial standards were not in effect in 1823, the chief justice was obviously cognizant of the need to avoid conflicts of interest and the appearance of impropriety, since he previously absented himself from two appeals in another case involving a land title dispute in which he owned an interest. However, for some reason he did not recuse himself in *Johnson*, even though he stood to benefit from the rulings of the Supreme Court in that case.

The Marshall family had a variety of other long-standing interests in upholding the validity of Virginia's land grant system. Thomas Marshall had brought suit in *Marshall v. Clark* (1791) to confirm veteran land rights in the military warrant lands under Virginia's land grant system.[46] *Marshall* upheld the state's power to grant those interests in land. Under the Virginia Supreme Court's decision in *Marshall*, ownership of military warrant land became perfected once Indian title was extinguished. *Johnson* could resolve, once and for all, Virginia's power to convey land still owned and occupied by Indian tribes. Both father and son had worked hard to develop, implement, and protect that land grant system. John was a beneficiary of that system, with a preemptive right in military warrant land with a personal stake in upholding the legality of the market. Thomas surveyed military warrant lands and administered that state program. Both were deeply involved in legislation and litigation, such as *Marshall v. Clark*, to develop, implement, and protect Virginia's legal ability to convey preemptive rights to veterans in land occupied by tribes before their title had been extinguished. On a broader level, as a land speculator who gobbled up 240 square miles of land, Marshall had compelling reasons to be deeply concerned about protecting the booming American preemptive market. By 1823, the preemptive market was an important engine driving the economy. A vast number of land titles were completely dependent upon the market's validity, and that validity hinged upon the states' ability to convey legal interests in land still occupied by Indian tribes before their title was extinguished by the federal government.

In short, John Marshall had a great love of the land—which he bought and sold in enormous amounts. Those interests and activities led historian Newmyer to conclude that Marshall's "economic self-interest and dedication to public service were inextricably linked," and that Marshall advanced them "as an ambitious, upwardly mobile, professional lawyer with business connections and a passion for land speculation" and "by serving first in the army, then in the state legislature."[47] *Did Marshall also advance those self-interests in Johnson v. M'Intosh?*

If Marshall or his family still owned interests in the above land or possessed wealth from its sale when *Johnson* came before the Supreme Court, the chief justice arguably had an economic interest in the outcome of the case that required his disqualification, at least under modern rules of judicial ethics. Canon E(1) of the Code of Judicial Ethics requires judges to disqualify themselves in cases where their impartiality "might be reasonably questioned." That situation arises when a judge or his family has "an economic interest in the subject matter in controversy" or "any other more than de minimis interest that could be substantially affected by the proceeding." Is it fair to apply today's standards? Since *Johnson* is still relied upon by courts today, it seems fair to judge the decision maker by today's standards. Marshall was aware of the need to avoid conflicts of interest and the appearance of impropriety. He should have disqualified himself.

Instead, by enlarging the issues presented in the case, *Johnson* offered Marshall an opportunity to confirm Virginia's land grant system once and for all. To do that, he had to stray far beyond the narrow, prewar issue presented by Harper in order to address and uphold *Virginia's* postwar preemptive market and to confirm the land titles obtained under that market. By recasting the case from one involving a prewar land purchase into one that addresses the postwar preemptive market, Marshall could affirm his own land grants and those of his family, assigns, and other non-Indians. In the same breath, he could protect the family fortune amassed from a life spent buying and selling land. The far-reaching decision in *Johnson* achieved those goals. As I discuss next, the *Johnson* decision held that the United States—not Indian tribes—owns legal title to Indian land and the tribes are merely tenants whose "right of occupancy" can be extinguished at the government's will. This outcome, however harsh for the Indians, protected Marshall's self-interests and preserved all land titles obtained through the preemptive market.[48] Along the way, Harper's interests were subordinated even though the crafty counselor represented land speculators; and in a nation that otherwise worships private property rights, the land rights of an entire race of people were dispossessed by the stroke of the pen in a single opinion.

The Opinion in Johnson v. M'Intosh

Writing for a unanimous court that he ruled with a firm hand, the chief justice said the validity of the land sales turned on "the power of the Indians to give, and of private individuals to receive a title which can be sustained in the Courts of this country."[49] With this particular question, Marshall turned the case from a narrow inquiry into the legality of a prewar sale under British law into an inquiry into the legality of the postwar preemptive market under American law, including Virginia's land grant system, based upon trade in land still owned and occupied by Indians.

Similar to disclaimers in the slave cases, Marshall began the inquiry into the nature of Indian landownership by saying his analysis cannot examine "principles of abstract justice," nor could the Court question rules by which property is acquired.[50] This is judicial code for "something very unjust is about to happen." Without constraints imposed by justice, those property rules, of course, worked against the Indians since they were made by the colonizers. Marshall could then restrict ownership rights of the "savage tribes" without blame. His opinion held that under Europe's doctrine of discovery, England obtained "the exclusive right of the discoverer to appropriate the lands occupied by Indians" and this "right" was inherited by the United States and the original thirteen states, as the successors to the British.

> It has never been doubted that either the United States, or the several States, had a clear title to all the lands within the boundary lines described in the treaty (with Great Britain), subject only to the Indian right of occupancy, and that the exclusive power to extinguish that right, was vested in that government which might constitutionally exercise it.[51]

In short, the discovery of Indian land by Europeans operates to transfer legal title from the Indians to the government, according to Marshall. This title was variously described by the Court as the "fee," "absolute title," or the "absolute ultimate title," and the Indian right was described as a "right of occupancy" or "right of possession," which could be extinguished by the government through purchase or conquest.[52]

The legal precedent for this holding was Marshall's expansive interpretation of the European principles of discovery. Those principles, according to him, operated to transfer legal title "to the government by whose subjects, or by whose authority, [discovery] was made, against all other European governments, which title might be consummated by possession."[53] In short, indigenous sovereignty and land rights were automatically diminished upon the "discovery" of Indian country by Pilgrims or other lucky Europeans. This rule is astounding for several obvious reasons. But first and foremost, neither English nor Spanish law entertained the notion that discovery grants title to Indian land.[54] Marshall introduced a greatly expanded version of the doctrine into American jurisprudence. For precedent, he pointed to Virginia's assertion of exclusive preemption rights over Indian lands and Virginia's practice of prohibiting Indians from selling their land to anyone except the government.[55] He justified this remarkable holding by reasoning that "our whole country [has] been granted by the crown while in the occupancy of the Indians" (which was not true) and the colonies did the same thing—after all, "every title within those governments [is] dependent on these grants" and they "cannot be considered as nullities."[56]

Thus, the Indians went from landowners, as recognized by the British colonists for over 150 years, to tenants whose occupancy can be terminated by purchase or conquest at the will of the American government, which is clearly a second-class property right.

We are at once confronted with a manifestly unjust outcome. This posed a major problem for Marshall. He could not afford to ignore the elephant in the room altogether, even though his opinion eschewed principles of abstract justice, because *an unjust decision could be seen as illegitimate, couldn't it?* How could this inequitable result be justified? Was the dispossession of Indian legal title just? Since Marshall would not "enter into the controversy, whether agriculturists, merchants, and manufacturers, have a right, on abstract principles, to expel hunters from the territory they possess, or contract their limits," he was left with a half-hearted justification that rested only upon a bald statement that

> Conquest gives a title which the Courts of the conqueror cannot deny, whatever the private and speculative opinions of individuals may be respecting the original justice of the claim which has been successfully asserted...It is not for the Courts of this country to question the validity of this title, or to sustain one which is incompatible with it.[57]

Reduced to playing the race card, the chief justice also asserted that the "character and religion" of the Indians "afforded an apology for considering them as a people over whom the superior genius of Europe might claim an ascendancy."[58]

Marshall also had to explain why the outcome of the case was seemingly at odds with international law. Otherwise, his inequitable treatment of Native Americans might make the United States look like an illegitimate outlaw nation in the eyes of the world. Under international law, according to Marshall, when conquest is complete, the conquered usually blend with the conqueror and become incorporated into the new nation, where they must be treated fairly and their property rights normally "remain unimpaired."[59] Though the ruling does impair Indian property rights, Marshall explained that the "character and habits" of the "conquered" Indians provided "some excuse, if not justification" for acquiring their title, despite the international law norms to the contrary. The behavior of the American Indians made it impossible for the United States to protect their property rights and treat them fairly:

> [T]he tribes of Indians inhabiting this country were fierce savages, whose occupation was war, whose subsistence was drawn chiefly from the forest. To leave them in possession of their country, was to leave the

country a wilderness; to govern them as a distinct people, was impossible, because they were a brave and as high spirited as they were fierce, and were ready to repel by arms every attempt on their independence.[60]

Accordingly, Marshall claimed that the nation had no choice in how it dealt with the tribes and that the normal rules of international law did not apply.

> The Europeans were under the necessity either of abandoning the country, and relinquishing their pompous claims to it, or of enforcing those claims by the sword, and by the adoption of principles adapted to the condition of a people with whom it was impossible to mix.[61]

Thus, the normal rules governing the relations between the conqueror and the conquered were simply "incapable of application" in the United States.[62] *It was the Indians' own fault.*

Finally, Marshall had to grapple with another elephant in the room, the problem of absurdity; that is, whether the doctrines of discovery and conquest were absurd principles, since most of the Indian tribes had never been conquered at all and, furthermore, discovery cannot logically be equated with conquest. *We cannot afford for the Court to become the laughingstock of the legal world; its decisions must be taken seriously.* Unfortunately, no amount of persuasive argument could mask the absurd and arbitrary nature of the inequitable doctrines. In the end, he was therefore forced to conclude that it did not matter whether the doctrines were arbitrary and absurd or not.

> However extravagant the pretension of converting the discovery of an inhabited country into conquest may appear; if the principle has been asserted in the first instance, and afterwards sustained; if a country has been acquired and held under it; if the property of the great mass of the community originates in it, it becomes the law of the land, and cannot be questioned. So, too, with respect to the concomitant principle, that the Indian inhabitants are to be considered merely as occupants, to be protected, indeed, while at peace, in the possession of their lands, but to be deemed incapable of transferring the absolute title to others. However this restriction may be opposed to natural right, and to the usages of civilized nations, yet, if it be indispensable to that system under which the country has been settled, and be adapted to the actual

condition of the two people, it may, perhaps, be supported by reason, and certainly cannot be rejected by Courts of justice.[63]

Accordingly, Marshall adopted the international doctrine of discovery of the European nations that colonized North America as the law of the United States. Under *Johnson*, the tribal land sales to Murray did not convey good title to the land companies. Only the United States (or the original thirteen states prior to the Nonintercourse Act of 1790) could grant good legal title to Indian lands to folks like M'Intosh and Marshall, because the governments owned title to the land—not the tribes. After the adoption of the Constitution, the Natives were mere tenants of the United States. The federal government now held legal title to Indian land along with the exclusive preemptive right to extinguish the Indians' occupation by purchase or conquest.[64]

Thus ends the story of *Johnson v. M'Intosh*—one of the ten worst cases ever decided—about how the Indians lost legal title to America. From 1823 onward, the law accorded Indians second-class land rights. In the stroke of a pen, they became tenants of the government and their occupancy of land was subject to dispossession by sale or sword at the government's discretion. They could either cede their land or fight for it, a Hobson's choice that the law placed on no other landowners. In either case, the American Indian tribes were preordained to dispossession.

To Marshall's credit, it should be noted that he largely repudiated the discovery doctrine a few years later, after he saw how it was being used by states, like Georgia, to seize Indian land throughout the eastern seaboard and to remove an entire race of people to distant reservation enclaves beyond the Mississippi River. Distressed at the legacy of cases like *Georgia v. Tassels* (1830),[65] The Definer of the Nation, as his biographer called him, significantly narrowed, if not overruled, the doctrine in *Worcester v. Georgia* (1832), which was decided in the twilight of his distinguished career.[66] Unfortunately, shortly after his death, the Jackson Supreme Court reinstated the doctrine in five cases decided between 1836 and 1842.[67] The long-lived doctrine remains alive and well today. It is relied upon by the Supreme Court to forestall Native American legal efforts to recover lost land and sovereignty, most recently in 2005,[68] and *Johnson* is used for similar purposes by courts in other nations.[69]

There is a wise saying among lobbyists: "You do not want to know how sausages or laws are made." The same can be said for the landmark federal Indian law cases that embody the dark side of the law. Believe it or not, *Johnson* has taken on a divine quality over time, as if handed down by God himself. The principles espoused in *Johnson*, like those in *Dred Scott*, are tainted by colonialism and overt racism. Like other unprincipled decisions of the past, *Dred Scott* is no longer cited by the Supreme Court as precedent and the same should be the fate of *Johnson*. We should no longer give credence to *Johnson* simply for its ethical violations alone. There is no doubt that under today's standards the *Johnson* case is far too unethical for its opinion to be given any serious effect. The American judicial system of 1823 was clearly cognizant of ethical concerns, even though formal codes of ethics may not have been promulgated by that date. This is evident in *Fletcher*, where the Supreme Court admonished against feigned cases; in Judge Parke's reluctance to preside over *Johnson* in the district court because of his conflict of interest in previously representing the land companies; in Georgia's efforts to eradicate land corruption in the Yazoo scandal in *Fletcher*; in the outcry made by cabinet officials concerning Harper's shenanigans in *Johnson*; and, finally, in Chief Justice Marshall's reluctance to decide the *Hunter's Lessee* appeals, which involved his own property. We cannot turn a blind eye, then, to the ethical conduct in *Johnson* simply because it occurred in the 1820s, especially if courts use *Johnson* to decide Native American cases today.

The Impacts of *Johnson* on Native Americans

Leaving legal niceties aside for a moment, the Indians say that white men kept only one promise: "They said they would take our land, and they took it."[70] The appropriation of legal title under *Johnson* was a milestone in that process. In the end, *Johnson* worked numerous hardships on the Indians. Land was their paramount asset. It provided their identity, culture, and religion as well as their ability to sustain themselves as indigenous peoples.

By 1955, the indigenous land base had shrunk to just 2.3 percent of its original size. *Johnson* paved the way for this tragedy. Its doctrine granted enormous power over Indian lands to the US government and accorded only a diminutive, second-class land right to the tribes—the aboriginal right of occupancy. The loss of legal title was a serious blow. Dispossession followed in the process set in motion, initially, by European colonialism and then consummated by homegrown Manifest Destiny. Since the United States already owned the absolute legal title to Indian lands under *Johnson*,

Congress could enact numerous laws over the next century that had the effect of dispossessing the Indians of their land. By 1881, Indian landholdings in the United States had plummeted to 156 million acres. By 1934, only about 50 million acres remained (an area the size of Idaho and Washington) as a result of the General Allotment Act of 1887.[71] During World War II, the government took 500,000 more acres for military use.[72] Over one hundred tribes, bands, and Rancherias relinquished their lands under various acts of Congress during the termination era of the 1950s.[73] In the 1960s, tribal landholdings constituted just 50.5 million acres.[74]

The "Indian right of occupancy" proved meaningless against the United States over the next 150 years, as the occupation of indigenous homelands by one tribe after another was extinguished by the government through various means, including treaty cessions, coercion, wars, and outright confiscation. In *Tee-Hit-Ton v. United States* (1955), the Supreme Court allowed the government to confiscate aboriginal land interests with impunity.[75] Justice Stanley Reed coldly held that the Indian right is "not a property right" at all—it is nothing more than "permission of the whites to occupy" territory that can be terminated "without any legally enforceable obligation to compensate the Indians."[76] He impatiently explained to the Tee-Hit-Ton Band of Tlingit Indians that 350,000 acres of their aboriginal lands, where they lived, hunted, fished, and gathered since time immemorial, were forfeited to the government. "No case in this Court has ever held that taking of Indian title or use by Congress required compensation."[77] Relying on *Johnson,* Justice Reed held that Indian occupancy "may be extinguished by the Government without compensation," after all,

> Every American schoolboy knows that the savage tribes of this continent were deprived of their ancestral ranges by force and that, even when the Indians ceded millions of acres by treaty in return for blankets, food and trinkets, it was not a sale but the conqueror's will that deprived them of their land.[78]

Land loss was not the only consequence of *Johnson.* Shortly after it was decided, the states seized on the discovery doctrine and the diminished Native land rights espoused by Marshall as the legal basis for evicting the Indian race from the eastern seaboard and relocating the tribes to reservations west of the Mississippi—just like the Japanese American removal during World War II, only on a larger and permanent scale. *Johnson* undercut Native American efforts to remain in their homelands. *Since we already own their land, we can extinguish their occupancy and order the Indian squatters to leave.* Unlike the Japanese American removal, no apology or reparations were made for removing Indians.

Finally, what do we make of Marshall's discourse on conquest? In *Johnson* he equated the act of discovery with conquest, even though it is admittedly absurd to do so. As a matter of historical fact, very few Indian tribes were ever actually conquered by the United States or anyone else. This term is defined in most dictionaries as the appropriation of territory by war or the subjugation of a people through the use of raw military force. Such examples are rare in US history. Certainly the Indians in *Tee-Hit-Ton* were never conquered by any definition of the term. Yet by 1955, the false notion of equating discovery with conquest was firmly embedded in Justice Reed's mind. On a darker note, *Johnson* can be read between the lines to sanction the use of the sword as a legitimate and lawful means for acquiring Indian land and for effectuating the nation's Indian policies. Did Marshall's discourse provide a legal foundation for warfare against Native Americans, including various massacres conducted without any discernable legal basis? In those instances, was *Johnson* the *sole* legal basis for killing Indians? These largely unexplored questions about the legality of the Indian wars will be examined in chapter six.

This chapter, however, is primarily concerned about land loss and its attendant impacts upon the property rights, cultural integrity, and sovereignty of American Indian nations. My own nation, the Pawnee, provides an example of these impacts. Our homeland lies in the Great Plains, where four bands of Pawnee Indians—the *Skiri* (Wolf), *Chaui* (Begging-for-Meat), *Piitahauirata* (Man-Going-Downstream), and *Kitkahaki* (Little Earth Lodge)—inhabited earth lodge villages along the major rivers in present-day Nebraska and Kansas. Throughout this domain the Pawnee built towns, grew corn, hunted buffalo, and offered prayers to *Atius Tirawahut'* (Father Sky) and *Atira Huraatsa* (Mother Earth). For nearly three hundred years, we repulsed the Spanish conquistadors (*Custarus*, Hairy Noses) and kept French fur traders (*Cariks Taka*, White People) at bay. But it was not to be so with the Americans (*Resi Kutsu*, Big Knives). With the coming of Lewis and Clark's Voyage of Discovery in 1804, the doctrine of discovery was presumably imported into Pawnee country and operated on paper to "conquer" the Pawnee and divest title to their lands under Big Knife law, leaving them with a right of occupancy.

Knowledge of this inequitable doctrine would surely have changed the character of the early encounters and relations between the two worlds. They would not have been as friendly, and early Big Knives would have been expelled, or worse, by the powerful and more numerous Pawnee. For example, in 1833 as the Americans approached a *Chaui* village on the *Kitskatus* (Platte River), a member of the small party named John Treat Irvin observed that surrounding hills "were black with masses of mounted warriors...yet they stood motionless and in silence, watching the approach of the mission."[79] Irvin recorded the colorful encounter.

At length a single horseman detached himself from the mass, and came galloping down the hill and over the prairie to meet us. As he approached there was a wild, free air about him, and he governed his gigantic black horse with great ease. I could not help but think that if the rest of these warriors were of the same mould, any resistance of our band, however desperate, would avail but little against an attack of these proud rulers of the prairie.

Upon reaching the party, he sprang from his horse, and shook hands with Mr. Ellsworth. He then gave directions through the interpreter, that the band should be drawn up in as small a compass as possible, to avoid all contact with his warriors. After spending some time in completing this arrangement, he galloped back, and gave the signal to the rest. In an instant the hills were deserted, and the whole mass of warriors were rushing toward us, across the broad bosom of the prairie. It was a moment of intense and fearful expectation. On they came; each mad horse, with erect mane and blazing eye, urged forward by the bloody spur of an Indian master. They had reached within two hundred yards of the party, but still the speed of their horses was unchecked, and the powerful tramp of their hoofs rang like thunder upon the sod of the prairie. At a signal, however, from the chief, the band separated to the right and left, and commenced circling around us, in one dark, dense flood. Their whoops and yells, and the furious and menacing manner in which they brandished their bows and tomahawks, would have led a person unacquainted with their habits, to have looked upon this reception as anything but friendly. There is something in the fierce, shrill scream of a band of Indian warriors, which rings through the brain, and sends the blood curdling back to the heart. Their ornaments, though wild, were many of them beautiful. The closely shaved heads of some were adorned with the plumage of different birds. Others wore an ornament of deer's hair, bound up in a form resembling the crest of an ancient helmet, and a plume of the bald eagle floated from the long scalp-locks of the principal warriors.

Some few wore necklaces of the claws of the grisly bear, hanging down upon their breasts. The bodies of some were wrapped in buffalo robes, or the skin of the white wolf; but the most of them wore no covering, save a thick coat of paint. This they profusely smeared over their bodies and arms, and many had even bestowed it upon the heads and limbs of their horses. After dashing around us for some time, the chief waved his hand, and the turmoil ceased. The warriors sprang from their horses, and seating themselves round in a large circle, waited for the arrival of the chief of the [*Chaui*] Pawnees.[80]

After the Big Knives arrived, the Pawnee struggled to retain their domain and way of life. In 1822, just one year before *Johnson* was decided, *Piita Reesaaru'* (Man Chief) told President Monroe:

We have plenty of buffalo, beaver, deer and other wild animals—we have also an abundance of horses—we have every thing we want—we have plenty of land, if you will keep your people off of it.[81]

Man Chief's plea was in vain. After a series of land cessions, Pawnee hegemony ended fifty years later when the *akitaru* (tribe)—decimated by smallpox, hunger, and warfare—was marched to Indian Territory in Oklahoma to a small reservation, which now consists of just one square mile.

Though the Pawnee were removed from their homeland in 1872, tribal memories remain embedded in the songs, ceremonies, history, sacred places, and oral traditions of the Pawnee who frequently return to aboriginal places. In the spring of 2006, I accompanied a small delegation of Pawnee chiefs who traveled from Oklahoma to visit that homeland. Our task was to arrange the repatriation and reburial of eight hundred tribal dead, disinterred from Nebraska graves by the Big Knives after the Pawnee relocation. Standing in the midst of an old village located on a high bluff overlooking the Loup River, we gazed upon our beautiful homeland, which stretched before us in all directions far off into the green haze. In 1600, this town contained almost two thousand *Skiri* living in eighty earth lodges. Today it is nothing but a cornfield, full of pottery shards, arrowheads, and stone scrapers—the evidence of Pawnee life long before Europeans and Americans arrived.

On that spring day, our delegation experienced a feeling known only to Native Americans—the great sadness of a dispossessed, displaced people who have experienced "the loss of a country," in the words of anthropologist Martha Blaine.[82] She aptly captured the forces legalized by *Johnson*:

> From the Beginning, one purpose of New World colonization and settlement was acquisition of land for establishment of town sites, ports, roads, farms, and later railroads. Individuals who had no land of their own in the Old World, or who had owned land, wanted to possess it on the American continent. This and other motivations and subsequent actions came at the expense of the original users and owners, the Native Americans, or Indians. Treaties of friendship, followed closely by requests for purchase and cession of Indian land, began in the seventeenth century. The land coveted extended from the Atlantic Coast to the Pacific Ocean.
>
> Acquisition of a continent was not made without coercion and military force, used when necessary as one tribe after another resisted the westward push of the strangers into their homelands. At the end of the nineteenth century, very few Indian tribes remained on their aboriginal lands with access to their villages, hunting grounds, cemeteries and sacred places.[83]

Efforts to Reclaim Land and Overcome Hardships Imposed by Johnson

During the Native American sovereignty movement of the past several decades, the Indian tribes halted the massive one-way transfer of property made possible by *Johnson*. In fact, they *reversed* that trend. Since the nadir of the 1960s, tribes in the lower forty-eight states expanded their land base to 58 million acres, an increase of 7.5 million acres—an area much larger than Massachusetts.[84] An additional 44 million acres were set aside for Alaska Natives pursuant to a federal statute enacted in 1971.[85]

This remarkable feat was accomplished by various means made possible by a wide variety of federal laws, regulations, and policies during the modern era of federal Indian law that encourage land acquisition and growth of the Indian land base. Some land was recovered through enormous efforts to recover tribal spiritual sites, such as Taos Pueblo's crusade to recover its sacred Blue Lake. Other lands, which had been illegally taken, were recovered through landmark litigation, such as the historic land claim cases brought by the Native American Rights Fund (NARF).[86] That trend continues today, despite backlashes in the courts and Congress.

In the spring of 2006, I stood on the banks of the Loup River in Nebraska, along with the Pawnee chiefs, Roger Welsch, the noted Nebraska folklorist, and his wife, Linda. We gazed upon the Welsch's beautiful sixty-acre farm spread along the river. The lush rural property has been completely restored to its native grasses and plants, and it lay in the heart of the former Pawnee homeland. The Welsch family is *giving the land back* to the Pawnee Nation, and I was to represent the Nation in this historic transaction as a NARF attorney. We asked Roger why the family made this unprecedented decision. "We knew this was Pawnee country and we were moved by something deep in the land to return it to the Pawnee people." The Welsch family has lived closely on the land for many years and listened to its rhythm. Is this part of the process of becoming indigenous, more native to the place where we live? Maybe so. In any event, the family's act is subversive. After all the enormous efforts that went into dispossessing the Indians through cases like *Johnson v. M'Intosh* and the wars, laws, and policies that accompanied the settlement of the American West, Roger and Linda are simply *giving the land back* to the Indians.

Unfortunately, the dark cloud of *Johnson* continues to hang over Indian Country, with its outmoded doctrines of colonialism and racial superiority ready for use by any court. Just like blacks were "a subordinate and inferior class of beings" in *Dred Scott,* Indian "heathens" are an "inferior race of people" in *Johnson*.[87] The unsavory and unethical history of *Johnson* compels a fundamental reexamination of its holdings and tainted principles. We cannot turn back the clock. But there exists ample reason to restrict future applications of this case. In 2007, the United Nations approved the Declaration on the Rights of Indigenous Peoples, a historic international convention that sets "minimum standards for the survival, dignity and well-being of the indigenous peoples of the world."[88] Article 28 recognizes the legal right of indigenous peoples "to the lands...which they have traditionally owned, occupied or otherwise used or acquired" and requires states to "give legal recognition and protection to these lands...with due respect to the customs, traditions and land tenure systems of the indigenous peoples concerned." Article 28 seemingly repudiates the discovery doctrine of *Johnson v. M'Intosh* and requires US law to recognize and protect Native American land rights and tenure. Indeed, Article 39 requires the United States to "take the appropriate measures, including legislative measures, to achieve the ends of this Declaration." These standards imposed by the UN declaration surely caused John Marshall to roll over in his grave, and they provide a benchmark for reforming his odious doctrine.

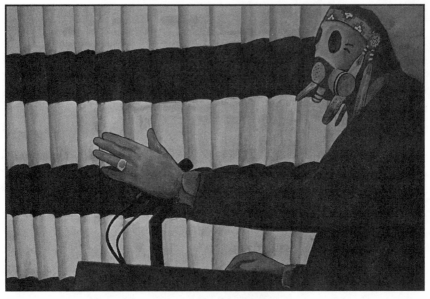

State of the Union

CHAPTER FIVE
Cherokee Nation v. Georgia:
Shutting the Courthouse Doors

IT WAS A RAINY DAY in Georgia when they hung Corn Tassels. After midnight on a cold December night in 1830, an urgent message from Governor George R. Gilmer arrived ordering Sheriff Eberhart to execute the Indian immediately. George Corn Tassels had been convicted by the state courts of killing another Indian within the Cherokee Nation. He was prosecuted under a set of state laws enacted to harass, intimidate, and drive the Cherokee Nation out of Georgia. The Georgians wanted Cherokee land. And they wanted the Cherokee to leave. The so-called Cracker State was using all of its available legal and police powers to rid the state of Native Americans.[1]

Since Corn Tassels's appeal to the United States Supreme Court had been granted, his execution should have been stayed. However, defiant and fearful Georgia could never allow the high court to review the state's spurious race laws. Meeting in emergency session, the legislature decried "interference by the Chief Justice of the Supreme Court of the United States, in the Administration of the criminal laws of this State," and directed state officials to execute the Indian.[2] Corn Tassels had to die posthaste so Georgia could safely evade federal judicial review and continue its repugnant policies without outside interference from Washington do-gooders. Corn Tassels was hung the very next morning before a large crowd, including many Cherokee—he was lynched, really, because Georgia lacked any jurisdiction over Indian activity within the Cherokee Nation, as was belatedly determined by the federal courts. Afterward, the body was turned over to distraught relations who buried him nearby. Though legalized by Georgia laws and courts, the state's actions in killing Corn Tassels, defying the US Supreme Court and persecuting a race of people through government machinery geared to abolish the Cherokee government, stripping the Cherokee of their human rights, confiscating their property, and, ultimately, removing and relocating them were acts of genocide rarely seen in American history.[3]

Sadly, the Supreme Court stood by and allowed this injustice to occur in *Cherokee Nation v. Georgia*, one of the ten worst cases ever decided.[4] *Cherokee Nation* marks the first time that an Indian tribe went to federal court in a major lawsuit to protect the political, human, and property rights of an American Indian tribe and its members from destruction by a state. As you will see, this case involves an especially egregious set of facts: ethnic cleansing in the antebellum South via the machinery of the state. The Supreme Court dismissed the action, holding that it raised "political questions" that courts are not empowered to decide and, in addition, Indian tribes cannot bring suits in the courts of the United States. The Court turned its back on the Cherokee Nation during its time of need, in a decision that simultaneously denied full nationhood status to Indian tribes, prevented their access to the courts, and relegated them to a second-class wardship status under American law, all of which proved highly injurious to Indian tribes over the next 175 years. The decision spurred the national Indian removal movement and contributed to the removal of more than eighty thousand Indians from the eastern United States between 1828 and 1838,[5] making the Cherokee Nation's struggle to remain in its homeland during this chilling ethnic cleansing campaign one of many tribal histories that tug at the heartstrings.

To grasp these events, we must confront southern racism and consider the plight of minority groups when they are persecuted through the power of the state—that is, that menacing side of democracy described by Alexis de Tocqueville as "the tyranny of the majority." What is the role of the courts when these factors come into play? This chapter explores the role of the Southern judiciary in the removal of the Indians from the eastern United States and the injustices that occur when Indian tribes are denied timely and meaningful access to the federal courts.

Today, everybody wants to be a Cherokee, and with good reason, given the rich culture and colorful history of that popular tribe. This esteemed American Indian tribe is one of the largest in the United States. I do not know how many people have proudly confided to me, over the years, that they are part Cherokee. "My great-grandmother was a Cherokee princess," so the story goes, "but she was ashamed of being Indian so she never taught us anything about that side of our family; do you know how I can find my Indian roots?" Many notable Americans are reputed to be Cherokee, such as Elvis, Cher, Jimi Hendrix, Jesse Jackson, Rita Coolidge, Dolly Parton, Willie Nelson, Val Kilmer, Will Rogers, Oral Roberts, and Chuck Norris, to name a few.[6] However, this phenomenon was not always so.

There was a time when many whites so reviled Cherokees that they recoiled at the very thought of living next door to supposed inferior Indian "savages." Whites commenced an ethnic-cleansing program to remove the entire Indian race from the South. During this dark time, known as the removal era (1815–1846), the Cherokee bravely resisted forcible resettlement for many years. In the end, they were overwhelmed in the face of government-sanctioned racism from all quarters, backed by raw state police power, due to the lack of timely and enforceable legal protections. As a result, the Cherokee were dispossessed of their homeland and ultimately were marched at bayonet point out of their homes into temporary stockades for relocation. Hundreds hid in caves and remote mountainous regions, fleeing the Georgia militia and federal troops—just like Anne Frank and her family hiding in German-occupied Holland—but thousands more became refugees on the infamous Trail of Tears, where one-fourth of the tribe perished. It was all perfectly legal. Here is how it was done...

The Roots of the Cherokee-Georgia Conflict

The aboriginal Cherokee homeland extends throughout the mountainous Allegheny region of the American Southeast in present-day Georgia, Tennessee, Alabama, Virginia, Kentucky, and the Carolinas. This beautiful domain comprises over 40,000 square miles, bounded on the north by the Ohio River of Kentucky and Virginia and extending southward into northern Georgia and Alabama. This important tribe has a long diplomatic and legal history. In the colonial era, 20,000 to 25,000 Cherokee resided in over fifty towns throughout Cherokee territory. They greeted the Hernando de Soto expedition when it penetrated the interior in 1540, and they were courted as valuable allies by all the European colonial powers during their tumultuous struggles for hegemony over the region.[7] Strategically located between territories claimed by the warlike English, French, and Spanish, the Cherokee Nation was drawn into the chronic warfare among these colonial powers. They participated in the French and Indian War (1754–1763), the Revolutionary War (1776–1782), hostilities against intruding American squatters following the Treaty of Hopewell of 1785, and the Creek War of 1812, while at the same time suffering several smallpox epidemics.

By 1800, the Cherokee numbered twenty thousand people. They occupied over forty thousand square miles of aboriginal land reserved for the Cherokee Nation in the Treaty of Hopewell, which guaranteed "the remainder of their country forever."[8] Half of the nation lay in Tennessee, while the rest was in Georgia and Alabama, with a sliver in North Carolina. The nation was governed by a national council composed of prominent chiefs and headmen from the Cherokee towns. Significant strides toward becoming a bicultural people were made under the federal policy to "civilize" Indians. In 1827, the Cherokee Nation adopted a constitutional government modeled after the United States', with three branches and a capitol located at New Echota, close to present-day Calhoun, Georgia. During this time, several religious missions spread the Christian gospel within the borders of the Cherokee Nation, and the people shifted to an agricultural economy. After Sequoyah invented the talking leaves—the Cherokee alphabet—tribal members quickly became versed in reading and writing their language. The Cherokee government founded the country's first tribal newspaper, the *Cherokee Phoenix,* in 1827, with national and international circulation.[9] The Cherokee had adapted to the new American republic and were poised to prosper as an influential American Indian tribe in the southeastern United States, but a clash was brewing between this ancient culture and newcomers in the Georgia region of the Cherokee Nation.

Georgia was founded in 1732 as a penal colony, in a bizarre penological experiment to permanently rid England of its unwanted criminals and poor.[10] By sending convicts to America, England's swelling jails and harsh debtor prisons could be relieved and the inmates could provide labor and other needed services in the colonies.[11] Unfortunately for the Cherokee, who lacked stringent immigration laws, north Georgia became the new home for the deportees. They were persons who were, by definition, undesirables that could not pass muster under today's immigration standards. The idea was to resettle the convicts, then teach them how to become useful and self-supporting through labor. That laudable rehabilitation goal, like most penology experiments, failed. After African slavery was introduced, the slaves soon replaced indentured British convict labor, and the scheme to teach the former prisoners how to become industrious fell apart. The ex-prisoners became harsher slave drivers than their more aristocratic neighbors.

Since these folks lived at the very bottom of their own society—as an underclass composed of undesirable criminals or impoverished inmates— they needed someone that they could look down upon. Indians and blacks became scapegoats over whom these unfortunates could assert supposed racial superiority. Into this mixture came other poor white southerners, variously derided as "crackers" or "corn-crackers," nicknames meant to label them as lawless, rootless rascals with a reputation as "boaster[s]" and "braggart[s]."[12] *Well, there goes the neighborhood.* As one can imagine, early race relations among indigenous and these nonindigenous Georgians did not go well.

It was only a matter of time before the immigrants began to yearn for Cherokee land and want the Natives to leave. In the early decades of the nineteenth century, several forces supported their desire to rid the South of Indians. Cotton was king and cheap land (preferably free) was needed to grow the ever-increasing quantity demanded by the textile industry. Expansionism was the order of the day, with opportunistic states' rights politicians driving the bandwagon. Political power in Washington shifted to the South and West following the nation's expanding population trend. With court rulings such as *Johnson v. M'Intosh*, whites were seemingly right when they expropriated Indian land. *After all,* went the common stereotype, *Indians do not farm their land like God intended.* In addition, widespread racism in the South played a significant role in animating the settlers' anti-Indian sentiments and justifying their dispossession and removal of the Indians.

As a result of these abject prejudices, federal Indian policy began to shift from the work of assimilating tribal Indians into American society, which had been the goal from the beginning of the republic, to removing them from it altogether. By the late 1820s, these factors combined to make removal of the Indians from the South a popular imperative in the Cracker State. As you will see, instead of being bulwarks against ethnic cleansing, the southern courts and the Supreme Court in *Cherokee Nation v. Georgia* became willing instruments in the removal process. The southern judges acceded to the will of the popular anti-Indian movement and issued opinions that fanned the flames of prejudice and undercut the Indian tribes' struggle to remain in their homelands.

Of these mounting forces, southern racism was the most destructive and invidious element that powered the removal movement, as Anglo Americans began in earnest to consider themselves racially superior to nonwhites. During this period, southern whites were becoming increasingly concerned, according to historian Tim Alan Garrison, with developing "putative racial distinctions between themselves and blacks and Indians."[13] Race and ethnicity have always been important concepts in America, with Georgia and other southern states usually in the forefront of the good-ol'-boy brand of American racism. Southern discourse on race was strongly influenced in the early 1800s by leading scientists and intellectuals of the day, along with court opinions that tagged Indians as "savages" and blacks as "inferior." Early southern thought developed during this period was later used to justify slavery in national debates before the Civil War.

Leading antebellum scientists, such as Dr. Samuel G. Morton and Dr. Charles Caldwell, conducted experiments and wrote texts attempting to prove the racial superiority of whites. Their findings supplied a scientific justification for slavery and the dispossession of American Indians. As president of the Academy of Natural Sciences, the influential Dr. Morton ranked the races by measuring human skulls.[14] Between 1820 and 1851, he acquired hundreds of human skulls to perform bizarre eugenics studies. In *Crania Americana* (1839), he proclaimed whites as the master race. "This race," according to Morton, "attains the highest intellectual endowments" and "peopled the finest portions of the earth, and [has] given birth to its fairest inhabitants."[15] Native Americans ranked very low on his pseudoscientific scale. Among their many innately inferior racial flaws, Morton found, "in their mental character the [American Indians] are averse to cultivation, and slow in acquiring knowledge; restless, revengeful, and fond of war, and wholly destitute of maritime adventure"; and his "scientific" findings asserted they are savages—that is, they have intellectual faculties "of a decidedly inferior cast" and are a "warlike, cruel and unforgiving" people who "turn with aversion from the restraints of civilised life, and have made but trifling progress in mental culture or the useful arts."[16] Blacks barely made the scale, because Morton was unsure whether they were the same species as whites. By assigning them "the lowest grade of humanity," he supplied a supposedly scientific basis for slavery.[17]

Dr. Charles Caldwell also contributed to the racial "science" of the day. As founder of the University of Louisville Medical School, he sprinkled a heavy dose of barefooted religion into the pseudoscientific discourse. In *Original Unity of the Human Race* (1852), Caldwell argued that God created four separate races—white, brown, red, and black—and placed them into a hierarchy, with whites at the top of the scale.[18] After comparing the crania of these races, Caldwell determined that red Indians were inherently inferior beings who are biologically incapable of civilization and doomed to extinction, like "wild animals."[19] According to Caldwell, "animal propensities" rule Indian morality and intelligence, and this trait renders them more "animal than of a human being."[20]

These "findings" provided scientific justification for removal. If wild savages cannot be absorbed into civilized society, shouldn't they be separated and removed from white society? *They are inferiors who cannot be civilized; they must be removed from civilization for their own good.* Morton and

Caldwell provide classic examples of scientific racism because they lent the veneer of science to support the racist paradigm of the day. Their findings resonated with southerners since they supported notions of racial superiority, justified slavery, and allowed them to rely upon science to justify the dispossession and removal of Native Americans. Thus, Georgia's governor George Troup was actually spouting conventional science, not simply redneck prejudice, when he maintained that Indians are fixed "in a middle station, between the negro and white man" but will gradually sink "to the condition of the former" if allowed to remain in the East.[21] These ingrained attitudes on race explain anthropologist James Mooney's observation that, unlike Spanish and French colonists who frequently lived among and intermarried with Native Americans, the English and Americans were highly race-conscious settlers. For them, racial separation was the rule of the day. Mooney described the settlers' attitudes as follows:

> [I]t never occurred to the man of Teutonic blood that he could have for a neighbor anyone not of his stock or color…Indians were regarded as an encumbrance to be cleared off, like the trees and wolves, before white men could live in the country. Intermarriages were practically unknown, and the children of such union were usually compelled by race antipathy to cast their lot with the savage.[22]

Georgians were filled with racial prejudice in the antebellum South. "The idea of Indians residing around and among whites," according to historian Garrison, was simply "not acceptable to citizens in Georgia"—they wanted racial separation "until it shall please God to bleach [their] skin."[23]

Against this backdrop, the seeds of the Cherokee-Georgia crisis were planted. At the outset, the new republic made too many conflicting promises about land. First, the United States signed the Treaty of Hopewell in 1785 to make peace with the Cherokee Nation and to reserve land for it in northern Georgia "forever." That promise was promptly broken. In the Compact of 1802, the fork-tongued government promised to extinguish all Indian land title in Georgia in exchange for a cession of land in western Georgia, as soon as Cherokee title could be "peaceably obtained, and on reasonable terms."[24] This thoughtless act of expediency broke the word of the United States in the Treaty of Hopewell and prompted one of the cruelest episodes in American history.

No one asked the Cherokee Nation about the deal. It flatly refused to cede any land in Georgia.[25] To support their entreaties, the federal authorities argued that whites already owned Cherokee soil under the right of discovery.[26] Resting on their treaty, the Cherokee rejected the doctrine of discovery espoused in *Johnson v. M'Intosh*, arguing that "[o]ur title has emanated from a *supreme* source, which cannot be impaired by the mere circumstance of discovery by foreigners; neither has this title been impaired by conquest or by treaty."[27] Tribal leaders informed the president that the "Cherokee Nation have now come to a decisive and unalterable conclusion, not to cede away any more lands" and suggested that other arrangements be made to accommodate Georgia's desire for land.[28] In the face of a dogged, nonviolent Cherokee resistance campaign to remain in their homeland, which included pacifism and noncooperation, sophisticated legal and moral arguments, public relations, and political lobbying in the nation's capital, the federal government balked at using force to remove the Cherokee. (That would be "unjust" and "revolting" to the sensibilities of the American people, according to President James Monroe.[29])

By the late 1820s, Georgia had grown impatient.[30] Governor Troup maintained that racially inferior Indians could never be assimilated or allowed to remain in Georgia. He warned in 1827 that if the federal government would not remove the Cherokee, Georgia would assume authority over them and drive them out. The state legislature bleated, "[t]he lands in question *belong* to Georgia—she *must* and she *will* have them."[31] It cried, "the time must come when the soil of Georgia shall no longer be imprinted with the footstep of the savage."[32] The irate lawmakers warned that nothing in the Compact of 1802 prevented Georgia from "resorting to force" and threatened the Cherokee Nation with the dire consequences of turning "a deaf ear to the voice of reason and of friendship."[33] The shrill cries became absolutely hysterical with the discovery of gold in Cherokee country. In 1828, the Cracker State mobilized. Emboldened by the election of Indian fighter and removal advocate Andrew Jackson to the presidency, Georgia launched its legal scheme to bring about a final solution to the Indian question. It used the law to force the Cherokee Nation to relinquish its sovereignty, lands, and gold, and make life so intolerable and repressive that the recalcitrant Indians would become demoralized and emigrate to a more racially tolerant place.

Extending the Law of the Crackers over the Cherokee Nation

The legislative blitzkrieg began in the late 1820s with the enactment of a series of anti-Indian laws. Georgia's 1827 Indian policy called for an all-out assault on the Cherokee Nation.[34] It formulated what was to become "the legal ideology of removal," in the apt words of historian Garrison. The policy began by protesting the federal government's failure to extinguish Indian title despite repeated appeals by Georgia. Next, it provided a disingenuous and self-serving rationale for the state's ownership of Indian land. The rationale rested, first and foremost, on the bald assertion that "*force* becomes *right*" under a homegrown, backwoods theory of "domain and empire."[35] Georgia's theory posited the false notion that British law only allowed Indians to possess land with permission by the Crown and assumed that this royal prerogative passed to Georgia as Britain's heir (a dubious presumption given the humble origins of the penal colony). Guided by these notions, the policy asserted that Georgia may legally exercise sovereignty over the lands and citizens of Indian nations within her chartered limits and take their land, since Indian title is "only permissive and temporary" under American law.[36] The policy urged the federal government to extinguish all Cherokee title to land in Georgia, protested the adoption of the Cherokee Constitution of 1827 by the Cherokee Nation, and announced that Georgia would not recognize that government.[37] In response to northern moral concerns, a more humanitarian gloss was placed on the mean-spirited policy in 1827. Georgia argued transparently that removal *is for the Indians' own good* and began burping out a bevy of anti-Indian race laws to bring the Cherokee Nation to its knees.[38] These Jim Crow laws are part of the dark side of the law. They illustrate such ill will and hostility against Indian tribes witnessed during much of the nineteenth century that the Supreme Court was prompted to oust the states from the administration of Indian affairs in later years to protect the tribes, because the states had become—in the eyes of the Supreme Court—their "deadliest enemies."[39]

To prevent Indian opposition to Georgia's policy, several statutes were enacted to prevent their access to state and tribal courts. The 1826 law stated: "no Indian and no descendant of an Indian, not understanding the English language, shall be deemed a competent witness in any court of justice created by the constitution or laws of this State."[40] This bar was expanded two years later:

[N]o Indian, or descendant of an Indian, residing within the Creek or
Cherokee nations of Indians, shall be deemed a competent witness, or
a party to any suit, in any court created by the constitution, or laws of
this state, to which a white man may be a party.[41]

Nor could Cherokees resort to their own courts, since Georgia declared all
Cherokee laws null and void, prohibited the application of those laws in
Georgia courts, and outlawed the use of Cherokee courts for any purpose.[42]

Other civil liberties were restricted in laws that isolated Cherokees
from contact with other peoples. An 1828 law prohibited neighboring Creek
Indians from entering Georgia without a permit since they were seen as sup-
portive of the Cherokee cause.[43] White males could not reside in the Cherokee Nation without a permit issued only after a loyalty oath was sworn.[44]
To discourage commercial intercourse, contracts between Cherokee Indians
and white persons were declared null and unenforceable.[45] As you will see
below, the rights of assembly and property ownership were abolished under
increasingly harsh martial laws.

The legislature extended Georgia laws over the Cherokee Nation in three
annexation laws. The first annexed part of the Cherokee Nation lying within
two counties.[46] Remaining portions of Cherokee territory were gobbled up
by subsequent extension laws that declared all Cherokee laws in the annexed
territories "null and void, as if the same had never existed."[47] To fill the void,
martial law was provided by magistrates specially empowered to hear legal
matters in the annexed territory. They could "call out a sufficient number of
militia...to aid and protect [them] in the execution of [their] duty."[48]

Removal—the final solution—crept into the picture in an 1828 resolution of the Georgia House of Representatives. It instructed the governor
to ask the president of the United States to remove "every Indian, whether
Creek or Cherokee, who may be found residing within" a boundary area
between the two nations.[49] To encourage removal, Georgia outlawed the use
of Cherokee law or courts to prevent or punish Indians from "enrolling as
an emigrant or actually emigrating, or removing from said nation" or selling
or ceding their land to the United States.[50] On the national level, Georgia's
laws were supplemented by its incessant urging that the federal government
remove the Indian nations across the Mississippi River. The branches of the
federal government began lining up in the late 1820s. A receptive President
John Quincy Adams lamented that Indians refused to assimilate or accept

Christianity and were instead intent on forming independent sovereignties. His secretary of state, Henry Clay, added that Indians were "inferior to the Anglo-Saxon race" and "not worth preserving"; to him, "their disappearance from the human family will be no great loss to the world."[51] In the late 1820s, government plans for removing the Cherokee and other Indian tribes were presented to Congress by the administration, complete with a chilling deportation list that inventoried the tribes, tallied their populations and acreage, and slated 129,266 Native Americans for emigration.[52]

Congress finally agreed to act. With the election of President Andrew Jackson in 1828, it passed the Indian Removal Act of 1830, despite strong opposition by the Cherokee Nation and its supporters, authorizing the president to make the necessary arrangements.[53] Though emigration was supposedly voluntary, the Indians were advised that "refusal to emigrate meant the end of federal protection and abandonment to state jurisdiction."[54] President Jackson made it clear that tribal sovereignty in the East was quickly coming to an end, and tribes were no longer welcome in that part of the nation.

By the time the national Indian Removal Act was signed into law, Georgia's removal program was already in full swing. To hamper Cherokee resistance, the assembly of tribal officials was criminalized by a law that prohibited,

> any person, or persons, under colour or pretense, of authority from said Cherokee tribe, or as head men, chiefs, or warriors of the tribe, to cause or procure by any means the assembly of any council, or other pretended Legislative body of the said Indians, or others living among them, for the purpose of legislating, (or for any other purpose whatever).[55]

The offense was punishable by imprisonment at hard labor for four years. (Georgians had by this time forgotten their penal roots and were running harsh prisons of their own.) To enforce Georgia's growing body of anti-Cherokee laws, a special paramilitary force was created—the infamous Georgia Guard. It's mission was to enforce state law within the Cherokee Nation, arrest violators, "protect" Cherokee gold mines, and otherwise harass and intimidate the Indians.[56]

Georgia was now poised to confiscate Cherokee land, water, and gold. This was accomplished by two remarkable statutes. The first created a lottery system for disposing of Cherokee land.[57] It divided the Cherokee Nation into four sections, and subdivided each into ninety-six districts containing plots of various sizes. The plots were surveyed under military protection and any interference was strictly prohibited. The lottery allowed white males to draw lots for the land. Indian homes were supposedly protected, but no Indian could "rent, sell or convey, his right of occupancy to any person or persons, unless it be to the government of this State, or of the United States," or to a lottery winner.[58] No compensation for taken Cherokee land was provided. As elated lottery winners entered the Cherokee Nation to take possession of the land, "some Cherokees fled in bewilderment," according to historian Walter Conser, while "others stubbornly refused to leave their homes and lands until they were evicted."[59]

The same law also turned regulation of navigable waters within the Cherokee Nation over to the state. The second law confiscated Cherokee gold mines. They were declared "the property of Georgia."[60] The governor was directed to "take immediate possession of all the gold, silver and other mines...in the said Cherokee country," by "military force" if necessary. Unauthorized digging by any "white man, Indian, negro or mulatto," or slave was prohibited (the latter could "be confiscated and sold"). *Now, all that remains is to run out the redskins, if only the feds would put military teeth behind their Indian Removal Act.*

By 1830, the crisis came to a head. The Cherokee government had been outlawed and its citizens stripped of their civil liberties and property. The Georgia Guard was goose-stepping its way into the Cherokee Nation, intimidating Indian residents, making arrests, seizing their land, and stationing guards at confiscated gold mines. The Cherokee Nation was overrun by prospectors, surveyors, militia, lottery winners, squatters, and other trespassers. Chaos and intimidation ruled the day. The Cherokee government protested the anti-Indian laws and trespasses, stating that "the Cherokee people [are not] prepared to submit to [Georgia's] persecuting edict" and appealed to the United States "for justice and protection."[61] Federal troops were dispatched to the tumultuous region, but withdrew as soon as the state complained about their presence, leaving the Cherokee Nation vulnerable to trespassers and the Georgia Guard. Were Georgia's actions legal?

In the Courts of the Crackers: Enforcing Georgia's Extension Laws

With all other avenues closed, the Cherokee leaders retained legal counsel to seek relief in the US Supreme Court. As the struggle spilled into the courts during the summer of 1830, the *Cherokee Phoenix* explained:

> If we are to be removed…by the United States…we wish to leave in the records of her tribunals, for future generations to read, when we are gone, ample testimony that she acted justly or unjustly.[62]

William Wirt, a famous litigator and former US attorney general, was picked to direct the legal offensive. As Wirt was figuring out how to get the Cherokee cause before the Supreme Court, the Georgia Guard arrested George Corn Tassels in Hall County, a chaotic place in the annexed region where Indians were frequently detained and incarcerated. Under Wirt's direction, Corn Tassels's lawyers challenged the constitutionality of the state's actions, making *Georgia v. Tassels* (1830) the perfect vehicle for taking the matter to the high court.[63]

In *Tassels,* the defendant contended that the extension laws were repugnant to the Constitution, because they violated the Treaty of Hopewell, which was the supreme law of the land, and infringed upon the sovereignty and right of self-government of an independent Cherokee Nation.[64] In reply, the state denied the Cherokee held any political or property rights. It asserted, first, that "Indian tribes are inferior, dependent, and in a state of pupilage to the whites," and, second, that the treaty is "void, because the general government had no right to treat with Indians within the limits of the State."[65]

The state court accepted Georgia's bigoted states' rights argument and upheld Georgia's laws in a bizarre opinion that turns the foundational principles of modern federal Indian law on their head. At the outset, the judges complained that the issue would never have surfaced except for outside political agitation, but promised that it would not influence their decision.[66] Relying on *Johnson v. M'Intosh*, they ruled that Cherokee sovereignty and land rights were destroyed by the doctrine of discovery and, as heir to Great Britain, Georgia could appropriate land belonging to the Indians.[67] *Shucks, since Georgia already owns the disputed lands, it must have jurisdiction over them.*

To support its circular logic, the *Tassels* court held that Indian tribes are not considered sovereignties by the US Constitution and the federal government erroneously entered into treaties with them.[68] Even if the United States could enter into Indian treaties, they become void, according to the court, when they conflict with states' rights or property.[69] Furthermore, the court announced that Cherokees are under a "state of pupilage" by Georgia and no treaty "could change that relation" or provide them with "the right of independent self-government."[70] Thus, treaties cannot obstruct "the act of Georgia, extending jurisdiction over the country in the occupancy of the Cherokee Indians."[71] In coming to this conclusion, the court found it patently unfair that everyone else took Indian land, "but so soon as the State of Georgia pursues the same course, a hue and cry is raised against her, and a lawyer residing near 1,000 miles from her borders has been employed to controvert hers and obstruct her laws."[72] Furthermore, Indians are merely "a savage race, and of imbecile intellect," according to the court, "incapable of complying with the obligations [of] civilized society."[73] The state laws were upheld and Corn Tassels was sentenced to death.

The idea of halting the state's onslaught against the Cherokee Nation never occurred to any of the Georgia judges. Their *Tassels* opinion espoused a dark southern view of Indian rights—an amoral world where aboriginal affairs are governed exclusively by the states without federal interference, in which Indians are an underclass; a place where treaties are void and tribes hold no political, property, or human rights. In this dark vision, states wield "plenary" power over Indians—unrestrained by constitutional limitations—because they are savages with an "imbecile intellect," incapable of civilization, and exist only under state tutelage as wards of the state without rights of citizenship. No one can accuse the judiciary of holding enlightened views in this case.

Nevertheless, *Tassels* did pave the way for appeal to the US Supreme Court. On December 12, Chief Justice Marshall granted a writ of appeal and ordered Governor Gilmer to appear before the Supreme Court. The appeal alarmed the state government. Governor Gilmer called the legislature into an emergency joint session. Preaching to the hastily assembled choir, he ranted that Marshall had no jurisdiction to intrude on Georgia or control its courts, and he promised to disregard Marshall's order. Outraged, the legislature directed Gilmer "to disregard each and every mandate" of the Supreme Court and to "resist and repel, any and every invasion, from whatever quarter upon the administration of the criminal laws of this State."[74] The disgruntled lawmakers vowed not "to become a party" to the appeal and ordered Corn Tassels's immediate execution—provocative acts calculated to moot the appeal, defy and forestall federal judicial review, and create a constitutional crisis.[75] Corn Tassels's death ended the appeal, but not the Cherokees' resolve to seek Supreme Court review. Three days later, Wirt amended the *Tassels* pleadings and refiled the case as an original action in the Supreme Court brought by the Cherokee Nation against the State of Georgia, entitled, *Cherokee Nation v. Georgia*.[76]

Cherokee Nation v. Georgia: How the Cracker State Got Away with Injustice

The Cherokee Nation appeared before the Supreme Court as a "foreign state, not owing allegiance to the United States, nor to any state of this union."[77] Its lawsuit sought to protect Cherokee sovereignty, self-government, and Indian-owned land derived "from the Great Spirit" from encroachment by Georgia.[78] By challenging the constitutionality of Georgia's extension laws—together with their underlying legal doctrines, fictions, and prejudices—the lawsuit called the foundation of colonialism into question.

The petition declared that Georgia lacked legal authority to seize Chreokee land. It asserted that the Georgia Charter and the doctrine of discovery do not clothe the state with the power to usurp Indian land, because these authorities are at odds with natural law. How can sailing along the coast possibly operate to appropriate Cherokee title, the petition asked? Cherokees "never assented" to the discovery doctrine; nor is it "a principle of the natural law, or obligatory on them."[79] Similarly, Georgia cannot disturb Cherokee self-government. British and American law never granted that authority to Georgians, and the numerous treaties between 1775 and 1819 recognize the Cherokee Nation as a "sovereign and independent state" with a right of self-government free from state interference.[80] The petition pointed to the Cherokee constitution, courts, laws, schools, and churches, and described how the people of the nation have become "civilized Christians and agriculturalists."[81] We are not savages, it urged; the Cherokee are just like "their white brethren around them."[82] Relying on American law, the petition reminded the Court that "treaties are the supreme law of the land; and all judges are bound thereby"—no state may pass laws impairing treaties.[83] Taking aim at Georgia's extension laws, the petition asserted that their invidious purposes were to parcel out the territory of the Cherokees; to extend the laws of Georgia over the same; to abolish the Cherokee laws, and to deprive the Cherokees of the protection of their laws; to prevent them, as individuals, from enrolling for emigration, under the penalty of indictment before the state courts of Georgia; to make it murder in the officers of the Cherokee government to inflict the sentence of death in conformity with Cherokee laws, subjecting them all to indictment therefore, and death by hanging; extending the jurisdiction of the justices of the peace of Georgia into the Cherokee territory, and authorizing the calling out of the militia of Georgia to enforce the process; and, finally, declaring that no Indian, or descendant of any Indian, residing within the Cherokee nation of Indians, shall be deemed a competent witness in any court of the state of Georgia, in which a white person may be a party, except such white person who resides within said nation.[84]

The petition decried the United States' failure to protect the Cherokee Nation from these unconstitutional acts, telling the Cherokee instead that federal troops "would co-operate with the civil officers of Georgia in enforcing their laws upon them."[85] The petition also informed the Court of the hanging of Corn Tassels in defiance of the chief justice in order to evade judicial review; recounted the most recent bevy of state laws enacted to confiscate Cherokee land and gold mines, and to abolish their right to assemble, including the stationing of armed forces at Cherokee gold mines; and, finally, it pointed out ongoing acts of violence and injustice by Georgia officers and agents within Cherokee territory under color of state law.[86] Georgia's laws are intended to force the Indians from their territory, the Cherokee Nation asserted, *in direct violation of the Cherokee treaties and the US Constitution.*

The lawsuit requested the Supreme Court to declare Georgia's laws null and void and enjoin the state "from interfering with the lands, mines and other property, real and personal, of the Cherokee nation, or with the persons of the Cherokee people."[87] These actions would "annihilate the Cherokees as a political society, and...seize, for the use of Georgia, the lands of the nation which have been assigned to them by the United States in solemn treaties repeatedly made and still in force."[88] Appealing to the conscience and sense of justice of the Court, the Cherokee sought "to be left in the undisturbed possession, use, and enjoyment of [their property], according to their own sovereign right and pleasure, and their own laws, usages, customs, free from any hindrance, molestation, or interruption by the state of Georgia, her officers, agents, and servants."[89]

How could the courts of the conqueror entertain such claims? Like the slaves in the *Dred Scott* case, Indians were at the courthouse doors asking a court that had not previously even recognized their standing to sue to strike down laws and principles that subjugated them. Furthermore, Georgia warned it would not participate in or obey the Supreme Court, creating a potential constitutional crisis. These factors sorely tempted the Marshall Court to side-step the issues. After all, under Article III of the US Constitution, no one could sue Georgia due to its sovereign immunity from suit secured to the states by the Eleventh Amendment. The only way this could be done was if the Cherokee Nation was treated as a foreign nation because foreign nations are not barred from suing states.[90] The Cherokee Nation therefore had vital jurisdictional, as well as substantive, reasons to appear as a foreign nation, especially since Georgia had successfully blocked other avenues for Supreme Court review.[91] Thus, the nation's legal status became a central issue as the case came before the six black robes on the Marshall Court.

The Court voted 4-2 to deny the Cherokee Nation standing to sue Georgia in four different opinions. A majority agreed the nation was a state, with the right of self-government and owned-property rights that could not be disturbed, but did not consider it a foreign state. Jurisdiction was also denied because the majority considered the request to protect Cherokee self-government from interference by Georgia to be a "political question" courts may not decide.

Chief Justice Marshall acknowledged that the nation is "a distinct political society, separated from others, capable of managing its own affairs and governing itself," and determined that federal treaties and laws "plainly recognize the Cherokee nation as a state."[92] However, he did not consider it a foreign state for purposes of suing a state of the union in federal court, despite the general rule that "nations not owing a common allegiance are foreign to each other."[93] Resorting once again to bare racial stereotypes, Marshall denied that the founders intended to allow Indian tribes to sue in federal court as foreign states. Considering Indian "habits and usages," he wrote, the framers of the Constitution did not have "tribes in view, when they opened the courts of the union to controversies between a state...and foreign states"; nor did it enter "the mind of an Indian" to use American courts because "[t]heir appeal was to the tomahawk."[94]

Justice Thomas Johnson rejected Cherokee nationhood status on racial grounds. Admitting no concern for "the morality of the case," he disagreed that Indian tribes are sovereignties because they are, in his eyes, "so low in the grade of organized society."[95] To him, tribes were a lowly "race of hunters connected in society by scarcely a semblance of organic government" and composed of a "restless, warlike, and signally cruel" people with "inveterate habits and deep seated enmity."[96] How could "any nation on earth treat them [as] a member of the community of nations?" he asked.[97] Like the *Tassels* decision, Johnson expressed deep-seated racial prejudice and animosity throughout his opinion—denigrating Cherokee land claims (their territory is "allotted to them as a boon, from a master or conqueror"),[98] scoffing at their nationhood ("the law of nations would regard [them] as nothing more than wondering hordes, held together only by ties of blood and habit, and having neither laws or government, beyond what is required in a savage state"),[99] and chiding them for going to court (they should not "appeal to any arbiter but the sword").[100] This tirade was joined by Justice Baldwin, who warned that if we allow Cherokees into the courthouse, "countless tribes…will rush to the federal courts in endless controversies, growing out of the laws of the states or of congress."[101]

Upholding the doctrines of colonialism, Marshall denied that Indian nations can be considered foreign nations under American law, because the indigenous nations "occupy a territory to which we assert a title independent of their will" and "they are in a state of pupilage" in their relations to the United States that "resemble that of a ward to his guardian."[102] In this imperialistic setting, he coined the phrase "domestic dependent nations" to denominate Indian tribes—a distinctly second-class political status since it meant that Indian tribes would not have attributes of external sovereignty in international relations and are nations subjugated by and subsumed into the domestic political system of the United State.[103] The holding also incorporated the trust doctrine first articulated in Victoria's law of nations into American law through Marshall's "state of pupilage" language, spawning the federal Indian trust doctrine—another second-class political status for Indian wards. Both of these principles remain foundational principles of federal Indian law today. Though some commentators assume they benefit Native Americans, it must be remembered that they were not espoused in *Cherokee Nation* to help Indian tribes, but rather to deny access to the courts.

Significantly, two justices considered the Cherokee Nation a foreign state and would have ruled in its favor.[104] Because the majority did not consider it a foreign state, the case was dismissed for lack of jurisdiction. The Court held that "an Indian tribe or nation within the United States is not a foreign state in the sense of the constitution, and cannot maintain an action in the courts of the United States."[105] It also described Georgia's assault on Cherokee sovereignty as a political question beyond "the proper province of the judicial department."[106] Turning a blind eye to the destruction of Cherokee self-government, Marshall sidestepped the issue with the following platitudes forever etched in records of the nation's judiciary:

> If it be true that the Cherokee nation have rights, this is not the tribunal in which those rights are to be asserted. If it be true that wrongs have been inflicted, and that still greater are to be apprehended, this is not the tribunal which can redress the past or prevent the future.[107]

Foregoing an opportunity to prevent manifest injustice, the Supreme Court ducked the issue in *Cherokee Nation*. In an opinion dominated by prevailing prejudices against Native Americans, the court closed its doors to the Cherokee during a pivotal time in their struggle to remain on their land as an independent people. By sending a signal that now all branches of government were lined up against the Cherokee people, the black robes paved the way for dispossession and forcible removal and became part of the process.

The Impacts of *Cherokee Nation* on Native Americans

The *Cherokee Nation* decision had several devastating impacts on Native Americans, most of which linger today. The most immediate was on the tribes in the South, because it encouraged the dispossession and removal fervor sweeping the region. Encouraged by the decision, other states joined Georgia in extending their laws over the Cherokee Nation and other Indian tribes in the South to rub out their independence and force them to leave.

By closing its eyes to bald aggression against a Native American minority, the Supreme Court sent a larger message to Pilgrims everywhere that was to guide their relations with Indians during the rest of the nineteenth century: *Indian tribes*, in Marshall's words, "*cannot maintain an action in the courts of the United States.*"[108] Following that ruling, the tribes ceased being litigants in the courts of the conquerors as Manifest Destiny ran its course. They were not welcome in the courthouse. Neither were their members, individual Indian wards of the government who, as noncitizens, were without the right to use American courts. It was not until the 1890s that Indian tribes began to reappear in the federal courts. Seemingly without reliable access to court, the tribes were forced to cede their land and sovereignty to land-hungry states or fight for their rights. In creating that perception, if not that reality, *Cherokee Nation* did far more to advance the goals of Manifest Destiny than divine intervention, as violence, warfare, and intimidation became coequal partners with the law as the principal means for moving indigenous peoples aside.

Cherokee Nation's guardianship doctrine and "domestic dependent nation" status were not espoused to help the Cherokee Nation, but to avoid ruling on its case. These doctrines have become cornerstone principles of federal Indian law since 1831. As we will explore in subsequent chapters, they often worked hardships on Indian tribes until advocates in the modern era of federal Indian law converted them into a shield as tools to protect Native American sovereignty, property, and human rights. On the dark side, trusteeship is a common feature in colonialism that means the government owns title to your property and guardianship is easily abused when unchecked by the courts—the government "can do things" to wards of the state that it could never do to citizens. In modern federal Indian law, the guardianship principle is supposed to inure to the benefit of the wards, as I will discuss in chapter fifteen. In that context, whenever the government is called upon by Native Americans to live up to the fiduciary standards of conduct normally imposed upon trustees in its management of Indian trust property or resources, federal agencies strenuously deny any trust obligation or responsibility to act like a trustee.[109] And what do we make of the "domestic dependent nation" status of American Indian tribes? At first blush, the loss of independence and the normal attributes of nationhood are obvious. For those Indian tribes who had not been conquered or, for that matter, who had not even encountered whites to any significant degree by 1831, the imposition of this subordinate political status by the Supreme Court was conquest by judicial fiat, especially when done without their consent to join the United States duly expressed in appropriate treaties. The second-class nature of this governmental status within our political system is seen today in the ease by which the Supreme Court trims the sovereignty rights and jurisdiction of tribal governments in recent years, making it painfully evident that the existence, scope, and nature of tribal sovereignty in the United States is vulnerable because it depends upon judicial fiat in the courts of the conqueror.[110]

Our immediate concern, however, is the struggle of the Cherokee people. Southerners rejoiced at the *Cherokee Nation* decision. Georgia had successfully bullied the high court and was now free to continue its vitriolic Indian policy. Alabama quickly jumped into the fray as Cherokee refugees fled into the Creek Nation within that state by enacting its own extension laws to assume jurisdiction over the Creek Nation. Relying heavily upon *Cherokee Nation* and the doctrine of discovery, the Alabama Supreme Court upheld those laws in *Caldwell v. State* (1832) in an opinion that also provided a legal justification for Indian removal.[111]

In *Caldwell*, a white farmer was charged with murdering an Indian in the Creek Nation. He asserted that Alabama's extension law was unconstitutional because it interfered with the sovereignty of the Creek Nation and the United States' power over Indian affairs. The Court rejected Creek sovereignty as no more than a "high pretension to savage sovereignty."[112] Applying Southern notions of international law, it held that Indian tribes are too savage and "ignorant of the customs and usages of civilized society" to have sovereignty and observed that treaties with these inferiors might as well be done with a "beast of the...forest."[113] They do not even own their own land, under *Johnson v. M'Intosh,* the court explained; and state extension laws are needed to carry out the Indian wardship principle of *Cherokee Nation.*[114] Such laws may legally destroy tribal sovereignty because whites conquered the tribes and obtained their national rights, the court reasoned, even though it admitted most tribes had never in fact been conquered.[115] *Fiddlesticks. We would have conquered them if they resisted.*

The moral consequences of abject colonialism were completely lost on the *Caldwell* court. Siding steadfastly with the colonizers, it asserted "our forefathers were justifiable in clearing away the forests and cultivating the fields formed by their industry, and in bringing the Indians into subordination to them...let us continue to act in the same way."[116] If Indians disliked living under the thumb of the state, they should leave. After all, Alabama "has looked with the deepest solicitude" upon "the removal of the Indians, and the opening of the territory occupied by them to a valuable population" and "to the time...when the whole state would be freed from its Indian population."[117] These inferiors are naturally bound for extinction, in any event, the Alabama judges predicted, and will be replaced by cheerful "cities, smiling fields, and happy habitations."[118] The Court rejoiced that "our happy political institutions and the religion of the Bible have displaced their barbarous laws, and wretched superstitions" and ended its opinion on a self-righteous religious note: "Are we not compelled to admit that the superintending providence of that Being who first formed the earth, is to be seen in this mighty change?"[119]

Thus, encouraged by *Cherokee Nation,* the Alabama courts eagerly lined up with the Christian God, the Georgia judiciary, and Congress to force Indians from the South. To evade Supreme Court review, Alabama did not expedite Caldwell's execution, like Georgia. Instead, the governor pardoned him to moot any possible appeal from the *Caldwell* decision.[120] In 1836, the United States army marched 14,000 Creek Indians out of Alabama to Indian Territory in present-day Oklahoma.

Cherokee resistance remained steadfast in the face of these crippling setbacks. William Wirt returned to court shortly after *Caldwell* was decided in a last-ditch legal effort to seek judicial protection. On this occasion, the Georgia Guard arrested several missionaries living in the Cherokee Nation without a state permit. They were convicted and sentenced to four years in prison at hard labor under Georgia law. The missionaries challenged their conviction on the same grounds used in *Cherokee Nation.* Their appeal became a vehicle for bringing another test case to the US Supreme Court, where Wirt reargued the merits of the Cherokee cause in the famous case of *Worcester v. Georgia* (1832).[121] This time, Wirt scored an astounding victory.

Worcester came in the twilight of Chief Justice Marshall's distinguished career, at a time when his thinking about the place of American Indians in society and law had fully matured. By 1832, he had seen—to his surprise and dismay—how his prior rulings in *Johnson* and *Cherokee Nation* had been used to gravely harm American Indians. As you will see, Marshall was now prepared to address the Cherokee issues head-on and set a path for correctly understanding Native American rights.

Deeply moved by Wirt's eloquent and forcible argument in *Worcester,* the Marshall Court struck down Georgia's extension laws.[122] Rejecting the South's dark version of Indian law, the Marshall Court ruled that Georgia had no right to tread on the sovereignty of the Cherokee Nation or take its land. Abandoning derogatory racial stereotypes, the majority simply described American Indians as "a distinct people, divided into separate nations, independent of each other and of the rest of the world, having institutions of their own, and governing themselves by their own laws."[123] The landmark decision ridiculed and restricted the doctrine of discovery as "an extravagant and absurd idea."[124] The king's royal charters and the doctrine of discovery do not transfer Indian land title to anyone, the Court ruled. They simply granted England and its successor, the United States, an exclusive right to purchase such land as the Natives were willing to sell, and nothing more; and this power does not affect tribal sovereignty, much less empower states to govern Indian tribes or intrude into their self-government.[125] Laying to rest Georgia's pompous claims to "domain and empire," the Court observed that the goal of Georgia's royal charter was simply to enable England's incarcerated poor "to gain a comfortable subsistence by cultivating lands in the American provinces," and this charitable purpose is "incompatible with the lofty ideas of granting the soil, and all its inhabitants from sea to sea" to the penal colony.[126]

Worcester established the principle that the borders of Indian reservations form an inviolate barrier to intrusion by state laws. The Court stated, "[t]he treaties and laws of the United States contemplate the Indian territory as completely separated from that of the states; and provide that all intercourse with them shall be carried out exclusively by the government of the union."[127] Thus, Georgia's laws were declared a nullity, because the "Indian nations had always been considered as distinct, independent political communities, retaining their original natural rights, as the undisputed possessors of the soil, from time immemorial" and treaties made with Indian nations are "the supreme law of the land."[128] The Court concluded:

> The Cherokee Nation, then, is a distinct community occupying its own territory, with boundaries accurately described, in which the laws of Georgia can have no force, and which the citizens of Georgia have no right to enter, but with the assent of the Cherokees themselves, or in conformity with treaties, and acts of congress.[129]

Accordingly, the Court reversed the missionaries' conviction and ordered their release. The ruling no doubt absolved the conscience of many of the justices for encouraging the removal fervor in *Cherokee Nation*. A relieved Justice Story wrote shortly afterward, "[t]hanks be to God, the Court can wash its hands clean of the inequity of oppressing the Indians and disregarding their rights," adding, "[t]he Court has done its duty. Let the Nation now do theirs."[130]

Unfortunately, the belated decision did the Cherokee little good, for it came too late in the day to deter the Indian removal movement. By 1832, federal removal policies were entrenched. Upon learning of the *Worcester* decision, President Andrew Jackson reputedly said, "John Marshall has made his decision, now let him enforce it" and did nothing to enforce the judgment.[131] Georgia, of course, ignored the ruling and defiantly refused to release Samuel Worcester and his fellow missionaries from prison. The rest of the South had already lined up under the green light given in *Cherokee Nation*. In fact, one southern court repudiated *Worcester* in *State v. Foreman* (1835).[132]

Foreman arose in 1835 during a period of turmoil and confusion within the Cherokee Nation. Tribal unity was at last beginning to crumble under incessant removal pressures, the invasion of frenzied white trespassers, and the oppressive conditions of Native life under southern rule. By then, their only judicial champion, John Marshall, had died. His court was now under the leadership of Chief Justice Roger Taney, a stalwart slavery proponent and Jackson appointee. Against this backdrop, one Cherokee was charged in *Foreman* with murdering another in the Tennessee portion of the Cherokee Nation—a reputed political assassination of a removal advocate. The prosecution was brought under a state law extending criminal jurisdiction over the Cherokee Nation. To breathe life back into the southern doctrines of Indian law rejected in *Worcester*, the prosecuting attorney attacked that decision as being contrary to all of Marshall's prior holdings and repeated the old arguments against tribal sovereignty made in *Tassels*, *Caldwell*, and *Cherokee Nation*. In a rambling 2-1 decision, the Tennessee Supreme Court embraced the arguments. Chief Justice Catron handed down the decision of the court in one of the most racist judicial opinions ever written.

Describing Pope Alexander VI's papal bull of 1493 as the law of nations, Catron contended that none of the inhabitants of the New World "were allowed any rights" under international law and casually observed that European claims in the New World were "enforced by the sword."[133] North America should "be peopled by Europeans," he declared, rather than be "the haunt of savage beasts, and of men yet more fierce and savage."[134] We cannot allow "mere wandering tribes of savages" to own land, because they are infidels without rights in Christian courts, as held by Lord Coke in *Calvin's Case*.[135] Absolutely livid with hate, the court ranted that nonagricultural peoples "deserve to be exterminated as savage and pernicious beasts."[136] Embracing the racist element of Manifest Destiny, Catron predicted that Indians will melt away "under the influence and superior powers, mental and moral, of the white man, as did the savages of Europe, Asia, and Africa"—they must "accept a master or perish."[137] How can Cherokees possess sovereignty and soil when "North American savages...had no government"? Rejecting *Worcester,* the court reinstated the harsh settler-state law of the South:

> Our claim is based on the right to coerce obedience. The claim may be denounced by the moralist. We answer, it is the law of the land. Without its assertion and vigorous execution this continent never could have been inhabited by our ancestors. To abandon the [doctrine of discovery] now is to assert that they were unjust usurpers, and that we, succeeding to their usurped authority and void claims to possess and govern the country, should in all honesty abandon it, return to Europe, and let the subdued parts again become a wilderness and hunting ground.[138]

Despite *Worcester,* the court held that Indian treaties are void if they conflict with state's rights.[139] In short, pejorative racial stereotypes of American Indians controlled the *Foreman* decision.

Thus, the courts of Tennessee, Georgia, and Alabama enthusiastically supported the South's legal framework for dispossessing the Cherokee people and destroying their government. The dark trilogy of legal opinions in *Foreman, Caldwell,* and *Tassels* not only fanned the flames of prejudice against Native Americans, but set an ugly malignant tone for anti-Indian racism in the South. This trilogy became the de facto law of the South in flagrant disregard for the belated decision in *Worcester.* In the meantime, Indian tribes throughout the East were being relocated, one after the other, to Indian Territory far beyond the borders of existing states under the federal removal policy.

Demoralized and disillusioned by the overwhelming removal pressures that were engulfing the Cherokee Nation, the people's resolve faltered and a few succumbed. Under constant harassment by the Georgia Guard, who arrested and detained Principal Chief John Ross without charge and seized the *Cherokee Phoenix,* national unity began to splinter. While the Ross government was negotiating with President Jackson to find a compromise solution that would allow the Cherokee to remain in their homeland, a tiny removal faction of individual Cherokees approved the administration's Treaty of New Echota. Even though this "treaty" was not entered into by the Cherokee government, the bogus document quickly supplanted all prior treaties entered into between the Cherokee Nation and the United

States. Signed on December 29, 1835, it purported to require all Cherokee to "remove to new homes within two years."[140] A petition protesting the so-called treaty was signed by nearly 17,000 Cherokee and the tribal government bitterly repudiated the document. However, in the eyes of the United States, that nefarious treaty—part of the dark side of the law—completed the legal framework for removal. The president refused to consider the Cherokee petition and directed that no further assembly would be allowed for the Cherokee government to discuss the matter.[141] The law of the conquerors now required the Cherokee to leave.

After tidying up the paperwork, the bureaucrats turned the distasteful task of forcible removal over to the military. The unpleasant job fell to General Wool, the commander of federal troops in the Cherokee territory. His first step was to disarm the Cherokee and quell any further tribal opposition to the removal treaty. The departure deadline came and went. However, only a handful of Cherokee voluntarily removed. Thus, Wool's successor, General Winfield Scott, assembled 7,000 soldiers in May of 1837 to forcibly remove nearly 17,000 Cherokee. His proclamation warned every man, woman, and child to remove in one month or face the consequences:

> My troops already occupy many positions…and thousands and thousands are approaching from every quarter to render resistance and escape alike hopeless…Will you, then, by resistance compel us to resort to arms…or will you by flight seek to hide yourselves in mountains and forests and thus oblige us to hunt you down?[142]

Stockades were built throughout Cherokee territory for holding the prisoners. From these posts, the soldiers rounded up every Indian they could find. Mooney describes the sickening hunt from eyewitness accounts:

> [S]quads of troops were sent to search out with rifle and bayonet every small cabin hidden away in the coves or by the sides of mountain streams, to seize and bring in as prisoners all the occupants, however and wherever they might be found. Families at dinner were startled by the sudden gleam of bayonets in the doorway and rose up to be driven with blows and oaths along the weary miles of trail that led to the stockade. Men were seized in their fields or going along the road, women were taken from their wheels and children from their play. In many cases, on

turning for one last look as they crossed the ridge, they saw their homes in flames, fired by the lawless rabble that followed on the heels of the soldiers to loot and pillage. So keen were these outlaws on the scent that in some instances they were driving off the cattle and other stock of the Indians almost before the soldiers had fairly started their owners in the other direction. Systematic hunts were made by the same men for Indian graves, to rob them of the silver pendants and other valuables deposited with the dead. A Georgia volunteer, afterward a colonel in the Confederate service, said: "I fought through the civil war and have seen men shot to pieces and slaughtered by the thousands, but the Cherokee removal was the cruelest work I ever knew."[143]

Amid the brutality, some Indians were shot and hundreds escaped into hiding as fugitives. After the people were herded into General Scott's concentration camps, the death toll and dirty work of removal began. By the time it was over, more than 4,000 Cherokee exiles had died as a direct result of removal.[144] The sickness, heartbreak, malnutrition, exposure, dispossession, and death that accompanied the six-month winter journey known as the Trail of Tears illustrate the staggering cost in human suffering that forcible removal causes.[145]

The removal of the Indian race from the South is one of the greatest tragedies found in American history, marked by terrible injustice, broken treaties, discriminatory laws, unenforced court rulings, greed, and abject racism. It is hard to fathom the great capacity for evil that lies in the human breast, for we cannot tarry long at that doorstep without being utterly repulsed. In 2000, one descendent of those who were removed, Joy Harjo, the Muscogee Creek poet and musician, posed a universal question that seems apt as we contemplate the harm brought about by the Indian removal movement. She wrote:

> Why does evil exist? I ask the question we all continue to ask. And why does evil often sit in the chairs of rulers, presiding over history, over human and other lives they are charged to protect? We are the ones who give these people power. Andrew Jackson was made president after being medaled with high war honors by the US Government for killing Mvskoke women and children who were resisting being forced from their homelands.[146]

What can be said of the legal framework that made the tragic Trail of Tears possible? Two observations can be made.

First, though it was all very legal, we know it was wrong. Government removal of indigenous groups from their aboriginal lands is considered an act of genocide in the world today. To what extent does the legal structure for Cherokee removal resemble the legal framework for removing the Jewish population from German society? There are uncomfortable parallels. In both instances, the roots of removal began with the development of putative racial distinctions that justify the supposed racial superiority of the dominant majority group. This racism was fermented in the South by politicians, scientists, and intellectuals and supported by statutes and judicial opinions until it was deeply embedded in the minds of most Southerners. Similarly, in Germany the vitriolic writings of Hitler and others contributed to widespread prejudice against Jews. Nazi laws singled them out from the rest of the population by requiring Jews to wear yellow armbands and stars. In both places, the target group was stripped of its civil liberties during the second phase of removal. We have seen how thoroughly this was done by Georgia law. Similarly, German statutes disallowed Jewish access to the courts, removed them from the professions and economy, and severely restricted interracial contact. The third phase involved state confiscation of property. This was accomplished in both instances through the law. Thereafter, the target populations were incarcerated pending deportation, and the victims were rounded up by force if necessary and taken away. Ghettos were established for those purposes throughout Europe, similar to the military stockades in Cherokee territory. Finally, the exiles were physically removed to their final destinations by the machinery of the state. Removal was perfectly legal in both places.[147] Not a judge could be found in Germany or Georgia to declare the framework for removal illegal, as their tribunals were effectively closed to Indians and Jews. Instead, the courts in both instances enthusiastically supported the legal framework for removal. The law was employed as an instrument for evil in both instances. The biggest difference between the two removal programs is that the deplorable actions of the Nazis are burned into the public consciousness while the framework for Indian removal is barely remembered.

Second, the legal framework for Cherokee removal illustrates the pivotal role of the courts in democracies in protecting minority rights from what Alexis de Tocqueville and John Stuart Mill described as the "tyranny

Legal Framework for Removal*

Phase of Removal	Georgia	Germany
1. The ideology for removal is developed	White superiority espoused by politicians, scientists, intellectuals; anti-Cherokee policy of the Senate Resolution of 1827.	Widespread prejudice against Jews engendered by writings of Hitler and others, supported by state propaganda, and Nazi party program (1920) (p. 3).
2. Minorities are singled out by the law	Cherokee ethnicity self-apparent; state law directed specifically against the Cherokee.	Jews must wear yellow armbands and Jewish star in public so they can be identified. Law defines Jew and requires them to register with state and carry ID cards; state issues special names and passports marked with a J (1935, 1938–39 and 1941 Decrees at 139, 223, 233, 237, 244, 347).
3. The target group is stripped of civil liberties	Indians cannot testify or sue whites in state court, use Cherokee laws or courts (Acts of 1826, 1828–1830); contact with others circumscribed (Acts of 1828, 1830); commercial intercourse discouraged, contracts annulled (Act of 1830); self-government banned (Acts of 1827–1829); assembly prohibited (Act of 1830); special police created to enforce anti-Cherokee laws (Act of 1830). Cherokee Nation denied access to federal court in *Cherokee Nation*.	Intermarriage banned (1933 and 1935 laws and decrees at 3, 122, 127, 139–40); Jews removed from government, education, medicine, army, law, farming (1933 and 1935 laws at 12, 17–8, 53, 115–6; 1934 and 1936–8 decrees at 98, 104, 173–4, 187–8, 234, 242); nationality and citizenship revoked (1933 and 1935 Acts at 36, 127); assembly restricted (1935 Decree at 141); racial mixing banned (1937 Edict at 191–2); radios banned (1939 Decree at 305).
4. The state confiscates property	Cherokee land awarded to lottery winners, state takes control of water, limits right of Indians to sell or lease their land (Act of 1830); gold mines and precious metals confiscated (Act of 1830).	Jewish businesses are banned, banking accounts regulated and rescinded (1938 Decree at 254–5).
5. The target populations are incarcerated pending removal	Indian Removal Act (1830) and nefarious Treaty of New Echota (1835) lay federal foundation for removal. Process begins with General Scott's proclamation (May 1837) and building of stockades to house Cherokee pending deportation.	Jewish right to travel restricted (1939 Decree at 244); Reich Office for Jewish Emigration formed (Edict of 1939 at 276); ghettos established in European cities to incarcerate Jews pending removal.

*All page citations to German law in this table are to the Nazi statutes, decrees, and regulations that appear in Joseph Walk, ed., *Das Sonderrecht fur die Juden im NS-Staat: Eine Sammlung der gesetzlichen MaBnahmen und Richtlinien—Inhalt und Bedeutung* (Heidelberg, Germany: C. F. Muller Juristishcer Verlag, 1981) (meaning *Rights of Privilege for the Jews in the Nazi State: A Collection of the Legal Measures and Directives—Content and Meaning*), which have been translated for the author by Joanne Hayes of the University of Colorado.

of the majority." These nineteenth-century thinkers pointed out that one of the biggest challenges in a democracy is to protect minority rights and liberty from the excesses of majoritarian rule. Every form of government carries an inherent danger of intrusion upon individual liberty. For democracies, it is the absolute power of the majority. When every institution of democratic government gives sway to the daily passions of the majority that are hostile to minority liberty, as in the case of the Georgia-Cherokee conflict, it falls to the courts to control these excesses of democracy. The Supreme Court in *Cherokee Nation* failed to discharge that function. The Court closed its doors, shut its eyes, and allowed the tyranny of the majority to dispossess and remove the Cherokee people from their homeland. It is important to safeguard the rights and liberty of indigenous peoples who are often permanent minorities in settler states. They can never hope to become part of the majority without shedding their indigenous rights, values, and way of life and quietly assimilating into the settlers' society. For democratic settler states who prize free institutions, an independent judiciary must provide a legal bulwark against encroachments upon Native peoples. When they fail to do so, the tyranny of the majority can do great harm, even in a democratic form of government.

Could the Supreme Court have forestalled these events with a timely declaration of tribal rights in *Cherokee Nation*? We shall never know. An injunction in 1831 might have changed the political equation by dampening Georgia's assault and stopping the other southern states in their tracks, or at least made it clear to the nation at a pivotal time that their actions were illegal. On the other hand, the belligerent states' rights mood of antebellum southern states willing to secede to preserve their slave-based way of life may have rendered any decision impotent. We do know that the *Cherokee Nation* Court deftly sidestepped the issue when it was first presented in an opinion that encouraged the movement, and that it was too late in the day for *Worcester* to rectify those mistakes. There is wisdom in the adage "justice delayed is justice denied."

Native American Efforts to Overcome Hardships Created by *Cherokee Nation*

Toward the end of the nineteenth century, Indian tribes slowly gained reliable access to the federal courts, years after Manifest Destiny had spent itself on the Pacific Rim. The celebrated case of *United States ex rel. Standing*

Bear v. Crook (1879) sparked renewed interest in litigation as a means to protect Indian rights.[148] In *Standing Bear*, Judge Elmer Dundy ruled that a Ponca Indian chief was a "person" under the habeas corpus law and could therefore maintain an action in the courts of the United States to challenge the legality of his tribe's confinement, despite the argument by the US attorney that none but free American citizens are entitled to bring such cases in federal court. The Ponca Tribe had been removed to Indian Territory, but Standing Bear's band escaped and returned to their Nebraska homeland, where they were arrested by General George Crook. The court set Standing Bear's people free, after holding that Crook lacked the authority to incarcerate them, and allowed them to remain in their homeland. This decision opened Indian eyes to the possibility of protecting their rights through litigation.

A handful of tribes became litigants in the 1890s. This trend increased dramatically with the passage of twentieth-century laws increasing tribal access to the courts, such as the Indian Claims Commission Act of 1946, which established a special forum to hear Indian claims against the United States.[149] In 1966, another statute authorized Indian tribes to bring suit in federal court to protect rights arising under the Constitution, laws, or treaties of the United States.[150] From then on, the courthouse doors were open and tribes took full advantage of their right to sue. During the modern era of federal Indian law, tribes scored a number of astonishing legal victories as they reclaimed their sovereignty and held America accountable for obligations owed to Native people under the law.

In closing the courthouse doors to the Cherokee Nation at a crucial time, *Cherokee Nation* illustrates that justice delayed is justice denied. Today, the United Nations Declaration on the Rights of Indigenous Peoples (2007) makes it clear that denial of access to the courts on indigenous land issues is a human-rights violation. Articles 26–28 require states to recognize and protect indigenous lands, to implement "a fair, independent, impartial, open and transparent process...to recognize and adjudicate the rights of indigenous peoples pertaining to their lands," and to afford them a right to participate in that process. None of these human-rights protections were available to the Cherokee Nation in 1831. Further, when indigenous land has been "confiscated, taken, occupied, used or damaged without their free, prior, and informed consent," as done to the Cherokee people, Article 28 requires the state to give restitution of lands equal in size and quality or other appropriate redress. Failure to provide those protections, processes, and remedies amounts to a clear-cut human-rights violation under the UN declaration. Though this international law development comes too late in the day for the Cherokee Nation, it leaves little doubt about the injustice done in 1831 and may help forestall future landgrabs. The declaration also leaves no doubt that the Indian removal policy promoted by *Cherokee Nation,* the southern judiciary, and Congress in the 1800s amounts to a massive violation of human rights, if executed today under current international standards. Article 10 states: "Indigenous peoples shall not be forcibly removed from their lands or territories."

The remarkable holdings in *Worcester* helped Native Americans mitigate the hardships imposed by *Cherokee Nation*'s doctrines of colonialism. *Worcester* arose in the wake of *Cherokee Nation*, during a frightening time when the nation was aligned to oppress, dispossess, and remove the Cherokee. As the single shining beacon from that dark period, *Worcester* established several important legal principles that endure today: (1) the Indian tribes enjoy a sovereign right of self-government free from interference by the states; (2) their treaties must be honored as the supreme law of the land; (3) the doctrine of discovery and edicts from Europe do not divest Indian land or sovereignty; and (4) reservation borders are protective barriers against hostile states and land-hungry settlers. Although belated and ineffectual in 1832, *Worcester* eventually became the law of the land over time under principles of stare decisis. Today, *Worcester* is cited every time a court protects tribal sovereignty. On the other hand, the bigoted trilogy of the southern judiciary is no longer cited as legal precedent. *Tassels, Caldwell,* and *Foreman* fell into obscurity and cannot be found in modern treatises, such as *Cohen's Handbook on Federal Indian Law*. Access to the courts has made a difference in the lives of Native Americans, who even use the courts to confront vestiges of racism in public life that have been so injurious in the past.[151]

At the same time, *Cherokee Nation* remains good law today, but in a mitigated form. It is relied upon by the courts mainly to denominate Indian tribes as "domestic dependent nations"—the second-class political classification became the legal basis used by Indian tribes during the Native American sovereignty movement to solidify their remaining sovereignty within the American political system. It is cited also for espousing the federal Indian trust doctrine, which tribal litigants converted into a shield for protecting tribal rights during the modern era of federal Indian law. The dark side of *Cherokee Nation*—it's noxious use of the discovery doctrine and prevailing racial prejudice to place Indian tribal nationhood into a colonial legal structure—has been largely obscured, superseded, and mitigated over time by *Worcester*. Thus, when those two decisions are read together by modern-day courts, powerful principles of federal Indian law emerge. Those principles solidify the presence of tribal governments in the American political system, which comprises over five hundred federally recognized Indian tribes who are fully functional "domestic dependant nations" in the eyes of the law, including three Cherokee governments—the Cherokee Nation, United Keetoowah Band, and Eastern Band Cherokee Tribe. In short, after lawyering up, tribal litigants made the best out of a bad case and turned a sow's ear into a silk purse. Unfortunately, the dark side of *Cherokee Nation* still resides in the law, ready for use by any jurist who wishes to impose harsh colonial doctrines upon Indian tribes.

The human spirit is hard to snuff out. Few acts of genocide are entirely successful, due to the human will to survive. Despite the United States' efforts to remove every Cherokee from the South, many escaped. These fugitives were befriended by W. H. Thompson, a longtime friend of the Indians. A man of goodwill able to rise against the anti-Indian sentiments of his day, Thompson was an orphan who had been adopted by a Cherokee chief and given the name *Wil-Usdi'*. Under his protection, over one thousand Cherokee found refuge in North Carolina.[152] Today, 13,400 of their descendants remain in the South. They reside deep in the Smoky Mountains on an Indian reservation of 52,000 acres governed by the Eastern Band of Cherokee Indians, a federally recognized Indian tribe.[153] The presence of this flourishing Indian nation represents victory over the Indian removal movement. It gives testament to the determined will of indigenous peoples to remain in their homeland.

Those Cherokee emigrants who survived the Trail of Tears managed to flourish in dusty Oklahoma. With a diverse tribal membership comprising more than 200,000 Cherokee Indians, Delaware Cherokees, Shawnee Cherokees, and former slaves known as Cherokee Freedmen, the Cherokee Nation is located in northeast Oklahoma, where 70,000 real, live Cherokee Indians reside in a territory spanning fourteen counties. The Nation continues to exercise self-government with a strong cultural and economic base.[154] Today, everyone wants to be a Cherokee, even movie stars. Many prominent Americans proudly belong to this popular tribe of Indians.

In the fall of 2008, I journeyed to the heavily forested mountains of Cherokee, North Carolina. I came to address a historic joint council held between the Cherokee Nation of Oklahoma and North Carolina. As I looked out upon the Principal Chiefs and council members of this great people assembled in the luxurious casino auditorium, there was no doubt that I was in the midst of a handsome and vibrant people with a rich, storied past. Perhaps God smiles on those who have suffered great misfortune, because the resilient Cherokee people have largely overcome the immense burdens placed on their ancestors by the harsh law of the South. Looking back on the tragic events surrounding *Cherokee Nation*, my nephew Taylor Keen, a former member of the Cherokee National Council, observed in 2008:

> The Cherokee Nation suffered greatly from the tyranny of Georgia and its Harassment Laws, as each of our sovereign capacities as a Nation were systematically stripped from us. These events were mirrored once again by the State of Oklahoma at the end of the allotment period. But all of these events help galvanize the resolve of the Cherokee Nation, who has time and time again learned to survive, adapt, and prosper.[155]

And what became of Georgia's vainglorious dreams of domain and empire? Shucks, they never amounted to much.

ᎠᏂᏣᎳᎩ ᎠᏂᎳᏬᎾ, ᎣᏍᏓ Ꮟ ᎨᏤᏛ ᏤᎭ

(Cherokee People, it is good you are still here.)[156]

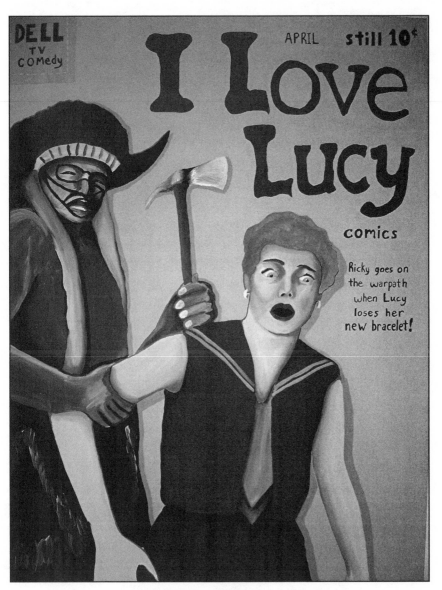

You Got Some Explaining To Do

CHAPTER SIX

Connors v. United States and Cheyenne Indians: Were the Indian Wars Legal?

THE LAND CAN SPEAK to those who listen. The stories it tells are not always pretty. There is a bluff near Chivington, Colorado, overlooking Big Sandy Creek where you can hear women and children crying in the wind. This remote spot is the place where 160 Cheyenne and Arapaho Indians were murdered by Colonel John M. Chivington's militiamen. The dead were horribly mutilated. Afterward, their scalps and body parts, including genitalia and fetuses, were paraded about Denver by the troops as grisly trophies before cheering crowds. Skulls of decapitated victims were sent back East to the Smithsonian Institution. In Indian Country, the Sand Creek Massacre created shock waves of anger among the Plains Indian tribes, because the Cheyenne and Arapaho villagers were mainly unarmed women, children, and the elderly who were at peace. They were camping at the site under the protection of the US flag when the unprovoked surprise attack took place. Subsequent government investigations determined that the assault was unauthorized, but no one was ever punished, not even a sacrificial corporal.

The 1864 massacre cut deep wounds into fragile race relations on the Great Plains and Rocky Mountain region, prompting bloody retaliation between Indians and whites for years to come. Only recently have those wounds begun to heal. Today, this haunting place lies peacefully hidden among the sand hills and grasslands of southeastern Colorado, populated mainly by antelope, coyote, and prairie dogs. It is hard to imagine the terror of that day, among the cottonwood timbers in the valley below the bluffs, where howitzers fired down into the village. In 2007, the US Park Service and Cheyenne Nation officially dedicated this place as the Sand Creek Massacre National Historic Site before a large crowd of descendants, dignitaries, and onlookers who gathered to pay tribute to the dead and memorialize this tragic episode in American history. One tribal speaker observed, "They say the event of Virginia Tech was the deadliest shooting rampage in American history. I think this was the deadliest shooting rampage in American history."

I have always admired the Cheyenne people. Over the years, I have enjoyed many friends, relatives, and clients among this fabled tribe.[1] In many respects, the Cheyenne Indians are American icons. Their history, way of life, value system, and spiritual outlook provide a rich example of

Plains Indian culture. For many people around the world, their striking images, proudly adorned in beautifully beaded buckskin and regal eagle-feather warbonnets, transcend the art of one tribe and symbolize the heart and soul of Native America itself. The history of my own people, the Pawnee Indians, is closely intertwined with that of our Cheyenne neighbors.[2] They call themselves *Tsis tsis' tas*, meaning the "Human Beings." Our Pawnee name for them is *Sahi*, and they are referred to in sign language as "Cut Fingers," after their mourning practice of making flesh offerings upon the death of a loved one. Though our two tribes were once traditional enemies who competed for hegemony over buffalo hunting grounds in the headwater country of the Republican River valley, each regarded the other as a brave people, and our numerous epic encounters are recorded in song,[3] stories,[4] buffalo hide paintings, and ledger book drawings.[5]

Violence often follows when two proud peoples collide. The Cut Fingers refused to bend when confronted by the warlike Americans, who are called *Reesi Kutsu'* ("Big Knives") by the Pawnee. The Human Beings steadfastly opposed the Big Knife incursion into the Great Plains. With only four thousand tribal members in 1875, they engaged the army in at least eighty-nine fights.[6] Their homeland is filled with haunting places where they fought and died—along the far-flung banks of the Washita, Sappa, Platte, Little Bighorn, Arikaree, and Republican rivers, in the Red Fork valley of the Powder River, at the Summit Springs refuge hidden deep within the Great Plains, and killing grounds like the infamous Sand Creek site and Fort Robinson stockade. In the end, the Cheyenne Nation settled on two reservations in Oklahoma and Montana—like other Plains Indian tribes dispossessed of their aboriginal lands by various means and placed onto the reserves that dot the American heartland.

During the nineteenth century, warfare was virtually constant for nearly fifty years on the Great Plains, where the resolve and warlike prowess of the indigenous peoples matched that of the Big Knives. At the height of the Indian wars, white fighters fervently longed to exterminate the Indian race altogether. "Nits breed lice," according to Colonel John M. Chivington, the fighting preacher who led the grisly Sand Creek Massacre in 1864.[7] As General William Tecumseh Sherman remarked in 1869, "the only good Indians I ever saw were dead."

What was the legal basis for the Indian wars? This subject has largely been ignored by scholars. In our legalistic nation, even something as brutal as war must be done in accordance with the law. Despite its medieval Christian origins, the law of war is part of the dark side of the law, because it legitimizes naked violence, invasion, and conquest. This chapter explores the legal basis for the use of force against Native Americans in the Indian wars. Interestingly, no case squarely addresses the issue. In *Connors v. US and the Cheyenne Indians* (1898), the court examined the facts surrounding the extermination of Cheyenne exiles led by Morning Star and Little Wolf during their epic fifteen-hundred-mile exodus in 1878–79.[8] Unfortunately, the court did not address the legality of those killings.

Connors is included as one of the ten worst Indian law cases ever decided, not because of its outcome, which is favorable to the Indians, or its legal precedent, but because the fact that it had to be decided at all illustrates larger problems in the law that warrant discussion. One cannot read the opinion without being overwhelmed by the grave subject matter addressed by the court on several levels. First, *Connors* draws attention to the need to confront and clarify the far-fetched notion of "conquest" in federal Indian law. Exactly what is the law of conquest and how has it shaped federal Indian law? A second problem arises on the international level. Is there an unspoken double standard in the law of war that allows settler states to wage war against indigenous peoples without observing the limitations and protections secured by the law of nations? Above all, the horrific facts etched in *Connors*'s evidentiary record raise a much larger, heartbreaking human-rights question: were the Indian wars legal? The answer to this question is significant. If those conflicts were authorized by law, then the killing and destruction were perfectly legal acts of war. If not, it was murder.

In exploring the role of law and judicial tribunals in the Indian wars, we will begin by examining the notion of conquest in federal Indian law, then describe the law of war that was applicable to the Indian wars, using an actual military conflict between the United States and the Northern Cheyenne as a case study. From this exploration, legal standards will emerge for judging the use of force against Native people in the United States.

The Notion of Conquest in Federal Indian Law

Conquest is not normally considered to be a legitimate source of governmental power in a democracy. Democracies rely instead upon constitutional law to govern their citizenry and to guide relationships with their political subdivisions. Yet unlike any other segment of society in the United States,

Native America is subject to the extraconstitutional law of conquest. The Supreme Court has relied upon doctrines of conquest to divest Indian tribes of title to their land and to uphold government extinguishment of aboriginal title, confiscation of aboriginal land, and laws that exercise dominion over Indian peoples and their property. This is an anomalous situation because everyone else is governed by the powers invested in federal and state government by the Constitution.

In this sense, Native Americans are excluded from the ideas of Thomas Hobbes and John Locke in Western political theory that the power to govern is derived from the consent of the governed or of individuals who entered into a social contract, as society emerged from anarchy, to be governed for the common good. Under this theoretical basis of democracy, non-Indians are subject to the power of government by virtue of their citizenship or, in the case of immigrants, their place of residence, and the government exercises authority over them pursuant to ordinary civil and police powers found in the Constitution. Likewise, political subdivisions, like states, have social contracts by which they voluntarily joined the union—either when the Constitution was formed or later, by democratic processes. No one suggests that by coming into the union, the fifty states were conquered (except perhaps the State of Hawaii), or that states or their citizens must be ruled under principles of conquest. It is only Indian tribes and their members who live under that supposed basis for governance.

This anomalous situation prompts a string of questions. What is this notion of conquest all about? What is the factual and legal basis for the doctrine of conquest in federal Indian law? Were Indian nations really conquered, and if so, when and how? Is it legally or politically necessary (or desirable) for the United States to rely on bare conquest to govern Indian tribes, rule Indian people, and exercise dominion over their property? Finally, if Native America was never really conquered, what were the Indian wars all about?

We will explore these questions briefly to provide a backdrop for considering the law pertaining to the Indian wars. As you will see, the notion of conquest is embedded in federal Indian law, but it rests on flaky legal grounds—a legal fiction articulated in *Johnson v. M'Intosh* (1823) and then rejected by the same court in *Worcester v. Georgia* (1832)—and on shaky factual grounds, if we apply the commonplace definition of *conquest* to the facts at hand. Furthermore, there is no apparent need for the United States to rely upon conquest in its relations with the tribal governments that exist within its territory, to control Native Americans or exercise power over their property. Ample power over Indian affairs is provided by a far more legitimate source: the US Constitution. As such, the doctrine of conquest is superfluous and should be expunged from federal Indian law as an outmoded and injurious vestige of our colonial past.

Talk of conquest started early. It began in the courts with *Johnson v. M'Intosh* (1823), when John Marshall crafted the rules for acquiring Indian land under the doctrine of discovery. According to *Johnson*, the multipurpose doctrine did several things. It operated to vest legal title to Indian lands in the United States; it granted the United States limited sovereignty over Indian nations; and it empowered the government to obtain Indian land by purchase or conquest.[9] *Purchase* is a straightforward concept. Indeed, nearly every aboriginal acre acquired by the United States was purchased through treaties made during times of peace—sometimes fair and square, often by hook or crook.[10] But *conquest* is an ugly word. It conveys a darker, more menacing connotation that requires greater explication. After all, conquest is aggression in its worst form.

Marshall wrote in *Johnson* that "title by conquest is acquired and maintained by force" and the "conqueror prescribes its limits."[11] This rule flew in the face of international law of the era, since bare conquest has never been considered sufficient to convey good title under international law. The law of nations has always forbade the use of force simply to acquire territory. Thus, Marshall was forced to devise a creative exception to the rule that conquerors must respect property rights in the lands they invade (i.e., we do not own Iraq merely because we invaded that nation). He said that the normal rules of international law governing the relations between the conqueror and conquered are "incapable of application" in the United States. Why? Because the settler state was confronted by Indian nations composed of "fierce savages, whose occupation was war." He therefore considered it impossible to mingle with Indians, to incorporate them into a colonial social structure, or to govern an Indian nation as a distinct people, because the Indian nations "were ready to repel by arms every attempt on their independence." Thus, "frequent and bloody wars, in which the whites were not always the aggressors, unavoidably ensued." According to Marshall, these factors forced the settler state to "resort to some new and different rule, better adapted to the actual state of things." The new rule fashioned in *Johnson* was an outlandish legal fiction that converted "discovery of an inhabited country into conquest."[12] Even if it looked good on paper, Marshall's new rule meant nothing to Indian nations. *It was a paper conquest by the Supreme Court in name only.* The United States' extravagant legal claims to land and sovereignty over any unwilling Indian nations remained to be won the hard way—"by the sword."[13]

Following *Johnson*'s discourse on conquest, Indian law opinions quickly began to fill with metaphors of war.[14] The early opinions were written during wartime with an unmistakable military mind-set, sometimes by judges who were themselves veterans of military conflicts with Indian tribes. In *Cherokee Nation v. Georgia* (1831), Justice Thomas Johnson reiterated that discovery grants rights of dominion over the country discovered, and that conquest provides such rights in case of war. He described Georgia's assertion of legal rights against the Cherokee Nation as "war in disguise."[15] The southern judiciary wrote jingoistic opinions in the extension cases discussed in chapter five that drip with hostility against Indians.[16] By 1955, the myth of conquest was so prevalent in the law that the Supreme Court assumed every American Indian and Alaska Native tribe had been conquered, even though few actually lost their land or independence by force of American arms. Justice Stanley Reed stated in *Tee-Hit-Ton Indians v. United States* (1955):

> Every American schoolboy knows that the savage tribes of this continent were deprived of their ancestral ranges by force and that, even when the Indians ceded millions of acres by treaty in return for blankets, food, and trinkets, it was not a sale but the conqueror's will that deprived them of their land.[17]

The legal and factual basis for the doctrine of conquest rests on dubious ground. One can argue that the Indian tribes were conquered and are subject to the law of conquest, because (1) *Johnson* says discovery by Europeans means all Indian tribes are automatically conquered; (2) Indian nations lost their independence and sovereignty by force of arms or they became domestic dependent nations through treaties; and (3) the territories of Indian nations were appropriated by the United States in war. An examination of each argument shows that none hold water, except in rare instances.

First of all, conquest cannot be equated with discovery. A legal fiction is an assumption of fact made by a court as the basis for deciding a legal question. The legal fiction used in *Johnson* bore no relation to reality in 1492 or 1823, when the case was decided—it was simply not true. Importantly, that legal fiction was at issue and rejected in *Worcester v. Georgia* (1832), when the Supreme Court discarded the absurd ideas about conquest and dominion found in the doctrine of discovery:

> This soil was occupied by numerous and warlike nations, equally willing and able to defend their possessions. The extravagant and absurd idea, that the feeble settlements made on the sea coast, or the companies under whom they were made, acquired legitimate power by them to govern the people, occupy the lands from sea to sea, did not enter the mind of any man.[18]

Unjust legal fictions in the law that are wrong and injurious should be rejected, not perpetuated by modern courts. Just like the legal fictions used in *Plessy v. Ferguson* (1896) that blacks are racially inferior and segregation is not harmful or denigrating were finally rejected in *Brown v. Board of Education* (1954), it is time to retire the foolish legal fiction that European discovery of an inhabited continent can be equated with the conquest of that continent.[19] Whether conquest occurred is best determined on a case-by-case basis, rather than by a sweeping assumption.

Second, the domestic dependant nation status of Indian tribes is not considered conquest when it is established through treaty agreements. When *Worcester* put flesh on that political classification, the court explained that treaty agreements placing Indian nations under US protection do not conquer or deprive them of their sovereignty, because "[p]rotection does not imply destruction of the protected."[20] The protectorate relationship is frequently found in international relations. It is simply one "nation claiming and receiving the protection of one more powerful: not that of individuals abandoning their national character, and submitting as subjects to the laws of a master."[21] *Worcester* emphasized that "the settled doctrine of the law of nations is, that a weaker power does not surrender its independence—its right to self government, by associating with a stronger, and taking its protection."[22] Furthermore, the Indian protectorate relationship described in *Worcester* creates "no claim to [Indian] lands, no dominion over their persons" at all—it merely binds Indian tribes to a stronger nation "as a dependent ally, claiming the protection of a powerful friend and neighbor, and receiving the advantages of that protection, without involving a surrender of their national character."[23] Justice John McLean astutely observed:

> Every state is more or less dependent on those which surround it; but unless this dependence shall extend so far as to merge the political existence of the protected people into that of their protectors, they may still constitute a state.[24]

Thus, *Worcester* held that the Cherokee Nation, which placed itself under the protection of the United States in treaties, retained its self-government and had never been conquered. Rather, the Cherokee Nation continued to exist as a separate and distinct people "being vested with rights which constitute them a state, or separate community—not a foreign community, but a domestic community—not as belonging to the confederacy, but as existing within it, and of necessity, bearing to it a peculiar relation."[25] In short, domestic dependent Indian nations are not conquered nations under federal Indian law or international law; they continue to exist as separate self-governing communities within our domestic political system.

This leaves us with the factual contention that Indian tribes lost their land or sovereignty by conquest. To assess this argument we must first define the term *conquest*. Strictly speaking, *conquer* means "to acquire by force of arms" according to *Webster's* and *conquest* refers to "something conquered," especially "territory appropriated in war."[26] Applying this narrow definition, few American Indian tribes and no Alaska Native tribes were conquered. First, in virtually every instance, Indian land was purchased through treaties or statutes, not appropriated in war.[27] The motive and goal of many Indian wars was to remove noncompliant bands and tribes to reservations established by the treaties as their homelands, and tribes fought to remain in ceded areas. But the fact remains that those acres were acquired by purchase, and force was not employed until later and then only to enforce the sale agreements. The Indians' territory in those instances was not appropriated in war. At most, armed force was a tool used to enforce treaty cessations; that is, in those circumstances it was a questionable police action to be sure, but not conquest as that term is normally understood. Second, it is difficult to find many tribes who lost their sovereignty by force of American arms since, as discussed above, most tribes agreed to come under the protection of the United States and assumed their domestic dependant nation status through treaties. In that sense, the treaties are analogous to the social or political contracts by which other political subdivisions joined the union because they are the instruments by which the signatory tribes came under the protection of the United States and exist within the political system as separate communities with the right of self-government.

Indian wars did occur, but few were outright wars of conquest, fought to appropriate Indian territory or reduce tribal sovereignty, since this was accomplished primarily through treaties of peace, trade, and friendship. To be sure, some Indian nations were defeated militarily, but whether they actually lost any of their land or sovereignty as a result of those particular conflicts requires a careful case-by-case examination yet to be conducted on any comprehensive basis. Until then, we cannot simply assume those tribes were conquered as that term is used in *Webster's* dictionary or commonly. Furthermore, the notion of a wholesale military conquest of every Indian nation by force, as is sometimes implied in federal Indian law, is plainly wrong. For example, no shots were exchanged in Alaska. No wars were waged against many tribal nations, such as the Pawnee and others. And many who were in fact defeated militarily did not lose a single acre or suffer reduced sovereignty as a result of the conflict. It would be a misleading fantasy to think conquest occurred in these situations. The law should not arbitrarily sanction the government of those tribes by conquest when it never happened as a mater of fact or law. This wrongly suggests that the United States' power to govern Indian tribes is derived solely from an extraconstitutional source—military conquest. The United States need not rely on that raw principle to rule Indian tribes, since the Constitution provides a far more legitimate source of federal power to regulate Indian affairs. Though some land was no doubt appropriated in war, no wholesale conquest occurred unless we define *conquest* far more broadly than *Webster's* to include the subjugation and dominion of Indian nations by means other than armed force. Indeed, there were arguably vehicles of conquest other than military force as Manifest Destiny engulfed the Indian nations during the nineteenth century: the use of law, germs that spread disease, culture conflict, destruction of game, habitat, and natural resources, theft and avarice, and so on. But these agents are not comparable to invading, seizing, and ruling another country by raw force of arms, nor are any of these destructive agents, standing alone, capable of conquering a continent inhabited by indigenous nations.

Admittedly, all Indian tribes are subject to rule by armed force, but no more so than any other segment of society—*we are all subject to military force if the legitimate need arises.* If mistaken and misplaced ideas about conquest are allowed to linger in the law, they can be dredged up at any time by politicians and jurists to exercise unwarranted control over Native people, property, and political institutions, or, worse yet, by other nations who look to federal Indian law to justify warfare against indigenous peoples free from the restraints, protections, and obligations imposed by international law. It is better to be factually clear: relatively little appropriation of Indian territory in war occurred as a matter of fact. For the most part, tribes entered into a protectorate relationship with the United States by treaty agreements, not as a result of military conflict, and the law does not treat the resulting domestic dependent nationhood status as conquest any more than a state that has joined the union through other constitutional means. The misleading and sweeping pronouncements by jurists like the late Justice Reed should be set aside, along with mistaken notions of conquest in the law. We are no longer in a state of war with Indian nations and the judicial mind-set of conquest derived from wartime jurisprudence no longer serves any apparent purpose—judicial saber rattling is highly inappropriate and outmoded in contemporary times. After all, the Indian wars ended in 1890. The last vestiges of those conflicts expired in 1913, when the Chiricahua Apache POWs were released from Fort Sill, Oklahoma, after twenty-seven years of imprisonment.

For the above reasons, the idea of conquest is dubious. The continued use of the law of conquest by federal courts to decide Indian legal questions today is highly questionable—unless the courts still believe they are courts of the conqueror. As seen, the notion of conquest is as complex in federal Indian law as it is in other arenas. Nations may lose wars and not be conquered. And there is a troubling reciprocity. No conquest is permanent, since occupation by the victors is often short and even the most powerful empires fade over time. Today's conquerors can become the conquered tomorrow. This reconnaissance-level discussion is not intended to provide definitive answers, but to highlight an area of inquiry. Given this minefield, jurists should tread lightly before applying sweeping notions of conquest to decide legal questions.

Turning now to the law of war, the judicial discourse on conquest in federal Indian law leads one to wonder about the role of war in federal Indian policy and whether the rules of war apply to the Indian wars or, for that matter, to settler-state warfare against indigenous peoples in general. American cases strongly hint that loopholes may exist when it comes to war against indigenous peoples. For example, in *Montoya v. United States* (1901), a case involving Indian hostilities, the Supreme Court observed:

> While, as between the United States and other civilized nations, an act
> of Congress is necessary to a formal declaration of war, no such act is
> necessary to constitute a state of war with an Indian tribe.[28]

Despite this language, disparate standards in the law of war should not be applied to the Indian wars. If federal Indian law is construed to sanction a double standard in the law of war, this would establish precedent for other nations to employ violence and military force against indigenous peoples in other lands without the need to observe the rights, protections, and limitations normally imposed upon combatants by the law of nations. That double standard would legitimize wars of genocide against indigenous peoples to be quietly waged by settler states in their backyards. We could not lightly place such a malevolent construction on federal Indian law, which tends to be looked upon and followed by settler states throughout the world as legal precedent for their relations with indigenous peoples. I argue in this chapter that the ordinary rules of war are applicable to the United States' Indian wars during the nineteenth century and should have been applied, just as they were applied to any other American war.

What was the role of warfare in federal Indian policy? In some instances, the United States commenced defensive wars to repel attack or other immediate threats by Indian bands, nations, or confederacies. Some were waged to put down rebellions. Others were offensive wars of aggression waged to punish Indian nations and bands for a range of alleged just, and sometimes unjust, causes. Some were race wars, pure and simple. From the tribal standpoint, Indian nations waged war for a variety of reasons. They waged defensive wars to repel attack, wars of independence, insurrection, and rebellion, and they waged offensive wars to punish legal wrongs committed against them, such as treaty violations, since resort to American courts to redress legal grievances was generally unavailable during the nineteenth century. The wars were fought in many places by warriors with strong warrior traditions that defined their place in the world, often to achieve personal honor, wealth, and to extract revenge or punishment for wrongs committed against their families and tribes.

At bottom, the Indian wars—regardless of their causes—were part and parcel of a relentless program of Manifest Destiny waged generally to clear Indian nations from the path of white settlement and to force them onto reservations established as their permanent homelands by treaty. US military policy during this period is aptly described in *Cohen's Handbook of Federal Indian Law* as follows:

> United States military policy was designed to bring natives under control and support the civilian dream of open lands for white settlement. From Indians battling Gen. Armstrong Custer at the Little Big Horn to Geronimo evading the cavalry in Arizona's hills and deserts, these were battles to the death. Geronimo and his Apaches were imprisoned and exiled to Florida; the Lakota who earlier fought Custer were gunned down at Wounded Knee. By the final years of the nineteenth century, Indian military resistance was no longer a viable option for any tribal groups.[29]

The Definition of *War* and an Overview of America's Indian Wars

The United States is no stranger to the use of force. It has waged war almost continuously since its inception.[30] Judging from that history, we are the most violent people on the planet. The Republic fought Indian nations, separated from the settlers by race, ethnicity, religion, and language, for more than one hundred years (1776–1890), perhaps killing over fifty thousand Indians. During this period of protracted warfare, a military mind-set dominated Indian affairs and found its way into the foundational cases of federal Indian law.[31] While on this extended war footing, Indian affairs and policies were administered by the War Department from 1776 to 1876. Indian affairs were conducted as an aspect of military and foreign policy, outside the realm of domestic civilian concern. The use of military force to control Indian tribes was a tool that dominated federal Indian policy as Manifest Destiny swept the continent.[32] Even though these measures left indelible marks on Native America, no one has performed a comprehensive legal analysis of the Indian wars and surprisingly little has been written about American Indians and the law of war.

Of course, what constitutes a war is a matter of perspective as well as law. Killing and destruction can be described as a great victory or horrific massacre, depending upon one's point of view; and there is a thin line between war, murder, and genocide. What is war? We think we know it when we see it, but war is a complex legal condition often surrounded by technical uncertainties. For example, the courts are unsure of the exact amount, level, and stage of hostilities that give rise to a state of war, and it is sometimes hard to know precisely when war actually starts or ends.[33]

War is defined in American jurisprudence as the contention of external force between two nations authorized by the legitimate authority of the two governments. A lawful public war is either "perfect" or "imperfect." The Supreme Court explained this dichotomy in *Tingy v. Bas* (1800). Perfect war is general, unconditional war initiated by a formal declaration of war:

> [E]very contention of force between two nations, in external matters, is not only war, but public war. If it be declared in form, it is called *solemn*, and is of the perfect kind; because one whole nation is at war with another whole nation; and *all* the members of the nation declaring war, are authorized to commit hostilities against all the members of the other, in every place, and under every circumstance. In such a war all the rights and consequences of war attach to their condition.[34]

Imperfect war is more limited in scope, as may be authorized and circumscribed by Congress, but very much war in every other respect:

> But hostilities may subsist between two nations more confined in its nature and extent; being limited as to places, persons, and things; and this is more properly termed *imperfect* war; because not solemn, and because those who are authorized to commit hostilities, act under special authority, and can go no farther than to the extent of their commission. Still, however, it is *public war*, because it is an external contention of force, between some of the members of the two nations, authorized by the legitimate powers. It is a war between the two nations, though all the members are not authorized to commit hostilities such as in a solemn war, where the government restrains the general power.[35]

Tingy's definition of war was the law throughout the nineteenth century, when the Indian wars occurred.[36] The Indian wars were classified as limited or imperfect war by the Supreme Court.[37]

The United States' use of force was an important tool of Manifest Destiny. More than forty so-called Indian wars were fought by the government, according to the Bureau of the Census in 1894.[38] The clash between cultures produced warfare on a vast scale. Untold thousands of Indian people died in the Indian wars, according to the census report:

> The Indian wars under the government of the United States have been more than 40 in number. They have cost the lives of about 19,000 white men, women, and children, including those killed in individual combat, and the lives of about 30,000 Indians. The actual number killed and wounded Indians must be very much larger than the number given, as they conceal, where possible, their actual loss in battle, and carry their killed and wounded off and secret them.

Applying this data, anthropologist Russell Thornton estimates that 53,500 American Indians were slain in the United States between 1775 and 1890, including 8,500 reported deaths from individual conflicts.[39] The body count might easily double if we add the numerous Indian wars that occurred before 1775. Some tribes, hit harder than others, were nearly annihilated by conflict with the Big Knives.

Between 1850 and 1890, fighting Indians was almost a daily occurrence for Americans, according to historian Gregory Michno.[40] His startling survey of major armed conflicts discloses an unrelenting forty-year military campaign conducted against Native Americans throughout a vast theater of war. His data for the American West alone (not including extensive warfare east of the Mississippi River before 1850) reveals a nation fully at war with its indigenous peoples:

Indian Battles/Skirmishes between 1850–1890*

Year	No. of Battles	Location
1850	24	CA, NM, TX
1851	13	AZ, CA, ID, NE, OR
1852	12	AZ, CA, NM, OR, TX
1853	13	CA, OR, TX, UT
1854	23	CA, CO, ID, NM, OK, OR, TX
1855	22	CO, ID, NE, NM, OR, TX, WA
1856	36	NE, NM, OR, TX, WA
1857	28	AZ, CA, IA, KS, NE, NV, TX, UT
1858	25	AZ, ID, KS, NM, OK, TX, WA
1859	23	AZ, ID, KS, NM, OK, TX, UT
1860	42	AZ, CA, CO, ID, NE, NV, NM, OR, TX, UT
1861	24	AZ, CA, NM, OK, TX
1862	45	AZ, CA, ID, MN, NV, NM, ND, OK, OR, TX, UT
1863	58	AZ, CA, CO, ID, MN, NE, NV, NM, ND, WY
1864	64	AZ, CA, CO, IA, KS, NE, NM, ND, OR, TX, WY
1865	72	AZ, CO, ID, KS, MN, MT, NE NV, NM, ND, OR, TX, UT, WY
1866	63	AZ, CA, CO, ID, MT, NE, NV, NM, ND, OR, TX, WY
1867	139	AZ, CA, CO, KS, MT, NE, NV, NM, ND, OR, TX, UT, WY
1868	118	AZ, CO, ID, KS, MT, NE, NV, NM, ND, OK, OR, TX, WY
1869	101	AZ, CO, KS, MT, NE, NM, ND, SD, TX, WY
1870	58	AZ, CO, KS, MT, NE, NM, ND, OK, TX, WY
1871	43	AZ, CO, KS, NE, NM, OK, TX
1872	60	AZ, CA, KS, MT, NE, NM, ND, OK, OR, TX, WY
1873	49	AZ, CA, MT, NM, ND, TX
1874	52	AZ, KS, OK, TX, WY
1875	15	AZ, KS, MT, NM, OK, TX
1876	32	AZ, MT, NE, NM, OK, SD, TX, WY
1877	43	AZ, ID, MT, NM, SD, TX, WY
1878	43	AZ, ID, KS, MT, NM, OK, OR, TX, WY
1879	32	AZ, CO, ID, MT, NE, NM, TX
1880	44	AZ, MT, NM, TX
1881	13	AZ, MT, NM, TX
1882	8	AZ, MT, NM, WY
1883	6	AZ, MT, NM
1884	1	CO
1885	11	NM
1886	4	AZ
1887	2	AZ, MT
1888	2	AZ, MT
1889	1	AZ
1890	5	AZ, MT, ND, SD

* Source: Gregory F. Michno, *Encyclopedia of Indian Wars* (Missoula, MT: Mountain Press, 2003)

Military might was not the only source of violence against Native Americans during this period. Civilians were also prone to violence. They took up arms against Indians so frequently that Michno could not tally their acts of aggression. He simply stated that thousands of reported deaths went uncounted since they were not part of an organized military action.[41] Acts of hostility by gun-toting settlers, legal or otherwise, contributed greatly to the carnage:

> Whites killed Indians in every state and territory, but perhaps most dramatically along the Pacific coast. In Washington, Oregon, and California, Indian populations declined as if a biblical flood had swept them from the land. The army may have accounted for several hundred fatalities, but thousands more perished from disease, malnutrition, and murder. Next to disease, white civilians with guns were the most dangerous threat to Indian survival.[42]

No other ethnic group in the United States has faced the muzzles of American guns like the American Indians. Modern Native Americans are the descendants of survivors who were spared.

What drove Indians and whites to war? No one has comprehensively examined with particularity the causes and objectives of the many Indian wars found in US history. Any such analysis would likely reveal finger-pointing among the combatants, with each side blaming the other for war. We can only supply legal guidelines for judging those contentions, beginning with the *Connors* case study.

The Cheyenne Indians Are *kaki suriru'*—A Very Brave People

It is fitting that we examine the legal basis of the Indian wars through a Cheyenne case study. They are a people with strong warrior traditions who migrated to the plains in the 1600s from as far away as the Hudson Bay region of present-day Canada. The *Tsis tsis' tas* originally lived in earth lodge dwellings like their aboriginal Plains Indian neighbors, but later took up a nomadic way of life with the acquisition of horses. This far-flung tribe ranged throughout the western plains in pursuit of the buffalo herds from Montana through Wyoming, South Dakota, Nebraska, Kansas, Colorado, and Oklahoma. They bore more than their share of war with the Big Knives. "As a child growing up among two Cheyenne women," remarked Richard

Williams in 2007, "I was often told that the Cheyenne were the bravest of all warriors and were willing to fight when others feigned bravery, causing them to withdraw from the battlefield." Many Pawnee war stories of my own tribe confirm from firsthand experience the valor and fighting spirit of the strong-hearted Cheyenne warriors, brave men and women who pledged to defend their people and way of life. The following story, which is important among my own family, recounts events that set the stage for those described in the *Connors* case.

At dawn, in the winter of 1876, my great-grandfather, *Tawi Hisi* (meaning, "Leader-of-the-Group"), and ninety-nine other Pawnee scouts trotted along the red earth trail toward Morning Star's village. Morning Star was the Cheyenne chief known in history books as Dull Knife. His village lay well hidden in the Bighorn Mountains of Wyoming. The Pawnee scouts were positioned in the center of the command with orders to take the village. On their left flank, one hundred Shoshoni scouts climbed the ridge while the white soldiers rode on the right flank, across the stream, as the command proceeded up the little valley.

The Cheyenne had been prominent, along with their Sioux allies, in the Battle of the Little Bighorn, when Custer was killed in one of the greatest military victories ever achieved by the Plains Indians. During that summer, the army came under enormous pressure to find and punish the Indian victors, yet they could not be located. Thus, the famed Pawnee scouts were recruited to assist in locating their hereditary foes, the *Sahi* (Cheyenne) and *Pariksukat* (Sioux). And now, five months after Custer's defeat, the Northern Cheyenne Tribe had been found at last!

Blowing their eagle-bone war whistles, the Pawnee stripped down and went into the fight on painted ponies recently captured from the Lakota Sioux. The ensuing battle raged all day as the Cheyenne put up a fierce resistance against their multiple attackers. Many were lost on both sides, but in the end the Pawnee scouts occupied the village and captured the *Sahi* pony herd.[43] Afterward, the snow began to fall and many Pawnee soldiers received new names to mark their hard-won victory, as was their tribal custom. That was when Leader-of-the-Group became Echo Hawk (*Kutawikucu' Tawaaku'a*), the name that my family bears to this day. Morning Star's people escaped but surrendered that spring. Many were removed to Fort Reno, in the Indian Territory of Oklahoma, to live with their Southern Cheyenne relatives, bringing the Sioux War of 1876 to a close.

From this and many other encounters, we know Cheyenne Indians are *kaki suriru'*, "without fear." The Cheyenne are respected among the Plains Indians as a remarkable, courageous people. I can recall a particular dawn morning in my youth when I sat in a canyon watching the Morning Star rise with my friend Raymond Spang, a Northern Cheyenne. Trading stories, I told him about our Pawnee beliefs concerning the mighty Morning Star, who rises in the dawn sky to chase the other stars before him. He replied, "We also have a Morning Star: the man better known as Dull Knife in history books." This chapter concerns Morning Star, the man.

The *Connors* Case and the Flight of Morning Star

On October 1, 1878, Morning Star and Little Wolf were leading their people across western Nebraska when they came upon Milton Connors's ranch. The fleeing Indians, who had escaped from the Cheyenne and Arapahoe Indian Reservation near Fort Reno, Indian Territory, located on the Canadian River in the present-day state of Oklahoma, where they had been sent after their surrender at the end of the Sioux War, were being pursued by soldiers. So far, they had outfought and outgeneraled the generals who pursued them on their exodus. Since September, they had traveled northward across the Cimarron, Arkansas, Sappa, Republican, Arikaree, and Platte rivers on a remarkable fifteen-hundred-mile journey to freedom in their Montana homeland. Often traveling at night, they were guided by an elderly woman blessed with a mysterious power to see in the dark. On this day, the hungry refugees made off with forty horses, forty steers, and one mule from the ranch.

Many years later, the Nebraska rancher sued the United States and Cheyenne Indians to recover damages for his lost livestock. The claim in *Connors v. the United States and the Cheyenne Indians* (1898) was brought under the Indian Depredation Act of 1891.[44] This law allowed the Court of Claims to hear citizen claims for property taken or destroyed by Indians. Specifically, it granted the court authority to determine all claims arising after 1865 "for property of citizens of the United States taken or destroyed by Indians belonging to any band, tribe, or nation, in amity with the United States, without just cause or provocation on the part of the owner." Under the act, a citizen could recover damages *only* if the tribe to which the Indians belonged was at peace (or "in amity") with the United States at the time the property was taken. Thus, the threshold inquiry was whether the Indians' tribe was at peace or war with the United States when the injury occurred. If the tribe was at peace, the citizen was entitled to recover money damages and the award could be deducted from tribal annuities. However, if the tribe was determined to be at war with the United States, the obligations of peace did not pertain and the claim would therefore be disallowed.

Connors was heard by Charles J. Nott, a judge nominated to the bench by President Abraham Lincoln in 1865. The New Yorker was a former cavalry officer in the Union army. During the Civil War, he spent thirteen months as a prisoner of war in a Confederate prison. By the time he retired from the bench at the beginning of the twentieth century, Nott was the chief justice of the US Court of Claims and the longest-serving federal judge in the country. This judge had seen war and was eminently qualified to hear cases on that subject. The United States and Cheyenne defendants were represented by an assistant attorney general. The findings of fact recited in Judge Nott's opinion are summarized as follows.

The court began its opinion by observing that the Northern Cheyenne Indians "had borne a distinguished part in the Sioux War of 1876, but had surrendered and made peace with the United States."[45] At the time of their surrender, in May of 1877, they numbered about 1,800 persons. About half were allowed to stay in their tribal homeland and ultimately settled on the Tongue River Reservation in Montana.[46] However, 937 persons led by Morning Star, Little Wolf, Wild Hog, and Old Crow were removed to the Southern Cheyenne and Arapaho Reservation at Fort Reno, Indian Territory. They went reluctantly, but with the understanding that if their new home proved unsatisfactory they could return to their native country.[47] After a year of sickness, starvation, and death, and repeated requests to return, "320 of them in September, 1878, broke away from the reservation."[48]

Under the leadership of Morning Star and Little Wolf, the tiny, starving group of Indians slipped away under the cover of darkness, leaving their tipis standing before the watchful soldiers. The Cheyenne were overtaken 120 miles from Fort Reno and a parley ensued. The commanding officer demanded that they return, but "Little Wolf, whom Captain John G. Bourke characterizes as 'one of the bravest in fights where all were brave,' said 'We do not want to fight you, but we will not go back.'"[49] Up to that time, the Cheyenne "had committed no atrocity and were in amity with the United States and desired to remain so."[50] Unfortunately, the "troops instantly fired upon the Cheyenne and a new Indian war began."[51] The court commented on that fateful incident:

That volley was one of many mistakes, military and civil, which have been the fatality of our Indian administration, for the officer who ordered it thereby instituted an Indian war, and at the same instant turned hostile savages loose upon the unprotected homes of the frontier and their unwarned, unsuspecting inmates. The Cheyennes outgeneraled the troops. They fought and fled, and scattered and reunited. They fought other military commands and citizens who had organized to oppose them, and in like manner they again and again eluded their opponents, making their way northward over innumerable hindrances. They had not sought war, but from the moment they were fired upon they were upon the warpath—men were killed, women were ravished, houses were burned, crops destroyed. The country through which they fled and fought was desolated, and they left behind them the usual well-known trail of fire and blood.[52]

The Human Beings split into two groups soon after they crossed the Platte River in Nebraska. By then, hundreds of American troops had been called into action to hunt them down.[53] The group led by Little Wolf escaped and successfully made the fifteen-hundred-mile journey to freedom in Montana. However, the troops captured forty-nine men, fifty-one women, and forty-eight children of Morning Star's band on October 3, two days after the raid on the Connors ranch, and placed them into custody at Fort Robinson, Nebraska. Though incarcerated, the prisoners of war still refused to return to the detested Indian Territory. By January, Captain Henry Wessells, the frustrated commander, turned to means used by "animal tamers" to subdue "wild beasts" and soon resorted to massacre.[54] Quoting from army reports, Judge Nott wrote:

In the midst of the dreadful winter, with the thermometer 40 degrees below zero, the Indians, including the women and children, were kept for five days and nights without food or fuel, and for three days without water.[55] At the end of that time they broke out of the barracks in which they were confined and rushed forth into the night. The troops pursued, firing upon them as upon enemies in war; those who escaped the sword perished in the storm.[56] Twelve days later the pursuing cavalry came upon the remnant of the band in a ravine 50 miles from Fort Robinson. "The troops encircled the Indians, leaving no possible avenue of escape." The Indians fired on them, killing a lieutenant and two privates. The troops advanced; "the Indians, then without ammunition, rushed in desperation toward the troops with their hunting knives in hand; but before they had advanced many paces a volley was discharged by the troops and all was over." "The bodies of 24 Indians were found in the ravine—17 bucks, 5 squaws, and 2 papooses." Nine prisoners were taken—1 wounded man, and 8 women, 5 of whom were wounded. The officer in command unconsciously wrote the epitaph of the slain in his dispatch announcing the result: "The Cheyennes fought with extraordinary courage and firmness, and refused all terms but death." The final result of the last Cheyenne war was, that of 320 who broke away in September, 7 wounded Cheyennes were sent back to the reservation.[57]

Like red and black ants, the Indians and whites fought until every last Cut Finger lay dead or wounded in the crimson snow. The Indians died fighting for their freedom, while the soldiers died fighting for Manifest Destiny. Captain Wessells, who instigated the tragedy by his mistreatment of the prisoners of war, was shot in the head, and Sargent William B. Lewis was awarded the coveted Congressional Medal of Honor, the highest tribute the nation can pay to a soldier in wartime, for his actions that day.[58] The survivors included wounded men such as Old Crow, Wild Hog, Left Hand, Tangle Hair, Porcupine, and Noisy Walker. Seven of these *Tsis tsis' tas* soldiers were taken to Kansas, where they were tried for murder in 1879 in civilian courts, but acquitted for lack of evidence.[59] In contrast, none of the white soldiers or citizens who killed Cheyenne noncombatants were tried for murder, presumably because folks naturally assumed their acts were lawful acts of war.

Though Judge Nott was himself a seasoned war veteran, one can almost hear him gasp as he wrote the opinion. He was troubled by several factors that illustrated "the extraordinary difficulty which the court has had to encounter in dealing with these Indian depredation cases."[60] If this were an ordinary case, he wrote, "there would really be no defendant before the court, for these bands had utterly ceased to exist before the suit was brought."[61] *Virtually everyone in Morning Star's band had been killed.* Moreover, Nott was confounded by the uncertain Cheyenne legal status.

These Indians, indeed, in 1878 occupied an anomalous position, unknown to the common or civil law or to any system of municipal law.

They were neither citizens nor aliens; they were neither free persons nor slaves; they were wards of the nation, and yet, on a reservation under a military guard, were little else than prisoners of war. Dull Knife and his daughters could be invited guests at the table of officers and gentlemen, behaving with dignity and propriety, and yet could be confined for life on a reservation which was to them little better than a dungeon, on the mere order of an executive officer.[62]

Above all, Judge Nott was troubled by the acts of the military. He wondered whether their actions were legal and whether the Human Beings had a lawful right to leave Indian Territory and travel peaceably to their native land. In fact, those questions were strenuously argued by the parties.

It has been argued in this case with great earnestness that these Cheyennes had a lawful right to leave the reservation and travel peaceably back to their old homes; and that they did not begin the conflict, and merely resisted force by force; that their acts were lawful and the action of the pursuing troops unlawful.[63]

Nott did not rule on these questions since it was "impossible to define their status from a legal point of view" and his central inquiry under the Indian Depredation Act was simply to determine whether the Cheyenne bands were "in amity" with the United States in order to decide the citizen's property claim. Thus, Nott sidestepped the issue, stating, "Whether they could have sued out a writ of habeas corpus and been set free by judicial authority is not for this court now to decide."[64]

As implausible as it may have seemed to Judge Nott in 1898, the Human Beings did have legal rights that courts could recognize. For example, *United States ex rel. Standing Bear v. Crook* (1879) involved a similar situation concerning the Ponca Indians of Nebraska.[65] They, too, had been removed to Indian Territory, where 158 died within a year or so. A small band led by Chief Standing Bear fled the reservation without permission of the government and returned to their Nebraska homeland. They were arrested shortly after their arrival by General George Crook at the request of the secretary of the interior and incarcerated pending their return to Indian Territory. Standing Bear sued for his freedom in a habeas corpus action that challenged the legality of their confinement. Judge Elmer Dundy allowed the suit, holding that Indians are "persons" within the meaning of the federal habeas corpus act with standing to bring such cases.[66] He then examined the legal basis for the Indians' incarceration and could find no authority whatsoever.[67] Since no war existed and no crime had been committed, the government had no power to confine the Ponca Indians. The *Standing Bear* court aptly observed that if Indians could be forcibly removed to a reservation in Indian Territory by the government without any apparent legal authority, why not place them in prison?

> I can see no good reason why they might not be taken and kept by force
> in the penitentiary in Lincoln, or Leavenworth, or Jefferson City, or any
> other place which the commander of the forces might, in his judgment,
> see proper to designate. I cannot think that any such arbitrary authority
> exists in this country.[68]

In the absence of any authority for confining or removing the Ponca Indians back to Indian Territory, the court ordered their release from custody.

Under *Standing Bear*'s rationale, Morning Star's people had a lawful right to leave Indian Territory and peaceably return to their native land, since they were at peace and had committed no crime in 1878. By the same token, the soldiers had no apparent legal authority to demand their return or fire upon them. Since the soldiers' acts in provoking the conflict were most likely unlawful under *Standing Bear*, it is no wonder that Judge Nott was uncomfortable.

Nott denied Connors's claim since the Indians had been driven to war by the time of their raid on his ranch. In such instances, the court held, neither the United States nor the Indians are liable for damages under the act. This is a correct result, which was affirmed by the Supreme Court on appeal. However, the *Connors* case leaves us to wonder about the elephant in the room.

Could the tragic events of 1878–79 have been prevented by the courts? As demonstrated in the *Standing Bear* decision of 1879, contemporary courts could have protected Morning Star's right to travel peaceably to Montana since the *Tsis tsis' tas* left the reservation during a time of peace and had committed no crime, according to *Connors*. Unfortunately, access to the courts was generally unavailable to American Indians during this period. Their predicament was captured in the book *Cheyenne Autumn* (1953), in which author Marie Sandoz recounts the thoughts of Little Wolf as he surveyed his worn-out people moving across the plains that winter.

> The Indian is left without protection of law in person, property or life. He has no personal rights. He may see his crops destroyed, his wife and children killed. His only redress is personal revenge.[69]

They had no recourse to American courts. Connors also raises a larger question: to what extent was America's use of force against Indians lawful? Were the military's actions at Fort Robinson legal? Was the Sioux War of 1876 a legal conflict? What about other conflicts, like the Sand Creek Massacre and the forty Indian wars referenced by the Bureau of the Census? Definitive answers must await future research by scholars into the facts and circumstances leading to each conflict and the documents, if any, that authorized them. Then, we can apply the law of the conquerors as a measuring stick. To encourage that research, some legal principles and tentative conclusions are discussed below.

The Law of War in the Americas

Only men and ants engage in war. Ants have an excuse: they are driven into all-out warfare by biological imperatives that are regulated by the law of nature. Similarly, a nation's use of military force is governed by immutable principles of natural law. That body of law is called the "law of war." It is "founded on the common consent as well as the common sense of the world" and firmly embedded in international law.[70] For centuries, this component of international law has allowed nations to use force legally, both defensively against attack and offensively to punish wrongdoers or exact compensation for legal wrongs.[71]

It is ironic that naked force can be clothed in the law. Warfare is the supreme expression of violence and destruction among our species. Large-scale violence *must* be governed by law, with rules of war adhered to by every nation. Otherwise, the antlike carnage would constitute horrific criminal conduct, if not crimes against humanity. Warmongers could be prosecuted as common criminals, along with foot soldiers who do their bidding. To protect those folks, the law of war distinguishes between violence committed as part of a public war and violent acts committed without the sanction of war. In the first instance, the killing is justified if done within the proper bounds of warfare; in the latter, individuals who commit acts of violence are considered terrorists and murderers who are subject to punishment under domestic law. For example, if I shoot a roomful of people during wartime as a lawful belligerent, the killing is lawful and I might receive a medal. The same act is murder if committed in times of peace. *We need rules of war to legalize violence.*

In international law, war can only be conducted by nations. It is usually waged between two or more independent nations, but a state of war can also exist when one of the warring parties is not an independent nation in the ordinary sense, as in the case of civil wars or rebellions[72] and wars between settler states and indigenous tribes within their borders.[73] Though Indian tribes are not considered independent nations by international or federal law, they still retained the power to wage war as domestic dependent nations, according to the Supreme Court.[74] Thus, the law of war is fully applicable to the United States' Indian wars. During the nineteenth century, American law defined *war* as the use of force between two nations authorized by the legitimate authority of the two nations, and the law distinguished between general and limited war.[75] The Indian wars were considered limited or imperfect wars.

In all the above circumstances, the use of military force by nations is governed by the law and usages of war as set forth in international law. The well-established customary rules of war are peremptory norms—that is, higher laws based upon long-standing state practice that cannot be altered by treaties or domestic law.[76] They govern every nation's decision to go to war (*jus ad bellum*) and the manner in which it is conducted (*jus in bellum*). The rules governing American warfare, in particular, are derived from international and domestic sources. Thus, to understand rules applicable to the Indian wars, we must first examine principles of international law pertaining to war, and then look at US law.

International Law

The law of nations is the starting place for our analysis. No country can disregard international norms regarding the use of force without being branded an outlaw. Thus, to determine questions of war, the Supreme Court wisely consults the law of nations as well as the Constitution.[77] As discussed earlier, international law originated in Europe as a product of medieval Christian thought. It was conceived to define relations among the nations of Europe, guide their dealings with the non-Christian world, and provide rules for colonizing the New World.

Rules of war were espoused early on by founding jurists, such as Franciscus de Victoria, Alberico Gentili, and Emmerich de Vattel, to provide guidelines for invading the Americas.[78] Many of their legal principles—such as the doctrines of discovery, conquest, and just war—were readily incorporated into the fabric of American law in cases like *Johnson v. M'Intosh*, *Cherokee Nation v. Georgia*, and other jurisprudence. In particular, the law of war was adopted in whole cloth. In the *Prize Cases* (1862), for example, the Supreme Court consulted international law to determine whether a legal state of war existed during the Civil War. The Court applied it to evaluate President Lincoln's decision to go to war (*jus ad bellum*) and the belligerents' use of force (*jus in bellum*) during that conflict.[79]

The decision to go to war (*jus ad bellum*) entails consideration of several fundamental concepts. First and foremost is the distinction between a war of defense and an aggressive war. A nation can lawfully use force in only two circumstances: (1) defensively, to repel attack or invasion and (2) offensively, to punish legal wrongs.[80] Defensive war may be waged immediately without a declaration of war. It is done solely in self-defense when necessary to repel attack or other immediate threats. In those circumstances, the use of force is the unquestioned right of every sovereign nation. By contrast, stringent requirements must be observed before an offensive war can be waged.

Offensive wars are those of aggression and invasion. They may be waged only when just cause exists, that is, when one nation commits a legal wrong that injures another. Legal wrongs can be numerous and sometimes suspect, depending on how they are defined and by whom,[81] but they do not include religious or ideological differences, racial or ethnic animosity, or the bare pursuit of empire, domain, or conquest. In the absence of bona fide legal wrongs, none of those illegitimate motives provide just cause for war. After all, the just-war doctrine springs from Christian concepts of morality and justice—essential notions that mark right from wrong—which are intended to place in check the immoral dark side of human nature. Under Christian doctrine, certain evils can never justify making war, such as the lust for power, cruelty, or a desire to do wrong.[82] Victoria labeled three causes of war as inherently unjust: (1) differences of religion, (2) extension of empire, and (3) personal glory of the prince.[83] That is why customary international law does not consider jihad, holy wars, ethnic-cleansing campaigns, Iraq's invasion of

Kuwait, and Hitler's Blitzkrieg to be just wars. In all instances, the law of nations requires an acceptable legal basis for commencing offensive war. In this sense, a lawful just war resembles a "judicial procedure" between nations to redress wrongs and vindicate justice, except generals, not judges, decide the outcome.[84] In short, the just-cause doctrine requires aggressor nations to justify their use of violence, as seen in the George W. Bush administration's attempt to identify legal wrongs committed against the United States by Iraq that justify our invasion of that country. Many are not persuaded that just cause exists, since no weapons of mass destruction were ever found, and the bare idea of bringing democracy to an utterly foreign land with a vastly different cultural and political heritage is not a just cause for war because it is tantamount to the extension of ideological empire.

Due to the grave consequences that attend war, international law imposes procedural safeguards on the use of offensive warfare.[85] First, the proper body in each nation invested with the power to wage war must make findings of (1) just cause to identify the wrong committed and (2) a prudential judgment that war is actually in the national interest.[86] These findings are akin to findings of a court of law that must be made before a judgment is entered to exact punishment or compensation under domestic municipal law.[87] Next, the nation must issue a formal declaration of war before commencing an offensive war.[88] The declaration serves important purposes. It gives notice to the offender of the legal wrong and a demand for satisfaction to allow it opportunity to settle the dispute peaceably. It notifies citizens and other nations of the change in legal relations occasioned by the existence of war and, finally, it sets the parameters for the armed conflict. Japan disregarded these obligations in the infamous surprise attack on Pearl Harbor, executed before a declaration of war on the United States. That is why its attack was deplored by the world.[89] In short, a declaration of war is the legal equivalent of a judicial judgment that legally ushers in an offensive war to redress wrongs done to a nation. After World War II, the United States seems to have dispensed with this formality. It invaded Korea, Vietnam, Iraq, and other places without issuing a declaration of war, leaving scholars to debate the legality of those murky wars of aggression, which are beyond the scope of this book. It seems we can declare war on most other things, like poverty, crime, drugs, and terrorism, but not the actual countries we invade.

Finally, offensive war must be conducted according to several elements of just war. Under the principle of right authority, the initiation of offensive war can only be done by the entity vested by domestic law with the power to make war.[90] The use of force must be in proportion to the wrong done since it is compensatory punishment for an injury inflicted upon a nation, and nothing more.[91] It must be waged only as a last resort after peaceful means for resolving the dispute have failed.[92] Finally, even if all of the above elements are present, a war is unjust if waged out of hatred, prejudice, or other improper motives.[93]

International law also regulates the conduct of war by the foot soldiers (*jus in bellum*). It prescribes a wide variety of rules pertaining to the rights, treatment, and punishment of captured soldiers as belligerents; rules for capturing and confiscating enemy property; prohibitions against killing innocents and noncombatants; the treatment of debts, contracts, and treaties among enemies and belligerents during wartime; and all other facets of war. These rules provide acceptable boundaries for combat, mitigate the horror and cruelty of war, and prevent escalating retaliation among combatants. War quickly turns into atrocity and genocide when they are not observed. Consequently, violations constitute war crimes punishable in appropriate international, military, or other tribunals.

US Domestic Law

The Indian wars were public wars under US law, just like any other American war during the nineteenth century.[94] The courts of the era recognized that war can exist when one belligerent is an Indian nation.[95] They acknowledged that the United States can wage war on domestic dependent Indian nations who, by the same token, retained legal power to wage war on the United States.[96] Felix S. Cohen, the father of federal Indian law, observed in 1942 that the power to make war, which is a fundamental attribute of sovereignty in international law, was recognized in Indian nations well into recent times. He stated:

> This power has been recognized in Indian tribes down to recent times, and there are still on the statute books laws which contemplate the possibility of hostilities by an Indian tribe. The capacity of an Indian tribe to make war involves certain definite consequences for domestic law. Acts which would constitute murder or manslaughter in the absence of a state of war, whether committed by Indians, or by the military forces of the United States, may be justified as acts of war where a state of war

exists. Hostile Indians surrendering to armed forces are subject to the disabilities and entitled to the rights of prisoners of war.[97]

The Indian wars were considered wars of the imperfect or limited kind, but war nevertheless in the legal sense.[98] Judge Nott used this test to define the Indian wars in a case involving the Apaches:

> The books hold that when war exists every citizen of one belligerent is the enemy of every citizen of the other. Conversely, this court holds that when every white man, at a given time and in a certain territory, is found to be the enemy of every Indian, and every Indian is found to be the enemy of every white man, a condition of amity does not exist within the meaning of the fifty statutes which employ the word "amity" to prevent war upon the frontier. If a party of bad white men or a party of bad Indians engaged in rapine and murder and the remainder of the white community and of the Indian tribe did not take up arms, it was crime, but not war. If, on the contrary, the condition of affairs was such that every man on the one side stood ready to kill any man on the other side and military operations took the place of peaceful intercourse, hostility so far existed that amity ceased to exist...[99]

The normal rules of war apply to the Indian wars, just as they did to every other public war in the same period. During the nineteenth century, American courts routinely applied them to every type and facet of public war. It did not matter whether the war was against foreign nations[100] or rebels at home,[101] or whether the war was a general one commenced by a declaration of war or limited warfare authorized by Congress. Since the Indian wars were recognized as public war, there is no reason why the rules should not apply. There is no basis to assume that some sort of exception in the law existed for Indian wars. Researchers should, therefore, apply normal American rules of war to the Indian wars. Some of those rules, which were well settled in the nineteenth century, are discussed next.

America's decision to go to war in the nineteenth century was governed by international law (*jus ad bellum*) and the War Power Clauses of the US Constitution, which allocate war powers between Congress and the president. Under the Constitution, only Congress may declare war, whereas the president is empowered to conduct war.[102]

The just-war doctrine was adopted by statute. The Northwest Ordinance was enacted by the Continental Congress in 1787 to govern the Northwest Territory and reenacted by Congress two years later.[103] Article 3 provides:

> The utmost good faith shall always be observed towards the Indians; their land and property shall never be taken from them without their consent; and in their property, rights and liberty, they never shall be invaded or disturbed, *unless in just and lawful wars authorized by Congress.* (emphasis added)

This law makes the just-war doctrine of the law of nations applicable to Indian wars waged within the Northwest Territory, and those wars must be "authorized by Congress." For the sake of uniformity, these same requirements arguably pertain to other territories subsequently obtained by the United States, such as the Louisiana Purchase, especially in the absence of a clear expression of congressional intent to the contrary. Otherwise, the American landscape would be subjected to a strange, checkerboard law of war.

A review of the Indian wars will reveal that many, but not all, were authorized, or at least mentioned, by statutes passed by Congress, primarily appropriation laws enacted after hostilities commenced. However, the inquiry does not end there, since the Northwest Ordinance also requires those wars be just. Thus, one must determine whether the conflict passes muster under the just-war doctrine. Furthermore, in the case of an offensive war of aggression against an Indian tribe, international law requires us to evaluate the sufficiency of sometimes cryptic language employed in those statutes to see whether it provides sufficient notice to fulfill the important purposes of declarations of war. For example, the "Act to increase the cavalry force of the United States, to aid in suppressing the Indians" (August 15, 1876) merely appropriates money and authorizes the president to employ more troops "in existing Indian hostilities." Such language does not provide minimal information normally required in declarations of war.

American law also recognized the distinction between offensive and defensive war. The president could wage defensive war to repel attack without a formal declaration of war.[104] However, he could not initiate offensive war. Invasion and general wars of aggression could only be initiated by a formal declaration of war issued by Congress.[105] And, in the case of Indian wars, the Northwest Ordinance required them to be "just and lawful wars authorized by Congress."

The conduct of American warfare during the nineteenth century was governed by *jus in bellum*, regardless of whether the war was of the general or limited kind.[106] As illustrated in *Tingy*, international law applied with full force to limited wars, even though their limits and operation were circumscribed by parameters set by Congress. Thus, when a limited war is involved, such as an Indian war, one must consult pertinent acts of Congress to learn who is authorized to commit hostilities, where those hostilities may be committed, against whom, and other limitations imposed by Congress.[107] Combatants in domestic warfare were clearly required to observe the customary rules of war. It is therefore fair to conclude that those same rules were equally applicable to Indian wars.[108] Those rules were adopted in the US Army's Lieber Code of 1863 to guide the military in the proper conduct of warfare under international law.[109]

The Lieber Code prohibited American soldiers from killing unarmed civilian noncombatants.[110] It granted captured soldiers all of the accepted legal rights and protective status as prisoners of war, and it bestowed upon them the rights of belligerents—exempting warlike acts committed by captured soldiers in wartime as criminal offenses.[111] The code prohibited mistreatment of prisoners of war, such as the infliction of suffering by cruelty, want of food, or other barbarity.[112] It required them to be fed and treated with humanity.[113] While escaping prisoners could be shot and killed, their attempted escape was not considered a crime.[114] Finally, the killing or inflicting of additional wounds upon an enemy already wounded was an offense punishable by death.[115] As you'll see, the code was not followed by the US Army during its pursuit and capture of Morning Star's people.

The Use of Military Force against Morning Star's People Was Illegal

Based upon Judge Nott's findings of fact made in the *Connors* case, it is evident that the United States' use of force against the Northern Cheyenne was illegal in several important respects.

First, it was an unconstitutional *offensive* war initiated and conducted without the required authorization by Congress. The bluecoat troops were not repelling an attack or invasion when they instigated the conflict. Their assault was not waged in self-defense. *The Northern Cheyenne were at peace and had committed no crimes or atrocities when the firing began.* They were lawfully traveling to Montana, as established in *Standing Bear*, and nothing more. The bluecoats lacked any apparent legal authority to order them back to the reservation or fire on them. As such, this was not defensive warfare. Only Congress can initiate offensive war. Since it did not do so, the use of force, though perhaps authorized by General Philip Sheridan, was *not* authorized by the legitimate authority prescribed by the Constitution. The government's use of force was therefore illegal because it violated both domestic law and international law's principle of right authority—the very rules made by the conqueror.

By contrast, under the same rules, the *Tsis tsis' tas* were lawful belligerents waging a defensive war. They repelled armed attack in self-defense, as allowed by the law of nations. Domestic law fully recognized their power to wage war as a domestic dependent Indian nation. Indeed, their capacity to maintain relations of war and peace was recognized by treaty.[116] From their standpoint, the incidents in *Connors* met the criteria for a defensive Indian war. As stated by Judge Nott, "every white man, at a given time and in a certain territory, is found to be the enemy of every Indian, and every Indian is found to be the enemy of every white man."[117]

Second, the United States lacked just cause to wage an offensive war against the Human Beings. The just-cause requirement was imposed upon the government by the Northwest Ordinance and international law: *a nation can wage offensive war only to punish legal wrongs.* As Judge Nott found, the Northern Cheyenne were at peace and had committed no crime. They were engaged in lawful conduct, as illustrated in the analogous *Standing Bear* case. The *Connors* opinion does not disclose the reason why the soldiers fired on the Indians. However, historians determined that General Sheridan, the commanding general of the Division of the Missouri, feared that the government's failure to stop Morning Star would be viewed as a sign of weakness by other Indian tribes, which could jeopardize the government's reservation system.[118] *After all, if Indians can simply leave their reservations, the government's apartheid system would be undermined.* This policy concern motivated Sheridan throughout the affair. In November of 1877, he communicated his concerns to Washington:

> [U]nless these Indians are sent back, the reservation system will receive a shock which will endanger its stability. If Indians can leave without punishment, they will not stay on reservations.[119]

Despite this policy concern, leaving an Indian reservation was lawful—a far cry from committing a legal wrong against the United States.[120] In the absence of just cause, the war was illegal under both the law of nations and the statutory command of the Northwest Ordinance that no war be waged against Indian tribes without just cause.

Third, the domestic rules for conducting war were violated by the troops. Once Morning Star's people were captured, they were entitled to the treatment and privileges of prisoners of war provided in the Lieber Code, which required the military to conduct warfare within the bounds of acceptable international norms. The deprivation of food, water, and fuel in the Fort Robinson stockade by Captain Wessells violated Section 3, which expressly forbade the infliction of suffering "by cruel imprisonment, want of food…or any other barbarity."[121] The Cheyenne POWs were required to be fed and treated with humanity, not starved, deprived of water, nor subjected to freezing temperatures. Above all, the Lieber Code required that unarmed persons "be spared in person, property, and honor as much as the exigencies of war will admit."[122] *Was it necessary to kill the unarmed women and children who escaped from the stockade into the winter storm?* Further, the code strictly forbade the infliction of additional wounds upon an enemy already wounded—an offense made punishable by death—but that rule was ignored during the breakout from the stockade.

Finally, we must consider the rights of belligerents that the Lieber Code bestowed upon the Cheyenne soldiers. It provided that "killing, wounding, or other warlike acts" committed by captured soldiers in wartime are not considered criminal offenses.[123] This legal protection for captured soldiers was violated by the government when it sent the seven surviving Cheyenne soldiers to Kansas in chains to be tried for murder for lawful acts of war. Even though acquitted for lack of evidence, the POWs should never have been tried in the first place under the rules of war. This made a mockery of the Lieber Code by creating a double standard in the law of war, because none of the American soldiers were tried for violating the Lieber Code or civilian laws by their illegal conduct. No wonder Judge Nott was troubled by the facts before him in the *Connors* case—*there was no legal basis for the war and it was conducted illegally.*

The rules of war were not followed by the United States in many of its wars with the Cheyenne and perhaps other tribes. For example, there is no apparent legal basis for the massacre of the Cheyenne and Arapaho villagers

at Sand Creek. Those Indians, too, were at peace when attacked. Several government investigations were conducted to determine whether the assault on
the village was conducted according to the rules of civilized warfare.[124] The
House of Representatives report concluded that the villagers were "deliberately murdered" and "the soldiers indulged in acts of barbarity of the most
revolting character."[125] It branded Chivington and his men as war criminals.

> As to Colonel Chivington, your committee can hardly find fitting terms
> to describe his behavior. Wearing the uniform of the United States,
> which should be the emblem of justice and humanity; holding the
> important position of commander of a military district, and therefore
> having the honor of the government to that extent in his keeping, he
> planned and executed a foul and dastardly massacre which would have
> disgraced the veriest savage among those who were the victims of his
> cruelty. Having full knowledge of their friendly character, having him-
> self been instrumental to some extent in placing them in their posi-
> tion of fancied security, he took advantage of their inapprenhension and
> defenceless condition to gratify the worst passions that ever cursed the
> heart of man...Whatever may have been his motive, it is to be hoped
> that the authority of this government will never again be disgraced by
> the acts such as he and those acting with him have been guilty of com-
> mitting...[T]he truth is that he surprised and murdered, in cold blood,
> the unsuspecting men, women, and children on Sand Creek, who had
> every reason to believe they were under the protection of the United
> States authorities, and then returned to Denver and boasted of the brave
> deeds he and the men under his command had performed...[F]or the
> purpose of vindicating the cause of justice and upholding the honor of
> the nation, prompt and energetic measures should be at once taken to
> remove from office those who have thus disgraced the government by
> whom they were employed, and to punish, as their crimes deserve, those
> who have been guilty of these brutal and cowardly acts."[126]

No one was punished. By contrast, Indian combatants of the various conflicts such as the one described in *Connors* were tried in both civilian courts
and military tribunals for their acts of war.[127] But that's just the way it goes
in the courts of the conqueror. Further research will shed more light on the
extent to which the law of war was violated in the nineteenth century.

Have the Indians Overcome the Hardships Imposed by War?

The Northern Cheyenne Indians successfully returned to their beloved homeland. This remarkable feat was accomplished against overwhelming odds at enormous cost, as described in *Connors*. Lame Deer, Montana, is the capital of the Northern Cheyenne Reservation, which sits in the beautiful Tongue River valley. It is one of the last best places in the American West—a spectacular homeland well worth fighting for. We can only regret the death toll, suffering, and legal wrongs perpetrated against the Human Beings in 1878–79 and mourn the bloodshed. The survivors' descendents still lament those tragic events, as Richard Williams poignantly observed in 2007: "the Cheyenne's heartbreaking little-known story is one of America's saddest tragedies—decent people annihilated simply because they wanted to return to their homeland; if left undisturbed, they would have retired to their homeland and lived peacefully ever after."[128] Regardless of the hardships, the Cheyenne Nation stands proud today under the Creator's original instruction to the Human Beings: *the Cheyenne Nation shall be strong so long as the hearts of the women are not on the ground.*

In the winter of 1973, Native American Rights Fund (NARF) attorneys John Echohawk and Roy S. Haber were called into Wounded Knee, South Dakota, shortly after the occupation of that village by the American Indian Movement (AIM) and traditional tribal leaders began. Wounded Knee was an impoverished and oppressed community on the neglected Pine Ridge Indian Reservation so desperate for social change that it gave rise to hostage taking and an armed stand-off. When the attorneys arrived, it was a war zone. A few hundred Indians in the isolated village were surrounded by a large force of US marshals, FBI agents, and BIA police armed with shotguns and automatic weapons and supported by a dozen armored personnel carriers. The task of the NARF attorneys, who were the first outsiders allowed into the besieged area, was to open lines of communication for negotiations between the parties so no one would be killed. After a series of meetings with AIM leaders in the village church, a tipi was erected on neutral ground in the demilitarized zone between the lines, and negotiations began. It was to be the last armed confrontation between Indians and Big Knives in the twentieth century.

Recalling the historical significance of the seventy-day Wounded Knee occupation, Echohawk observed, "it focused national attention on neglected Native American issues for the first time in many decades, and the nation began to constructively address long-overdue grievances."[129] Today, most modern-day Indian wars are fought in courtrooms and legislative hallways by several thousand Native American lawyers. They are foot soldiers in the remarkable Native American sovereignty movement, which has done so much to restore pride, sovereignty, and well-being in Indian Country. Today these attributes of freedom are sometimes taken for granted. However, indigenous rights are never voluntarily given by the conqueror. They must be demanded, wrested away, and earned in the first instance by the Native people themselves with support from people of goodwill. Native American rights were won in hard-fought legal battles and legislative campaigns during the modern era of federal Indian law.

Myths about the law of war and conquest must no longer be tolerated. When Chief Justice Marshall alluded to the right of conquest in his trilogy of decisions, he did not imply that it is an unfettered right free of legal restraints. Many carelessly assume that "might makes right" when considering indigenous affairs, as reflected in the infamous remarks of Justice Reed in *Tee-Hit-Ton Indians*.[130] Though invasion, war, and conquest are brutal acts, they are still governed by the law. The Indian wars were not free from legal restraint. No loophole or exception to the rules of war existed for warfare against indigenous people then, or now, even though a double standard may have been applied by the United States to judge its own conduct during those conflicts. Furthermore, if we define *conquest* as "the appropriation of land by force of arms," there was no wholesale military conquest of Native America as Justice Reed seemed to believe.

Were the Indian wars legal? Certainly not, at least in the case study described in *Connors*, nor at Sand Creek. Further research on other conflicts may demonstrate that some of the Indian wars were perfectly legal, while in others the violence committed against Native Americans was unlawful—indeed, murder that went unpunished. In the latter instances, much of the death and destruction could have been averted, or at least mitigated, had America observed the law of war.

But why should we care at this late date? The Cheyenne care. So do other indigenous peoples who have been harmed by war or live under its threat today. Much violence was committed against Native peoples in the nineteenth and twentieth centuries—amounting to world war against them in some years. Their concerns about violence are reflected in the United Nations Declaration on the Rights of Indigenous Peoples (2007), which protects indigenous peoples from acts of genocide and the use of violence by states, including the forcible removal of their children, forced assimilation or cultural destruction, and forcible removal from their lands.[131]

The legality of the Indian wars matters in the same way that the legitimacy of American wars in Korea, Vietnam, Afghanistan, and Iraq matter to many people, especially the veterans of those conflicts and their families. I believe it also mattered to Judge Nott, when the former prisoner of war examined the facts in *Connors* and asked whether the violence committed against the Cheyenne was lawful. Though *Connors* did not decide the issue, the case serves much the same stark educational purpose as *Cherokee Nation v. Georgia*, by leaving in the records of the courts of the conqueror, for future generations to read, ample testimony of the conduct of the United States toward its Native peoples. It memorializes the use of violence as part of the federal Indian policies of the nineteenth century.

The scars of war have slowly begun to heal on the Great Plains.[132] The remains of slain Cheyenne taken from the Sand Creek and Fort Robinson massacre sites by the government were repatriated to the Cheyenne people and reburied in the 1990s.[133] The moving Sand Creek dedication in 2007 is a telling step toward reconciliation between the red and white inhabitants of this region. In his eloquent speech, US Senator Sam Brownback of Kansas bravely admitted that the wrongs committed there, and elsewhere, were improperly tolerated by the US government. He backed his words by introducing Senate Joint Resolution 4 into the 110th Congress, which offers an apology to the Native Americans on behalf of the nation.[134] Regardless whether Congress actually passes this historic measure, outside of the District of Columbia's beltway a healing process is underway in the American heartland. It is spurred from stories told by the land, like the place that is now enshrined as a national historical site. Perhaps more members of Congress should come to Chivington, Colorado, and listen to the land.

CHAPTER SEVEN
Lone Wolf v. Hitchcock: Breaking the Treaties

THE WEATHER WAS BLISTERING HOT in western Oklahoma. Nevertheless, over fifty thousand sweaty-faced folks crowded into El Reno, Oklahoma Territory, to watch the lottery drawing. The government land office was opening the Kiowa, Comanche, and Apache Reservation to white settlement—a real boon. The dusty onlookers were quite a rabble, mainly down-and-out homesteaders, hucksters, and land sharks. These homeless sodbusters had lost out on five previous occasions to rivals who feverishly staked claims to Indian land in the Oklahoma land runs. The races carved up Indian Territory under the federal government's allotment policy to satisfy popular demand for Indian land. By 1902, this was the last intact reservation in the former Indian Territory. Despite the heat, two million acres would be divvied up today among 12,500 winners, and that would complete colonization of the Indian reservations in present-day Oklahoma, the Sooner State.[1] At the dawn of the twentieth century, Manifest Destiny had almost run its course, but not before these buckaroos got their land.

America was about to engulf the Kiowa, Comanche, and Apache people. These allied tribes were a tough bunch. Their confederacy once ruled the southern plains; the panhandle of Texas, Oklahoma, and New Mexico, extending into Kansas and Colorado, comprised the vast homeland. Mounted warriors from these buffalo-hunting nations barred Spanish, Mexican, Texan, and American settlement in the region for over 160 years. At the urging of a war-weary United States, they made peace in the Medicine Lodge Treaty of 1867.[2] The peace accord ceded the enormous region to the United States, but reserved buffalo-hunting rights in the ceded area and a permanent homeland "for the absolute and undisturbed use and occupation" of the three tribes in the Wichita Mountains of southwest Oklahoma, where the Indians settled and took up the reservation way of life.[3] This story is about Lone Wolf, a Kiowa warrior and chief, and his efforts to avoid the forced allotment of his reservation in the courts of the conqueror.

On that hot summer day in 1902, Lone Wolf grimaced as settlers streamed into the reservation for the land lottery. *This was illegal!* The treaty guaranteed that the reservation would never be taken away, unless by consent of a three-quarters vote of all adult male tribal members.[4] Despite that stipulation, Congress opened the reservation to settlers without the required vote.[5] To make it worse, the lawmakers *knew* the Indians did not want to sell their land and were against the bill and that the federal negotiators involved in the matter had acted in a fraudulent, underhanded way. In the words of one commentator, the process "stank to high heaven."[6] But Congress passed the law anyway, approving the heavily tainted Jerome Agreement. Incessant parochial pressure from land-hungry Oklahomans was more important to the lawmakers than Kiowa treaty and property rights—after all, Indians could not vote, they were just wards of the government.

Besides that, breaking up the reservation was supposed to be good for Indians, according to policy makers and social reformers. Indians could not become assimilated into society as useful citizens, it seemed, while still in a tribal state, and their communally owned tribal land was seen as an obstacle to the government's civilization efforts. Consequently, Congress passed the General Allotment Act of 1887 (known as the Dawes Act) to establish a process for breaking up reservation homelands by parceling tribal land owned by Indian tribes to individual members and selling the remainder to white settlers.[7] According to Rough Rider President Teddy Roosevelt, this law was "a mighty pulverizing engine to break up the tribal mass."[8] The allotment and sale process would benefit Indians, according to policy makers, by stamping out tribalism and savagery so the red race could be absorbed into mainstream society. This transformation would theoretically be brought about by incoming white neighbors bringing the gifts of civilization in buckboard wagons and teaching Indians the habits of civilized life; and once civilized, Indians would not need so much land. Indians must be "liberated" from the burden of owning too much land before these benefits could be bestowed upon them—whether they wanted them or not. In actuality, the land transfer from one race to another was nothing more than an affirmative action program for landless settlers done at tribal expense, and the program had devastating consequences on Indian tribes, causing the loss of almost ninety million acres of tribal land by 1934 (two-thirds of the land base in 1887), when the policy was abandoned as a dismal failure.[9]

Many Indian traditionalists, like Lone Wolf, were not persuaded of the benefits of civilization and assimilation at the cost of their homeland, culture, and way of life, and they resisted government destruction of the tribal land base. Lone Wolf was an old-time Kiowa warrior, a veteran of raids into Texas and Mexico and of hard-fought battles in the Llano Estacado ("Staked Plains")—places like Palo Duro Canyon and the Adobe Walls.

Originally named Walking Above (*Mamedaty* in Kiowa), he won the name Lone Wolf (*Gazpacho*), bestowed on him by none other than the great Kiowa war chief Lone Wolf the elder for counting coup on a Texas Ranger in the Llano Estacado during the Buffalo War of 1874 (also known as the Red River War). From that day on, Walking Above was known as Lone Wolf the younger, and upon the death of the elder chief in 1879, Lone Wolf the younger succeeded him.

During the soul-killing days of reservation life when missionaries and Indian agents tried to "civilize" the Kiowa, Lone Wolf became a staunch opponent of the government's allotment and assimilation programs. He would not accept forced allotment and the government's shenanigans without a fight. Relying upon the Medicine Lodge Treaty, Lone Wolf led a group of Indians in filing suit in 1901 to block the illegal allotment and sale of their reservation. As the case worked its way to the Supreme Court, President William McKinley opened the reservation on August 6, 1902, and the three tribes' land was soon parceled out to the motley crew at El Reno. Now only the Supreme Court could halt the destruction of the Indians' treaty-protected land base.

On January 5, 1903, the Supreme Court handed down the decision in *Lone Wolf v. Hitchcock* (1903).[10] Announcing the "plenary power" doctrine, the court allowed Congress to carve up the reservation against the Indians' will, in violation of the treaty. Writing for the unanimous Court, Justice Edward Douglas White explained that Congress possesses paramount power over Indian tribes and their property because it is their guardian. Strangely, this plenary power is not found in the Constitution, but was implied by the Court from the trusteeship doctrine. The Court declared that Congress's plenary political power over Indians is absolute—that is, beyond the rule of law—because it is not subject to judicial review, and it includes the raw power to abrogate treaties. The sole check on that unlimited power was a bare presumption that Congress will exercise it in "perfect good faith."[11] The plenary-power doctrine was seemingly plucked out of thin air by the Supreme Court against the backdrop of federal guardianship of a dependent, supposedly inferior race of people—a dubious basis upon which to sanction the rule of Native people by unlimited power, a despotic power aimed at no other Americans in US history. Under this extraordinary doctrine, the *Lone Wolf* Court held that Congress can lawfully dispose of Indian property any way it sees fit, even by laws that abrogate treaty stipulations, and the Indians have no legal recourse in the courts.

Lone Wolf is one of the ten worst Indian law cases ever decided. Much has been written about this infamous decision by legal scholars analyzing the many disturbing ramifications of the landmark case, but the fact remains that this notorious case is not well known to the general public.[12] One federal court ruefully observed, when looking back on *Lone Wolf* many years later, that "[t]he day Lone Wolf was handed down, January 5, 1903, might be called one of the blackest days in the history of the American Indian, the Indians' *Dred Scott* decision."[13] Indeed, the parallels to the infamous slavery ruling are chilling. Both cases turned on patently racist notions of white supremacy, both refused to address claims of the plaintiffs, and both placed these racial groups beyond the pale of judicial and constitutional protection under the political-question doctrine.[14] Though *Dred Scott* and its progeny have been repudiated and are no longer cited as legal authority by the courts, the essence of *Lone Wolf* and its philosophy remain with us in many frightening respects. For these reasons, it is important to understand the genesis of *Lone Wolf*'s legal doctrines lest they be applied to other people, here or abroad, and to forestall the continuing vitality of the *Lone Wolf* mentality in the courts of the conqueror when Native American issues are concerned.

Though many aspects of *Lone Wolf* can be decried, the uppermost concern addressed in this chapter is honor. "Great nations, like great men, should keep their word."[15] With these words, Justice Hugo Black underscored the importance of good faith and fair dealing in making and keeping treaties with Indian nations. Over 360 Indian treaties were negotiated by American diplomats, signed by the president, and ratified by the Senate pursuant to the Treaty Clause of the US Constitution.[16] The Constitution proclaims that all treaties made "shall be the supreme Law of the Land," including those made with Indian nations.[17] Despite the lofty constitutional status of treaties, history is replete with instances like *Lone Wolf* in which the United States did not keep its word. As noted by Senator Daniel K. Inouye, the longtime chairman of the Senate Indian Affairs Committee during the modern era of federal Indian law:

> Too few Americans know that the Indian nations ceded millions of acres to the United States, or that while the terms of the treaties naturally varied, the promises and commitments made by the United States were typically made in perpetuity. History has recorded, however, that

our great nation did not keep its word to the Indian nations, and our preeminent challenge today as lawmakers is to assure the integrity of our treaty commitments and to bring an end to the era of broken promises.[18]

The hundreds of treaties made in the nineteenth century were vitally important to the signatories, both the United States and Indian nations. An entire continent was transferred to the fledgling republic through treaties struck with Native peoples. Through them, the republic obtained the enormous land cessions that allowed settlement of Indian lands, demarcated boundaries between sovereigns, and set aside reservation homelands for the tribes.[19] The treaties are equally important to Indian nations because they are the foundational documents by which they entered into the protection of and a political union with the United States, as "protectorate" nations, which will be elaborated upon in chapter fifteen.

The treaty agreements, which were struck in solemn councils between official representatives of the negotiating parties, guided formal political relationships in Indian affairs throughout most of the nineteenth century. Indeed, the treaties were the only legal means for dealing with Indian tribes during much of the nation's early history. Until 1871, when Congress ended the treaty-making practice by statute, treaties were one of the principal means by which the United States interacted with Indian nations.[20] Through these diplomatic agreements, the federal government established peace, trade, and friendship with Indian nations; developed mutual assistance pacts; brought the tribes under the protection of the United States; engineered the removal of tribes from their homelands to the reservation system; and advanced myriad Indian policies intended to promote American ideas about civilization, education, and assimilation. The treaty agreements embody hard-fought deals made by Native Americans, together with the promises made to indigenous peoples by a grateful though often overreaching nation during the colonization period. Today, the treaty accords constitute a major source of federal Indian law that defines the rights, relationships, and responsibilities among indigenous and nonindigenous peoples in the United States.

This chapter examines the diplomatic and legal history of the Medicine Lodge Treaty that conveyed a large portion of the southern plains to the United States while retaining a reservation homeland in western Oklahoma. The *Lone Wolf* story illustrates how treaties with Indian nations were made, why they were vital to each signatory, and how treaties were broken, with the blessing of the Supreme Court, by lawmakers who callously disregarded the rights of a few Indians in order to pander to popular political positions. In examining the plenary-power doctrine of *Lone Wolf*, we must consider the moral obligations that rest on lawmakers when they exercise absolute power over an Indian minority and confront the dangers of the "tyranny of the majority"—feared by thinkers such as Alexis de Tocequeville and John Stewart Mill—that can arise in the midst of a democracy when courts fail to carry out their antimajoritarian function to place in check the abuse of power. As you will see, the *Lone Wolf* mentality sounds a warning to democratic values.

The Treaty Negotiations

Our story begins in the "Great American Desert," as the Indian Peace Commission made its way across the open prairie, cutting deep tracks in the tall buffalo grass. The little caravan was a small army, really. The contingent was led by seven top-level diplomats appointed by the president, with an entourage of Indian chiefs, local politicians, and a gaggle of reporters embedded in a wagon train bearing gifts, food, and supplies. With guidons flying in the wind, the Seventh Cavalry escort accompanied the party with orders to protect the group, but not provoke the waiting tribes gathered at Medicine Lodge Creek, Kansas. In all, the caravan numbered about 600 souls—diplomats, interpreters, sundry officials and staff, soldiers and civilian scouts, and teamsters—with 211 wagons and 1,250 animals in the column.[21] The seven diplomats named to the Indian Peace Commission were Senator John B. Henderson, the chairman of the Senate Indian Affairs Committee, the commissioner of Indian Affairs, Samuel F. Tappan, and three generals: Major General William S. Harney, Major General C. C. Augur, and Major General Alfred H. Terry.

Their mission was of grave importance. Congress wanted to make peace with the Plains Indians and create permanent homeland reservations for the nomadic tribes where over time they could be assimilated into the republic—all so that the march of Manifest Destiny, which had faltered in these southern plains amid fierce tribal resistance, could resume its course peaceably. The Indian Peace Commission was created by Congress in 1867 to ascertain the causes of war, remove those causes, and accomplish the nation's peace and reservation objectives through a great treaty-making process.[22] Emphasizing the gravity of the situation, section five of the act authorized the president and secretary of war to gather four thousand volunteers, should the commissioners fail to establish peace and secure the Indians' consent to remove to the reservations, "for the suppression of Indian hostilities."

As the delegation entered tribal hunting grounds populated by grazing buffalo in the Kansas prairie, the escort of Indian chiefs provided safe passage. Among them was Satanta ("White-Bear-Person"), the flamboyant Kiowa war chief—a man who lived in a flaming-red tipi and carried an army bugle to confuse US troops on the battlefield. Known as the "orator of the plains," the large-sized warrior entertained, and perhaps intimidated, the reporters with his tales of many exploits.

Just two days out of Fort Larned, Kansas, a pale of foreboding swept over the skittish travelers as they encountered a prairie fire burning in the distance. "Was it torched by warriors protesting our arrival?" asked nervous reporters (dressed variously, in trim waistcoats from their train ride to Kansas or duded up in buckskin fringes with brand-new revolvers strapped to their sides). The southern plains of Kansas, Oklahoma, Texas, New Mexico, and Colorado can be a forbidding place to newcomers, frequented as it is by violent thunderstorms and life-threatening tornadoes. These arid, windswept prairies are bitter cold in winter and baking hot in summer. Water is scarce unless you know where to find it, especially in Llano Estacado, where only the hardy (or very desperate) survive. The baldies were hardly fit for colonization. Most immigrants scurried quickly through the region to friendlier, more habitable destinations.

In 1867, this wide expanse was more than inhospitable. It was a danger zone occupied by mounted Comanche, Kiowa, Apache, Cheyenne, and Arapaho, fiercely determined to prevent unwanted intrusions into their domain. These allied tribes ruled this vast empire on horseback, like the Mongol and Arab horse cultures living in other unfenced lands suited mainly for a nomadic way of life. They were especially opposed to the construction of railroads and telegraph lines through the buffalo commons, which disturbed and drove away the herds upon which the tribes depended. Even less did they accept the building on Indian land of permanent white settlements, which were invariably destructive of the Indian way of life. These tribes were fighting harder for their land and way of life than any others had done before. They made westward immigration downright dangerous and settlement all but impossible. The Comanche repulsed Spanish, Mexican, and Texan expansion for 150 years. The Texas frontier was scoured by raiders who swept through hapless settlements under the Comanche moon in search of horses and captives. Colorado towns were burned to the ground by angry Sand Creek Massacre survivors and their allies in 1865. Pilgrims fled to Denver as forts, ranches, and way stations burned along the South Platte River during this period. During Red Cloud's War (1865–1868), the army retreated from the Powder River country, abandoning forts and the Bozeman Trail to victorious Cheyenne, Arapaho, and Sioux warriors in the Fort Laramie Treaty of 1868.[23] The previous year, Dog Soldiers attacked an Iron Horse (a steam locomotive) and wrecked the westbound Union Pacific train near Plum Creek Station, Nebraska, and their war parties roamed central Kansas at will throughout the 1860s. The Kiowa, who possessed more horses per capita than any other Plains tribe, were notorious for their frequent raids into Texas and Mexico. The Plains Indians—said to be the best light cavalry in the world—fought on their own terms and were forever cutting telegraph lines, attacking railroad construction crews, forts, and buffalo hunters, not to mention isolated ranches. In 1867 alone, Indians and whites fought 139 battles throughout the West.

Peace—that's what the war-weary nation wanted in 1867. With the end of bloodletting in the Civil War, America was undergoing reconstruction and reconciliation in the war-torn South. Eastern cities were bustling, and the continent lay before millions of immigrants who began streaming westward as railroad and telegraph lines inched toward connecting the coasts. The only obstacle to progress and prosperity was the western Indian tribes who formed a barrier to white settlement. The Republic could either conduct a race war of extermination or negotiate and assimilate the Indians into settler society. After national debate and more than a few violent confrontations, the country chose the latter approach—it was more humane and less costly. Hence, the United States launched its Indian Peace Policy on the Great Plains in 1867 with the creation of the Indian Peace Commission.

And now, over five thousand hostile Indians awaited the American negotiators at the treaty grounds in western Kansas—camped in a remote valley where the Medicine Lodge Creek flowed through ceremonial land dotted with Kiowa Sun Dance lodges. It was the largest gathering of Plains Indians ever assembled and everyone was skittish. The Americans were jumpy as they bravely entered the vast encampment. The Indians were leery of the soldiers and on guard against marauding Pawnee and Kaw who were prowling about the valley after the large pony herds. And everyone—Indian and white alike—worried about the large band of Cheyenne Dog Soldiers who were camped several miles away on the Cimarron River with intentions unknown. There was good reason for the commissioners to be nervous upon entering the camp. Lieutenant Colonel Douglas C. Jones sized up their situation:

> [F]ifty soldiers were able to offer but little protection. The Cheyennes had stopped raiding, but most of them were still staying away from the treaty grounds—assembled within easy striking distance. The Kiowas were traditionally unpredictable, and certainly [General] Harney must have been aware of their reputation. These fine, delicate-featured horsemen were claimed to be the most vicious, ruthless, unprincipled Indians on the Great Plains. If trouble should develop, most assuredly the Comanches would throw their lot behind Indian friends—although there were not overly fond of the Cheyennes, their loyalty to the Kiowas was already well known. Only the Arapahoes could be considered trustworthy, and many of them were not resigned to peace.[24]

One thing was clear, the lords of the southern plains did not come as supplicants as the two cultures met under the council arbor to hear proposals and promises made by the Peace Commission.

It had been a painstaking feat to assemble the tribes, a task accomplished by Indian Superintendent Thomas Murphy. At last, on October 14, the Peace Commission arrived. After being welcomed by a party of chiefs, the commission made its camp within a wagon barricade on the banks of Medicine Lodge Creek, amidst the braying of government mules and barking Indian dogs. Guards were posted and the treaty party settled down for the night. The next few days were spent in the customary treaty rituals—gift giving and welcome speeches, posturing, and other preparations for the treaty councils as the correspondents strolled through the Indian camps. Many participants wanted to wait until the Cheyenne Dog Soldiers came in, but the Human Beings were making medicine on the Cimarron, and this would take several days. Separate treaties would be negotiated with different tribal confederacies. On the evening of October 15, eighty Dog Soldiers rode into the camp, led by Tall Bull, to make preliminary arrangements for the arrival of the Cheyenne contingent from the Cimarron. Their sudden appearance, singing as they rode splashing through the water into the commissioners' camp, sent jitters throughout the encampment.[25] The Kiowa were impatient to conduct their business and depart for their winter camps, so they and the Comanche agreed to talk in four days, allowing Indians and whites to testify before the commission about the causes of war in the meantime.

With interpreters at the ready, the Kiowa and Comanche treaty negotiation began on October 19. Since the Kiowa language was the least known among the seven spoken by the parties and they had no interpreter of their own, the Kiowa delegation relied upon the Comanche's interpreter, Phillip McCusker, a frontiersman married to a Comanche woman. He translated English into Comanche (the trade language of the southern plains understood by most neighboring tribes) into Kiowa, and then vice versa.[26] Because additional tribes were also present, the laborious process required speakers to pause after each sentence to allow translation into several different languages.

The treaty council was held under a brush arbor constructed in a cottonwood grove where the tribal representatives seated themselves on logs, "garbed in their best blankets and fine buckskin jackets, and many wore neck pieces of bear claws and elk teeth, while others sported breast plates of polished quills and bones" and others yet were "fitted out in army coats."[27] The prominent chiefs lined the front rows, with lesser chiefs and warriors filling the back rows, and in the shady grove alongside the Medicine Lodge, "the women tended children and horses."[28] One reporter described the Kiowa delegation in the half circle of Indians facing the treaty commissioners:

> The Kiowa were on the left, with Satanta sitting in front on an army campstool, probably commandeered from some frontier post. The chief wore an army coat General Hancock had given him earlier in the year. Behind him were Kicking Bird and old Satank. Satank wore about his neck a silver medal with the profile of President Buchanan. The old Kiowa was sixty-seven years old, and streaks of grey marked his long, straight-hanging hair. His mustache was a dirty white.[29]

The Comanche delegation was headed by Ten Bears.[30] Cheyenne, Arapaho, and Apache onlookers were present, even though they were to negotiate their treaties at a later date.

As negotiations got underway, Senator Henderson spoke first for the United States, greeting the tribal delegates: "Friends of the Cheyenne, Comanche, Kiowa, Arapaho, and Apache Nations! The Government of the

United States and the great Father has sent us seven commissioners to come here and have a talk with you."[31] He explained that the government was concerned about incessant warfare in the region and wanted to correct the underlying root causes:

> What has the government done of which you complain? If soldiers have done wrong to you, tell us when and where, and who are the guilty parties. If these agents, whom we have put here to protect you, have cheated and defrauded you, be not afraid to tell us. We have come here to hear all your complaints and to correct all your wrongs...we intend to do justice to the red man. If we have harmed him, we will correct it; if the red man has harmed us, we believe he is brave and generous enough to acknowledge it and to cease from doing any more wrong.[32]

He promised many things to bring about peace on the plains:

> We...would give...all the comforts of civilization, religion, and wealth, and now we are authorized by the great Father to provide...comfortable homes upon our richest agricultural lands. We are authorized to build for the Indian school-houses and churches and provide teachers to educate his children. We can furnish him with agricultural implements to work, and domestic cattle, sheep, and hogs to stock his farm.[33]

Senator Henderson's remarks were met with complete silence. At last, the mercurial Satanta arose and spoke for the Kiowa. He stated the Kiowa and Comanche were not at war, but had come "to listen to the good word," and he rejected the gifts proffered by the United States.

> All the land south of the Arkansas belongs to the Kiowas and Comanches, and I don't want to give away any of it. I love the land and the buffalo, and I will not part with any. I want you to understand also that the Kiowas don't want to fight, and have not been fighting since the treaty. I hear a good deal of fine talk from these gentlemen, but they never do what they say. I don't want any of these Medicine homes [churches] built in the country. I want the papooses brought up just exactly as I am. When I make peace, it is a long and lasting one, there is no end to it... I have heard you intend to settle us on a reservation near

the Mountains. I don't want to settle there. I love to roam over the wide prairie, and when I do, I feel free and happy, but when we settle down we grow pale and die.[34]

The next day, Ten Bears expressed similar sentiments for the Comanche.

You said you wanted to put us upon a reservation, to build us houses, and to make us Medicine lodges. I do not want them. I was born upon the prairie where the wind blew free and there was nothing to break the light of the sun. I was born where there were no enclosures, and where everything drew a free breath. I want to die there, and not within walls. I know every stream and every wood between the Rio Grande and the Arkansas. I have hunted and lived over that country. I lived like my father before me, and like them, I lived happily.[35]

Senator Henderson persisted, urging that the reservations would be for the Indians' own good, and he offered the tribes buffalo-hunting rights in the ceded area so they could continue the chase and ways of their fathers while the great herds lasted. He proposed to make their home on the Red River around the Wichita Mountains of their ancestral homeland, which would provide a spot to bury their dead and to farm for those who wished to do so.[36] Based on these promises, the chiefs relented at last and reluctantly touched the pen to the treaty on Sunday, October 21, with the addition of an off-reservation hunting clause, ceding sixty thousand square miles of tribal land to the United States in exchange for a reservation homeland, hunting rights, and the other amenities promised by the United States. Most of that day was devoted to church services (many Indians showed up drunk or hungover, to General Harney's chagrin—he thought it was a foolish idea to bring Plains warriors to church in the first place) and to explaining the treaty provisions to the chiefs.[37] Senator Henderson reiterated that, "[t]he treaty is for the purpose of giving you more goods than you received before. It is solely for your good and not for the good of the whites."[38] The reluctant Satanta expressed misgivings about reservation life and Kiowa dependence upon the government for food that was promised by Senator Henderson:

This building of homes for us is all nonsense; we don't want you to build any for us. We would all die. Look at the Penntatus. Formerly they were powerful but now they are weak and poor. I want all my land even from the Arkansas south to the Red River. My country is small enough already. If you build us houses, the land will be smaller. Why do you insist on this? What good can come of it? I do not understand your reason. It is time enough to build us houses when the buffalo are all gone…This trusting to the agents for my food, I do not believe in it. Too many things have been promised.[39]

He added, "I have no little lies hid about me, but I do not know how it is with the commissioners."[40] Lone Wolf the elder was present, but the war chief refused to touch the pen and make his mark upon the treaty.

On October 22, the Kiowa and Comanche assembled to receive their treaty gifts, which were stacked in great bundles upon the ground. During this respite, the Comanche performed feats of horsemanship for the correspondents. The newspapermen also discovered that the Kiowa had two captive white women in their camp, but the captives refused repatriation and opted to stay with the Indians. As the Kiowa broke camp, Satank rode to the commissioners' camp to say his farewell. Standing before them and speaking through the translator, McCusker, the Kiowa chief made an eloquent speech urging the government negotiators to keep their word. His words had a profound impact upon those present.[41] One reporter wrote this about Satank's farewell speech:

> I have heard the re-echoing eloquence of statesmen, as it warbled through the House and Senate of our national capitol. I have heard and felt the influence of ministerial oratory as it came from the rostrum…When the last goodby fell from his lips, it was not the voice of college culture, of prejudice, of partisan strife; it was the voice of nature and of God.[42]

After shaking hands, the elder mounted his pony and rode off with his waiting family to winter in their aboriginal homeland—a land no longer owned by them.

Breaking the Treaty of Medicine Lodge

It is interesting to see how soon promises are forgotten. Though the treaty promised that no unauthorized persons "shall ever be permitted to pass over, settle upon, or reside" in the tribes' reservation, their homeland lasted only thirty-five years.[43] Early reservation years were marked by turmoil and strife, leading to the Buffalo War of 1874–75, as the Indians saw their herds in treaty areas diminish and found adaptation to reservation life difficult. During the hostilities, Lone Wolf the elder fought alongside of the Swan, a medicine man who received his power from buffalo bulls. Following military defeat, the tribes returned to the reservation at Fort Sill, where they were disarmed and dismounted. Lone Wolf was the last chief to come in from the Staked Plains in February 1875.

Upon surrender, President Ulysses S. Grant directed the War Department to pick tribal leaders for confinement. Seventy-two were sent in chains to Fort Marion in Saint Augustine, Florida—including Lone Wolf and the Swan—where they were incarcerated for three years as prisoners of war.[44] This was done summarily, without a trial.[45] Shortly following his release in 1878, Lone Wolf passed away, marking the end of an era. The Kiowa now took up the reservation way of life in earnest under the firm hand of Bureau of Indian Affairs (BIA) agents and government missionaries.

During reservation days, Lone Wolf the younger lived in an isolated reservation area near Rainy Mountain Creek, where as the new chief he upheld the old ways and participated in Kiowa ceremonial life—the Ghost Dance, Sun Dance, and the Peyote Religion—and resisted government assimilation efforts to stamp out Kiowa culture. As a traditional leader, he and his followers were called "The Implacables" by the Indian agents.[46] To resist the assault on Kiowa culture, they used nonviolent means to interfere with the government farming program, missionary work, and school attendance, and found other ways to outwit the federal agents.[47] Unfortunately, resistance was an uphill battle since the assimilation onslaught was backed by the machinery of the government. In the end, troops were called in to halt the Kiowa Sun Dance in 1887.[48] Using the full power of law as an assimilation tool, the BIA enacted its infamous Code of Indian Offenses, which banned traditional Native American religious beliefs and practices across the country and established a special court to enforce its dictates with the invidious goal "to end Indian culture."[49] And the missionaries' zealous religious work among the Kiowa to proselytize, convert, and provide religious education among them was sponsored by the government, despite the prohibition against government-sponsored religion in the Establishment Clause of the First Amendment to the US Constitution. The legality of these efforts to remake the Kiowa people shall be discussed in other chapters.

However, it was the establishment of the Jerome Commission in 1889 to open the reservations in Indian Territory to white settlement that concerned Lone Wolf and his followers the most.[50] The commission was one of fifteen working throughout the nation to negotiate with the Indian tribes to break apart their reservations. Composed of ruthless negotiators, the Jerome Commission had successfully concluded nine agreements to cede and allot Indian reservations by the time it arrived at the Kiowa, Comanche, and Apache Reservation in 1892. This time the negotiations would be far different from the treaty negotiations of 1867, which led to the Medicine Lodge Treaty. There would be no pretense of equality between the parties. As Chairman Jerome told the Indians, "Congress has full power over you, it can do as it is a mind to with you." And he warned them that "Congress has determined to open this country."[51] The government envoys would dictate terms to the three tribes and resort to falsehoods, intimidation, and bribery to browbeat the Indians into an agreement. Scholars have thoroughly chronicled the threats, fabrications, and fraud employed by these negotiators.[52]

The central legal flaw in securing the so-called agreement was the fraudulent manner in which Indian signatures were obtained by the government. The treaty required that no cessations of the reservation could occur without the consent of at least three-fourths of the adult male population of said reservation, and the commissioners could not persuade that many Indians to sign. Thus, the commissioners lied to the Indians about the purchase price, claiming they would receive more money by selling out (twenty-five dollars per person) than by their current lease income (which was, in reality, seventy-five dollars per person annually).[53] Desperate, the commissioners and their interpreter began working behind the scenes to coerce those Indians who worked for the government to sign the agreement, some were simply ordered to sign, and the interpreter signed for those who refused.[54] Troops were called in to quell the Indians' outrage at the fraud, but despite the work of the commission to simply add Indian names to the document, the three-fourths consent of the adult males was never obtained. Nevertheless, the tainted agreement was sent back to Washington, where, incredibly, "the commissioners switched versions of the agreement, substituting their altered copy for that which had been partially signed at the councils" and it "ultimately contained only counterfeit signatures."[55] The heavy-handed negotiations were a travesty, running roughshod over Indians who opposed the allotment and sale of their reservation.

There is no pleasant way to violate a treaty, but the Jerome Commission process stank to high heaven by any measure. The Indians strenuously opposed congressional ratification of the tainted agreement for eight years. Lone Wolf and various tribal delegations made repeated pilgrimages to Washington, DC, hat in hand, to lobby against bills to ratify the Jerome Agreement. But in the end, Congress approved the measure in 1900.[56]

Lone Wolf turned to the courts to overturn that law, relying upon the Treaty of Medicine Lodge. The legal initiative was supported by local cattlemen who were opposed to opening reservation pastures to homesteaders and by the Indian Rights Association, a precursor to modern-day Native American advocacy groups. The Indians hired William M. Springer to bring the case. The well-known lawyer, a former Indian Territory judge and former congressman, was an interesting choice because during his time in Congress he had been instrumental in creating the Jerome Commission, declaring in 1888 that "no portion of this continent can be held in barbarism to the exclusion of civilized men."[57] But this controversial past also meant that Springer was intimately aware of the issues and well-suited to challenge the law on the grounds that the allotment and sale of the reservation was done fraudulently, against the Indians' will and in violation of their treaty. Suit was filed in 1901 to halt the government sale in the face of widespread popular clamor for opening the reservation.

Lone Wolf: The Spawn of Legal Doctrines for Ruling American Colonies

Lone Wolf and his legal team were optimistic as the case came to the Supreme Court. Their case involved seamy facts and a clear-cut treaty violation. No court had ever sanctioned the taking of tribal land against the Indians' will under such circumstances. Unfortunately, the appeal came before justices who had, only a few years earlier, decided *Plessy v. Ferguson* (1896), the unjust case that legalized racial segregation.[58] They gave short shrift to Lone Wolf's arguments in the Court's first case involving the power of Congress to administer Indian property.

In a unanimous opinion, the *Lone Wolf* Court held that Congress has "[p]lenary authority over the tribal relations in the United States," and that political power "is not subject to be controlled by the judicial department."[59] This remarkable power is not found in the Constitution. Rather, the justices reasoned that:

> Congress possessed a paramount power over the property of the Indi-
> ans, by reason of its exercise of guardianship over their interests, and...
> such authority might be implied, even though opposed to the strict let-
> ter of a treaty with the Indians.[60]

Writing for the Court, Justice Edward White explained that the sole check on this absolute power over Indian people is a bare moral obligation of Congress "to act in good faith."[61] The Court precluded Indian challenges to congressional action by citing the convenient political-question doctrine, explaining that "the judiciary cannot question or inquire into the motives which prompted the enactment of this legislation."[62]

The decision thus placed American Indians outside the rule of law in their relations with the federal government, leaving them protected only by a thin hope that the government would act in "perfect good faith"—a cruel gesture in a case challenging bad faith on the part of the government that leaves one to wonder when Congress's moral obligation might come into play if not in circumstances involving "fraudulent misrepresentations," "conceal-ment," and treaty violation. Hiding behind the political-question doctrine, Justice White brushed the sordid facts aside, explaining "these matters, in any event, were solely within the domain of the legislative authority, and its action is conclusive upon the courts."[63] Instead, he asked Indians to trust the government as their sole recourse under the law:

> We must presume that Congress acted in perfect good faith in the deal-
> ings with the Indians [and] that the legislative branch made its best
> judgment in the premises. In any event, as Congress possessed full
> power in the matter, the judiciary cannot question or inquire into the
> motives which prompted the enactment of this legislation.[64]

Without judicial review, no meaningful remedy could be hoped for by the Indians. Justice White allowed the fox to guard the henhouse—if Indians are injured by Congress, they must ask that same body for relief.[65]

The miscarriage of justice in *Lone Wolf* is best understood against the backdrop of the American law of colonialism developed in the *Insular Cases* (1889–1905).[66] During the turn of the century, the nation was in a patriotic fervor as an emerging world power embroiled in imperialist wars to acquire oversees colonies or quell rebellions in the new American possessions. The

Spanish-American War (1898–1902), the overthrow of the Kingdom of Hawaii (1887), the American-Philippine War (1899–1913), and the Boxer Rebellion in China (1900–1903) raised a series of new constitutional questions about the relationships and responsibilities of the American government with colonized people in far-flung parts of the world. These were the questions that the Court was preoccupied with when the Kiowa case came to it in 1903.

Justice White, the author of the *Lone Wolf* opinion, was deeply embroiled in the judicial debate over how the colonies should be ruled. In the *Insular Cases,* he argued that Congress has plenary power over colonies unfettered by the Constitution, because it does not follow the flag into new territories and is inapplicable to them unless and until Congress so declares. In *Downes v. Bidwell* (1901), the precursor to *Lone Wolf,* Justice White espoused the view that constitutional protections are not applicable to overseas possessions without express congressional approval. He reasoned that the nation has inherent power to acquire and rule territories by conquest, discovery, or cessation under the law of nations.[67] Relying upon the harsh law of conquest and various Indian cases, like *Johnson v. M'Intosh* (1823) and *Kagama v. United States* (1886),[68] he wrote that "the conqueror, by the completion of his conquest, becomes the absolute owner of the property conquered from the enemy nation or state," and Congress can impose any conditions it sees fit "relating to the rights of the people then inhabiting those territories."[69] According to White, though a colony belongs to the United States, it is not part of the nation and can be governed by terms imposed by Congress regardless of the Constitution.[70] This doctrine, which leaves the civil rights and political status of native colonial subjects up to the sole discretion of Congress, prevailed against Justice John Harlan's minority view that the rule creates a dangerous double standard for governance in our democracy.

Justice Harlan warned that the doctrine gave Congress an "omnipotent" power to "withhold fundamental guarantees of life and liberty from peoples who have come under our complete jurisdiction" and could allow those rights, including property rights, to be taken by laws "inconsistent with the Constitution of the United States."[71] He argued that unless the Constitution follows the flag into the new possessions and takes effect immediately, a serious double standard in constitutional law will arise in which "the Constitution is the supreme law of the land in the states…and organized territories of the United States," but not in the colonized lands of native peoples "over which the United States had acquired all rights of sovereignty of whatsoever kind."[72] "It would mean," he wrote in 1903, "that the United States may acquire territory by cessation, conquest, or treaty, and Congress may exercise sovereign domain over it, outside of and in violation of the Constitution, and under regulations that could not be applied to the organized territories of the United States and their inhabitants" and thereby cause "the American people [to] lose sight of, or become indifferent to, principles which had been supposed to be essential to real liberty."[73]

These concerns were unpersuasive to the majority. Indeed, Justice White feared any result that would endow colonized inhabitants with the rights and protections of citizenship. This would "inflict grave detriment" on the nation by bestowing citizenship on those "absolutely unfit to receive it."[74] Voicing the worst fears of every colonizer, he warned that if millions of uncivilized inhabitants of alien lands were "immediately and irrevocably incorporated into the United States...the whole structure of the government [could] be overthrown."[75] To him, it was far better to vest Congress with plenary power over the colonies and not worry about their constitutional rights. *We will assume that Congress will not abuse its power and be faithful to constitutional ideals, even though those limits are inferred, not expressly required.*[76]

Justice Harlan predicted that as the American empire grew, an abhorrent double standard would become engrafted upon our constitutional form of government. He wrote, "a colonial system entirely foreign to the genius of our government and abhorrent to the principles that underlie and pervade the Constitution" will result. There will be "two governments over the peoples subject to the jurisdiction of the United States—one, existing under a written Constitution, creating a government with authority to exercise only powers expressly granted" and "the other existing outside of the written Constitution in virtue of unwritten law, to be declared from time to time by Congress, which is itself only a creature of that instrument."[77] Harlan could not assent to such a system that allowed the exercise of absolute and arbitrary legislative power over an underclass in our constitutional democracy.[78]

Despite the dangers described by Justice Harlan, the majority view prevailed. The *Insular Cases* allowed Congress to make laws to govern colonies without being subject to the restrictions normally imposed when it passes laws for the United States. The majority vested Congress with the absolute, unfettered plenary power to determine the civil rights and political status of the inhabitants of those lands.

Justice Harlan did not express the same concerns in *Lone Wolf,* decided the same year that he dissented in the *Insular Cases* and under the same principles. He silently concurred as *Lone Wolf* applied the plenary-power doctrine at home, allowing Congress to ignore treaties with Indian tribes and govern their lands as it wished, just like colonized peoples in overseas possessions. Indeed, the similarities between *Lone Wolf* and *Insular Cases* are striking. Both sanctioned Congress's plenary power to govern Native peoples without the limitations imposed by the Constitution. Both denied Native people any recourse under American law and asked them to trust that Congress would only exercise its immense power in good faith and be faithful to the spirit of the Constitution in its dealings with native inhabitants. And both imposed a double standard for governing peoples and lands under the United States' jurisdiction: on the one hand, a constitutional government for citizens of the states and organized territories of the United States, complete with judicial review of legislative acts and, on the other hand, an extraconstitutional form of governance for Native peoples, one engrafted upon the Republic as a far-flung colonial system, and the other embedded at home on Indian reservations within the boundaries of the United States.

Implications of *Lone Wolf* and Hardships Imposed on Native Americans

Lone Wolf is a frightening case on many levels. First, it marks a low point in American jurisprudence defining the political and legal status of Indian nations and their members within the boundaries of the United States. At the beginning of the nineteenth century, Indian nations had been largely independent sovereigns functioning outside the boundaries and sphere of interference of the United States. As Manifest Destiny overran the tribes, the law shifted away from treating them as domestic dependent nations with the right of self-government described in *Worcester v. Georgia* (1832),[79] to treating them in *Lone Wolf* as a weak, dependent, inferior people—simple wards of the government ruled by plenary power not subject to judicial review. By 1903, the law treated Native Americans as a fully colonized people. It is unfortunate that as the nation surrounded the tribes and engulfed their lands, the turn-of-the-century Supreme Court deliberately rejected the opportunity to welcome Native peoples into the body politic on a much more equitable basis. Instead, the *Lone Wolf* Court chose to treat Native America like the colonized subjects in the *Insular Cases,* without recourse to the courts of the conqueror. Even though Indian tribes and their territories were undeniably part of the United States by 1903, the law accorded the First Americans lower legal status than immigrants.

Second, by legitimizing the forced government allotment of the Kiowa, Comanche, and Apache Reservation, *Lone Wolf* opened the door to the most massive, uncompensated seizure of private property ever seen in US history—an abhorrent and anomalous proposition in a nation that is otherwise religiously devoted to the protection of property rights.[80] After *Lone Wolf,* Congress no longer needed Indian consent to allot reservations and sell the remaining lands to homesteaders. Nothing stood between Indian land and the power of the federal government to acquire it. Oklahoma history became a microcosm of colonialism, complete with all the trappings. Within two years of the Court's decision, Congress enacted six laws disassembling other Indian reservations without tribal consent, or even negotiations.[81] By 1906, Oklahoma Territory was neatly organized into counties, enabling Congress to burp out the State of Oklahoma.[82] Just three decades after *Lone Wolf* opened the frontier, the sea of grass in the wild Oklahoma prairie had been destroyed by steel plows pulled across the country. Within a single generation, the sodbusters' land turned to dust and blew away, leaving only a dust bowl.

Third, empowered by *Lone Wolf,* Congress was free to abrogate treaties made with Indian nations with impunity. This dark political power was wielded with a heavy hand until nearly every treaty ever made was in some fashion unilaterally broken, along with the word and honor of a nation.[83]

Above all, *Lone Wolf* sanctioned a deplorable use of despotism in our democracy. Its holding rendered carefully negotiated treaties subject to the plenary power of Congress and left the treaties unenforceable should Congress choose to breach them. On a larger scale, vulnerable nonvoting Indians were placed into the hands of lawmakers, who were granted absolute control over them simply because they were wards of the government. This extraconstitutional power created the double standard in governance feared by Justice Harlan in the *Insular Cases* and perhaps helped the public to "lose sight of, or become indifferent to, principles which had been supposed to be essential to real liberty" when American Indians are concerned. There is no other word to describe governance under the *Lone Wolf* doctrine except *tyranny,* as that term is commonly understood—the exercise of absolute power beyond the rule of law. Indeed, tyranny was exercised in the facts of the

Kiowa case: The Indians' land base was unilaterally taken against their will by an act of Congress, ostensibly to assimilate them, also against their will, into the dominant society. In upholding such a law, the Court sanctioned a radical congressional experiment in social engineering that used American Indians as subjects against their will. The proud warriors and hunters of the southern plains would be made to become yeoman farmers and barefooted Baptists by the government.

The presence of unbridled legislative power in a constitutional democracy seriously ruptures democratic principles, because it unleashes an all-powerful majority. This is a prescription for totalitarianism, as J. L. Brierly noted in *The Law of Nations*:

> [A] majority rarely is, and never ought to be, all-powerful. No Democrat if he is true to his principles can believe that there ought somewhere in the state to be a repository of absolute power, and to say that such a power resides in the people is to deny that either minorities or individuals have any rights except those that the majority allow them. That is totalitarianism, for autocracy is autocracy whoever the autocrat may be.[84]

Absolute power is dangerous, especially to minorities. In the past, Congress used this potent power to enact laws harming Indian tribes, sometimes when Indians could not vote, but always when this tiny, impoverished minority could not defend its interests before that branch of government.[85] *Lone Wolf* asked only that lawmakers be required to act in "perfect good faith." Under that good-faith standard, what working principles should guide lawmakers when crafting laws affecting Native Americans? John Stuart Mill and Alexis de Tocqueville provide some answers from classical Western thought on the nature of liberty and minority rights in democratic society. At minimum, their guideposts for protecting individual liberty and minority rights should be followed by lawmakers when legislating in "perfect good faith" for Native peoples or other minorities in our democracy.

Mill defined *liberty* as protection against the tyranny of political rulers in any form of government. His essay *On Liberty* (1859) explains that harmony between authority and liberty is achieved only when social control over individual freedom is imposed to prevent harm to others.[86] Unwarranted intrusions upon liberty arise when individuals are forced to do something against their will, even if it is for their own good.[87] He cautioned that political despotism can occur in democracies when popular government oversteps those bounds. Mill described this condition as the "tyranny of the majority," observing that society itself can become the tyrant

> if it issues wrong mandates instead of right ones, or any mandates at all in things with which it ought not to meddle, it practices a social tyranny more formidable than many kinds of political oppression, since, though not usually upheld by such extreme penalties, it leaves fewer means of escape, penetrating much more deeply into the details of life, and enslaving the soul itself.[88]

The lawmakers' paramount ethical challenges to avoid such tyranny are to realize there is a "limit to the legitimate interference of collective opinion with individual independence," to find that limit, and to "maintain it against encroachment…as indispensable to a good condition of human affairs" and "as protection against political despotism."[89]

In a similar vein, Alexis de Tocqueville observed that Congress is particularly susceptible to the tyranny of the majority because its members are swayed "even to the daily passions, of their constituents."[90] He warned that liberty is endangered when the omnipotent power of the majority in a democracy goes unchecked. Unlike Justice White, Tocqueville held no myopic views about "good faith" in the exercise of absolute power by any form of government:

> Unlimited power is in itself a bad and dangerous thing; human beings are not competent to exercise it with discretion, and God alone can be omnipotent, because His wisdom and His justice are always equal to His power. But no power upon earth is so worthy of honor for itself, or of reverential obedience to the rights which it represents, that I would consent to admit its uncontrolled and all-predominant authority. When I see that the right and the means of absolute command are conferred on a people or upon a king, upon an aristocracy or a democracy, a monarch or a republic, I recognize the germ of tyranny, and I journey onward to a land of more hopeful institutions.[91]

To avoid a slide toward despotism, Tocqueville urged that laws be confined to that which is just and courts must enforce limits on the exercise of legislative power.[92] Above all, the exercise of omnipotent power from any quarter must be resisted and checked in a democracy.

Lone Wolf sanctioned just such evils. It legitimized majoritarian intrusions upon the liberty and property of the Kiowa, Comanche, and Apache. Freed from the antimajoritarian principles represented by the judiciary, lawmakers chose to act, not in "perfect good faith" toward the Indians, as Justice White presumed, but in blatant disregard of the principles elucidated by Mills and Tocqueville in a clear-cut case of the tyranny of the majority.

Efforts to Overcome Hardships Imposed by *Lone Wolf*

In 1955, the Kiowa, Comanche, and Apache were awarded $2 million in damages against the government for taking their land at an unconscionable price below the fair market value.[93] And in 1998, almost one hundred years after *Lone Wolf*, the Supreme Court recognized and protected the sovereign attributes of the Kiowa tribal government, which, despite this history, is flourishing in western Oklahoma.[94] However, *Lone Wolf* provides sober lessons in American honor, liberty, and governance.

During much of the twentieth century, Congress ruled Native America with unchecked plenary power. That unbridled power has been partially fettered in the modern era of federal Indian law as Indian nations struggled to reclaim their sovereignty in the United States. As the tribes gained increasing reliable access to the courthouse, the judiciary began to trim the hard edges from *Lone Wolf*'s doctrines. First, the political-question doctrine was repudiated in *Delaware Tribal Business Committee v. Weeks* (1976).[95] That case held that Congress's power is not absolute; rather, it is subject to judicial review and constitutional limitations. Next, the decision in *United States v. Sioux Nation* (1980) rejected Justice White's stupid conclusive presumption of congressional good faith.[96] *Sioux Nation* held the government liable for taking Indian property under the Fifth Amendment, making its power over Indian property as trustee subject to constitutional limitations.[97] Yet, core principles of *Lone Wolf* remain embedded in the law, ready for use at any pendulum swing. Congress still has plenary power over Indians. As held in *Santa Clara Pueblo v. Martinez* (1978), Indian tribes enjoy the sovereign right of self-government, with the power to make their own laws in internal matters, but "Congress has plenary authority to limit, modify or eliminate the powers of local self-government which the Tribes otherwise possess."[98] And no act of Congress has been struck down no matter how deeply it abrogated an Indian treaty without consent of the Indians. In short, the Supreme Court has only partially repudiated *Lone Wolf*'s notion that the Constitution places no limits on Congress's power over Indians.[99]

A new legislative era began in 1970, once Congress became accountable to the courts and the Constitution and after Indians gained voting rights and lobbying expertise. During that age of Indian self-determination, which was inaugurated by President Richard Nixon, the legislative branch passed remedial Indian legislation to protect tribal sovereignty and self-determination, land and natural resources, and the human and culture rights of Native Americans. On the legislative front, it is still possible today to witness the abuse of power in the halls of Congress by beltway bigots who routinely place holds on Indian legislation in the dark corners of the US Senate or by weak souls in the House of Representatives who lack the spirit to speak honestly to majorities back home. And, frightening periods of backlash sometimes arise when the majority party exudes hostility or indifference toward Native American interests. These episodes are harsh reminders that Native Americans are a permanent minority—political captives, so to speak, who, without a strong and courageous judiciary, are forever subject to the tyranny of the majority.

And what about the treaties? Early Native American Rights Fund litigation in the tribal sovereignty movement sought to breathe life back into the treaties.[100] Recognizing that "Congress chose treaties rather than conquest to acquire vast Indian lands," the federal courts began to limit the ways in which Congress may abrogate treaties—requiring clear congressional intent to do so—and to actually *enforce* treaty promises, sometimes in the face of bitter local opposition.[101] The sweeping decision in *Washington v. Fishing Vessel Association* (1979) upheld Indian fishing rights reserved in the treaties that relinquished the Pacific Northwest to the United States in exchange for reservations and a right to fish at usual and accustomed fishing sites.[102] The case affirmed that a treaty is "a contract between two sovereign nations" and began a new era of treaty enforcement.[103]

That legacy allowed me to stride to the podium in 2003 (one hundred years after *Lone Wolf*) to deliver my argument before the Ninth Circuit Court of Appeals, carrying with me the Klamath Treaty of 1864. My purpose in *Braren v. United States* (2003) was to defend the lower court's vibrant interpretation of the treaty, a holding that recognized the Klamath Tribes' treaty-protected water rights for habitat needed to support tribal hunting, fishing, and gathering activities. While the court dismissed the case on procedural grounds, it was careful not to disturb the vitality of the treaty, the promises made in that document, or the legal status of treaties with Indian nations—ideals deeply engrained in federal Indian law.[104]

When judges enforce treaties, they uphold solemn promises made by our nation to its Native peoples and restore honor to the words spoken by American diplomats. That gives meaning to Justice Black's remark that great nations, like great men, should keep their word. In the final analysis, we must consider the import of words, whether spoken by a great man or a great nation. Lone Wolf the younger was a Kiowa warrior and chief who became a plaintiff in the courts of the conqueror. He attempted to hold the nation to its words spoken on the banks of the Medicine Lodge Creek. Lone Wolf was buried in 1923 in Kiowa country, near Rainy Mountain in western Oklahoma, but his memory lives on. One of his descendants is none other than N. Scott Momaday, the acclaimed Pulitzer Prize winner and poet laureate of Oklahoma.[105] His observations about the nature of a word are apropos to the promises of a nation:

> A word has power in and of itself. It comes from nothing into sound and meaning; it gives origin to all things. By means of words can a man deal with the world on equal terms. And the word is sacred.[106]

On September 13, 2007, the United Nations approved the United Nations Declaration on the Rights of Indigenous Peoples, which, among other things, requires every nation to recognize, observe, and enforce indigenous "treaties, agreements and other constructive arrangements concluded with States or their successors and to have States honor and respect such treaties, agreements and other constructive arrangements." Time will tell whether and to what extent this international standard is observed in the courts of the conqueror.

CHAPTER EIGHT

United States v. Sandoval: Rule by Guardianship

IMAGINE YOU LIVE IN A NATION where the government owns your property. It has a powerful agency called the Bureau of Caucasian Affairs to control wards of the state, including you. The agency supervises your family and decides what is best. It handles your money, enforces morals, personal appearance, and manner of dress. It provides state-approved religion, schooling, and food for your community. This is all done by the superintendent—a government bureaucrat placed in charge of your community with complete control over it. *No one can leave without his permission.* Like a god, he makes the laws and acts as the police, prosecutor, judge, and jury. The courts cannot review his actions, for they are all, by definition, perfectly legal. Sound like totalitarianism? Nope, it is the abuse of guardianship. For several generations, the Bureau of Indian Affairs (BIA) used its trustee powers to become an intolerant and all-powerful ruler of Indian people, and the courts allowed this anomaly to happen.

This chapter explores the dark side of the guardianship principle in federal Indian law, when federal agencies supplanted tribal authority. During a frightening period in American history, the BIA's guardianship powers were absolute and went unchecked by the courts. Earlier chapters focused on the role of the courts in appropriating Indian land. We turn now to the role of the courts in governing Indians. We shall pay particular attention to the period between 1886 and 1934, when the government's guardian powers over Indian tribes reached their zenith and bureaucrats subjected Indians to what Felix S. Cohen called "the greatest concentration of administrative absolutism in our governmental structure."[1] How did the rule of guardianship over a race of people arise? What are its attributes and limits? And how did Indian wards fare under government tutelage as minors in the eyes of the law? Though numerous cases address these questions, we shall examine three—a dark trilogy that, when taken together, must be included in the ten worst Indian law cases ever decided.

The lead case in my study is *United States v. Sandoval* (1913), which extended federal jurisdiction over Pueblo Indian land.[2] While *Sandoval* reached the right result, it focused primarily upon racism to justify the decision. In so doing, *Sandoval* created confusion about the source of federal power in Indian affairs, leading many to think that it rests upon abject racism and unbridled contempt for tribal religion, culture, government, and way of life. The racist atmosphere fostered by *Sandoval* was unnecessary, because the Court could have focused on principled reasons found in federal Indian law.[3] Instead, we are left with the impression that federal police and guardianship power can arise whenever the government considers Indians racially inferior and their way of life barbarous. Such a judicial mind-set is dangerous precedent for controlling minorities who are out of favor with the government; and the mischief arising from that mind-set is seen in the decisions that allowed federal power to run amok on Indian reservations. The other two cases, *United States v. Clapox* (1888) and *In re Can-ah-couqua* (1887), show how the unfettered abuse of guardianship operates in real life.[4] They let us look into the face of absolute power and ponder the excessive lengths to which the government programs of "tutelage" and "civilizing the Indians" went to stamp out Native culture and traditional life—even to the extremes of taking children and banning tribal religions. As described by legal commentators:

> In the late nineteenth century, coercive attempts at assimilation were applied to almost all aspects of Indian life. Local agents were charged with pressing white civilization upon native peoples by controlling such details as hair length, funeral procedures, hunting and fishing practices, and beef slaughtering. As late as 1921, new regulations were enforced punishing those who engaged in specified dances and ceremonies. The federal government even adopted a "renaming" program to substitute proper European-style personal names for difficult to pronounce or remember tribal names.[5]

Such serious intrusions into Native life must be described as ethnocide or cultural genocide because they contributed to the disappearance of Native American culture, even though its bearers are not physically destroyed.[6] Though the government's conduct in *Clapox* and *Can-ah-couqua* was plainly unconstitutional if applied to citizens, it was upheld as an act of guardianship over Indian wards of the state.

Strong legal doctrines were needed by the government during this period to consolidate the gains of Manifest Destiny, especially to support any further land acquisition from Indian reservation enclaves, to control the internal affairs of Indian tribes, and to guide assimilation of Indians into settler society. Guardianship furnished the answer. In cases like *Clapox* and *Can-ah-couqua*, the courts allowed the guardian government to place a heavy yoke on its Indian wards, stifling their traditional ways of life with a soul-killing bureaucracy engaged in an experiment in enforced acculturation. The tribal sovereignty over the internal affairs and social relations of Indian tribes that had been recognized and protected by the Marshall Court was displaced by an intrusive and unaccountable federal bureaucracy bent on destroying tribal culture. And it was done ostensibly to "civilize" the Indians and prepare them for citizenship. The government's ethnocide was described as "tutelage" or "pupilage." It was legitimized by the courts as federal guardianship over a weak and dependent people who were seen as backward, uncivilized, and deeply in need of paternalistic guidance from a superior society to prepare them for citizenship in their own land.

The Origins and Growth of the Trust Doctrine's Guardianship Principle

On an international level, guardianship is a venerable instrument of colonialism. At its core, this institution simply means, "I own your property and can control your person any way I see fit." This principle quickly becomes noxious when abused by the government and unchecked by the courts. It originated in Franciscus de Victoria's law of nations at the dawn of the colonial era, as Europe developed the legal bases for colonizing the Western Hemisphere. Pointing to a duty to civilize and Christianize the backward people of the New World, Victoria suggested that European nations "might undertake the administration of [the Indians'] country, providing them with prefects and governors for their towns, and might even give them new lords, so long as this was clearly for their benefit."[7] That handy arrangement facilitates colonization goals—land acquisition, controlling the local populace, and extracting wealth—because guardianship mechanisms make it easier to acquire, manage, and exploit the colonial resources available for the taking.

Premised on the presumed racial, religious, and cultural superiority of Europeans, guardianship has been used extensively by colonizing nations to manage Native people and control their property in colonies around the world while they shoplifted their resources and wealth. James Anaya observed in *Indigenous Peoples in International Law* the extensive use of the guardianship and trusteeship doctrines to rule Native peoples in colonized lands:

As colonizing states and their offspring consolidated power over indigenous lands, many such states adopted trusteeship notions akin to those proposed earlier by Vitoria as grounds and parameters for the nonconsensual exercise of authority over indigenous peoples...Pursuant to this philosophy, associated with the now infamous school identified as "scientific racism," the objective of trusteeship was to wean native peoples from their "backward" ways and to "civilize" them.[8]

Civilizing or uplifting local Natives as part of the guardianship principle was done "for their benefit," but not altogether out of altruistic motives. Tutelage was simply a pretext for asserting control over them. It furnished an excuse for expropriating land, resources, and wealth from colonized lands and justified these actions in the minds of the colonizers. What's more, it also made for better relations. As Lord Gladstone explained in 1837, it was far better for colonists to deal "with civilized men rather than barbarians," because "[s]avages are dangerous neighbors and unprofitable customers, and if they remain as degraded denizens of our colonies they become a burden upon the State."[9]

Such an intrusive and oppressive doctrine necessarily rests upon raw power, and it requires justification lest it be condemned as immoral. Because governance of Natives by guardianship was permissible under Victoria's law of nations as long as it was done "for their benefit," colonizing nations assumed a self-imposed duty of "tutelage" as a component of guardianship. That duty required them to oversee the moral and material well-being of Native tribes and to improve their morals, habits, and spiritual well-being—in short, to transform them from barbarians to civilized people for their own good. Tutelage, done under watchful government eyes, would instruct, convert, and uplift Native "pupils" in preparation for eventual citizenship in the new society brought by the colonists to their conquered lands. Colonial governments also assumed a duty to "protect" aborigines from themselves, as improvident, childlike people with primitive customs, and from settlers and civilized nations that would exploit them. Sometimes called "the white man's burden," these altruistic justifications for guardianship rest on notions of racial supremacy and extreme cultural ethnocentricity in which indigenous peoples must be viewed as inferior, backward, and uncivilized heathens without the capacity of self-government—folks who require missionary and other guidance by outsiders from distant lands.

The self-imposed duties of tutelage were necessary components of the guardianship principle in the eyes of international law, and the US government was a full-fledged subscriber. A 1919 State Department study explained that colonizing nations have a "positive duty...to undertake directly the education and training of the aborigines in the arts and sciences of civilization and in the political principles on which all civilized societies is based."[10] Continuing, the study laid out the accepted basis for ruling colonized peoples:

> [D]omination of distant communities by a Republic [is] permissible when needful and to the extent needful, but only provided the State recognized and fulfilled the positive and imperative duty of helping these dominated communities to help themselves by teaching and training them for civilization, as the wards and pupils of the nation and of the society of nations...[C]ivilized States have recognized that guardianship of aboriginal tribes implies not merely protection, not merely a benevolence toward private missionary, charitable, and educational effort, but a positive duty of direct legislative, executive, and judicial domination of aborigines as minor wards of the nation and of equally direct legislative, executive, and judicial tutorship of them for civilization, so that they may become in the shortest possible time civil and political adults participating on an equality in their own government under democratic and republican institutions.[11]

Thus, during the early decades of the twentieth century, America was busy uplifting the Natives throughout its empire in Micronesia, the Philippines, Puerto Rico, San Domingo, Panama, the Virgin Islands, Guam, the Wake Islands, Midway, the territories of Hawaii and Alaska, and on Indian reservations at home.[12]

Tutelage and civilization efforts used Christianity to uplift Native wards and convert them in most colonies. Archbishop Desmond Tutu recounts how this process worked in Africa:

> There is a story, which is fairly well known, about when the missionaries came to Africa. They had the Bible and we, the natives, had the land. They said, "Let us pray," and we dutifully shut our eyes. When we opened them, why, they now had the land and we had the Bible.[13]

In the United States, the program went to great lengths and included determined government efforts to replace tribal religious beliefs and practices with Christianity.[14] Beginning with President Ulysses S. Grant's Indian Peace Policy (1869–1882), the government and church groups worked hand in hand to destroy tribal religion. The goal was to Christianize the Indians as part of the civilizing process. To realize these objectives, the government funded missionary efforts and conveyed Indian land to missionary groups to establish reservation churches. From 1869 to 1882, church leaders were appointed as government Indian agents in charge of entire Indian nations on many reservations. By 1886, 278 government boarding schools, operated by church groups, actively proselytized schoolchildren through required religious instruction.[15] Christianization efforts were enforced by government suppression of Native religion in 1883 with an outright government ban on tribal religious practices, including ceremonial dances, in the Code of Indian Offenses. Ultimately, military force was used to halt the Ghost Dance in 1890, when three hundred Sioux Indians were killed by US troops.[16] Those prohibitions continued until 1934. It is difficult to imagine these excesses today, but the legal infirmities of that onerous program are clear. One legal commentator summed up those problems:

> With the help of Christian churches, the government also endeavored to suppress Native American religious beliefs and practices: the goal of both church and state was to assimilate the Indians by destroying Indian religion and culture and replacing them with Christianity and "American" culture. From a twentieth-century perspective, these joint efforts to destroy Native American beliefs and practices and replace them with Christianity raise serious constitutional concerns. Yet this entanglement of church and state went largely unquestioned for most of the nineteenth century...The government was deemed to have authority to suppress traditional religious practices and establish Christianity among the Indians, the Constitution notwithstanding...The agents assumed that the government had the authority to suppress specific religious practices of its Native American wards, because their practices were not Christian and were obstacles to civilization. They simply took for granted that the "Great Father" had the authority to forbid his children their religion and to punish them for any disobedience in this regard.[17]

The program was fraught with human rights and constitutional violations arising from (1) the ban on tribal religion, (2) the use of military force to suppress religion, and (3) entanglement of church and state in a joint effort to suppress tribal religions while at the same time establishing Christianity among Native Americans. These actions, done in the name of guardianship, disregarded the Free Exercise and Establishment clauses of the US Constitution.[18] They created a double standard that commonly plagues colonies and settler states: pressing a state-approved religion onto citizens infringes upon their religious liberty, but it is entirely permissible when done to colonized wards of the state.

The guardianship principle, together with its ethnocentric trappings, excesses, and assumptions of plenary power, was the international norm throughout the age of colonialism. All colonizing nations relied on guardianship as the central legal principle for governing relations with tribal inhabitants. Nearly four hundred years after it was first expounded by Victoria, the State Department survey found "definite acceptance and application by all civilized States of the principle of guardianship of aborigines."[19] It also found that American law contains "the fullest recognition and most complete application of the principles of guardianship and tutorship of aboriginal tribes."[20] Those principles are described in typical Supreme Court cases of the period, such as *United States v. Ricketts* (1903), which observed that "Indians are wards of the nation in a condition of pupilage or dependency, and have not been discharged from that condition" by Congress; they occupy land with the consent and authority of the United States as "part of the national policy by which the Indians are to be maintained as well as prepared for assuming the habits of civilized life, and ultimately the privileges of citizenship."[21] What this preparation for citizenship entailed was explained in the State Department survey, which summarized the central role of guardianship in colonial governance: "Where aboriginal tribes are located in a country suitable for permanent settlement by citizens of civilized States, the modern practice is to discourage tribal organizations and to deal with the aborigines as individuals under guardianship."[22]

In the United States, the guardianship principle was adopted as a cornerstone principle of federal Indian law by the Marshall Court. *Cherokee*

Nation v. Georgia (1831) declared that Indian tribes are domestic dependant nations "in a state of pupilage" with a relation to the United States that "resembles that of a ward to his guardian."[23] *Worcester v. Georgia* (1832) described that relationship as a government protectorate familiar in international relations.[24] *Worcester* explains that the relationship is simply that of "one nation claiming and receiving protection of one more powerful: not that of individuals abandoning their national character, and submitting as subjects to the laws of a master"; and it emphasized that tribes retain their sovereignty under that relationship "as distinct, independent political communities" with governmental power over their internal affairs and social relations in accordance with "the settled doctrine of the law of nations... that a weaker power does not surrender its independence—its right to self government, by associating with a stronger, and taking its protection."[25] *Worcester* analogized that relationship to a protectorate situation commonly seen in the international context:

> A weak state, in order to provide for its safety, may place itself under the protection of one more powerful, without stripping itself of the right of government, and ceasing to be a state. Examples of this kind are not wanting in Europe. "Tributary and feudatory states," says Emmerich de Vattel, "do not thereby cease to be sovereign and independent states, so long as self-government and sovereign and independent authority are left in the administration of the state." At the present day, more than one state may be considered as holding its right of self government under the guarantee and protection of one or more allies.[26]

Similarly, when Indian tribes came under the protection of the United States through treaty agreements, they retained most rights of self-government in their relation to the United States:

> By various treaties, the Cherokees have placed themselves under the protection of the United States: they have agreed to trade with no other people, nor to invoke the protection of any other sovereignty. But such engagements do not divest them of the right of self government, nor destroy their capacity to enter into treaties or compacts. Every state is more or less dependent on those which surround it; but unless this dependence shall extend so far as to merge the political existence of the

protected people into that of their protectors, they may still constitute a state. They may not exercise the powers relinquished, and bind themselves as a distinct and separate community.[27]

Thus, the terms *protectorate* or *suzerainty* as used in international relations more accurately describe the relationship between Indian tribes and the US government envisioned by the Marshall Court than the guardianship principle used in private law.[28] These foundational cases establish the core principle in federal Indian law that the United States has a special, sui generis (unique) trust relationship with Indian tribes.

Under now well-established principles of federal Indian law, the federal government wears two hats in its trust relationship with Indian tribes: as guardian and trustee. As the guardian of Indian tribes and their members, it exercises control over them as wards of the state; as the trustee of their property held by the United States in trust, it manages that property for their benefit. That fiduciary relationship, with these dual roles of guardianship and trusteeship, has characterized Indian affairs since the early days of the Republic, arising from treaties, early statutes, and decisions like *Cherokee Nation* and *Worcester*. Trusteeship is a necessary function of federal ownership of millions of acres of Indian land acquired by the United States under the rule of *Johnson v. M'Intosh* (1823).[29] That Indian land is held in trust by the government for Indian landowners. As trustee, the government has fiduciary obligations to manage that land and related income for the Indian beneficiaries' advantage. As guardian, Congress exercises plenary power over Indian tribes, people, and property with a self-imposed duty to protect them as wards of the government with fiduciary obligations to manage their affairs, property, and general well-being.

Federal protection of Indian tribes as domestic dependant nations from unwarranted intrusions and predation by the states remains as essential today as when Chief Justice John Marshall adapted this doctrine in the 1832 to protect the Cherokee Nation from destruction by Georgia. The guardianship relationship between Indian tribes and the United States, as it was initially conceived by the Marshall Court, was meant as a protectorate or suzerainty relation in which semi-independent tribes agreed by treaty to become protectorates of a stronger power while retaining sovereignty as domestic dependant nations over their internal affairs and social relations.[30] The tribes were left to their own rules and traditions in those matters, to be exercised under the protection of the United States, including major crimes committed by one Indian against another in Indian Country.[31]

Unfortunately, the guardianship principle was later expanded by the Supreme Court to permit the extension of plenary federal power over those internal affairs. That trend began in *Kagama v. United States* (1886), which allowed Congress to exercise police power over Indian tribes, treating them as dependent wards of the nation, rather than self-governing communities with power over their internal affairs.[32] That shift supplanted tribal authority with federal guardianship whenever it was deemed necessary to protect Indians or to justify increasing federal hegemony over their lives, property, and affairs. As stated in *Kagama*:

> These Indian tribes *are* the wards of the nation. They are communities *dependent* on the United States,—dependent largely for their daily food; dependent for their political rights. They owe no allegiance to the states, and receive from them no protection. Because of local ill feeling, the people of the states where they are found are often their deadliest enemies. From their very weakness and helplessness, so largely due to the course of dealing with them, and the treaties in which it has been promised, there arises a duty of protection, and with it the power…The power of the government over these remnants of a race once powerful, now weak and diminished in numbers, is necessary to their protection, as well as to the safety of those among whom they dwell.[33]

Such guardianship could be assumed even without Indian consent and can be maintained as long as Congress sees fit. It gave rise to the unchecked plenary power of Congress over Indian affairs.[34] As explained in *Lone Wolf v. Hitchcock* (1903), that power over Indian tribes is derived from Congress's "exercise of guardianship over their interests."[35]

Immense power can be used for good or bad. As such, the Indian trust relationship is a double-edged doctrine. On the good side, it was intended to shield and protect tribes as domestic dependant nations, as envisioned in treaties, early statutes, and cases like *Worcester*. To be sure, the trust relationship has been effectively used by Congress to protect Indian tribes in a variety of settings over the years. As guardian, Congress can protect tribes from interference by states in order to protect their use of tribal property and right to self-government as a dependent people.[36] Congress has passed numerous laws to safeguard and provide for Indian health, education, safety, and employment.[37] The federal government also has ample power, as the guardian of Indian tribes, to protect their cultures and religious practices.[38] Used as a shield for these protective purposes, federal guardianship is very much like a protectorate of dependent nations envisioned in *Worcester*. However, on the dark side, beginning with *Kagama* the guardianship principle was twisted into a sword by the courts to justify excessive government intrusion into the internal affairs of Indian tribes and to exercise unwarranted control over the lives and property of American Indians in a slide toward despotism. Cloaked in immense guardianship powers, an all-powerful bureaucracy found that nothing could stand in the way of ethnocide enforced in tribal communities in the name of "tutelage" and "civilizing the Indians." The trilogy of cases discussed in this chapter shows that the creation of frightening, state-run, Orwellian societies on Indian reservations was perfectly legal in the courts of the conqueror, because it was done in the name of guardianship.

United States v. Sandoval and Guardianship of a Racially Inferior People

In 1897, Congress enacted a law prohibiting the sale of intoxicating liquor to any Indian owners of allotted trust land or wards of the government over whom guardianship is exercised.[39] Pursuant to the police power of Congress, such sales in Indian Country were punishable by imprisonment and fine. Shortly after New Mexico was admitted into the Union in 1910, Felipe Sandoval was indicted for introducing liquor into Santa Clara Pueblo in violation of the act. He moved to dismiss the charges, claiming the act did not apply to Pueblo Indians since they are citizens—not wards of the government—and their land was not held in trust by the United States. Therefore, he argued, there was no statutory or other basis for Congress to exercise guardianship or police power over Pueblo Indians for acts that are normally subject to state police power.

Sandoval's argument had legal support from two nineteenth-century court decisions. The US Supreme Court and the Supreme Court of New Mexico Territory had previously examined the Pueblos' legal status and ruled they are citizens, not wards of the government.[40] In *United States v. Joseph* (1876), the Supreme Court reviewed Pueblo history and society. It found Pueblo Indians have lived in permanent villages with their own governments for centuries as agricultural people who manufacture their clothing and implements, speak Spanish, and have Catholic missions in every Pueblo community.[41] The Court heartily approved their character, finding virtue and integrity fostered among a people who "are as intelligent as most nations or people" and it lauded them as "a peaceable, industrious, intelligent, honest, and virtuous people."[42] The *Joseph* Court could find no basis to assign ward status to such people: they are Indian "only in feature, complexion, and a few of their habits," according to the Court, and have "nothing in common" with the class of semi-independent, wild nomadic tribes—such as the Apache, Comanche, and Navajo—for whom guardianship is intended by the federal laws.[43] As such, neither their race nor their land tenure (involving communal ownership of fee land) alone justified classifying them as wards. Similarly, in *United States v. Lucero* (1869), the New Mexico court ruled that the Indian Department had no legal authority to appoint an Indian agent for the Pueblo Indians, because they are citizens of the United States, not wards of the government subject to management by that agency.[44] *Lucero* and *Joseph* were wrongly decided and the resulting lack of federal protection led to white exploitation of Pueblo peoples and lands. Fortunately, they were later overturned by *Sandoval*, though it did so primarily on racial grounds, as you'll see.

Relying on *Joseph* and *Lucero*, the trial court in *Sandoval* ruled that Pueblo Indians are citizens, not wards of the government in a state of tutelage, and therefore it dismissed the criminal prosecution, holding the law was inapplicable.[45] In so doing, it found no source for Congress to legislate for the Pueblo Indians, since they were not parties to any treaties and their land was not held in trust by the United States. Nor did Congress's power to regulate commerce seem applicable, since no interstate commerce was regulated. Finally, the court determined that the plenary authority of Congress arising from the guardianship of Indians as a dependent people is not a basis for the liquor law, because the Pueblo Indians were long considered citizens of the United States—and no act of Congress had ever changed their status from citizens to wards. Consequently, the trial court concluded that "the sole basis upon which federal jurisdiction may be retained over these people, [is] the fact that they are of Indian lineage."[46] It rejected the idea that race alone can provide a basis for exercising the plenary power of guardianship.[47] It held that the national government cannot assume guardianship rights over a citizen simply because Indian blood runs in his veins.

The Supreme Court overturned this decision upholding federal jurisdiction over Pueblo land, because the political branches had recognized the Pueblos as domestic dependent Indian communities and confirmed title to Pueblo land. However, the opinion is startling because it is filled with undisguised racism that distorts the meaning of federal power over Indian tribes. In one of the ten worst Indian law cases ever decided, the court did correctly overrule *Joseph*, but its heavy reliance upon racially disparaging invectives hurled at the Pueblo Indians suggests that federal guardianship exists because they are a racially inferior people. The paramount fact was that the people of Santa Clara Pueblo are "Indians in race, customs, and domestic government," and the court branded all Pueblo Indians of New Mexico as "inferior people...adhering to primitive modes of life, largely influenced by superstition and fetishism, and governed chiefly according to crude customs inherited from their ancestors."[48] These findings were made by justices who never met a Pueblo Indian or visited their villages. The jurists relied solely upon selected excerpts taken from Indian Department reports for their findings. Those excepts describe Pueblo Indians as "intellectually and morally inferior" people who are "easy victims to the evils and debasing influence of intoxicants."[49] The government reports cited in the opinion roundly condemned all aspects of Pueblo life, customs, government, and civilization, variously asserting that they cannot vote intelligently, are not civilized enough for citizenship, and would be exterminated without federal protection; the government reports condemned their religious ceremonies as a drunken and "ribald system of debauchery," calling them "great evils" that must be given up as pagan customs. The reports also criticized their governments as authoritarian, cruel, and inhuman and charged that Pueblo communal life and heathen customs contribute to immorality and laxness in their family relations.[50]

The disparaging characterizations approved in *Sandoval* are at odds with the high praise accorded them in *Joseph*. Somehow, the Pueblo Indians went from an intelligent, virtuous, self-governing group of upstanding communities to a degraded bunch of vile inferiors in just a few short years! In any event, the *Sandoval* Court reiterated that under the guardianship principle, American courts vest in the United States "as a superior and civilized nation the power and duty of exercising a fostering care and protection over all dependent Indian communities" within its borders as Congress sees fit. And it upheld the assertion of guardianship over the Pueblo Indians—stating that given their "Indian lineage, isolated and communal life, primitive customs and limited civilization, this assertion of guardianship over them cannot be said to be arbitrary."[51] As such, the federal liquor law was applicable to them as wards of the government, notwithstanding their citizenship and ownership of their own land.[52]

So what forms the basis for guardianship? Under *Sandoval*, it can seemingly arise based solely upon race if the government deems Indians racially inferior or disapproves of their way of life. The heavily racist language employed by the Court clouds the legitimate power of the political branches to enter into a protectorate relation with Indian tribes and exercise federal jurisdiction over dependent Indian communities.[53] As you will see in the next two cases, Big Brother can and did "do things" to Indians as their "guardian" that it could never do to regular citizens.

United States v. Clapox and the BIA's Code of Indian Offenses

In the spring of 1888, Minnie was sitting in a BIA jail on the Umatilla Indian Reservation. The Indian agent had ordered her arrest for violating the Code of Indian Offenses. The wife of an Indian man in a customary plural marriage, Minnie was accused by the agent with "living and co-habiting" with another Indian other than her husband, which he deemed a misdemeanor under special BIA rules for Indian conduct promulgated by the secretary of interior "for the improvement of morals of the Indians on this reservation"—especially the ban on plural marriages "peculiar to the Indian in his savage state."[54] As Minnie awaited trial, friends and family boldly broke into the jail with armed force and set her free! For their daring act, the rescuers were charged with violating a criminal law prohibiting jailbreaks.[55] Thus begins the story of reservation romance, rescue, and repression in *United States v. Clapox* (1888), one of the worst cases (Indian or not) ever decided.

For more than ten thousand years, numerous bands of Indians have inhabited the Columbia River valley. In treaties of the 1850s, they were consolidated onto various reservations in present-day Washington and Oregon. My wife, Pauline, is one of those people—she was raised in a traditional way by her great-aunt, a tribal elder, on the Umatilla Indian Reservation, located in the rolling hills of northeast Oregon. As a child, she spoke Umatilla with her great-aunt in their little household. They lived an old-time lifestyle on top of a big grassy foothill along the Oregon Trail. Every morning, young Pauline rode her horse down to a corral, where she caught the school bus to nearby Pendleton. Though Pauline belongs to three Columbia River bands, the Wyam ("Waterfall"), Wanapum ("River"), and Palouse ("Horse") bands, the tribes that inhabit the reservation of her childhood are the Cayuse, Umatilla, and Walla Walla—a group of well-known horsemen and fishermen of the Columbia River basin.

At one time, these proud people were ruled as wards of the government by Indian agents bent on destroying their culture. Like other Indian tribes, they were subject to the national policy of tutelage and civilization, when the federal government sought to acculturate and Christianize them. The program was carried out by bureaucrats who managed all aspects of the Indians' daily lives, including their morals, habits, and religious beliefs in a program enforced with the full power of the law. Cases like *Clapox* illustrate Indian life under these oppressive conditions and reveal the role played by the courts in enforcing the assimilation process.

Police power for the assimilation program was founded most visibly on the infamous Code of Indian Offenses, promulgated by Secretary of the Interior Edward Teller in 1883. The code created Courts of Indian Offenses for each reservation. It also established rules for those courts that defined those Indian offenses for which reservation Indians could be arrested, tried, and incarcerated.[56] Teller said his code sought to eliminate "heathenish practices" and his court system was intended to bring about the end of Indian culture—the final solution to the Indian question.[57] However, Teller's courts were not "real" ones, because they were not created by the Constitution of the United States or any act of Congress, but simply by administrative fiat. They functioned like crude kangaroo courts under the Indian agent's guidance without any written processes. As explained in *Clapox,* "no written warrants are issued by said court, and no written record is kept of its findings or judgments"; however, those shortcomings were excused as the "first effort in the administration of justice [and] written process and proceedings could not have been expected."[58]

The Code of Indian Offenses warrants close review.[59] It directed each Indian agent to establish an agency tribunal called the Court of Indian Offenses and "strictly enforce" rules specified in the code. The courts were empowered to hear all matters presented to them by the agent, who also appointed the judges and had jurisdiction over Indian offenses specified in the code. The agent could compel attendance and enforce court orders "with the aid of the police," and all court orders were subject to his approval or disapproval, with any appeals heard by the Indian Office. Rule four of the code is a complete ban on the practice of tribal religion. It reads:

> The "sun-dance," and all similar dances and so-called religious ceremonies, shall be considered "Indian offenses," and any Indian found guilty of being a participant in any one or more of these "offenses" shall, for the first offense committed, be punished by withholding from him his rations for a period not exceeding ten days; and if found guilty of any subsequent offense under this rule, shall be punished by withholding his rations for a period not less than fifteen days nor more than thirty days, or by incarceration in the agency prison for a period not exceeding thirty days.[60]

Rule five prohibits plural marriages as offenses punishable by a fine of twenty dollars or hard labor for twenty days, or both, and the deprivation of rations so long as the marriage exists.[61] Rule six bans the practices of medicine men. Their powers were outlawed because the government feared they would hinder civilizing efforts and "prevent Indians from abandoning their heathenish rites and customs." Thus, their mysterious practices and powers were punishable by not less than ten days in the guardhouse.[62] Other rules prohibited Indian "give-away" customs at funerals and other events and outlawed the marriage custom of "paying" for the bride. Rule nine was a catchall provision giving the courts jurisdiction over any other unspecified misdemeanors. Sections 586 and 587 prohibited Indians from leaving the reservation except for "good conduct" or under other specified conditions, and those who failed to comply would "be looked upon and treated as hostile Indians, subject to arrest and punishment."[63]

In *Clapox*, the defendants pled not guilty. They argued that the BIA had no lawful authority to promulgate or enforce the Code of Indian Offenses. As such, Minnie committed no offense for which she could be legally arrested or detained, and the crime of breaking people out of jail did not apply since it only prohibited freeing a person jailed for or convicted of an offense.[64]

Federal Judge Matthew Deady rejected their contentions. He upheld the government's authority to enact the Code of Indian Offenses by an administrative edict. It did not matter that the Courts of Indian Offense were not real courts. It was sufficient that those tribunals were "mere educational and disciplinary instrumentalities" used by the government "to improve and elevate the condition of these dependent tribes to whom it sustains the relation of guardian." After all, the reservation was merely a "school," in the eyes of the court, where "Indians are gathered…under the charge of an agent, for the purpose of acquiring the habits, ideas, and aspirations which distinguish the civilized from the uncivilized man."[65] *Clapox* thus upheld the power to create these novel courts and make rules to improve "the morals of the Indians on this reservation."[66]

Consequently, Minnie's violation of the rules was treated as an offense against the United States, and she was properly incarcerated in the agency jail. As such, the jailbreak law applied and her rescuers were convicted. In the words of the court, they freed her in "flagrant opposition" to the United States' authority by "subversive" acts undermining the BIA's "laudable effort to accustom and educate these Indians in the habit and knowledge of self-government."[67] They fought the law, and the law won. The court enforced the code with zero tolerance.

The *Clapox* decision fostered an omnipotent, state-controlled social order on the Umatilla Reservation, imposed by the government in the name of guardianship. It sanctioned a chilling brave new world for American Indians that rivals the nightmarish dystopias described by George Orwell and Aldous Huxley.

In re Can-ah-couqua: Guardianship Alaska-Style

The poignant case of *In re Can-ah-couqua* (1887) shows how guardianship can run roughshod over personal liberty and parental rights.[68] Can-ah-couqua was a Tlingit mother who placed her five-year-old son into a Presbyterian mission school in Sitka, Alaska, supported by a BIA contract paying $11.25 per month to the school for each Indian student. She surrendered her son, Can-ca-dach, to the missionary school so he could be educated, but changed her mind three years later. When school officials refused to release him, Can-ah-couqua filed a petition for habeas corpus against the superintendent and chaplain alleging they were unlawfully restraining his liberty, contrary to her will and wishes as his mother.

The federal court denied the petition, stating, "the policy of the government is to aid these mission schools in the great Christian enterprise of rescuing from lives of barbarism and savagery these Indians, and conferring upon them the benefits of an educated civilization."[69] Case closed. The best interests of Can-ca-dach dictated that the child be detained by missionaries. If parents can simply withdraw their children from federally funded mission schools "at their own pleasure, this would render all efforts of both the government and missions to civilize them abortive."[70] The court relied upon the federal-trust doctrine to support its harsh ruling—even though only Presbyterians were being sued, the court obviously considered church and state to be one:

> These Alaska Indians are dependent allies, under the protection of the laws, and subject to such restraints in their tribal relations as may be deemed necessary for their own shelter, promotion, and protection, and they must realize the binding force of their obligations...I cannot escape the conclusion that the best interests of this child imperatively require that he should be remanded to the custody of the superintendent of the mission...sound morals, the good order and protection of civilized society, unmistakably demand it, the court has no alternative.[71]

The mother, who was considered "rude and untutored," living a "profligate and dissolute life," still had natural affection and a mother's love—she was granted visitation privileges "when her presence will not interfere with recitations or study...under surveillance of the superintendent or his subordinates a reasonable length of time, but shall not be permitted to take him away without order of the court."[72] Guardianship rights of the government and its Presbyterian proxies take precedence over those of parent and child when you are a ward of the government in Alaska. Life would never be the same for mother or child, a family broken, for the good of the government's "great Christian enterprise."

Efforts to Overcome Hardships Imposed by the *Sandoval* Trilogy

The United States seriously harmed Native Americans in the name of guardianship when that power went unchecked by the courts. The government invoked that principle to commit cultural genocide, to run roughshod over civil liberties, and to justify unwarranted intrusions into the daily lives, homes, and bedrooms of Native Americans. Compounding the problem, the courts allowed racism to infect the guardianship principle in *Sandoval* and failed to forestall government excesses in *Clapox* and *In re Can-ah-couqua*.

The judicial trend away from *Worcester*'s protectorate principle led to an abuse of power in the name of guardianship with shameful despotic results. During the twentieth century, the government suppressed Pueblo Indian dancing using guardianship powers ushered in by the *Sandoval* trilogy. As moral policemen, narrow-minded bigots in the BIA viewed Pueblo ceremonies as barbarous impediments to the government's tutelage and civilization program.[73] On a broader scale, straitlaced bureaucrats worked nights, weekends, and overtime exercising puritanical control over Indian life and morals on every Indian reservation and community, zealously peering into the bedrooms of an entire race of people. John Collier, an admirer of Pueblo culture, finally put a stop to these obnoxious practices in 1934, when he issued directives as commissioner of Indian Affairs to restore Native American religious freedom and curtail fervent missionary work in government-run schools.[74]

In short, every time the government acted during the period from 1886 to 1934 to expand hegemony over the internal affairs of Indian tribes or expand control over Indian property, it invoked the guardianship principle like an unabashed colonial power. The BIA was a zealous and efficient authoritarian when given puritanical control over Indian tribes. The paternalistic agency, however, proved to be notoriously sloppy and inept as trustee when actually managing and accounting for Indian property in its care. Its mismanagement of Indian trust funds has been described as "the greatest Indian scandal of the twentieth century" by legal commentators, and it remains "an unresolved crisis into the twenty-first century."[75] Whenever asked to be accountable, the BIA swiftly runs from its fiduciary obligations.

These blemishes on the Indian trust relationship must be reformed. They cannot be tolerated because the guardianship and trust principles are important components of the Indian trust doctrine. I have four recommendations. First, guardianship should be retained, but only as originally intended in the protectorate or suzerainty relation envisioned by treaties and the Marshall Court, because that political relationship affords beneficial protection to Indian tribes as domestic dependent nations when properly used.[76] Indeed, the use of federal guardianship as a shield for those purposes should be strengthened by the law. Second, the abject racism embedded into the guardianship principle by the courts in cases like the *Sandoval* trilogy must be rooted out. Third, by the same token, government abuse of its guardianship powers to intrude into tribal life and culture and trod upon civil liberties must be curbed, not promoted, by the courts. The time is overdue for the courts to emerge from the age of colonialism and strengthen the US trust relationship with Indian tribes in a manner more keeping with the postcolonial era. And, finally, federal trusteeship must be reformed. The system is broken. As the owner and trustee of Indian trust property, the law must require the government to act like a fiduciary and be accountable for centuries of mismanagement of Indian trust property. Many of these reforms are under way, with varying degrees of success, but significant legal and political challenges lie ahead.

Indian tribes have worked to achieve religious freedom for Native Americans and eradicate racism from the guardianship principle. Though John Collier curtailed overt government suppression of tribal religious freedom, problems continued throughout the twentieth century due to ingrained hostility toward indigenous religions in the United States and ignorance about the impact of government laws and activity upon those little-known religious practices.[77] In 1978, Congress found that widespread government infringement upon Native American religious beliefs and practices still continued. It enacted the American Indian Religious Freedom Act (AIRFA), which acknowledged that the First Amendment has not worked to protect traditional religious practices. This landmark law established an affirmative federal policy to protect and preserve the traditional religious beliefs and practices of American Indians, Alaska Natives, and Native Hawaiians.[78] Though the AIRFA policy has no enforcement teeth, it set a national Indian policy and identified a legislative agenda that has endured to the present.[79] The courts of the conqueror have been slow to embrace the new national policy, as I will discuss in more detail in subsequent chapters, clinging instead to nineteenth-century attitudes toward Native religious suppression.[80]

Racism is difficult to eradicate, because few openly admit to harboring those dark prejudices. It took enormous effort to overturn racial segregation ingrained in Supreme Court decisions, but that was accomplished in *Brown v. Board of Education* (1954).[81] *Sandoval* was dead wrong about the Santa Clara Pueblo people, and it was a mean-spirited decision that infected the principle of guardianship with abject racism. As for the open contempt for Indians expressed in *Sandoval*, that case remains good law today and those attitudes may well continue to play a role in modern-day cases, in less overt tones. Prejudice against Indians has largely been repudiated by the lay public. This is evident in the opening of the National Museum of the American Indian and other areas where Americans have come to appreciate Native art and admire Native culture. Though quick to accept prevailing prejudices, courts often lag behind society at large in accepting social change.

The Santa Clara Pueblo, though demonized in *Sandoval,* deftly used the umbrella of federal protection to develop and expand its tribal sovereignty during the modern era of federal Indian law. I have always admired the Indians of Santa Clara Pueblo, having spent considerable time there visiting friends in my younger days and later on as a Native American Rights Fund (NARF) attorney. I strongly disagree with the disparagement of these people in *Sandoval* by justices who never met a Pueblo Indian or visited a pueblo, much less Santa Clara Pueblo. Situated on the Rio Grande in northern New Mexico, Santa Clara Pueblo is widely respected. That beautiful adobe village predates the United States. Along with eighteen other Indian pueblos, the unique arts, government, traditional religion, and way of life of Santa Clara Pueblo truly make New Mexico a "land of enchantment." Yet, as wrong as *Sandoval* was, it did usher in federal guardianship that Pueblo leaders and litigators used to protect the Pueblo tribes from state interference, modeling the domestic dependent nations with rights of self-government over their internal affairs and social relations as envisioned by *Worcester.* Indians have a knack for adapting, making the best of a bad situation, and surviving.

The harsh rule by guardianship has lessened since the days of the *Sandoval* trilogy. Emancipation from the dark side of wardship became a quest for freedom from the soul-killing, heavy paternalistic rule of Indian tribes by the BIA, which is very similar to the quest for freedom from slavery by blacks. The trend toward restoring tribal control over the internal affairs and social relations of Indian tribes is seen in *Santa Clara Pueblo v. Martinez* (1978).[82] That case protects Santa Clara's self-government power to determine its tribal membership according to its unique cultural and religious traditions. The historic decision did several things.

First, the Court eschewed federal intrusion upon traditional values important to the pueblo's cultural survival. That deference restores *Worcester*'s principle that Indian tribes are distinct political communities with self-government power to regulate their internal and social relations.[83] Second, the Court expressly applied Congress's new federal policies of furthering Indian self-determination and tribal self-government. Its decision strengthens tribal courts and extends governmental immunity from suit to the

Pueblo. The case thus lifts the yoke of federal management over pueblo lives and culture. Contrary to *Sandoval*, the *Santa Clara* Court avoided interference with internal Pueblo affairs and strengthened the Pueblo's ability to maintain itself as a culturally and politically distinct entity. Reversing the trend set in motion by *Kagama*, the Court limited the power of the government to intrude upon tribal sovereignty unless and until Congress expresses a clear intention to do so.[84]

For these reasons, the *Santa Clara Pueblo* decision is clearly part of the trend toward getting Big Brother out of the internal affairs of Indian tribes. That trend began in the Indian Reorganization Act of 1934 (IRA).[85] The IRA repealed the General Allotment Act, restored any remaining unallotted land to tribal ownership, and replaced federal management of internal tribal affairs with the establishment of tribal governments. After the passage of the IRA, in addition to the Indian Citizenship Act of 1924, and Commissioner Collier's directives of 1934, it became harder for the Great Father to peer into his children's bedrooms, especially after courts began to place limits on federal guardianship powers during the modern era of federal Indian law.

One important gain won in the Native American sovereignty movement is the national policy of Indian self-determination and self-government, which has been embraced by every president and Congress since 1970. Those branches of government have advocated these important national policies over the past generation, as seen in numerous executive orders and statutes enacted during that period. The dark rule of Indian tribes by the plenary power of federal guardianship has largely been replaced by tribal self-government. Today, the principle threat to *Worcester*'s protectorate principle and tribal sovereignty comes not from these branches of government, but from an entirely different quarter—the US Supreme Court. In recent decades, the conservative court, stacked with jurists indifferent or hostile to Native America, has relegated to itself the role of arbitrator and definer of tribal sovereignty (a role eschewed by courts for over 150 years under the political-question doctrine) and embarked upon an ad hoc, case-by-case approach to limiting, redefining, and destroying tribal sovereignty. In a series of cases, the Supreme Court has trimmed the criminal-justice powers of tribal governments over reservation crimes committed by non-Indians and nonmember Indians, and it has allowed intrusion by state authorities into reservation boundaries that once were barriers to the states.[86] In the postmodern era of federal Indian law, the Supreme Court has resurfaced as the court of the conquerors. Indian tribes frequently petition Congress and the president to check the excesses of the Supreme Court in order to protect tribal self-government, Indian self-determination, and even the fundamental human right of worship, as discussed in other chapters.

After the Indian tribes lawyered up, attention turned to the federal trusteeship system. The chickens came home to roost at the BIA. The BIA manages about $2.9 billion in tribal trust funds and collects nearly $378 million in revenue derived from income-producing tribal land every year. It also manages about 300,000 individual trust fund accounts for individual Indians, which includes income earned from their trust lands. The autocratic agency was never subjected to judicial review during the height of the guardianship era, even though the agency has long been heavily criticized for mismanaging Indian money entrusted to its care as trustee.[87] Today, both Congress and the courts are deeply involved in efforts to reform the federal trusteeship system.

Congress passed the Indian Trust Management Reform Act of 1994.[88] When the recalcitrant agency failed to comply, NARF filed a massive class action lawsuit in 1996 on behalf of 300,000 Indians against the federal government for mismanagement of their trust funds. *Cobell v. Kempthorne* charged breach of trust—the government breached its duty as trustee to properly manage trust funds derived from the Indian beneficiaries' allotted trust lands across the country over the past 125 years. The suit asserts that billions of dollars are missing from trust accounts controlled and managed by the government. NARF asked the federal court to order an accounting, to reform the system, or to put management of Indian money into a private receivership, where it can be properly managed. If the BIA wants to exercise trusteeship power, the *Cobell* plaintiffs demanded that the agency act like a trustee, be competent, accountable, and, above all, become a real fiduciary—just like every other financial institution that handles other people's money. In 2008, the *Cobell* court held that the government must pay $455.6 million to individual Indians for mismanaging income earned from their trust lands.[89]

The circle closed around the hapless agency on December 31, 2006, when 103 lawsuits were filed by NARF and a large number of Indian tribes against the agency, charging mismanagement of tribal trust funds as well. NARF's case, *Nez Perce Indian Tribe, et al. v. Kempthorne, et al.*, is a class action brought by twelve Indian tribes on behalf of all Indian tribes who have not filed potential trust mismanagement claims against the government trustee—potentially 225 Indian tribes.[90] Then attorney general Alberto Gonzales estimated in congressional testimony that the United States' potential liability for tribal trust fund mismanagement may exceed $200 billion. Mismanagement of tribal money on that scale strikes at the core of the federal trust responsibility and has created a national financial crisis for Indian Country and the United States. John Echohawk, one NARF attorney in *Nez Perce*, told Congress in 2007:

> Imagine the widespread outcry if banks, savings and loan companies, and investment houses that were chosen by investors were to fail to meet their fiduciary obligations. Undoubtedly such harm would be corrected.[91]

Cobell, *Nez Perce*, and the other 102 lawsuits have triggered an all-out modern-day Indian legal war, pitting all Indian tribes and American Indians in the nation against the United States over federal trust accountability. The bevy of lawsuits seeks to reform the government's shoddy system for managing Indian trust funds and to make the beneficiaries whole.

Thus far, in the protracted, hard-fought *Cobell* litigation, the court has determined that the Indian trusts are enforceable and the United States was derelict in discharging its fiduciary obligations by mismanaging the trust accounts of the plaintiff Indian beneficiaries.[92] The court observed that the United States assumed elaborate control over their lands and moneys, creating some 300,000 trust accounts covering an estimated eleven million acres of individual Indian trust land "over one hundred years ago through an act of Congress (General Allotment Act of 1887)" and those accounts "have been mismanaged nearly as long."[93] The government confessed it does not know how many trust accounts are in its system or the proper balance of those accounts and cannot locate records to determine their value.[94] The agency must now pay the piper. The *Cobell* court seems intent on applying the common law of trusts to impose stringent fiduciary standards upon BIA bureaucrats long accustomed to sloppy ineptitude—the agency's hallmark. That would create the bureaucrats' worst nightmare and a brand new white man's burden: real trusteeship and accountability. As stated by Donald Wharton, another NARF attorney involved in the *Nez Perce* litigation: "The time for lame excuses is over—it is time that the federal government finally becomes what it has always claimed to be, the trustee of the Indian tribes, and accept responsibility to act like a fiduciary without dodging its duties and placing blame for mismanagement elsewhere."[95]

Conditions have also changed on the Umatilla Indian Reservation since the *Clapox* decision. Despite the government assault on their culture under the Code of Indian Offenses, the Indians of that reservation resisted. Many continued their way of life and were not brainwashed. They are survivors of cultural genocide, and it is a miracle and a testament that any Native culture remains in the United States. Today the Confederated Tribes of the Umatilla Reservation have 2,400 citizens governed by a hardworking tribal government. Many still speak tribal languages, practice the traditional Seven Drums religion, and eat a rich diet of traditional foods like salmon, roots, berries, deer, and elk obtained through hunting, fishing, and gathering. Their government representatives work to preserve their cultural heritage. The Confederated Tribes maintain their original covenants with their Creator, and the land, water, animals, fish, and plants comprising their aboriginal habitat through spiritual practices and longhouse ceremonies.[96] At the same time, they have accomplished great economic growth, as seen in the Wildhorse Resort and Casino and other businesses. They are confidently poised to prosper in the twenty-first century as a successful and culturally distinct people in their aboriginal homeland.[97] I am grateful they resisted. Otherwise, I should not have been blessed with life alongside my wise and wonderful wife, Pauline—a traditional person with indigenous knowledge and ways.

The paramount challenge of the law is to protect what little remains in the surviving Native American cultures. The United Nations Declaration on the Rights of Indigenous Peoples prohibits ethnocide. Article 8 states, "Indigenous peoples and individuals have the right not to be subjected to forced assimilation or destruction of their culture." That new international standard outlaws the dark side of guardianship, with its invidious tutelage and civilization components.

What about the plural marriages in *Clapox*? The BIA ban rubbed them out. That is unfortunate. They were common among many tribes as part of traditional life, including the Pawnee and my own family.[98] As a descendent from a plural marriage, I continue to wonder about their merits. Can they really be so bad? The Puritan and Pilgrim idea of marriage has been under severe attack for many years, as seen in our stunning divorce rates, growing acceptance of same-sex marriages, and the millions who shun it altogether by just shacking up. Perhaps pagans can tutelage us through this family crisis. Why let Puritans, Pilgrims, and the BIA define marital relations? Romance was not their forte. Maybe the old-time Indians had it right all along. But what is most important is the right to choose.

It is hard to ignore the human tragedy brought about in the *In re Can-ah-couqua* guardianship case. Little can be said. Sometimes, it is hard to find words to express incredible sadness, especially the heartbreak that springs from humans' inhumanity to their fellow humans. The seizing of children presents one of those occasions. The government's "great Christian enterprise" was a legalized form of kidnapping that probably destroyed the lives of both mother and child, inflicting wounds that could never heal. Out of respect for them, nothing can be said. Silence seems appropriate to close the chapter on guardianship, that venerable instrument of colonialism.

CHAPTER NINE

In re Adoption of John Doe v. Heim: Taking the Kids

"The law is not a revolutionary force. It is a very conservative force that supports whatever system is in place."

—Bertram E. Hirsch, Association on American Indian Affairs attorney (1971–1977) and one of the authors of the Indian Child Welfare Act of 1978[1]

IT WAS BUSINESS AS USUAL in the Bernalillo County court system. Another Indian child was going to be adopted by a white family. As paperwork in the adoption proceeding was filed in the Albuquerque court, no one thought about placing the three-year-old with an Indian family so his cultural heritage and tribal ties could be preserved. The system blithely ignored these vital factors when placing Indian kids in 1975—a time when one in four Indian children in America were separated from their families and placed into non-Indian families, foster homes, or other settings.[2] After all, are Indians really fit to rear children—with all that alcoholism, poverty, and cultural mumbo jumbo? The adoption agency, judge, and social worker knew little about those things, and cared even less.

But that day an unusual thing happened. The boy's grandfather, a Navajo silversmith, would not give up his grandson without a fight. He filed a habeas corpus action to prevent the adoption and regain custody of his grandchild. Grandpa asserted custody under Navajo custom—a body of tribal traditions that accords grandparents custody of their grandchildren under the extended family structures and child-rearing practices of the Navajo Nation. "Grandfather Doe" simply wanted what most Indian elders cherish—the right to raise a family, to live together with the grandchild he raised since birth as an extended family, and to protect their cultural integrity as Native Americans.[3] His case pitted Navajo law, unique Indian cultural values, and the vital interests of Indian tribes in retaining their children against New Mexico state law, which recognized none of these things.

The trial court was unimpressed with Grandpa's claims. The judge dismissed his action and granted the adoption petition. So did the New Mexico Court of Appeals. Its decision, reported as *In the Matter of the Adoption of John Doe; Grandfather Doe, on behalf of John Doe, a child v. Heim, et al.*

(1976), is one of the ten worst Indian law cases ever decided.[4] The decision illustrates a destructive pattern widely followed by state courts in deciding Indian child custody cases—a pattern that produced such large-scale removal of Indian children throughout the nation by 1978 that Congress declared an "Indian child welfare crisis of massive portions."[5] As mounting numbers of Indian kids disappeared into state child-welfare systems, Congress investigated the causes and, in one of its finest hours, intervened to protect Indian families and the cultural integrity of Indian tribes.

It is unfortunate that some Indian children will unavoidably require placement due to their family circumstances, but the pivotal question is, who decides: state systems where they reside or their tribes of origin? Prior to 1978, most state courts ignored or failed to recognize the importance of tribal relations to the maintenance of Indian families and to the continued existence of Indian tribes. In exercising jurisdiction over Indian families, state judges blindly applied Anglo standards to Native settings, instead of more appropriate cultural and social standards derived from tribal customs and laws, to guide their removal and placement decisions. That judicial mind-set preordained the removal of Indian children from their families and tribal settings, in most cases, to be raised in an alien culture. It placed the power to decide the fate of Indian children and families into the hands of a bureaucracy unsuited to make those kinds of decisions—the system was composed of judges, social workers, and adoption agencies unfamiliar with Native cultures and often hostile or indifferent toward Indian tribes. As this process occurred, Indian tribes stood by helplessly watching their families break apart and kids disappear at the hands of state and local jurisdictions. Sometimes, no one realized what was happening as isolated family-by-family forced separations occurred. No one connected the dots until the enormity of the situation became apparent, causing outrage and alarm.[6]

By 1978, this system had produced a shocking result: the wholesale separation of Indian children from their families. The removal of one in every four Indian kids from their families and tribal settings not only robbed thousands of their cultural heritage, but seriously impaired the ability of Indian families and tribes to pass down Native language, history, traditions, and wisdom to future generations. The staggering loss of kids and culture reached crisis proportions in many Indian communities, exposing a faulty legal system so rigid in its refusal to incorporate Native American values into the law that it produced a system so abusive and destructive of Indian families and culture as to allow the twin specters of ethnocide and genocide to awaken and threaten the cultural survival of Indian tribes.

The alarming statistics ultimately prompted congressional action in 1978 to protect the best interests of Indian children and the cultural integrity of Indian tribes. Indian leaders had advocated legislative steps to address the crisis since the mid-1960s. Two years after *Heim* was decided, Congress passed one of the most sweeping and remarkable federal Indian laws ever enacted, the Indian Child Welfare Act of 1978 (ICWA).[7]

Taking its guardianship duties seriously, Congress decisively reversed the judicial mind-set illustrated by *Heim*. ICWA requires state courts to apply Indian cultural values as minimum federal standards when placing Indian children. Above all, the landmark law places decision-making authority into the hands of Indian tribes by recognizing the exclusive authority of tribes to decide cases involving Indian children living in the tribal community and by requiring state courts to transfer placement cases to tribal courts when requested. This extraordinary measure expands the jurisdiction of tribal courts far beyond reservation boundaries to every state where tribal children reside. Furthermore, the federal law restructured tribal/state relations by directing state courts to give "full faith and credit" to the laws, records, and judicial proceedings of Indian tribes.[8] The sweeping statute remains one of the most impressive human rights and tribal sovereignty laws ever passed by Congress.

This story deserves telling since many take tribal sovereignty over Indian children and families for granted. That is all too easy to do today, because every Indian tribe now exercises that power daily though their governmental agencies, codes, and courts. However, that important right did not always exist—it is a hard-earned attribute of sovereignty that had to be demanded and fought for by tribal leaders during the modern era of federal Indian law. In telling the story of *Heim* and the remarkable movement to bring the kids home that resulted in the passage of ICWA, I will focus on the legal career of one attorney, Bertram E. Hirsch. He litigated in *Heim* and many other cases of that era to reform the system, and he walked the halls of Congress, along with many others, to advocate the passage of ICWA.[9] Indeed, many tribal leaders and advocates in Indian Country worked hard to secure passage of that vital law as a legislative priority identified at the very beginning of the sovereignty movement in the mid-1960s. The *Heim* case fell victim to that movement. Taking Indian children away from their families and tribal settings is a practice that began shortly after the discovery of the New World. ICWA brought that practice to an end in the United States in 1978. Hirsch's important contributions during that historic period (1968–1978) illustrate how the work of one attorney can help change the world and make it a better place.

Why Taking Children Is Harmful to Indigenous Peoples

No nation or human society can survive for long when its kids are systematically taken away. Indian tribes are especially vulnerable, because children are the wellspring of their futures. Elders impart tribal language, songs, history, religion, skills, customs, beliefs, and practices to the young so the culture can be carried on by future generations. Youth thus become repositories of tribal wisdom and heritage gleaned over millennia. In the cycle of Native life, they ensure the survival of tribal cultures that are carried on through oral traditions. For these reasons, Congress made a finding in ICWA that "there is no resource that is more vital to the continued existence and integrity of Indian tribes than their children."[10]

When kids are removed from their extended family and tribe, twin harms occur: they become cultural orphans who suffer the loss of their heritage, and the tribe is diminished since fewer youth remain to learn and carry on the traditions.[11] When such losses occur on a large scale, cultures themselves become threatened.[12] As the world's remaining tribal cultures disappear, a treasure trove of ancient wisdom is lost and the diversity of the human family is diminished. Many factors contributed to the alarming decline and disappearance of the world's tribal cultures during the twentieth century, such as degradation of indigenous habitat, disease, the temptations of technological Western society, and sometimes ethnocide and genocide. The forcible taking of indigenous children is one factor that can be remedied—it should not be tolerated by the law in any nation.

International legal and human rights are implicated by the forcible removal of indigenous children from their families and communities. When that is done with the intent to destroy a tribal group, it amounts to the crime of genocide. The United Nations defines *genocide* as an act "committed with intent to destroy, in whole or part, a national, ethnical, racial, or religious group," such as "[f]orcibly transferring children of the group to another group."[13] It also amounts to a human-rights violation. The Declaration on the Rights of Indigenous Peoples recognizes the right of Native peoples to live as culturally distinct peoples, free from the forcible removal of their children to another group.[14]

It can be debated by historians and legal commentators whether the taking of Indian kids in US history was forcible or done with the requisite intent to violate current UN standards. (Any removal of a child from its family and tribal setting is forcible, in my view, if done against the will of the parents, extended family, tribe, or the child—even if done under the color of law; and it can hardly be said that removal of untold thousands was an accident.) History will decide that question. In any event, the widespread removal of indigenous children in the New World over the past five hundred years destroyed the lives of untold thousands and contributed to one of the greatest losses of world culture ever witnessed. Columbus himself may have initiated the practice, bringing children from the New World on his return voyage.[15] In the United States, government agents began snatching children from reservations in earnest during the late nineteenth century.

As part of the assimilation program, kids were rounded up on many reservations and sent to federal boarding schools, often hundreds of miles away, where they were kept for years. Under strict tutelage, the children were prohibited from speaking their languages, dressing in Indian clothes, wearing traditional hairstyles, and praying to the Great Spirit, while at the same time the government proselytized them.[16] The school officials tried to completely remake these vulnerable and impressionable youth by inoculating them with values from a foreign culture and assimilating them into the dominant settler society. Their motto was "Kill the Indian, Save the Man."[17] The homesick children incarcerated in these institutions were brainwashed. They were taught to be ashamed of their families, their cultures, and their tribes. Many lonesome kids ran away. Others adapted to institutional life, but reclaimed their identities later in life. Many were successfully indoctrinated by the government and became estranged from their families and tribes for the rest of their lives. In each instance, the heart and soul of every child was deeply affected by this life-altering experience of removal and separation by a government determined to raise Indian children in the place of their natural parents.[18]

Some courts upheld government custody of Indian children, even when they were being held against the parents' wishes.[19] Other courts required school officials to produce legal authority for holding children against their will.[20] Congress supported the program by allowing the secretary of the interior discretion to withhold rations, clothing, subsistence, and Indian monies from heads of Indian families who neglected to send their children to school.[21] When overzealous agents began coercing parents into allowing their children to be removed to off-reservation boarding schools, Congress had to pass a law in 1895 forbidding their use of compulsory means, demonstrating how widespread the problem was by the turn of the century.[22] Alaska and the Mormons also got in the act where Indian kids live in remote areas. Alaska had no schools in the bush, so kids from those areas were placed with white families at state expense to attend school, rather than furnish schools in their home communities.[23] Similarly, the Mormons placed 2,700 Indian kids with Mormon families in 1977 alone to attend school during the school year, and they fought to ensure that no federal law interfered with their "voluntary" placement program.[24]

In 1978, Congress finally saw how destructive the federal boarding school system was to Native American families. A House report declared that it "contribute[s] to the destruction of Indian family and community life."[25] By that time, 34,538 Indian children (more than 17 percent of all Indian schoolchildren) were living in institutional settings in seventy-four boarding schools, rather than at home.[26]

The federal mind-set was that Indian children are better off being raised by white families. From 1958 through 1967, the Bureau of Indian Affairs (BIA) funded the Indian Adoption Project, administered by the Child Welfare League of America. The BIA-funded project placed hundreds of Indian children from sixteen western states for adoption by white families in the East.[27] By the 1970s, state child-welfare systems were also contributing heavily to the destruction of Indian families and the separation of children from their tribes. Once Indian families moved away from reservations into the cities, a migration set in motion by the federal termination legislation and relocation program of the 1950s, the state systems could get their grips on the kids. Once ensnarled by those bureaucracies, most wound up in non-Indian homes or institutions.[28] By 1974, that was the fate of 25 to 35 percent of all Indian children.[29]

Based upon extensive evidence amassed in hearings, Congress indicted the state systems and courts for creating this crisis, stating, "[t]he wholesale separation of Indian children from their families is perhaps the most tragic and destructive aspect of American Indian life today."[30] Several root causes were identified by Congress. Much of the blame was laid at the door of non-Indian social workers untutored in Native culture. They deeply misunderstood the role of extended families in Native social structures, misinterpreted Indian child-rearing practices, and applied cultural biases or discriminatory criteria in evaluating Native family situations.[31] Hirsch, who was active in Indian child-welfare litigation during this period, observed that the agency's attitude was "no Indian parent is 'fit' to be a parent."[32] State courts compounded the problem by relying on the testimony of such folks. Congress found that the "abusive actions of social workers would largely be nullified if more judges were themselves knowledgeable about Indian life and required a sharper definition of the standards of child abuse and neglect."[33] Congress was also concerned that discriminatory placement standards applied by state systems "made it virtually impossible for most Indian couples to qualify as foster or adoptive parents, since they are based on middle-class values."[34]

In short, the state systems for protecting the best interests of children failed to incorporate the values and unique cultures of indigenous peoples in the United States. Discriminatory and ethnocentric standards were applied and enforced by social workers, agencies, and courts that lacked the training, insights, or motivation to make the system accountable and workable for Native Americans. The system naturally produced racially disparate results—Indian children were removed at far greater rates than kids of other races more familiar to the social workers.[35] The ignorance, ethnocentricity, and bias built into those systems is a form of discrimination called *institutional racism* when those factors produce racially disparate results.[36] State courts were an integral part of the problem. At the judicial stage of the process, the tribunals decided the fate of the Indian children and families in child custody, dependency, and termination of parental rights proceedings—no kid can be permanently removed without court approval. Foster care, which is designed to be a temporary condition, often became permanent in this system.

The New Mexico case is significant in three ways. First, it illustrates the role of state courts in removing Indian children during the pre-ICWA era. Second, rather than passively submit to the system, the child's natural father and grandfather mounted an all-out legal assault on the system in a determined effort to keep their extended family together.[37] With legal support from the Navajo Nation and the Association on American Indian Affairs (AAIA), they presented the Court of Appeals with all the right arguments for reversing the decision below and for calling New Mexico's child welfare system into question.[38] The court chose to reject their arguments in a decision that provided a poignant example of the need for a federal law to reform the system and place decision-making into the hands of Indian tribes.

Third, one attorney involved in the appeal was a young lawyer named Bertram E. Hirsch. Born in 1947, the New Yorker attended Queens College during the 1960s and earned a law degree from NYU School of Law in 1971. As a child of the 1960s, when young people were more concerned about social justice than playing video games, Hirsch participated in the civil rights movement. During college, he became a member of Congress of Racial Equality and participated in marches, including the 1968 march on Washington, DC, when Martin Luther King Jr. proclaimed, "I have a dream." During that period, his interest turned to Native American justice issues. In 1967, the college student obtained a part-time job with AAIA, which was then headquartered in the Big Apple. It was there his odyssey began, which would take him throughout Indian Country, into courtrooms in thirty-seven states, including the Supreme Court Chamber, and finally into the halls of Congress to confront and help defeat the system that took the kids. The *Heim* case was one stop along the way. Hirsch was to play a pivotal role in bringing down the system upheld in *Heim* through a landmark act of Congress, the Indian Child Welfare Act of 1978. ICWA would reverse the principles that underpinned *Heim* and forever change the power of the state agencies and courts to unilaterally determine the fate of Indian children. The *Heim* court was seemingly oblivious to the national movement to obtain those federal reforms, which was well under way in 1976, when it handed down its short-lived decision and provided Congress with a perfect example of the need for the law. Through vigorous legislative advocacy in the hallways and hearing rooms of Congress in 1974–78, the young attorney would make sure that decisions like *Heim* would never happen again.

Heim Shows How the Courts Contributed to a System Bent on Taking Kids

Gallup, New Mexico, was bustling in 1975. Navajo Indians could be seen everywhere, strolling the streets or riding in pickups up and down Route 66. The border town sits in the heart of Indian Country, next to the Zuni, Hopi, and Navajo Indian reservations. Sometimes called the Indian Capital of the World, Gallup is filled with pawnshops, liquor stores, and beer joints. It has a checkered history of Indian/white relations. Gallup is home to the Navajo family in *Heim*.

"Grandfather Doe" was a man with a more colorful name than that assigned by the court. He was a decorated veteran during the Korean War. In 1975, Grandpa was considered one of the leading Navajo silversmiths, an artist carrying on a family tradition for making outstanding silver and turquoise jewelry from a prominent Navajo family of well-known silversmiths. He lived off the reservation in nearby Gallup, a border town long occupied and frequented by his people. Grandpa was in his mid- to late forties at the time, according to Hirsch, one attorney in the *Heim* case, who observed, "he was absolutely fine in everyone's eye—except perhaps to a prejudiced eye."[39]

In 1972, Grandfather Doe's extended family household included his daughter. Unmarried, the pregnant woman had just split the sheets with her child's father. Shortly after the child's birth, in March of 1972, the father, a traditional Navajo, moved into the household from the reservation. He was booted out six months later by the mother—the two had difficulties getting along. According to the *Heim* opinion, from the time of the child's birth, Grandpa "provided in his own house for the care, custody and control, shelter, food and clothing of the child."[40] During the three-year period until the mother turned his grandson over to the adoption agency, Grandpa "gave the child his personal care and attention, 'including feeding, changing diapers, washing and bathing,'" and "was 'primarily' responsible for the care, custody and control of the child."[41] The child was in Grandpa's care under Navajo custom and tradition, which, according to the *Heim* court, "confers upon grandparents, particularly maternal grandparents, the status of guardians of the grandchildren," and his care for the boy "was in accordance with this tradition."[42] There was no question that Grandpa "had a right to custody under Navajo custom."[43]

In the spring of 1975, several events occurred in rapid succession. In March, Mom moved out and took the three-year-old with her. Unable to care for the child, she turned him over to an adoption agency a few days later. She testified in *Heim* that she felt she could not provide her son with a proper upbringing on her own and she considered Grandpa's household unsatisfactory because of his alleged "alcoholism and the instability of the home."[44] The woman had been raised by non-Indian relatives until age sixteen. As a result of her upbringing, she did not speak her Native language or practice Navajo customs, and she identified more with non-Indian culture than the Navajo Way. The acculturated mother requested placement with a non-Indian family.[45] The agency placed the boy with a non-Indian family, who promptly filed a petition in Albuquerque to adopt the child a few weeks later. To prevent the loss of his grandson, Grandpa countered five days later by filing a petition for habeas corpus on behalf of the child. Both cases were heard by Bernalillo County District Court Judge Rozier E. Sanchez.

Judge Sanchez dismissed Grandpa's case, holding that he was not a custodian of the child under New Mexico law and had no standing to challenge the adoption.[46] The court did let Grandpa participate in the adoption proceedings, along with the natural father, as persons eligible for possible placement. Following a hearing on the placement issue, the court found that the best interests of the boy required his placement with the non-Indian family and granted their petition. The non-Indian family had "great love and concern" for the child (acquired in just six months) and could provide a suitable home, whereas Grandpa (who raised the boy for three years) merely "sells Indian jewelry for a living and spends a substantial portion of his time away from his home."[47] Returning the child to Grandpa "would cause trauma" to the child and would not be in his best interest, according to the Albuquerque judge.

Throughout the proceedings, Grandpa maintained his right to custody of minor children in an extended family under Navajo custom (especially where the mother has rejected that culture) and his desire to raise the child to maintain Navajo culture, ethnic heritage, and customs.[48] In extended families, not just one parent can dispose of a child, because many members must participate in such decisions. Furthermore, on appeal, the Navajo Nation and AAIA maintained that New Mexico courts do not have jurisdiction over adoption cases involving Navajo children, urging that such matters should be decided by Navajo tribal courts because the Navajo Nation maintains a *parens patriae* relation with all Navajo children, wherever they are located.[49] They also maintained that Judge Sanchez disregarded testimony concerning cultural factors of placement.

The Court of Appeals agreed that Grandpa was entitled to custody under Navajo law and had standing to challenge the adoption, but refused to apply Navajo law in New Mexico courts or extend full faith and credit to tribal law. The court stated:

> New Mexico need not subordinate its own policy to a conflicting Navajo custom...The grandfather had a right to custody under Navajo custom; he had no such right under New Mexico law.[50]

As such, his rights were not superior to those of the non-Indian family—they "not only have a right to custody [under New Mexico law], but actual physical custody of the child...obtained from [the adoption agency] who in turn obtained custody from the mother."[51] The court went on to decide the child's fate and confirmed the adoption in the best interests of the child. In so doing, the decision rejected the Navajo cultural interests at stake, Navajo law, Navajo Nation jurisdiction, and the role of extended families in Navajo social structure.[52] Even though the parents, child, and grandfather all belonged to the Navajo Nation, none of that mattered at all.

Grandfather Doe passed away in 2005, at the age of seventy-three. He was born into the Towering House People Clan for the Red House People Clan and buried on the Navajo Reservation in Lupton, Arizona, on the New Mexico border. We do not know whether he ever reconnected with his grandson, a boy named John Doe by the courts of the conqueror. The boy became a tragic statistic as one of the Indian kids who disappeared into the system before ICWA became law, despite the best efforts of his extended family, the Navajo Nation, and the AAIA litigants to prevent his removal. But the winds of change were blowing.

During the pre-ICWA period, Hirsch and AAIA litigated extensively to protect Native American families and reform the system. Some cases were won, others lost. Some hearings occurred in rural courtrooms packed with Indians and whites, where the air was so thick with tension and racial animosity that it could be cut with a knife. One judge angrily ordered the return of a child to his natural parents with the caustic statement, "I'll return the child and I don't care what they do with it—they can barbeque him for all I care."[53] That effort took the young attorney to the US Supreme Court, where he argued *Decoteau v. District Court* (1975) at the age of twenty-eight.[54] While the AAIA litigation effort was valuable, the problem was too massive, and asking state courts to fix a problem that they themselves created could not be expected to bring immediate change—it would take an act of Congress to reform the system. The cases litigated during this period, however, would inform the provisions of the law.

At the same time, AAIA was deeply involved in the national grass-roots movement occurring in Indian Country to get a federal law passed to resolve the child welfare crisis. In 1968–69, Hirsch did a national survey of county welfare practices, developing statistic evidence on a state-by-state basis that documented the problem. AAIA supplemented that evidence with the development of a powerful body of expert-opinion evidence on the impacts of the system on Indian children and families, and the Native rights group participated in national press conferences and local workshops to educate the public on the issue. Eyes turned to Washington, DC, in 1974, when congressional oversight hearings began. A deeply concerned senator from South Dakota, James Abourezk, opened the hearings with the following remarks.

> We have called these hearings today to begin to define the specific problems that American Indian families face in raising their children and how these problems are affected by Federal action or inaction...[T]here are few who are knowledgeable about the difficulties American Indians face in a matter of vital concern to them; namely the welfare of their children and families...It appears that for decades Indian parents and their children have been at the mercy of arbitrary or abusive action of local, State, Federal, and private agency officials. Unwarranted removal of children from their homes is common in Indian communities. Recent statistics show, for example, that a minimum of 25 percent of all Indian children are either in foster homes, adoptive homes, and/or boarding schools, against the best interest of families, tribes, and Indian communities. Whereas most non-Indian communities can expect to have children out of their natural homes in foster or adoptive homes at a rate of 1 per every 51 children, Indian communities know that their children will be removed at rates varying from 5 to 25 times higher than that...
>
> Because of poverty and discrimination Indian families face many difficulties, but there is no reason or justification for believing that these problems make Indian parents unfit to raise their children; nor is there any reason to believe that the Indian community itself cannot, within its own confines, deal with problems of child neglect when they do arise. Up to now, however, public and private welfare agencies seem to have operated on the premise that most Indian children would be really better off growing up non-Indian. The result of such policies has been unchecked, abusive child-removal policies...Officials would seemingly rather place Indian children in non-Indian settings where their Indian culture, their Indian traditions and, in general, their entire Indian way of life is smothered. The Federal Government for its part has been conspicuous by its lack of action. It has chosen to allow these agencies to

strike at the heart of Indian communities by literally stealing Indian children, a course which can only weaken rather than strengthen the Indian child, the family and the community. This, at a time when the Federal Government purports to be working to help strengthen Indian communities. It has been called cultural genocide.[55]

Over the course of the two-day hearing, witness after witness told their tales and Indian Country presented its case. The South Dakota senator would be their champion, and the days of unilateral power of state regimes to decide the fate of Indian children were numbered.

Efforts to Overcome the Hardships Imposed by Cases Like *Heim*

The *Heim* decision became final on October 21, 1976. As the ink dried on the adoption petition, political events in Washington, DC, were rapidly occurring. The stars began to align that year. Presidential candidate Jimmy Carter recognized the crisis and he made a campaign pledge, at the urging of Indian Country representatives, to address it.[56] That fall, Senator James Abourezk (D-SD), chairman of the Senate Subcommittee on Indian Affairs, introduced Senate Bill 3777 in the waning hours of the 94th Congress. It was an exploratory bill drafted by Hirsch and his AAIA colleagues.[57] The South Dakota senator urgently wanted to lay a legislative proposal on the table to generate feedback from Indian Country and set the stage for action in the 95th Congress.[58] Tony Strong, a Native Alaskan attorney who was on Abourezk's personal staff at that time, recalls the day Hirsch strode into his office with the legislative proposal in hand, saying, "We gotta get this bill introduced."[59] It was introduced three weeks later.

Momentum grew when the American Indian Policy Review Commission submitted its final report to Congress on May 17, 1977.[60] The report confirmed the existence of a crisis that could destroy Indian Country.[61] It found institutional racism in state regimes that made decisions "inherently biased by the cultural setting of the decisionmaker," and it offered legislative recommendations.[62] Two weeks later, Senator Abourezk introduced Senate Bill 1214, which would become the vehicle in the 95th Congress for the final law.

The provisions of Senate Bill 1214 (as well as its counterpart in the House) were informed by the oversight hearings and the policy review report and were carefully drafted to take advantage of the positive outcomes won in the Indian child-welfare litigation by incorporating those holdings and to craft language that would make it impossible for the negative outcomes to ever happen again.[63] For example, the extended family provision and the transfer to tribal court provision, in addition to other provisions of ICWA, ensure that the outcome in *Heim* would be different if decided in the post-ICWA era. Senator Abourezk wanted every provision of the law to be supported by case law or an existing state statute, and he wanted political support for the measure from states with large Indian populations—which Hirsch helped deliver, through legal research and agency advocacy, which were chores performed in addition to his congressional testimony (hearings are largely window dressing for the unsung work that goes on behind the scenes, outside of the hearing room).

True to his word, President Carter signed ICWA into law on November 8, 1978. He signed the bill at the urging of Indian Country and congressional leaders, over a veto threat by four cabinet heads from the Justice Department, the Department of the Interior, the Office of Management and Budget, and the Department of Health and Human Services. The Justice Department argued the law was unconstitutional; the Interior Department quibbled with it, as did the Mormons; and the Child Welfare League of America, an umbrella group for adoption agencies, staunchly opposed the measure—all to no avail. (Sometimes we do not want to know how laws or sausages are made.) In any event, Congress determined that it had ample power to enact ICWA under its plenary power over Indian affairs, because there is no greater threat to essential tribal relations and no greater infringement upon tribal sovereignty than interference with tribal control over Indian children.[64] The president agreed.

In placing the decision-making power over the fate of Indian children in the hands of their tribes of origin, ICWA does protect the essential tribal relations and sovereignty of Indian tribes over their internal affairs. Like *Cherokee Nation v. Georgia* (1831), the *Heim* case illustrates the harm state power can cause when it is allowed to intrude into that zone.[65] It is a grave reminder of the need for federal protection in the modern context. As the Supreme Court observed long ago in *Kagama v. United States* (1886), federal protection of dependent Indian tribes from unwarranted intrusions by state and local jurisdictions is a necessary feature of the American political system, because "the people of the states where they are found are often their deadliest enemies."[66]

The courts of the conqueror should have fulfilled that bulwark function. Instead, they allowed states to usurp and supplant tribal control over essential tribal relations, which created the threat of cultural genocide in the American heartland toward the end of twentieth century. Congress rid the nation of that dark cloud; and we have people like Bertram E. Hirsch to thank for their tireless efforts during the period when Indian Country went to Congress to take back the kids.

Today, the statutory protections of ICWA are being followed throughout the nation. Since 1978, thousands of reported and unreported cases have been resolved under the act.[67] Section 1911(b) grants tribal courts jurisdiction over children beyond reservation boundaries. This remarkable provision, which sprang from *Heim* and cases like it, was and is transformative, going beyond what any other law has ever recognized—a truly amazing feat that continues to be of major importance to every Indian tribe and has helped to retain thousands of kids within their tribal communities who would otherwise surely have been raised away from their tribes and extended families as a lost generation. Since 1978, the system has changed. A generation of tribal lawyers and administrators has worked in state and tribal courts and tribal child-welfare agencies across the nation to implement the law.

One evening, years later in Manhattan, Hirsch reflected on the past. Over dinner, he said that ICWA may not be perfect, but it has never been amended, and it is fulfilling its objectives. As we drank coffee, he urged tribes and practitioners to view the law as merely setting *minimum* standards, adding: "They should take advantage of their opportunity to incorporate the full measure of tribal culture and traditional law into tribal family codes." Indeed, by directing state courts to apply Indian cultural standards in making removal and placement decisions, ICWA is truly a culturally based federal Indian law with an Indian heart. As I walked back to my downtown hotel, I felt increased awe for ICWA and the historic movement that went into its making.

Times of adversity test the best in us, but in every crisis champions emerge. In his younger days, attorney Hirsch took a soldier's stance and confronted the system that took the kids. In so doing, he looked institutional racism in the face. At a very young age, he helped rid the nation of cultural genocide. We owe a debt of gratitude to him and AAIA. If it be true that contemporary tribal attorneys stand on the shoulders of giants, he is one of those giants in the field of federal Indian law. Much of what the Native American sovereignty movement sought to achieve was the halt and reversal of historical patterns that have been destructive to Native life. It is fitting that one of the early goals was to bring the children home. Many legal practitioners worked hard to make the world a better place during the modern era of federal Indian law, to be sure.[68] To me, Bertram E. Hirsch is a hero. For his work, one grateful client, the Sisseton-Wahpeton Sioux Tribe, adopted him at a General Council ceremony in 1975 and named him *Maka teca hoksina* (New Earth Boy).

Medicine Men

PART THREE
The Spirit World

CHAPTER TEN

Wana the Bear v. Community Construction:
Taking the Dead

STOCKTON, CALIFORNIA, IS ONE PLACE WHERE conquest really did occur. Founded in 1849, the town is named for Robert F. Stockton, a naval officer who drove the Mexican forces out of California during the Mexican-American War (1846–1848) and became California's first military governor. Stockton was a violent place during the gold rush, as miners systematically drove the Miwok Indians from their lands between 1850 and 1870, forcing them to leave their burial grounds behind.[1] Before the gold rush, at least 100,000 Indians inhabited California. By 1870, some 70,000 had died from disease and homicide.[2] Miwoks fled Stockton and the survivors found refuge with other bands in the region.

In 1979, bulldozers showed up at the burial ground and began clearing the land for a housing project. In the process, the remains of two hundred human beings were unearthed from the well-known Miwok graveyard.[3] As the numbers mounted, one of the descendants, Wana the Bear, attempted to halt the mass grave desecration and protect remaining burials. He filed suit for an injunction under an 1854 California statute protecting cemeteries. The law stated: "Six or more human bodies buried in one place constitute a cemetery."[4] The issue to be decided was whether this statute applied to the Indian burial ground.

Thus begins the story of *Wana the Bear v. Community Construction* (1982), one of the ten worst Indian law cases ever decided. The California Court of Appeals held that the Miwok burial ground is not a cemetery under California statutes since it was not used continuously as a graveyard without interruption for five years. The ruling that Miwoks failed to use the burial ground for the prescribed period failed to take into the account the fact that they had been *driven away* by the whites, and their cessation of use was involuntary, because the Indians fled from the barrels of gold-miner guns. Accordingly, the burial ground did not qualify for protection, and the court allowed the remaining graves to be dug to make way for the housing development. The public policy of protecting "places where the dead are buried" did not apply to this burial ground or those dead according to the court.[5]

The decision is notable not for its narrow and arguably ethnocentric construction of a cemetery statute, but because it illustrates something larger—the failure of lawmakers and the courts, who interpret the laws, to address, incorporate, take into account, and protect indigenous interests. That failure is anathema to any legal system that must be accountable to every segment of the society it is intended to serve, even the indigenous people. It is important to understand the root causes of this shortcoming, since the law ought to be accountable to every segment of society, lest any be left in an unprotected class. In addition, the failure in *Wana the Bear* to take into account the forcible displacement of the Indians when interpreting the cemetery law has other far-reaching implications. Like the Miwok, many Indian tribes were removed, relocated, or driven away from their homelands and forced to leave their dead behind. Those burials became subject to protection, if at all, by incoming settlers. But their laws seldom protected Indian burials. Consequently, uncountable numbers of graveyards became subject to despoliation after the removal of the tribes. On the Great Plains, my own people suffered this fate. No sooner were the Pawnee removed from their Nebraska homeland then settlers poured into their cemeteries to dig and cart away the contents.[6]

Wana the Bear illustrates that the courts were ill-equipped to apply an established body of statutes and common law to the circumstances and needs of Native Americans. The result was to leave Indian burial grounds in an unprotected legal status. Some legal commentators assert that the failure of the law to take into account legitimate indigenous interests is ethnocentric or at worst discriminatory. Others, such as lawyer H. Marcus Price III, point out that indigenous interests were simply outside of the realm of non-Indian experience when statutory and common law were being developed in the eighteenth and nineteenth centuries. Indeed, most disputes between Indians and whites in that formative period were settled on battlegrounds rather than courtrooms. Price states:

> At a sensitive time when American courts were developing an experience-based common law and legislators were enacting specific statutes for cemeteries and burials to account for American requirements, the courts and lawmakers were not allowed the benefit of considering practical issues related to the appropriate disposition of prehistoric aboriginal remains and grave goods or regarding the property rights of Indians to these items. Thus, when issues later surfaced in the courts, the judicial system was forced to apply an established body of statutes and common

law to situations that law had not previously considered and with which it was ill suited to deal. This resulted in decisions like *Carter v. City of Zanesville* (Ohio, 1898), in which the court held that decomposed skeletal remains of prehistoric Indians did not constitute a body as contemplated at law, and *Wana the Bear v. Community Construction, Inc.* (California, 1982), in which an established Miwok traditional cemetery was held to not constitute a cemetery for purposes of the California state statute.[7]

According to Price, when the law is confronted with new situations that it has not previously encountered or had the opportunity to consider, "seemingly bizarre and anomalous legal resolutions can occur."[8] That may be so, but his conclusion begs the question, how could a legal system overlook the basic interests of an entire race of people in its midst during the development of the law? This is puzzling, because indigenous people were not invisible, and their issues and circumstances were known to the public, if not well understood. *Wana the Bear* thus illustrates either an ethnocentric judicial mind-set or some other shortcoming in the development of the law. I shall argue here that it is the product of much larger forces at work—the legacies of conquest and colonialism imprinted upon the legal system.

Regardless of the causes, the impact of the legal system's failure to reflect or take indigenous needs into account is the same: little or no legal protection was afforded for Native American burials. The loophole in legal protections allowed hundreds of thousands of Native American dead to be dug up and carried away in disregard of the sensibilities of affected Native American communities.[9] This mass appropriation amounted to a glaring double standard in the law, since non-Indian graves have never been treated in such a manner anywhere in the United States. Over time, the double standard affected every Indian tribe, Alaska Native village, and Native Hawaiian community in the nation. Each suffered an invasion of body snatchers of every description—tourists, developers, pothunters, treasure seekers, amateur or professional archaeologists, museum collecting crews, soldiers, and federal agencies—in a bizarre national pastime first set in motion by Pilgrim landing parties at Plymouth Rock in 1620. The looting continued unabated until state lawmakers began closing loopholes in the 1980s, and Congress finally put a stop to it on a national level in 1990 with the enactment of the Native American Graves Protection and Repatriation Act (NAGPRA).[10]

In this chapter, I will summarize the history surrounding the disturbance of Indian graves and the appropriation of cultural patrimony from tribal communities in the United States. I will probe the forces at work that explain the double standard in the law illustrated by *Wana the Bear*. My analysis will expose shortcomings in the legal system that allowed manifest injustice and permitted unequal treatment of Native Americans to reach massive proportions by the 1980s. Finally, I examine the national grassroots movement that arose in Indian Country to seek legislative reforms on the state and national levels. By the 1980s, shortcomings in the legal system highlighted the need for new laws.

A remarkable grassroots movement took hold in Indian Country during the 1980s. The state and federal laws passed in the ensuing years today comprise a considerable body of law that increases legal protections for Native American graves, establishes national procedures for the repatriation of Native dead, and provides guidelines for recovering other cultural items illegally taken from Indian Country during the colonization period in Manifest Destiny when staggering amounts of cultural property were taken from burial grounds, battlegrounds, and communities in one of the most massive transfers of movable property ever seen. The legislative movement culminated in 1990, with the passage of NAGPRA. This landmark human-rights law continues to be implemented almost one generation later, often over the fervent opposition of some scientists, museum workers, and universities who see themselves as the self-appointed guardians of Native American dead and cultural patrimony.

In examining these issues, it will be necessary to review the historical relationship between Native Americans, anthropologists, and museums. There has often been a fascinating love-hate relationship between these communities since the founding of anthropology and American museums in the United States. On the good side of the Indian/museum relationship, museums play an important role in educating the public about Native Americans, and they have preserved much of the cultural patrimony from earlier periods when the federal government was otherwise bent on destroying Native culture. Many close, mutually beneficial relationships have been forged in recent years between these communities, and numerous tribes own and operate their own museums. On the dark side, historical museum collection practices have often been rapacious until recent decades and included collecting human remains and other sensitive cultural material from tribal areas under dubious circumstances; and museums have been slow to return material improperly acquired when requested by the Native owners and descendants of the dead, sometimes taking as long as fifty years to decide repatriation requests. Since the passage of NAGPRA, these parties have improved their relationships during the consultation and repatriation processes. Many anthropologists devoted to the study of Native Americans are members of a discipline, which includes archaeology and physical anthropology, that has frequently exploited and harmed Native peoples in their research, collection, and publication practices in sensitive areas, by placing their professional interests over the well-being of the peoples that they study, especially when it came to the taking of the dead. In recent years, many in that profession have improved their ethics and attitudes toward the people they study. Unfortunately, some museum and anthropology workers refuse to accept the social changes mandated by NAGPRA, preferring to darken relationships with Native America for reasons of their own, which shall be examined in the postscript section of this chapter.

In examining the interplay between the sacred and the secular and the need for the law to be accountable to all social values in a community, one legal and religion scholar, Wallace H. Johnson, observed that justice can be measured by the way society mediates these diverse, sometimes competing ingredients:

> All communities are defined by the values which hold that group together. A key value that defines the quality of a community, either ancient or modern, is respect and protection for the rights of all, whether in the majority or those on the fringe. A challenge for us in contemporary society is to understand that our 'community' includes indigenous peoples; the burial practices and 'rites' associated with passage to the afterlife are as important to them as the Christian beliefs of our majority population are to us. We will be judged as a culture by how we react to protecting those beliefs.[11]

The Spiritual Dimensions of Human Burials and the Afterlife

Up until now, our inquiry into the dark side of federal Indian law has examined how law and the courts affect mundane Indian affairs—that is, the earthly affairs of the living. Beginning with this chapter, we depart to another plane. We shall examine how the spiritual side of Native American life is impacted by the legal system. That investigation takes us into the Spirit World, a mysterious realm where immense mystical power abides and profound explanations about our place in the cosmos can be found.[12] The logical starting place for this journey is that sacred moment in everyone's life when we give up the ghost, the time when the spirit leaves the body at the cessation of life and travels to the Land of the Dead.

What happens when we die? Nobody really knows. But the question has concerned and confounded humans since the dawn of time. Myriad answers have been handed down through the ages by every culture, religion, and place where mankind has contemplated mortality and impending death. Does human consciousness end at death? Dust to dust, and nothing more? Or do we somehow pass into the mysterious beyond? The afterlife is variously described by laymen as passing through the pearly gates to a heavenly place where winged angels strum harps upon the clouds; going to the happy hunting ground, for the heartier hunter/gatherer souls among us; or sailing off into the sunset to Valhalla by Vikings and old soldiers who fade away. Many fear the prospect of afterlife in an intolerable inferno where improvident souls, wretches, and most lawyers are consigned. Or do we return to this earth—like a bad penny—reincarnated in the form of an animal, plant, or person?

Religion was founded in large part to answer these questions. One commentator observed:

> After a lifetime of investigation of the origin of religious structure, the great Sir James G. Frazier concluded that awe toward the dead was probably the most powerful force in forming primitive systems for grappling with the supernatural.[13]

Unfortunately, world religions cannot agree on the answer. Illustrating the perplexing diversity of religious belief, one man's article of faith seems utter folly, and perhaps rank heresy or superstition to another. Perhaps, viewed in their best light, all of the answers supplied by the world's religions are correct, or none at all. We cannot *really* know if there is but one right answer, as insisted by the true believers of each faith. "There are many tickets to heaven," explained the late Wallace Black Elk, a Lakota medicine man, when referring to the bewildering variety of churches. Besides, how can one choose, and what if the wrong choice is made? Black Elk counseled, "the safest bet is to buy all the tickets." At the end of the day, every belief is entitled to respect. Only those completely secularized minds that have long been estranged from the magic side of human life will dismiss beliefs in life after death as barbarous superstition. Yet even secularized Americans must stop short of treading on the sacred so long as First Amendment values continue to adhere and be cherished.

Two things from world religion are clear, however. First, awe and respect toward the dead is widespread. Second, many religions and cultures do believe in an afterlife in a spiritual world (however described) as a central article of faith. Indeed, much time is spent by clergy imparting the necessary wisdom and rules for finding the path to the Spirit World and staying there. Both of these attributes of religion are common in Native America. As an example, my family got a glimpse of the afterlife from my great-grandfather Echo Hawk. It is said that in 1923, the old warrior fell ill and died, but recovered shortly thereafter and came back to life. He explained what he saw in his vision:

> I was walking upon the prairie, when all at once I heard singing coming from over the next hill. When I came to the hilltop, I saw a great Pawnee earth lodge village on the other side of a river and my folks were standing on the far bank—healthy, young, and dressed in fine Indian clothes. I hurried down to the river and naturally wanted to cross to be with my family, but my relatives said, "No, my son, you cannot cross this river until you grow your hair long and in braids."[14]

One year later, after Echo Hawk grew his hair into braids, he passed away. The afterlife has always been central to Pawnee belief. The existence of life after death was confirmed many times during the Ghost Dance. Adherents frequently fell into trances, went to the Spirit World, and saw visions that are memorialized in our Ghost Dance songs about the afterlife. The belief in life after death goes far back in time, to the days in Nebraska when priests sent spirits of Pawnee dead to the North Star, who placed the souls of the departed upon the Milky Way (then called the Spirit Trail) to be blown by wind to the Spirit Star in the southern sky—a celestial Spirit Chief who received the spirits and oversaw the Land of the Dead located in the heavens, below the southern horizon. Tobacco-smoke offerings are still made to those ancestors in the southern sky. Hence, the old-timers not only believed in the afterlife, but knew where it was and how to get there. Those ancient beliefs in life after death are corroborated and strengthened by the Christian churches that have sprung up in Pawnee Country and they continue to be observed today in tribal ceremonies, such as the Pawnee funeral feast.

All Native American tribes and communities have a rich variety of traditional spiritual beliefs surrounding death, the spirit, and the afterlife.[15] Ceremonies have always been held to prepare the dead, consecrate their remains and make them holy, and to place sacred objects in the grave with the body to help the dead make their sacred journey to the Land of the Dead so relatives there will know that they were well-cared for on Earth. Even today, Indian "undertakers" perform vital services in their tribal communities. Respect and awe command that, once buried, the dead, their place of burial, and their burial possessions not be disturbed, as this can harm the dead, cause their spirit to wander, and even bring harm to the living who allow this to happen.[16] These beliefs prohibiting disturbance of the dead are similar to rules followed by Orthodox Jews and many other peoples in all ages, cultures, and places around the world. One legal commentator on these commonly held religious beliefs has correctly observed:

> The sepulture of the dead has, in all ages of the world been regarded as a religious rite. The place where the dead are deposited all civilized nations, and many barbarous ones, regard in some measure at least, as consecrated ground. In the old Saxon tongue the burial ground of the dead was "God's acre."[17]

Indeed, the laws in every state prohibit grave robbing, mutilation of and tampering with the dead, unlawful possession of human bodies and body parts, and grave desecration.[18] This demonstrates that the sanctity of the dead and the sensibilities of the living are deeply ingrained in our own mainstream society, even though many consider themselves secularized folks with rational outlooks that eschew superstition and dismiss the supernatural, often even the sacred.

What do courts have to do with death and the afterlife? The law exists to serve its host society and protect the system, and it is supposed to reflect the values and ideals held by members of society. Since mankind's beliefs surrounding death, the afterlife, and the proper treatment of the dead are embodied by every society into a set of taboos, protocols, mores, and sensibilities, it becomes the chore of law to protect that belief system. The law thus prescribes the appropriate treatment of the dead, including their human remains, burial possessions, and place of sepulture. A significant body of law exists in the United States for these purposes.[19]

Even though Native Americans share the same reverence, respect, and religious sensibilities concerning death, the afterlife, and the proper treat-ment of the dead as the rest of humanity, the law has not always protected those beliefs and practices. Since the landing of Pilgrims, who opened the first Indian graves, American history has been marked by a bizarre double standard: American law strictly protected the graves of non-Indians, while allowing, even encouraging, hundreds of thousands of Indian graves to be looted.[20] Unless we deny that Indians are human beings or adopt the pre-tense that their religious traditions regarding death do not amount to reli-gion, it is difficult to explain the discrepancy and impossible to justify treat-ing dead Indians any differently from the dead of any other group. Is this a case of simple religious discrimination, or are there larger forces at work?

Factors That Spurred the Appropriation of Dead Indians and Cultural Patrimony

Much has been written about the Native American repatriation movement in recent years. A burgeoning body of literature, both here and abroad, analyzes the array of dynamic, sometimes competing, social interests at stake, such as human rights, race relations, religion, science, scientific racism, education, museums, ethics, law, and social change.[21] This section focuses on the two causative factors that gave rise to the repatriation movement. They remain at the heart of the problem, as threads that tie all the issues together: the first is the double standard in law and social policy concerning treatment of the dead in the United States; and the second is the social mind-set that accom-panied America's scramble for cultural patrimony, taken from colonized Native American communities when the government's guardianship powers over Indian wards of the government were at their zenith (circa 1880–1934). These causative factors can only be understood against the background of the twin themes studied in this book, colonialism and conquest.

Colonialism is a political and economic institution devoted to a one-way transfer of all forms of property from Native to non-Native hands. The very purpose of colonialism is to extract land, resources, and wealth from colonized lands. Those goals continued to be pursued in settler states, and in most colonies and settler states, that even included the appropriation of indigenous dead, grave contents, and other movable cultural property taken from indigenous communities. The hard evidence lies in the British Museum, Smithsonian Institution, the Louvre, and other large museums of the colonizing powers, which are filled with dead bodies and cultural patrimony seized from colonized lands.[22] These pursuits in harvesting the works of Native peoples and their dead most assuredly followed the flag into Indian lands colonized at home and other possessions of the American empire in distant lands overseas. As noted by Franz Boas, an anthropologist and avid museum collector, imperialism "imposed upon our scientific institutions a duty of familiarizing the American people with the inhabitants of the countries for whose welfare we have made ourselves responsible, for whose future developments and progress we shall be held to account before the judgment of history."[23]

Notions of conquest also added fuel to the one-way transfer of property. Conquerors typically view cultural property belonging to the vanquished as spoils of war, available for the taking by the conqueror. Plunder and pillage are as old as war itself, as seen in the looting of occupied lands by victorious conquerors all over the world—done by Babylonians, Romans, Vikings, Crusaders, Cortés, Pizarro, Napoleon, English shoplifters in Africa, and, most recently, in the systematic plunder of Europe by the Nazis.[24] Sadly, much of the world's art and cultural property has been displaced by war. This has created potent political issues and prompted decades of hard work since 1946 by postwar European nations to repatriate millions of objects, unfinished business that occupies those nations well into the twenty-first century.

In the United States, a similar process occurred. The Indian wars (1776–1890) took place over a vast theater of war in which untold thousands were killed and displaced. Spoils of war were taken from battlefields and burial grounds during that period, and later, more systematically, from subjugated communities.[25] Despite the explicit US Army prohibitions against the looting of private property, religious objects, and works of art that were promulgated by President Abraham Lincoln in 1863 in the Lieber Code, the bluecoats amassed wagonloads of battlefield booty from Indian villages and the bodies of slain Indians.[26] The Cheyenne Dog Soldier ledgerbook drawings taken from the Battle of Summit Springs, Colorado, may be one prominent example.[27] That practice was followed by civilian combatants in individual acts of violence as well. The soldiers and settlers established precedent for the fervid "rip and run" operations conducted by museum collecting crews in later years when it was safe to do so. While the collectors conquered no one, they took advantage of the fortunes of war, if not the spoils.

The Role of the Scientific Community in Fomenting Appropriation of the Dead

Scientific interests played several pivotal roles in fomenting the massive transfer of dead Indians and cultural patrimony from Native communities that was set in motion by the forces of colonialism and conquest found in Manifest Destiny. The scientific community created the demand for this material, provided legitimizing rationales for the appropriation of it from tribal areas, and anesthetized the way Americans viewed Native American dead and allowed them to reconcile disparate racial treatment. Furthermore, the mantle of science is used today by some in the museum and anthropology communities to justify retention of Native American dead in the collections of museums, universities, and federal agencies. The central role of the scientific community is therefore fundamental to understanding the forces at work that led to the taking of the dead.

First of all, the early fields of phrenology, archaeology, and anthropology and the newly established American museums created an insatiable demand for dead Indians and other cultural booty.[28] Scientists needed crania and other Native American body parts as specimens for their studies and experiments on race. Before the Civil War, Dr. Samuel Morton hired gravediggers to obtain hundreds of Indian skulls to support his research.[29] Then the search for Indian body parts was joined by the US Army. The Surgeon General's order of 1868 directed army personnel to procure Indian crania and other body parts for the Army Medical Museum.[30] In ensuing decades, thousands of heads were taken from battlefields, burial grounds, POW camps, hospitals, fresh graves, and burial scaffolds across the country as the military decapitated Indians in haunting places and ghastly events like the Sand Creek Massacre and the Fort Robinson Breakout.[31] At the end of the Indian wars, when the army ended its head-hunting policy, museum collecting crews rushed in and competed with one another to see how fast they could take bodies and cultural property from tribal areas. One skeleton collector, Franz Boas, remarked that stealing bones from Indian graves is "repugnant work" but "someone has to do it."[32] One account of robbing Blackfeet graves in 1892 is chilling.

I collected them in a way somewhat unusual: the burial place is in plain sight of many Indian houses and very near frequent roads. I had to visit the country at night when not even the dogs were stirring…after securing one [skull] I had to pass the Indian sentry at the stockade gate which I never attempted with more than one [skull], for fear of detection…On one occasion I was followed by an Indian who did not comprehend my movements, and I made a circuitous route away from the place intended and threw him off his suspicions. On stormy nights—rain, snow & bitter cold, I think I was never observed going or coming, by either Indians or dogs, but on pleasant nights—I was always seen but of course no one knew what I had in my coat…The greatest fear I had was that some Indian would miss the heads, see my tracks & ambush me, but they didn't. I regret the lower maxillae are not on each skull, I got all I could find, and they are all detached save one. There is in the box a left radius & ulna of a woman, with the identical bracelets that were buried with her. The bones themselves are nothing, but the combination with the ornaments makes them a little noticeable.[33]

As late as the 1930s, one Smithsonian anthropologist, Ales Hrdlicka, traveled to Kodiak Island, Alaska, and over the objections of the Native residents, removed more than three hundred remains from a local burial site.[34]

Historian Douglas Cole documented the heyday of collecting in the Pacific Northwest, between 1875 and 1925, and concluded:

During the half-century or so after 1875, a staggering quantity of material, both secular and sacred—from spindle whorls to soul catchers—left the hands of their native creators and users for the private and public collections of the European world. The scramble for skulls and skeletons, for poles and paddles, for baskets and bowls, for masks and mummies, was pursued sometimes with respect, occasionally with rapacity, often with avarice. By the time it ended there was more Kwakiutl material in Milwaukee than in Mamalillikulla, more Salish pieces in Cambridge than in Comox. The city of Washington contained more Northwest Coast material than the state of Washington and New York City probably housed more British Columbia material than British Columbia herself.[35]

Even today, American museums, with the help of private collectors, are the major source of world demand for the cultural patrimony of indigenous peoples from other lands—causing a massive transfer of cultural heritage from the Third World to suburban living rooms and museum showcases in America.[36]

The scientific community toiled to legitimize the process by providing the nation with a set of very rational scientific justifications for the seemingly rapacious acts of colonialism and conquest. In a classic case of scientific racism, pseudoscientific theories generated during this period animated widespread belief in the supposed racial inferiority and lack of humanity of indigenous peoples, making it easier to stomach the unpleasant invasion of graveyards and clandestine pillaging of ceremonial houses.[37] *Scientific racism* is a term that commonly denotes (1) obsolete scientific theories on race developed by the mainstream scientific community in the nineteenth and twentieth century, (2) contemporary racist propaganda, disseminated by governments, institutions, and individuals, disguised as scientific research or argument, and (3) politically motivated research aimed to scientifically justify racist ideology or discriminatory treatment.

When the appropriation of Native America took place in the nineteenth and twentieth centuries, scientific racism was at its zenith. It was manifested by the mainstream scientific community through the use of physical anthropology, craniometry, phrenology, eugenics, physiognomy, and other disciplines concerned with the classification of humans into distinct races and racial categories. Supposedly innate traits—such as intelligence, morals, habits, and the capacity for civilization—were assigned to the races as immutable facts discernible to scientists from the study of human body parts, mainly skulls. Their findings supported master-race ideologies, and their theories postulated notions of racial superiority. By paying close attention to race and physiological differences, these disciplines provided the world with scientific support for popular racism of the day.

The immense harm caused by this work was not limited to Native America. The scientific fodder was eagerly embraced by segregationists and supremacists, who harbored racial prejudice. The pseudoscientific theories provided support and ideological justifications that were endorsed by governments, institutions, and individuals to justify mistreatment of racial and religious groups around the world. Science was thus enlisted to uphold slavery and quell moral doubts about that institution, to anesthetize the mass removal of American Indians from their homelands, to clothe colonialism in the mantle of the white man's burden, to numb the mind to systematic Nazi persecution and destruction of the Jews, to sustain unjust apartheid governments, and to underpin judicial doctrines that supported the foregoing activities and, in the United States, to legitimize slavery, racial segregation, and dispossession of American Indians in the courts of the conquerors.

Of most interest here, during the colonial era, researchers earnestly claimed to prove scientifically that Caucasians are superior to indigenous peoples. Though anathema today, the many books, studies, findings, and claims of scientific racism were widely endorsed in the nineteenth and twentieth centuries. They clothed simple prejudice and base racism with the imprimatur of science. That made it much easier in the minds of the conquerors and colonizers to stigmatize, marginalize, and dispossess people who inhabited the lands they invaded. Also fundamental to scientific racism during that period was the undisputed assumption from medieval times that Western culture is the pinnacle of social evolution in the entire world, an ethnocentric idea that underpinned colonization in every corner of the Earth. Though repudiated today by the mainstream scientific community, it is hard to unring the bell. Scientific racism was the undergirding for the double standard in American law and social policy that allowed the mass invasion of Indian burial grounds to be carried out by a society that would never violate the sanctity of its own graves, and it also fueled the rapacious collection of cultural patrimony documented in historian Douglas Cole's *Captured Heritage*.[38]

The scramble for bones and patrimony in the United States mirrors European collection practices in other indigenous lands during the colonial era.[39] Today, the museums of those nations are the principle holders of the cultural treasures, bones, and patrimony of the Third World primarily because of their colonial histories. In the United States, the massive transfer that stripped Native America clean was justified by museum collectors at the time by the mantra of the white man's burden, which they said placed a duty upon the colonizers to collect as much as possible before the red man disappears into extinction. That justification proved to be incorrect. Native America did not vanish. However, it was denuded of its material culture.

Science anesthetized the way that secularized Americans view Native American dead and allowed them to treat Indian dead in ways they would never treat their own. *Our dead are human beings, but their dead are specimens that should be retained for study by scholars and experiments in laboratories.*

This doublethink allows the public to reconcile disparate treatment in laws and policies that protect the sanctity of the dead for everyone, except Native Americans. In the scientific viewpoint, there is no evidence that Indians have a relationship to departed spirits, and tribal beliefs or experiences relating to the dead, or spirits of the dead, are mere superstition. According to the late Vine Deloria Jr., a well-known theologian, attorney, and author, the secular mind "denies the possibility or importance of the after-life and limits human responsibilities to tangible things that we can touch."[40] Yet, at one time, that attitude was not prevalent—all cultures once viewed the dead and their places of burial with great religious awe, and disturbance was strictly taboo. American law still reflects those religion-based sentiments when applied to non-Indian burials, just as strongly as it did in Pilgrim days.

The gradual elevation of science over religion in the United States produced a secularized society that can comfortably view dead Indians as specimens that rightfully belong to scientists, rather than as human beings who are dead persons entitled to rest in peace. Thus, teachers and schoolchildren could view opened Indian cemeteries in tourist attractions without batting an eye.[41] Deloria traced the trend toward secularism in a series of articles that even today comprise the intellectual foundation for the Native American repatriation movement.[42] That trend deserves some elucidation because it defines the current climate for considering Indian efforts to repatriate their dead, which will be examined later.

Medieval Europe once followed two traditions of thought that regarded faith and reason as "equally viable paths to truth."[43] The organized religions in that part of the world were gradually overtaken, for a variety of reasons, by secular science in demonstrating truth. By the time of the writing of the US Constitution, it was felt necessary to rein in the organized religions to curb religious abuse, conflicts, and persecution in the religion clauses of the First Amendment and to separate church from the secular affairs of the state. Even so, during early colonial times, the organized churches played a significant role in everyday life. They addressed social issues, such as education and charity for the poor, and influenced the literature and policies of the day. Over the decades, churches withdrew from active involvement in the public arena and confined themselves to weekly services, membership/fund-raising drives, and bingo. The organized churches did make occasional pronouncements on issues such as abortion, birth control, and the death penalty. Sometimes they ventured forth into political contests in the harness of right-wing candidates. But for the most part, the everyday business of education, health, welfare, culture, and government was left to others.

Deloria thus observed that a "major phenomenon of this century has been the erosion of the power and influence of organized religion in American society."[44] This demise gave birth to what he and others have described as the rise of a new "civil religion" in which organized church groups took a backseat to a melding of scientific, secular, and bureaucratic thinking by administrators and institutions that hold purely secularized views and see the world through the eyes of the hard sciences. This outlook becomes base scientism when it rejects all other sources of knowledge, as I will further discuss in chapter eleven.

The civil religion views birds, plants, and animals of the natural world and human beings predominately as phenomena that can be subjected to scientific study. Since no other values are recognized, it is easy to believe in a need "to use Indian human remains for scientific work, teaching material, and public displays" as a central article of faith.[45] Hence, Native Americans were confronted with the widespread attitude of federal agencies, museums, and universities that Indian remains are "resources, comparable in most respects to timber, oil, and water, belonging to the federal agency on whose land they were found," or in museum storage boxes.[46] Indeed, the Antiquities Act of 1906 and the Archaeological Resources Protection Act of 1979 declare that dead Indians found on federal lands are "archaeological resources" belonging to the federal government, which can be excavated with permits, so long as they are permanently curated in museum or university repositories.[47] Historian Robert E. Bieder observes that the human body in science has become depersonalized and desacralized: "Gradually liberated from its religious moorings, the body—according to scientists—ceased to be a temple of the soul and became data," and any religious scruples compromised in the names of science or medicine in the acquisition, retention, and treatment of that data "proved even weaker when the bodies involved belonged to other races."[48]

In this climate, Native Americans would have to justify repatriation of their dead to the new civil religion. Deloria predicted tough sledding:

> The power of civil religion and the inability of organized religion to articulate a set of values superior to those of the state combine to define the present situation in the following manner: Religious behavior must be justified on secular grounds in order to be protected.[49]

To the high priests of civil religion in museums, repatriation of the dead was akin to book burning—that is, the unwarranted destruction of data. As stated by James Hanson, director of the Nebraska State Historical Society in 1988, "a bone is like a book…and I don't believe in burning books."[50] He demanded proof that the soul actually uses burial offerings in the next life and challenged the Pawnee to "prove that their religion is being affected by our possession of [Pawnee dead and their burial offerings]."[51]

The mantle of secular science continues to be used today to justify retention of dead Indians, only the arguments are different in the postcolonial era. It is harder to defend the legacies of conquest and colonialism, because it is no longer credible or kosher to claim that Indians are savages doomed to extinction, to appeal to notions of racial or cultural superiority, or to assert a birthright to harvest dead bodies and movable cultural property from tribal areas. Those arguments are vestiges of scientific racism, repudiated at the close of the colonial era. Thus, apologists and defenders needed to produce new reasons to retain the Indian dead who have lain in their collections for over a century. This is the new white man's burden, and one that is nearly impossible to sustain. Why? The retention of bones and cultural patrimony of other peoples can be rationalized on almost any grounds, but none can completely ignore the mode by which these things were acquired. Against the secular arguments stands the other and older pathway to truth—religion. And the validity of the sacred in this debate is buttressed by another value that is larger than the state—the human rights principle. Against these pillars, the secular arguments made from behind the curtain of science are themselves in for a rough time in the postcolonial age.

Religious Discrimination, Ethnocentricity, or Were Larger Forces at Work?

The root causes of the double standard in American law that effectuated the mass transfer of dead Indians and cultural material are clear. To be sure, lawmakers and courts were ill equipped to prevent that pattern. But it was not simply because the needs of indigenous peoples were obscure to them when formative law developed. It is hard to imagine that the legal system was altogether blind to the needs and experiences of the marginalized Native peoples living in its midst. Their needs were known or knowable, but they were simply ignored or considered unimportant out of a combination of ignorance, ethnocentricity, and, above all, the malaise commonly found in colonies and settler states during periods of colonization and conquest. This conclusion emerges as the most plausible explanation when the forces of conquest and colonization are examined.

Against the background of those forces, indigenous dead were fair game in the public mind. That mind-set also created a duty to appropriate as much Native patrimony as possible as part of the white man's burden. These forces simply marched unopposed through loopholes created by lawmakers, who made cemetery, archaeology, and other laws pertaining to the dead that ignore or fail to consider Native American interests. In interpreting those laws, courts like the one in *Wana the Bear* failed to serve as a protective bulwark. A double standard emerged because the legal system would never permit the rapacious taking of non-Indian dead in the same manner and scale. It would take a sea change in public opinion to halt the destructive process set in motion by this potent combination of forces and reverse it through means of repatriation, tasks that would fall to Congress during the modern era of federal Indian law.

The lessons that can be learned from the seemingly bizarre outcome in *Wana the Bear* are important for those legal systems that have the complicated task of serving democratic societies composed of diverse peoples with different cultures and needs. Inequitable treatment can easily arise from the simple lack of knowledge of marginalized segments of society, as pointed out by Price. Manifest injustice can also arise from the insensitive and inflexible enforcement of policies implementing a variety of laws designed for worthwhile purposes that fail to take into account their impact upon the needs of indigenous peoples, as seen in the Indian child welfare crisis of the 1970s and the mistreatment of Indian dead from 1620 to 1990. The anomalous outcome in *Wana the Bear* bespeaks a pressing need for the law to be consciously responsive to every segment of society, so that it is attentive to the needs and circumstances of even the weakest and most misunderstood among us. That is the weighty responsibility of all three branches of the federal government, as well as every state: to ensure that the laws are made, administered, interpreted, and enforced in a manner that is accountable to all groups that comprise our diverse society. It is the defining role of the judicial branch and the legal profession to remain ever vigilant to ensure that this is done. Failure to achieve these goals caused unwarranted disturbance in the Land of the Dead.

The Native American Grave Protection and
Repatriation Movement

As Indian tribes gradually regained control over their sovereignty and solidified their place in the American political system, they were increasingly better positioned to demand legislative attention to the mistreatment of their
dead. By the 1980s, it could not be ignored since virtually every tribal community was affected and the problem began to worsen. During that decade,
pothunters continued to pour into private and public lands to dig graves,
discard bones, and cart away the contents to sell in art, museum, and antiquity black markets. Shocking incidents were widely publicized in the press,
which plastered onto front pages across the nation photographs of hundreds
of open graves on private land, strewn with bones. Reporters also caught
developers digging out thousands of bodies to make way for resort hotels
in Hawaii and other parts of the nation, or housing projects, as seen in the
Wana the Bear litigation. The overt disregard for the dead witnessed by the
public in these incidents shocked the conscience and turned the stomach of
many in Indian and non-Indian communities alike.

At last, society began to rethink the treatment of Native American
dead. Awakened by the startling *Wana the Bear* decision in 1982, California lawmakers sprang into action by passing a law to protect Indian burial
grounds the same year. Price noted:

> Prompted by increased looting and vandalism of Indian burials and
> monuments, and by the example of dramatic cases such as *Wana the
> Bear v. Community Construction, Inc.*, California has enacted one of the
> most sweeping and severe "unmarked burial" laws in the nation.[52]

Other states soon fell into line as lawmakers confronted similar problems in
other parts of the nation. Lawmakers quickly grasped the need for new laws
after being educated about the problem by the Native American communities.[53] By 1990, thirty-four states enacted similar measures in a national trend
toward closing loopholes in grave protection laws, and state courts handed
down decisions upholding the new laws.[54] The process marked a significant
social change in attitude as society began to view Native American dead in
a new light, as human beings. Though some old-school archaeologists accustomed to viewing Indian graves as their personal property opposed the grave
protection movement, it was by and large supported by the mainstream

scientific community, although for different reasons than those of Native American communities (we want to preserve Indian graves for our studies and these "resources" should not be despoiled by common looters).

During the 1980s, concern also focused on museums as facts about their enormous collections of the dead came to light. In the mid-1980s, tribes and organizations began demanding information about those collections and filing repatriation claims. In Washington, DC, Indians learned the Smithsonian Institution alone housed over eighteen thousand Native American skeletal remains and footage of the long, green boxes stacked from floor to ceiling shocked Indian Country.[55] Would those institutions give back the dead? Not without a fight.

All of Indian Country gathered for the repatriation struggle, which resulted in the passage of several groundbreaking state repatriation laws in Nebraska, Kansas, and Arizona in 1989 and 1990.[56] During that movement, which eventually culminated in the enactment of NAGPRA, many current and former staff members of the Native American Rights Fund (NARF) worked alongside tribal leaders and clients, community members, and local, regional, and national Native organizations, such as the National Congress of American Indians (NCAI) and the Association of American Indian Affairs, to litigate the issues, educate the public, and lobby for new federal and state laws.[57] By the end of the decade, all Indian tribes, Alaska Native communities, and the Native Hawaiian people worked together to change the way America views their dead and to make social change.

Numerous bills were introduced in Congress between 1986 and 1990. My closest associate on the national level during this pivotal time was Suzan Shown Harjo, a former NARF legislative specialist and longtime repatriation advocate, who was then serving as the executive director of NCAI. Since the 1960s, Harjo has been one of the predominant figures in Indian Affairs within the Beltway—a seasoned veteran with fingerprints on over five hundred laws passed during the modern era of federal Indian law, including the American Indian Religious Freedom Act of 1978.[58] Only a handful today know from an inside perspective how the landmark laws of that era were made, and she is one of them. From our side of the table, she deftly guided the strategy for navigating NMAIA and NAGPRA through political waters in the nation's capital, avoiding pitfalls and booby traps in the backwaters, hallways, and hearing rooms of Congress. It was an honor to work at her side during that time. I proudly call my dear friend and associate "sister."[59]

The numerous federal repatriation bills did not move far in Congress over the opposition of the museum and science communities until two things happened. The first was the temporary derailing of the effort by Washington insiders to obtain the enormous Hyde collection of American Indian cultural materials and to make out of that collection a brand new museum within the Smithsonian Institution chain devoted to the American Indian. Native American repatriation activists threw a stick into those cogs, which frustrated efforts in the Senate to grease the wheels for the new museum. They demanded that the Smithsonian agree to include a repatriation requirement as part of the legislative package it so desperately wanted and needed to build the new museum as a condition for obtaining Native American support. How, in good conscience, could Native America support a new Smithsonian museum devoted to its heritage with all those skeletons in the closet? This eleventh-hour demand to address the skeletons in the nation's attic led to a repatriation agreement finalized at the Coyote Café in Santa Fe, New Mexico, in a meeting between the Indian negotiators—Suzan Shown Harjo, executive director of the National Congress of American Indians, and myself—Bob Adams, the secretary of the Smithsonian Institution, and Senator Ben Nighthorse Campbell. The agreement was incorporated into the pending bill and signed into law as the National Museum of the American Indian Act of 1989 (NMAIA).[60] This law created a federal precedent for NAGPRA, enacted a year later. NAGPRA applied the Coyote Café policy to the rest of the nation.

The second development that broke the case in the national repatriation debate was the human-rights principle agreed to by Native American, museum, and science leaders during a yearlong dialogue (1989–90) sponsored by Senator John McCain (R-AZ) at the urging of museum representatives. The dialogue centered upon the appropriate treatment of human remains, funerary objects, and cultural patrimony held by museums. The major principle agreed to by the participants was that "the process for determining the appropriate disposition and treatment of Native American human remains, funerary objects, sacred objects, and objects of cultural patrimony should be governed by respect for Native human rights."[61] The report from this dialogue was presented to Congress and became the framework for NAGPRA. The rest, as they say, is history.

Are Any Arguments for Keeping Native American Dead Valid These Days?

A final word is in order before we leave the Land of the Dead. Any major civil-rights or human-rights law takes generations to fully implement. This is true for NAGPRA, especially given the national scope of the problem and massive numbers of dead Indians involved. As the nation set about the task of repatriation, the initial step required federally funded museums, universities, and federal agencies to identify and conduct an inventory of the dead Indians, Alaska Natives, and Native Hawaiians in their collections. This took several years, but 150,887 persons were identified. (This figure does not include additional human remains held by institutions that receive no federal funding, or museums in foreign countries, because those institutions are not covered by NAGPRA.) Of these 150,887 persons, museum researchers identified the name, tribe, or cultural affiliation of 32,054 dead persons by 2008. They were duly repatriated, along with 669,997 associated funerary objects, to their kin and appropriate Native American communities under the NAGPRA process.[62]

However, the vast majority—118,833 individuals—had not been repatriated by 2008. Why? The museums, universities, and federal agencies are unable to ascertain their identities—that is, their cultural affiliation to particular American Indian and Native Alaskan tribes. Consequently, they are America's unknown Native American dead. The issue now confronting the federal government is to determine the proper disposition of these unknown dead, because NAGPRA commands that a process be developed for their disposition. After years of consultation with the Native American, science, and museum communities, the secretary of the interior published a proposed rule in 2007 that would require their repatriation to specified Native American communities whenever museums, agencies, and universities cannot establish their "right to possession," which is defined in the proposed rule as "possession obtained with the voluntary consent of an individual that had authority of alienation."[63] This disposition has generated sharp debate. On the one hand, Native America widely supports that disposition, because it comports with mainstream values in Native America and is also consistent with the laws and social policies of mainstream society that guarantee a decent burial for each person, whether or not their identities are known. On the other side of the debate, some scientists and museums would like to keep these dead, even when there is no "right to possession," on the grounds that they are valuable scientific data. They urge that these dead are specimens that must never be buried, but should be permanently retained for future scientific studies or scholarly research.

The scientific value of most of these 118,833 dead is highly debatable. Most of these persons died in recent historical times. Unfortunately, their identities and provenance are currently unknown for a variety of reasons, such as: (1) government removal of Indian tribes from their aboriginal lands and the shuffling of Indian tribes across the country during the course of American history; (2) the loss over the years of pertinent museum records by staff or inadequate curation practices (like stuffing remains in boxes and forgetting about them for sixty or seventy years); (3) the lack of provenance information furnished by the persons who turned these dead over to museums and agencies; (4) inadequate museum consultation with Indian tribes concerning the cultural affiliation of these dead; and (5) though most are simply unknown Indians who died in recent historical times, in some instances the antiquity of some of these Native American remains makes their cultural identification difficult.

Thus, despite the much-heralded miracles of science, the finest university minds and museum professionals who have spent their entire careers studying these dead Indians now profess they do not know who they are and could only identify 20 percent of the dead Indians in their collections. This abysmal figure is puzzling. Their seeming inability to identify these dead (i.e., assign a reasonable relationship between them and appropriate Native American groups based upon a simple preponderance of the evidence) stands in *stark contrast* to proven ability of forensic specialists in the American military to speedily, efficiently, and accurately identify the human remains of nearly all American war dead from foreign combat zones. This is successfully done by the military under far more trying and complex circumstances: sometimes decades after the dead died in POW camps; sometimes after individuals were killed and their remains scattered on the battlefield; sometimes when commingled remains were recovered from common graves, and often with only a few body parts to work with. However, the military is *highly motivated* to make those identifications, for the sake of families and communities at home, whereas the academics are not. To the contrary, they resist making straightforward identifications under NAGPRA since that means those dead must be repatriated and they will lose control over their "specimens" and "data." Thus, the reluctant scientists charged with the statutory task of identifying these dead spend more time, energy, and brainpower thinking of reasons *not* to repatriate them, especially ancient dead, than identifying them in a timely manner. Hamstrung by conflicts of interest, they are the last opponents of the national repatriation policy. Very much like the last Japanese soldiers to surrender years after hostilities ceased in World War II, the custodians of these 118,833 dead Indians are caretakers of one of the last vestiges of colonialism in the land and the heirs to a dubious legacy of scientific racism that underpinned that bygone era.

Given their conflict of interest, the scientists' new justifications for permanently retaining these dead should be carefully scrutinized. Instead, they are uncritically accepted by most people, and the press, as an article of faith simply because they are pronounced by scientists from behind the cloak of science. *It must be correct, if scientists say so.* But once the cloak is removed, the reasons are frail and unpersuasive.

Many justifications ignore the elephant in the room and shrivel when considered in the larger social context: quite simply, the right of burial is a social norm uniformly guaranteed by mainstream society to every person who dies by the statutes in all fifty states. This extends to known and unknown dead, as well as to persons buried by their family or friends, or if none exist, by the state. It includes unclaimed dead, unknown strangers, paupers, and indigents, and even prison inmates or other institutionalized persons who die without friends, funds, or next of kin. While some laws allow medical or scientific study of the dead in narrow circumstances, they uniformly require burial in every instance within a reasonable time after study.[64] In no instance does the law allow anyone to permanently withhold any human remains from burial within a reasonable time. Consequently, it would be unprecedented and highly extraordinary in mainstream society to permanently deny the burial of Indians simply because their identities are unknown. As you will see, the radical departure from this norm that is urged by the museum and science communities is simply not supported by the kind of compelling justifications that one would expect.

Why Some Museums and Scientists Want to Keep Dead Indians

The following is a list of the top ten justifications given by some museums and scientists for keeping dead Indians in the twenty-first century, with accompanying analysis.

1. Indian remains are a national resource: they have great value to science; profound and sophisticated experiments are being conducted on them with the promise of great things for Indians and all of humanity. There are three criticisms of this claim. First, where are the profound studies? Without substantiation, this justification is simply a bare appeal to science. Many tribes have been sorely disappointed in the lack of significant relevant information produced by the mass disinterment of their cemeteries. For example, after nearly a century of secretly studying thousands of dead taken from Pawnee graves, without the knowledge or consent of the Pawnee Nation and without permits normally required by state law, leading scientists proclaimed that "Pawnees ate corn." We could have told them that. They also concluded that "Pawnee have lived in the region a long time," but they do not know for how long, or where we came from. We could have told them we were placed in the Great Plains by the Creator during the Creation and have lived there ever since. But then, the secular mind dismisses the sacred and demands proof that religious beliefs are true. Turnabout, then, seems fair play. Can we now insist that science be made to prove its claims?

Second, the scientific community has never convincingly identified or explained the peculiar characteristics of Indian bones and body parts that make them more valuable for study than the remains of other races. What can possibly be learned about the human condition, diet, the prevalence of disease, and most other pressing subjects by the exclusive study of Indian bones that could not be gleaned just as well, if not better, from the bones of other races? Indeed, the remains of other races stand to yield better information since more is known about their identities, provenance, and circumstances. Taken to its logical conclusion, the endpoint of the argument that Indian bones can yield interesting information applies with equal force to the human remains and cemeteries of every racial, ethnic, and economic group in the nation; and this conclusion strongly suggests that they, too, should be dug up and retained for scientific study, if we are to take this argument seriously. But it is only Indians who are targeted and placed into laboratories. And the stockpiling of Indian bones seems hardly necessary to plumb reliable information about Native America, because most information on things like their diet, social and economic conditions, and history are readily available in voluminous historical accounts, ethnographies, and Bureau of Indian Affairs annual reports, and from the oral traditions of the people themselves. By contrast, the contributions to knowledge about Native America found in the conclusions, conjectures, and theories about the more distant past that is drawn from the study of bones have proven to be very speculative.

Assuming for the moment that Indian remains are a one-of-kind national resource, there still remains the thorny matter of consent to study the dead. There is no unfettered scientific right to study human body parts. Permission has always been required by science to study the dead of any other race. Scientists cannot simply appropriate and study human body parts in any nation without first securing the donor's voluntary consent, permission from the next of kin, or otherwise complying with strictly regulated procedural safeguards in a legitimate manner. There is no question that scientific research done at the expense of human rights is inherently immoral, as seen in the German medical experiments performed upon involuntary subjects during World War II.[65] Sure, interesting things were learned, but at what cost? That society cannot abide such conduct is well illustrated by the laws in all fifty states that comprehensively regulate the medical or scientific use of dead bodies. Those statutes permit such research only under socially acceptable and carefully prescribed conditions involving informed consent by the deceased, next of kin, or other authorized representative, such as those safeguards that are provided in the anatomical-gift laws and the criminal laws that prohibit grave robbing, desecration, mutilation of the dead, and the unlawful possession of dead bodies. Thus, even if the 118,833 Indian dead are important to science, this does not automatically confer an unfettered right upon scientists to retain them. Dennis Baak, a senator in the Nebraska legislature, made these observations in 1990 when supporting the repatriation and reburial of Pawnee dead, despite the avowed historical importance of those human remains:

> The way I look at it, we will be burying a part of history, but we probably didn't have the right to dig up part of Native American history to start with. I became convinced that the artifacts are such a part of their religious beliefs that we have no right to keep them. Their religious beliefs are also part of our history. By putting them back, we are honoring part of our history, rather than reburying it.[66]

2. The ancient past is not just the heritage of a single group—it belongs to the whole world. We are all the same species, and no one living culture, religious group, interest group, or biological population

has any moral or legal right to the exclusive use of ancient skeletons. Hmmm. The "we are all one" argument is a completely different song than the one sung by scientists in the nineteenth and twentieth centuries, when scientific racism claimed that Indians and Negroes were not the same species as Caucasians—or if some relation exists, there are vast differences in the scale of intelligence, morals, habits, and capacity for civilization. Moreover, in the age of colonialism the doctrines of Manifest Destiny and the white man's burden allowed one single group to take control of the ancient, as well as recent, remains of all colonized peoples. Leaving aside this change in tune, many today would dispute the underlying premise of this argument that there is a common humanity, saying there is no such thing due to the great diversity that splinters our species into many independent and concrete historical locations, cultural moorings, and religious outlooks. Besides, how is *common humanity* defined and who gets to define it? But, getting down to the nitty-gritty, the argument is flawed because (1) it is legally infirm; (2) the circular argument defies logic; and (3) it is at odds with other anthropological interests and the human rights of indigenous peoples.

First, the contention that human remains, ancient or otherwise, can be "owned" by the whole world is legally incorrect. It flies in the face of the common-law rule that dead people are not property that can be bought or sold in the marketplace as chattel.[67] The common-humanity argument that bones are the cultural heritage of all of human society and cannot therefore be controlled by any one nation is at odds with the laws of every nation that strictly control the cultural heritage and cultural property found in its territory.[68] Thus, the notion that cultural property and archaeological resources are the property of no one and can be controlled by no single nation or group is simply not the law. The Archaeological Resources Protection Act and the Antiquities Act vest the ownership of archaeological resources, including bones, found on federal and Indian land in the United States.

Aside from legal infirmities, the circular argument defies logic. By asserting that scientists can keep Indian bones since no one group, nation, or culture can own or control them is a transparent argument that disguises their own property ownership claims. *Gee, if no one owns these things, we get to keep them.* The reasoning is like the legal fiction employed by Australian colonists to appropriate aboriginal land—this is vacant land owned by no one.

Finally, the argument ignores other paramount anthropological interests entirely. The contention that no single living culture can own or control ancient human remains ignores cultural continuity to the past—the well-spring of every living culture—and the relationship between the living and the dead found in the sacred side of every indigenous culture where those remains were obtained. The ability to discard those well-known anthropological cultural interests so that the interests of physical anthropology can be served shows the lengths to which the proponents are willing to go to retain their specimens. They would throw the baby out with the bathwater. During the colonial era, the cultural interests of the indigenous peoples in their own past were subordinated. However, the United Nations Declaration on the Rights of Indigenous Peoples closed that loophole in 2007.[69]

The declaration protects indigenous people from the destruction of their culture and actions that deprive them of their integrity, cultural values, or ethnic identities. Importantly, it recognizes their right to maintain, protect, and develop the past, present, and future manifestations of their culture, including archaeological sites. In that regard, states are required to develop mechanisms to return property taken without their free and informed consent or in violation of their laws, traditions, and customs. In particular, Article 12 recognizes "the right to repatriation of their human remains," and it requires states to repatriate both "ceremonial objects and human remains in their possession through fair, transparent and effective mechanisms developed in conjunction with indigenous peoples concerned." The argument that indigenous dead belong to or can be controlled by no single group or culture is refuted by the declaration; and violations of the minimum standards set forth in the declarations are considered human-rights violations.

Dr. Jeanette Greenfeld, an international expert on cultural property (which includes archaeological remains) examined the "we are all one" argument in the international context and concludes:

> Generally speaking it is clear that cultural property is most important to the people who created it or for whom it was created or whose particular identity and history it is bound up with. This cannot be compared with the scholastic or even inspirational influence on those who merely acquire such objects or materials. The current arguments about the retention of major objects on the grounds of scholarship are no longer tenable. In most instances the task of learning has been satisfied, as for example with the Rosetta Stone, whose hieroglyphics have already been deciphered. The Parthenon and its marbles continue their hold on the imagination

but they no longer have a relevancy significant for twentieth-century Europe. The continued scholastic value of keeping the marbles in Britain is debatable...Scholasticism can be a high-sounding motive for a selfish and unrelated purpose. Museum claims of universality are also suspect because...they cannot be invoked unilaterally but must be determined by the international community...The retention of art treasures can be rationalized on almost any grounds, especially the sanctity of the 'collection.' However this ignores the fact that when the international collections were made, they were done at the cost of destroying the completeness of the 'collections' of other peoples, and it chooses to ignore completely the mode by which many treasures were acquired.[70]

3. We must keep Indian remains permanently for future studies, because new techniques might be developed and new questions might be asked. What can possibly justify keeping human remains for more than a century, much less forever? There comes a time when objects have been so thoroughly studied that scholars can no longer justify retaining them. This applies even to world treasures, such as the Elgin Marbles and the Rosetta Stone. Indian remains are simply not a world treasure like the Rosetta Stone; they are first and foremost human beings. Are there so many studies that scientists must keep these remains for more than a hundred years? Or are these dead being retained so each new generation of scholars can simply repeat old studies with new techniques? The laws in the United States that do allow the medical or scientific study of dead people in narrow circumstances provide guidance. They sometimes allow indigent prison inmates, paupers, or wards of state institutions who die without friends or next of kin, and who thus must be buried at state expense, to be used for medical or scientific study before burial—but they uniformly require that those remains be buried after study. In no instance do any of those laws allow scientists to keep those remains permanently. Those limits are placed out of respect for the dead and they should be adhered to in the case of the American Indians as well. If the argument of the scientists is carried to its logical conclusion, the paupers, unclaimed dead, and institutionalized persons to be buried at state expense in their labs should never be buried—because doctors and scientists can always think of more studies or new questions to ask; nor should the dead of any race be buried, because over time, their remains will become ancient—yet we never hear the voice of science crying over the burial of those dead. Nor do the scientists contribute their own dead to museums in the hope that new techniques and questions will someday in the distant future make them valuable to science.

4. Archaeologists have an ethical obligation to the past. Ancient remains cannot speak for themselves, so we have to tell their story; and our ethical obligation to do this is more important than any rights of the descendants. This appeal to high-sounding scientific ethics to subordinate conflicting indigenous interests is contrary to the Principles of Professional Responsibility of the American Anthropological Association (1971), which state: "In research, an anthropologist's paramount responsibility is to those he studies. When there is a conflict of interest, these individuals must come first."[71] Thus, the "archaeologist's burden" cannot justify retaining the dead when it conflicts with the expressed interests of the very indigenous peoples they study. Native America has clearly said it wants these Native American dead to receive a decent burial consistent with their mainstream cultural mores and religious sensibilities, which fall within the ambit of the United Nations Declaration on the Rights of Indigenous Peoples, as well as the policies that underlie the laws in all fifty states respecting the treatment of the dead, including unclaimed and unknown dead. Whatever obligations are assumed by archaeologists, whenever their professional or private interests conflict with the interests, rights, and well-being of the Native people they study, the interests of the Native people must come first under the controlling ethics of their own profession.

Many secular minds simply assume that this self-imposed obligation "to speak for the dead" is sacred, because it is part of the civil religion, but this scientific interest is neither sacred nor does it rise to the level of religion. What is at stake are very real religions and sacred obligations of indigenous people in the United States that extend deeply into the Land of the Dead in ways that the secular mind lost track of many generations ago. Taken to its logical conclusion, the secular interest in science can run roughshod over human rights under this argument, because the plain implication is: even if Indians may have religious connections to the dead, or to the spirits of the dead, which is doubtful to the purely scientific mind-set, the secular interests and perceived obligations of a small group of scientists and scholars take precedence. The flaws and contradictions in the crude attempts by the scientific and museum communities to dismiss Native religious interests in this fashion were soundly criticized by Deloria in 1989:

The human remains of American Indians are, to this way of thinking, an important national resource over which [scientists] alone must have custody. They do not and will not admit the proposition that Indians have any sentiments at all towards their dead. And if such a belief is true, the attitude is that it really doesn't matter and that the secular claims of a small group of scientists and National Park Service museum directors should have precedence over the religious beliefs and practices of American Indians...The schizophrenia here is painfully clear. How can people hold these contradictory views? Either Indian religions are a real tradition to be experienced and protected and from which it is possible to learn, or they are not. If they are valuable, there should be no question that they should be protected in the fullest capacity of the law as rapidly as possible, without any debate whatsoever. If Indian religions are not valuable, then scholars and theologians and the general public should stop the traffic in Indian artifacts, cease visiting reservations for research and spiritual enlightenment, and return all of these worthless things lying around museums and art galleries to the simple people who do, in their primitive ignorance, cherish these things.[72]

5. Just who do these Indians represent? Since identities of these 118,833 dead are unknown, how can Indian tribes speak on their behalf, and what interest do they have concerning the disposition of these dead? It does not matter that the identities and particular cultural affiliations of these 118,833 Native American dead are unknown, because American law in most jurisdictions allows unrelated friends of the dead to undertake the responsibility for burial when the next of kin cannot be found. The law takes great pains to see that even unknown dead will receive a decent burial, if by no one else, then by the state. We need look no further to find support for this proposition than the Tomb of the Unknown Soldier in Arlington National Cemetery, where thousands assemble daily to honor unknown war dead, even though no one knows who is entombed there.

The NCAI represents over 250 tribal governments. Their position is expressed in a 2003 resolution, which states that the disposition of these unknown Native American dead "must be made by the appropriate Tribes and Native Hawaiian organizations in concert with the group's customary traditional practices, wishes and beliefs," and those dead should be "speedily repatriated to Native peoples in accordance with procedures to be determined by contemporary Native American groups."[73] The tribal governments assert the widespread belief in Native America that these 118,833 unknown dead are related to contemporary Native Americans as their nearest culturally connected relatives and they have undertaken the governmental responsibility for their disposition. There is nothing unusual in that at all, because governments undertake the responsibility to bury unclaimed and unknown dead every day under American statutes. There is no dispute that these are Native American dead, but the "who do you represent" argument ignores the continuity to the past maintained in traditional Native American communities and the close spiritual ties to the Land of the Dead that bind indigenous people to these dead, no matter how ancient they may be, as an important part of their histories and cultural and religious traditions—attributes of indigenous life that are recognized and protected in the United Nations Declaration on the Rights of Indigenous Peoples, the human-rights policy that underlies NAGPRA, and by the federal trust responsibility to preserve and protect the culture and traditional religious beliefs and practices of Indian tribes.

If the scientists' concern that no one has standing to undertake the responsibility for burial of unknown dead is taken seriously, then why not let them dig older sections of American cemeteries to exhume persons without next of kin simply because their relation to any living person is unknown? This argument, if taken to its logical conclusion, would place large numbers of those dead into the keeping of scientists.

6. We spent our time and money and invested our reputations obtaining and studying these 118,833 specimens. Why should we give them to folks who made no such efforts to retrieve them? Besides, we will lose our livelihood if we return this material. This self-interest argument must be given short shrift under the conflict of interest ethical statement in the Principles of Professional Responsibility of the American Anthropological Association (1971), discussed earlier. The livelihood justification surely drives the folks who depend most heavily upon the study of Native American dead for their income, but that self-interest is not discussed much in public due to the conflict of interest prohibition that governs the study of anthropology. Native America should not be made to subsidize career choices with its dead at the cost of its cultural integrity, religious freedom, and human rights. In those instances where museums, universities, and agencies cannot establish their right to possession under the rule proposed by the Department of the Interior, the remedy for scientists with particular study interests in specific dead is to present their case for studying them to the appropriate Native American communities who are granted control over those dead by the proposed rule. If a convincing presentation is made, further study might be granted. Indian tribes are not antiscience when their human rights are not trammeled. To the contrary, they commonly employ archaeologists and work closely with anthropologists every day as part of their daily governance, and they enjoy close working relationships with scientific staff. However, the truth of the matter is that the physical anthropologists who have spent their careers in laboratories studying dead Indians, often against the wishes of their tribes of origin, are afraid to speak to living Indians in tribal communities, much less in tribal government settings.

7. It does not matter how these dead were obtained, or why Indians want them back, because the study of the bones promotes enormously important values, such as education, scholarship, and science. Let's forget about the way the bones and patrimony were obtained—the past is ancient history and Indians cannot unring the bell. This utilitarian argument puts the proponents on dangerous moral ground, because it says theft and looting are okay so long as the end justifies the means. Even the civil religion must be accountable to morality, which is one value higher than the state itself. Study done at the expense of human rights is both immoral and illegitimate. This includes study done through the clandestine taking of the dead, as the Dr. Frankenstein literature and films lecture to us. He produced a scientific marvel, bringing life to the dead, but was still hounded and persecuted by the appalled townsfolk for his reprehensible scientific conduct. We cannot put science upon such a great pedestal that its work and interest become sacrosanct regardless of the means by which it is performed. The mass appropriation of Native American dead was unscrupulous then as it is indefensible today. This places the defenders and would-be caretakers of those dead today in a difficult moral position to justify further, much less permanent, retention of those dead. As stated by Greenfield, "The wholesale looting and plundering and (sometimes fraudulent) 'purchasing' of objects by dominant countries is a continuing blot on the saga of the growth of archaeological learning."[74] The ends do not justify the means, and it is impossible to ignore how these dead were obtained. Though that history of past events cannot be changed, the tide of history that previously favored taking the dead now favors repatriation, and it should not be dismissed by arguments that would have us ignore how the bones were obtained. Though some may argue that the bones were obtained legally and in accordance with society's mores at the time they were taken, they will have a full opportunity to test that contention on a case-by-case basis under the right-of-possession standard in the proposed rule.

8. Indians are religious fundamentalists, anti-intellectuals, and antiscience. They are being unreasonable—they want to destroy collections, which are like libraries. The only good Indian is an unburied Indian. When all else fails, these name-calling arguments and personal attacks resort to rabble-rousing and making bare appeals to inflammatory prejudices to bring public sentiment and animosity against Native people. This smacks of the old-fashioned scientific racism employed by their predecessors; and it certainly has the press marching to the beat of their drums. Native Americans will survive those attacks, but they are unwarranted. Hopefully, an attack by secular science upon one of the last remaining traditional religious groups in the nation will not be supported by mainstream America.

9. We know what is best for you. Indians should spend their time on other problems. Your descendants might condemn you for burying these dead, whose remains might be of interest to them in future generations. This is a paternalistic argument. Native Americans must look to their own tribal governments and spiritual leaders to know what is best for us. Thanks anyway, but we cannot rely upon scientists in laboratories who have never spoken to living Indians or interacted with living tribal communities for guidance in our affairs.

10. Burial goods should not be returned. As a last-ditch effort, this argument says "At least let us keep the funerary objects." In some cases, this interest in coveted grave objects of great monetary value and scholastic interest (like the peace medals interred in Pawnee graves) is a strong motivating factor in museum resistance to repatriation claims.[75] Yet this argument ignores the role of funerary objects in Native American mortuary traditions, as well as the common law rule that funerary objects are not "abandoned" property available for the taking (otherwise graves would be subject to despoliation as soon as the next of kin leave town). The proposed rule should not sanction simple grave robbing by exempting associated funerary objects from repatriation along with the human remains they were interred with. It is a common practice of everyone to inter their dead with personal possessions— clothing, religious items, and mementos of every description. We do not need to prove that the dead really need any of these things or that they actually use them in the afterlife for them to be protected from looters. The living reasonably expect that once those items are placed in the grave with the dead that they shall stay with the dead. No exceptions should be made for Indians, as long as those sentiments and expectations are shared by Native Americans.

With these observations about the top ten reasons given by scientists and museums to keep dead Indians, our examination of how the law and social policy impact the Land of the Dead comes to the end of the trail. Since the days of *Wana the Bear*, the disturbance of that spiritual realm has been slowed by NAGPRA. Someday, all Native dead will be reburied, just like all other American dead. When the living close that double standard in the law once and for all, the dead can rest in peace.

McBelieve

CHAPTER ELEVEN
Employment Division v. Smith: Taking the Religion

Reuben Snake was one of the greatest tribal leaders of the twentieth century. He realized if *Smith* were allowed to stand, it could be the death knell of the Peyote Religion of the Native American Church. He created a coalition to go to Washington and fight for his religion. The goal seemed impossible: overturn the highest court of the land without a dime in his coffers! When asked how he proposed to do this, he replied: *With a frequent flier coupon and a prayer.* Then he added with a soulful smile: *We'll find good friends along the way.*

—James Botsford, attorney for the late Reuben A. Snake Jr.[1]

THE REMARKABLE STORY about how Reuben Snake overturned a Supreme Court decision deserves to be told. He led an improbable movement in the 1990s to overturn *Employment Division v. Smith* (1990), one of the most unpopular cases of the twentieth century.[2] This tale is about the human spirit. It will uplift freedom-loving people everywhere because it involves a quest for religious liberty. Many books and articles have been written about the *Smith* decision and its far-reaching implications, but little has been reported about the Native American movement that overturned *Smith* through the passage of the American Indian Religious Freedom Act Amendments of 1994.[3] That story will go down in history as one of our nation's finest hours. I know. I was there. This chapter tells how it was done.

In the late 1980s, the United States Supreme Court heard four Native American religion cases that changed the face of the law.[4] Each of these cases refused to apply extant First Amendment principles to Native American free exercise of religion claims. The cases were decided by the conservative axis of the Ronald Reagan Court led by Chief Justice William Rehnquist. The axis backed away from the task of protecting tribal religious practices. The doctrines announced in those cases made it clear that the First Amendment will never be interpreted by the Rehnquist Court to protect tribal religions. The rulings, of course, devastated Native America. They impacted every tribal community in Indian Country—one of the most marginalized segments of our society already marked by a long history of religious discrimination. The rulings emphatically rejected any constitutional protection for them. This chapter exposes the factors that led to this anomalous situation in the "land of the free" and how Indian Country responded to the utter lack of legal protection by the courts toward the end of the twentieth century.

Historically, American courts had a poor track record in protecting Native American religious liberty during the nineteenth and twentieth centuries. In the absence of judicial protection, the government enjoyed free rein to restrict tribal religious liberty for almost two hundred years, as if no constitutional protection existed for Native America at all. By 1990, the Supreme Court gave up that task entirely in the *Smith* case and referred the matter to Congress. The judicial mind-set that allowed this loophole in religious liberty is puzzling because the protection of individual liberty is the defining role of the courts. In our system of government, the task of safeguarding minority rights and personal freedom from the excesses and abuses of majoritarian will expressed by the political branches falls to the judiciary. James Madison explained the special obligation of the courts as the guardian of the Bill of Rights when he presented that foundational document to Congress.

> If they are incorporated into the Constitution, independent tribunals of justice will consider themselves in a peculiar manner the guardians of those rights; they will be an impenetrable bulwark against every assumption of power in the Legislature or Executive; they will be naturally led to resist every encroachment upon rights expressly stipulated for in the Constitution by the declaration of rights.[5]

This critical check on the balance of governmental power in our democratic system collapsed when it came to Native American worship. How can any religious faith be excluded from the ambit of the First Amendment? Was it a simple legal anomaly, or something darker?

Several forces explain the judicial system's nearly complete failure to protect tribal worship in Native America. If viewed narrowly, the Indian religion cases are seen only as products of an insensitive court system that experienced inordinate difficulty understanding and protecting a set of religions vastly different from those more familiar to American judges. That explanation, however, is not entirely correct, as the courts have protected exotic faiths imported from other lands, such as the animal slaughter rituals of the Santeria religion, of African origin, imported from Cuba or the sacramental ingestion of the hallucinogenic *hoasca* tea imported from the Amazon rain forest by white Americans who belong to the O Centro Espírita Beneficente União do Vegetal Church.[6] Thus, we cannot explain the courts' failure to protect indigenous religion by the apology, "Gee, I can't understand your religion."

In the case of Native American religion, the courts were captive to larger, more powerful forces that resulted in the near eradication of tribal religion—that is, settler-state policies animated by religious discrimination against tribal religions. This form of discrimination and intolerance was particularly pronounced because it was propelled by the forces of conquest and the mind-set of colonialism. No other religious group in the United States has been subjected to these forces, which virtually preordained the suppression of tribal religion as a matter of government policy and pressing social imperatives in a settler-state society. Historian Patricia Limerick concluded that the government's campaign against Indian religions was an integral part of the conquest of the American West.

> By the 1890s, the wars of conquest were officially over; but the power politics of conquest remained unsettled. The actual battles were, in many ways, only a prelude to this campaign on the part of the agents to convince the Indians that...the Government is supreme, and will do what it pleases with them or theirs...In this context, the suppression of religious freedom carried down-to-earth meanings of power and dominance. To the agents of the 1890s, religion could rebuild a people's morale; religion could make them defiant; religion could make them hard to rule. In those terms, suppressing religion was as vital a part of conquest as sending troops out to engage in direct military combat.[7]

The government also sought to eradicate tribal religion as part of its program to end Indian culture in the late 1800s as part of the assimilation, civilization, and tutelage policies. These policies prevailed when the federal government ruled Indian tribes by guardianship.[8] Rule by guardianship was common in colonies and settler states during the age of imperialism, where it was popularly referred to as the white man's burden. The will to suppress tribal religion during the conquest, colonization, and guardianship processes was animated by religious intolerance. Europe's history of religious intolerance was carried to the New World by Columbus. It informed the goal of colonialism to supplant colonized people. It was easier to marginalize and dominate Native people by discounting their religion and replacing it with a supposedly superior one. The legal systems in colonized lands supported that work, or at least turned a blind eye toward the destruction of tribal religion. These forces rubbed out many tribal religions around the world in the nineteenth and early twentieth centuries.

Even after the colonial era came to a close, American courts continued to retain many nineteenth-century attitudes seen in Indian religion cases. That continuing failure to understand and respect Native American religious beliefs and practices is partially due to the progressive secularization of American society during the twentieth century, which has pushed all religions aside. *Smith* completed the secularization process insofar as the law is concerned by placing the sacred firmly under the control of secular political institutions. In short, against the forces of conquest, colonialism, guardianship, religious intolerance, and secularization, the courts cast aside their bulwark function during the nineteenth century and allowed the American legal system to become part of the process of marginalizing and supplanting tribal religion. Together, these potent forces molded a legal system that allowed the government to infringe upon and destroy tribal religions in ways the courts would never tolerate for other religions. The end result was a loophole in religious liberty that lingered in the courts of the conqueror many decades after those policies were repudiated by the larger society. Ultimately, that judicial mind-set produced noxious legal doctrines in *Smith* so out of step with mainstream values that the task of protecting religious liberty has largely been taken away from the courts and placed into the hands of Congress.

The legal doctrines of *Smith* spring from two Supreme Court decisions decided in 1988 and 1990. In *Lyng v. Northwest Indian Cemetery Association* (1988), the Supreme Court began the process of eviscerating Native religious freedom. *Lyng* allowed the US Forest Service to destroy a tribal vision questing site located on Forest Service land by building a dirt logging road through the holy place.[9] Even though the Court conceded the road would destroy the holy place and associated religions of three tribes that were dependent upon visions and other activities performed there, it held that no burden was placed upon Indian religious practices within the meaning of the First Amendment. That astounding leap of logic was achieved by narrowing the reach of the First Amendment to almost minute proportions—the

Court reasoned that government can destroy an entire religion without burdening any religious practices so long as it does not (1) punish someone for practicing his religion or (2) force a person to violate his religion. Only in those narrow circumstances does the First Amendment apply, according to the *Lyng* Court. Thus, the government can destroy a holy place and render worship impossible *without burdening anyone's religious worship*, so long as it does not punish people for practicing their religion, nor force them to violate their religion. This remarkable judicial sophistry rests upon a pure legal fiction: that the government can destroy an entire religion without burdening any religious practices. It strips Native American holy places of any constitutional protection and frees the government to destroy religions, so long as government does not punish the practitioners nor force them to violate religious tenets. *Lyng* deserves (and will receive) further analysis in its very own chapter.

Smith continued the slide down the slippery slope greased by *Lyng*. *Smith* held the First Amendment does not protect the sacramental use of peyote in religious ceremonies of the Native American Church (NAC). In *Smith*, the controversy was over a small cactus that grows in the United States only in the Rio Grande valley of Texas. The plant has naturally derived mind-altering properties from mescaline. When ingested, it can produce psychoactive effects. Though medical studies have not documented any adverse medical or psychological problems among American Indians due to their religious use of this plant, peyote was outlawed as an illicit drug as part of the war on drugs.[10] These laws have produced controversy over the ceremonial use of this plant by tribes—a religious practice that may span ten thousand years.[11] Archaeological radiocarbon dating dates Peyotism in the Rio Grande valley to 5000 BC, long before Columbus arrived and the United States was founded.[12] This religious tradition is much older than Christianity. Due to its antiquity, Peyotism is classified as one of the "primal" religions of the world (i.e., one of the oldest religions that came before the rise of the historical religions).[13] Today, some 250,000 American Indians practice the Peyote Religion. It is perhaps the oldest, most continuously practiced religious tradition in the western hemisphere. The NAC is the modern, organized embodiment of this indigenous religion, called The Peyote Road. The central tenet is the belief that the peyote plant has a spirit, just like us. Through the Creator, peyote is a profound plant of power that can communicate with people, assist their prayers, heal the sick, and help

Indians lead a better life. Because of these attributes, peyote is considered a holy sacrament given to the Native people and is part of the body of the Creator. Profound religious ceremonies have amply demonstrated the mystical powers of the peyote plant to untold thousands of American Indians over centuries of ceremonial use.

It was a tall order to exclude an entire religion with 250,000 members from the ambit of the First Amendment. That feat was accomplished only by conducting major surgery on the First Amendment and associated legal precepts. First, the Court exempted all criminal laws and all civil laws of general application that restrict religious liberty from the reach of the First Amendment. This enormous new exception *rewrote* the First Amendment to read: Congress shall make no law prohibiting the free exercise [of religion], *except all criminal statutes and all civil statutes of general applicability.* Second, *Smith* discarded the legal test developed by the Supreme Court in earlier cases for protecting religious liberty under the First Amendment, known as the "compelling government interest" test. Under that test, government may not infringe upon a religious practice unless it is necessary to protect a compelling government interest of the highest order and there is no less restrictive way to protect that interest. The Court was concerned that this test was too stringent—that is, too many religious practitioners might benefit from such a strict test and carve too many exceptions to general laws necessary to accommodate their religious practices. Thus, the Court scrapped the test, saying that American religious diversity is a "luxury" our nation cannot afford.[14] Third, the Court raised the bar for constitutional protection of religion by adding new requirements that worship will not be protected when the government burdens religious liberty unless that action also violates some other additional First Amendment freedom, such as freedom of speech, association, or the press. This new requirement has no legal basis and was pulled out of thin air to arbitrarily place additional hurdles in front of citizens seeking to protect their religious liberty. Finally, *Smith* prohibited courts from accommodating religious practices. It told minority religious practitioners to go to Congress, instead of the courts, when general laws infringe upon their religious practices. The defining role of the courts as protectors of religious liberty was brought to an end in *Smith*, even though the Rehnquist Court knew that unpopular minority religions have little chance of securing political relief from the very institutions that threaten them.[15] As noted in the dissent, religious liberty is threatened when it is placed alongside other, private interests that must be lobbied for in the political arena.

In short, the new rules announced in *Lyng* and *Smith* snuffed out hope that tribal religion will be protected by the First Amendment. Why did the Supreme Court go so far in the Indian cases to trash the First Amendment? Legal scholars have analyzed the remarkable gymnastics used by the Court to restructure and restrict First Amendment jurisprudence in the *Smith* line of Indian cases.[16] The Court did not tiptoe through the tulips. Rather, the conservative axis brazenly ignored established legal precedent, openly abandoned legal tests that it considered too tough on the government, and carved gaping exceptions that place nearly every kind of statute beyond the protective reach of the First Amendment.

In the end, these gyrations rationalized such a diminutive view of the Constitution that *almost no protection for worship remained for anyone!* American Indian religion was the miners' canary. The doctrines of the Indian religion cases threatened the rest of the nation, because they severely restricted the entire body of law that protects American religious liberty in general. Indeed, the rulings hearkened the decline and fall of the First Amendment as the primary basis for protecting freedom of worship in the United States. In so doing, *Smith* emphatically ended an era in American life when religious freedom was considered an inherent human right and foundational principle of the Republic.

The Indian cases thus placed the Court on a collision course with Congress in a dispute between these two branches of government over the vitality and extent of religious freedom in our modern society. After *Smith*, the First Amendment would no longer be the primary means for protecting religious freedom. All of America would have to depend upon politicians instead. Religious liberty is now dependent on the outcome of elections, the political vicissitudes of lawmakers, and lobbying in the dark corners of Congress. *Smith* precipitated a stampede to Congress. Church groups of every description immediately left their pews, toiling nights and weekends to pound down the doors of Congress for new laws to create statutory protections for their freedom of worship. The panic-stricken pilgrimage to Washington, DC, sparked an epic struggle between Congress and the Supreme Court over the nature and extent of American religious liberty—a pitched battle that lasted the rest of the twentieth century.[17] *Smith* has never been repudiated by the Supreme Court to this date. However, the deeply divided Court remains splintered by repeated calls from numerous justices urging reconsideration of the *Smith* ruling.[18] During that internal squabble among the justices, Congress passed laws that flatly repudiated *Smith* as being sorely out of step with the Bill of Rights and the needs of a modern society comprising virtually every religion known to the human race. As I will discuss, Reuben Snake led the Native American coalition that secured passage of one such law that overturned *Smith* and legalized the religious use of peyote by Indians in all fifty states.

The failure of the courts to protect Native American worship is very sobering. The judiciary has experienced inordinate difficulty in applying routine First Amendment principles to Native American religious freedom claims over the years. *Smith* epitomizes the courts' failure to apply that body of law to tribal religions. In the absence of judicial protection, the government took tribal religion away from Native peoples with impunity in the nineteenth and twentieth centuries. In order to protect what little remains, the courts must come to grips with the forces that allowed that unjust travesty to happen and repudiate the judicial mind-set that led to *Smith*. Several profound questions must be addressed. First, how should we comport ourselves, as members of a modern, industrialized society, toward the surviving indigenous religions in the United States? In former colonies and settler states, what are the roles of law and the courts of the conqueror? On a larger scale, how should the modern world comport itself toward the last surviving primal religions of the world? Finding the proper balance between the sacred and the secular in the modern world is a compelling issue for all of us.

In order to provide a context for understanding the forces that led to *Smith*, it is necessary to remind secular minds of the nature of religion— that is, authentic faith held by people for whom religion still matters—and why religion matters in the modern world. Accordingly, we shall first examine the nature of religion and explain how indigenous religion fits into the religious traditions of the world. We shall glimpse into the mystical side of Native American life and explore the relationship between humans and the plant world in Native North America as the backdrop for understanding the sacramental use of peyote at issue in *Smith*. We must also trace the historical suppression of tribal religion in the United States and identify the root causes of religious intolerance and discrimination that worked their way into the machinery of government. The rise of secularism that marginalized the sacred in American life is another pathway to *Smith* that will be explored. Finally, after detailing *Smith* as one of the ten worst Indian cases ever decided, I will chronicle the amazing movement led by Reuben Snake to overturn that case with the passage of a historic law that reverses the forces that produced the *Smith* mind-set—a remarkable feat that gives hope for the survival of the world's remaining primal religions.

Do Indians Have Religion?

On October 12, 1492, on his first day in the New World, Christopher Columbus recorded in his diary that Indians "would easily be made good Christians, because it seemed to me that they had no religion."[19] He was wrong. However, the early colonizers brought similar attitudes to North America. Many wondered whether Indians had souls. Most were convinced that tribal beliefs and practices were barbaric superstitions held by "heathen savages," or at best the New World religions were inferior and needed to be replaced by Christianity. These attitudes indicate religious intolerance or religious discrimination, and they marked race relations and government policy in the United States in the nineteenth and most of the twentieth centuries. This mind-set proved to be highly injurious to Indian tribes when enforced through the machinery of government and the legal system. The goal of this chapter is to dispel misconceptions about indigenous religion, beginning with the fact that Indians do have religions.

What is religion? We think we know it when we see it, but many people cannot fathom religious beliefs and practices that are vastly different from their own. This problem blinded the early colonists, settlers, and government policy makers who were unable to see that Indians had religion, when in fact North America was teeming with profound tribal religions of great antiquity. Many federal judges in the twentieth century shared this problem. They were seemingly baffled when confronted by Native American religion claims. Despite clear testimony from practitioners themselves, courts had great difficulty discerning whether tribal beliefs and practices actually amount to a "real" religion.[20] Many claims were erroneously branded as "cultural preferences" or desires "to express pride in heritage" that did not rise to the level of religion.[21] Some tribal religions were described as "holistic worldviews" too broad to be a religion as Anglo Americans categorize it.[22] Others were not considered a religion because medicine men did not meet regularly or often like the leaders of Christian churches do.[23] Holy places, like cemeteries, were described as "cultural," not religious places;[24]

and tribal attempts to protect worship at holy places were frequently seen as "property rights" claims, not religion claims.[25] The problem of recognizing tribal religious activity in our midst is further compounded today by a secular mind-set, held by many, that has lost sight of authentic religious faith and the nature of religion as one path to understanding the world around us. Thus, since 1492, Native North America has been seen by many newcomers as a place of superstition, largely devoid of any real religion.

North America has never been a vast land without religion, as Columbus thought. Religion is a mark of humanity. It has shaped *every* human society since the beginning of time, including Native North America. The sacred is not only embedded in the human mind, but has been cherished in every age by all races and cultures, because the spiritual side of life uplifts the human spirit. Religion not only provides identity, but answers ultimate questions about life, death, and the world around us. It addresses questions about the human spirit that science cannot answer.[26]

Belief in the higher powers allows people to confront the supernatural, understand its magic, and peer into the Great Mystery. It is through faith alone that we are brought into contact with the spiritual realm, propelled by religious ceremonies that enrich our lives. Furthermore, for most of human history, religion was the primary path toward truth and the nature of reality—that is, it guided our understanding of the world around us. It explained the things we can see, touch, and feel and, more important, those we cannot. It gave meaning to the forces of nature and of the universe. And it allowed us to fathom the spiritual world that lies beyond our view. The articles of faith found in world religions are a treasure trove of wisdom. They provide sound advice for conduct, values, and ethics, and they espouse enduring theological and metaphysical truths. When considered collectively, this sacred knowledge is the sum of mankind's wisdom traditions compiled by the human race over millennia.[27] This is so, even though no religious belief can actually be proven by facts or other hard evidence discernable to the secular mind! For all of these reasons, individual religious conscience is widely considered inviolable in lands where Hinduism, Buddhism, Confucianism, Taoism, Islam, Judaism, and Christianity abide, as well as aboriginal places where primal religions are found.

Though long overlooked by scholars, religion obviously exists among America's Native peoples. Huston Smith, a leading authority on world religion, classifies Native American religions among the "primal religions" of the world. In 2001, this beloved figure sheepishly explained why he revised his classic text, *The World's Religions*, to include tribal religion among the religious traditions of the world:

> "My God, Huston," I heard myself saying in the car, "for three decades you have been circling the globe trying to understand the metaphysics and religions of worlds different from your own, and here's one that has been right under your feet the entire time—and you haven't even noticed it." That was the moment when the significance of this totally new area of world religions, supposedly my field of study, just clicked… So thirty-five years after the first edition of my book had appeared, I added a chapter about the primal religions, making it eight, instead of seven, religions covered in the book…To omit them from the first edition of my book was inexcusable, and I am glad I will not go to my grave with that mistake uncorrected. The added chapter honors the primal religions as fully equal to the historical ones.[28]

Smith defines tribal religions as primal because they came first and are the oldest religious traditions of the human race. These religions, according to Smith, represent "human religiousness in its earliest mode" and allow tribal people to "retain insights and virtues that urbanized, industrialized civilizations have allowed to fall by the wayside."[29] The primal religions differ from the large historical religions in several major respects. They are tribal in nature, that is, they normally consist of small groups who practice according to the oral, not written, tradition.

The tribal religions cannot be considered in a vacuum, but must be understood within the context of the primal world, for tribes in their aboriginal places are embedded into their indigenous habitats so solidly that the line between nature and the tribe is not easy to establish. For example, when the first early explorers came into Klamath Indian Country in southern Oregon, they were amazed how closely the Indian hunters, fishers, and gatherers merged with their environment: "Almost like plants, these people seem to have adapted themselves to the soil, and to be growing on what the immediate locality afforded."[30] Unencumbered by materialism, the primal world has no sharp lines dividing humans from animals and plants—as all are thought to possess the same spirit. As Black Elk, a Lakota, put it:

> All things are the works of the Great Spirit. He is within all things; the trees, the grasses, the rivers, the mountains, and the four-legged animals, and the winged peoples. He is also above all these things and peoples.[31]

In totemism, animals are like people who talk, plants have spirits just like us, and humans can exchange forms with their opposites in the natural world. Humans are kin to animals and plants, connected by physical, social, and spiritual ties. These close connections are illustrated by tribal names. Many Indians are commonly named after animals and plants from their tribal areas. My family members, for example, carry such Pawnee tribal names as Blue Corn Woman, Acorn, Young Buffalo Calf, Eagle Woman, Mother Corn Goes Inside, New Horse, Fighting Bear, Good Horse, Big Crow, Hill of Corn, Coming Horse, Blue Hawk, Roam Eagle, Flying Eagle, Echo Hawk, Male Elk, Eagle-Flies-High, Hawk, Screaming Eagle, Crazy Horse, Stallion, Spotted Horse Chief, White Eagle, and She-Is-Leading-A-Horse-Inside-To-Give-It-Away. In this tradition, people are relatives to the plants and animals that comprise their world.

Similarly, no sharp lines exist between this world and the next. Smith observes that "the most important single feature of living primal spirituality" is the "symbolist mentality" that "sees things of the world as transparent to their divine source."[32] He points out that "modernity recognizes no ontological connection between material things and their metaphysical, spiritual roots" like primal peoples who are "better metaphysicians" in this sense, even though their metaphysics is "naturally of mythic cast."[33] In this regard, to the primal mind physical appearances and reality are never entirely as they seem. Instead, the landscape, forces of nature, and the animals and plants in the primal world have a spiritual side; and that reality presents a "'spiritual dimension' which escapes modern man."[34]

Smith categorizes the tribal religions in the United States among the primal religions of the world, along with indigenous religions in Africa, Australia, Oceania, Siberia, Southeast Asia, and the other Indians of North and South America; and he ranks them alongside the major historical religions. He found that no one religion is superior: "[N]o one alive knows enough to say with confidence whether or not one religion is superior to the others—the question remains an open one," but "this book has found nothing that privileges one tradition above the others."[35] The best advice is to view all religious traditions as a single mosaic "in a stained-glass window whose sections divide the light of the sun into different colors" as the Spirit appears to different peoples, because religious differences have inherent worth and for God to be understood in all parts of the world, "divine revelations would have had to be couched in the idioms of its respective hearers."[36]

Within the primal religion framework described by Smith, Native Americans are heir to religious traditions with amazing diversity that rank high among the world's religions for their rich spirituality, ceremonial life, profound beliefs, and ritual practices.[37] That includes the Peyote Religion at issue in the *Smith* case. Much has been lost due to the forces that have eroded the spiritual powers of nearly every religious tradition, including secularization, religious intolerance, and the lack of legal protections against infringement and religious discrimination by the government. Nonetheless, even today the surviving aboriginal religions in the United States exist on a scale that surpasses Middle Eastern diversity. Our soil is quite literally sacred ground—that is, a land that is home to older and more numerous holy places than those described in the Old Testament and the Koran. Many tribes continue traditional rites in our own land throughout the ceremonial year. The challenge is to protect what remains.

The intrinsic value of Native American religions extends far beyond the religious sphere. Based upon centuries of close observations of the natural world by a race of hunters, fishers, and gatherers with cultures that evolved from their indigenous habitats, the unique American religions bring depth and beauty to our country's cultural heritage. These primal religions contain environmental teachings and ethics sorely needed in today's industrialized society, which has polluted large parts of the nation, driving away the fish, animals, and plants that once inhabited those regions. That trend is the direction we are headed unless the nation finds a clear ethic for addressing the natural world. The sacred symbols, music, art, and religious objects found in Native American religion are prized cultural patrimony and intellectual property that are increasingly appreciated for their intrinsic beauty. To Native peoples, the traditional religions are the glue holding Indian tribes and Native communities together over the centuries, often in the face of great adversity. Even today, the bundle of legal rights enjoyed by Indian tribes, including casinos and bingo halls, can be quite meaningless unless their political, property, and human rights are informed by a vibrant language, culture, and traditional religion.

The Role of the Plant World in Primal Religion

To understand the Peyote Religion at issue in *Smith*, one must ponder the spiritual relationships between Native peoples and the Plant World found in the aboriginal American religions. What is our relationship to the plants that comprise our environment? Many in today's secular world have become estranged from the natural world or were never in tune to the ties between humans and plants that deeply shape human cultures.

We mostly interact with plants only when they are on the dinner plate or when we water potted plants in the home, and few maintain close ties to Native plant communities in the wild. Melvin Gilmore was an early ethnobotanist who studied the extensive plant knowledge of the Plains Indians at the turn of the nineteenth century. He noted that native plants and their uses as food and medicine were largely overlooked by incoming settlers who displaced them:

> The people of the European race in coming into the New World have not really sought to make friends with the native population, or to make adequate use of the plants or the animals indigenous to this continent, but rather to exterminate everything found here and to supplant it with the plants and animals to which they were accustomed to at home. It is quite natural that aliens should have a longing for the familiar things of home, but the surest road to contentment would be by way of gaining friendly acquaintance with the new environment…We shall make the best and most economical use of all our land when our population shall have become adjusted to the natural conditions. The country cannot be wholly made over and adjusted to a people of foreign habits and tastes. There are large tracts of land in America whose bounty is wasted because the plants which can be grown on them are not acceptable to our people. This is not because these plants are not in themselves useful and desirable, but because their valuable qualities are unknown.[38]

By contrast, the Native people were intimately familiar with the plants that lived in their tribal habitats, and the vegetation of their region was an important factor shaping their cultures. Their relationships with the plant world ran deep and were maintained on a metaphysical level.

Among indigenous peoples, it is often said that animals and plants can give knowledge and power to those who listen. As the late Vine Deloria Jr.

observed, "Stories abound in which certain plants talk to people or appear in dreams to inform humans of their uses."[39] This feature of primal religion was noted by Smith. The primal mind reveres beings, such as animals and plants, according to their proximity to their divine source, and the division between animal, plant, and human is muted, "for plants have spirits like the rest of us."[40] Like animals, they can take pity on humans, place them under their protection, and teach them their secrets. As Brave Buffalo, a Lakota, explained in 1918:

> All people have a liking for some special animal, tree, plant or spot of earth. If they would pay attention to these preferences and seek what is best to make themselves worthy of that to which they are attracted, they might have dreams which would purify their lives.[41]

These relationships in the primal world produce the kind of joy expressed by another Lakota, Standing Bear, that is rarely found in the modern world:

> The Indian tried to fit in with nature and to understand, not to conquer or rule. Life was a glorious thing, for great contentment comes with the feeling of friendship and kinship with the living things around you.[42]

This kinship extends to all creatures great and small. As Pete Catches, Lakota, explained in 1973: "All animals have power, because the Great Spirit dwells in all of them, even a tiny ant, a butterfly, a tree, a flower, a rock."[43] Nothing is overlooked in primal religion, as Black Elk astutely observed: "One should pay attention to even the smallest crawling creature for these may have a valuable lesson to teach us, and even the smallest ant may wish to communicate to a man."[44]

This spiritual relationship extends to relatives in the Plant World. As one Lakota pointed out in 1894, "The tree is like a human being, for it has life and grows; so we pray to it and put our offerings on it that God may help us."[45] When traditional Klamath Indians enter a forest, they are taught to introduce themselves by approaching the largest tree and telling that ancient being their name, tribe, and clan and asking its blessing to be welcomed into the forest and all of its surroundings. If done in a good way, the tree will grant one's prayer. The Plant World communicated to my family members in times past. My great-grandfather Echo Hawk, who was then named Big

Crow (*Kaa'ka' Raarihuuru*) told this story about a cedar tree to James Murie in 1903.

> In olden times a war party went out to the west to find the enemy. For many moons they traveled. At last they came to a rough country. There they made a camp. In the night these warriors heard a woman crying. Three warriors were selected to find the woman. They went in the direction of the crying, which became fainter as they drew near to it. They went away, and again the crying was heard. They followed the sound again and all came to a cedar tree. It was the cedar tree that was crying like a woman. When they found it was the cedar tree that was crying, one man said: "Warriors, let us go home." They would not listen to the man, but continued their march. The man would not go with them, but lingered behind, for he was afraid to go on the war-path after he had heard the cedar tree weeping, for he thought it was a bad omen. The next day they were attacked by the enemy. The lone man watched from a distance. All were killed, so the lone man went home and told the story.[46]

For millennia, the human cultures in North America have paid close attention to the plants and animals in their habitats—just like all good hunting, gathering, and fishing societies must do in order to survive and flourish. As a result, diverse religions arose from those observations. In those religions, plants and animals are considered sacred. This continues today by aboriginal hunters, fishers, gatherers, and their descendants—that is, traditional folks who live in tribal communities and continue to maintain the close spiritual relationships that were forged long ago with the plants and animals of their world. Though little understood by non-Indians, these bonds are commonplace among tribal people around the world, especially those who continue life in aboriginal habitats. In many American Indian, Alaska Native, and Native Hawaiian communities, the spiritual side of life continues to be enriched by teachings and spiritual power received from animals and plants. As Reuben Snake explained in 1993:

> When you look at all the other parts of creation, all the other living creatures—the Creator endowed them with gifts that are far better than ours. Compared to the strength of the grizzly bear, the sharp sightedness

of the eagle, the fleetness of the deer, and the acute hearing of the otter, we're pitiful human beings. We don't have any of those physical attributes that the Creator put into everything else. For that reason, we have to be compassionate with one another and help one another—to hold each other up.[47]

Traditional ceremonies are held in those communities to honor these spiritual relatives, to communicate and receive blessings or knowledge from them, and to otherwise worship the Creator in the natural world.

The Makah Indian whaling culture is one striking example. For thousands of years, this seafaring tribe has looked to the ocean for food, tools, and clothing. Whaling became the core of Makah culture, art, identity, economy, and way of life. The rituals, songs, ceremonies, and legends surrounding whales have deep spiritual significance in Makah life.[48] Similarly, the animals, plants, and sea life of southeastern Alaska pervasively affect Tlingit society, just like the flora and fauna in Hawaii deeply influence the Native Hawaiian communities. The Columbia River tribes revere salmon and the women of those tribes maintain close religious connections to the plants, roots, and berries that comprise ceremonial foods. Their religion holds that those creatures and plants voluntarily gave themselves to the people at the time of creation as gifts so that humans can sustain their lives in this world. The Great Plains region furnishes another example, where big-game hunters evolved into complex buffalo-hunting cultures with a rich set of rituals, songs, ceremonies, and powers related to Father Buffalo. The plant life of the prairies also deeply shaped the cultures of the Plains Indians.[49]

My Pawnee ancestors were deeply influenced by the plants and animals of the prairie.[50] Corn, cedar, tobacco, sweetgrass, and sage are sacred plants that help humans get in touch with higher powers. Mother Corn (*Atira' rikiisu*) is especially holy, since she was given to the Pawnee by the Evening Star at the time of Creation.[51] The Pawnee not only revered the buffalo and other animals, but also grew crops and gathered many wild roots, berries, and plants for food, medicine, and an amazing variety of other purposes in Nebraska. During this period, animals and plants frequently communicated with the Pawnee through a power given to them by a mysterious star that stands in the northeast quadrant of the heavens—a male star named *Upirit raarihuuru katitkusu* (Big Black Meteoric Star).[52] The Creator placed him there to hold up that portion of the sky and gave that celestial being a wonderful power—to let animal and plant spirits communicate with human beings. Through Black Star, plants could tell people their secret properties and prairie animals could teach their ceremonies and give mystical powers to Pawnee medicine men.

Examples of these mysterious communications abound in Pawnee oral traditions.[53] In one, the Crows (*Kaa-ka'*, in Pawnee) took pity upon a man and shared their mysterious powers to find buffalo. They gave the Pawnee the Crow-Lance Society powers in hunting and war.[54] In another, a female kernel of corn lying upon the ground, cried out to a man. She taught him that Mother Corn is sacred and how to place it in holy bundles, because Mother Corn represents Mother Evening Star on Earth.[55] Even roots communicated directly to the Pawnee, through the power of the Black Star, to tell humans where to find them and what their secrets are.[56] The animal spirits were said to reside in animal lodges in the Loup and Platte rivers—places where deserving Pawnee could go to receive knowledge and power about the spiritual side of life directly from the animal beings of the Great Plains. Our Young Dog Dance, Doctor Dance, and all society dances were given to the Pawnee from the animals, along with the power to heal the sick.

Sound incredible? All encounters with the higher powers of the supernatural world are incredible and must be taken as an article of faith. These tribal traditions are no more incredible than the burning bush that spoke to Moses as the voice of God. Most religious folks accept that encounter as true. Likewise, it is true that animals and plants can and have talked to those who listen in Native North America. Until recently, many scientists believed that animals were incapable of thought or communication—simple automatons lacking the ability to think, feel, or communicate; however, today, many are amazed as they learn more about animal intelligence.[57] Indians could have told them that animals are relatives, with powers of their own, who are capable of thought, feeling, and communication to those who listen. The same can be said for roots, berries, certain trees, and plants of power, all of whom must be approached and gathered in a sacred way in order to receive their benefits and blessings according to tribal teachings. This indigenous belief system comprises what Huston Smith terms the "primal world" in Native North America and the spiritual way of life he classifies as "primal religion," and this belief system forms the metaphysical background for the Peyote Religion at issue in the *Smith* case.

The Peyote Road Is a Profound Primal Religion in Native North America

One of the most remarkable primal religions found in the United States is the Peyote Religion of the NAC. It is often called the Peyote Road by practitioners, because it teaches a spiritual way of life with all of the theology, values, moral code, and ethics needed to fulfill a meaningful life—making it a complete religion in every respect. Though little known to most Americans, the history, ceremonies, teachings, beliefs, practices, and importance of this religion are well-documented.[58] It may be the oldest, most continuously practiced religious observance in the New World that is still in use today. Dating back ten thousand years, the Peyote Religion dwarfs most other world religions in antiquity.[59] A leading researcher, the late anthropologist Omer C. Stewart, observed:

> We can assume with assurance for millennia they used [peyote] in the same manner they used it in early historic times: as a medicine to be taken internally or as a poultice on sores; to foretell the future; to find lost objects; as a stimulant in strenuous activity, such as travel or war; and in group religious ceremonies when supernatural aid was sought through group participation. At the time of the Spanish Conquest of Mexico and our first written records of its use, peyote was known far beyond its natural habitat [along the Rio Grande and in Mexico].[60]

One early account of the discovery of peyote comes from the Aztecan people of central Mexico, where legends says that long ago a pregnant woman went berry picking and got lost from her band.[61] The woman gave birth to a child and lay helpless in the hot sun after she cut the navel cord. With buzzards flying overhead, the weakened woman heard a voice: "Eat the plant that is near you, for it is life and a blessing for you and your people." After eating the plant, strength returned immediately to save the woman and child. Upon returning, she told her relatives about the plant, thus beginning the Native peoples' long relationship with peyote as it is known today.

Over the centuries, many tribes discovered this plant of power. The religious use of peyote spread northward. Each tribe has stories about how the people received this religion. One in my own family says the Pawnee received it from great Comanche Chief Quanah Parker, in the 1890s. During that period, according to this family tradition, Pawnee priests and medicine men still had their traditional powers obtained from centuries of living on the open prairie. When Quanah came to the Pawnee reservation, he told the religious leaders, "I have brought you a new religion. Let me show you my powers." Being polite, they invited Quanah to their medicine lodge. "Wait a minute," they said, "then come into the Earth Lodge." When Quanah entered the lodge bringing the peyote medicine and sacred instruments of the NAC, he saw the Pawnee priests assembled—but they were no longer men. Reclining on the first mat, he saw a grizzly bear; on the second mat lay a wolf; on the third, a mountain lion; and next lay a wildcat. *The Earth Lodge was filled with animals!* "Come on, guys," Quanah exclaimed in sign language, "We do not do that in this religion!" Then, all at once, the animals turned back into men! And the Pawnee doctors told Quanah, "Okay, now show us your new religion."[62] In this remarkable way, our people received the Peyote Religion. It continues to be prevalent among the Pawnee and many other tribes to this date.

The early Spanish conquistadors observed Peyotism among Indians in Mexico. Spain tried to stamp it out, but the religion survived the medieval cruelties of the Spanish Inquisition. Despite nearly a hundred prosecutions over the next two hundred years, it persisted and spread. Peyote converged on the southern plains in the 1890s, during the early reservation period. By the early 1900s, the Peyote Road was firmly established on most Oklahoma reservations. It helped tribes cling to cultures that the government sought to destroy. During that troubling period, missionaries and Indian agents chipped away at tribal heritage by day. But at night, the language, songs, dress, and ceremonies returned through clandestine peyote meetings held in tipis, safely hidden from the authorities. To combat persecution in Oklahoma, tribal elders chartered a church in 1918 to make their religion more recognizable to lawmakers. They named it the NAC. By 1990, over 250,000 Indians followed the Peyote Road in scores of NAC chapters, located in twenty-four states.[63] The importance of the NAC in their lives is evident in the personal testimonials provided in *One Nation Under God: The Triumph of the Native American Church* (1996).[64]

> Throughout all the years that I had lived on earth, I now realized that I had never known anything holy. Now, for the first time, I knew something holy.
>
> —John Rave (Hochunk), after first Peyote meeting

Vegetation and trees, the rivers, sunshine, the moon in the night, thunder and lightening, birds flying in the air—it seems like God made this world and left it just the way he made it. And we found this Medicine. I'll be ninety-four on my next birthday, so if there's an example of someone who's been using Peyote all his life, I guess I'm he. I feel that I would die for this Medicine, it has meant so much to my life. My people use it and find spiritual guidance in it.

—Truman Daily (Otoe-Missouri)

We talk to the Medicine in the same way that we talk to trees and rivers.

—Parish Williams (Ponca)

In the first creation God himself used to talk to people and tell them what to do. Long after, Christ came among the white people and told them what to do. Then God gave us Indians Peyote. That's how we found God.

—A Kiowa

When you eat it, your mind turns to the Great Spirit. In one song I can learn what might take twenty or twenty-five years in school.

—Bernard Ice (Oglala Lakota)

All of the important things that life requires are woven into the ceremony. The entire ceremony is symbolic of our dependence on and use of things in our environment: fire, water, plants, and animals.

—A Crow

During the meeting the singing sounded lovely, the Indian dresses looked very beautiful, and in the morning the sun rose on the best world I ever saw. I felt young and good in every way.

—A Chiricahua Apache

There are certain times in a meeting when you can feel a presence. A feeling comes in the meeting—it's a holy feeling, the presence of the Spirit of God that's in the midst of these people. You feel that presence. It makes you want to pray deep in your heart.

—A Menomini

About that time in the meeting the old roadman told the story of our origins. It seemed like I lived right through it. To understand it I had to live through it.

—Anonymous

Our music, our songs, the ceremonial objects that we use in our tepees—these are all good for us Indian peoples. I'm going to stand up for our Indian ways—that's number one. I'm going to continue to teach my children and grandchildren our Indian culture and try to be a role model for them. Our religion is too beautiful, too refined, too rich to abandon. This is where I communicate with my Creator.

—John Emhoola (Kiowa)

I don't think that those who are not Native Americans can understand our Holy Sacrament. We Indians are close to fire and the fireplaces that protect the Medicine and its effect on our minds. The Medicine brings us closer to God the Spirit, who gives us good lives and good outlooks on the future.

—Robert Billie White Horse (Dine')

We burn incense for purification, and we eat Peyote to come into communication with the Great Spirit. But we also have to have something to offer to the Great Spirit. He accepts our offerings through the ascending smoke of our sacred tobacco. That's why it is so special for us. We try to keep the drum going during our sermons. We try not to talk too long, or pray too long. Just keep the heartbeat drum going. Then, through our Medicine, we have this spiritual experience.

—Johnny White Cloud (Otoe-Missouri)

The great beauty of the human race is found in the amazing ways that we reach for the heavens. One quarter of a million Native Americans are connected to the peyote plant through the profound religious ceremonies of the NAC. This is a remarkable display of connectivity to human religiosity in one of its earliest forms. *They carry on one of the oldest religious traditions still practiced by the human race.* Those who are not in tune with the Plant World may never completely understand primal religious beliefs and practices, much less the Peyote Religion. The central ritual observance in all-night NAC prayer ceremonies is the ingestion of peyote. This sacramental use is not dissimilar from other traditional cultures in aboriginal lands where hallucinogenic plants have been ingested for religious or healing purposes by tribal people for thousands of years.

While the Peyote Religion is little understood by the public, this unfamiliar faith is a bona fide religious tradition nevertheless. As such, it is entitled to the same respect and legal protections enjoyed by the better-known religions. The hallmark of religious tolerance—which is the cornerstone of a pluralistic society built upon individual liberty—is respect for every religion, especially unorthodox faiths not shared by the majority. A tolerant society recognizes that in the realm of religious belief "the tenets of one man seem the rankest error to his neighbor," according to *Cantwell v. Connecticut* (1940), but the law nonetheless protects those differences as liberties necessary "for a people composed of many races and creeds."[65] The defining role of the First Amendment is to protect unfamiliar or unpopular faiths, since the majority in constitutional democracies rarely intrudes upon mainstream religion. One constitutional scholar observes:

> One rarely sees laws that force mainstream Protestants to violate their consciences. Judicially enforceable exemptions under the free exercise clause [of the First Amendment] are therefore needed to ensure that unpopular or unfamiliar faiths will receive the same consideration afforded mainstream or generally respected religions by the representative branches.[66]

In the pre-*Smith* era, most courts protected the Peyote Road when Indians were charged with violating drug laws prohibiting peyote use. In the landmark case of *People v. Woody* (1964), three Navajo were arrested during a peyote ceremony and charged with illegal use of peyote.[67] California claimed that peyote use was harmful to Indians and that a religious exemption for them would adversely impact the enforcement of state drug laws. Following a widely publicized trial, the Indians were convicted. On appeal, the California Supreme Court reversed their convictions and set them free. It ruled the First Amendment protects their right to use peyote for religious purposes. In a straightforward application of the law, the *Woody* Court found that the state's case rested upon "untested assertions" and the Indians' worship did not harm any compelling government interest.

We have weighed the competing values represented in this case on the symbolic scale of constitutionality. On the one side, we have placed the weight of freedom of religion as protected by the First Amendment; on the other, the weight of the state's "compelling interest." Since the use of peyote incorporates the essence of the religious expression, the first weight is heavy. Yet the use of peyote presents only a slight danger to the state and to the enforcement of its laws; the second weight is relatively light. The constitutional scale tips in favor of the constitutional protection.[68]

As a result, the Navajos were freed. In granting a religious exemption from the California law to protect their free exercise of religion, the *Woody* Court described the larger interests at stake:

We know some will urge that it is more important to subserve the rigorous enforcement of the narcotic laws than to carve out of them an exception for a few believers in a strange faith. They will say that the exception may produce problems of enforcement and that the dictate of the state must overcome the beliefs of a minority of Indians. But the problems of enforcement here do not inherently differ from those of other situations which call for the detection of fraud. On the other hand, the right to free exercise of religious expression embodies a precious heritage of our history. In a mass society, which presses at every point toward conformity, the protection of a self-expression, however unique, of the individual and the group becomes ever more important. The varying currents of the subcultures that flow into the mainstream of our national life give it depth and beauty. We preserve a greater value than an ancient tradition when we protect the rights of the Indians who honestly practiced an old religion in using peyote one night at a meeting in a desert Hogan near Needles, California.[69]

Woody is a classic example of American justice at its best. That landmark decision, which is solidly grounded in the First Amendment doctrine, was followed by other state courts in later years.[70] Soon after the *Woody* case was decided, Congress passed the Drug Abuse Control Amendments of 1965 and in 1966 peyote was added to the list of controlled substances with an administrative exemption for the religious use of peyote by the NAC.[71] Relying upon the federal Indian trust doctrine, the courts upheld the

government's power to accommodate the Peyote Religion through administrative exemptions and regulatory means, as necessary tools to protect
minority religion in a tolerant society. In *Peyote Way v. Thornburgh* (1992), a
federal court upheld the power of Texas and the Federal Drug Enforcement
Administration (DEA) to grant religious exemptions from federal and state
drug laws for the religious use of peyote by Indians in the religious ceremonies of the NAC and to regulate the harvest and distribution of peyote in
Texas for Indian religious use.[72] When non-Indians complained this was
unconstitutional special treatment, the court upheld the system based upon
the federal government's trust relationship with Indian tribes, stating:

> We hold that the federal NAC exemption allowing tribal Native Ameri-
> cans to continue their centuries-old tradition of peyote use is rationally
> related to the legitimate government objective of preserving Native Ameri-
> can culture. Such preservation is fundamental to the federal government's
> trust relationship with tribal Native Americans. Under [*Morton v. Man-
> cari*, 417 US 535 (1974), non-Indians] are not similarly situated to…NAC
> [members] for purposes of cultural preservation and thus, the federal gov-
> ernment may exempt NAC members from statutes prohibiting possession
> of peyote without extending the exemption to [non-Indians].[73]

The *Peyote Way* Court added that this Indian-only exemption, which was
created under the federal government's trust relationship with Indian
tribes as a tool to protect their cultures, does not violate the Establishment
Clause's prohibition against the establishment of religion nor the separation
of church and state requirement:

> The unique guardian-ward relationship between the federal govern-
> ment and Native American Indian tribes precludes the degree of separa-
> tion of church and state ordinarily required by the First Amendment.
> The federal government cannot at once fulfill its constitutional role as
> protector of tribal Native Americans and apply conventional separatist
> understandings of the establishment clause to that relationship…Thus,
> we hold that the federal NAC exemption represents the government's
> protection of the culture of quasi-sovereign Native American tribes and
> as such, does not represent an establishment of religion in contravention
> of the First Amendment.[74]

Unfortunately, the *Woody* line of cases was short-lived. It came to an end in 1990 with the *Smith* decision. Because *Smith* never disturbed the government's legal power to *voluntarily* accommodate the Peyote Religion under *Peyote Way*'s federal Indian trust doctrine, that religion is protected today by legislative and administrative fiat, rather than as a constitutional right enforced by the courts.[75] The courts' retreat from the bulwark role envisioned in the Constitution when it came to protecting tribal religion is puzzling. How do we account for that retreat in a pluralistic society that still professes religious tolerance? The paths to the *Smith* mind-set are many. They will be explored, beginning with American religious history.

The Suppression of Native American Religion in the United States

Discrimination, like other forms of racism and human evil, can take many shapes. The dark side of religion is that age-old tendency toward intolerance, which sometimes takes virulent forms. This brand of discrimination can be pronounced, even in America, as explained by Justice William F. Murphy:

> No chapter in human history has been so largely written in terms of persecution and intolerance as the one dealing with religious freedom. From ancient times to the present day, the ingenuity of man has known no limits in its ability to forge weapons of oppression for use against those who dare to express or practice unorthodox religious beliefs...[E]ven in this nation, conceived as it was in the ideals of freedom, the right to practice religion in unconventional ways is still far from secure... To...religious minorities, befalls the burden of testing our devotion to the ideals and constitutional guarantees of religious freedom.[76]

That shortfall in our mental makeup caused much of the human suffering, war, and misery found in world history. American Indians have not been spared from the forces of religious intolerance. That history of religious discrimination was described by Senator Daniel K. Inouye, chairman of the Senate Select Committee on Indian Affairs, in 1992:

> Religious intolerance and suppression of tribal religions of Native Americans in the United States is not new. In fact, this form of discrimination

has characterized the relationship between our indigenous population and newcomers from Europe for the past 500 years.[77]

The roots of American religious intolerance were planted long ago. One scholar traces the origins of Christian intolerance to the early struggles of this nascent religion to survive in a polytheistic world and to the rhetoric forged in the canonical scriptures to defend the Christian experience of monotheism.[78] When Christianity was founded, the dominant religious system in the ancient world was polytheism. To survive, carve an identity, and justify its monotheistic outlook, the new cult asserted absolute truths and demonized the "false gods," "false religions," and "false prophets" of the day. In ancient times, conventional debate typically included slanderous attacks upon rivals, which were not necessarily taken literally in the Hellenistic culture.[79] As a result of these historical circumstances and ancient rhetorical conventions, strong rhetoric of intolerance and theological absolutism found its way into the New Testament. Unfortunately, subsequent Christian readers took that language literally. They read the texts as "direct divine revelations expressing propositional truths about reality," and not as "human writings generated by specific social and historical circumstances."[80] This misreading produced tragic consequences—the long history of Christian religious intolerance.

Whatever the root causes of intolerance may be, it is truly amazing how long it took for the Christian nations of Europe to move from base religious intolerance to bare tolerance and, finally, to authentic religious liberty and the attendant accommodation of religious differences that eventually took hold in twentieth-century Europe. That path was long and torturous, as described by one historian.

> It cannot be denied that for more than a thousand years the history of Christianity was marked by intense intolerance and persecution of Jews and all religious dissenters, who were readily branded as "heretics." It is no exaggeration to say that in the broad sweep of history more wars have been fought, more persecutions have been carried out in the name of religion than for any other single cause.[81]

Intolerance would also have dire implications for the peoples of the New World. In the Dark Ages, parochial notions that Christianity is the only true religion and that it is binding upon the rest of humanity took hold in

Europe.[82] Extreme claims were put forth by the papacy in Boniface VIII's bull, *Unam sanctam* (1302), which declared: "It is altogether necessary for every human creature to be subject to the Roman pontiff."[83] In this medieval view, all other religions are inferior, if not barbarous, and should be replaced by Christianity. Much of early European history was driven by those ill-conceived ideas of religious intolerance and superiority.

By 1492, Spain was fresh from centuries of religious crusades against infidels for possession of holy places in the Middle East. It was an emergent nation filled with religious intolerance. The king expelled the Jews that year and unified Spain as a Christian nation by defeating the Moors and expelling the Muslims. The Inquisition, which lasted well into the 1800s, was in full swing in 1492. It used torturous means to rid Spain of undesirable religious influences. Heretics, Africans, Gypsies, and others faced persecution, imprisonment, torture, and death because of their spiritual beliefs. That gut-wrenching wave of religious persecution is darkly reminiscent of the medieval witch hunts that burned thousands at the stake in an effort to stamp out all vestiges of primal religion from Europe. As the evil handmaidens of intolerance, the Crusades, extreme papal claims, expulsions, witch hunts, and the Inquisition epitomize the dark side of religion. They spawned an especially virulent form of religious discrimination.

The history of European religious intolerance accompanied the colonists to the New World as their cultural baggage. It characterized their relations with Native people for centuries to come. Senator Inouye noted how the religious prejudices of early colonists became the foundation for relations with Native people:

> In the minds of Europeans, tribal religions of the New World were inferior…Thus, it is not surprising—especially given Europe's own heritage of religious discrimination among unpopular Christian denominations and against non-Christian world religions—that intolerance became a basic feature in the Pilgrims' and other colonists' relationship with the Indians. Indeed, although early settlers came to America to escape religious persecution, Old World prejudices were transplanted in the Colonies, where discrimination became commonplace.[84]

These attitudes are prominently reflected in the foundational documents of colonialism. They list the bringing of Christianity to the New World as one of the primary purposes of the colonies. The Papal Bulls of 1493 declare that indigenous people can easily be made Catholic. They expressly conveyed the hemisphere to Spain so Ferdinand and Isabella could convert Indians to the Catholic faith.[85] Similarly, the royal charters that establish British colonies *commanded* the colonists to propagate Christianity among the North American "savages" who "live in Darkness and miserable Ignorance of the true Knowledge and Worship of God."[86]

Nothing could be clearer: a central purpose of the American colonies was to convert Indians to Christianity. This imperial imperative overwhelmed the liberties later enshrined in the First Amendment for the nineteenth and most of the twentieth century. Apparently, those liberties were meant only for colonists, and not the Indians, since constitutional protection seemed to apply only to the Christian faiths during this period. Alternatively, the settlers did not see the tribal religions as religions at all and the idea of First Amendment protection did not even come up—nobody in the settler state therefore felt a tension between their religio-political values and their practices in dealing with Native religions. In any event, by the beginning of the twentieth century, colonization and the propagation of Christianity went hand in hand in the United States and other colonized lands as the age of imperialism reached its zenith around the world.[87] As one religion scholar noted, "Nowhere does the name of God and justice appear more frequently than on the banner and shield of the conqueror."[88]

Given these deeply rooted attitudes of pronounced religious intolerance and the use of the cross to colonize and rule the Indian tribes, it is not surprising that the practice of tribal religion would be in for hard sailing in the new republic. These attitudes and associated practices would usher in a shameful history of religious suppression carried out by the federal government, with help from fervent missionary groups. Historians have studied how the US government suppressed tribal religions in the nineteenth and twentieth centuries.[89] They document a sixty-five-year period of overt government suppression, beginning with President Ulysses S. Grant's Peace Policy in 1869, that lasted until 1934, when the commissioner of Indian Affairs John Collier lifted the ban on tribal religion and issued orders to protect Native American religious liberty and curtail government-sponsored missionary efforts. During this period, the government aimed at Christianizing Native America. The Christianization policy had two prongs, both of which were conducted in facial violation of the free exercise and establishment clauses of the First Amendment to the US Constitution.

The first prong promoted Christianity among the tribes and converted Native Americans with the active help and cooperative involvement of Christian churches. Working hand in hand with church groups, the government established Christianity among the tribes by (1) conveying Indian land to church groups to establish missions among the Indians, (2) proselytizing Indian youth in government boarding schools or church-run Indian schools operated at government expense, and (3) allotting Indian tribes among Christian groups who were appointed as Indian agents with complete power over the reservations for proselytization purposes.[90] By these means, secretary of the interior Columbus Delano proclaimed in 1872 that "The missionary authorities have an entire race placed under their control, to treat with in accordance with the teachings of our higher Christian civilization."[91] These startling measures were, of course, a radical departure from constitutional principles unprecedented in the history of American church/state relations. Yet the Establishment Clause presented no obstacle to overt government entanglement with church groups, nor their joint efforts to establish Christianity among the tribes. This constitutional protection was ignored by government officials who felt it was okay to violate church/state prohibitions in Indian affairs. They simply assumed they had authority to install Christianity among the Indians. That prevailing attitude is reflected in the 1869 Report of the Board of Indian Commissioners:

> The legal status of the uncivilized Indians should be that of wards of the government; the duty of the latter being to protect them, to educate them in industry, the arts of civilization, and the principles of Christianity...The establishment of Christian missions should be encouraged, and their schools fostered...The religion of our blessed Savior is believed to be the most effective agent for the civilization of any people.[92]

Government education was seen as a tool that "cuts the cords that binds [Indians] to Pagan life," according to one superintendent in 1887, "places the Bible in their hands, substitutes the true God for the false one, Christianity in place of idoltry...cleanliness in place of filth, [and] industry in place of idleness."[93] As historian Limerick notes, nineteenth-century Americans were blinded by notions of religious superiority, and no thought was given to Native American religious liberty during this era:

For government officials as much as for missionaries, Christianity was so manifestly the right religion—indeed, the only religion with a claim on truth—that the question of religious liberty for Indians never entered their minds.[94]

Limerick explains the mind-set behind this prevailing prejudice, which seems so odd from a twenty-first-century perspective:

> To nineteenth century white Americans, the First Amendment protected the exercise of *religion*, while what the Indians practiced was superstition, primitive rites, and peculiar customs—practices that, to the nineteenth century Anglo American mind, did not deserve the First Amendment's guarantees of liberty.[95]

As a result, an unprecedented anomaly in church/state relations developed in American religious history in which an entire race was proselytized through the machinery of the government. Such a startling exception to settled constitutional principles in a democratic nation could only occur in a settler state intent upon stamping out vestiges of indigenous religion, as that conduct would never be tolerated if perpetrated against other minorities, then or now. Sadly, the courts upheld those singular practices in the rare instances when Native American church/state issues came before them, as previously discussed, in cases like *In re Can-ah-couqua* (1887).[96] What else can a legal system do if its purpose is to sustain the system that is in place, rather than serve as a bulwark to protect personal liberty?

The second prong of the Christianization policy was much darker. It involved active government suppression of Native American religious practices through the unprecedented use of the law, incarceration, and raw military force. In 1883, secretary of interior Edward Teller promulgated the Code of Indian Offenses, which established a reservation criminal code and court system with the avowed goal to eliminate, once and for all, "heathenish practices" and bring about the end of Indian culture.[97] Rule Four was a complete ban on the practice of tribal religion. It reads:

> The "sun dance," and all similar dances and so-called religious ceremonies, shall be considered "Indian offenses," and any Indian found guilty of being a participant in any one or more of these "offenses" shall, for the

first offense committed, be punished by withholding from him rations for a period not exceeding ten days; and if found guilty of any subsequent offense under this rule, be punished by withholding his rations for a period not less than fifteen days, or by incarceration in the agency prison for a period not exceeding thirty days.[98]

Rule Six banned the practices of medicine men and outlawed their powers, because the government feared medicine men would hinder the civilization and Christianization program. This infamous code was upheld in *United States v. Clapox* (1888), under the United States' guardianship powers over Indian tribes.[99] Clothed with this extraordinary power, the Bureau of Indian Affairs worked zealously throughout Indian Country until 1934 to suppress tribal religious ceremonies and ceremonial dances by arrests and other means.[100] Troops were brought in to enforce the ban against the Ghost Dance, leading to the slaughter of nearly three hundred Sioux men, women, and children at Wounded Knee.[101] That use of force was apparently condoned as legal, since no one was ever charged with murder or any other crime; but the mass killing at Wounded Knee was clearly illegal under the law of war, outlined in chapter six. Nonetheless, simply because the Sioux were worshipping a tribal religion on their own reservation:

> The Hotchkiss guns were fired on the tepees, where the women and children were gathered, and "poured in 2-pound explosive shells at the rate of nearly fifty per minute, mowing down everything alive." Most of the men were killed near the front of the camp, but the bodies of the women and children were scattered along a distance of two miles, evidence that many were killed while fleeing.[102]

This low point in American religious history shows the extreme government measures taken to suppress tribal religion in the "land of the free." Religious genocide is frightening wherever it exists, but especially in a democratic nation.

In short, "the federal government's efforts to convert Indians to Christianity became a cornerstone of its federal Indian policy," according to Inouye, and "[a]s may be expected, government violation of Indian religious freedom in respect to the Establishment Clause was soon followed by an incursion on these freedoms alternatively protected by the Free Exercise Clause, which prohibits governmental intrusion on the practice of religion."[103] An administration report to Congress concluded in 1979 that separation of church and state was entirely disregarded in the government's treatment of Indians.

> That Christianity and federal interests were often identical became an article of faith in every branch of the government and this pervasive attitude initiated the contemporary period of religious persecution of the Indian religions. It was not, to be certain, a direct attack on Indian tribal religions because of their conflict with Christianity, but an oblique attack on the Indian way of life that had as its by-product the transformation of Indians into American citizens. Had a Christian denomination or sect, or the Jewish community, been subjected to the same requirements prior to receiving affirmation of their legal and political rights, the outcry would have been tremendous. But Indians, forming an exotic community which few understood, were not thought to be the proper subjects of this concern.[104]

John Collier lifted the outright government ban on tribal religion in 1934. However, serious government infringements continued well into the 1970s. Religious discrimination was firmly embedded in the public mind and the courts continued to describe Indian tribes as "savage."[105] Inouye observed that the history of religious discrimination continued long after 1934:

> This ban was not lifted until 1934, more than one generation later. Unfortunately, our government still persisted in infringing upon tribal religious practices. Federal agents arrested Indians for possessing sacred objects such as peyote, eagle feathers, and they cut hair of Indian children. By authority of the federal government, these agents also prohibited school children from speaking their native languages, prevented native access to holy places located on public lands, destroyed Indian sacred sites, and interfered with tribal ceremonies.[106]

After hearings held in 1978, Congress finally recognized the need for a law to protect Native American religious freedom. To remedy this long-standing problem, Congress enacted the American Indian Religious Freedom Act of 1978 (AIRFA).[107] This law sought to reverse the history of religious discrimination and suppression by establishing a new federal policy:

> To protect and preserve for American Indians their inherent right of freedom to believe, express, and exercise the traditional religions of the American Indian, Eskimo, Aleut, and Native Hawaiians, including but not limited to access to sites, use and possession of sacred objects, and the freedom to worship through ceremonials and traditional rites.

The House and Senate committees that advanced this measure proclaimed:

> America does not need to violate the religions of her native people. There is room for and great value in cultural and religious diversity. We would all be the poorer if these American Indian religions disappeared from the face of the earth.[108]

Although AIRFA was a landmark, it only announced a congressional "policy." As such, AIRFA's efficacy depended upon implementation and enforcement by all three branches of government. Regrettably, that support never materialized in the intervening years leading to *Smith*. In 1992, Inouye declared that the AIRFA policy proved unenforceable and inadequate:

> [AIRFA] requires cooperation from all three branches of government in our system to effectively implement a Congressional policy. Unfortunately, such support was not forthcoming, and the enlightened attitudes expressed in the Act in regard to Indian religious freedom have never been effectuated. The federal courts have since ruled that this policy has no mechanism for enforcement.[109]

This checkered religious history demonstrates that Native Americans have shared a common fate with most indigenous societies. Since the dawn of the colonial era, the world's indigenous peoples have suffered what amounts to religious genocide. That history springs from the dark sides of colonialism and religious prejudice. To colonize Indians, it was necessary to take their religion. That task was justified, if not mandated, by widespread religious intolerance and discrimination that animated policies of suppression carried out by settler states. This hostility raises a pressing question: can such nations adequately protect surviving tribal religions in the postcolonial era? If so, what social, structural, and legal changes will assure their survival in the modern world?

Policies alone will not strengthen the ability of primal religion to survive. It will take a fundamental social change to eradicate all vestiges of religious prejudice in every quarter, including the courts of the conqueror, and to extend the ideals and principles of religious tolerance to aboriginal religion. Those changes must be enforced by the courts through effective laws and legal doctrines with teeth. Professor Huston Smith provides an alternative, non-legalistic, and more humanistic answer to the question how industrialized peoples should comport themselves toward the primal religions in what seems the short time they have left on the planet. This gentle scholar believes we were mistaken in our assessment of tribal people: "Primal peoples are not primitive and uncivilized, much less savage. They are not backward; they are different."[110] He advises us to put aside prejudices and stereotypes and simply listen.

> [P]erhaps we can live out our numbered years of planetary partnership in mutual respect, guided by the dream of one primal spokesman that "we may be brothers after all." If we succeed in doing this, there is still time for us to learn some things from them. [As John Collier] said of his charges: *They had what the world has lost: the ancient, lost reverence and passion for human personality joined with the ancient, lost reverence and passion for the earth and its web of life. Since before the Stone Age they have tended that passion as a central, sacred fire. It should be our long hope to renew it in us all.*[111]

Unfortunately, neither paradigm has been achieved in most settler states. Hope does glimmer, however, in the United Nations Declaration on the Rights of Indigenous Peoples (2007). It beckons each nation to strengthen its laws and social policies to protect religious freedom of the world's tribal peoples. As will be seen, *Smith* shows the need for the UN human-rights standard.

Given this religious history, the path to the *Smith* judicial mentality can be seen through the lens of conquest and colonialism in a settler-state society. In this view, propagating Christianity was the avowed purpose of the British colonies. To occupy the continent, they first had to pacify and dominate Native America. No conquest is complete until the foundation of Native culture is undermined and the people are thoroughly demoralized. In colonialism, rulers supplant, marginalize, and transform the aborigines.

Founded upon these principles, it was necessary for the settler state to suppress tribal religions. The legal system could either support or curb the government's suppression of primal religion occurring right under the nose of the courts. Since the goal of the legal system is to make everything "perfectly legal," it *had* to foster suppression, or at least turn a blind eye. In this view, *Smith* and *Lyng* merely culminated the settler-state process set in motion by conquest and colonization. Irrespective of the root causes, the fate of the Peyote Religion would be determined by the courts in *Smith* against the ugly backdrop of religious discrimination.

The Judicial Climate for *Smith* Was Foreboding in the 1980s

In the late 1980s, additional factors were brewing in the marble chambers. They created a hostile judicial climate, as the Indian religion cases were making their way to the Supreme Court. Four of those factors that set the stage for the oral argument in *Smith* are mentioned here.

First, modernity—it supplies the contemporary social context for protecting religion in a distinctively secular world. Secularization is the cultural process by which the area of the sacred is progressively diminished and pushed aside. In traditional times, religion was the primary pathway to truth about the world around us. This human condition existed for thousands of years before the rise of the industrial world. Religious liberty was therefore considered a bedrock social principle in the 1700s, when the Constitution was written. *But today, religion is just not that important!*

By the late 1980s, significant social changes had diminished its overall importance in American life. The courts booted religion out of the schools in the watershed Scopes Monkey Trial in 1925.[112] Increasing numbers of secularized folks began to wonder if god was dead by midcentury, when Julian Huxley pronounced, "it will soon be impossible for an intelligent or educated man or woman to believe in god as it is now to believe that the earth is flat."[113] By the end of the century, the sacred was largely banished from public life.

Progressive secularization remade hometown America. It relegated religion to the margins of society. Smith analyzed how science and technology colonized religion in the universities, strongly influenced mass media, and replaced religion with scientism as the primary path to truth and knowledge about reality. Not to be confused with science, scientism asserts that science is the only, or best, path to knowledge capable of describing all of reality, with authority over all other interpretations provided by religion, philosophy, mystical or metaphysical, or humanistic explanations.[114] The legal system's contribution to this secularization process is to help push religion to the side. The *Smith* decision illustrates the role of law in this process by stripping away constitutional protections for the freedom of worship and placing that liberty firmly under the control of secular political institutions.[115]

Though many Americans profess to hold religious beliefs, they are largely practiced in the private sphere, leaving the scientific worldview to hold sway in the public arena. In this climate, it becomes far too easy for the courts to dismiss the value of religion and subordinate worship to the secular interests of the state, no matter how trivial. Judges can pronounce doctrines that strip protection for unorthodox religions or religious minorities without ruffling many feathers. Courts might even shrink the constitutional scheme for protecting religious liberty, as done in *Smith*—after all, the Great Spirit cannot be proven by science.

In short, secularization created an insensitive, if not hostile, social climate for deciding *Smith*. In this environment, almost any governmental interest, real or imagined, can trump a fundamental religious interest. Modernity and the unprecedented growth of the state during the twentieth century have increased conflict between the secular and the sacred. As one leading constitutional scholar puts it, the state now represents the greatest threat to religious liberty:

> The most important religious conflict in the United States is not the conflict of one religion against another, but of the secular against the religious. On one side are all those people who take religion quite seriously, for whom religion still makes a substantial difference in their lives. On the other side are all those people who do not take religion seriously, who cannot imagine why these superstitions persist, and who cannot understand why religious minorities are demanding special treatment from the secular administrative state.[116]

As government regulation of human affairs has become more detailed and pervasive, the Supreme Court notes that religious ways of life run "into conflict increasingly with requirements of modern society exerting a hydraulic insistence on conformity to majoritarian standards."[117] How that conflict is resolved by the legal system fundamentally shapes our society.

The second factor that contributed to a hostile judicial climate for the Indian religion cases was the Supreme Court's trend toward restricting American religious liberty in general. Beginning in 1987, the trend toward eroding religious liberty began in the dark corners of American prisons. In two back-to-back cases, the Supreme Court carved out an exception for prisons to the traditional legal test for protecting religious liberty—the compelling-state-interest balancing test, which had been applied for decades to protect American worship. In its place, the Court created a new, lax reasonableness test that granted judicial deference to wardens. That watered-down test effectively stripped prison inmates of any meaningful free-exercise protections. *Turner v. Safley* (1987) involved prison restrictions on correspondence and the right to marry. The *Turner* Court announced the new test for prisons: "when a prison regulation impinges on inmates' constitutional rights, the regulation is valid if it is *reasonably related* to legitimate penological interests."[118] This test was soon applied to Islamic worship in *O'Lone v. Estate of Shabazz* (1987).[119] The weak reasonableness test empowers wardens to infringe upon religious freedom at will, based upon almost any justification.[120] By allowing restrictions on worship based on speculation, rather than truly important prison concerns, *O'Lone* opened the door for unwarranted state intrusions upon religious liberty.

History teaches that once noxious legal doctrines are espoused for one group, they begin a life of their own and are hard to contain. Thus, whenever one segment of society falls outside the ambit of the law, others soon follow. Shielded from public view, the crack in individual freedom that began in American prisons went largely unnoticed by the public. It quickly widened. We cannot easily separate ourselves from any segment of society, however marginalized, because everyone's freedoms derive from the same source, the US Constitution.[121] The late Justice William Brennan prophetically warned that differential constitutional treatment in the prisons places the nation on a slippery slope:

> Once we provide such an elastic and deferential principle of justification [for impinging upon religious freedom in prisons], "[t]he principle…lies about like a loaded weapon ready for the hand of any authority that can bring forth a plausible claim of an urgent need. Every repetition imbeds that principle more deeply in our law and thinking and expands it to new purposes."[122]

American Indians would shortly become the next victims in the erosion of free-exercise rights.

The third factor contributing to a hostile judicial climate was the rise of judicial conservatism to dominance in the Supreme Court under the leadership of the late Chief Justice William H. Rehnquist. In the late 1980s, the conservative axis of the Reagan Supreme Court assumed control of the Court. The familiar champions of individual rights from the Warren and Burger Courts were replaced with a slew of conservative Republican appointees: William H. Rehnquist, Anthony Kennedy, Antonin G. Scalia, and Sandra Day O'Connor. By the late 1980s, the civil libertarian wing of the Supreme Court had dwindled to three dissenters: Thurgood Marshall, William Brennan, and Henry Blackmun. They comprised an articulate, but largely ineffectual minority on the Court. Thus comprised, the Supreme Court would seriously weaken the body of law protecting American religious liberty in a string of cases decided between 1987 and 1990, the very time when *Smith* and *Lyng* were working their way through the legal system. The conservative axis would hardly be sensitive to religious minorities, especially during America's war on drugs, waged by state law enforcement officials. These justices would breathe new life into the court of the conquerors.

The fourth factor was Justice Scalia, a 1986 Reagan appointee. As a hard-core conservative, Scalia distrusted the ability of federal judges to balance individual religious conscience against the majority will expressed in laws. As part of the Court's new majority, he could use the marble chamber as a bully pulpit to advocate his ideology. As *Smith* and *Lyng* made their way to the Court, the junior justice was poised to restrict the reach of the First Amendment. He would write a majority opinion in *Smith* with such a pint-sized picture of the First Amendment that an entire religion with 250,000 members would fall through the cracks.

Mr. Smith Goes to Washington (Twice) and Gets a Spanking

I made my second trip to the Supreme Court in this particular controversy in 1989. The case entailed a conflict between a protected liberty—religious freedom—and law enforcement over the use of peyote by Galen Black and Alfred Smith, a white man and his Indian sidekick. The two were alcohol counselors who got fired for ingesting the cactus plant in a religious ceremony. After they were fired, both men applied for unemployment compensation benefits and were denied by the State of Oregon. Oregon's drug laws made peyote use illegal despite the fact that Indian peyote use is one of the oldest religious practices in the hemisphere.[123] Further, since 1963, a string of Supreme Court cases made it clear that denial of unemployment compensation for persons fired for religiously motivated conduct impermissibly burdens their freedom of religion.[124] Relying on that precedent, the disgruntled counselors appealed the decision, asserting that it infringed upon their religious freedom.

In a straightforward application of the law, the Supreme Court of Oregon agreed with Smith and Black.[125] In so doing, it joined several other state courts in protecting the religious use of peyote in the ceremonies of the NAC under the First Amendment to the US Constitution.[126] The stage was thus set for review by the US Supreme Court. It sprang into action at the insistence of Oregon's attorney general, David B. Frohnmayer—who was notable in the 1980s for combating religious minorities like Indian Peyotists, Islamic prisoners, and sects from other lands.[127] In this instance, he sought to rid Oregon of the Peyote Religion in the name of the drug war. Using that rubric, he would argue in court that peyote is a drug, its use is criminal conduct, and any exemption to Oregon's criminal law for the religious use of peyote would undermine America's war on drugs.

We managed to dodge a bullet on that first trip to the Supreme Court.[128] When confronted with the Oregon Supreme Court's decision protecting this indigenous religious practice under the First Amendment, the incredulous Rehnquist Court bounced the entire case back to the Oregon court, asking it: "Did you *really* mean to protect this religion?"[129] On remand, the state court answered, "Yep, we really did," and it reaffirmed its holding. After efforts to end the controversy at that stage broke down, the State successfully petitioned the Supreme Court to review the case a second time.[130] The return of *Smith* to the Rehnquist Court in the wake of the *Lyng* decision raised mounting concerns among many onlooking NAC leaders. Though the interests of their 250,000 members were at stake, the NAC did not control the case, and neither Smith nor Black belonged to the NAC.[131]

So now, we were back in the marble chambers once again. And Justice Scalia was pounding Craig J. Dorsay of Oregon Legal Services—the two men's new attorney—with hostile questions.[132] Like a bull terrier, the jurist grabbed him by the pant leg and would not let go of the hard-pressed attorney: "Should the First Amendment allow human sacrifice by the Aztecs?"[133] Chiming in, Justice Sandra Day O'Connor asked: "How about marijuana use by a church that uses that as part of its religious sacrament?"[134] *The oral argument was not going well.* As concerned NAC elders watched the courtroom drama unfold, their worst fears were being confirmed: their ancient religious way of life was about to become an innocent victim of the drug war in the landmark case of *Employment Division v. Smith* (1990), one of the ten worst Indian law cases ever decided.[135]

In a 6-3 decision, a majority of the *Smith* Court held the First Amendment does not protect the sacramental use of peyote in religious ceremonies of the NAC. The Court went to extraordinary lengths to reach this result, going far beyond the issues necessary to decide the case. Its stunning decision departed from settled First Amendment jurisprudence and weakened religious liberty,

First, Scalia's opinion carved a huge exception to the First Amendment by placing all criminal laws and civil laws beyond the reach of its protection. As Justice O'Connor pointed out in her concurring opinion, such a narrow reading renders First Amendment protection virtually meaningless, because "only the extreme and hypothetical situation in which a State directly targets a religious practice" is covered.[136] Second, *Smith* discarded the compelling-state-interest test used by courts for decades to protect American religious liberty.[137] According to Justice Scalia, that test is too stringent. It would court anarchy, since "many laws will not meet the test."[138] To avoid that specter, he scrapped the test. *(After all, we cannot allow religion to threaten the most powerful government on Earth.)* This restructuring of the law sees religion as a threat to a well-ordered society that must be reined in, controlled, and dominated by the secular. *Smith*'s new rule weakening religious liberty was a crowning victory of the secular over the sacred. Third, distrusting the ability and power of judges to carve exceptions to statutes to protect religious liberty, Scalia got the courts out of the business of accommodating religion altogether. Declaring religious diversity a "luxury" that our nation cannot afford, he told religious groups to go to Congress, not the courts, to protect their right to worship.[139] Like Justice White in *Lone Wolf v. Hitchcock* (1903), Scalia believed lawmakers will "do the right thing" once freed from judicial oversight.[140] Scalia wrote:

> It may fairly be said that leaving accommodation to the political process will place at a relative disadvantage those religious practices that are not widely engaged in; but that unavoidable consequence of democratic government must be preferred to a system in which each conscience is a

law unto itself or in which judges weigh the social importance of all laws against the centrality of all religious beliefs.[141]

Under Scalia's hard-edged judicial philosophy, if you are a religious minority, tough luck—move to a more tolerant region.[142] In one of the rarest displays of insensitivity in recent court history, Scalia's opinion contained no discussion about the NAC or the importance of the peyote sacrament to Indian religious practitioners, and it did not even give lip service to the importance of religion in American life at all. The dissenters, however, voiced those values and were deeply concerned about the impacts of the decision on Native America. Justice Brennan stated that those impacts "must be viewed in light of the federal policy reached in reaction to many years of religious persecution and intolerance—of protecting the religious freedom of American Indians," and he warned that the Court's failure to apply well-worn rules to Indian religion claims will render the First Amendment "merely an unfulfilled and hollow promise."[143]

Needless to say, the majority opinion created a firestorm of criticism. Dissenting justices ranted, legal scholars raged, and all of organized religion rushed headlong to Washington to lobby lawmakers. In the frenzy, nearly everyone forgot about the Indians directly harmed by the unpopular decision. They would have to address their plight on their own. That is exactly what they did. Left behind in the dust, a grassroots movement began brewing on Indian reservations when Rueben Snake received word about the *Smith* decision.

Back in Washington, four justices in *Smith* believed the majority went too far. The majority's approach "dramatically departs from well-settled First Amendment jurisprudence," wrote Justice O'Connor, "appears unnecessary to resolve the question presented, and is incompatible with our Nation's fundamental commitment to individual religious liberty."[144] She would not have granted talismanic effect to all criminal and general civil statutes to automatically restrict religious liberty, even in a drug war.[145] Above all, four justices rejected Scalia's vision of a nation that disfavors religious minorities as an "unavoidable consequence" of its system of government and leaves accommodation of their religious liberty to the political process. O'Connor wrote:

> [T]he First Amendment was enacted precisely to protect the rights of those whose religious practices are not shared by the majority and may

be viewed with hostility. The history of our free exercise doctrine amply demonstrates the harsh impact majoritarian rule has had on unpopular or emerging religious groups such as the Jehovah's Witnesses and the Amish..."The very purpose of a Bill of Rights was to withdraw certain subjects from the vicissitudes of political controversy, to place them beyond the reach of majorities and officials and to establish them as legal principles to be applied by the courts. One's right to life, liberty, and property, to free speech, a free press, freedom of worship and assembly, and other fundamental rights may not be submitted to vote; they depend on the outcome of no elections."[146]

The dissenters vehemently rejected the idea that preservation of religious liberty in a pluralistic society is a "luxury."[147] Justice Blackmun stated:

> I do not believe the Founders thought their dearly bought freedom from religious persecution a "luxury," but an essential element of liberty— and they could not have thought religious intolerance "unavoidable" because they drafted the Religion Clauses [of the First Amendment] precisely in order to avoid that intolerance.[148]

Three justices suspected the ruling might be a shortsighted overreaction to drug-war hysteria fanned by Attorney General Frohnmeyer, especially given the paucity of evidence actually offered to support his arguments. Because Oregon failed to present a compelling state interest in prohibiting the religious use of peyote in their view, they would have ruled in favor of Black and Smith under the traditional legal test normally applied in such circumstances.[149] The state's failure to justify its ban was troubling, because bare religious intolerance "harkens back to the repressive federal policies pursued a century ago" to suppress tribal religions.[150] The 6-3 decision reflected the deep division that would characterize the Supreme Court throughout the remainder of the twentieth century.[151]

Scholars condemned *Smith* as "one of the most unpopular decisions in the Court's recent history."[152] They variously described the ruling as being inconsistent with the original intent, meaning, and text of the First Amendment;[153] as giving unwarranted, talismanic effect to criminal laws;[154] as a troubling use of precedent "bordering on the shocking";[155] and as the case that destroyed "traditional concepts of individual liberty."[156] With one voice, they condemned *Smith* for wreaking havoc on the law and undermining religious freedom.[157]

After 1990, lower courts had to deny constitutional protections that most Americans once took for granted. One court pulled a decision protecting Hmong religious beliefs against disturbance of the dead through autopsies, stating: "It is with deep regret that I have determined that the [*Smith*] case mandates that I recall my prior opinion."[158] As similar cases mounted, religious liberty shrunk to tiny, unrecognizable proportions. One disgruntled judge ruefully observed: "*Smith* does not alter the rights of prisoners; it simply brings the free exercise rights of private citizens closer to those of prisoners."[159]

When Pilgrims and Puritans began to complain, Congress took notice of the growing crisis in religious liberty. Mainstream religion and civil libertarian groups began working nights and weekends, pounding down the doors of Congress demanding a new law to overturn *Smith* and restore stringent legal protections for American worship. This coalition drafted the Religious Freedom Restoration Act (RFRA) bill, but that measure contained no protection for the NAC. In their rush to Congress, RFRA Coalition leaders shunned the NAC as too controversial, telling the Indians, "Form your own coalition and get your own law passed." So two coalitions were formed—one was a Native coalition led by the late Hochunk tribal leader Reuben Snake and the NAC groups, and the other was the RFRA coalition for everyone else. Two bills were presented to Congress and both passed.[160] When President Bill Clinton signed RFRA into law in 1993, he noted the need for an additional law to protect Native American religious freedom:

> The agenda for restoration of religious freedom in America will not be complete until traditional Native American religious practitioners have received the protection they deserve. My administration has been and will continue to work actively with Native Americans and the Congress on legislation to address this issue.[161]

Sometimes, the coyote laughs last. Unfortunately for the RFRA folks who shunned the Indians in their drive to Congress, the RFRA was subsequently declared unconstitutional by the Supreme Court in 1997 as applied to the states. But the Indian law, which is described next, passed in 1994 and remains in full force and effect today.[162]

Mr. Snake Goes to Washington in the Battle to Overturn the *Smith* Decision

Have you ever worshipped with fear of a knock on the door? Without legal protection in the wake of *Smith*, 250,000 NAC members became subject in twenty-two states to arrest, incarceration, and discrimination solely because of their form of worship.[163] One NAC leader stated, "When we want to pray, we have to look up to see if someone is watching us. That means we pray in fear."[164]

The injustice of *Smith* slapped many Native Americans in the face. One woman tearfully decried the decision:

> It's hypocritical, this Supreme Court Decision against our Church. I have many relatives who served in Desert Storm. We prayed for them regularly. One of my cousins, a quiet man who was brought up in our Church, ran one of the computers that fired missiles in that war. For him to defend his country like that, and then have his country forbid him to pray—pray in the way he believes, which is the only way you can pray sincerely—it's not right.[165]

Alienation engulfed one lifelong NAC elder, a Korean War veteran:

> As I understand things, the Constitution of the United States guarantees that we all have certain human rights, among which is the right to worship as we deem right. But it has worked out that everybody seems to have these rights except Indians. That's the part I don't understand.[166]

Returning veterans from Iraq were outraged to find their faith endangered:

> Now I find that my Church is in trouble. When I entered military service I took an oath. I raised my right hand and said, "I am an American fighting in the armed forces, which protect our country and our way of life. I am prepared to give my life in its defense." I lived up to that. I laid my life on the line, in Operation Desert Shield/Desert Storm and the highway of death. I think I deserve the right to my religion—the right for it to continue the way we want it to without outside interference.[167]

From among these voices, a leader arose with the Great Spirit by his side—a man named Reuben Snake. In the book he coedited with Huston

Smith, *One Nation Under God: The Triumph of the Naive American Church* (1996), he introduced himself with these remarks:

> I am a Hochunk; other people refer to us as Winnebagos. My English name is Reuben Snake, but I also have an Indian name, *Kikawunga*, which means a great deal to me, for it is a very old traditional name for my clan of the Winnebago people. On Easter Sunday morning, 1939, my grandmother's uncle, my great-grandfather, baptized me into the Native American Church and christened me *Kikawunga*, a name that is remarkable not only for its antiquity but for its connotations, for it means "To Rise Up"...I came to see that in giving me that name my great-grandfather was commissioning me to help resurrect the heritage of my people.[168]

Snake bore both names with dignity and they defined his mission in life.

> I have tried to fulfill that commission, particularly as it relates to the Native American Church. There is a great deal of chaos and confusion in today's world, but God's truth (as it comes to us through our Church) is eternal and always available to us...Sitting on the ground tokens humility, and my name, Reuben Snake, makes me more conscious of that virtue than usual. Snakes are not the most exalted of creatures; they are earth-bound, they hug the earth. In playful moments, I sometimes introduce myself as Reuben Snake, your humble serpent.[169]

History will show that Reuben Snake lived up to all of his names. In the dark days following *Smith*, he put together the largest coalition of NAC organizations ever seen and led it to the halls of Congress.

Snake would devote the rest of his life to the enormous task of overturning a Supreme Court decision. During this crucial period in Native American history, he provided inspirational spiritual guidance to propel a tribal grassroots movement to Washington, DC, in an unlikely quest to overturn *Smith* against all odds. Snake was uniquely qualified to lead the people in this quest for religious freedom. He was at once an accomplished orator, a profound thinker, fearless warrior, humorist, religious leader, educator, diplomat/statesman, writer, ambassador, singer, and humble servant, as well as a revered spiritual leader of the NAC.[170] Despite these gifts, Snake walked in deep respect while meeting the challenges of his day. All of these attributes would be needed by this humble man to transcend differences and provide vision for a people in need. Yet, Snake rose to the challenge as a truly great leader for any race in any age.

> Each one of us is endowed by the Creator with his spirit. The spirit that makes you stand up and walk and talk and see and hear and think is the same spirit that exists in me—there's no difference. So when you look at me, you're looking at yourself—and I'm seeing me in you.[171]

During this crisis, the "humble serpent" became Indian Country's Martin Luther King Jr., Nelson Mandela, and Chief Joseph—all coiled up into one remarkable Snake.

The story of how the NAC overturned *Smith* through Congress's enactment of the American Indian Religious Freedom Act Amendments of 1994 is chronicled in various sources, but it is not well known to most Americans.[172] From a legal standpoint, it is far more complex to secure passage of landmark legislation than to litigate a case, because there are few rules to follow in Congress and one must convince hundreds of lawmakers and their staffs, as opposed to a single judge, of the merits of one's cause. The political process can also be daunting, because adversaries often have more resources and political pull than Indians, a distinct advantage that was normally present in the modern era of federal Indian law. What chance would Snake's unorthodox faith have in this arena?

Immediately after news of the *Smith* decision arrived in Indian Country, Nebraska NAC leaders asked Snake to take the lead in overturning the ruling. He rose to the challenge, put aside his other commitments, and devoted his remaining years to that task. His first move was to establish the Native American Religious Freedom Project, staffed by his adopted brother, attorney James Botsford, an experienced Native rights veteran in First Amendment battles. After uniting the NAC organizations, Snake's project participated over the next two years in a national grassroots campaign, along with the rest of Indian Country to address the crisis precipitated by Indian religion cases. Snake's project joined with Chairman Peterson Zah of the Navajo Nation and Patrick Left Hand of the Salish and Kootenai Tribes of the Flathead Reservation to establish an unprecedented national coalition that powered the human rights movement from Indian reservations to

Washington, DC. The movement marched through six congressional field oversight hearings, the making of a movie, and the establishment of alliances with swelling numbers of new friends along the way.

In early 1993, omnibus legislation was introduced by Senator Inouye, chairman of the Senate Select Committee on Indians Affairs. Senate Bill 1021 addressed the full array of religious problems created by the Indian religion cases, including the lack of legal protection for the Peyote Religion. That comprehensive legislation stalled in 1994 due to mounting opposition over the sacred-sites provisions. As the death of that vehicle seemed imminent in late 1993, a core team came together to develop a strategy for the enactment of stand-alone peyote legislation. This team consisted of the unprecedented NAC coalition led by the NAC of North America, tribal leaders, Navajo Nation lobbyists, NARF attorneys, and Botsford. Armed with strategic advice from Franklin Ducheneaux and Pete Taylor, two talented Beltway veterans during the modern era of Federal Indian law, the team charted the course toward passage of the law in 1994. The plan focused on House legislation developed in consultation with Congressman Bill Richardson (D-NM), the current governor of New Mexico, who was then chairman of the Native American Affairs Subcommittee. A separate bill would avoid the probable death trap of multiple committee referrals in the House, and it could move quickly if supported by the DEA and the Department of Justice.

Once the elements were in place, the process moved swiftly. In the Second Session of the 103rd Congress, Chairman Richardson introduced House Bill 4230 on April 14, 1994. This followed a March 16, 1993, hearing that laid the foundation and secured support from the DEA and Justice Department. A hearing on the bill was held on June 10, when NAC, DEA, administration, and Indian Country testimony was received. With speed that amazed Beltway insiders, the bill advanced through the committee levels and passed the House on August 8. After a number of anonymous Republican holds on the bill in the Senate were lifted, as a result of NAC lobbying over the August recess in the home states of the holdouts, the measure passed the Senate in September and was signed into law by President Clinton on October 6, 1994, in the last hours of the 103rd Congress—at a pivotal time, just before the political window of opportunity closed. The Democrats would lose control of the Congress and the White House for years to come, when the Capitol would be run by a mean-spirited bunch, preoccupied with war abroad and with little sympathy for Indian causes.

The law expressly overturned the *Smith* decision, legalized the religious use of peyote in all fifty states, and prohibited discrimination against Indians on account of this religious practice. It was passed pursuant to Congress's protectorate powers as the guardian and trustee of American Indian tribes—powers emanating from *Worcester v. Georgia* (1832).[173] In establishing stringent statutory protections for this ancient religion, the law brought to an end a prolonged epic struggle of NAC members. Its passage gave rise to victory celebrations throughout Indian Country in 1994, as relieved NAC elders counted their blessings. As the dark cloud of *Smith* was laid to rest, Abraham Spotted Elk Sr., president of the NAC of Wyoming, exclaimed: "It's a great day for members of the Native American Church to finally be able to pray without fear."[174] Frank Dayish Jr., president of NARF's client, the NAC of North America, proclaimed: "It is right and just that the First Americans will finally have the freedom to worship with the peace and dignity they deserve."[175]

The American Indian Religious Freedom Act Amendments of 1994 are a Magna Carta for the NCA—a law with teeth. Beyond that, the law helps reverse a shameful religious history, repudiates intolerance, and carries the nation beyond the legacies of colonialism and conquest into a new era. It demonstrates that aboriginal religious freedom can be protected in a nation with colonial roots. As such, it signals the way to a time when America sheds the trappings of a settler state and becomes a more just society that is native to place. Looking back, the courts of the conqueror may have done the nation a favor in *Smith*. That is certainly true for the Peyote Religion. One Omaha elder, the late Elmer Blackbird, suggested that the NAC write a thank-you letter to the Supreme Court stating:

> We were unhappy about it at the time, but in the long run you did us a favor. With all the problems that seem to be coming our way, we were beginning to wonder if we should continue to worship in our Native American ways. You sent shockwaves through our Church. The threat your decision posed—that it might do us in—made us realize how much the Church means to us. It mobilized our energies. We went to work, and in four years won back our rights through Congress. So thank you, Supreme Court. Your blow against us turned out to be a blessing in disguise.[176]

Reuben Snake's untimely death in 1993 came during the latter legislative stages of the movement he set in motion. The fallen inspirational spiritual leader was sorely missed by NAC leaders who carried the campaign to its successful, historic conclusion. While Reuben did not live to see the enactment of the law, his spirit undoubtedly guided its passage from the Spirit World. Shortly after his death, I strode to the witness table in the congressional hearing room. In halting fashion, I began my testimony in support of the bill:

> Mr. Richardson: Counselor Echo-Hawk, my thanks to you for all the work you have done on this issue. Probably no one—at least in this city and country—probably knows more about this issue than you do. I will ask you to please proceed. Remember that your statements are part of the record, and I look forward to your testimony.
>
> Mr. Echo-Hawk: I appreciate those kind remarks this morning. Good Morning to you, sir, as well as to the members of the subcommittee. I am a staff attorney with the Native American Rights Fund and I am very pleased and deeply honored to appear before the subcommittee today on behalf of the Native American Church of North America. I am very pleased also to offer testimony in support of the HR 4230 on behalf of the Native American Church of North America...[177]

The thoughts of most witnesses in the hearing room drifted to Reuben, as it was impossible to ignore his spiritual presence. His sage wisdom filled the room. Even now, many years later, Reuben's teachings ring true for all of us...

> I believe that the foundation of all of our lives should be our spirituality. No matter what one plans to do with one's life, one should develop a spiritual relationship with the Creator and the Divine Creation. To do so means one has to listen from the elders...They're going to say things to us and show us things that are vital for us to develop our spirituality.[178]

Reuben A. Snake's primal legacy transcends his day. His lessons in life, leadership, and love for the Creator are valuable for every people and age. They came from that small cactus plant that grows only in the Rio Grande valley, and nowhere else in the world. The beloved Humble Serpent is missed, but his legacy shines the light, as we stride toward a more just society.

Throws-The-Book

CHAPTER TWELVE
Lyng v. Northwest Indian Cemetery Association: Taking the Holy Places

"For the Yurok, Karok, and Tolowa peoples, the high country
constitutes the center of the spiritual world."

—Judge Stanley A. Weigel, United States District Court,
Northern District of California, in 1983

HAVE YOU EVER WALKED ON HOLY GROUND to a spot where the world was created or made your medicine in a holy place? Nowhere is the cultural divide between tribal and nontribal people so vast as the way that we look at the land. In ancient times, all of humanity revered the sacred found in the natural world. Today, many have forgotten how to listen to spiritual power that springs from the land; however, the Bible reminds us that sacred places exist. Moses's vision on Mount Sinai comes to mind. His vision shaped the destiny of the Jewish people and transformed a desert mountain into their revelatory center of the world:

> There the angel of the Lord appeared to him in a flame of a burning bush. Moses noticed that, although the bush was on fire, it was not being burnt up: so he said to himself, "I must go across to see this wonderful sight. Why does not the bush burn away?" When the Lord saw that Moses had turned aside to look, he called to him out of the bush, "Moses, Moses." And Moses answered, "Yes, I am here." God said, "Come no nearer, take off your sandals; the place where you are standing is holy ground."[1]

In this chapter, we shall journey to the center of the spiritual world in Native North America. It is a beautiful, primordial place called the High Country. Located in the wilderness peaks and high meadows of the Siskiyou Mountains, it lies in the heart of the aboriginal homeland of several Indian tribes of northwest California—rare communities that still practice an ongoing indigenous religious system.

For centuries, tribal mystics went to the High Country for the same reason that Christian contemplatives sought out isolated places in the

Middle Eastern deserts: to be alone with themselves in a sacred place and, ultimately, with God.[2] In this place, some of the prehuman "beforetime" spirits departed to the heavens or turned into animals or rocks upon the coming of human beings; and this is where the souls of the great Indian doctors reside. It is possible in this place of many spirits to acquire power, fly through the hole in the sky into the heavens, catch a song, or learn esoteric knowledge. And, here is where we shall study how the laws of men and the laws of the Great Spirit intersect.

How are holy places treated by the courts of the conqueror? American law provides surprisingly little legal protection for them. In *Lyng v. Northwest Indian Cemetery Association* (1988), the Supreme Court declared that no First Amendment principle exists that can protect tribal worship on holy ground.[3] In that case, Yurok, Karok, and Tolowa Indians asked the federal courts to protect worship in the High Country in the Six Rivers National Forest, where the nearby tribes have worshipped since time immemorial. Their religious traditions, which are aimed at the renewal of the world, depend on the immense spiritual powers found in the High Country to carry out their religion. But their ties to the High Country would be threatened by the coming of the US Forest Service. Surrounded by virgin forest and shrouded in the mountain mists, the High Country stood in the path of logging and road construction. The agency bureaucrats saw the area merely as "733 million board feet" of timber. They wanted to harvest the timber and build a road to haul it out of the wilderness.

Following an extensive trial, the lower courts forestalled the Forest Service. They found that its plan would "virtually destroy" the Indians' religion and halted the destruction under the First Amendment.[4] On review, the Supreme Court accepted that crucial finding of fact. Indeed, Justice William Brennan was appalled at the agency's brutally insensitive conduct. He found it difficult "to imagine conduct more insensitive to religious needs than the Government's determination to build a marginally useful road in the face of uncontradicted evidence that the road will render the practice of respondents' religion impossible."[5] Nonetheless, the Supreme Court still ruled in favor of the agency in a 5-3 decision.

Five justices were confounded by the Indians' claim. They could find no constitutional basis to protect their religion. Justice Sandra Day O'Connor wrote, "the Constitution simply does not provide a principle" to protect the claims.[6] Writing for the majority, she declared that the First Amendment did not apply to the dire circumstances in the case where the existence of an entire religion was at stake. In her technical view, no "burden" is placed on a religious practice unless the government (1) "punishes" people for worshiping or (2) "coerces" them to violate their faith. She engaged in hair-splitting distinctions to argue that the word *prohibit* in the First Amendment does not mean "destruction." As I will explain, this strained parsing harkens us back to a bare level of religious tolerance that was accorded to heretics during the Middle Ages—when nascent nations first agreed not to punish or coerce religious dissidents, and nothing more. That reading of the First Amendment falls short of the vibrant religious liberty expected by most people in modern times.

Under *Lyng*'s minimalist vision of religious liberty, the Forest Service can literally destroy a holy place *and* the associated religion of some five thousand people without "burdening" anyone's religious practices in the eyes of the law, so long as Indians are not punished for worshiping or forced to violate their faith. Of course, it is pure fiction that a religion can be destroyed without burdening peoples' religious practices—one of several unjust legal fictions found in federal Indian law. The remarkable legal fiction in *Lyng* produces a "cruelly surreal result," according to Justice Brennan: "*Government action that will virtually destroy a religion is nevertheless deemed not to 'burden' that religion.*"[7]

As steward of the national forests, the US Forest Service is too often prone to political cronyism, or it becomes the hapless captive to moneyed special-interest groups. During these unfortunate periods, pork-barrel projects take precedence over stewardship in the minds of agency leaders. As a result of the 1988 decision, the agency is free to destroy and desecrate holy ground throughout the American West at will. Few nations are guilty of systematically destroying their own holy places, but some Forest Service leaders think that is the American way, and their shameful abuse of stewardship is executed with complete impunity.[8] There does not appear to be an antidote, for Congress and the courts rarely hold those government agents in check.

On a deeper level, the *Lyng* controversy was about two vastly different ways of looking at the land. The settler state still views land in economic terms, as a resource to be exploited. This is a hangover from our rapacious colonial origins and frontier mentality; and no place is sacred in this view. In 1948, Aldo Leopold, the influential ecologist, forester, and father of wildlife management in the United States, lamented: "There is as yet no ethic dealing with man's relation to land and to the animals and plants which grow upon it."[9] Planting seeds for that ethic, he urged us to decolonize the way we look at the land and evolve a land ethic as the social product of a mature society. He predicted that ethic will fundamentally change our role from conquerors of the land—and the animals and plants that grow on it—to members of a biotic land community:

> In human history, we have learned (I hope), that the conqueror role is eventually self-defeating. Why? Because it is implicit in such a role that the conqueror knows, *ex cathedra*, just what makes the [land] tick, and just what and who is valuable, and what and who is worthless...It always turns out that he knows neither, and this is why his conquests eventually defeat themselves.[10]

Unfortunately, Leopold's land ethic has not taken root. Even many foresters who followed Leopold's footsteps have lost sight of his ideals in their stewardship of the public lands. To them, the natural world must be quantified only for its value to the conquerors as a natural resource. By contrast, the Native experience on the land teaches that some places are holy ground. That experience gave rise to an indigenous belief system that "holds land sacred."[11] These different worldviews are at the heart of a longstanding conflict between two disparate cultures.

Ironically, many Americans revere holy places in lands far away from North America, but they are completely unaware of the ones right under their feet at home. The late congressman Morris Udall called attention to that blind spot in 1978 and urged the nation to respect holy places in our own country.

> For many tribes, the land is filled with physical sites of religious and sacred significance to them. Can we not understand that? Our religions have their Jerusalems, Mount Calvarys, Vaticans, and Meccas. We hold sacred Bethlehem, Nazareth, the Mount of Olives, and the Wailing Wall. Bloody wars have been fought because of these religious sites.[12]

Unfortunately, his ringing words have largely fallen upon deaf ears. Since 1978, government agencies *intentionally* destroy holy places, *even when they know they are holy ground*. To make matters worse, the other branches of the federal government knowingly condone it. Why? Because the government views the land through the eyes of the settler state, and the task of the legal system is to justify that viewpoint. The *Lyng* doctrine does just that: agencies destroy Native American holy places in a land that professes religious liberty. In stark contrast, Congress passes laws that strictly protect church property owned by non-Indian religious groups so that they can be protected from such unthinkable conduct.[13] This doublethink leaves tribal holy places in an unprotected legal status at the mercy of the Forest Service or other like-minded agencies.

This chapter examines the *Lyng* doctrine. To appreciate this case, we must clearly understand the nature of holy places in world religion, and especially the role of the High Country in the religion of the Yurok, Karok, Hoopa, and Tolowa Indians who worship in the Siskiyou Mountains. Finally, we will ask: does an antidote to *Lyng* exist?

What Is a Holy Place?

Holy places cannot be approached safely in many authentic religions without the necessary purification, protection, and ritual preparations. Thus, before our story begins, we must prepare by reviewing the nature of holy places in world religion. Otherwise, we cannot fathom the sacred sites located in our midst.

It is stating the unremarkable to say that all world religions have holy places. From the beginning, humanity's wisdom traditions have shared a unifying dependence, in varying degrees, upon sacred sites. Worship at special religious sites is a basic attribute of religion itself. However, when thinking of sacred sites, most Americans think only of the well-known Christian, Jewish, and Islamic holy places in the Middle East that are familiar to the Judeo-Christian tradition, such as Mount Sinai, Bethlehem, the Wailing Wall, or Mecca. None doubt that these important sites are entitled to stringent legal protection for the practitioners of those faiths. The preservation of such places is the responsibility of each nation. Indeed, the laws of Israel do just that.[14]

Across the world, there is a common human theme of seeking direct spiritual contact at sacred geographical points. The holy places form a rich tapestry where humans can experience direct communication from God, divine beings, or spirits. Each year, the modern world's many places of power attract millions of pilgrims seeking enlightenment, esoteric knowledge, or spiritual communication with God in visionary forms. In the folklore of the eastern Christians, the summit of Golgotha is sacred because that is where Adam was created and buried. It is a cosmic mountain where heaven and earth meet at the center of the world.[15] In Jerusalem, monks from six sects faithfully guard the Church of the Holy Sepulcher, built on the very site where Jesus was crucified. A ladder has stood near the entrance since 1852, awaiting Jesus' prophesied return—it is a sacred space of fundamental importance for all of Christianity. Judaism's most sacred spots are the Wailing Wall, where Hebrew blessings are whispered, and Mount Sinai, where Moses received his lifelong power to communicate with God—the revelatory center of the world where Jewish people ritually return each year. Millions pilgrimage annually to Mecca, the holiest place in all of Islam, to pray at the Kaaba. Even American tourists reverently walk in the footsteps of the prophets in the Holy Land abroad, with camera in hand.

Across the Indian Ocean, the Hindus revere the Ganges River. It is the pathway to salvation. Millions make pilgrimages to Varanasi, the holiest city in Hinduism. Whereas Buddhists seek enlightenment under the Bodhi Tree, because that is where Siddhartha sat in meditation many years ago, attained nirvana, and became the Buddha. Sikh worshipers pray toward the Golden Temple, a holy site that sits upon a sacred pool. In other parts of the world, sacred mountains, waterfalls, caves, and lakes dot the Philippines, Indonesia, Hawaii, Australia, and South America where indigenous people pray. For the primal religions of the world, which are deeply embedded in their indigenous habitats, the religious ties to place are longstanding. As Huston Smith, author of the *The World's Religions*, notes, "Many historical religions are attached to places," but no historical religion "is embedded in place to the extent that tribal religions are."[16]

In short, the modern world is filled with holy places. The renowned religious historian Mircea Eliade defines the tie between visions and holy places that form the basis for many world religions as hierophany, the manifestation of the sacred.[17] He notes that many religions are based upon these dramatic encounters with supernatural beings that manifest themselves in natural places, like the sky, mountains, stones, and water bodies. Hierophanies can reveal esoteric knowledge or convey broader revelations for groups of people or nations, and they often transform the ordinary places where these extraordinary events occur into a spiritual center of the world, in the religious sense, for the community involved. Thus, ordinary spots become revered as primal ground where the first or most important revelations occurred, forming sacred geography demarcated from the mundane world. At the end of the day, however, a full understanding of a sacred place is experiential. You must go there, feel the power, and be instructed in the context of the site in order to appreciate it—otherwise it is possible for one people to destroy or desecrate a place that others consider holy.

Given this widespread pattern of hierophany, can it be that America alone is bereft of holy places? Is ours a vast land where the sacred cannot be found except in man-made places, like churches, the Denver Mint, or Wall Street? "Be attentive," say Native Americans. "Many places in the natural world are hallowed. It is impossible to confine the Great Spirit in man-made artifacts." Recent literature documents that America is home to holy places that rival those in the Middle East.[18] When Moses climbed Mount Sinai, on this side of the world Sweet Medicine ascended Bear Butte. That venerated Cheyenne prophet faced the Creator on a sacred mountain, where he received spiritual gifts and teachings, including the sacred arrows. Upon Sweet Medicine's return, like Moses, he instructed the people in the sacred laws, covenants, prophesies, and ceremonies that shape the Cheyenne Nation to this very day. (The only difference between the two mountains is Bear Butte has no legal protection under the laws of man.)

When thinking about holy places in our corner of the world, it is necessary to begin with man's relationship to the sky. In North America, Father Sky (*Ati'as Tiirawaahat,* in Pawnee) has religious significance. To many tribes, the Sky World forms a great, arched, sacred dome, within which all can live and walk with goodness that comes from the heavens. In the Pawnee origin story, the first woman and man were children of the stars. At Father Sky's direction, these celestial beings placed them upon the earth by a whirlwind funnel cloud in the Great Plains of Nebraska. From that geographic center, the heavens extend outward in all of the sacred directions, as shown in the starry night sky.[19] The vault of the heavens is full of celestial beings who influence the way things are on Mother Earth. They form one vast constellation called the Wildcat, so named after its polka-dot hide. Father Sky sits at the top, in a special place where people can direct their prayers. For this reason, the old-time Pawnees said we can be glad: anywhere you go, we are in a holy place—"Just look up" (*suks riiwataa*). In short, the entire American sky is one vast holy place—one "inexhaustible hierophany," in Eliade's words, and anything that happens there (such as lightning, thunder, or the movement of the stars) "is a moment in that hierophany."[20]

Beneath Father Sky is our home, a land called Mother Earth (*Atira' Huraaru'*) that is filled with holy places. One scholar organized American holy places into seven categories.[21] In no particular order, the first category is religious sites associated with ancient myths from primordial times involving the creation and the way things are, or spots important in migration traditions. Rainbow Bridge is such a place. The natural sandstone bridge is formed by the union of two ancient beings who produce the rain, rainbows, clouds, and moisture that spread over the Dine' Reservation. Out of the Grand Canyon, the Zuni people emerged at the beginning of time. The second category comprises pilgrimage routes through sacred landscapes used by Native people for millennia. The route to Zuni Heaven, where all Zuni go after death, is one such pilgrimage route. The Karok follow a sacred route in order to conduct their World Renewal ceremonies on the banks of the Klamath River. And then there is the mysterious Golden Stairs leading to the High Country in the Siskiyou Mountains, which goes all the way to heaven, as I will discuss later. The third category covers gathering places for especially sacred plants, materials, and minerals. The Peyote Gardens in Texas, the pipestone quarry in Minnesota, and a certain cave in Colorado where all colors of the sacred Ute paints can be found, are examples. Artifacts, like shrines, altars, cairns, and ancient ruins, form the fourth category. This includes places like the Bighorn Medicine Wheel (our corollary to Stonehenge) and the Pueblo shrines that dot New Mexico. Another category consists of burial grounds and massacre sites that are revered in much the same way as the Gettysburg battlefield and Arlington National Cemetery are considered consecrated sacred ground by the American public. Sixth are vision-questing sites, where Native people go to communicate directly with the spirit world, just like Moses and Sweet Medicine did in times past.

And finally, there are the great American sacred centers where many spirits and divine beings live. These are often mountain summits located at the spiritual center of the world for the surrounding tribes where heaven and earth meet, or other prominent natural places on the landscape. These are special places of profound power that combine many of the qualities from the other categories all in one. A partial list of the holy places in this category, published in existing literature, includes: The Four Direction Mountains that surround the Dine' Nation located in Colorado, New Mexico, and Arizona; Bear Lodge (Wyoming), the sacred place of twenty Plains Indian tribes; Pahuk (Nebraska), the home of Pawnee animal spirits; Bear

Butte (South Dakota), where Crazy Horse and Sweet Medicine received their visions and many Indians today still do; Mount Graham (Arizona), the home of Apache mountain spirits; San Francisco Peaks (Arizona), the religious center of the world for all of the southwestern tribes; Mount Shasta (California), the home of supernatural beings and a way station for Indian souls on their way to the Milky Way; Kootenai Falls (Montana), a powerful waterfall vision-questing site and home of primal spirits of the Kootenai Nation; Blue Lake (New Mexico), where the Taos people emerged and founded their pueblo around AD 1300; Sweet Grass Hills (Montana), a living entity and holy place of the Blackfeet; Badger-Two Medicine (Montana), the vision-quest and ceremonial center of the Blackfeet Nation; among others too numerous to name. These places form the center of the world for tribes who practice human religiousness in its earliest mode in America.

In short, our nation is home to numerous Native American holy places. The government is well aware of that fact. In 1979, the secretary of the interior submitted a report to Congress following a one-year study of traditional Native American religions. The report found:

> The Native peoples of this country believe that certain areas of land are holy. These lands may be sacred, for example, because they contain specific natural products, because they are the dwelling place or embodiment of spiritual beings, because they surround or contain burial grounds or because they are sites conducive to communicating with spiritual beings. There are specific religious beliefs regarding each sacred site which form the basis for religious laws governing the site.[22]

The High Country in *Lyng* is one of those places. It is the destination of our case study, and we go there now.

The Land of the Yurok, Who Live at the Base of the High Country

I want to take you to a place of immense beauty—a pristine region so teeming with life that it overpowers the imagination. It's right here in the United States. In March of 2008, I went on a remarkable journey, traveling the entire length of the Klamath River. It started in the Oregon headwaters on the banks of the Williamson River, near Crater Lake and Klamath Marsh, the ancient Klamath Indian settlement.[23] The trip entailed about three hundred miles, descending downstream through breathtaking country and several Indian reservations to the mouth of the Klamath, where it empties into the Pacific Ocean on the Yurok Indian Reservation at Requa, California.

My purpose was to visit the land and people involved in the *Lyng* litigation. The Native American Rights Fund (NARF) had filed a Supreme Court amicus brief to support their cause in 1987, and we attended the oral argument in Washington, DC, to watch Marilyn Miles, a Kickapoo, of California Indian Legal Services argue the case. (She was the second Native American to argue a case before the Supreme Court.)[24] Even though I have litigated water rights for many years in the headwaters of the river for the Klamath Tribes in Oregon, I never spent much time in the lower reaches of California, where the case arose. I would journey into the land of the Yuroks as a guest of Amy Bowers, a NARF attorney and tribal member, and her family. After meeting up near the scenic Klamath River Highway, we would go to Requa, then boat upriver to the confluence of Blue Creek, which originates in the High Country and empties into the Klamath River.

The river begins to run swiftly along the Klamath River Highway, and our entrance into the narrows was welcomed by hunting eagles flying overhead. Sparsely populated, this beautiful valley is hidden in the Klamath Mountains. It is one of America's best-kept secrets—a land that time forgot. Along the way, we spent the night on the Hoopa Valley Indian Reservation at the home of Amy's relations—Susan and Leonard Mastens. Susan is a former president of the National Congress of American Indians and was previously a chairwoman of the Yurok Tribe; Leonard is currently vice-chair of the Hoopa Tribe. Their home in Hoopa sits on the banks of the Klamath, and we feasted that night upon freshly caught steelhead trout. It rained hard during our visit. The next morning, fresh snow lay in the passes. We descended into the coastal rain forest, where the massive redwood trees grow as tall as 379 feet and live to be two thousand years old. They are the longest-living organisms on earth. To Yuroks, the redwood beings are guardians of the sacred places.

Shortly, we arrived at the Yurok Reservation. It fronts the Pacific Ocean and straddles the Klamath River for forty-four miles upstream, extending a mile on either side of the waterway. It is a coastal but distinctly riparian reservation that winds its way into the Siskiyou Mountains. The Yuroks have occupied the valley for millennia, because it is located within their ancestral territory. Numerous historic and prehistoric villages dot the area.

Since the beginning, they have been Salmon People. Each year, major runs of coho, chinook, and steelhead stream into reservation waters, where the sea lions, eagles, and Yurok compete for the catch. Their stewardship of this well-endowed land is strongly evident in the largely undisturbed landscape, clear waters, and teeming populations of fish, birds, and animals of all kinds. These attributes make this reservation one of the last best places in the Pacific Northwest. Where others have despoiled their communities in the span of a few short decades, Yurok Country remains largely unsullied after thousands of years of continuous human habitation.

How is this so? That remarkable feat is no doubt a product of Yurok religion, which fosters a clear land ethic—the hallmark of tribal communities living in their indigenous habitats. The five thousand tribal members carry on an indigenous religious system with numerous ceremonies, such as the First Salmon Ceremony, Doctor Dance, White Deerskin Dance, Jump Dance, Brush Dance, Kick Dance, Boat Dance, and Flower Dance. Some are for healing. Others are World Renewal ceremonies, held to maintain good relations with all of the relatives in the natural world, to protect the earth from catastrophe and maintain the stability of the world, and to pray for the well-being of the land itself. World renewal theology is a feature of primal religion found only rarely in the religious outlook or land stewardship ideals in the modern world. "For the religious man of the archaic cultures," Eliade writes, "the world is renewed annually; in other words, with each new year it recovers its original sanctity, the sanctity that it possessed when it came from the Creator's hands."[25] Stewardship takes on an entirely deeper meaning among tribes that carry on World Renewal ceremonies.

Only those deeply embedded in the land can fathom such a theology—that is "embeddedness," in the words of Smith, to the extent that "order reverses itself and we begin to think, not of primal peoples as embedded in nature, but of nature...extending itself to enter deeply into them, infusing them in order to be fathomed by them."[26] The world renewal outlook in primal religion transcends our lineal conception of time and history, which starts from the time of creation and runs to the end of the world. By contrast, in Yurok time, the community has the freedom to begin the world anew each year and take part in nature's "eternal return."[27] Yurok ceremonies help the world recover all of its powers intact. This primordial stewardship ethos is an archaic treasure from the past that few can fathom today.[28] In this religious worldview, nature recovers with the help of humans, who take part in creation. The Yurok and neighboring tribes along the Klamath River are an exceptionally spiritual people. They reach for the spiritual side of the natural world. Like salmon, they navigate waters that most people can only glimpse. The Yurok way is tied to the High Country, deep in the Siskiyou Mountains.

Two Yurok fishery technicians from the tribal fishery department met us at the dock, Scott Gibson and Steve Nova. We were to motorboat to Blue Creek. Circling out into the bay, where sea lions gathered on the delta by the sea, we made our turn and headed inland, bouncing lightly over the current. (As the only landlubber in the group, I gripped the rails tightly, secure in my life vest and cowboy hat, with braids flying in the wind!) Accompanied by the ever-present eagles, we left the sunny beach behind and swiftly made our way upstream, navigating the misty mountain reaches through the lush streamside reservation landscape, largely unsullied by the hand of man. It was like traveling back in time to a place where the world is young.

At last, we reached our destination. Blue Creek is an azure stream. It originates in the High Country and plummets nearly five thousand feet through old-growth forest to empty into the Klamath at the foot of the mountains. If you snorkel the cool, crystal-clear waters of this incredible stream, you will see large groups of salmon lying in the deep holes.[29] Eagles line the lush banks where abundant wildlife resides. The pristine creek is simply "doing what it is supposed to do," according to Scott. As we bobbed in the water, the Yuroks gazed reverently toward the blue stream and offered their prayer, for ahead lay a pilgrimage trail into the High Country, the mysterious Golden Stairs...

The High Country, the Spiritual Center of the World in Yurok Religion

One does not lightly enter the High Country, for the immense power that abides there can be dangerous for the unprepared. Based on evidence presented in the *Lyng* trial, when medicine people prepare for the World Renewal ceremonies, first they must fast, cleanse, and purify themselves and observe certain taboos so the dances will not fail.[30] Purification cleanses the mind and rids bad thoughts so one can become holy. Power can only be acquired if the spirits recognize your sincerity.[31] Once purified, a medicine person ascends into the High Country to pray and obtain power.

There are several pilgrimage routes used by the nearby tribes. The seeker approaches the High Country in a sacred manner by walking these trails, or running; each step is important because "every step of the way you learn something."[32] The quest is done for the entire community that depends upon the powers received in the High Country for the success of the ceremonies held in the river valley below. The particular trail near Blue Creek is called the Golden Stairs, a pathway followed by Yurok doctors. Like us, doctors from downriver places go by boat to Blue Creek, then follow the stream to the Golden Stairs, where they ascend into the High Country. One Yurok elder said, "One sees where it starts, but not where it is ended," because the trail is a corridor between heaven and earth that leads all the way to heaven; and nobody has ever got to the end of it.[33]

Once in the High Country, one enters into a remarkable haven of wilderness and natural beauty—meadows, valleys, and a pristine old-growth forest where towering Douglas firs grow over three hundred feet tall. Several outcroppings on Medicine Mountain, such as Chimney Rock and Doctor Rock, are special places where seekers can contact the Spirit World. Rhythm sticks help induce a trancelike mental state to be receptive to the spirits, until, at last, direct contact is made! One place along the ridge, known as Peak 8, is at the heart of the spiritual world for the Indians of northern California. This mysterious peak at the crest of the mountain has the most powerful medicine in the area. Only a few people (one person in each generation) possess sufficient power to use Peak 8 safely, for there one can achieve contact with the cosmic universe. Peak 8 "is located below the 'hole in the sky' and…an individual could fly through the hole in the sky and into the heavens."[34] Knowledge obtained there is esoteric and restricted, but medicine people using the peak are "in extreme danger and can be easily hurt."[35]

During the mythic age, the prehuman beforetime spirit people lived in the lowland. They gave early humans all things necessary for life. Later, these spirits retreated to the High Country, where many continue to reside, while others departed to the heavens from one of the mountain meadows. Those spirits, together with the souls of Indian doctors who also reside in the High Country, help the living to make medicine there. The Indians undergo the arduous journey to pray for the renewal of the world and for the whole human race. Since time immemorial, the spiritual well-being of the tribes has depended upon the success of these quests to the High Country.

The High Country lies in the Six Rivers National Forest (SRNF). In 1976, during the Gerald Ford administration, the Forest Service determined to build a logging road right through the middle of this area so that 733 million board feet of timber could be harvested, primarily through clear-cutting.[36] Since 1930, some logging roads had already been built into sections of the SRNF, but the High Country in the center of the national forest remained a roadless wilderness. By 1982, all that remained to connect the roads, access new timber, and haul logs to mills at either end of the forest was a six-mile section through the High Country.

The agency clearly understood the religious importance of the area. It had commissioned an independent study to provide definitive information on the Indian cultural and religious sites in the vicinity. The study, which was completed in 1979, documented all of the aforementioned facts from 166 tribal informants. It concluded that the proposed development would have devastating impacts on the High Country and the attributes that made it a sacred place. The study "found that the entire area 'is significant as an integral and indispensable part of Indian religious conceptualization and practice.'"[37] It pointed out that "[s]pecific sites are used for certain rituals, and 'successful use of the [area] is dependent upon and facilitated by certain qualities of the physical environment, the most important of which are privacy, silence, and an undisturbed natural setting."[38] For these reasons, the study recommended against the project and concluded that it "would cause serious and irreparable damage to the sacred areas which are an integral and necessary part of the belief systems and lifeway of Northwest California Indian peoples."[39]

Imagine the outcry if the government destroyed your place of worship. It would be intolerable for our government to cause "serious and irreparable damage" to sacred sites integral to the belief system of the Christian churches—and unthinkable. Nonetheless, despite this information, the agency adamantly rejected the recommendation of its own study. The regional bureaucrats decided the road was more important for developing "timber and recreation resources and to the economies of Del Norte and Humboldt Counties."[40] Following various appeals, R. Max Peterson, chief of the Forest Service, affirmed the decision and ordered implementation of the plan.[41] He wrote, the Indians "have not shown a compelling reason to forego the benefits that will accrue to the general public from completion of the road as planned," adding that the "Constitution prohibits the government from giving preferential treatment to any religion."[42] Peterson's decision was made during the heyday of clear-cutting the national forests in the 1980s, when government "stewardship" stockpiled forest resources only until it became politically expedient to exploit them. Individuals always act for an institution. Those responsible for the agency decisions in *Lyng* disserved the tribes and brought about a lawsuit in the courts of the conquerors.

The Trial: Indians Go to Court to Protect Worship on Holy Ground

As road construction drew near in the summer of 1982, the Indians filed a lawsuit in federal district court in San Francisco to halt the destruction of the High Country. The Indian plaintiffs were tribal elders Jimmie Jones, Sam Jones, Lowana Brantner, and a young man named Christopher H. Peters, together with the Northwest Indian Cemetery Protective Association, composed of sixty-five Tolowa, Yurok, Karok, and Hupa. They were joined by various environmental groups, and the State of California filed a separate complaint to oppose the Forest Service plan by and through two state agencies, the Resource Agency and Native American Heritage Commission. Among other things, the two consolidated cases asserted that the project would impermissibly destroy the religious area and infringe upon the Indians' ability to practice their religion, in violation of the First Amendment to the US Constitution. Together, the plaintiffs sought to protect Native worship on holy ground under the First Amendment in the courts of the conqueror.

The case was assigned to the late Judge Stanley A. Weigel (1907–1999), one of the most famous federal district court judges of his day. Weigel was appointed to the bench in 1962 by President John F. Kennedy and had reached senior status by the time the case came to him. According to the press, he was considered "a tough judge with a short fuse, but he was also known for his independence and his courage to render decisions regardless of their popularity."[43] To many unfortunate lawyers, the San Francisco judge "was renowned for being a great curmudgeon and being particularly tough on attorneys," but he had a reputation for "being a fair jurist."[44] Representing the Indians was a young Native staff attorney of the California Indian Legal Services (CILS), Marilyn B. Miles (who is now a distinguished judge on the California Superior Court). This case was her first major federal court litigation, just two years out of University of California at Davis School of Law, and it would take her all the way to the highest court in the land.

Judge Weigel denied the plaintiffs' motion for a temporary restraining order (TRO) to halt the project, but scheduled an expedited evidentiary trial on the merits, giving the attorneys just six weeks to prepare. The first day of trial in the packed courtroom was rough sledding for Miles. Her opening statement was repeatedly interrupted and criticized by Judge Weigel, and, worse yet, he threatened to exclude crucial evidence—every young attorney's worst nightmare![45] But the tide began to change on the second day, when Judge Weigel admitted crucial evidence from the administrative record and Miles's Indian witnesses began to tell their stories in their own words.

The lead witness was the youthful Chris Peters, the grandson of one of the Indian doctors.[46] The long-haired Indian man presented a slide presentation in open court as plaintiffs' Exhibit 1 to allow the judge to visualize the pristine beauty of the holy places. He began his testimony in the San Francisco courtroom:

> The Yurok, Karok and Tolowa Indian Tribes live in the northwestern corner of California. These tribes share the use of a very special religious area. That area is located in the southern portion of the Siskiyou Mountains, and referred to by the Indian people as the "high country." Doctor Rock, Chimney Rock, Peak 8 and Little Medicine Mountain are located within this religious area and are some of the more sacred places within the high country. They have been used throughout the years by Indian people who go there to pray for special purposes [or] special powers, or medicine. The high country was placed there by the creator as a place where Indian people could seek religious power...This area is our church: cannot be moved or disturbed in any way.[47]

The young man testified that "any adverse changes in the high country will have a direct impact on the practice of our religious beliefs" and this holy place is not only "essential to our religious beliefs," but is "the very core of our cultural identity."[48] One by one, the tribal witnesses shared their profound religious experiences in the High Country with Judge Weigel and explained how the development would destroy the religious efficacy of that place. One witness explained:

> That area belongs to a spiritual world that was put there by a creator or a spirit for Indian people to use. It is the core, it is the very center of our cultural identity. It is where we get the power that makes our religious ceremonies significant. Where we get personal power that reaffirms our Indianess and our way of life. To disrupt it and to destroy it, as the Forest

Service is proposing to do, would definitely have an impact on the regeneration of Indian people. Currently it would totally destroy any hope of our grandchildren from knowing what that area has for them.[49]

Another elder testified about the project's destructive impact on the holy place.

The high country is like our church. In building a road through our church would really be destructive in my frame of mind…[The Indians] have to pray. When the medicine [women] go out there to pray, they stand on these rocks. They call them Doctor Rock and Chimney Rock and they meditate. I mean the forest is there looking out. They talk to the trees and rocks, whatever is out there. Our people talk in their language to them and if it's all logged off and all bald there, they can't meditate at all. They have nothing to talk to and after they get through praying, their answer comes from the mountain. The medicine lady that goes there or man will see a light or a phantom or whatever they see and then their prayers are answered.[50]

The eloquent witnesses testified from the heart. Their stories had a powerful impact on Judge Weigel, who began to connect with the elders. "With each new witness," according to observers, "slowly but surely, Judge Weigel was starting to grasp the significance of the Sacred High County."[51] Having set the stage, Miles then played her ace card. The last witness was a grand medicine woman, Lowana Brantner, who clearly entranced Judge Weigel. Before the packed courtroom, she asked him to close his eyes and accompany her to the High Country. What happened next is a remarkable moment in the modern era of federal Indian law.

The room was deathly still as Judge Weigel and Lowana Brantner embarked on their journey. As the clock ticked on and seconds became minutes, the silence deepened even further and the only sound was the occasional muted cough. Finally, Lowana opened her eyes and commanded Judge Weigel to return. She turned to him and said, "Now do you know what we mean?" His response was simply, "Yes, I do."[52]

For all intents and purposes, the case was won. The courtroom erupted into applause, cheers, crying, and laughter as the judge turned to the defendants and secured their promise not to construct the road until he issued his decision. "Judge Wiegel, a most careful preserver of decorum, let the celebration go on for some time as he and Lowana smiled at each other," according to observers. "Those of us who were there that day will never forget it."[53]

Looking back today on this moving experience in her first major case, Judge Miles attributes the successful outcome in the district court to the power of the elders: "I have always believed that it was because we focused on the spiritual, religious, the power of the places and the people, that this particular case played out as it did."[54] Paying tribute to her clients, Judge Miles stated, "Knowing it was my first case, they were so gracious and confident with our goal for the trial: to allow elders to tell their story and to warn those who did not know or understand the harm that comes from destroying sacred and powerful areas."[55] Her strategy (which was to find a tough, but fair-minded judge, then let the elders and medicine people tell their stories) was a winning formula followed in the great trials during the modern era of federal Indian law that produced a remarkable track record.[56]

The Lower Courts Protected Indian Worship in the High Country

Judge Weigel handed down a landmark decision in 1983. The opinion begins by noting that the "unorthodox character" of the tribal religious beliefs is no basis for denying constitutional protection.[57] The district court found that the High Country is "considered sacred by members of the Yurok, Karok, and Tolowa Indian tribes."[58] Judge Weigel summarized the undisputed evidence established at the trial:

> Ceremonial use of the high country by the Yurok, Karok, and Tolowa tribes dates back to the early nineteenth century…and probably much earlier…Members of these tribes currently make regular use of the high country for several religious purposes. Individuals hike into the high country and use "prayer seats" located at Doctor Rock, Chimney Rock, and Peak 8 to seek religious guidance or personal "power" through "engaging in emotional [and] spiritual exchange with the creator" (Tr. at 79). Such exchange is made possible by the solitude, quietness, and pristine environment found in the high country. Certain key participants in tribal religious ceremonies, such as the White Deerskin and Jump Dances must visit the high country to purify themselves and

make "preparatory medicine." The religious power these individuals acquire in the high country lends meaning to these tribal ceremonies, thereby enhancing the spiritual welfare of the entire community. Medicine women in the tribes travel to the high country to pray, to obtain spiritual power, and to gather medicines. They then return to the tribe to administer to the sick the healing power gained in the high country through ceremonies such as the Brush Dance and Kick Dances.[59]

Based on the evidence, Judge Weigel determined that "for generations" the tribes "have traveled to the high country to communicate with the 'great creator,' to perform rituals, and to prepare for specific religious and medicinal ceremonies," which uses are "central and indispensable" to their religion.[60] He concluded:

> For the Yurok, Karok, and Tolowa peoples, the high country constitutes the center of the spiritual world. No other geographical areas or sites hold equivalent religious significance for these tribes. Further, use of the high country is essential to performing the "World Renewal" ceremonies, such as the White Deerskin and Jump Dances, which constitute the heart of the Northwest Indian religious belief system. Finally, use of the high country in training young persons in the tribes in traditional religious beliefs and ceremonies is necessary to preserve such practices and to convey them to future generations. Degradation of the high country and impairment of such training would carry "a very real threat of undermining the [tribal] communities and religious practice[s] as they exist today."[61]

The court found that Forest Service logging and road construction would place a burden upon the Indians' religious practices by violating the sacred qualities of the High Country and impairing its religious uses by the tribes in several respects. First, the road would destroy pristine conditions in the roadless wilderness area that are essential for its religious use. Second, noise from logging and traffic would impair the vision quests. (Even Moses could acquire no vision under those circumstances.) Third, environmental degradation from the road would erode the religious significance of the area. (Similarly, if the Israeli government built a road through the Church of the Holy Sepulcher, it would erode the religious significance of the site where Jesus was crucified.) Finally, the religious use of the area would be impaired by increased recreational use resulting from the new road (just like tourists could interfere with Muslim prayers at the Kaaba if allowed to picnic and play touch football in that holy place during times of prayer). Accordingly, the court ruled that the road construction and logging would "seriously damage" the qualities of the High Country necessary for tribal worship and were "potentially destructive of the very core of Northwest [Indian] religious beliefs and practices."[62]

Finally, Judge Weigel proceeded to apply the compelling-government-interest legal test to see whether the Forest Service's logging and road interests were of sufficient magnitude to override the burden that the project would place upon tribal religious practices. He found that those interests were marginal at best and speculative. The road would provide no net increase in jobs, no material increase in timber harvest, and only speculative improvements in forest administration, and any recreational benefits were cancelled by resulting environmental degradation.[63] Thus, under the constitutional test, the Forest Service action would unlawfully burden the Indians' freedom of religion protected by the Free Exercise Clause of the First Amendment to the US Constitution. Judge Weigel therefore enjoined the construction of the road and the plan to log the area. In so doing, he also rejected the Forest Service's argument that this relief would create a "government-managed 'religious shrine' in violation of the Establishment Clause of the First Amendment."[64]

In 1986, Judge Weigel's decision was affirmed by the Ninth Circuit Court of Appeals in a 2-1 decision written by Circuit Judge William C. Canby Jr., who is himself a distinguished scholar in federal Indian law.[65] While the case was on appeal, Congress enacted the California Wilderness Act (1984), which placed most of the area into protected wilderness status, leaving open only a twelve-hundred-foot corridor for the completion of the G-O road.[66] The act reduced the issue of logging, "although it does not disappear," and Congress did not take a position on whether the road should be completed, but left that dispute to the courts.[67] The court of appeals agreed with Judge Weigel that the proposed project would impermissibly interfere with the Indians' free exercise of religion rights for two reasons. First, the High Country was a religious place of central importance to the tribes:

> There is a great deal of evidence in the record that the high country is
> indispensable to a significant number of Indian healers and religious

leaders as a place where they receive the "power" that permits them to fill the religious roles that are central to the traditional religions. There is abundant evidence that the unitary pristine nature of the high country is essential to this religious use. Finally, there is much evidence that the religious lives of many other Indians depends upon the services of those leaders who have received the necessary "power" in the high country. On all of these points, there is virtually no evidence to the contrary.[68]

Second, evidence admitted at the trial "amply supports, indeed virtually compels, the conclusion that logging and the construction of logging roads would be utterly inconsistent with the Indians' religious practices."[69] The court of appeals concluded that the project would "virtually destroy" the Indians' ability to practice their religion.[70] The court rejected the Forest Service's argument that there is no burden upon religion unless the government actually penalizes religious practices. That argument was based upon a holding in an earlier Indian religion case, *Bowen v. Roy* (1986), which held that a government social security number assigned to an Indian child for purposes of providing government benefits does not burden any religious practices, because the parents were merely attacking a purely internal government operation that offended their religious sensibilities.[71] By contrast, the *Lyng* Court distinguished *Roy* since the plaintiffs had proved that logging and road construction would "virtually destroy" their ability to practice their religion and, in addition, "logging and road-building on public lands, to which the public has access, is not the kind of internal governmental practice that the Court found beyond free exercise attack in *Roy*."[72]

With a landmark victory firmly in hand, the Indians readied for the ultimate test of their claims, because their cause was now poised to go the Supreme Court. The hard-fought victory in the lower courts would soon be reversed by the Supreme Court in one of the worst Indian cases ever decided.

The Supreme Court Denies Protection for Worship in the High Country

The fate of tribal worship in the High Country would be determined by the Rehnquist Court. As I discussed in the previous chapter, during the late 1980s, that Court was preoccupied with restricting twentieth-century notions of American religious liberty established by the Stone, Vinson, Warren, and Burger Courts. That expansive vision of religious liberty in a constitutional democracy came to an abrupt end shortly after President Reagan appointed three new justices during the 1980s—Sandra Day O'Connor, Antonin G. Scalia, and Anthony M. Kennedy. To lead this conservative cohort, Reagan promoted William H. Rehnquist to succeed Warren Berger as the chief justice in 1986. Thus, the *Lyng* case came before the most archconservative Supreme Court in the twentieth century. As a newly constituted majority, the conservative axis of the Court was eager to flex its muscle and make its mark on American society.

Given the strong evidentiary record established at trial by Marilyn Miles and the findings of fact made in the lower courts, it would be difficult for the Rehnquist Court to rule against the Indians under existing law without doing some mighty fancy footwork, and that is exactly what the majority did in a 5-3 decision. The majority opinion was written by Justice O'Connor. As I will explain, the infamous decision turned on a couple of unjust legal fictions bolstered by judicial sophistry and hair-splitting distinctions of the highest order.

First, the majority ruled that federal land management of public lands cannot burden anyone's religious practices as a matter of law. O'Connor reasoned that land management is purely an internal government affair that, by its very nature, can have no more impact upon anyone's religious practices than the color of government filing cabinets.[73] She supported this irrational presumption of fact by expanding the holding in *Bowen v. Roy* (that purely internal government operations cannot by their very nature burden religious practices) to control much different facts in the *Lyng* case.[74] While the facts in *Roy* obviously warranted such a holding since that case involved an internal agency office's computerized numbering system and it is hard to see how that function can possibly affect any religious practice, O'Connor failed to see any difference between the two cases. She concluded: "The building of a road or the harvesting of timber on publically owned land cannot meaningfully be distinguished from the use of a Social Security number in *Roy*."[75] Her failure to distinguish the different factual situation in *Roy* from the facts in *Lyng* is disingenuous; but that sophistry effectively placed Indian worship on federal lands outside the purview of cognizable First Amendment claims.

In his dissenting opinion, Justice Brennan found O'Connor's professed "inability to differentiate *Roy* from the present case" to be "altogether remarkable."[76] The fallacy of applying *Roy* to the facts at hand was readily apparent to him: the social security numbering system used in government computer systems at issue in *Roy* was clearly an internal matter—just like the color of office filing cabinets, that internal governmental administrative matter was highly unlikely to affect anyone's religious practices. By contrast, federal land-use decisions "have substantial external effects that government decisions concerning office furniture" do not have.[77] Because land-use decisions can actually, in fact, place a burden upon religious practices as demonstrated by the evidence, Brennan persuasively argued that the application of *Roy* is "wholly untenable"; and it produces the "cruelly surreal result" that "government action that will virtually destroy a religion is nevertheless deemed not to 'burden' that religion."[78] In short, the majority's assumption that federal land-use actions are merely internal government matters that cannot affect religious practices is an unwarranted legal fiction. Brennan pointed out the fallacy of that fiction:

> The land-use decision challenged here will restrain respondents from practicing their religion as surely and as completely as any of the governmental actions we have struck down in the past, and the Court's efforts simply to define away respondents' injury as nonconstitutional are both unjustified and ultimately unpersuasive.[79]

Second, the sharply divided court enunciated a hard and fast rule that so severely restricted the reach of the First Amendment to such rare circumstances that little room for constitutional protection against government actions that infringe upon religious liberty remains. It declared that no burden is placed upon religious practices unless the government also punishes a person for practicing religion or forces one to violate his religion. Only those narrow circumstances trigger First Amendment protections. Under this restrictive vision of religious liberty, government can destroy an entire religion with constitutional impunity, so long as it does not go further and punish anyone in the process nor coerce practitioners to violate their religious tenets. Under that crabbed standard, it did not matter that the Forest Service project will "virtually destroy the Indians' ability to practice their religion," because the agency is not punishing Indians for practicing their religion, nor forcing them to violate any of their beliefs.[80] O'Connor wrote:

> Even if we assume that we should accept the Ninth Circuit's prediction, according to which the G-O Road will "virtually destroy the Indians'

ability to practice their religion," 795 F.2d at 693 (opinion below), the Constitution simply does not provide a principle that could justify upholding [the Indians'] claim.[81]

Of course, it is a legal fiction that an entire religion can be destroyed without placing a burden upon religious practices. The Court reached this harsh result by construing the First Amendment in the narrowest terms possible. Splitting hairs, O'Connor distinguished the word *prohibit*, as used in the Free Exercise Clause, from *destroy* and under her narrow parsing of the term any government action that places indirect coercion or penalties upon the free exercise of religion and makes it more difficult to practice religion is not covered by that term.[82] Under this fine distinction, it was perfectly legal to log the High Country and build a road through the holy places even though that activity would "have devastating effects on traditional Indian religious practices."[83] While the constitution itself draws no fine distinctions between the types of restraints on religious exercise, that's just the way it goes in the courts of the conqueror when it comes to protecting worship on holy ground.

The fancy footwork in *Lyng* was driven by the Court's apprehension that recognizing the Indians' religion claim might someday bring civilization to its knees. Justice O'Connor sought to forestall an imaginary parade of horribles. If the Forest Service had to accommodate tribal worship in the High Country, she worried that crafty Indians might someday parlay that protection into a "veto over public programs" or in the future "seek to exclude all human activity but their own from sacred areas of the public lands." Or, worse yet, she feared that Indian entrepreneurs might somehow acquire "de facto beneficial ownership of some rather spacious tracts of public property" (just like ranchers, miners, and ski resort owners who use vast amounts of public lands) and bring about a "diminution of the Government's property rights, and the concomitant subsidy of Indian religion"—and in her worst nightmare, these subversive horribles could even "divest the Government of its right to use what is, after all, *its* land."[84] These unsubstantiated fears of barbarians at the gate motivated a ruling that would above all safeguard the government against these apprehensions, no matter how remote. This paranoid mind-set sees Indian religious practitioners much like the early European rulers saw religious heretics in their midst—as traitors to the state; and it would be unthinkable to extend a significant measure of religious liberty to Indians under these circumstances. It is a far better judicial policy to sacrifice those ideals and nip these fears in the bud than to subject the state to the alarming hardships imagined by the Rehnquist Court.

Lyng's Far-Reaching Impacts Left Indelible Marks on American Society

After *Lyng*, no constitutional principle exists to protect Native worship on holy ground located on public land. These holy places are preexisting ancient sites deemed sacred by indigenous peoples many centuries before they came into federal ownership. Though each nation is responsible for protecting holy places located within its borders, the *Lyng* ruling leaves American holy places at the complete mercy of the federal government and lets agencies destroy them with constitutional impunity. Under this loophole in religious freedom, there is no enforceable legal protection for this universal form of worship at holy places in the American legal system.[85]

Native American efforts to secure legislative protection for tribal worship at American holy places have been steadfastly opposed by the federal government since 1988. Instead, Congress created a double standard for statutory protection of holy places in the United States in 2000. The Religious Land Use and Institutionalized Persons Act of 2000 (RLUIPA) protects the religious use of church property only if the claimant "has an ownership, leasehold, easement, servitude, or other property interest in the regulated land."[86] While the RLUIPA standards help to ensure that no church, synagogue, mosque, cathedral, Sunday school, church school, camp, or parking lot will be bulldozed, the property ownership requirements of that law operate to exclude all indigenous holy places that are no longer owned by Native people dispossessed by the conquest and settlement of the frontier. This oversight not only gives rise to second-class treatment of Native American holy places, but this markedly disparate statutory treatment may run afoul of the Equal Protection and Establishment Clauses of the Constitution by impermissibly fostering and favoring one category of religious places while excluding another category. As a result, indigenous religious sites have been bulldozed, flooded, paved over, clear-cut, commercialized, and desecrated by agencies and tourists, and shelled by the military. In 1995, forty-four sites were threatened by development, tourism, resource exploitation, looting, and vandalism.[87] Such an onslaught would shock and outrage the nation if committed against church or government-owned religious property.

In contrast to the stringent RLUIPA protections for other religious property, the only protection afforded to Native American holy places is an unenforceable "policy" promulgated by President Bill Clinton encouraging federal agencies to accommodate tribal worship at holy places on federal land and to avoid harming those places "to the extent practicable, permitted by law, and not clearly inconsistent with essential agency functions."[88] This policy has not prevented the Forest Service from desecrating important tribal holy places, as most recently seen in *Navajo Nation v. US Forest Service* (2008), in which the agency is proposing to pour fecal matter on a tribal holy place in order to make artificial snow from recycled sewer water in order to subsidize a privately owned ski resort.[89]

There obviously remains a pressing need for law reform to protect Native worship on holy ground in the United States. Relief can be provided by a new federal law. Alternatively, advocates must develop a sound constitutional theory rooted in the Free Exercise Clause, which can only be accomplished by overturning *Lyng*. Otherwise, advocates must look elsewhere in the Constitution for a new source of protection for the last remaining tribal cultures that are dependent upon worship at holy places.

As suggested by the Indian religion cases of *Bowen*, *Lyng*, and *Smith*, it may well be that the First Amendment does not and was never intended to include religious freedom for American Indians. Our legal and religious history seems to bear this conclusion out. When the framers drafted the Constitution, Indians were not citizens and few were subject to US law. The framers recognized that Indians were members of distinct political sovereigns and treated the Indian tribes as such in that organic document.[90] Perhaps the time has come to discard the notion that the framers intended to include tribal religion in the Bill of Rights, since most of them would not recognize those religions as anything other than rank superstition. As I will discuss in chapter fifteen, we can look elsewhere in the Constitution to find a more reliable basis for protecting tribal religions. The government has ample constitutional authority to protect holy places and accommodate Native worship on public lands *when it wants to*.[91] Yet, the survival of those places cannot depend solely upon voluntary government accommodation. Instead, the protectorate relationship assumed by the US government under the *Worcester* doctrine ought to *require* the government to protect those places as the guardian of domestic dependent Indian nations.[92] Because the culture, religion, and very identity of Indian tribes is often dependent upon worship at tribal holy places—as seen in the Yurok World Renewal Religion—the protectorate principle of federal Indian law should impose an affirmative and enforceable obligation to protect those places from harm, as an integral part of the trust responsibility necessary to the well-being of the domestic dependent Indian nations. Failing that, Congress should enact a new federal statute for that purpose.

Without legal protection, the last remaining sacred places left in the natural world will continue to be destroyed by the government until the land has been wiped clean of its spiritual dimension, leaving our people with a sterile landscape where the Great Spirit can be found only in the concrete and steel structures built by man. Why should we care whether an antidote to such a future exists? At first blush, the infamous *Lyng* case places a yoke only upon Native American communities since they alone hold religious ties to holy ground in the natural world. The attitude of many mainstream religious groups is: *we have protection for our religions; let the Indians fend for themselves—it's every man for himself.* Yet the *Lyng* mentality affects everyone in several important ways. As I will discuss, *Lyng* contributed to the frightening slide to *Employment Division v. Smith* (1990) and the resulting demise of the First Amendment. Despite that upheaval, *Lyng* remains the law of the land—it has never been rooted out of the law like *Smith*, which was soundly repudiated by Congress in fairly short order. On a metaphysical level, *Lyng* impedes our search for the spiritual side of Mother Earth. Environmentally, it bars the pathway for developing a meaningful land ethic needed by our nation. Socially, it stymies social evolution from a settler state.

The *Lyng* doctrine has never been reversed by the Supreme Court nor repealed by Congress. Aside from the devastating impact upon Indian tribes and Native Hawaiian communities, the doctrine has inflicted two deleterious impacts on general American religious liberty that should not be tolerated.

First, the weakening of religious liberty in *Lyng* led directly to the slide toward the infamous *Smith* decision in 1990 that precipitated the outbreak of an unprecedented religion crisis in the 1990s.[93] *Smith* was soundly repudiated by several acts of Congress, but *Lyng* still lies in the weeds as a blemish on the same ideals that exhorted Congress to repudiate *Smith*. Legal advocates should seek to overturn the *Lyng* doctrine, like the opponents of racial segregation who toiled to overturn the noxious separate-but-equal doctrine that perpetrated injustice for so many for so long.

Second, by drastically curtailing the scope of the First Amendment, the *Lyng* doctrine has fundamentally altered the nature of American society. We now have less constitutional protection for religious liberty than most other democracies. It should deeply concern us all that the minimalist vision of religious liberty emanating from *Lyng* is one of bare toleration of religion in a secular society. The rule allowing religious freedom to exist in our diverse society as a protected liberty only to the extent that one is not punished or coerced, and no more, is a medieval principle that is sorely out of step with the needs and ideals of twenty-first-century America.

That crabbed principle is also at odds with the intent of the framers of the Constitution. It must be remembered that when the Founding Fathers wrote the First Amendment, they sought to enshrine freedom of worship as a foundational principle of the Republic and to radically depart from the repressive religious history of Europe. In a later case, Justice O'Connor herself, after tracing the historical development leading to the writing of the Free Exercise Clause in 1791, concluded that "around the time of the drafting of the Bill of Rights, it was generally accepted that the right to 'free exercise' required, where possible, accommodation of religious practice."[94] *Accommodation* is a revolutionary concept in human history that requires much more than simple tolerance of religion—it is the affirmative and robust protection of full and free religious exercise, rather than a bare commitment not to punish a person for practicing religion or coercing one to violate relief tenets.

James Madison, one of the principal architects of the Bill of Rights, strenuously objected to the use of the word *toleration* during the drafting of the Bill of Rights. He contended that word implied that the right to practice one's religion was merely "a government favor, rather than an inalienable right."[95] For Madison, simple "tolerance" countenanced too much state interference in religious conscience. He advocated a shift toward the language of rights because, *"all men are equally entitled to the full and free exercise of [religion or the duty we owe our Creator], according to the dictates of conscience."*[96] Justice O'Connor correctly observed that in the days when the Bill of Rights was drafted "it was accepted that government should, when possible, accommodate religious practice." The new republic was inhabited by people of deep religious conviction who expected their government to uphold their religious exercise, especially at a time when government was far less intrusive than it is today. The accommodation principle of the revolutionary leaders—including Madison, Thomas Jefferson, and George Washington—radically departed from the long history of European religious intolerance and rose above the bare level of tolerance that was just emerging in the kingdoms, aristocracies, and theocracies of Europe.[97]

In abandoning a bare tolerance standard as the guideline for the First Amendment, Justice O'Connor aptly noted in 1997 that the Founding Fathers took a profound step that has deeply shaped the character of this nation:

> The Religion Clauses of the Constitution represent a profound commitment to religious liberty. Our Nation's Founders conceived of a Republic receptive to voluntary religious experience, not of a secular society in which religious expression is tolerated only when it does not conflict with a generally applicable law. As the historical sources discussed above show, the Free Exercise Clause is properly understood as an affirmative guarantee of the right to participate in religious activities without impermissible government interference, even when a believer's conduct is in tension with a law of general application. Certainly, it is in no way anomalous to accord heightened protection to a right identified in the text of the First Amendment.[98]

The *Lyng* doctrine simply does not comport with the vibrant standard for religious liberty intended by the framers. Instead, *Lyng's* tolerance standard harkens us back to the medieval ages, when the nascent nations of Europe merely tolerated the existence of heretics in the community without being punished or coerced into abandoning their dissident religious beliefs.

The emergence of religious liberty in human history is a relatively recent phenomenon. Even though the original teachings in all world religions preach respect for the beliefs of others, few lived up to those ideals.[99] Religious liberty existed nowhere in Europe during the Middle Ages. Historians have marked the long and tortuous path that the emergence of religious liberty took in Europe, where an immense change was required to rid itself from centuries of religious intolerance and to rise up to a minimal level of tolerance.[100] During that period, heretics were seen as traitors to the state, religious differences were demonized, and it was unthinkable to grant "religious freedom" to heretics, to infidels, or those thought to be held captive by demonic forces.[101] Inquisitions were the order of the day, until the crowned heads and pointy-headed potentates of Europe finally realized that for religion to be authentic, articles of faith cannot be rammed down the throat by the church or the state. Instead, belief must be accepted as a voluntary, personal, and free choice; and a coerced or forcibly imposed faith is an absurd contradiction in terms.

However, it was not until the middle of the sixteenth century onward "that a few voices were raised in defense of genuine religious freedom," according to one historian, and finally, "the execution of Servetus for heresy in Calvin's Geneva (1553) evoked a response from Sebastian Castellio, *On Heretics, Whether they Should be Prosecuted* that provided the first full-scale argument for freedom of conscience."[102] This radical new idea did not take hold for over a century, when English pamphlets began to condemn persecution and demand real religious liberty for all, not just toleration for one particular group. The rise from bare tolerance to religious liberty was slow in coming. One historian recounts the many years it took to make that vital transition to the kind of vibrant religious liberty that many take for granted today.

> By the end of the seventeenth century, reasonably adequate theories of religious rights had been formulated. Implementing them took much longer. Persecution became more sporadic in the eighteenth century, but it was not until the liberal revolution of the nineteenth century that freedom of religion became widely established in the constitutions of Western states and not until the twentieth century that the major Christian churches proclaimed religious rights as an essential feature of the Christian faith itself.[103]

The birth of true religious liberty, as it is known today, took place in large measure on our shores, as documented in the historical sources surrounding the writing of the Bill of Rights in 1791. That is why ours is the land of the free.

Unfortunately, *Lyng* would take us back to a time when society begrudgingly tolerated religious differences and refrained from punishing or coercing religious minorities. We should not accept that retreat from religious liberty. Nor should we allow the legal system to disclaim responsibility to protect Native American worship on holy ground. On the contrary, affirmative remedial protection is required to protect and preserve the last endangered religious sites in Native North America as irreplaceable national treasures. Lest there be any hesitation, the UN Declaration on the Rights of

Indigenous Peoples (2007) asks each nation to protect the inherent right of indigenous peoples "to maintain, protect, and have access in privacy to their religious and cultural sites."[104] This tall order is the unfinished business of the next generation.

Beyond the religious human-rights sphere, it is important to decolonize the way we look at the land before the last holy places are gone, if we are ever to become a distinctively American people. The presence of aboriginal holy places makes our nation distinct from any other land. We cannot shed the trappings of the settler-state mentality until we cast aside the role of the conqueror and evolve a land ethic as the social product of a nonsettler state, just like the Native people who came to terms with the land centuries ago. To be sure, our disparate peoples cannot fully adapt to the landscape until we recognize the spiritual side of Mother Earth and take the indigenous perspectives into account. Long ago, the peoples of Europe took God out of nature in that part of the world during the rise of the modern secular age; but the tribal peoples of America tell us that this land is still sacred and the Great Spirit does abide in the natural world. The challenge is to hold the legal system accountable to that reality. After all, in a more just society, it is not hard to imagine the descendants of settlers and Natives joined in a rich, viable relationship that encourages their joint experience living on the land where they were born. *Lyng* stands as a legal barrier to these social changes. The law should foster, not impede, the negotiation of that new relationship. Hence, this chapter argues for a retreat from injustice manifested in the *Lyng* doctrine.

The law should take Indigenous religious needs into account so valuable Native American wisdom can be shared about the spiritual side of Mother Earth, the need for a land ethic, and so that our joint experience on the land can be celebrated. A Mohican prophecy shines the way to the mountaintop:

> A long time ago the Creator came to Turtle Island and said to the Red People: "You will be the keepers of Mother Earth. Among you I will give the wisdom about Nature, about the interconnectedness of all things, about balance and about living in harmony. You Red People will see the secrets of Nature...The day will come when you will need to share the secrets with other people of the Earth because they will stray from their Spiritual ways. The time to start sharing is today.[105]

There is one fitting postscript to the *Lyng* decision: the Forest Service was ultimately foiled by Congress. In 1990, the agency's plan to destroy the High Country was blocked by the passage of the Smith River National Recreation Area Act.[106] This act was spurred by the Indians' attorneys from the California Indian Legal Services. It added the twelve-hundred-foot G-O Road corridor into the protected Siskiyou Wilderness, ending the misguided project once and for all. The prehuman beforetime spirits had the last word in this matter; and they were more interested in the World Renewal ceremonies of the Yurok, Karok, Tolowa, and Hoopa Indians than the nefarious plans of insensitive Forest Service officials. Consequently, it is still possible for the mystics among these tribes to ascend into the High Country, just as their forbearers have done for centuries, to meet the Great Spirit and obtain the power to help the natural world renew all of its powers intact—a feat for which all of humanity should be grateful. These tribes still retain a rare indigenous religious system, which is a national treasure we should strive to preserve, not destroy.

What Lies Beneath The Water

CHAPTER THIRTEEN

Tee-Hit-Ton Indians v. United States:
Confiscating Indigenous Habitat

THE PEOPLE WERE MIGRATING downstream, searching for a better life. Following the banks of a mountain stream, they came upon a glacier! The vast field of ice blocked their trek. Seemingly impassable, it was too steep to climb and too far to go around. Yet, the river flowed beneath the deep crevasses, so the people decided to build a raft and float underneath the glacier. Once the vessel was built, they asked, "Who will go?" Two elderly women volunteered. "We have lived a long life. We will go." The pair boldly floated into the mountain of ice and disappeared.

When they emerged on the other side, the elders discovered a wondrous land. It was an immense temperate rain forest beside the sea, a maritime paradise teeming with awesome creatures, edible plants of all kinds, and bountiful waterways in one of the most beautiful places in the world.[1] This *terra nullius* (land belonging to no one) was a Garden of Eden, located right on the shores of Native North America. The people identified this spectacular place as *Haa Aaní* (Our Land), the Land of the Tlingits.

The Tlingit Indians are one of America's rain forest tribes who reside in the great Pacific Northwest. After ten thousand years, these aboriginal hunters, fishers, and gatherers merged closely with *Haa Aaní* and evolved a striking culture that mirrors their habitat. In mythic times, little difference existed between early humans and the animals and fish that inhabited *Haa Aaní*, except in form. In those days, spirits freely transformed from animal to human, and back. This metaphysical kinship relationship shaped Tlingit society. Over time, the people's relation to the animals created the fabric of Tlingit society. Crossing the line that sometimes divides humans from animals, the people called themselves Eagles or Ravens, and they still do. The Animal-Fish People organized into clans respectfully named after exalted animals or fish who took pity upon early humans, such as the Killer Whale, Dog Salmon, Wolf, Frog, and Bear Clans. Together, the clans make up present-day Tlingit society and provide identity for the people.

The Tlingit inhabit America's largest rain forest—an area about the size of West Virginia. Tribal villages dot shorelines along the islands, bays, rivers, and fjords of southeast Alaska. This homeland forms one of richest environments on earth. It is a place inhabited by whales, salmon, moose, deer, bears, eagles, and many other creatures. Berries of all kinds grow along the streams, and the beaches provide a cornucopia of seafood. This amazing habitat produced an astounding aboriginal culture. Tlingit art, architecture, dance, music, spirituality, technology, and the subsistence way of life arose from the rain forest, rivers, and sea; and they comprise a culture that reflects the rich coastal habitat nestled against snow-covered mountain peaks. In addition to the influences of land and sea, this society is heavily shaped by the animals and plants of southeast Alaska, as seen in the abstract Tlingit art forms, such as carvings, totem poles, masks, and painting style. This beautiful animistic art is surreal, as if produced from another world. It is at once imbued with a powerful spirituality deeply rooted in the natural world. Similarly, the hunting, fishing, and gathering way of life is also based upon the same spirituality. Tlingit ties to tribal habitat run deep, because the two are one in the same.

In 1909, the United States Forest Service arrived. With a vastly different cosmology, heavy-handed agency rulers asserted control of *Haa Aaní* as the new landlords. No Indian treaty or agreement was reached to authorize agency occupation of aboriginal land. The Forest Service simply *usurped* the forest. It was the mother of all landgrabs, accomplished under a turn-of-the-century decree issued by President Theodore Roosevelt at the zenith of the age of imperialism, when the United States ruled a far-flung colonial empire. By executive fiat, his proclamation created the Tongass National Forest right in the heart of Tlingit Country, where the people had lived, hunted, fished, and gathered since ancient times. No need to consult the Indians. After all, His Majesty, the Emperor of Russia, "sold" Alaska to the United States in 1867.[2] That treaty specified that the "uncivilized tribes will be subject to such laws and regulations as the United States may, from time to time, adopt in regard to aboriginal tribes of that country."[3] Under the treaty, "uncivilized tribes" were without citizenship, property, liberty, and religious rights. Those tribesmen, including the Tlingit, were deemed colonial subjects to be ruled by the US government as it saw fit—similar to other colonies in the American empire.[4]

Colonization of Native land is invariably accompanied by destroying the habitat that supports the tribal way of life. Colonies displace the Natives, extract natural resources from the land, and remake the natural world for agriculturists and manufacturers. Thus, conquest of nature often accompanies the settlement of Native territory. In *The Conquest of Paradise*, historian Kirkpatrick Sale examined the astounding level of environmental degradation that accompanied European colonization of the New World.[5] In 1823, Chief Justice John Marshall described the ebb and flow of colonization in the United States:

> As the white population advanced, that of the Indians necessarily receded. The country in the immediate neighborhood of agriculturalists became unfit for them. The game fled into thicker and more unbroken forests, and the Indians followed. The soil…being no longer occupied by its ancient inhabitants, was parceled out according to the will of the sovereign power.[6]

In just a few short decades, for example, the plains habitat of my own tribe—the Pawnee Nation—was virtually destroyed as countless millions of buffalo and wolves were slaughtered and steel plows were pulled through native plant communities. When Native peoples resisted, the law invariably supported the destruction of their indigenous habitat, often with harsh, life-altering results. The depopulation of American Indians and destruction of their cultures following European contact has been attributed, in part, to the accompanying destruction of indigenous habitats.[7] Simply put, deforestation, dewatering, and destruction of the wild animals and plants that sustained Indian tribes, led to their collapse. Many went extinct following the conquest of nature in North and South America since 1492.

In *Haa Aaní*, Forest Service czars soon began turning the rain forest into a lumber, pulp, and paper industry. As the agency attacked the old-growth forest occupied by the Tlingit, the bureaucrats did not even bother to remove the Indians. In the headlong rush to cut the forest, they would simply clear-cut around villages and burial grounds—including the most sacred shaman burial sites—and loggers would destroy remote hunting camps where they felt necessary, as if the Indians were invisible. In this mentality, the Tlingit way of life must give way to pioneers—that is, to the timber and pulp mill investors and salmon industry interests from Seattle. Juneau businessmen were clamoring for commercial growth. They saw the forest as money in the bank for themselves and jobs for sourdough misfits from the Lower Forty-eight who stampeded north to get rich in Alaska, the last frontier.

In the ensuing decades, the battle for the Tongass rain forest pitted the Tlingit's aboriginal Indian title to their tribal homeland against the United

States' title by "conquest." The battle came to a head in 1951, when the agency sold all of the merchantable timber in a 350,000-acre tract of aboriginal land in the Tongass National Forest to a pulp and paper company. This was land occupied by the Tee-Hit-Ton Clan of Tlingit Indians.[8] They depended upon the habitat for hunting, fishing, gathering berries and roots, and harvesting trees for large tribal houses and canoes from time immemorial for their subsistence and cultural survival. They challenged the massive timber sale in the Court of Claims, asserting that it constituted a taking of their property by the government without just compensation, as required by the Fifth Amendment to the US Constitution.

In the end, aboriginal property rights to the *Haa Aaní* meant nothing to the courts. In *Tee-Hit-Ton v. United States* (1955), the Supreme Court upheld the government timber sale without any need to compensate Indians for the taking of aboriginal property.[9] In one of the ten worst Indian cases ever decided, the Court tersely explained that American title to *Haa Aaní* is derived from raw conquest:

> Every American schoolboy knows that the savage tribes of this continent were deprived of their ancestral ranges by force and that, even when the Indians ceded millions of acres by treaty in return for blankets, food and trinkets, it was not a sale but the conqueror's will that deprived them of their land.[10]

Under this rule of law, government confiscation of aboriginal land is lawful in a conquered land. The Court explained, "after the coming of the white man" the Indians' aboriginal land title merely becomes "permission from the whites to occupy" the land at the pleasure of the government, and nothing more.[11]

Tee-Hit-Ton was decided in the waning years before the modern era of federal Indian law. The rule was announced during the low point in American Indian history. It is the logical extension of the dark side of federal Indian law, as formulated by cases like *Johnson v. M'Intosh* (1823) and *Lone Wolf v. Hitchcock* (1903): Indian homelands can be taken by outright confiscation.[12] *Tee-Hit-Ton* did not mince words. Land held by the Indian "right of occupancy" of *Johnson* can be seized by the government "without any legal obligation to compensate the Indians."[13]

Confiscation is a repugnant word that chills landowners. It is anathema to capitalism because it undermines economies built on private property. Most

Americans safely assume their property cannot be seized by the government. The Bill of Rights guarantees that no person shall be deprived of property "without due process of law…nor shall private property be taken for public use, without just compensation."[14] How can such a contrary rule be imposed upon Indian land? Justice Stanley Reed based his holding on conquest:

> After conquest [Indian tribes] were permitted to occupy portions of territory over which they had previously exercised sovereignty, as we use that term. This is not a property right but amounts to a right of occupancy which…may be terminated and…fully disposed of by the sovereign itself without any legally enforceable obligation to compensate the Indians…This position of the Indians has long been rationalized by the legal theory that discovery and conquest gave the conquerors sovereignty over and ownership of the lands thus obtained.[15]

Strangely, Reed's "conquest" never occurred. History records that the Tlingit united militarily to defeat the Russians in 1802 for their attempts to bully the locals, but discloses no war of conquest waged to appropriate Tlingit land by force of American arms. Though the Forest Service's history in southeast Alaska may be high-handed, it hardly amounted to a war of conquest waged against the natives.[16] One legal commentator, Nell Jessup Newton, says there was no "functional equivalent of a declaration of war followed by conquest."[17] Because Alaska Natives never fought a skirmish with the United States, but instead welcomed the Americans with open arms, Newton rejects Reed's assertion that Alaska Natives were subjugated by conquest, because it "stretches the imagination too far." Newton concludes that the only "act that can be said to have conquered the Alaska Native was the *Tee-Hit-Ton* opinion itself."[18] Since no land was appropriated by military force, Reed's far-fetched notion of conquest is a legal fiction. Most Alaska Native groups never even encountered or made contact with the Russians. But that's just the way it goes in the courts of the conquerors.

This chapter examines *Tee-Hit-Ton*'s novel doctrine of confiscation and its grave impacts upon Native America, particularly tribal efforts to protect indigenous habitat in ancestral territory, needed to support hunting, fishing, and gathering ways of life. As used here, the term *indigenous habitat* refers to the lands, waters, animals, and plants in ancestral homelands traditionally occupied by indigenous tribes and used by them to support their aboriginal cultures and ways of life—that is, vital habitat without which aboriginal cultures and ways of life cannot survive. While the *Tee-Hit-Ton* case addressed the concept of *aboriginal title* to traditional tribal land, the underlying facts involved the destruction of indigenous habitat by the US Forest Service.

As you will see, the *Tee-Hit-Ton* mind-set hampers tribal efforts to protect indigenous habitat and thereby places the ancient ways of Native American life into jeopardy. While some recent encouraging progress has been made to protect those habitats, federal Indian law falls short of protecting vital aboriginal interests in indigenous habitat—interests crucial to the survival of the world's remaining hunting, fishing, and gathering cultures. However, as I will explain, emerging international law and recent court decisions in other lands do recognize and protect such interests, to wit: the rights of indigenous peoples to own, use, protect, and control ancestral land and natural resources that are critical to their cultural survival. That emerging body of law may point the way for law reform needed in the United States, one of the last remaining hard-core settler states in the postcolonial world.

Why the *Tee-Hit-Ton* Tale Is Important and Must Be Told

The *Tee-Hit-Ton* story is a classic tale of colonization that deserves telling. It relates how *Haa Aaní* was colonized by the Forest Service (circa 1908–1955) and how the outright confiscation of Tlingit aboriginal property used for hunting, fishing, and gathering was given the air of legitimacy by the courts. In many ways, the story is a microcosm of Manifest Destiny. By 1950, Native America had slumped to its nadir. Most Indians were living in abject poverty as marginalized persons upon the fringes of a nation bent on stamping out all vestiges of tribal culture during the termination era.[19] During this period, judges could dispense with niceties in Indian cases and simply tell it like it is. A reading of the unvarnished *Tee-Hit-Ton* opinion does just that—in hard-edged, bone-chilling words.

Though the same court desegregated America in *Brown v. Board of Education* (1954) under the leadership of Chief Justice Earl Warren, it was not ready to reverse doctrines of conquest and discovery in Indian cases.[20] Instead, the US Supreme Court was still bent on conquering America in 1955, if we take Justice Reed at his word in the bald-faced *Tee-Hit-Ton* opinion, written just ten months after *Brown* was handed down. His *Tee-Hit-Ton* opinion brings the law of colonialism into a harsh, modern-day context. It illustrates how easily the manifestly unjust confiscation of Native land can be justified by leading jurists as the law of the land in the courts of the conqueror.

The *Tee-Hit-Ton* case, with its misplaced notions of conquest, has never been reversed.[21] It raises several sobering questions that are critical to the cultural survival of Indian tribes and their aboriginal way of life in modern-day America.

The ruling shows that Indians cannot rely upon the Fifth Amendment or aboriginal property rights to protect indigenous habitat from destruction at the hands of the government. Indeed, discussion of aboriginal title is largely a moot point today, since most aboriginal property rights were extinguished long ago by voluntary treaty cessions, myriad government takings, or outright confiscation as in *Tee-Hit-Ton*. While some Indian owners were eventually compensated for takings and confiscated land by various congressional remedies in laws like the Alaska Native Claims Settlement Act (ANCSA) or Indian Claims Commission Act, monetary compensation for damages does not protect a way of life.[22] How can Native Americans meaningfully protect indigenous habitat in ancestral homelands from destruction when that habitat remains vital to their hunting, fishing, and gathering existence? Few Indian treaties reserved off-reservation hunting, fishing, and gathering rights in ceded land, and those that did often left those rights vulnerable to later invasions by development. None of those treaties expressly reserved water needed to support hunting, fishing, and gathering in ceded habitat or other protection from environmental harm. Thus, federal Indian law offers few protections for indigenous habitat in ancestral territory no longer owned or controlled by Indian tribes. *Tee-Hit-Ton* illustrates the difficulties encountered in the courts when tribes attempt to protect a way of life dependent upon aboriginal habitats.

Today, most remaining land owned by Native communities is held under treaties, executive orders, or statutes. Although some Indian land includes indigenous habitat, most of that habitat is no longer tribally owned or controlled after aboriginal title was extinguished. Nevertheless, many tribes still maintain a hunting, fishing, and gathering way of life, especially in the Pacific Northwest. Much of the critical habitat that produces fish, animal, and plant populations necessary for that way of life is now federal land or lies in navigable streams, riparian zones, and ocean waters beyond the outer continental shelf. Thus, the last remaining hunting, fishing, and gathering cultures have largely been divested of habitat critical to their survival. The law offers little protection for that habitat or way of life. Why should we care? After all, we "mostly" paid the Indians for their ceded or confiscated territories.

Huston Smith, the religion scholar, describes the ties to indigenous habitat in religious terms. One distinguishing feature of primal religion is "embeddedness" in nature. That occurs, according to Smith, to such a degree that we think "not of primal peoples as embedded in nature, but of nature...extending itself to enter deeply into them, infusing them in order to be fathomed by them."[23] For them, the sanctity of nature is taken seriously. They venerate ancestral habitat through the World Renewal ceremonies and belief systems found in Native America that transcend our lineal conception of time.[24] This "ensoulment" of nature, as described by Professor Gregory Cajete, a Tewa, is the result of long human experience with the natural world by people who have interacted with a particular landscape so long that their identity is inseparable from the land.[25] This helps explain why Native people lament loss of ancestral land, removal, or destruction of tribal habitat, for this amounts to "a loss of part of themselves."[26]

> Relationships between Native peoples and their environments became so deep that separation by forced relocation in the last century constituted, literally, the loss of part of an entire generation's soul. Indian people had been joined with their lands with such intensity that many of those who were forced to live on reservations suffered a form of "soul death." The major consequence was the loss of a sense of home and the expression of profound homesickness with all its accompanying psychological and physical maladies. They withered like mountain flowers pulled from their mother soil.[27]

On another level, a different kind of battle took place in the struggle for the Tongass—one that raises profound questions. Government colonization of *Haa Aaní* pitted two conflicting cosmologies against each other. The way tribes look at animals and plants in natural habitats—as the world's remaining hunting, fishing, and gathering cultures—is vastly different from the way settlers view colonized land. At one time, all of humanity was a race of hunters, fishers, and gathers who lived in the natural world and depended upon cooperation with nature to survive. This cosmology respects life and reveres animals and plants in human habitats. This worldview is still carried on by indigenous peoples embedded in ancestral habitats. Some ten thousand years ago, an opposing cosmology began to emerge among those humans who began domesticating animals and plants in agrarian societies. Agriculturalists had to combat the natural world, control the plants, and dominate domesticated and wild animals to survive. They evolved a new cosmology that sanctifies domination of the land and the conquest of nature. The two ways of life would collide in *Haa Aaní* and compete for control of the rain forest.

Thus, as the Alaskan struggle spilled into the federal courts fifty years ago, it raised what has become the paramount question facing indigenous people in the world today: can a hunting, fishing, and gathering way of life derived from tribal habitats survive in the colonized lands of modern nations? Many dismiss this way of life as "inferior" or "primitive." Environmentalists wonder whether those habitats themselves can survive. How should modern society comport itself toward the world's last remaining hunting, fishing, and gathering cultures? Do they have a right to exist? If so, what is the best political model for democratic majority control of minority cultures in the postcolonial world: domination, accommodation, or some form of cultural self-determination or other model for coexistence? Given the wide cosmological gulf that exists between agrarian and primal cultures, answers will test the tolerance of settler-state societies and the limits of their legal systems and will reveal the character of modern society.

As we strive to find a just balance of rights, relationships, and responsibilities in the twenty-first century, the fate of the few surviving cultures that depend upon the integrity of indigenous habitat hangs in the balance. The world now insists that these questions be addressed and answered by each nation. The United Nations Declaration on the Rights of Indigenous Peoples (2007) specifies that indigenous peoples must be given the right to own, control, and use ancestral territories and be provided effective means to protect the environmental integrity of indigenous habitat.[28] These standards seek to protect the well-being, dignity, and human rights of hunters, fishers, and gatherers who carry on the oldest way of life of the human race. These are some of the gravest matters addressed by international institutions. *Genocide* is defined by the United Nations as the deliberate destruction of a racial, ethnic, or cultural group; and genocidal acts include "inflicting conditions of life calculated to bring about a group's destruction in whole or part."[29] Where indigenous peoples are concerned, some researchers interpret such acts to include "destruction of the habitats utilized by indigenous peoples."[30]

The challenge is to protect surviving indigenous groups. To paraphrase Justice Reed, today every American schoolboy deplores clear-cutting the world's remaining rain forests. The world knows that destruction of the Amazon rain forest, for example, will destroy the Indian tribes who live there. Public opinion insists that those cultures be preserved. Yet few realize that rain forest tribes exist in our nation and their way of life depends upon healthy indigenous habitats. They inhabit the Pacific Northwest, from Yurok Country in northwest California to Tlingit villages on the Chilkat River and Yakutat Bay.

Conflicting Cosmology: How Humans View Animals and Plants

To put the *Tee-Hit-Ton* story into context, we will review humanity's two age-old competing ways of life and the conflicting cosmologies that arise from those worldviews. As used here, *cosmology* is the foundation for how a culture understands the natural order of the universe and the world around us, as derived from its religious, social, and political orders. From that vantage point, we can better grasp interests at stake in the struggle to colonize *Haa Aaní*. As you will see, when spurred by the forces of colonialism, the Western agrarian-based cosmology aggressively dominates the natural world, including the peoples who live there.

The underlying cosmological tension in *Tee-Hit-Ton* was over the way humans view animals and plants. The timber sale would reduce a rain forest homeland to pulp and paper. The occupants "were in a hunting and fishing stage of civilization," according to the Supreme Court.[31] The area contained their burial grounds, towns, houses, smokehouses, and hunting camps. The Tee-Hit-Ton Clan used the land "for fishing salmon and for hunting beaver, deer, and mink," and gathering "wild products of the earth."[32] In contrast, the government was determined to establish timber-processing operations for the manufacture of pulp and paper. Protecting the Tlingit way of life would "seriously delay, if not prevent, the development so earnestly desired by Alaskans" (meaning everyone *except* the people who lived in Alaska for millennia).[33]

How a society views animals and plants in the natural world defines its character, culture, and reveals its innermost feelings about the living world around us. Cosmology can be divided into two venerated ways of life: (1) the hunting, fishing, and gathering existence is the oldest way of life lived by humans since the dawn of our existence. It gave rise to primal cultures that dominated human evolution for hundreds of thousands of years and although endangered, this lifeway continues to prevail in a few isolated tribal habitats around the world. (2) The agricultural way of life emerged about ten thousand years ago. Over time, it swept the planet, except for isolated pockets. It informs the mind-set for viewing nature in modern societies. The two outlooks differ significantly. To inhabit a natural world, primal people must cooperate with animals and plants and encourage natural processes to survive, while agriculturalists living in a man-made world must control and dominate nature to survive. These differences account for much atrocity, discrimination, and conflict found in human history during the conquest of nature.

The Animal-Peoples' Cosmology

For all of human evolution and most of our history, the entire human population subsisted as hunters, fishers, and gatherers.[34] For 160,000 years, this way of life dominated our species as we spread across the planet. Life in this lengthy period instilled gut instincts that shaped our biology, minds, and spirit. The relationships formed with animals during this period wired the human spirit. The habits of animal behavior and plant knowledge were instilled in people. Ancient humans amassed in-depth traditional ecological knowledge about the Natural World that parallels modern man's fascination with Western science. Appropriate conduct for living with them guided human behavior. Hunting brought us into the wild and awakened our awe of animals, beings with remarkable attributes and powers. That awe may have inspired the first religions and art—as suggested by the animal spirits drawn in caves twenty thousand years ago.

Spiritually, human hunters were animistic. People believed animals are endowed with spirits and souls. As animal spirits gave or offered themselves to humans, harvesting and eating them required hunters to reciprocate by making offerings to them to ensure their return the following year. As illustrated by Native American beliefs, protection and reciprocity came from a sacred covenant forged between humans and the animals in mythic times in which animal relatives willingly gave themselves to people in exchange for our prayers, reverence, and respect. We pledged to thank the animals, to respect them through song, dance, art, and story, and to call upon their spirits and seek their eternal return through ceremonies.[35] Those beliefs and practices sanctified our relationship with mystical animals and plants as hunters, fishers, and gatherers and legitimized our presence in their world.

Pockets of this belief system remain in Africa, North America, South America, Asia, and Oceania. One of the largest concentrations of these surviving cultures is in North America. They survived long enough to be studied by anthropologists.[36] Information gleaned from the Yup'ik, Inupiat, Cree, Bella Bella, Tsimshian, Kwakiutl, Nootka, Quileute, Quinault, Makah, Tlingit, Haida, Yurok, Hoopa, Klamath, Salmon Tribes of Puget Sound, Columbia River Tribes, Southwestern Diné, Apache, and Pueblo Tribes, and hunter-gathers of the northern plains tells us much about mankind's earliest existence. These contemporary hunters, fishers, and gatherers provide a glimpse of human existence in its earliest mode. Their way of understanding the world is a human legacy. Unfortunately, this cosmology has been forgotten, dismissed, and sometimes demonized by the modern world.

Chapters eleven and Twelve described religion in Native American cultures. Those cultures derive from a hunting, fishing, and gathering way of life. It produced a cosmology well described by Cajete in *Native Science: Natural Laws of Interdependence*.[37] That worldview revels in Mother Earth's remarkable ability to support life. It proclaims Mother Earth as the foundation for human culture. That is, ethics, morals, religion, art, politics, and economics derive from the cycles of nature, behavior of animals, growth of plants, and human interdependence with all things endowed with a spirit of their own.

In the cosmology of Native American gatherers, plants hold an honored place as the foundation for human and animal life. They are called *Toharu* in Pawnee, which is a sacred concept for the "living covering" of Mother Earth.[38] Across North America, plants are venerated in creation stories that tell us who we are, why we are here, and what our place in the world is. They are honored in ceremony, song, art, lore, and religion as foods, medicines, and materials. As explained in chapter eleven, plants have talked to people in Native North America and sometimes become their guardians. Accordingly, gatherers approach wild roots, berries, peyote, corn, tobacco, cedar, sage, and other medicines in a ritual way, just as humans have done throughout evolution. The prayers, ritual preparation, and pilgrimages that accompany gathering make subsistence profound. They place restraints upon gatherers in their use of plants and govern conduct in the Plant World.

The women of the Columbia River Tribes—my wife's people—remember the covenant with plants. They know that plants came first and took pity upon humans. They hold longhouse ceremonies to honor plant relatives before the first roots can be dug or the first berries can be picked. Unlike the products available at the corner grocery store, plants are sacred food with spirits of their own that cannot be approached without the proper ritual preparation. Though illogical to Western minds, for the women of these tribes, gathering demands a respectful participation with plants as spiritual beings in a natural environment; and it is carried out on a distinctly spiritual plane.

Similarly, the Native American perception of animals mirrors hunting cultures around the world. Hunting is an ancient way of life in North America—a tradition much older than the ten-thousand-year-old Clovis sites. This tradition evolved songs, dances, ceremonies, art forms, and a spiritual reverence for animals. It produced an elaborate cultural context for hunting and a worldview that explains how humans should conduct themselves with animals.

As noted by Smith, Cajete, and Mircea Eliade, the wall that separates humans and animals in the primal world is thin. Like most hunting cultures, the widespread kinship with animals found in Native America was established through covenants, dreams, visions, and lore. Through those means, many animals endowed with power communicated with humans and shaped their cultures. The "conversation of death," in the words of author Barry Lopez, between hunter and prey, which takes place in this context, takes on a primal meaning; and meat thus acquired becomes "sacred meat."[39] Today, Indian hunters often put a pinch of tobacco in the mouths of their kill to assist it on its spirit journey. It is part of the covenant made in mythic times. One Santee Dakota explained: "The animals long ago agreed to sacrifice their lives for ours, when we are in need of food or of skins for garments, but we are forbidden to kill for sport alone."[40]

The pervasive animal influence in Pawnee culture provides an example of the revered place of animals in Native America. Animals predominate in Pawnee names, stories, songs, ceremonies, hunting, and in the tribal social order itself.[41] In mythic times, the early Pawnee gained wisdom and knowledge about the spiritual world from the animals. As Eagle Chief explained in 1907:

> In the beginning of all things, wisdom and knowledge were with the animals, for *Tirawa,* the One Above, did not speak directly to people. He spoke to people through his works, the stars, the sun and moon, the

beasts, and the plants. For all things tell of *Tirawa*. When people sought to know how they should live, they went into solitude and prayed until in a vision some animal brought wisdom to them. It was *Tirawa* who sent his message through the animal. He never spoke to people himself, but gave his command to beast or bird, which came to some chosen person and taught him holy things. So it was in the beginning.[42]

At birth, every child came under the influence of a particular animal, which became its guardian in life. That tie could also arise when kindly humans took pity on helpless animals—like bear cubs, puppies, and orphaned horses—who returned kindness with animal powers.

Animal spirits are said to dwell in medicine lodges. Their councils could take pity on deserving humans, teach them secrets, and give them power or protection. This view of reality is illustrated by a story told in my family.

Once long ago, a youth from our family was on the warpath (*raawiir-akuuru'*) somewhere in south Texas. In this hot, arid land, he got lost. After food ran out, the horse raider began to suffer greatly from hunger and thirst. At last, he fell weakly to his hands and knees, rolled into a ravine, and passed out. Later, he was awakened by singing and a gourd-like rattle. The warrior saw that a wolf was singing and flicking his wolf claws together in time to the music! It spoke to him. "I have been watching you for several days and I will take pity on you and give you a power to you and your descendants." The wolf blessed him and said, "Wherever you go, you will never starve. You will always find something to eat when you need it. From now on, you will be taken care of." So the warrior arose and climbed out of the ravine. He did find food, recovered his strength, and made his way home.[43]

Birds are also helpers who mediate between humans and *Tiirawaahat* (God, or the mighty all-pervasive power in the expanse of the universe). In mythic times, there was a world without birds, only animals and people; however, some families turned into the birds we see today.[44] Among them, hawks are guardians of warriors and messengers for the Morning Star; and the crows, eagles, magpies, owls, bluebirds, meadow larks, and roadrunners carry messages from the beyond. The mystical power of messenger birds is illustrated in a family tale.

An Echo Hawk youth accompanied a war party a long ways from home on his first raid, when he was wounded by an arrow and left for dead. Before he finally collapsed several days later, he prayed for help from the Creator (*Ati'as Tiirawaahat*), then he fell into unconsciousness. As he came to, an eagle stood before him. It said, "I am from *Tiirawaahat*, who has taken pity upon your prayer, so I am here to help you." The messenger bird told the youth, "Nearby you will find a buffalo carcass. Though it is old, it will not make you sick. Eat and remember the blessings of *Tiirawaahat*, be sincere in your prayers, and from now on you and your descendants will never get sick from the food you eat." After the sacred bird flew away, everything it said came to pass. The people were surprised and thankful when the boy returned home, for they thought he was a dead warrior, killed upon the prairie.[45]

Even clams are regarded as wonderful beings in this worldview. They have a cleanly nature, though they live in the mud.

Animal-human relations in Native America are intimate on many levels, as illustrated in Pawnee society. In many stories, for example, Pawnee marry buffalo or other animals, and transformation between humans and animals often occurs. They teach that humans are closely related to the animals who voluntarily offer themselves to people as food. Thus, entire societies can be shaped by the animals in tribal habitats. Pawnee social fabric consisted of societies that originated from animals in visions. It was a society built upon the Crow Lances, Horse Society, Deer Society, Crazy Dogs, Brave Raven Lance, Young Dog, Otter Lance, and Iruska Society. The Pawnee received many tribal religious ceremonies from the plains animals, such as the Bear, Buffalo, Horse, White Beaver, and Young Dog Dances. Even medicine came from the animal beings who formed bonds with Indian doctors and taught humans their medical secrets, how to heal, and gave deserving doctors special powers. Through these many avenues, the traditional Pawnee way of understanding the world is heavily influenced by the spirits of animals.

In short, in tribal cosmology, animals help hunters, fishers, and gatherers become fully human and they are regarded as holy. Identification with animals runs deep on many levels. For example, the Pawnee admire the wolf, imitated its ways, and "became" wolves when scouting or at war. For this kinship, they are called Wolf People by neighboring tribes. Similarly, many tribes, bands, and clans are named after animals that shaped their cultures. They include Salmon People, Buffalo Nations, Snakes, Crows, Wolf-People, Crayfish Eaters, Whaling People, and the Tlingit Eagles, Ravens, and Wolves. They are the Animal-People of Native North America. Because they walk in the tracks left by our ancestral hunters, their cosmology remembers and understands human interdependence with animals and plants as the natural order of the universe. As hunters, fishers, and gatherers, they are still related to a living world where everything has a spirit. The worldview of Animal-People strongly encourages natural processes so that animals and plants can flourish and will return to habitats shared with humans. As such, their values and lifeways are still imbued with mankind's ancient conservation ethic. That ecological imperative is evident in nearly every tribal habitat in North America, because those places *teemed* with animal and plant life, even after thousands of years of occupation by hunters, fishers, and gatherers.

The Agriculturalists' Cosmology

The Western view of the world and how we should live in it is based upon a ten-thousand-year-old agrarian culture. Agriculture was a major revolution in human history. As used here, *agriculture* is a farming culture that tames, domesticates, and breeds plants and animals; reorders natural features; and controls natural processes to make nature more productive and beneficial to humans. Over time, Western farming civilizations underwent industrial, scientific, and technological revolutions. But they still retained an agriculturalist cosmology. The pervasive effect of agriculture on modern society is described by Jim Mason, an American authority on animal-human relations:

> For nearly 10,000 years people of the West have farmed—that is, manipulated nature for human benefit. Ponder for a moment this long human experience and how deeply it influences our thinking and culture. This is a hundred centuries of controlling, shaping, and battling plants, animals, and natural processes—all things of the world around us that we put under the word *nature*. Controlling—and alternately battling—nature is a very old way of life to us. It is a stance with nature so deeply ingrained in us that we are rarely conscious of it. Controlling nature is second nature to us. We are people of an agrarian culture, and we have the eyes, ears, hearts, and minds of agriculturalists. Whether or not you have ever been a farmer, or even a visitor at a farm, if you

are a Westerner you are imbued with the culture of the farmer and it determines virtually everything you know and think about the living world around you.[46]

Agriculturalists must control the natural world to survive. It is impossible to farm virgin land or breed untamed animals for food. So, land must be significantly altered to produce crops. Natural hydrology must be reordered for irrigation. Local wildlife must be suppressed, because insects, birds, predators, pests, and vermin kill farm animals or eat crops. Native plant communities must be destroyed to make way for crops grown by man. In the end, nature is conquered.

At its heart, the genius of agriculture is animal husbandry and mass crop production. This requires utter domination of plants and animals. Their biological processes, genetics, behavior, and lives are altered. Strict control is necessary to tame, domesticate, breed, and cultivate them. In this regime, animals and plants lose their stature. They become property with a slavish existence for man's benefit. This form of enslavement is at odds with the animal-human relation in hunting cultures, as seen in Lakota Standing Bear's remarks:

> The animals had rights: the right of man's protection, the right to live, the right to multiply, the right to freedom, the right to man's gratitude. In recognition of these rights, people never enslaved the animals, and spared all life that was not needed for food and clothing.[47]

Because agriculturalists must constantly battle the living world to sustain their way of life, their cosmology must support, rationalize, and romanticize the conquest of nature; and it must exalt human domination of all other forms of life. That cosmology is described by Mason as a God-given domination of the natural world.[48] He coined the term *dominionism* to describe the exercise of human supremacy over all living things.[49]

This way of thinking has deep religious and intellectual roots in the Western world. Our exalted place in the world is a foundational religious principle of early agrarian cultures. It was strengthened by secular thinkers during the industrial, scientific, and technological revolutions, as Western civilizations morphed into modern societies. Animal-human relations in modern society were summed-up by Sigmund Freud in 1917:

> In the course of his development towards culture man acquired a domi-
> nating position over his fellow-creatures in the animal kingdom. Not
> content with this supremacy, however, he began to place a gulf between
> his nature and theirs. He denied the possession of reason to them, and
> to himself he attributed an immortal soul, and made claims of divine
> descent which permitted him to annihilate the bonds of community
> between him and the animal kingdom.[50]

Freud described our supposed supremacy as "human megalomania."[51]

In the book of Genesis, biblical scribes wrote down the religious traditions of Judaism and Christianity in the early agrarian societies of the Middle East. In the foundation myth of Western civilization, the Creation story
of Genesis tells agriculturalists why they are here. After creating the world,
plants, and animals, God made humans in his own image and granted them
"domination over the fish of the sea, and over the fowl of the air, and over
the cattle, and over all the earth, and over every creeping thing that creepeth
upon the earth."[52] God ordered humans to multiply and "have domination
over the fish of the sea, and over the fowl of the air, and over every living thing that moveth upon the earth."[53] God gave these early agricultural
people all living things—the herbs, trees, fruits, seeds, beasts, fowl, and
crawling creatures. In turn, animals would "fear" and "dread" humans, as
the natural order of things:

> And the fear of you and the dread of you shall be upon every beast of
> the earth, and upon every fowl of the air, upon all that moveth upon the
> earth, and upon all the fishes of the sea.[54]

In Genesis, there is no religious restraint in man's relation to animals and
plants. Rather, it is God's will that humans should own, rule over, and
exploit all living things. This divine mandate, according to Mason, "tells
the sacred story of how we came to have dominion over all of nature."[55]

Over the ages, the Western intelligentsia contributed to the biblical
version of domination. A long line of thinkers—beginning with Aristotle
through Roman thinkers, to Saint Augustine and Saint Thomas Aquinas—
heartily endorsed the theme.[56] Aquinas taught that animals have no souls.
He departed sharply from hunter thinking.[57] Western science helped pave the
way for the conquest of nature. In the 1600s, Sir Francis Bacon said nature

is a slave to man and can be conquered by science. René Descartes classified animals as dumb, unfeeling beasts that are incapable of thought, sensation, speech, or communication, animated only by machinelike reflexes. This idea freed us from moral guilt in our interactions with animals, since they are lowly, mindless beings without souls. It severed any lingering human connection with animals and detached us from their world. As the only sentient spiritual beings on the planet, humans can treat animals and plants as they see fit. According to Mason, this opened the door for unbridled exploitation:

> Descartes's decoupling from, and desensitizing of, nature blew away any remains of timidity or remorse a person might have in carrying out the ruthless, often violent, deeds of nature conquest.[58]

Thus, science "freed" Westerners from kinship with other living things. They could now dominate life on earth without moral restraint. Absolute human control of the living world, then, rests upon a solid religious, scientific, and philosophical foundation in Western cosmology. As Cajete observed, Western culture "disconnected itself from the natural world in order to conquer it."[59]

Carried to its logical conclusion, dominionism creates a brave new world for animals and plants. They live in bondage, subject to the dark side of agriculture. We dare not think about the abject cruelty involved in mass animal husbandry, with the stomach-turning treatment of food animals in factory farms, or how untold millions of them are killed in mechanized slaughterhouses.[60] Hidden away from public view, these nightmarish animal factories are haunting places where man's ruthless application of technology has outpaced our current ethical horizon.[61] Unlike hunters-fishers-gatherers, we are totally estranged from our food supply. Monstrous treatment of nonhuman life is second nature to people anesthetized by a cosmology that safely distances humans from animals and plants. We cope by thinking, "That's alright, they're only animals—*this is the natural order of things*." This outlook assaults wild animals and plants with even less compunction; and we do not hesitate to destroy their habitat, so long as it benefits a human interest. Governor Sarah Palin chanted that mantra in 2008, when she told the American public, "You bet we will drill, baby, drill. And we will mine, baby, mine."[62]

Unfortunately, dominionism does not stop at animal-human relations.[63] It sometimes spills over into human relations. *If we can enslave or exploit animals, why not people?* When people view others as animals, racism quickly surfaces. Discrimination, dispossession, and violence usually engulf vilified people who are branded as subhuman "vermin," "monkeys," "savage beasts," "pigs," "baboons," "vipers," "curs," "cockroaches," or "insects"— especially when these animal stereotypes are reinforced by scientific racism.[64] That climate breeds injustice—racism, intolerance, and colonialism—and fosters socially acceptable violence normally reserved for pests. In this context, animal exploitation leads to exploitation of people. It provides a mental analogue for injustice.

Dominionism in human relations becomes strident when fueled by the forces of colonialism. As Europe colonized the world, its notions of racial, cultural, and religious superiority joined forces with its long tradition of dominating the living world. That potent combination of forces produced one of the most destructive cosmologies in human history. It set in motion a perfect storm that engulfed indigenous peoples and the natural world. The modern legal systems of those aggressive societies produce cases like *Tee-Hit-Ton.*

We can only regret the aggression and great harm done to tribal peoples and habitats as human cosmologies collided during the conquest of nature in the past five hundred years. Ancient ways of life and the habitats upon which they depend are nearly extinct. In the modern world, much depends upon curbing the excesses found in those legal regimes and recapturing the values, relationships, and cosmologies of the hunters, fishers, and gatherers who live in ancestral habitats. Unless the avowed goal of the modern world is to eradicate our oldest way of life, the law in each nation should justly mediate between those differences so that all of human culture can survive and coexist. Today there is hope that this can be achieved, because many now admire, not despise, the world's remaining hunting, fishing, and gathering cultures. Even hardened city dwellers find walks in the woods to be therapeutic. People grow lawns and gardens not because they need food, but because it somehow feels good and reconnects them, and animals bring out the humanity in autistic children when all other forms of therapy fail. Those urges promote human well-being and assist in recovering balance in our lives. Thus, the inbred connection to the natural world is not entirely dead, even in urban dwellers living in an industrialized land. After all, in our hearts we are still Animal-People as a result of our biological upbringing, though it may dimly beat in the modern world.

To preserve the hunting, fishing, and gathering cultures, the unwarranted excesses found in agrarian societies that threaten the existence of hunters, fishers, and gatherers must be curbed. To do so, we must identify those excesses, reconcile differences that separate farmers from hunter-gatherers, and protect the best in both worldviews. This path offers the best hope for rekindling human spirituality after colonialism has run its course and the spiritual wells that fueled the conquest of nature have run dry. Indeed, this may be the *only* path to a more just culture in settler states that joins indigenous and nonindigenous people together for peaceable coexistence on the same planet.

Against the backdrop of the world's competing cosmologies, we return to our journey in the land of the Tlingit Indians.

A Journey to *Haa Aaní*—the Land of the Tlingit Indians

The rain fell down as we trudged up the gangplank. The waiting ship was anchored north of Juneau. *Good thing I have new rain gear!* Tonight, we would cross Icy Straits. We were bound for Hoonah, Alaska. This Tlingit village sits on the coast of Chichagof Island, due south of Glacier Bay. Our destination: the heart of the Tongass National Forest. The annual Grand Camp of the Alaska Native Brotherhood (ANB) and Alaska Native Sisterhood was taking place, and we wanted to witness this gathering.

My seafaring companions were family: wife Pauline, niece Susan Johnson (of the Forest Service), cousin Helaire Echo-Hawk, and friend John Autrey (also of the Forest Service). We made for a happy crew. I was a guest of the Forest Service at Hoonah and looked forward to attending the Grand Camp. As we rolled on ocean swells toward the island, I reflected on our journey. I had come to see *Haa Aaní* and visit the people involved in the *Tee-Hit-Ton* litigation. The trip surpassed my highest expectations. But how can this enchanting land be described on paper? The waterfalls, glaciers, immense mountains, and water bodies defy description. Whales steam across the horizon while large brown bears gallop through the tideland, among crowds of eagles feasting on salmon, not to mention the marine life that congregates along the shorelines. Here, humans talk to the trees. "The trees are alive," says Tlingit attorney Tony Strong. "You cannot cut them without asking permission before they can be used for any purpose."[65] Even today, Sealaska—the Native corporation created by federal law for southeast Alaska—holds an annual Tree Ceremony to give thanks to the spirits of the trees. I found Nirvana in the Chilkat River valley, a home to every known race of salmon. In Klukwan, Tlingit women hunt moose in the bush and lead rich traditional lives, while artists carve spellbinding animals in wood. In this land, Eagles and Ravens imitate animals as they dance; and humans are engulfed by the Natural World.

I wanted to find out what I could about a Raven named William Paul who lived from 1885 until 1977. This remarkable Tlingit Indian attorney brought *Tee-Hit-Ton* as a test case.[66] Prior to 1970, Indian attorneys were rare, but Paul advocated Native rights for over fifty years. His groundbreaking career is a prototype for Native American lawyers today, even though he is not well-known outside of *Haa Aaní*.

My path led to Tony Strong. A longtime friend, he is an Eagle from Klukwan who belongs to the Wolf Clan and practices law in Juneau. As a Tlingit attorney since 1980, Strong is a veteran of modern-day legal battles. He guided the work of the Native American Rights Fund (NARF) from 1988 to 1994 as a member of its board of directors. Soft-spoken but self-assured, Strong carries the mantle of William Paul well. A renaissance person, he is at once a versed lawyer, accomplished hunter-fisher, well-known chef, and a cultural practitioner deeply knowledgeable about tribal ways. Strong took us under his wing.

Given my interest in Paul, Strong ushered me to the doorstep of Dr. Walter Soboleff—one of the great twentieth-century Tlingit leaders.[67] It was my good fortune to meet this esteemed figure. He is a Raven, born into the Dog Salmon Clan in 1908, when the Tongass National Forest was created. Soboleff was a comrade-in-arms with Paul. During that movement, Soboleff was ordained as a Presbyterian minister in 1940 and was an ANB leader, serving as Grand Camp President many times. Today, this one-hundred-year-old elder is revered in *Haa Aaní*. If Reverend Martin Luther King Jr. pressed Christian morals into the cause of justice, he marched to the beat of Soboleff's drum. I took an immediate liking to this kindly, wise man. What a wonderful pair to guide me into the world of William Paul!

In 1885, William Paul was born at Tongass Village, Alaska, into the Tee-Hit-Ton Clan. He became a charismatic orator with many accomplishments, supporters, enemies, victories, and defeats. During the 1920s, this Tlingit lawyer emerged as a force. He attacked school segregation in *Haa Aaní*, won citizenship for his people, secured the right to vote, and fought to protect salmon fishing. He helped build ANB—founded in 1912 as the nation's first Native American civil rights organization—into a potent political voice. He launched a newspaper in 1923 to press the ANB political agenda, and, in the same year, Paul was elected to the territorial legislature as the first Native legislator. These victories set the stage for a long and distinguished career in the face of great adversity.

Despite the controversy that surrounded his work, Paul was a "good man and real hero, who did much of his legal work pro bono," according to Soboleff. "He was unliked by the whites because of his inroads on voting rights and school desegregation."[68] Paul's feats are remarkable, because they were accomplished before the Indian Citizenship Act, at a time when Native Americans were a subjugated and demoralized race. Even though ANB was founded in 1912 to fight for civil rights, Soboleff recalls that the culture lay hidden underground until the late 1950s, when an awakening in cultural pride occurred. Rosita Worl, a Tlingit scholar who began her studies with Paul at the age of ten, heralds him as the "Father of Alaska Native Land Claims."[69]

In 1929, Paul confronted the biggest challenge of his day: the fight for Native land rights. At an ANB convention, he urged, "This is your land, fight for it!" During the 1930s, Paul lobbied for legislation authorizing land-claim litigation in the Court of Claims to secure compensation for the taking of aboriginal land. A law was passed in 1935, but it required suit by a central body representative of Tlingit and Haida Indians, even though *clans* are the landowners in Tlingit society. This proviso created internal debate over the best litigation approach. At last, in the 1940s as the Indians were organizing for litigation, Paul broke ranks from the debate and began filing cases to test his theory that the clans are the proper parties to litigate land rights, instead of the intertribal organization designated in the claims statute. By that time, the controversial litigator had been disbarred from the practice of law in Alaska, but he guided land-rights litigation conducted by his two sons, attorneys William Paul Jr. and Fredrick Paul.

Thus, in the 1940s a formidable Tlingit Raven emerged. He would challenge the destruction of *Haa Aaní* and litigate to protect his way of life. Early victories sent shockwaves to the agencies that were disturbing the use and possession of Tlingit land.[70] With the help of his sons, he would fight on as the architect, instigator, and star witness in the *Tee-Hit-Ton* test case, which was filed by the Paul litigation team in 1951.

The Rule of *Haa Aaní* by the Forest Service

The Tongass National Forest (TNF) was carved out of Indian land. In 1908, nearly every inch was owned by Tlingit clans, and their Haida Indian neighbors. Eighteen federally recognized Indian tribes live within TNF boundaries. The TNF was created subject to any existing property rights.[71] However, Indian land rights were ignored as the Forest Service began its operations. Indian rights, if any, could be determined later.

In the early years, from 1908 to 1920, the major agency tasks in Alaska were to finalize national forest boundaries, reconnoiter the natural resources, and map possible dam sites, mill sites, and pulpwood possibilities.[72] A young forester, B. Frank Heintzleman, came to Alaska in 1917 to help inventory the forests. The Pennsylvanian was a high-toned dresser, who dreamed of riches in timber paper products. He would later become regional forester and the nemesis of William Paul. who led agency efforts to oppose Native land rights in the TNF. Ultimately, he became the governor of the Territory of Alaska from 1953 to 1957.

In 1920, twenty million board feet of timber were cut, primarily along Alaskan shores.[73] President Warren G. Harding called for the development of a pulp industry in Alaska.[74] The Roaring Twenties saw agency growth and flourishing timber sales. Visiting industrialists eyed the pulp possibilities of *Haa Aaní* after two staggering sales of 1.6 billion feet of timber caught their attention in 1927.[75] They wanted a piece of the pie before all the trees were gone.

Thus, by 1929, when Paul issued the battle cry to protect Tlingit land rights, the frenzy to extract natural resources from *Haa Aaní* was full-blown. The frantic pace slowed during the Great Depression, but resumed in the 1940s, as Regional Forester Heintzleman marched toward an empire made of pulp. By then, he governed a vast fiefdom. The agency exercised unquestioned power in the TNF to parcel out water rights, homesteads, special-use permits for mines, canneries, fox farms, and to build reservoirs, pipelines, and tunnels, like an omnipotent ruler.[76]

The clash with the Indians was inevitable, as rangers made destructive sweeps into the forest from the 1930s to the 1950s to burn or destroy Native subsistence camps and remove their structures from the land. Foresters, loggers, and homesteaders often treated Indians "as trespassers on their own lands as if these lands had been abandoned or ceded."[77] In 1946, Tlingit people complained about "instances of violent confrontation" and a pattern of "being driven out due to intimidation or competition."[78] As *Haa Aaní* became a de facto colony of the Forest Service, "Government appropriation and restrictive regulation of traditional Native lands [were] a source of tension."[79] A 1944 memorandum describes timber sale procedures:

> Exterior boundary of area is surveyed and blazed. Strips are then run through the area and a ten to twenty percent sample of the timber is cruised. Any improvements of importance on the area are readily seen, and special clauses are inserted in timber sale contracts which state measures to be used in protecting these improvements.

Disruption of Native subsistence, land use, and occupancy was unavoidable in the rip-and-run operations that clear-cut into, among, and around homesites, villages, burial grounds, subsistence camps, and gardens. During the 1940s, the Tlingit Indians were living on the land. According to Soboleff, "many came home and found their camps or cabins fenced off—they were just trying to survive."[80]

During the Heintzleman administration (1937–1953), the pitched battle began. In 1944, the Department of the Interior woke up and began developing protections for aboriginal land and subsistence rights in *Haa Aaní*. Following various petitions and hearings, secretary of the interior Harold Ickes issued a 1945 decision that recognized significant aboriginal land claims, together with hunting, fishing, trapping, and gathering rights, in the TNF and adjacent waters.[81] The department resolved to establish Indian reservations on those aboriginal lands within the TNF. This proposal shocked foresters. They vigorously opposed the creation of Indian reservations in their fiefdom: "Yikes! Just give them money, but no permanent rights in the land—anything else would disrupt the orderly development of the forest."[82]

The Heintzleman administration fought hard to protect the agency's regime. Forest service records from this period show a determined effort to rally administrative, political, and public opposition against aboriginal rights and to lobby in Washington against recognition of those rights.[83] Sounding the battle cry, the regional forester wrote, "with not less than 18 Indian groups in the National Forest…very substantial portions of the National Forest would be split off for Indian use"—besides, their land is the best in the TNF and the rest "would hardly be worth retaining."[84] Playing the race card, the secretary of agriculture argued it is "extremely improbable" that Congress would subordinate "non-Indian rights, equities and interests."[85] He opposed any relief that would disrupt the "industrial possibilities" of the TNF.[86] The interdepartmental squabbling produced a standoff. This allowed the agency to continue timber sales in aboriginal areas in 1946 and ignore the Interior Department's determination until ordered otherwise by Congress.[87]

By 1947, the Natives were in open revolt. The ANB defiantly charged the Forest Service and pulp corporations with trespassing on aboriginal lands. Even more alarming to agency bigwigs, several villages threatened the regime's timber monopoly by negotiating *Indian* contracts to sell timber on aboriginal land. The Forest Service scrambled to quell the revolt. The besieged foresters began spying on village timber activities, interrogating the Indians, and threatening villagers with trespass actions to curtail the subversive sales.[88] In turn, the Indians *dared* the Forest Service to arrest them for exercising their property rights.[89] The tug-of-war between the Forest Service, Interior Department, ANB, and the Tlingit villages, which lasted well into the 1950s, scared away bewildered pulp paper companies.

In the midst of this turmoil, Paul scored a stunning legal victory in *Miller v. United States* (1947) that stopped the confiscatory rule of *Haa Aaní* in its tracks.[90] The Ninth Circuit's *Miller* decision affirmed the existence of congressionally recognized aboriginal land in *Haa Aaní* and ruled that it cannot be seized by the government against the consent of Tlingit landowners without paying just compensation.[91] Unfortunately, the *Miller* rule was short-lived. It produced backlash just five months later, when Congress enacted a classic settler-state law. To combat the *Miller* decision, the lawmakers passed a joint resolution that authorized the secretary of agriculture to sell timber and land within the TNF "notwithstanding any claim of possessory rights" based upon "aboriginal occupancy or title."[92] Thus, Heintzleman could sell aboriginal timber and land, so long as the receipts were maintained in a special account "until the rights to the land and timber are finally determined." Though it took no position on the validity of Tlingit land rights, the ramrod measure authorized the immediate sale of their property—it allowed the involuntary sale of *Haa Aaní*. The final-ownership-determination provision was a cruel and meaningless gesture, since there would be little hope of recovering alienated land, much less restoring habitat destroyed by industrialists. Despite Tlingit opposition to the act, Congress sidestepped the *Miller* decision—it is all too easy for insiders to change the rules in a system run by confiscators.[93] The Supreme Court would later describe the 1947 law as a "congressionally approved taking of land."[94] This is a euphemism for *confiscation*. The 1947 law amounted to theft. This rain forest was stolen in a classic tale of North American colonialism.

The Tlingits Bring Suit in the Courts of the Confiscators

Under the authority of the 1947 act, the agency sold sixty million board feet in 1950.[95] Pulp investors formed the Ketchikan Pulp Company and, in 1951, won a contract to buy 1.5 billion cubic feet of timber at bargain-basement prices to manufacture pulp over a fifty-year period.[96] The sweetheart deal was a long-awaited triumph. At last, agency dreams of a pulpwood industry would come true![97] The sale of all the merchantable timber would destroy an immense area in the vicinity of Wrangell, Alaska, the aboriginal homeland of William Paul and the Tee-Hit-Ton Clan. They would resist confiscation of their property by filing *Tee-Hit-Ton v. United States* to test the nature and extent of Tlingit land rights in Alaska. They crossed the line where few dared to go, into the courts of the confiscators.

The early 1950s were bad times for Indian test cases. As law professor Charles Wilkinson points out, those years marked the low point in Native American life, when Indian tribes faced a legal, social, economic, political, and cultural nadir.[98] While Indians were being ruled as colonial subjects, America was busy romanticizing its past. Moviegoers thrilled to low-budget Westerns, as singing cowboys raced through the Wild West punching cows, chasing bad guys, and shooting Indians. Conquest was a swell children's game among little buckaroos playing cowboys and Indians. The nation was not ready to face its dark history. It was still ridin' the wide open range at the Saturday matinee. Besides, real blood was being spilled in North Korea. Cold war cowpokes needed strong morale, as soldiers marched to protect the American Way from the communist threat. The circle-the-wagon mentality of the 1940s that produced the Japanese interment cases still guided the nation in the 1950s.[99]

During the Korean War era, many civil liberties were thrown under the bus as Washington purged suspected communists in our midst. At this time, the national Indian policy worked to terminate federal Indian trust responsibilities, extend state power over Indian reservations, and assimilate Indians into mainstream society. The last thing on Washington's mind was to protect a divergent way of life, much less Tlingit property rights in far-away *Haa Aaní*. The Supreme Court began the century with the law of colonialism in cases like *Lone Wolf v. Hitchcock* (1903) and *United States v. Sandoval* (1913).[100] As John Wayne, Gene Autry, Roy Rogers, Hopalong Cassidy, Gabby Hayes, Lash LaRue, the Lone Ranger, and Tonto paraded across the silver screen in 1955, the Supreme Court could hardly be expected to row against the tide. That would go against the cowboy code.

Justice Stanley Reed wrote the *Tee-Hit-Ton* opinion. This wealthy Kentuckian traced his heritage to early colonial roots of the nation. He joined the Sons of the American Revolution and Sons of the Colonial Wars and married into the Daughters of the American Revolution. He came to the bench as a devoted agriculturalist, as a weekend farmer who raised prize-winning Holsteins, and as a lawyer for big agricultural interests.[101] On the high court, Reed voted against the Japanese Americans in the World War II interment cases. He was a conservative member of the Warren Court. As the lone holdout in *Brown v. Board of Education* (1954), he planned to dissent, but ultimately joined the majority so that a unanimous decision could be issued.[102] However, Reed's reluctance stemmed from a shaky commitment to civil rights, since he reputedly belonged to an all-white club and owned a home with a restrictive all-white covenant.[103]

Thus, the cosmological roots of dominionism and colonialism are evident influences in Justice Reed's background. It is not surprising that he expressed the prevalent views about American Indians, when America was consumed with glorifying its frontier history. In 1946, he opined that Indians who occupy aboriginal land without congressional permission are like "paleface squatters on public lands without compensable rights if they are evicted."[104] No one better on the Warren Court could be found to write the *Tee-Hit-Ton* opinion about aboriginal land rights.

The Supreme Court took the case to resolve two conflicting decisions concerning Tlingit land rights. The decision in the court below held that no rights exist because Congress has not recognized aboriginal land rights in Alaska, whereas *Miller* held several laws confirm such rights.

In the Supreme Court, the Indians advanced two arguments. First, they claimed absolute ownership of the land by virtue of aboriginal occupation since time immemorial. This original Indian title in Alaska is just like ordinary real estate owned by white people, despite the doctrines in *Johnson v. M'Intosh* (1823) and its progeny that espouse inferior Indian land rights. They argued that *Johnson*'s doctrines of discovery and conquest are inapplicable in Alaska, because the historical, political, and legal background in Alaska is fundamentally different from that of the lower forty-eight states. After all, Russia never conquered any Alaska tribes; and the Tlingit possess a highly developed culture and well-defined system of land ownership. Alternatively, the litigators claimed Tlingit land rights under two federal laws pertaining to Alaska that confirm aboriginal possessory interests in land, as recognized by the Ninth Circuit in the *Miller* case.[105] A congressionally recognized possessory right to the land arises under the Alaska Organic Act of 1884:

> Indians...shall not be disturbed in the possession of any lands actually
> in their use or occupation or now claimed by them [with title to be
> acquired in a manner prescribed by] future legislation by Congress.[106]

Similarly, the act of June 6, 1900, reads: "Indians...shall not be disturbed in the possession of any lands now actually in their possession."[107] Under either theory of land ownership, William Paul's team argued that Tlingit property may not be taken against their will without just compensation; and, thus, the sale of timber from Tlingit land is an unconstitutional taking. The government denied all of the Indians' contentions.

The Supreme Court rejected the Tlingit arguments. It went to great lengths to avoid blame and extend the usual apologies about injustice that are commonly found in unjust decisions. First, the opinion repeats *Johnson*'s excuse: "Conquest gives a title which the Courts of the Conqueror cannot deny."[108] To avoid blame for injustice under the doctrine of conquest, the Court hid behind a presumption of good faith.

> It is to be presumed that in this matter the United States would be
> governed by such considerations of justice as would control a Christian
> people in their treatment of an ignorant and dependent race.[109]

In any event, justice is irrelevant and immaterial, because "the propriety or justice of their action towards the Indians with respect to their lands is a question of governmental policy and thus is not a matter open to discussion."[110] Even though justice and morality are beyond the pale when it comes to dispossessing Indians, we should not be alarmed, for "American people have compassion for the descendants of those Indians who were deprived of their homes and hunting grounds by the drive of civilization" and they would like to "share the benefits of our society" with Indians.[111] (That goodwill, however, does not "allow the tribes to recover for wrongs." It is extended only as "a matter of grace, not because of legal liability."[112]) After the Court upheld the outright confiscation of Tlingit property, it defended its ruling with a bald claim that "Our conclusion does not uphold harshness as against tenderness toward the Indians."[113] Justice Reed doth protest too much. Despite lengthy apologia, it is hard to hide manifest injustice. Platitudes filled with ethnocentric notions of racial and cultural superiority bring little comfort and rarely result in "tenderness."

The Court held that Indian land rights are subject to the doctrines of discovery and conquest. Under those doctrines, those rights disappear "after the coming of the white man" and thereafter Indians can inhabit land only with "permission from the whites."[114] Like Marshall, Justice Reed equated discovery with conquest. He reasoned that (1) conquest is a legitimate means to extinguish aboriginal title; (2) the government conquered all Indian tribes, as a matter of fact—either through warfare or by forcing treaties upon Indians involuntarily; and therefore (3) all aboriginal title in the United States had been extinguished by conquest prior to the *Tee-Hit-Ton* case, with the sole exception of any lands that Congress had chosen to grant back to the Indians.[115] Consequently, the opinion reads like a paperback Western:

> Every American schoolboy knows that the savage tribes of this continent were deprived of their ancestral ranges by force and that, even when the Indians ceded millions of acres by treaty in return for blankets, food, and trinkets, it was not a sale but the conqueror's will that deprived them of their land.[116]

Conquerors do not have to compensate Indians when they seize conquered land. Under a rule supposedly derived from *Johnson*, the Court held that original Indian title is not a property right in a conquered land and Indian occupancy of aboriginal land that is "not specifically recognized as ownership by action of Congress, may be extinguished by the Government without compensation."[117]

The Court rejected the argument that the *Johnson* doctrines do not apply in Alaska. The Tlingits were in a "hunting and fishing stage of civilization" and the use of their land for hunting, fishing, and gathering "was like the use of the nomadic tribes of the United States."[118] In addition, contrary to the holding in *Miller*, the *Tee-Hit-Ton* Court found "nothing to indicate any intention by Congress to grant to the Indians any permanent rights in the lands of Alaska occupied by them by permission of Congress."[119] Consequently, Tlingit property rights "may be extinguished by the Government without compensation" just like Indians in the lower forty-eight states.[120] Relief for the Indians, if any, must come from Congress, not the courts— "no other course would meet the problem of growth of the United States."[121]

The *Tee-Hit-Ton* Court made it plain that its doctrines serve the dominant purpose of colonization in the United States. While tribal land rights are respected in other American colonies, such as the Philippines, the purpose of those colonies is much different—that is, "to administer property and rights for the benefit of the inhabitants thereof."[122] By contrast, in the United States "'the dominant purpose of the whites in America was to occupy the land.'"[123] Alaska Native land rights stood in the path of that goal. Thus, the law was placed into the service of colonialism. Doctrines of discovery, conquest, dispossession, and confiscation were marshaled to destroy Tlingit land rights in *Haa Aaní*. The *Tee-Hit-Ton* story is a classic tale of American colonialism in the twentieth century.

Efforts to Overcome the Impacts of the *Tee-Hit-Ton* Decision

Federal Indian law hit rock bottom with the 1955 decision. The *Tee-Hit-Ton* opinion sanctioned one of the greatest land heists in American legal history, and certainly the largest in the twentieth century. In the eyes of the law, outright confiscation of land is normally considered abhorrent and that kind of taking is prohibited by the Bill of Rights. Consequently, legal principles that sanction outright confiscation are suspect. They come from the bottom of the barrel—the very floor, beneath which the law can sink to no lower depths.

In the wake of *Tee-Hit-Ton,* the Forest Service stepped up timber sales in the TNF. In 1959, a second pulp mill opened in Sitka, Alaska. The decision unleashed habitat destruction throughout *Haa Aaní* by the government with impunity. The way of life of Tlingit hunters, fishers, and gatherers was placed into jeopardy as the dispossessed Indians helplessly watched their homeland being turned into paper and pulpwood. Public concern mounted in the ensuing decades as clear-cutting began to injure the habitat and the salmon runs.[124]

Several vital challenges lay ahead for the Tlingit during the modern era of federal Indian law. First, the Indians were determined to obtain damages for the seizure of their property. Second, they needed legal protections for their hunting, fishing, and gathering existence and to regain self-government in *Haa Aaní*. Third, the Tlingit needed legal protection for indigenous habitat in the TNF. On a broader scale, all Indian tribes in the lower forty-eight states, and especially in the Pacific Northwest, needed to secure habitat protection for their ancestral habitats before the last remaining hunting, fishing, and gathering cultures in the United States disappeared. Finally, these primal cultures needed to secure a reliable body of law to protect their right to exist as distinct cultures in a modern-day settler state as a matter of cultural survival. This would be a tall order for a generation of modern-day warriors who followed in William Paul's footsteps.

Compensation for the taking of *Haa Aaní* came from two sources. In 1968, the Tlingit and Haida received $7,546,053.80 in damages in *Tlingit and Haida Indians v. United States* (1968) as compensation for aboriginal land "taken from them by the United States without payment of any compensation therefore."[125] This action was filed under the 1935 act mentioned earlier, obtained by William Paul, which gave the Court of Claims authority to award damages for Tlingit and Haida land claims.[126] In 1971, Congress contributed additional millions in compensation as part of an elaborate settlement of all aboriginal land claims and hunting and fishing rights in Alaska. Congress extinguished those rights in ANCSA in exchange for $962.5 million and forty-five million acres distributed to Native corporations.[127] The Indians of *Haa Aaní* received their share of these assets, and over half a million acres of their ANCSA lands came from the TNF—no doubt to the foresters' chagrin.[128] The Indians of *Haa Aaní* would be governed by their federally recognized tribes and villages, with a corporate structure created by ANCSA. The rule of *Haa Aaní* as a de facto Forest Service colony came to an end, though many Native Alaskan challenges remain to protect Tlingit existence in a land where aboriginal natural resources are mostly owned and controlled by others.[129]

Though ANCSA extinguished aboriginal hunting, fishing, and gathering rights in Alaska, Congress expected the secretary of the interior to protect traditional hunting and fishing practices.[130] In 1980, a statutory scheme for protecting traditional Native subsistence practices on public lands—including the TNF—was created by the Alaska National Interest Lands Conservation Act (ANILCA).[131] As a result of these statutory protections, the Tlingit are able to exercise a measure of cultural self-determination in our modern society. They continue to hunt, fish, and gather in much the same way as their ancestors. That subsistence lifestyle is a living treasure, because it provides a rare link to the human past in a modern-day world.

ANILCA also curbed rampant timber sales in the TNF. It created fourteen wilderness areas in the national forest, totaling over five million acres. Habitat protection increased in 1990 when the Tongass Timber Reform Act designated five additional wilderness areas and several roadless areas in order to retain the wilderness characteristics of the TNF. The last pulp mill closed in 1997. By 2001, employment in the timber industry had fallen to just 780 jobs. Today, 13.2 million acres of the 16.8-million-acre TNF are in a protected, nondevelopment status. In the end, the Forest Service's dream built upon rip-and-run clear-cutting operations failed. Any logging done today on Native land in TNF borders is carried out by Native villages or corporations at a pace of development controlled by the Native peoples themselves, and it is done commensurate with the oldest way of life known to the human race, for the indigenous habitat of *Haa Aaní* maintains viable populations of fish, wildlife, and plants necessary to support the Tlingit way.[132] Today, traditional food obtained from tribal habitat remains at the center of Tlingit culture.

These amazing successes would not be possible without significant intervention by Congress. As interpreted by Justice Reed, the doctrines of federal Indian law lacked sufficient vitality to protect a lifeway dependent upon tribal habitat in *Haa Aaní*. To their credit, lawmakers filled the void with statutory protections. However, the shortcomings in federal Indian law raise concern for the fate of the other primal cultures in the Pacific Northwest. Can they protect ancestral habitat in ceded areas vital to their lifeways? Two hopeful threads in federal Indian law spring from NARF cases— *United States v. Washington* (1974) and *United States v. Adair* (1983).[133]

United States v. Washington enforced a treaty right to fish at off-reservation locations, which was reserved by Puget Sound Indian tribes in the Stevens Treaties. The holding produced later decisions that may establish an enforceable treaty right to protect indigenous habitat. In 2007, Judge Ricardo S. Martinez held that the treaty fishing right imposes a duty upon Washington State to refrain from diminishing fish runs by building or maintaining culverts that block salmon passage to spawning and rearing grounds.[134] The court explained the duty "arises directly from the right of taking fish that was assured to the Tribes in the Treaties, and is necessary to fulfill the promises made to the Tribes."[135] Thus, treaties might be a legal basis for protecting habitat in concrete instances. Because habitat protection can be expensive, legislation to fund remedies for the violation of treaty habitat rights will be needed to help give effect to the treaties.

The *Adair* decision held that a treaty hunting, fishing, and gathering right includes an implied water right to support adequate habitat for those purposes. Today, the amount of water needed for that habitat is being quantified by the State of Oregon. It is measured by "enough water to assure that a viable and self-renewing population of the treaty species will exist to the extent necessary to enable the exercise of the Tribal rights to fish, hunt, trap, and gather."[136] The *Adair* cases are in line with a growing number of cases that recognize that fish need water and other habitat requirements to survive and flourish. Many cases protect fish habitat in the Pacific Northwest when necessary to fulfill Indian fishing rights.[137] This line of cases provides another key toward protecting indigenous habitat. That habitat protection increases when the Endangered Species Act (ESA) comes into play for treaty fisheries that contain endangered or threatened species.[138]

The marriage between federal Indian law and environmental law can also provide a strong legal tool to protect indigenous habitat. The ESA marks a major shift in dominionist thinking. It is the most comprehensive law for the preservation of endangered species ever enacted. It provides effective means to conserve critical ecosystems needed by endangered or threatened species to survive.[139] Unfortunately, this watershed statute is not triggered until a species falters on the brink of extinction, and then it acts to place them on a life-support system; whereas, the hunting, fishing, and gathering way of life in the Pacific Northwest depends upon a much higher standard—healthy habitats that produce viable animal and plant populations. However, the law may be moving in that direction. Significantly, federal law recognizes that the "[m]ajor cause of extinction is destruction of natural habitat," that animals and plants have intrinsic, incalculable value, and that the preservation of endangered species from extinction is more important than the projects of man.[140] It is but a short step for our society to protect animals and plants in their natural habitats *before* they become endangered. As a result of these developments, society is gearing up in the twenty-first century to remove dams in the Klamath River basin and other watersheds in the Pacific Northwest to protect endangered Indian treaty fisheries from extinction. That effort also requires supporting legislation to ease the way toward a modern society that lives in peace with the Natural World.

Despite these gains in the lower courts, the Supreme Court, with its *Tee-Hit-Ton* mind-set, has not yet addressed these emerging theories for protecting indigenous habitat. The need for the law to protect indigenous habitat is made clear by the United Nations Declaration on the Rights of Indigenous Peoples (UNDRIP). The UNDRIP asks nations to protect that habitat when Native people depend upon it to carry on their way of life. Article 26 provides: "Indigenous peoples have the right to the lands, territories and resources which they have traditionally owned, occupied or otherwise used or acquired" and requires legal protections for those lands, territories, and resources. Article 28 asks nations to affirmatively help indigenous peoples to conserve and protect that habitat. Thus, the United States has an obligation to strengthen laws to protect indigenous habitat in ancestral areas that are presently outside of tribal control. International tribunals and the high courts in other countries are already beginning to recognize and extend similar habitat protection. For example, in *Awas Tingini v. Nicaragua* (2001), the Inter-American Court of Human Rights held that Nicaragua violated tribal property rights by granting a logging concession to a foreign company to log traditional lands.[141] The court held that there is an international human right of indigenous peoples "to the protection of their customary land and resource tenure."[142] In *Maya Indigenous Community of Toledo District v. Belize* (2000), the Inter-American Commission of Human Rights recommended that logging and oil concessions on traditional tribal land be suspended to protect Mayan land rights.[143] It determined that Belize failed to protect that habitat. These international developments suggest that the *Tee-Hit-Ton* mind-set is outmoded and federal Indian law must be uplifted to comport with the United Nations' minimum standards.

Toward a New Land Ethic in the Postcolonial World

"Drill, baby, drill," chanted Governor Sarah Palin. "Mine, baby, mine!" Her mantra of dominionism fell short in the 2008 presidential race because America had other priorities. The conquest of Alaska has run its course. In *Haa Aaní*, I found a friend in John Autrey. This quiet, unassuming Alaskan is a professional forester. He is the US Forest Service's tribal relations manager for the TNF. John loves the land and works hard to maintain good government-to-government relations with the Indian tribes that inhabit the national forest. The Forest Service has acknowledged the removal of Native fish camps in the twentieth century and wants to foster new relationships for an era of trust. To honor John, a Brown Bear (*Teikweidee*) Clan Mother—the late Ester Shea—gave him an Indian name, *Aanlatiní* (meaning, "Person who watches over the Land"), and adopted him.[144] Aanlatiní sometimes kayaks to work at Ketchikan, often accompanied by killer whales. In him, we can glimpse the next generation—Alaskans at peace with the Natural World and all of its inhabitants.

Everyone can celebrate the struggle to protect America's greatest rain forest. *Haa Aaní* is still inhabited by Eagles and Ravens. I sense there are millions who love the land, just like Aanlatiní; and they admire the hunting, fishing, and gathering ideals of the Pacific Northwest Indians. Their way of life is everyone's legacy. Let us take a vow borrowed from a Nez Perce patriot: *From where the Sun now stands, let us fight the Natural World no more, forever.* This is the path to a new American land ethic in a more just culture—one that embraces ancient values that spring from the land.

Chief Justice

PART FOUR

From the Valley of Darkness
to the Mountain Crest

Peaceful Negotiations

CHAPTER FOURTEEN
Was Genocide Legal?

THE TEN WORST INDIAN LAW CASES are pregnant with a question that demands our attention: was genocide against American Indians legal in the United States? We dare not ask, for any answer will prove troubling. However, we cannot leave our tour of the dark side of the law without some parting observations about the cases highlighted in this book. We will tarry long enough to ponder the meaning of *genocide* and explore how these cases pertain to that question.

Genocide continues to be a tremendous problem in the world today, just as it has been throughout human history. The purpose in studying genocide is not to demonize a particular society or condemn individuals responsible for committing crimes against humanity, but to understand the causes and consequences of those acts in order to develop early warning systems that can forestall the causes—racism, greed, bigotry, violence, and the abuse of power—*before* they escalate into acts of genocide or ethnocide. Legal systems can play a critical role in early warning systems to keep the dark side of every human heart in check. Where vulnerable groups are prone to ongoing violent acts of genocide, the more immediate question is not whether it can happen again, but, can it be stopped?[1]

Genocide is a familiar fate among the world's indigenous peoples.[2] For this reason, the United Nations Declaration on the Rights of Indigenous Peoples (2007) devotes considerable attention to protecting them from genocide. There is a debate among some scholars whether genocide against American Indians occurred in the United States. An analysis of the law might shed some light on that controversy. In places where genocide or ethnocide occur, the law plays various roles. The law can legitimize or legalize the deliberate and systematic destruction of a people or their culture, as in the case of Nazi Germany, where the legal system was part of the genocidal process. In this instance, the law is an instrument of the process. On the other hand, the law can prohibit genocidal acts. If it is interpreted and enforced to safeguard minorities from tyrannical acts of the majority, it is a bulwark against genocide and ethnocide. If those safeguards are unenforced, the legal system is not a bulwark, but a facilitator of the process.

This book has surveyed, as it must, the various forms of racism found at the heart of these ten unjust cases. To begin, we examined how medieval phobias, religious intolerance, and racial prejudice of the Old World informed early international law. That body of European law provided rules for the invasion, conquest, and colonization of the Americas. The royal charters of the original colonies imported those notions to our shores. Without any regard for Native rights, the charters established the American colonies, authorized the colonists to occupy the land, and instructed them to exploit natural resources for England and convert Indian infidels to Christianity. The charters initiated colonization processes that engulfed Native peoples. The processes of dispossession continued unabated in the new republic until they ran their course.

Next we examined how those European prejudices and principles were adopted into domestic American law as a foundation for Manifest Destiny. In *Johnson v. M'Intosh* (1823), they became foundational principles in American law. According to *Johnson*, Indians are "fierce savages" and their "character and religion" afford "an apology for considering them as a people over which the superior genius of Europe might claim an ascendancy."[3] That discriminatory judicial attitude runs throughout the cases in this book as the thread that ties them together.

Cherokee Nation v. Georgia (1831) examines the roots of homegrown American racism in the antebellum South. We saw how barefooted notions of white supremacy thoroughly infected the southern judiciary in the removal cases. That judicial mind-set saw Indians as a lowly "race of hunters connected in society by scarcely a semblance of organic government"—a "restless, warlike, and signally cruel" people, with "inveterate habits and deep seated enmity."[4] In *Connors v. US & Cheyenne Indians* (1898), we found the illegal use of force that nearly exterminated the North Cheyenne. There we examined notions of conquest and saw how a jingoistic, military mind-set derived from a one-hundred-year Indian war influenced federal Indian law. *Lone Wolf v. Hitchcock* (1903) carried the racial outlook into the twentieth century. It relied upon notions of white supremacy to give birth to the plenary-power doctrine and clothe Congress with absolute power over Indian property and affairs. *Lone Wolf* describes Indians as a weak, dependant people—simple wards of the government who can be ruled by fiat, as a fully colonized people. In the *Sandoval* trilogy (1887–1913), we examined the white man's burden, with its ethnocentric trappings of racial, cultural, and religious superiority. These discriminatory trappings justified government suppression of Native life, religious freedom, and culture in the dark side of guardianship.

These guardianship cases are filled with undisguised racism. Indians are "inferior people" who must be "civilized" by government "tutelage" to instill "sound morals" and "the habits, ideas, and aspirations which distinguish the civilized from the uncivilized man."[5] Institutional racism raised its head in *In re Adoption of John Doe v. Heim* (1976). That case illustrates the role of state courts in child-welfare systems underpinned by institutional racism and ethnocentrism so pervasive that one of every four Indian children was separated from their families. In *Wana the Bear v. Community Construction* (1982), scientific racism fueled a frightening double standard in the law so sweeping that it allowed the taking of hundreds of thousands of dead Indians from their graves. In *Employment Division v. Smith* (1990) and *Lyng v. Northwest Indian Cemetery Association* (1988), the courts went to great lengths to exclude tribal religious practices from First Amendment protection. This astounding body of law can only be understood against a long history of religious discrimination. Can it be that this sordid religious heritage still inhabits the dark corners of our judicial system, lingering hidden beneath the mind-set of leading jurists? Finally, in *Tee-Hit-Ton Indians v. United States* (1955), the doctrine of confiscation was based upon many of the above forms of racism brought to bear in a modern-day context. Once again, Indians are "savage tribes" and "ignorant" people, whereas Americans are a civilized, charitable "Christian people."[6]

As part of these diverse forms of racism found in the law, we turn to a larger problem. Genocide is racism in its darkest, most virulent form. It is the deliberate and systematic destruction of a group of people. Though the forms of genocide are diverse and the motives many, racism is always at the heart of the forces of destruction as a precondition that triggers crimes against humanity. It is the tie that binds.[7] When most Americans think of genocide, other faraway places come to mind. We are aghast at the systematic destruction of the Jewish peoples of Europe by Nazi Germany during the twentieth century. We blanch at ethnic cleansing in Bosnia, Treblinka, Auschwitz, Rwanda, Iraq, and too many other places. We mourn missing millions in communist dictatorships of Europe and Asia and smaller banana republics. However, genocide in North and South America rarely comes to mind.

Our history books do not mention genocide in the Americas. Many would rise up in anger at the uncomfortable thought of genocide in America. Yet how do we explain the impacts of colonization in the New World? Historians agree that colonization took a terrible toll. Every South

American civilization was systematically despoiled by Spain. Most islands in the Caribbean Sea were depopulated. In the United States, only 250,000 American Indians were left alive in 1900, after 125 years of warfare, land dispossession, removal, and enforced assimilation.

Nonetheless, many scholars vehemently deny that genocide took place in the United States. Carefully parsing the meaning of *genocide*, their quasi-legal argument is that it did not technically occur because (1) not all Indians were exterminated and (2) there was no intent to destroy them. In this view, the depopulation of Indians in the United States was not done deliberately. Rather, the holocaust, which brought the American Indian race to the very brink of extinction, was an accident, God's will, or possibly the Indians' own fault. Genocide researchers observe that "Indigenous peoples are often blamed for their own destruction."[8] In this view, the conquest and colonization of North America was genocide free, a very remarkable feat to be sure. Yet this argument has not taken the ten worst Indian law cases into account. Once we apply that legal framework to the debate, the picture changes into a disturbing genocidal process that was sanctioned every step of the way by the courts.

As you will see, the colonization of the Americas was accompanied by widespread acts of genocide and ethnocide that figure prominently in the astounding Native American population collapse since 1492. The millions who were tortured, slain, and enslaved by Spain during the brutal conquest phase of Mesoamerica (circa 1493–1550) comprise the world's largest holocaust by the sheer body count alone. In Latin America, the extinction of Indian tribes and disappearance of cultures continued well into the twentieth century. The threats of violence and extinction stalk those tribes to this very day. In North America, ethnocide and ecocide ravaged the surviving tribal populations in the twentieth century and endangered their remaining cultures. The preceding chapters demonstrate that colonization was lawful, according to the law of the colonizers. Indeed, the ten worst Indian law cases legalize specific acts or policies of colonialism in the United States. As shall become apparent, they also legalized several elements of genocide and ethnocide. While the courts did not themselves commit genocide or ethnocide, they are not innocent bystanders. Men in black robes created a legal climate that enabled the lawful commission of those acts by others.

What Is Genocide?

Genocide is defined by the United Nations in Article 2 of the Convention on the Prevention and Punishment of the Crime of Genocide (1948). It states:

> genocide means any of the following acts committed with intent to destroy, in whole or part, a national, ethnical, racial or religious group, as such:
>
> (a) Killing members of the group;
> (b) Causing serious bodily or mental harm to members of the group;
> (c) Deliberately inflicting on the group conditions of life calculated to bring about its physical destruction in whole or part;
> (d) Imposing measures intended to prevent births within the group;
> (e) Forcibly transferring children of the group to another group.[9]

To be genocidal, an act must be committed by states, agencies, companies, or individuals with the "intent to destroy" a group, in whole or part. Genocide experts interpret the "conditions of life" in subsection C that can bring about the physical destruction of indigenous peoples to include the intentional (1) prevention from practicing their traditional customs; (2) forced resettlement; (3) denial of access to food relief, health assurance, and development funds; and (4) destruction of the habitats utilized by indigenous peoples.[10]

Scholars describe diverse forms of genocide, but the Genocide Convention draws no distinction between those types of genocide. Forms of genocide include utilitarian genocide (mass killing to control economic resources), retributive genocide (to punish a group), cultural genocide or ethnocide (destroying a culture to assimilate a group), latent genocide (intentional activities with unintended consequences, such as spreading germs during an invasion), and developmental genocide (when perpetrators intentionally or unintentionally harm victims as a result of colonization or economic exploitation).[11] In every instance, racism provides a mental analogue for these acts. The motives for genocide are varied: (1) to eliminate competitors or potential threats; (2) to acquire wealth; (3) to implement a belief, theory, or ideology; (4) to create terror.[12]

Scholars point out that "genocide associated with expansion of economic wealth was closely associated with colonial expansion in Asia, Africa,

and the Americas."[13] And, they worry that the pace of genocide and ethnocide rose substantially in the twentieth century, when scores of indigenous
peoples were victimized by forms of genocide and ethnocide.[14]

We will apply the UN definition in examining whether genocide
against American Indians was legalized in the United States by the cases
studied in this book. While the convention's definition has been criticized,
it remains the most widely used. The convention was unanimously adopted
by the United Nations in 1948, but not ratified in the United States until
1988, long after the rest of the world agreed to its terms. This inaction
led the late Leo Kuper, one of the world's leading experts on genocide, to
wonder whether the United States' reluctance to ratify the convention came
from "fear that it might be held responsible, retrospectively, for the annihilation of Indians in the United States."[15] Raphael Lemkim was a prominent
proponent for the UN convention against genocide. In 1944, he coined
the term *genocide* by combining the Greek *genos* (race, tribe) and the Latin
cide (killing). He pointed out that genocide rarely succeeds in the complete
extermination of a group:

> Generally speaking, genocide does not necessarily mean the immediate
> destruction of a nation, except when accomplished by mass killings of
> all members of a nation. It is intended rather to signify a coordinated
> plan of different actions aiming at the destruction of essential founda-
> tions of the life of national groups with the aim of integration of the
> political and social institutions of culture, language, national feelings,
> religion, economic existence of national groups and the destruction
> of the personal security, liberty, health, dignity, and even the lives of
> the individuals belonging to such groups. Genocide is directed against
> the national groups as an entity, and the actions involved are directed
> at individuals, not in their individual capacity, but as members of
> the national groups...Genocide has two phases: one, destruction of the
> national pattern of the oppressed group; the other, the imposition of
> the national pattern of the oppressor.[16]

Though genocide is a systematic effort to destroy a group, genocide
experts Robert K. Hitchcock and Tara M. Twedt point out that in practice, genocidal acts rarely result in "total annihilation of the population."[17]
It is helpful to bear in mind the closely related concepts of ethnocide and

ecocide, because they are subsumed in Lemkin's definition of genocide. *Ethnocide* (sometimes called *cultural genocide*) refers to intentional acts that contribute to the disappearance of a culture, even though its bearers are not physically destroyed.[18] Acts of ethnocide include denying a group its right to speak its language, practice its religion, teach its traditions and customs, create art, maintain social institutions, or preserve its memories and histories. Genocide experts Hitchcock and Twedt point out:

> Indigenous populations frequently have been denied the right to practice their own religions and customs and to speak their own languages by nation-states, a process described as "cultural genocide" or "ethnocide."[19]

Ecocide is the systematic destruction of ecosystems by states, agencies, or corporate entities. Ecocide becomes genocidal when it is aimed at harming indigenous peoples or destroying their natural resource base. As made plain by researchers, tribal peoples can "be harmed through the destruction of their resource base, as occurred, for example, on the Great Plains of North America with the near extinction of the buffalo and in the equatorial zones of South America, Africa, and Asia with the purposeful destruction of tropical forests."[20] There is no question that the conquest of nature occurred in the United States during the colonization of Native lands. Was that done solely with a dominionist mind-set? Or was nature destroyed, in part, with the intent to destroy the subsistence base of Native people as competitors, as opponents to domionism, or as resistors to colonization processes? In the United States, for example, the premeditated slaughter of millions of buffalo was done in the mid-1800s to bring the Plains Indians to their knees. There was certainly competition over natural resources, and the courts viewed indigenous land uses as inferior and wasteful. Must farmers destroy hunter-gatherers to survive?

Genocide, Ethnocide, and Ecocide among Indigenous Peoples

Contact between settlers and indigenous people and the process of colonization frequently have tragic consequences. Hitchcock, a leading expert on genocide and ethnocide among indigenous peoples, writes that the world's indigenous peoples have been subject to genocides and massive human rights violations *in nearly every state where they reside.*[21] In over seventy countries, "indigenous peoples have experienced mass killings, arbitrary executions, torture, mental and physical mistreatment, arrests and detention without trial, forced sterilization, involuntary relocation, destruction of their subsistence base, and the taking of children away from their families."[22] Hitchcock says, "destruction of indigenous peoples and their cultures has been a policy of many of the world's governments"; and he correctly states that genocide "is neither accidental nor an unintended result of the actions of states, armies, private companies, or development agencies," because in virtually every case, genocide is "a calculated and generally premeditated set of actions designed to achieve certain goals such as the removal of competitors or the silencing of opponents."[23]

In settler states and colonies, indigenous peoples are especially vulnerable to genocide and ethnocide. The process of colonization is "often genocidal," according to Hitchcock and others. They correctly observe:

> Since the time of colonization, several million indigenous people have lost their lives either directly or indirectly as a result of the actions of other groups, states, or agencies.[24]

Researchers give several causes for the decimation of Native populations in lands settled by Europeans, including: "(a) diseases imported by settlers to which the local population lack immunity; (b) land usurpation and destruction of the indigenous economy; (c) deculturation and demoralization of indigenous groups, and alcoholism; (d) wars; and (e) slaughter by the colonists."[25] They emphasize that the major cause of the destruction is "colonization, especially in the 'conquest' and 'pacification' of indigenous groups."[26]

Genocide or ethnocide during colonization can occur in several contexts—as a struggle between a state and an indigenous group, as retributive genocide taken by states in payback for their behavior, or as conservation-related acts of purposeful environmental destruction. Native people are vulnerable when this occurs, because they are usually small in number, live in remote frontier areas, are particularly dependent upon vulnerable natural resources, and have little opportunity to defend their interests. Without adequate legal protections, they are often marginalized as invisible in the public mind, or frequently seen as the other (as in the low-budget Westerns or sci-fi films), or, worse yet, they are demonized as racially inferior, savage, animal-like peoples. Widespread racism is an early warning signal, according to Hitchcock and Twedt. They warn that government efforts to "vilify indigenous groups are frequently preconditions for genocidal action."[27] In most cases, genocide is justified and fueled by racism. Indigenous peoples are victimized by crimes against humanity partly because they are viewed as primitives, subhuman, savages, vermin, or nuisances for generations. Those pejorative stereotypes "reinforce the tendencies of governments to establish destruction and oppressive racial policies."[28]

The destruction of indigenous peoples and their cultures is accomplished not by a single, abrupt, deliberate act of genocide or ethnocide, but rather their populations and cultures collapse during a genocidal process sustained over a period of time. Genocide expert Kuper emphasizes that the "major cause" of their destruction is "colonization, especially in the 'conquest' and 'pacification' of indigenous groups," and he aptly describes how it occurs.

> Some of the annihilation of indigenous peoples arose not so much by deliberate act, but in the course of what may be described as a genocidal process: massacres, appropriation of land, introduction of disease, and arduous conditions of labor.[29]

Against this general overview, we shall explore the genocide and ethnocide of indigenous peoples in the New World.

Spanish Genocide in South America Planted an Enduring Legacy

We have already examined the self-serving law of Spain, which guided Spain's bloody conquest and colonization venture in the New World. The early legal scholars took the Saddam Hussein approach: *The law is whatever I write down on a piece of paper.* Under elastic legal principles, Spain butchered millions in the New World and committed the world's largest genocide. More than twelve million Indians died during the first forty years, as Spaniards killed, tortured, terrorized, and destroyed each group they encountered. The depopulation of the Americas was witnessed and chronicled by Bartolomé de Las Casas (1474–1566), who arrived in Hispaniola in 1503 and spent more than forty years in the colonies. This soldier/priest traveled widely throughout the Caribbean and mainland, chronicling the death of millions. He claimed that over forty million were killed by 1560.

In 1542, Las Casas reported to the king that mass murder was being committed in the New World, providing horrifying firsthand details.[30] The death toll reported is truly staggering.[31] In Hispaniola, almost two million Indians were killed. Between four and five million people were killed in Guatemala. In Venezuela, one million were sold into slavery. In Nicaragua, 500,000 to 600,000 were killed and more than half a million people were sold into slavery. In Honduras and the Yucatán, more than 200,000 were killed. In Peru, more than ten million were killed, and at least four million were slain in Mexico. The Bahamas and islands surrounding Puerto Rico were completely depopulated, while only a few survived in Cuba. The mammoth scale of this bloodbath is impossible for human minds to comprehend, but the vast majority of the peoples in the Western Hemisphere were exterminated at a staggering depopulation rate of 95 percent in most regions, as the demographers' rule of thumb.[32] One Spanish participant in this torrent of blood could not himself comprehend the cataclysmic magnitude of the destruction that was occurring around him, except to say there was neither "paper nor time enough to tell all that the [conquistadors] did to ruin the Indians and rob them and destroy the land."[33]

These Indians who died were nothing but primitive brutes in Spanish eyes, whereas the Spaniards saw themselves as civilized Christian masters who could conduct just wars to colonize Indian land.[34] The world shall never know how human knowledge and culture would have been enriched by the many amazing civilizations utterly destroyed by Spain. The legacy of genocide in Latin America continued well into the twentieth century, as Indian tribes in Brazil, Paraguay, and Peru were destroyed.[35] Columbus's "discovery" was a prelude to the destruction of Native peoples in the New World on a scale never before witnessed in the history of the world, or since. On this, our history is strangely silent. No museums mark the American holocaust.

The Destruction of American Indian Populations in the United States

Scholars have identified the interrelated factors that depopulated American Indians in the United States and destroyed their cultures. Demographer and anthropologist Russell Thornton identified and examined those factors. He concluded, "All of the reasons stemmed from European contact and colonization: introduced disease, including alcoholism; warfare and genocide; geographical removal and relocation; and destruction of ways of life."[36] Thornton's findings dovetail with the Doolittle Report (1867), which reported findings from a congressional investigation into the causes of the alarmingly rapid rate of population decline among American Indians after the Civil War. The report made the following conclusions.

> *First,* The Indians everywhere, with the exception of the tribes within the Indian Territory, are rapidly decreasing in numbers from various causes: By disease; by intemperance; by wars, among themselves and with the whites; by the steady and relentless emigration of white men into the territories of the west, which, confining the Indians to still narrower limits, destroys that game which, in their normal state, constitutes their principle means of subsistence; and by the irrepressible conflict between a superior and inferior race when brought into the presence of each other...
>
> *Second,* The committee are of opinion that in a large majority of cases Indian wars are to be traced to the aggressions of lawless white men, always to be found upon the frontier, or boundary line between savage and civilized life...From whatever cause wars...are very destructive, not only of the lives of the warriors engaged in it, but of the women and children, often becoming a war of extermination...The indiscriminate slaughter of men, women, and children has frequently occurred in the history of Indian wars.
>
> *Third,* Another potent cause of their decay is to be found in the loss of their hunting grounds and in the destruction of that game upon which the Indian subsists.[37]

In *American Indian Holocaust and Survival: A Population History Since 1492* (1987), Thornton painstakingly assembles the data on the population decline of American Indians in the United States and identifies the diverse causes for an astounding collapse of about 1.25 million persons per century from 1492 to 1890.[38] To each of Thornton's causes for the decline, I will add the legal doctrines highlighted in this book to determine whether those causes amounted to deliberate or intentional acts of genocide, ethnocide, or ecocide within the meaning of the United Nations Convention on the Prevention and Punishment of the Crime of Genocide.

Before the law is applied to Thornton's causes of population decline, the question of intent must be addressed. Those who deny that any genocidal acts occurred during the conquest and colonization of the United States contend that there was no intent to destroy Native people.[39] They admit that Indians were reduced to 250,000 persons by 1900. Their explanation goes as follows:

the colonists did not immigrate to America to exterminate Native Americans or destroy their cultures. The population collapse occurred because germs killed Indians, not the settlers. The Puritans had no premeditated plan to exterminate the neighboring tribes. Removal was not genocidal, because dispossession did not kill *that many Indians*. War did occur. It was merciless on both sides, but performed in conformity with the laws of war accepted at the time. Finally, the apologists argue that even if some isolated episodes tended to be genocidal, that does not justify condemning an entire society because it is unfair to apply today's standards to the past.

We cannot read the original colonists' minds. However, colonization was no accident. From the very beginning, it was a premeditated, deliberate, and systematic process to dispossess the Native Americans and displace their cultures, at whatever the cost. *Most of the early immigrants signed up to settle lands occupied by other people.* Unless we impute widespread stupidity among them, the colonists knew that the consequences of colonizing occupied Indian land would be dire: *colonization always entails the dirty task of dispossessing the aboriginal inhabitants.* The foundational legal documents that supported their venture could be no clearer about their destructive mission.[40] The papal bulls conveyed Indian land to Spain specifically to convert Indians and place their land under the sway of Spain. The Laws of Burgos, together with the *Requerimiento*, authorized the use of force to achieve these goals when the Natives opposed settlement, resisted the missionaries, or opposed Spanish domination. Similarly, the royal charters in North America *spelled out* a destructive mission. They authorized companies to establish colonies in non-Christian lands, with the avowed goals to convert infidels and savages, bring civilization and government to America, and exploit the natural resources. British law allowed just war against Native Americans if they violated English notions of natural law or were without a European-style religion. None of the Indian wars since the founding of these colonies were accidental. None of the legal opinions in this book were an accident. Instead, the predatory acts of conquest, colonization, and subjugation were deliberate. They were committed by the government, agencies, and individuals to dispossess and subjugate Native Americans at whatever the cost. Many of these acts and policies are the very factors identified by Thornton that led to the depopulation of American Indian tribes, the extinction of many tribes, and the widespread destruction of tribal culture. Sadly, those acts were legalized by the courts of the conqueror in the cases discussed in this book.

Warfare, Killing, and the Illegal Use of Force

The UN Genocide Convention lists "killing members of the group" as an act of genocide if it is "committed with intent to destroy, in whole or part, a national, ethnical, racial or religious group." Did such killing occur in the United States? Thornton estimates that 150,000 to 500,000 Indians were killed between 1492 and 1894. In this four-hundred-year period, these deaths resulted from: (1) forty wars between the United States and Indian tribes or bands, conducted almost continuously throughout the United States over a one-hundred-year period; (2) conflicts between Indians and civilian settlers, including systematic slaughter of Indians by settlers in California, Texas, and other places; and (3) intertribal warfare prompted in part by European or American involvement in tribal affairs or warfare among Europeans and Americans for continental hegemony.[41] Indians were killed intentionally in the military conflicts—that was the purpose of those campaigns and both combatants and noncombatants alike were slain. Colonial and territorial governments urged whites to kill Indians by paying bounties.

Although no comprehensive legal analysis of the forty Indian wars has been performed, the use of military force was both legal and illegal, depending upon the facts leading to each conflict. In chapter six, I applied the law of war to the adjudicated facts in *Connors v. US & Cheyenne Indians* (1898). I found that the United States' use of military force, which nearly exterminated the North Cheyenne Indians, was patently illegal under the applicable domestic and international law of war. Under those nineteenth-century legal standards, I also determined that the killing at the Sand Creek Massacre violated the law. Elsewhere, we discussed the infamous Wounded Knee Massacre, which Thornton describes as "the best-known genocide of North American Indians."[42] Though unlawful, none of the soldiers responsible for the killings at Fort Robinson, Sand Creek, and Wounded Knee were brought to justice. These episodes occurred at the height of the Indians wars on the Great Plains, when heated rhetoric calling for the extermination of the Indian race could be heard from military spokesmen, the press, civilians, and government officials.[43] The *Rocky Mountain News*, for example, issued an editorial in 1863 urging the extermination of the Indian race: "*They are a dissolute, vagabonish, brutal, and ungrateful race, and ought to be wiped from the face of the earth.*"[44] In such a climate, the unlawful killings committed by soldiers, militia, and civilians were acts of genocide. To explore the extent of genocidal acts committed by the military during the forty Indian wars, I have encouraged further factual and legal research into each war to identify any other illegal uses of force. If a widespread pattern of the illegal use of military force emerges over an extended period of time, this could provide strong evidence of genocide and a telling genocidal intent.

Thornton also documents the widespread slaughter of Indians by individual civilians, groups of settlers, or paramilitary groups. They killed untold thousands. For example, the California Indian population plummeted from 100,000 to just 30,000 persons during the gold rush (1849–1870).[45] In massacre after massacre, Thornton documents blatant acts of violent genocide in northern California and southern Oregon.[46] Many small tribelets went extinct, but not a single white man was prosecuted for any of these crimes.

Killing Indians was widespread. Some of it was legal under the law of war. In many instances, the killing was illegally done with impunity. Hitchcock and Twedt note:

> Given the prevailing attitudes toward indigenous peoples, it is not surprising that in the vast majority of instances the people responsible for killing them were never brought to justice.[47]

There was no bulwark against genocide in the nineteenth century.

Disease

There is no doubt that the germ was the primary agent of destruction. From 1620 to 1900, as many as ninety-three epidemics and pandemics spread among the Indians. Smallpox was the greatest killer in the nineteenth century. These were Old World diseases carried by settlers and slaves—diseases to which Indians had no immunity, such as smallpox, measles, bubonic plague, cholera, typhoid, scarlet fever, diphtheria, and whooping cough. There is a debate over how many times the settlers introduced these diseases intentionally, as through smallpox-infected blankets, or whether they carried disease to the Indians with the intent to destroy them. In any case, after the first two hundred years of epidemics and pandemics, nineteenth-century Americans *knew* white contact had deadly consequences for Indians, they *knew* that the germs they carried killed entire tribes, yet they still came among the Indian tribes *knowing* the potentially deadly consequences of infection upon tribal peoples. The agent of death by germs, then, was "the steady and relentless emigration of white men into the territories of the west," in the words of the Doolittle Report. The diseases they spread were the deadly by-products of the colonization process. If infection from whites during colonization was spread with the intent to destroy the Indians, it may properly be called genocide. Otherwise, the accidental infection of a tribe by unknowing whites was a simple negligent act committed during colonization, or infection would amount to gross negligence when settlers *knew* the risk of infection, but still contacted the tribes. The latter conduct amounts to callous disregard. In either case, negligence normally creates damages liability in tort law. In hindsight, a cultural tort for negligent conduct that is the proximate cause of harm to a tribal culture would have provided an effective remedy in the nineteenth century for the next of kin, and that potential liability may have caused settlers to act more responsibly. Had tort law accounted for that pressing social need, perhaps millions of lives might have been spared. Without such legal protection, millions died so that the land could be colonized.

Thornton correctly identifies disease as one of the interrelated causes for the American Indian population decline. Yet, disease does not displace responsibility for the near extinction of the American Indian race, because their destruction was neither inadvertent nor an act of God. Instead, disease was often combined with other factors, such as warfare, killing, slaughter, and dispossession, that brought about the destruction and decline of Indian tribes. Thornton states that the destruction of Native America was initially "a medical conquest, one that paved the way for the more well-known and glorified military conquests and colonizations."[48] Genocide experts would classify the spread of disease among tribal people by settlers during the course of colonial expansion as latent genocide (intentional activities with unintended consequences, such as spreading germs during an invasion or colonization) or as developmental genocide (the destruction of a group when perpetrators intentionally or unintentionally harm victims as a result of colonization or economic exploitation).[49] The decimation of indigenous peoples by diseases borne by immigrants is one of the tragic consequences of contact between immigrants and Indians in colonial settings. That destruction brought about during colonial expansion is predictable in the absence of any legal safeguards to protect tribal people from the spread of infection by germs carried by immigrants. The United States was well aware this caused the alarming American Indian population decline in the nineteenth century, as the Doolittle Report listed disease and colonial expansion as causes of the demographic collapse. In the absence of legal safeguards, it could be argued that the destruction of Indian tribes and their cultures through these means was a perfectly legal form of latent or developmental genocide.

Forcibly Transferring Children of One Group to Another

The UN convention lists "forcibly transferring children of one group to another" as genocide when it is done with the intent to destroy the group in whole or in part. During the nineteenth and twentieth centuries, it was the government's stated policy to destroy all vestiges of Indian culture, including the language, religion, dress, appearance, dance, and ways of life.[50] This "civilization" and "tutelage" process was carried out by taking the kids from their families and placing them into non-Indian institutions and settings where they could be brainwashed for assimilation.

Taking Indian children away from their families against the will of the child, family, and tribe was a widespread, perfectly legal practice in the United States until 1978. As demonstrated by the guardianship cases—*In re Can-ah-couqua* (1887) and *United States v. Clapox* (1888)—taking the kids was perfectly legal under the government's guardianship powers as part of "the great Christian enterprise of rescuing from lives of barbarism and savages these Indians, and conferring upon them the benefits of an educated civilization."[51] By 1978, one in four Indian children had been removed from their families and placed into the Bureau of Indian Affairs boarding schools or white foster families or institutions. *In re Adoption of John Doe v. Heim* (1976) illustrates the role of the state courts in producing that statistic. The widespread and systematic taking of kids amounted to genocide, as defined by the UN, when done to assimilate Indian tribes and break up the group's communities. It amounted to ethnocide when done to destroy Indian culture. This is not rocket science. No population can survive without progeny; and no tribal group can survive without its culture.

Removal and Dispossession

Genocide experts classify the removal of indigenous peoples, their forced resettlement, and the widespread dispossession of their land to be genocidal acts, because these acts inflict "conditions of life calculated to bring about a group's destruction" within the meaning of the UN convention. Thornton also identified these conditions as causes of American Indian population decline.[52] Removal was made legal by all branches of federal and state government. Whites wanted Indian land, and they wanted fervently to get rid of the Indians, as seen in the chapter five discussion of the southern removal cases leading to the passage of the Indian Removal Act of 1830.[53] Thornton estimates that over 100,000 American Indians were removed west of the Mississippi River from the southern and southeastern United States in the 1800s, and he chronicles the death toll that accompanied enforced removal.[54]

Many people died on the trails of tears from starvation, privation, and sickness along the way, and more died in the new settlements, unused to the climatic changes and primitive, refugeelike conditions. In my own Pawnee Tribe, many died from starvation, neglect, and disease after being displaced and removed to a new reservation in Oklahoma. My grandmother Martha Royce Blaine wrote in 1997: "When asked about these early years, Pawnees recall their grandparents telling them that in some tipis and mudlodges the family members still alive were too sick to bury those who had died."[55]

Likewise, the massive transfer of land from Indian to non-Indian hands was made possible by the courts in cases like *Johnson v. M'Intosh* (1823), *Lone Wolf v. Hitchcock* (1903), and *Tee-Hit-Ton v. United States* (1955). It was all perfectly legal in the courts of the conqueror, and the Indians who were plucked from their lands and indigenous habitats "withered like mountain flowers pulled from their mother soil."[56] By 1955, the Indian land base had shrunk to just 2.3 percent of its original size. The taking of Indian land was intentional. It accomplished the very purpose of colonialism. The courts were vital participants in that systematic process. They legalized a process every step of the way by which "the savage tribes of this continent were deprived of their ancestral ranges by force" and land cessions were wrung by "the conqueror's will that deprived them of their land."[57] Dispossession and removal contributed to the population decline in what experts describe as a genocidal process of colonization.

Ecocide and the Destruction of Indigenous Habitats

Genocide experts classify ecocide as one of those "conditions of life calculated to bring about a group's destruction in whole or part" within the meaning of the UN Genocide Convention.[58] "States sometimes engage in actions aimed at destroying the resource base in order to have effects on populations engaged in actions that they disagree with," according to Hitchcock.[59] He explains that ecocide, "the systematic destruction of ecosystems by states, agencies, or corporate entities, is a problem that indigenous peoples in many parts of the world have had to face."[60] Thornton includes ecocide as one of the interrelated causes of the American Indian demographic collapse.[61] In examining how the American Indian way of life was destroyed, which in turn caused mortalities, Thornton states:

> Most dramatic and perhaps most important, however, were the often deliberate destructions of flora and fauna that American Indians used for food and other purposes. Such destructions were "the strategy universally adopted by European troop commanders, who warred against Indians…destroying their crops, knowing that they thus destroyed the tribes' basic food supply" (Jennings, 1975:19). The most glaring example of animal reduction—probably the one most destructive to American Indians—was the near extinction of the buffalo, which culminated during the last half of the nineteenth century. The buffalo's destruction resulted in widescale starvation and the social and cultural collapse of many Plains tribes, particularly the Sioux.[62]

To the extent that the systematic killing of millions of buffalo was done to destroy the Plains tribes who stood in the path of settlement and opposed the colonization of their lands, it was genocide. Many Indians literally starved to death, including my Pawnee relatives, who expired during the harsh starvation years of the early reservation period in Nebraska and Oklahoma following the disappearance of the herds.[63]

Did genocidal acts of ecocide occur in the United States? If so, were those acts legal? It does appear that the slaughter of the buffalo was a genocidal act of ecocide. The facts in *Tee-Hit-Ton* also reveal what can only be described as the deliberate and systematic destruction of the *Haa Aaní* ecosystem by the US Forest Service over a lengthy period of time. Those acts were done to colonize the Tlingit rain forest homeland and extract timber resources for economic development. The Forest Service *knew* that Tlingit hunters, fishers, and gatherers depended upon their indigenous habitat to survive and carry on their culture and that they opposed the destruction of their tribal habitat, but that did not stop the headlong development of the forest into a de facto Forest Service colony dedicated to the pulp and paper industry. This smacks of latent or developmental genocide if the agency intentionally or unintentionally brought harm to the Indian people as a result of colonization or economic exploitation.[64] Was the agency's conduct, however defined, lawful? We need look no further than the *Tee-Hit-Ton* opinion for a clue. Today, the threat of ecocide in modern-day America prompts the Salmon People of the Pacific Northwest to fight with all of their might to protect the Salmon Nation, because their subsistence, cultural survival, and religion depend upon the return of the salmon to their indigenous habitats. They are fighting, quite literally, against ecocide in courts where the *Tee-Hit-Ton* mind-set still reigns.

Ethnocide: Intentional Destruction of Native American Culture

Where indigenous peoples are concerned, genocide experts classify ethnocide as one of those "conditions of life calculated to bring about a group's destruction in whole or part." Similarly, Thornton counts the intentional destruction of Native American ways of life as one of the causes of the American Indian population implosion.[65]

There is no question that the United States policy for most of the nineteenth and twentieth centuries was to stamp out the Native American way of life, including tribal religion, language, dance, song, dress, appearance, governance, child rearing, traditional education, customs, traditions, subsistence, and lifeways.[66] The avowed goals of that policy were to completely annihilate all vestiges of Native American culture and replace it with Christianity, Western dominionism, and instill Euro-American morals and values through enforced assimilation. Rebbecca Tsosie and Wallace Coffey write:

> Federal policymakers realized that by removing Native language and religion, the cultural core of the tribes would disintegrate, ensuring effective assimilation.[67]

This shove-it-down-your-throat policy is common in colonies and settler states. It is the hallmark of the white man's burden found in colonized lands.

The American courts legalized the enforced assimilation rules and policies at every turn throughout the nineteenth and most of the twentieth centuries. Under its guardianship powers originally espoused in *Cherokee Nation* and expanded over all Indians in *United States v. Sandoval* (1913), the government was able to place a firm hand on Indian culture. The lower courts acquiesced in the abuse of guardianship during the implementation of Indian ethnocide in cases like *In re Can-ah-couqua* (1887) and *United States v. Clapox* (1888). The Supreme Court ensured that Indians could not remove that yoke by enunciating the plenary power doctrine in *Lone Wolf v. Hitchcock* (1903). In clothing the government with unchecked guardianship and plenary powers, the courts worked hand in glove to smother Indian culture almost to death in the United States. Though most of the enthocide damage was done during the zenith of federal guardianship in the years from 1886 to 1934, the suppression of tribal religion continued to the end of the twentieth century. Constitutional law scholars worry that federal courts in the twentieth century continued to view tribal religious freedom through nineteenth-century eyes, as a hangover from the good old days when tribal religion was banned in the United States, in decisions that treat Native American worship as expendable.[68]

How does ethnocide cause mortality? The Indians—utterly demoralized and suffering from acute social anomy—died of a broken heart, and alcoholism. The cultural vitality of several generations was destroyed, and then it was recaptured by determined tribal people in the twentieth century who refused to see their way of life vanish from the face of the earth. This chapter is dedicated to them.

Was Genocide-At-Law Part of Our Legal System?

I agree with the genocide experts. Hitchcock and Twedt conclude that the United States (1) engaged "in cultural modification programs that led to the destruction of Indian societies"; (2) "employed ethnocide as its major indigenous peoples' policy"; and (3) resorted "to genocide if it was deemed desirable."[69] Thornton shows how these activities contributed to an alarming population decline among American Indian groups. In *American Holocaust* (1992), David E. Stannard examined the UN definition of *genocide* and concluded: "[I]t is impossible to know what transpired in the Americas during the sixteenth, seventeenth, eighteenth, and nineteenth centuries and not conclude that it was genocide."[70]

These findings and opinions are strengthened by a review of the ten worst Indian cases. The policies and processes of genocide and ethnocide that contributed to the population collapse were legalized and facilitated in very large measure by the decisions, legal doctrines, and interpretations of the law made in the cases discussed in this book. They show that the legal system was an instrument in the process. The resulting body of federal Indian law has a menacing dark side, which still lurks beneath the surface despite the historic gains made by Indian Country over the past two generations. The dark side of the law is very much like a loaded gun—ready to fire at any pendulum swing of federal policy.

The ten worst Indian cases ever decided figure prominently in the debate about genocide and ethnocide. They march in lockstep with the demographic collapse of the American Indian population, which teetered on the brink of extinction in 1900. They show how the courts worked hand in glove with the process. They upheld, or indirectly aided and abetted, many of the causes for that population decline. From all appearances, every act that led to the demographic collapse was perfectly legal. These cases show that the courts were willing instruments in the process. This harsh light has worrisome implications. We must identify the legal principles that made this shocking anomaly possible and reform them. In that process, however, it is important that federal Indian law should not be dismembered with a meat cleaver. It should be improved upon with a surgical scalpel, to remove cancerous parts, with the goal of strengthening its protective features to guarantee that federal Indian law will shield Native America, and not once again become an instrument of oppression.

Lessons can be learned from these ten cases. Let us first acknowledge that genocidal acts did occur. In the words of Professor Rennard Strickland, a renowned scholar of federal Indian law: "Genocide is the modern word for a long historical experience which is no stranger to the American continent."[71] He contends that in the nineteenth century, "law was a primary tool of genocidal extermination."[72] These ten cases provide fodder to develop an early warning system to prevent genocide and ethnocide from repeating in North America. Preventive measures are needed, even in the land of the free. The United Nations Declaration on the Rights of Indigenous Peoples asks all nations to develop mechanisms to protect indigenous peoples from genocide and its many virulent forms.

Courts should be the first line of defense in any early warning system, especially the Supreme Court. It was installed into the machinery of our democracy with the capability to curb excesses of power that are intolerable to human rights. During the modern era of federal Indian law, the Supreme Court did just that. In case after case, Indian Country reclaimed its sovereignty, dignity, culture, and pride. Nevertheless, after the hammering done by the Rehnquist Court (1986–2005) and the Roberts Court (starting in 2006), reform of the dark side of that body of law is the unfinished business of the next generation. Perhaps the tarnish will be scrubbed away by a new

Obama Court that is yet to be appointed. With the election of the first African American president, we can peer into a future free from the conditions that incubate genocide and ethnocide.

In Pursuit of Justice

CHAPTER FIFTEEN
Reforming the Dark Side of Federal Indian Law

If a man loses anything and goes back and
looks carefully for it he will find it.

—Sitting Bull (Hunkpapa Lakota Sioux)[1]

When there is much running about and the soldiers fall into rank,
it means that the critical moment has come.

—Sun Tzu, *The Art of War*[2]

WE MUST SET THE COURSE for future policy. The law is a living institution. It evolves over time to reflect changing social conditions. Every body of law has room for improvement. This is true for federal Indian law. It is a vibrant body of law with good and bad sides. During the modern era, it shielded American Indian tribes during their nation-building advances, even though the foundational principles were sorely battered by the Rehnquist Court. Despite the good side, a menacing side lurks near the surface. It stems from unjust doctrines of abject racism and unfettered colonialism that remain embedded in federal Indian law.[3] I heartily agree with the premises of law professor Robert A. Williams Jr. in *Like a Loaded Weapon* (2005).[4] These doctrines are "like a loaded weapon ready for the hand of any authority that can bring forward a plausible claim of an urgent need."[5] Because the law so strongly pervades all aspects of Native American life, we must improve and strengthen it. After my chapters of complaint, I cannot in good conscience rail against the dark side of federal Indian law manifested by the highlighted cases without offering constructive suggestions for legal reform. Here, I will offer a blueprint.

Reform is sorely needed despite the many hard-won legal victories in the modern era of federal Indian law. Since the late 1980s, the Supreme Court has steadily eroded the good side, which protected tribal sovereignty. The Rehnquist Court (1986–2005) ruled against Indian tribes in 88 percent of the cases. The Roberts Court appears to be following in the same tragic footsteps. The string of cases since 1986 rest on no discernable doctrinal footing, but are simply an ad hoc approach to destroying the protective shield of federal Indian law. This downward spiral has caused worried tribal leaders and legal scholars to ask, "Is the death of federal Indian law, as envisioned by the *Worcester* Court, at hand?"[6]

Despite this trend, I am optimistic that the stunning record of defeats will be reversed and the dark side of federal Indian law reformed in the twenty-first century. After all, the Supreme Court is rowing against the tide. It wants to *whittle* tribal sovereignty. By contrast, the other branches want to *bolster* tribal sovereignty through the self-government and self-determination policies that have been in place since 1970. The conflicting judicial policy comes at a time when millions of Americans are pouring into Indian reservations. They crowd the roads, colleges, and medical facilities. They tour the cultural and scenic recreational areas. They enjoy the museums, resorts, enterprises, and casinos. They also bring crime and the need for governance. In the face of this modern-day reality, the cases that gut tribal jurisdiction over those persons—*Oliphant v. Suquamish Indian Tribe* (1978) and its progeny—hamstring tribal government and discourage reservation economic growth.[7] They stymie self-determination by leaving tribal governments unable to pursue effective development strategies without jeopardizing their status or effectiveness as governments.[8] Thus, the Supreme Court is sorely out of step with national Indian policy since 1970. Ironically, the Supreme Court jumped on the bandwagon to dispossess and subjugate Native America in the nineteenth and twentieth centuries, but steadfastly resists current self-determination policies to foster sovereignty, economic growth, and cultural well-being today. However, the composition of the Supreme Court is ever changing. New appointments by President Barack Obama may begin to change its complexion and over time enable advocates to steer the Supreme Court back to *Worcester*'s foundational principles that are more in line with the United States' Indian self-determination and self-government policies.

Several factors have aligned to create a favorable climate for strengthening federal Indian law in the twenty-first century. First, Indian tribes are poised for the first time in over one hundred years to vigorously protect their rights. The great social movement launched in the modern era of federal Indian law firmly embedded tribal sovereignty in today's political landscape.[9] Today, 560 federally recognized Indian tribes exercise self-government powers recognized by all three branches of the national government. The federal government recognizes and fosters those powers, and the courts frequently protect them from unwarranted infringement. To be sure, setbacks abound and challenges to sovereignty lay ahead. But tribal government has grown sophisticated over the past generation. It provides the social unit, political infrastructure, and impetus for reforming the law.

Second, when given the chance, some Indian tribes have prospered within the contours of their sovereignty. Among other commercial endeavors, their amazing economic growth is strikingly seen in the gaming industry. This is uncharted territory. George Carlin, the late comedian, saw the irony of casino riches flowing into impoverished tribal communities:

> We steal their hemisphere, kill twenty or so million of them, destroy five hundred separate cultures, herd the survivors onto the worst land we can find…I am glad the Indians have gambling casinos now. It makes me happy that dimwitted white people are losing their rent money to the Indians. Maybe the Indians will get lucky and win their country back.[10]

Irreverent satire aside, this new wealth is an equalizer. It puts dollars for social justice into the hands of savvy tribal leaders. This wealth is a potentially significant source of funding to protect Native America in a society where justice costs money.

Third, the human resources that are required for sweeping legal change are abundant in Indian Country. Though small in numbers, the tribal population is big in heart and blessed with outstanding leadership. During the great social movement since 1955, Native America was led by remarkable tribal leaders, in my estimation. They were our Martin Luther Kings, Mahatma Gandhis, and Nelson Mandelas—except they were often named after animals and wore blue jeans and braids. They left a great legacy for the current generation of tribal leaders. In 2009, there were several thousand Native American lawyers, as opposed to the handful in 1970, and they were backed by thousands of other talented legal practitioners in the burgeoning field of federal Indian law. The tribes have lawyered up. There are more of them, they are better organized, and they are better funded than ever before. Native American intelligentsia thrives in universities and law schools across the land. Gifted artists and culture bearers flourish in the cultural revival that is sweeping Indian Country. They are cultural ambassadors from grassroots tribal colleges and remote reservation ceremonial grounds to the world at-large. In aboriginal areas, many traditional tribal communities still continue hunting, fishing, and gathering ways of life underpinned by age-old values from their land-based cultures. This time-tested cosmology provides them with a rock-solid grounding for cultural survival in the twenty-first century. In sum, Native America has the vitality to challenge the dark side of the law, inform its substance, and strengthen it. Our survival, security, and growth may depend upon it.

Finally, much larger social and cultural changes are afoot in the land. The world has changed. Colonialism has been repudiated, hard-core settler-ism persists only in isolated pockets, and the United Nations Declaration on the Rights of Indigenous Peoples is the new order of the day. At home, the winds of change bring hope that the millions who appreciate Native American contributions and want to coexist with indigenous peoples will lay aside settlerism and find a way to live in peace with the Natural World. For them, colonialism and settlerism have run their course, and they are ready to forge a more just culture. As America matures, so will the law. It will follow faithfully along. As we remake ourselves into a more just society, the courts will eventually be forced to abandon their role as the courts of the conqueror, for such courts have no place in nonsettler states. The bellwether election of Barack Obama as president of the United States may signal that this inevitable change is already underway.

As we chart the course for the future, we should keep in mind that Iroquois wisdom plans for seven generations out. Visionaries must develop a blueprint for reforming the dark side of federal Indian law. Given the dismal historical record, we cannot rest on good looks alone. Stringent legal protec-tions must be set in place to meaningfully safeguard Native rights. Even if a more just society emerges with a better moral compass, we cannot always count on good faith alone to prevent relapses by a nation recovering from settlerism. Good faith is no substitute for the rule of law.

Setting Goals for Legal Reform in the Twenty-First Century

To strengthen Native American legal rights, we set our sights on two high goals. First, let us elevate federal Indian law so that it comports with each minimum standard in the United Nations Declarations on the Rights of Indigenous Peoples (UNDRIP). If we steer our rudder by that bright star, Native America will find safe harbor. Many in Indian Country fail to see the relevance of international developments to tribal issues at home. This is short-sighted. Indian Country worked hard to support approval of the UNDRIP in the United Nations. That was done by leading organizations such as the National Congress of American Indians, the Native American Rights Fund (NARF), the Indian Law Resource Center, the International Indian Treaty Council, and many others. However, Indian Country cannot rest complacently upon bare approval of that historic instrument. As the saying goes, "it is easy to get a law passed, but hard as hell to implement it." The challenges are to (1) strengthen the interpretation of the UNDRIP standards by courts at home and abroad through strategic litigation support; (2) reform those areas of federal Indian law that fall below the UNDRIP standards so that our law comports with those standards; and (3) incorporate the UNDRIP itself into the domestic law of the United States as a binding legal document.

The UN approval of the UNDRIP is a watershed event. Though it is not yet a part of US law, the declaration at once strengthens all emerging norms of international law concerning indigenous peoples.[11] It sets forth standards of behavior that have immediate moral force within all countries in regard to their relations with indigenous peoples. Though those standards do not have binding legal force in the United States until our nation acts to accept them as its domestic law, the standards can still shape federal Indian law by providing international influence upon the courts for reinterpreting existing doctrines and by helping Congress set federal Indian policy in the twenty-first century.[12] For law reformers, the content of the UN standards provide a benchmark for measuring the adequacy of domestic indigenous law and for setting goals for reform. If the declaration retains its vitality as the standards are interpreted and adopted into law by nations around the world, it can provide binding domestic legal rights to safeguard the world's indigenous peoples and, eventually, become a binding international norm. Even now those standards can help set the course for future policy in the United States. As an international benchmark for protecting indigenous rights, the UN standards can guide Indian Country in setting a sound legislative and litigation agenda for reforming federal Indian law. For all of these reasons, reformers can organize efforts around the declaration to improve federal Indian law in the postcolonial age. This book invites Indian Country to evaluate the UNDRIP standards against Native American needs and aspirations. If they serve our needs, adoption of those principles and standards into US law and policy may become top legislative and litigation priorities, as a way to consolidate twentieth-century gains and reform the dark side of federal Indian law.

Second, the United States cannot meet the UN standards so long as doctrines of racism and colonialism are the law of the land. As such, several cases discussed in this book must be reversed and new legal theories developed to ensure that the law will shield Native America in the twenty-first century and beyond and will never again become a tool to harm indigenous peoples. In that process, great care should be taken, as explained below, so that federal Indian law is strengthened, not scrapped. While law reform in the courts is a slow process, litigation strategies and the legislative agenda for expunging the dark side of the law in the Congress can be developed now.

A Blueprint for Meeting UN Standards

The first goal poses an enormous task. It entails cutting-edge work to embed all of the UNDRIP standards into federal Indian law and to give the declaration itself binding legal force in the United States. But it is a task that will change the complexion of America for the better and, at long last, apply the lofty ideals proclaimed in the revolutionary period to the Native American tribal peoples. A comparison of federal Indian law with the UN standards reveals many shortcomings. For example, the Supreme Court has suggested that the Indian tribes' interest in self-government is not a "fundamental right" and in other cases has ruled that Congress may abolish tribal governments outright under the plenary-power doctrine.[13] Both of these notions are emphatically contradicted by the UNDRIP. Correcting these and other shortfalls in federal Indian law will demand the work of a generation, because many of our domestic deficiencies raise a set of knotty issues that will be hard to correct, such as protecting intellectual property rights belonging to tribal communities, preserving indigenous habitat, and protecting holy places, to name just a few challenges.

As we stand at the foot of the mountain, the incorporation of UNDRIP standards into American law calls for a focused social movement, one that is powered by a committed race of people and driven by the same urgent, impassioned necessity that fueled the epic civil rights movement that brought Jim Crow to its knees by overturning *Plessy v. Ferguson* in the consolidated cases of *Brown v. Board of Education*. The *Brown* decision was not an isolated incident in American legal history. It was the product of a planned strategy in a broad-based attack upon injustice that was waged by the NAACP for several decades on many fronts. *Brown* changed the face of America, and ultimately it set the nation upon a new path that made it possible for the first African American to be elected president of the United States. Indian law reformers should study the NAACP Legal Defense Fund's sustained legal campaign that ultimately produced that hard-won legal victory to appreciate the enormous time, resources, and labor that went into the making of that watershed event. Indian Country has not yet mounted such a focused national legal movement. Scholars have written about the "NAACP's legal strategy to destroy the doctrinal underpinnings of Jim Crow segregation."[14] Though Native America's goals may be somewhat different, the NAACP campaign provides a prototype for attacking the dark side of federal Indian law in strategic ways.[15] Buoyed by the hard-fought gains made since 1955, Indian Country has the experience, spirit, resources, infrastructure, and personnel to mount a renewed struggle similar to the NAACP campaign to systematically reform the dark side of the law once and for all, with help from all Americans of goodwill.

As a threshold matter, legal scholars should arm the Native American movement in the twenty-first century by identifying the shortfalls between federal Indian law and the UNDRIP. That thoroughgoing, comparative legal analysis should rival in ambition the sea-changing examinations of Indian policy, legal developments, and conditions of life done by the Meriam Report (1928) and the American Indian Policy Review Commission Final Report (1977), which became catalysts for change.[16] Then, Indian Country strategists can develop appropriate strategies to reform areas of law that fail to comport with UN standards. This mission requires tribal leadership, intelligentsia, and legal staff to organize into a national planning and action mode, similar to the many proactive litigation and legislative campaigns on particular problems that produced historic laws like the Indian Child Welfare Act of 1978 (ICWA), the American Indian Religious Freedom Act Amendments of 1994, Native American Graves Protection and Repatriation Act of 1990 (NAGPRA), the so-called Duro Fix, and many other remedial laws.[17] In this mother of all campaigns, strategists should develop appropriate legal, legislative, and social strategies implemented through a coordinated program of public education, national litigation, and legislation sustained over a long period of time.

As an Indian self-determination principle, the *content* of domestic legal reform called for above—that is, the particular policies, substantive law changes, new substantive law, principles, remedies, and legal theories— that are developed in this process must emanate from the heart of Indian

Country and be properly vetted there, rather than be unilaterally imposed from the outside by well-meaning do-gooders. Once developed, however, the implementation of these reforms will require enormous public education and effort by all corners of mainstream society. For openers, it will be necessary to confront and reverse the United States' embarrassing vote against the UNDRIP in the United Nations. This will be no small matter, because Congress may have to intervene and repudiate that George W. Bush administration stance through legislation that embraces the UNDRIP policy and directs the federal government to implement it in consultation with Native Americans.

The UNDRIP campaign should be conducted on several levels. On the international level, Indian law reformers must monitor how the international community is treating the UNDRIP in foreign nations and in international forums. The content of the UN standards are general. It is critical that those provisions be interpreted favorably on the international level to give strength to the meaning of the UNDRIP in our own land. This international law development therefore warrants strategic legal support from Native America, perhaps in the form of an international law development project modeled after NARF's Supreme Court Project, which monitors developments on that level and helps coordinate impact litigation in that court. Because the rest of the world has already embarked upon the process of interpreting and implementing the UNDRIP in other countries, that challenge is at hand. Failure to support those efforts may result in a watered-down document. Because that train is leaving the station, attention must be turned to the international front now.

Closer to home, every Indian tribe should enact tribal laws embracing the UNDRIP to provide precedent for the state and federal governments. On the state level, legislatures should be encouraged to pass similar laws. A grassroots legislative movement by tribal and state lawmakers can show Congress the way toward indigenous responsibility. In the courts, litigators should cite the UNDRIP as legal precedent in appropriate cases to carefully build a favorable body of UNDRIP law in the United States. It is appropriate for American courts to adopt international law principles to protect Native Americans today, just as they borrowed from international law to harm Native Americans yesterday. Socially and politically, all Americans should support this effort, because we should not be the last nation on earth to embrace the UNDRIP. If positive steps are taken in a timely manner, perhaps the United States can become a human-rights champion.

The Bush administration voted against the UNDRIP. During that administration, our human-rights leadership became tarnished and fell by the wayside. America cannot advance human rights as a foreign policy until it has cleaned up its backyard. As President Dwight D. Eisenhower said, "Whatever America hopes to bring to pass in the world must first come to pass in the heart of America."

Many in Indian Country are beginning to assess the implications and possibilities of the UNDRIP.[18] Some are working on bits of the blueprint in a piecemeal fashion, but I am unaware of any centralized organization dedicated to carrying forward a coordinated national campaign. That movement will not happen until the implementation of these standards into domestic law is seen as a priority, or until a further deterioration of Native rights occurs.

Eight Steps toward Discarding the Dark Side of Federal Indian Law

Federal Indian law and policy in the United States come closer than that of most nations in meeting the minimum standards set forth in the UNDRIP. Yet, our law falls short, because the doctrines underscored in this book are like lead balloons. They prevent the law from ascending to the level set by the United Nations, causing our legal regime to sink beneath the surface. These doctrines should be discarded, modified, or replaced by ones more buoyant in a postcolonial world. Federal Indian law certainly does not need to be scrapped in this process. It simply needs to be brought back into line with *Worcester*'s vision.

Worcester is the second buoy to steer toward in the twenty-first century. The legal reforms, remedial measures, and new legal theories for removing and replacing the dark side of the law should be aimed at returning federal Indian law to the original charter envisioned by Chief Justice John Marshall in *Worcester* and strengthening the nature of that charter.

The states voluntarily entered the Union by processes defined in the Constitution. As the early contours of the political system were taking shape, the Indian tribes also began entering the Union. They came through treaties with the United States made under the Treaty Clause. John Marshall, the definer of the nation, saw Indian tribes entering into the Republic in *Worcester* as separate political communities under a charter established by treaties, in which self-governing, domestic dependant nations exist free from unwarranted state intrusions in a protectorate safeguarded by a stronger nation. If we strive toward the protectorate described in *Worcester* and strengthen the relation intended by Marshall, much of the dark side of the law will fall away *and* the damage done by the Rehnquist Court in recent years can be repaired.

Here are eight steps for reforming the dark side of federal Indian law. They can be taken in tandem with the overall effort to elevate US law to the UN standards.

1. Set the theoretical framework for reform. At the outset, we should understand the theoretical framework for reforming the dark side of federal Indian law. It is found in the protectorate nature of the Indian tribes' political charter that was explained in *Worcester*. Conquest is not the means by which the tribes entered the Union. The treaty agreements that place Indian tribes under the protection of the United States did not conquer the tribes nor deprive them of their sovereignty. As set out in *Worcester*: "Protection does not imply destruction of the protected."[19] Thus, Indian tribes should *flourish* as protectorates within the *Worcester* framework. At the heart of the protectorate, each tribe is seen as one "nation claiming and receiving the protection of one more powerful: not that of individuals abandoning their national character, and submitting as subjects to the laws of a master."[20] *Worcester* intended that Indian tribes retain their sovereignty in this arrangement. Marshall explained:

> [T]he settled doctrine of the law of nations is, that a weaker power does not surrender its independence—its right to self government, by associating with a stronger, and taking its protection. A weak state, in order to provide for its safety, may place itself under the protection of one more powerful, without stripping itself of the right of government, and ceasing to be a state. Examples of this kind are not wanting in Europe...At the present day, more than one state may be considered as holding its right of self government under the guarantee and protection of one or more allies."[21]

While the stronger power gains an ally, it does not acquire the right to exploit or subjugate the weaker power. *Worcester* explains, the protectorate creates "no claim to lands, no dominion over their persons" and emphasized, as noted above, that "[p]rotection does not imply destruction of the protected."[22] Instead, the relation acts to bind Indian tribes, as domestic dependent nations, to the United States "as a dependent ally, claiming the protection of a powerful friend and neighbor, and receiving the advantages of that protection, without involving a surrender of their national character."[23] The Indian nations *continue* to exist as separate, self-governing communities within the American political system as a separate and distinct people "vested with rights which constitute them a state, or separate community—not a foreign, but a domestic community—not as belonging to the confederacy, but as existing within it, and of necessity, bearing to it a peculiar relation."[24]

Under this political charter for entering into the Union, *Worcester* ruled that (1) Indian tribes enjoy a sovereign right of self-government free from interference by the states; (2) their treaties must be honored as the supreme law of the land; (3) the doctrine of discovery and edicts from Europe do not divest Indian land or sovereignty; and (4) reservation borders are barriers against hostile states and land-hungry settlers that are protected by the United States.[25] The facts in *Cherokee Nation* and the southern removal cases are a constant reminder of the grave harm to Indian people that can arise when these rules are ignored or violated.

Reformers should direct the courts back to the protectorate envisioned by *Worcester,* define the contours of that relation, and strengthen it. Two bedrock features of that relation are clear. First, as the stronger power in the *Worcester* protectorate, the United States is both *obliged and empowered* to safeguard the above rules, to affirmatively advance tribal interests, and to protect the well-being of Indian nations, including their cultural and political integrity. The courts have upheld the United States' power to do all these things in a wide variety of contexts.[26] As noted in *United States v. Lara* (2004), Congress is empowered "to modify the degree of autonomy enjoyed by a dependant sovereign that is not a State…[and this] is not an unusual legislative objective," because it has been exercised in protectorate relationships with Hawaii, the Mariana Islands, the Philippines, Puerto Rico, and American Indian tribes for over one hundred years.[27] Reformers should reaffirm this protective feature and make the exercise of that power a legally enforceable *obligation* when necessary to protect and maintain the tribes' protectorate status in the *Worcester* setting. After all, protection of that status is the very purpose of the protectorate. Second, the protectorate relation described by *Worcester* does not give the United States license to prey upon, exploit, or destroy the Indian nations. This commandment from *Worcester* circumscribes the power of the protector. The prohibition against harm and concomitant obligation to do good are at the core of the protectorate relation, and these long-forgotten features of the guardianship doctrine should be imposed upon the United States, so long as it remains the guardian of Indian nations, by twenty-first-century courts as legally required mandates of federal Indian law.

The *Worcester* framework fundamentally shapes other doctrines in federal Indian law—plenary power, guardianship, and trusteeship—which have been abused in past legal history when considered in a vacuum. First, the protectorate relation should inform, if not replace, the plenary-power doctrine announced in *Lone Wolf*. In that case, the Supreme Court sought to arm Congress with tyrannical power over a supposed inferior race of weak dependent people—an awesome unfettered power that can be wielded unilaterally to break treaties, confiscate tribal property, and cause other mischief with impunity. The *Lone Wolf* Court created that power of darkness from Congress' guardianship over Indian people and property, not from the Constitution.[28] That source of power was misplaced.

Conceptually, the plenary power of Congress in Indian affairs does not derive from the guardianship principle of Victoria's law of nations, *Cherokee Nation*, *Kagama*, or *Lone Wolf*. It stems from the protectorate principle fashioned in *Worcester*, which provides constitutional grounding through the Treaty and Indian Commerce Clauses. The exercise of plenary power in the *Worcester* setting is available and proper only when the protector nation acts to safeguard the sovereignty and well-being of the weaker protectorate nation. *Protection does not imply destruction of the protected.* For these reasons, the word *plenary* should be replaced by *protectorate*, because the power of Congress in Indian affairs is more properly described as a "protectorate power" emanating from the *Worcester* framework.

Second, the protectorate principle informs and circumscribes the guardianship and trusteeship powers and obligations of the United States. These become derivative powers of a protector available to protect, not destroy, tribal sovereignty, property, cultural integrity, religious freedom, and traditional ways of life. In this framework, Indian tribes should flourish as the protectorates intended by *Worcester*, because the United States is *obliged* to safeguard them as a stronger power with fiduciary obligations; and plenary power, guardianship, and trusteeship are simply the tools by which affirmative protection is achieved.

Once safely tucked into the *Worcester* framework, these tools lose their potential for mischief. Marshall brought no dark side to the protector-protectorate relationship. Nothing in *Worcester* suggests a nefarious purpose. We should not impute the intent to exploit, oppress, and undermine the Indian tribes that entered into the Union under the *Worcester* charter any more than the courts or Congress would oppress states that joined the Union through constitutional processes. Importantly, *Worcester discarded* the discovery doctrine as "an extravagant and absurd idea." It held that discovery does *not* transfer Indian land title to anyone nor affect tribal sovereignty, much less empower states to govern tribes or intrude into their self-government.[29] Doctrines of dispossession thus have no place in the *Worcester* protectorate framework. Likewise, *Worcester dispensed* with the legal fiction of conquest. It ruled that discovery cannot be equated with conquest or dominion, because it found that the land was "occupied by numerous and warlike nations, equally willing and able to defend their possessions."[30] As such, there is no theoretical basis to rule Indian tribes by conquest or for courts to become courts of the conquerors. Those notions are at odds with a political charter intended to safeguard the integrity of Indian tribes in the American setting.

International law scholars can put more flesh on the rights, relationships, and obligations between the protector and the protectorate found in the relations among nations that guided John Marshall's great vision in 1832. Federal Indian law has always been heavily influenced by international law, which the Supreme Court adapted to the American setting, including *Worcester*'s concept of inherent tribal sovereignty.[31] A protectorate, in international law, is an autonomous territory that is protected diplomatically and militarily by a stronger nation. This form of amicable protection is extended by nations for a variety of moral and political reasons—like peace, trade, security, mutual protection, and other interests expressed in *Worcester*—in exchange for specified obligations from the protectorate, and those terms are often very favorable to the protectorate. *Worcester* emphasized the many vital needs of the United States and the Indian tribes served in this political arrangement and examined the amicable protection frequently extended by stronger to weaker powers in Marshall's day. In that form of international protection, the preexisting protectorate retains its fundamental sovereignty, except in external affairs, and the central duty of the protector is to help maintain the protectorate's status and integrity, as done in *Worcester*. Marshall borrowed directly from relations among the nations of his day and he adopted the protectorate relation to the American condition as the political charter for Indian tribes to enter the Union as domestic dependant nations.

Unfortunately, justices in subsequent Supreme Courts did not stay the course. They lost the thread during the mad dash to colonize the land. Judges embraced the prevailing notions of racism, colonialism, religious discrimination, and rapaciousness that underpinned Manifest Destiny, as seen in cases like *Clapox, In re Can-ah-couqua, Lone Wolf, Sandoval, Smith, Lyng*, and *Tee-Hit-Ton*. By the end of the twentieth century, *Worcester* lay on its deathbed, following a series of ad hoc rulings by the Rehnquist Court that nipped at the edges of John Marshall's great vision. In *Nevada v. Hicks* (2001), Justice Antonin Scalia painted a pint-sized picture of tribal sovereignty:

> State sovereignty does not end at a reservation's border. Though tribes are often referred to as "sovereign" entities, it was "long ago" that "the Court departed from Chief Justice Marshall's view that 'the laws of [a State] can have no force' within reservation boundaries. *Worcester v. Georgia*, 6 Pet. 515, 561, 8 L. Ed. 483 (1832)."[32]

With all due respect to Scalia, it is hard to imagine what business Nevada has in policing other jurisdictions. It has legalized practically every vice known to man and has plenty of sleaze to police in its own territory. In fact, tribal cops should help Nevada combat organized crime in Las Vegas, fight vice in Nevada's whorehouses, arrest sleaze in the quickie-marriage industry, and prosecute crimes against entertainment committed by Elvis imitators and aged crooners in the casino circuit. In any event, the diminutive vision of tribal sovereignty in *Hicks* restores the southern judiciary's dark version of Indian law that *Worcester* soundly rejected in 1832.[33] The *Worcester* vision must be reclaimed now that the land rush is over. After all, Indians are no longer demonized as "savages," or considered inferior childlike people who cannot govern themselves; and few would argue that we must govern Indians by conquest as abject colonized subjects.

2. Overturn *Johnson v. M'Intosh.* The doctrines of discovery and conquest in *Johnson v. M'Intosh* (1823) should be overturned by the Supreme Court. The Supreme Court still relies upon them.[34] For example, in *Nevada v.*

Hicks (2001), eighteen states sought to *expand* the doctrine of discovery. Their brief sent up the bat signal to the Dark Knight in the marble chambers. They claimed that the doctrine of discovery is the source of all federal Indian law and argued that it should vest plenary power in the states to intrude into Indian reservations.[35] Like Batman, Justice Scalia donned his black robe and answered the call. Even though his dark opinion in *Hicks* did not cite *Johnson*, he accepted their plea and sanctioned state intrusion into reservation homes. Hence, *Johnson* continues to undermine Indian tribes today, just like its doctrines "conquered" Alaskan tribes in 1955. There are four reasons why *Johnson* can and should be overturned.

First, the *Johnson* proceeding was crooked as a barrel of snakes, as made plain in Professor Lindsay C. Robertson's *Conquest By Law* (2005).[36] No attorney or judge should cite *Johnson* without first consulting this new research. The *Johnson* proceeding was infected by intolerable conflicts of interest among the attorneys. There was no "case or controversy" because the dispute was entirely *feigned* by the land speculators. The real parties in interest—the Indian tribes—were not present before the court as necessary parties. And, John Marshall should have been recused for a judicial conflict of interest. He decided the case and wrote the decision, even though he speculated in hundreds of thousands of acres near the case area with enormous interests at stake: his family fortune depended upon the outcome. In these disreputable circumstances, it is hardly any wonder that the Supreme Court burped out a gross miscarriage of justice. The decision is too heavily tainted to serve as legitimate legal precedent. Courts need not draw from the bottom of the barrel, especially in a nation that aspires in its organic documents to much higher values. Law professors should strip the unseemly case from property law and Indian law textbooks altogether for ethical reasons alone. At most, *Johnson* has instructive footnote value in the unpopular ethics courses. It illustrates how unchecked bad legal ethics and judicial conflicts of interest can impress bad law and miscarriages of justice into our legal system. In marked contrast to the crooked *Johnson* proceeding, the UNDRIP requires states to recognize and protect indigenous lands through "a fair, independent, impartial, open and transparent process."

Second, in *Worcester* Chief Justice Marshall rejected the discovery and conquest doctrines of *Johnson* as absurd legal fictions and circumscribed their reach. Unfortunately, his effort to erase them was short-lived. Soon after his death, the Supreme Court put together by President Andrew Jackson rushed to reinstate the doctrines.[37] Nonetheless, Chief Justice Marshall got it right: they are unjust legal fictions. The discovery of American Indian land by Europeans did not operate to transfer tribal title or sovereignty to anyone, nor can discovery of North America be equated with conquest of the continent. The outcome of no case should turn on these legal fictions.

Third, there is no question that the legal fictions in *Johnson* are wrongheaded. Their immoral purpose was to work great harm against Native Americans. Unjust legal doctrines have no place in legitimate legal systems. In *Mabo and Others v. Queensland* (1992), these concerns prompted the Australian High Court to overturn the doctrine of *terra nullius*, an unjust legal fiction for taking aboriginal land.[38] *Mabo* stated:

> [N]o case can command unquestioning adherence if the rule it expresses seriously offends the values of justice and human rights (especially equality before the law) which are aspirations of the contemporary Australian legal system. If a postulated rule of the common law expressed in earlier cases seriously offends those contemporary values, the question arises whether the rule should be maintained and applied. Whenever such a question arises, it is necessary to assess whether the particular rule is an essential doctrine of our legal system and whether, if the rule were to be overturned, the disturbance to be apprehended would be disproportionate to the benefit flowing from the overturning.[39]

Mabo determined that the doctrine of *terra nullius* should be overturned. It declared that when legal doctrines and fictions "depended upon a discriminatory denigration of indigenous inhabitants, their social organization and customs," which are "false in fact and unacceptable in our society," the courts can overrule them.[40] Otherwise, the law "would perpetuate injustice...and persist in characterizing the indigenous inhabitants of the Australian colonies as people too low in the social scale of social organization to be acknowledged as possessing rights and interests in land."[41] By the same token, the doctrines of discovery and conquest cannot command slavish adherence where they defeat the values of justice and human rights ideals in modern American life. The function of the law is to serve changing society, not to hold it prisoner to an unjust past.

Fourth, the UNDRIP standards abhor the doctrines of dispossession, which are the hallmark of *Johnson v. M'Intosh* (1823). Articles 28 and 39 repudiate the discovery doctrine by recognizing indigenous land rights and requiring states to "give legal recognition and protection to these lands…with due respect to the customs, traditions and land tenure systems of indigenous peoples." Article 39 would require the United States to "take appropriate measures, including legislative measures, to achieve the ends of this Declaration."

It does not take sophisticated legal rationale to overturn a doctrine of injustice that has outlived its time. When *Brown v. Board of Education* (1954) overturned the separate-but-equal doctrine, Chief Justice Earl Warren realized that the Supreme Court could not "turn the clock back to 1868 when *Plessy v. Ferguson* was decided."[42] However, the Court had to consider the importance of public education in modern American life. Relying upon the well-known deleterious psychological impacts of racial segregation upon African American children, the Court found that segregation solely on the basis of race "may affect their hearts and minds in a way unlikely ever to be undone."[43] Without demonizing the racist origins and purposes of the doctrine or delving deeply into technical constitutional analysis, the Court simply found that segregation retards the educational development of children and overturned the doctrine:

> Whatever may have been the extent of psychological knowledge at the time of *Plessy v. Ferguson,* this finding is amply supported by modern authority. Any language in *Plessy v. Ferguson* contrary to this finding is rejected. We conclude that in the field of public education the doctrine of "separate but equal" has no place. Separate educational facilities are inherently unequal.[44]

Similarly, the doctrines of discovery and conquest were espoused in 1823 to dispossess and subjugate American Indian tribes. They harmed the American Indian race and continue to undermine their governments, property, and well-being today. There is no place for those deleterious doctrines in American life today.

The overturning of *Johnson* will not cause our civilization to collapse. It is unlikely that a single acre of land will be returned if the doctrines of discovery and conquest are overturned. Mass land returns would be barred by the statute of limitations and laches principles. Furthermore, in virtually every instance, Indian lands were relinquished by treaty cession sale agreements and the outright takings or other unfair dealings associated with that process have largely been compensated by the Indian Claims Commission and Court of Claims cases. Voluntary steps can be taken to mitigate the legacy of *Johnson* by the United States, such as rectifying the plight of landless tribes and Native Hawaiians, and taking land acquired by Indian tribes back into federal trust status without putting up arbitrary bureaucratic barriers. The federal policy should be to *encourage* and *assist* Native American land acquisition efforts.

Congress has the power to overturn *Johnson*.[45] However, it is necessary for the Supreme Court to voluntarily do that job *itself* in a proper case so the justices can confront the dark side of the law and purge the Court. Like the High Court in *Mabo*, the Supreme Court must finally say, "We are no longer 'the Courts of the conqueror' in *Johnson v. M'Intosh (1823)*."

3. Insist that federal courts perform their bulwark function in a timely fashion. There are important, sober lessons to be learned from *Cherokee Nation* and the southern removal cases. The failure of the Supreme Court and the lower state courts to protect the Cherokee Nation from Georgia's aggression led to the forcible removal of a race of people—which was a genocidal act. Racial prejudice influenced the courts in these cases and the bench actually fanned those flames. By 1832, it was too late for *Worcester* to stem the tide of injustice that engulfed the Indian tribes of the eastern United States—and they were swept from the land.

Judicial courage to row against the tide of prejudice, racism, dispossession, and oppression of vulnerable minorities is, of course, an intangible human trait. Though bravery cannot be legislated, federal courts have a heightened duty to exercise their jurisdiction in Indian cases, whenever tribal sovereignty, Indian treaty rights, tribal property, or the human rights of Native Americans are at stake.[46] In those instances, the denial of timely and meaningful access to the court can bring about grave harm to living communities. In deciding such cases, litigators and judges should be sensitive to ferret out racism in any of its invidious forms: good-old-boy racism, scientific racism, institutional racism, ethnocentrism, legal racism, religious discrimination and intolerance, and aggressive dominionism that is harmful to the remaining hunting, fishing, and gathering cultures of the world. Indeed, it would be helpful to appoint Native American lawyers to the federal bench to break the race barrier in the federal courts and fully integrate the bench. In any case, the law should not fall prey to the dark side of human nature. Courtrooms should be the last place to manifest racism in any of its forms.

To their credit, Native Americans have lived with the domestic dependant nation classification and guardianship doctrine espoused by the *Cherokee Nation* court to avoid ruling upon the action brought by the Cherokee Nation to defend itself against Georgia. During the modern era, those doctrines were used to strengthen Native American rights; and in the twenty-first century they should be retained, strengthened, and exercised consistent with the *Worcester* protectorate described above. The temptation in the courts of the conqueror is to abuse these doctrines, as evidenced in the guardianship cases, or to cherry-pick them with the ad hoc approach taken by the Rehnquist and Roberts Courts to destroy the cardinal principles of *Worcester*. This disserves the bulwark function of the federal courts.

4. End violence against Native Americans. The power of tribal governments to protect their constituents against violence must be acknowledged and protected in the twenty-first century. Earlier, we examined the use of violent force against American Indians in the nineteenth century during a one-hundred-year race war. Important lessons are to be learned from that long history of violence. Scholars should determine the legality of that violence, as this research may form the basis for a congressional apology and reparations. That history should prompt US support for UNDRIP standards that prohibit violence and genocide against indigenous peoples through effective government mechanisms to prevent those crimes. Our immediate concern, however, is the escalating violence that is being committed against Native Americans in tribal communities today.

Native Americans live lives clouded by violence. They have significantly greater risk of becoming victims of violent crimes than any other Americans.[47] In this disturbing picture, Justice Department statistics show that the rate of violent victimization among American Indians is *more than twice* the national average.[48] Furthermore, they "are more likely to experience violence at the hands of someone of a different race."[49] The Rehnquist Court played a significant role in producing the escalation of interracial violence on Indian reservations. As you will see, it is responsible for lawlessness in tribal communities, where American Indians suffer violent crime at a much higher rate than any other group in the nation.

The *Oliphant* rule stripped Indian tribes of their ability to prosecute crimes committed by non-Indians on Indian reservations. Tribal courts do not even have jurisdiction to punish careless non-Indian drivers on reservation roads who harm or threaten the life and limb of residents under the ruling in *Strate v. A-1 Contractors* (1997).[50] Indian tribes were even stripped of criminal jurisdiction over nonmember *Indians* living on the reservation in *Duro v. Reina* (1990). This loophole forced Congress to intervene to restore inherent tribal sovereignty over nonmember Indians. In its headlong rush to whittle tribal sovereignty, the Rehnquist Court has left Indian tribes unable to protect their members from violence committed by outsiders. Indian tribes are the only governments in America without territorial jurisdiction over all persons coming within their territory. This anomaly was produced by an odd series of cases that treat tribal governments as nothing more than social clubs.

The judicial impairment of government on the tribal level "discourages lawfulness among non-Indians already present on reservations and acts as a perverse selection mechanism to attract precisely those non-Indians who might want the opportunity to be lawless," according to legal commentators.[51] Into this loophole in law enforcement come the meth cartels from Mexico that infest tribal communities across the nation, and violence abounds on the reservations as entire tribes are being devastated by crime. In 1995, Attorney General Janet Reno decried non-Indian violence being committed against American Indians under this loophole in governance:

> As a result, misdemeanor crime by non-Indians against Indians is perceived as being committed with impunity. This implicit message of lack of accountability deters victims from reporting crimes, and police from making arrests because they know there will be no prosecution. This, in turn, encourages the spread of crime and ultimately, the commission of even more serious crime.[52]

Professor Jacob T. Levy describes the harm done by the Rehnquist Court: "Tribes themselves are left powerless to provide one of the most basic of governmental functions: security for the life, limb, and property of their constituents."[53]

Given the long history of violence committed by non-Indians against Native Americans, reformers should seek to overturn the *Oliphant* line of cases in a more principled Supreme Court in the twenty-first century. Advocates can urge a return to the *Worcester* protectorate, explain how the *Oliphant* line violates the cardinal rules laid down by *Worcester*, frustrates the

Indian self-determination policy, and is at odds with UNDRIP standards that safeguard indigenous peoples from violence and protect their right to self-determination. Failing a return to *Worcester* in the courts, Congress can overturn the *Oliphant* line of cases, just like it reversed the *Duro* decision. As a protector, Congress is not only empowered to make necessary adjustments for the exercise of inherent tribal sovereignty, but it is obliged to restore that basic attribute of government.[54] An omnibus jurisdiction bill to overturn the *Oliphant* mind-set was drafted by Indian Country a few years ago, but it did not move in the unfriendly Republican Congress during the Bush administration. However, the protectorate obligation of the United States demands recognition of tribal jurisdiction over all persons that come within reservation borders. Congress should safeguard that inherent tribal sovereignty, if the courts do not, to protect Native Americans from escalating violence at the hands of outside criminals. The nation sorely failed to accord that vital protection during the madness of the nineteenth century, when genocide marched unabated through many tribal communities, and the legal system must not allow rampant violence to rear its head once again in the twenty-first century.

5. Fix the trusteeship system and reform the dark side of guardianship.
The *Sandoval* trilogy of cases introduced us to the frightening abuse of federal guardianship during 1886–1934, when the government's guardianship powers were at their zenith. It also exposed the national scandal created by the broken Bureau of Indian Affairs (BIA) trusteeship system that continues to mismanage Indian assets in 2009. The root cause of the guardianship abuses was plain old racism, while incompetence by BIA fiduciaries caused the financial crisis in which millions of dollars are unaccounted for. Both of these evils can be driven from the guardianship and trusteeship regimes and prevented from returning by the safeguards recommended here.

The shocking guardianship abuses identified previously have largely been corrected after Indians achieved citizenship, along with the demise of the infamous Code of Indian Offenses and the reining-in of moral policemen from the BIA. Those government abuses were premised on the notion that Indians were racially inferior people with contemptible religions, cultures, governments, and ways of life that needed to be stamped out and replaced with agrarian values and Christian beliefs. No other race has ever been subjected to the excessive lengths the government went to stamp out tribal culture and traditional life, including the extreme measures of taking children and placing them in institutions designed to obliterate their identity and banning the tribal religions. Ethnocide and cultural genocide was the result; and this was perfectly legal under cases like *United States v. Clapox* (1888), *In re Can-ah-couqua* (1887), and as late as the many pre-ICWA cases, like *In re Adoption of John Doe v. Heim* (1976).

The troubling legacy seems to lurk beneath the surface in the Indian religion cases of *Wana the Bear v. Community Construction* (1982), *Employment Division v. Smith* (1990), and *Lyng v. Northwest Indian Cemetery Association* (1988). The courts seemingly viewed twentieth-century American Indian free-exercise claims and tribal religious sensibilities through nineteenth-century eyes. To be sure, Congress has acted to repudiate those notions of racial and cultural inferiority, change the national policy, and afford statutory protections in Native American human-rights legislation, such as ICWA (1978), the American Indian Religious Freedom Act (AIRFA) (1978), NAGPRA (1990), and the AIRFA Amendments of 1994. But those attitudes lingered in the Rehnquist Court as the very mind-set that animated the "Courts of the conquerors" in the nineteenth and twentieth centuries.

Great care must be taken by twenty-first-century judges to ensure that the historical contempt for the Indian race and culture, which underpinned the abuse of guardianship, is swept from courthouse closets. Native Americans are still wards of the government, but today they are *also* citizens with constitutional rights. They should be able to rely upon constitutional law and a level playing field in the courtroom to protect against government abuse of the guardianship principle in the twenty-first century. In addition, the *Worcester* protectorate insists that all branches of the US government—including the courts—affirmatively *safeguard* tribal religions, cultures, families, and ways of life from unwarranted federal or state interference. Courts must join the rest of the country as we strive toward a more just culture. Their task is to become a bulwark for all segments of society, including Native Americans. That requires protection against the dark side of guardianship and fostering the use of that power to protect Indian tribes and their constituents as protectorates in our political system.

Apart from guardianship issues, Congress must fix the broken trusteeship system that continues to plague Indian Country. As shown by *Cobell*, *Nez Perce*, and the numerous companion cases brought by over one hundred

Indian tribes, the BIA system for managing and accounting for Indian and tribal trust property is broken. As John Echohawk said in 2007:

> Imagine the widespread outcry if banks, savings and loan companies, and investment houses that were chosen by investors were to fail to meet their fiduciary obligations. Undoubtedly, such harm would be corrected.[55]

Prophetically, many non-Indian financial institutions failed in 2008. Congress *rushed* to fix the financial crisis, as predicted by Echohawk, by working nights and weekends to pony up billions of dollars. Yet Indian Country has been in *precisely* that same dire situation for decades. When Indians were concerned, Bush administration trustees *fought* tooth and nail to deny government liability, to oppose reform, and to prevent a meaningful legislative fix. The effort to account for missing millions of dollars, make the tribes whole, and fix the system for managing Indian trust property deserves the *same* urgent concern that spurred Congress to work overtime with overwrought cabinet officials and Wall Street bigwigs to prop up, reform, and save the non-Indian financial sector. (Incidentally, no one asked BIA trust-fund-money managers for their advice in solving the crisis.) Why not ask these hotshots to find the missing millions of dollars at the BIA and fix the Indian financial sector? On a more serious note, tribal leaders do hope the Obama administration will fix the system under the leadership of Secretary of the Interior Ken Salazar and his assistant secretary for Indian affairs, Larry Echohawk. They are honorable men who take trusteeship seriously.[56]

6. Reform the dark side of *Lone Wolf*'s plenary-power doctrine. There is a theoretical and a structural approach for reforming the dark side of *Lone Wolf*'s plenary-power doctrine. Both approaches are supported by the UNDRIP standards. The goals should be to (1) preserve the plenary-power doctrine insofar as the United States exercises it to protect and safeguard the Indian nations as described in the *Worcester* protectorate; and to (2) discard the use of plenary power to harm Indian tribes and their constituents. As I will explain, once the plenary-power doctrine is placed within the theoretical framework of *Worcester*, both goals are accomplished.

The *Worcester* protectorate, as previously explained, is a political charter for Indian tribes fashioned by John Marshall from treaties, the Treaty and Commerce Clauses of the US Constitution, and widespread international practice among nations in 1832. It empowers the United States to protect the political, property, human, and cultural rights of Indian tribes and their constituents. As stated in *Lara*, treaties with Indian tribes made under the Treaty Clause "can authorize Congress to deal with 'matters' with which otherwise 'Congress could not deal.'"[57] The protectorate relation forms the real source of Congresss' plenary power to legislate for the benefit of Indian tribes. At the same time, the *Worcester* protectorate gives no license to destroy Indian tribes through the use of plenary power. The protectorate framework thus circumscribes the use of plenary power to harm Indian tribes that enjoy US protection. Theoretically, the *Worcester* charter trims away the dark side of the plenary-power doctrine. In this setting, the misuse of totalitarian power to harm Indian tribes envisioned by *Lone Wolf* has no place.

Substantively, the UNDRIP standards help shape modern notions about plenary power and provide rationale for trimming the negative from the *Lone Wolf* doctrine. They prohibit government conduct that violates the well-being of indigenous peoples. If adopted by the United States, those guidelines would unquestionably limit federal power over Indian tribes and individual Native Americans. Indeed, even under those standards as they now stand, plenary power may not be exercised today in derogation of the UNDRIP standards without facially violating the well-being of indigenous peoples as demarcated by the international community. By the same token, so long as plenary power serves those standards, it has international integrity. Thus, the role of the UNDRIP in defining the modern nature of plenary power in the postcolonial world cannot and should not be ignored. As an international barometer, it strongly suggests that plenary power cannot be used as a tool to harm indigenous peoples. The international standards encourage nations to uplift their law and policy to protect indigenous rights. In that regard, the UNDRIP supports Marshall's vision for the Republic. Recognition of the UNDRIP standards would curb the potential for abuse and reform *Lone Wolf*'s doctrine by preserving the beneficial side of plenary power, while discarding the harmful side.

Lone Wolf's ominous form of colonial rule is inappropriate in the postcolonial era. It called for totalitarian rule by Congress over a racially inferior, weak, and utterly dependent peoples. In this version of governance, the existence of tribal government is ignored, Indians are seen as noncitizen wards of the government who are without constitutional rights, and Congress's absolute power over them is unfettered by judicial review or constitutional limitations. In *Lone Wolf*, Congress may treat Indian subjects and their property any way it sees fit, even to the extreme of confiscating their land and unilaterally breaking treaties with impunity.

Lone Wolf sought to engraft this harsh form of colonial rule for Indian tribes upon our constitutional democracy in 1903. Today, none of these factors exist. Federal policy is built upon a government-to-government relationship, Indians have citizenship, and the exercise of plenary power is subject to judicial review and constitutional limitations.[58] Nor does the justification for *Lone Wolf*'s form of governance seem persuasive today. *Tee-Hit-Ton* justified this harsh form of control by distinguishing the United States' purpose in colonizing Indian land from more benign purposes in other colonies. It argued that "settlement of the white race in the United States" requires plenary power because "'the dominant purpose of the whites in America was to occupy the land.'"[59] *Tee-Hit-Ton* did not explain how that purpose can be reconciled with guardianship, which is the supposed source of the doctrine in *Lone Wolf*. The conflicting explanations arise because the Supreme Court simply cut the doctrine out of thin air as a pretext for confiscating Indian land.

The fundamental theoretical flaw in *Lone Wolf* and *Tee-Hit-Ton* is the failure to identify the correct source of Congress's plenary power over Indian affairs. *Lone Wolf* derived that absolute plenary power from the guardianship principle alone, since that extraordinary power is found nowhere in the Constitution. The Court stated:

> Congress possessed a paramount power over the property of the Indians by reason of its guardianship over their interests, and...such authority might be implied, even though opposed to the strict letter of a treaty with the Indians.[60]

As I argued earlier, the plenary-power doctrine stems not from the guardianship principle of *Cherokee Nation*, but arises more correctly from the protectorate relationship described in *Worcester*. Within the latter framework, plenary power may logically only be properly exercised to protect and safeguard, not destroy, that political charter. Guardianship alone is not inherently an extraconstitutional governmental power as *Lone Wolf* seemed to think. Rather, guardianship in fiduciary law is logically subject to the rule of constitutional law. Just like any other normal function of government, it is not above the law. Therefore if plenary power exists, and I agree that it does, it must come from another source. That source is found in the Constitution itself, namely, the Treaty Clause, which authorized treaties with Indian nations, and the Indian Commerce Clause. Those clauses clothe the national political branch with extraordinary power to enter into and maintain protectorate relations with Indian tribes and to legislate to safeguard the political, property, human, and cultural rights of Indian tribes as distinct political and cultural communities that exist in our nation under the protection of the United States. The political branches' power to enter into and maintain the protectorate relationship with Indian tribes, regardless whether they have treaties with the United States, has been described as "necessary concomitants of nationality."[61] Viewed in this light, plenary power must be retained to discharge the protectorate function, but that power cannot by definition be used to harm or destroy the protected tribal nations.

What is the appropriate theoretical framework for Congress's plenary power over Indian affairs in the postcolonial world? Our legal history in *Worcester, Lone Wolf, Tee-Hit-Ton,* and *Lara* suggests that there are two distinct kinds of governance in Indian affairs: the *Lone Wolf* model and the *Worcester* model. Clearly, the ingredients for *Lone Wolf* are gone. The *Worcester* protectorate, which was commended earlier, can be described as a benign protectorate, similar to other colonies where the United States was guided by the welfare of the Native peoples of those lands and administered property for their benefit. Such a protectorate for the Philippines was described in *Carino v. Insular Government of the Philippine Islands* (1909), where the United States respected tribal land rights, because the purpose of the Philippines colony was to "administer the property and rights 'for the benefit of the inhabitants thereof.'"[62] In this setting, *Carino* explained, "our first object in the internal administration of the islands is to do justice to the natives, not to exploit their country for private gain."[63] In so doing, *Carino* had to distinguish Philippine governance from harsher treatment of Indian tribes at home under *Lone Wolf* principles.[64] However, *Carino* could have looked at *Worcester* to reconcile the administration of that colony with American Indian protectorates at home. The administration of the Philippines "to do justice to the natives, not to exploit their country" is *precisely* the kind of protection envisioned in *Worcester,* where Georgia's annexation of tribal land and abolition of tribal sovereignty were declared illegal. *Worcester* protected the land base and political autonomy of the Cherokee

Nation as a culturally and politically distinct community in the American protectorate setting. This is similar to American purpose in the Philippines described in *Carino*. In both instances, the United States is a stronger power obliged to safeguard a weaker one under its protection.

This theoretical framework is a logical and legally sound pathway for curbing the dark side of the plenary-power doctrine. It places the doctrine into the framework established by *Worcester* and distances us from the abusive *Lone Wolf* and *Tee-Hit-Ton* mentality. The cases in this book illustrate the need for plenary power to protect Indian tribes and their constituents. It should be retained in a protectorate framework for that singular purpose only. Out of that framework, a new doctrine of plenary power emerges, one that is more in keeping with the postcolonial world.

We turn now to a structural framework for exercising plenary power in the modern world. Any form of plenary power in settler states is suspect, however, because it creates a structural problem that must be addressed to prevent the risk of abuse. Any government vested with plenary power over a minority runs the risk of unwanted oppression. John Stuart Mill and Alexis de Tocqueville described this inherent structural problem as the "tyranny of the majority." They explored the problem of minority liberty and rights in democratic society. Congress is particularly susceptible to the tyranny of the majority, according to Tocqueville, because lawmakers are swayed by "the daily passions of their constituents."[65] Minority liberty is endangered when omnipotent power driven by those passions goes unchecked. These thinkers held no myopic views about good faith in the exercise of absolute power. To avoid despotism in a democracy, Tocqueville urged that laws be limited to that which is just. He asked courts to enforce lawful limits upon the exercise of legislative power, wisely insisting that the exercise of omnipotent power be resisted and held in check.

How can we hold plenary power in check when it is exercised to maintain American Indian protectorates? All nations share the built-in risk of political oppression in indigenous affairs. Our history illustrates how unfettered plenary power worked to oppress Native America. The tyranny of the majority is strongly evident in the ten worst Indian cases. It caused incalculable human suffering, described in these pages. Justice Sandra Day O'Connor finally realized that Indians fare poorly when their unpopular minority causes are cast adrift in the political arena. Like Tocqueville, she decried the decision in *Smith* to place "the rights of those whose minority religious practices are not shared by the majority and may be viewed with hostility" into the hands of "majoritarian rule" as the sole means of protection in our democracy:

> The history of our free exercise doctrine amply demonstrates the harsh impact majoritarian rule has had on unpopular or emerging religious groups…"One's right to life, liberty, and property, to free speech, a free press, freedom of worship and assembly, and other fundamental rights may not be submitted to vote; they depend on the outcome of no elections."[66]

Institutional safeguards must be built into the political system to address this structural problem. When plenary power is concerned, reliable safety mechanisms are needed to reduce the risk of oppression in our system of government. We cannot always depend upon the goodwill of lawmakers, even in a protectorate relation. Someone needs to keep an eye on congressional power brokers when they go behind closed doors to make decisions that effect vital interests of the domestic dependent nations they are obliged to protect to make sure they get it right. Too often, Indian trust responsibility becomes an expendable trade bead in Congress.

The courts can keep an eye on Congress as a bulwark from afar. But that after-the-fact safety net will not always be there, as seen in the ten worst cases. A protectorate requires a stronger, more meaningful political arrangement to be viable. "We need more than just a government-to-government relationship; we need a nation-to-nation relationship," in the words of then president-elect Obama.[67] This heightened relationship in a protectorate is best accomplished in the political arena by providing the weaker power with a nonvoting seat in Congress. This is more in keeping with the protectorate status envisioned by *Worcester* and the nation-to-nation relationship that flows from the protectorate relation.

A seat in Congress was contemplated by some of the early Indian treaties in the Republic that provided the signatory Indian nations with a seat in Congress. In fact, the Cherokee treaty in *Worcester* does just that. American Samoa provides an example of this mechanism. It is an unincorporated territory of the United States in the South Pacific Ocean, acquired by the United States through a treaty with Germany in 1899. American Samoa is a self-governing indigenous territory with a land base of 76.8 square miles administered by the Department of the Interior.

The Honorable Eni Faleomavaega (D-American Samoa) is American Samoa's delegate to the US House of Representatives. He enjoys a nonvoting seat in Congress. Since 1989, he has advocated tirelessly for his people, Native Hawaiians, Oceania, and Native America in the legislative process as a nonvoting delegate. He participated in the hearings, development, and passage of historic Native American legislation during the modern era of federal Indian law. At vital times when Indian nations had no delegates of their own or other representation in Congress, he was an unwavering champion.

The US Constitution does not provide for congressional representation for territories or the District of Columbia, but those places elect nonvoting delegates to the House of Representatives. Thus, American Samoa, Guam, the Virgin Islands, Puerto Rico, the Northern Marianna Islands, and the District of Columbia elect nonvoting delegates to that chamber. They may participate in hearings, debates, and committee deliberations, as well as introduce bills, influence colleagues, provide access to Congress for their constituents, and otherwise participate in the nation's legislative process as nonvoting members of Congress. Indian tribes within the American protectorate are entitled to their own representation, even though a workable method for electing delegates from the domestic dependant nations to that chamber will have to be developed by political scientists. Indian tribes are unique political entities in our system of government. Since the inception of our republic, Indian affairs have entailed special government-to-government obligations on the part of the United States. Those obligations warrant similar treatment given by Congress to foreign protectorates to safeguard against the potential abuse of legislative power in the United States' relations with domestic dependent nations. Given Delegate Faleomavaega's impressive record, just a few delegates from Native America would change the face of Congress and ensure the success of the American Indian protectorate.

Within the theoretical framework for exercising and limiting the exercise of plenary power and the structural framework for protecting against the abuse of power, it is clear that we can replace the plenary-power doctrine of *Lone Wolf* with a doctrine more in line with the postcolonial world. Any vestiges of *Lone Wolf* and its mentality can be discarded. In summary, here are the reasons why the Supreme Court should overturn the *Lone Wolf* doctrine: (1) It relies upon the wrong source, guardianship, when it should have looked to the protectorate framework of *Worcester*, which springs from the Constitution. (2) The premise for *Lone Wolf*'s doctrine—that Indians are racially inferior people without constitutional rights—is no longer valid or acceptable. (3) *Lone Wolf* used plenary power to harm an Indian tribe and confiscate its property, which offends a bedrock limitation on the exercise of that power imposed by the *Worcester* protectorate. (4) *Lone Wolf* no longer has any vitality since all of the ingredients for ruling Indian tribes by the totalitarian power are gone and new features have emerged, such as the rise of tribal governments, which make the *Worcester* framework the most viable framework for federal power over Indian affairs in the postcolonial world. Many of the battles during the modern era of federal Indian law centered on the protection of tribal sovereignty of Indian tribes as domestic dependent sovereigns within the *Worcester* framework. The fruits of that labor, over the past thirty-five years, can be seen in the rise of the modern Indian nations, as the underpinnings of the *Lone Wolf* mentality have been assailed. It is now time to lay *Lone Wolf* to rest and change the name of its plenary-power doctrine to the protectorate-power doctrine, which more properly describes Congress's power over Indian affairs. (While we are changing names, we should use the Pawnee name for "Congress," which is *Pakskiciis Iriirarahkaaw,* meaning "the place where the bald ones are inside, i.e., the Capitol building.")

7. Overturn *Lyng* and strengthen cultural sovereignty. Tribal sovereignty has two sides, which form the pillars that support tribal life in the United States. The first is the political side: it focuses on tribal government and battles to maintain the Indian nations' protectorate status under the *Worcester* charter. The second is the cultural side of tribal sovereignty—that is, the indigenous ways of life that are defined not by federal Indian law, but derived from the cultural legacy of Native America. It is the glue that holds tribes together. It unites and inspires the people. It is a wellspring from within that gives hope for the future. It is the inherent spiritual power of Native America, handed down by the ancestors, answerable only to the Great Spirit and Mother Earth. This pillar is aptly described by Yaqui Rebecca Tsosie and Comanche Wallace Coffey as "cultural sovereignty," and it struggles to keep the forces that threaten the cultural survival of Indian nations at bay.[68] W. Richard West, a Cheyenne-Arapaho, the founding director of the National Museum of the American Indian, observed that political sovereignty and cultural sovereignty are "inextricably linked, because the ultimate goal of political sovereignty is protecting a way of life."[69]

The law must be reformed to strengthen cultural sovereignty. The goal is to allow Indian tribes and other Native groups a significant measure of cultural self-determination. *Cultural self-determination* is defined by Robert J. Miller as the right of a tribal group to "set the standards and mores of what constitutes its traditional culture and how it will honor and practice that culture."[70] Every Indian tribe and indigenous group "should have the same basic human right to live according to their cultural and religious beliefs as does the American dominant society," according to Miller, and "the issue of majority control over minority cultures arises" because it is the majority "that sets the laws and rules of society."[71]

The Rehnquist Court was not up to the task of protecting Native American religious liberty in the Indian religion cases. In the same way that the *Lone Wolf* and *Oliphant* mentalities imperil political sovereignty, the Indian religion doctrines undermine cultural sovereignty. While *Wana the Bear* and *Smith* were overturned by legislative measures, *Lyng* is still the law of the land. *Lyng* declared that no First Amendment principle exists to protect tribal worship at holy places on public land.[72] Nor is there any statutory protection for that form of worship, as held in *Navajo Nation v. United States* (2008).[73] Despite repeated pleas, Congress still has not passed a law to protect such worship twenty years after *Lyng*. In the meantime, holy places have been destroyed.[74]

Dire situations like this arise when the law is not accountable to every segment of society. American religious history shows how minority religious freedom can be oppressed when unchecked by the courts. Without legal restraints, our democracy went all the way. It banned tribal religions, imprisoned adherents, committed genocidal acts, and imposed government-sponsored religion upon Native peoples. Destroying holy places today is child's play. In the absence of legal protection, it is done without regret. Congress passed the Religious Land Use and Institutionalized Persons Act (RLUIPA) to protect hometown religious sites from the *Lyng* and *Smith* doctrines.[75] By contrast, every administration since 1988 has steadfastly opposed statutory protection for Native American holy places.[76] This double standard in federal law ignores Establishment Clause restraints in Indian affairs, just like nineteenth-century Indian policy.

The continuing vitality of *Lyng* says several things about modern society. First, the minimalist vision of religious liberty that protects worship only to the extent that one is not punished or coerced is one of bare toleration. In that, we have not managed to rise above medieval Europe, despite the effort by revolutionary leaders to give birth to true religious liberty by enshrining the accommodation principle into our organic documents. Second, *Lyng* completed the secularization process by placing religious accommodation into the hands of the secular political process as the sole means for accommodating religious freedom. Third, the *Lyng* standard stands as a barrier to social change. It prevents evolution from a settler state—and the way that conquerors view the land—into a society that takes indigenous religious needs into account and holds some places as holy ground. These changes are long overdue. The UN guidepost requires protection of indigenous holy places. That cannot be achieved until *Lyng* is reversed.

Lyng can and should be overturned. First, *Lyng* turned on an unjust legal fiction, described in the dissenting opinion by an incredulous Justice Brennan: "*Government action that will virtually destroy a religion is nevertheless deemed not to 'burden' that religion.*"[77] It is a pure legal fiction that a religion can be destroyed without burdening anyone's religious practices. No false legal fiction is entitled to talismanic effect when it perpetuates injustice, as demonstrated in *Brown* and *Mabo*. Second, this is not 1988. Federal agencies have much more experience in the past twenty years managing public land in ways that do not destroy holy places, and there are many success stories brought about by some federal land managers of goodwill. Furthermore, larger events since 1988 show that the minimalist vision of religious freedom of *Lyng* is not acceptable in modern American life. They include the laws passed to overturn the *Smith* case, the executive order promulgated by President Clinton directing federal agencies to accommodate Native worship at holy places, RLUIPA, and UNDRIP. Finally, the Rehnquist Court is no more. A newly constituted court in the twenty-first century will someday come to protect Native American religious liberty under extant law. Litigators should never accede to *Lyng* or perpetuate its doctrines. They must have gumption and courage to overturn *Lyng*.

Failing reversal of *Lyng*, Native Americans can always become skunks at the picnic as an unprotected religious minority. Taking the low road, reformers could study the anti-Indian litigation campaign of the Mountain States Legal Foundation. Using that model, Indian spoilers can conspire to undermine the religious liberty of other Americans by filing lawsuits that question the constitutionality of RLUIPA on Equal Protection or Establishment Clause grounds. More constructively, reformers can take the high road. Native America can renew efforts to ask Congress to repudiate *Lyng* with a new law that provides a cause of action to litigate to protect their holy places. In one of its finest hours, Congress repudiated *Smith* following a grassroots human-rights campaign that began on Indian reservations and ended in the White House, when the president signed the AIRFA Amendments of 1994 into law. Americans are fundamentally fair. They can be relied upon to confront injustice and do the right thing, once educated about pressing indigenous needs.

New theories are needed to protect Native American religious liberty in general. The Rehnquist Court said Native America cannot count on the First Amendment. Unlike most Americans who take First Amendment protection for granted, that has never been the case for American Indians. Rather than knock on a door marked No Indians Allowed, reformers should look elsewhere in the Constitution for a more reliable theory. The *Worcester* model for protecting political sovereignty is broad enough to protect cultural sovereignty. In that framework, the United States must protect, not destroy, the cultural integrity of American Indian protectorates. The courts routinely uphold the power of Congress and federal agencies to protect tribal religious practices under the "Indian trust relationship" when the United States *wants* to accommodate those practices. That is not enough. Case law should be developed to *require* US protection and *prevent* harm by the United States. That reform would bring UNDRIP principles into a modern *Worcester* model for a postcolonial world. It would protect cultural sovereignty by fostering the exercise of cultural self-determination by Indian nations as distinct political and cultural communities that exist within our political system under the protection of the United States.

Reformers should also look to tort law for possible legal theories to protect Indian tribes and Native American communities from cultural harm caused by agencies, corporations, and private individuals. Minority groups are often harmed by tortuous acts of groups and individuals. Hate groups and white supremacists, like the Ku Klux Klan or White Aryans, are an example. They were toppled by damages actions brought by the Southern Poverty Law Center, which awarded victims verdicts amounting to millions of dollars.[78] Similarly, Native American cultures have been harmed by corporations, groups, individuals, and agencies. Examples include: destruction of sacred sites and indigenous habitat; degradation of natural resources; digging up Indian graves; appropriating sacred objects, cultural property, or intellectual property rights; interfering with treaty rights; and disrupting traditional religious practices. Conduct in the ten worst cases provides further illustration. Forest Service destruction of *Haa Aaní* in *Tee-Hit-Ton* brought cultural harm to the Tlingits by destroying the indigenous habitat upon which their way of life depended. Mass grave excavation in *Wana the Bear* violated the religious rights and sensibilities of the next of kin Indian tribe. Taking a child against the mother's will in *In re Can-ah-couqua* diminished Tlingit culture by transferring a child from one group to another and brainwashing that tribal member into another culture.

This conduct might amount to a cultural tort, since it harmed tribal cultures. The facts in *Apache Tribe v. United States* (1978) provide another example.[79] In that case, the Chiricahua Apache filed a claim against the United States in the Indian Claims Commission for damages to the tribe arising from twenty-seven years of captivity as prisoners of war. The Apache contended that this prolonged confinement brought irreparable harm to their culture, as many died, children were taken to boarding schools, and the cultural integrity of the tribe crumbled. While the claim was dismissed for lack of jurisdiction, the cultural tort theory is compelling. Similarly, in 2002 the nation's largest salmon kill occurred. It took place in the Klamath River and was caused by irrigation water diversions. This tragedy is an example of a cultural tort committed against the Indian tribes whose culture, livelihood, and spiritual well-being depended upon that fishery.[80] Finally, the Exxon Valdez oil spill that caused ecological disaster in southeast Alaska might provide another example.[81] Tort law has not been sufficiently developed to encompass a damages claim remedy for tortuous conduct that inflicts harm upon the cultural integrity of Indian tribes.

Indian law reformers should study the legal framework for the Southern Poverty Law Center damages actions. That might provide thought for developing an appropriate legal framework for damages actions to redress harm to cultural sovereignty. In addition, a searching analysis of tort law might lead to a remedy that would deter tortuous behavior that harms tribal culture. Tort law evolves over time to constrain new forms of oppression and mediate social inequities as they arise; and the threat of money damages does create deterrence and send broad messages about what society deems important.[82] Tort principles can be fashioned to develop a cognizable cultural tort for negligent and intentional intrusions upon tribal culture that inflict emotional, cultural, economic harm. Such a theory should spell out that agencies, groups, and individuals have a duty to conduct themselves in a manner that avoids intentional or negligent harm to others, including tribal cultural communities. In short, reformers should develop extant elements of tort law (such as duty, duty to protect, standard of care, harm, foreseeable harm, proximate cause, the fact of damage, and amount of damages, and so forth) into a cognizable cultural tort as a tool to strengthen cultural sovereignty.

8. Protect indigenous habitat. One of the biggest challenges facing Indian tribes today is protecting the indigenous habitat located off the reservation that remains vital to their traditional hunting, fishing, and gathering ways of life. Traditional foods remain at the center of tribal culture especially in the Pacific Northwest and throughout Alaska. The songs, medicine, ceremonies, dress, spiritual beliefs, art, names, and social organization of tribal hunters, fishers, and gatherers are based upon the plants, animals, birds, and fish of indigenous habitats. These ancient relationships form the oldest human bonds with the Natural World left in North America. Those bonds are endangered.

Federal Indian law falls short of protecting indigenous habitat located outside of tribal control. The law development seen in *Adair* and *United States v. Washington* are encouraging possibilities for protecting indigenous habitat through treaties, especially when treaty rights are combined with environmental laws to form protective tools. That important work should continue. However, not all tribal groups in the Pacific Northwest have treaties, and that body of law is advancing too slowly to keep pace with the rate of habitat degradation that is rapidly overtaking the Pacific Northwest. The protections available from federal Indian law may be too little, and too late. Indigenous foods and natural resources are being diminished at a frightening pace, as the environmental viability of productive habitat in the land, rivers, and ocean is being destroyed by a society that is still engaged in conquering the Natural World and looks at the land only through the eyes of a settler state. Unless the law takes into account the needs of America's remaining tribal hunting, fishing, and gathering cultures, they will soon vanish from the face of Mother Earth. Once they are gone, no one will be left who can authoritatively articulate a sound environmental ethic for relating to the Natural World, which is vital traditional knowledge gleaned by human hunters, fishers, and gatherers long before the rise of agriculture.

Congress may have to intervene to save these endangered cultures. Despite their vitality, America's few surviving hunter-fisher-gatherer cultures are on the brink of extinction due to rampant habitat destruction that is beyond their control. The UNDRIP standards provide a guidepost for addressing this crisis. Developed in the United Nations over a twenty year period, Article 25 recognizes that *meaningful* stewardship can only arise from a *spiritual* relation to indigenous habitat.

> Indigenous people have the right to maintain and strengthen their distinctive spiritual relationship with their traditionally owned or otherwise occupied and used lands, territories, waters and coastal seas and other resources and to uphold their responsibilities to future generations in this regard.

Article 26 states: "Indigenous peoples have the right to the lands, territories and resources which they have traditionally owned, occupied or otherwise used or acquired." This provision realizes that the well-being and cultural survival of hunters, fishers, and gatherers are utterly dependent upon indigenous habitat, and nations must protect that relationship so that way of life can survive in modern nations, and not be destroyed. In this regard, Article 26 reads, "States shall give legal recognition and protection to these lands, territories, and resources." This tall order tests the will of each nation to protect indigenous habitat "with due respect to the customs, traditions and land tenure systems of the indigenous peoples concerned." As we learned in *Cherokee Nation,* justice delayed is justice denied. Unless these standards are embraced and implemented in a timely fashion, it will be too late to save indigenous habitat and the cultures that depend upon it. Immediate steps should be taken to bring the UNDRIP standards into American law. They can be folded into emergency measures to address the global warming crisis, as part and parcel of the effort to save humanity and the world in which we live. Ultimately, the declaration of peace with the Natural World will lead to a more just society that is more native to place.

Into the Twilight

In every civilization, the law is remarkable and indispensable. In the United States, the law forms a magnificent institution. It is vital to our grand experiment in democracy, and it always has been. As a man-made construct, it is nevertheless fraught with human frailties, and it sometimes falters. Because fairness in a legal system is vital to every individual, institution, and sector of society, a single miscarriage of justice concerns everyone.

When a miscarriage happens, we must pause and soberly diagnose the cause. The outbreak of injustice dampens the human condition. Its spread across the land places our highest ideals beyond reach. Against that evil, the impulse to resist life under unjust laws is strong. It is seen in the traditions of Thoreau, the wisdom of Gandhi, the words of Martin Luther King Jr., and the litigation of Thurgood Marshall. They followed Saint Augustine's maxim that "an unjust law is no law at all" and made the world a better place. The urge to reform an unjust law resonates in the Western tradition. I submit that on this side of the great ocean there is an inalienable right to justice in North America. It emanates from the land, perhaps planted by the Great Spirit to nurture human well-being.

The ten examples studied in these pages reveal serious problems afflicting the law pertaining to American Indians. I have attempted to explain why injustice is so prevalent in American Indian cases. In probing forces thought to be causal, I seek to better understand the nature of law and, on a personal level, purge disappointment. Hopefully, this soul-searching examination will provide a thought-provoking contribution to the law reform debate.

If this excursion into the dark nature of law contributes to a vision for improving our system of justice, it may not be in vain. The imperfections that skew the ability of our legal system to afford the right to justice for every litigant must be corrected. Once identified, the flaws should not be tolerated, for even one unjust act taints the system and shakes public confidence in the law. If allowed to linger and spread, unrest, civil disobedience, and other social upheaval are the results. More importantly, there is simply no place for injustice in a land that professes higher ideals; and that specter should not be allowed to stalk any of our citizens. For these reasons, it is fitting that federal Indian law reformers sharpen their swords. After all, the courts of the conqueror have not yet entered into their twilight. But their days are numbered, as they have outlived their time.

The sun must also set on every legal career. So in 2009, I turned in my spurs to the Native American Rights Fund. Today, I shall be found rocking on the front porch, and practicing law in Oklahoma. Our home sits on allotted Pawnee land beside the Cimarron River. Gazing upon the setting sun, perhaps I shall relive my days as a NARF staff attorney. The sun is called *Sakuuru'* by the Pawnee.

The sun also sets on the modern era of federal Indian law (circa 1959–1985). That heady time is gone, along with many giants of that day. The later years, under the Rehnquist and Roberts Courts, were long, hard, and dark, often marked by hostility from Congress and neglect in the White House. But in every long night, the Morning Star rises to bring light into the day. The fruits of the Native American social movement are seen today. However, Indian tribes cannot rest upon those achievements. In the twenty-first century, Indian Country may be embarking upon its greatest adventure of all time: to reform the dark side of the law, once and for all.

The American experience will be determined by we who are living in the twenty-first century. That history is yet to be written on how the American peoples will be judged. In those pages, the legal system will be shaped by this generation of Native American attorneys. As legal warriors they are like wolves, gathered at the doorsteps of the courts of the conqueror. I wish them well.[83] Into their hands fall the hopes and aspirations that were out of reach by their forebears. The final chapter on the American experience cannot be written until we embrace its indigenous heritage and harmonize that legacy with our own. The chapter on my own life as a NARF litigator closed when I bade farewell to my longtime comrades. As those days fade away, I am indebted to the Native American Rights Fund for my opportunity to serve. From where the Sun now stands, I shall litigate as a NARF attorney no more, forever.

AFTERWORD

As Walter Echo-Hawk explains in such compelling terms, American courts constructed a dark side of federal Indian law and it was no abstraction. The dry words on law book pages unleashed presidents and congressmen bent on Manifest Destiny, assimilation-minded federal bureaucrats, exploitive corporations, land-hungry settlers, state officials anxious to expand their jurisdiction, and Christian churches. They took most tribal land, suppressed the elaborate governmental structures developed over millennia, and clamped down on Indian spirituality, denying Native people the songs, dances, and stories that were the hallmarks of their cultures, of who they were. By the 1950s, Indian Country had hit rock bottom and tribes faced a hard-line Congress, which decreed a final termination—repeal of the treaties and the sell-off of those lands that remained.

Because Indian people are the most impoverished in the country, tribal leaders had few tangible assets, but they made up their minds to bring a revival to Indian Country—a last stand, as Vine Deloria Jr. called it. With a web of treaties, statutes, and administrative regulations dating back to pre-Revolution days, they had little choice but to rely on law. The dark side of Indian law posed the greatest obstacles and tribal leaders had to work around it by emphasizing the positive pockets of Indian law found in the original meaning of the treaties and some court opinions; petitioning Congress for new, progressive laws; and establishing strong tribal institutions on the reservations.

A broadly supported agenda emerged from Indian Country. Tribal leaders wanted permanency, protection of the essential things that had defined Native societies since the beginning of time. Permanent rights to land, water, and hunting, fishing, and gathering. Permanent sovereignty— self-determination, governance—in Indian Country. Permanent protection of their culture, their own sense and practices of spirituality.

Three generations ago, any such progress seemed impossible, except, that is, to tribal leaders. Of course, the modern Indian movement is incomplete. There is a painfully long way to go. Still, despite the stiff headwinds of the dark side of Indian law, the results have been stunning.[*] An overview of

*For works explicitly addressing the modern Indian revival, see Charles Wilkinson, **Blood Struggle: The Rise of Modern Indian Nations** (W. W. Norton: New York, 2005); **Rebuilding Native Nations: Strategies for Governance and Development** (University of Arizona Press: Tucson, 2007) (Miriam Jorgensen, ed.); Stephen Cornell, **The Return of the Native: American Indian Political Resurgence** (Oxford University Press: New York, 1988).

these successes exhibits the best side of America—that even the most marginalized among us can, with informed and determined leadership, greatly improve the well-being of their people.

On permanency of land and resource rights, tribes in the Puget Sound area achieved a decades-old dream in 1974 when US District Court Judge George Boldt put life into treaty promises with his monumental ruling that tribes had the right to harvest 50 percent of the salmon runs—a ruling that was affirmed by the Supreme Court in 1979. That led to similar affirmations of fishing, hunting, and gathering rights in the Rocky Mountains, Great Plains, Great Lakes region, and elsewhere. In related proceedings, courts also upheld expansive tribal water rights.

The determination of tribes has also been manifested in a deep-running development that has gone largely unnoticed: the tribal land base has been steadily growing. In the past half century, Indian land holdings in the contiguous states have gone from 50.5 to 58 million acres, an increase equal to one and a half times the size of Massachusetts. Most of that land has been laboriously purchased by tribes, parcel by parcel, often by reacquiring former reservation land that had been homesteaded by non-Indians under the forced allotment policy of the late nineteenth and early twentieth centuries. This will continue apace: nearly every tribe has an active land acquisition program.

Land acquisition is one of many areas where tribes have maneuvered around the dark side. In *Johnson v. M'Intosh*, one of Echo-Hawk's ten cases, the Supreme Court ruled that tribes lacked full ownership of their homelands. But Chief Justice John Marshall's opinion did not deny them all rights of land title: their land rights "were, in no instance entirely disregarded; but were necessarily, to a considerable extent impaired. They were admitted to be the rightful occupants of the soil with a legal as well as just claim to retain possession of it." Tribes, mostly in the East where almost all Indian land had been expropriated, seized on this "right of occupancy." In complex litigation and congressional settlements, they established land rights and won back some of their homelands. The dark side's impact on land and resource rights has hardly been erased—even in modern times, federal bureaucrats, forsaking their duty as trustees, drag their feet and make it difficult to place newly acquired tribal lands in trust—but creative and tenacious tribal leaders and their lawyers found a way to craft significant progress and achieve a measure of justice.

As for sovereignty, Marshall may have laid some of the foundations for the dark side, but his ruling and words in *Worcester v. Georgia* in 1832 acknowledged a fundamental truth about governance in America: Indian tribes were sovereigns. His central holding—good history, good political science, good anthropology—was that, before Europeans came, America "was inhabited by a distinct people, divided into separate nations, independent of each other and the rest of the world, having institutions of their own, and governing themselves by their own laws." Nothing in the treaties or federal laws changed that, the chief justice found, and tribal sovereignty remained intact. The Court held that Georgia had no right to enforce its laws within Cherokee territory, where tribal sovereignty prevailed.

The fact that Indian tribes were one of three sources of sovereignty in America along with the federal government and the states lay fallow for a century and a half as the Bureau of Indian Affairs (BIA) ruled Indian Country with an iron hand. But Marshall's words arced over the years and remained alive for modern tribal leaders to put to use.

Today, the tribes, not the BIA, govern Indian Country. As late as the 1960s, Indian tribes had four, two, or, more likely, no employees at all. Now the largest seventy or eighty tribes, which represent over 90 percent of all Indians, have 250 or more governmental employees, excluding gaming operations. Most of those tribal governments are larger than the nearby county governments. Even the smallest tribes typically have at least one hundred employees.

These are full-service governments. They have legislatures, courts, and police departments. They place a high priority on education, operating numerous preschool programs, over a hundred elementary and secondary schools, and thirty-six tribal colleges. They offer college scholarships. Some provide desktop computers to every family and laptops to every college student. Tribes operate health departments and many run clinics. New housing allows tribal members to return to the reservations. Tribal governments have family-services agencies to oversee adoptions and guardianships under the powerful Indian Child Welfare Act of 1978. Tribal leaders conceived and promoted that legislation in order to address *In re Adoption of John Doe v. Heim*, one of Echo-Hawk's ten cases, which epitomizes the child drain as white state-court judges regularly adopted Indian children into non-Indian homes; the Indian Child Welfare Act gives jurisdiction to tribal courts and social services agencies over all custody matters involving all tribal children residing on the reservations and many cases involving off-reservation children as well.

Tribal environmental and natural resources agencies cover numerous areas, including hunting and fishing regulation, timber and grazing management, and watershed management. Habitat restoration is a major focus. For example, tribes have been instrumental in numerous river cleanups and played a leadership role in major dam-removal efforts—the first in the American West—on the Elwha, Klamath, White Salmon, and Lower Snake rivers. Congress, responding to requests from tribal leaders, has adopted a treatment-as-states policy toward tribal governments. This recognizes tribes with authority as governments under the Clean Air and Clean Water acts and other environmental statutes, and many tribes, rather than the states, administer those programs within their reservations.

Tribal governments successfully argued to the Supreme Court that, as separate sovereigns, they should be able to conduct gaming operations, including casinos, under their own laws and beyond state authority. In a few cases, tribal members have become wealthy, but the predominant pattern has been for tribes to distribute only small percentages of casino income to individuals. Most of the proceeds are used by tribal governments to meet pressing social, health, and economic needs. Casinos have also provided much-needed job opportunities.

The permanence of tribal governments has been enhanced in recent years by the way that tribes have become entwined with state and local governments and citizenries. This has nothing to do with assimilation. It is a matter of strong, capable, independent tribal governments developing a network of influence.

The result is that non-Indian citizens are finding that Indian Country has much to offer. Tribes provide good jobs in tribal governments and business enterprises, including casinos. Cooperation, rather than the combat of litigation, has come to the fore and tribal officials regularly negotiate agreements with states, counties, and cities over subjects such as law enforcement, child custody, zoning, and hunting, fishing, and water—and usually establish permanent, coequal relationships to implement the agreements. Non-Indians receive health care in tribal clinics and attend classes in tribal colleges. The casinos make donations to local charities. Good tribal land management practices on the reservations and campaigns to combat bad timber, mining, and development practices have earned them respect as environmental stewards. Indian art, music, and cultural activities are admired and enjoyed by the outside public.

Tribal sovereignty in the early twenty-first century is real, not an academic theory or vague idea without substance. Tribes are the primary governments on an area nearly the size of Oregon. Yet tribal authority is incomplete in a number of areas, the most notable being tribal jurisdiction over non-Indians.

The primary case, which has led to several others, is *Oliphant v. Suquamish Indian Tribe*, a dark side ruling that easily could have qualified as one of Echo-Hawk's ten cases. In *Oliphant*, the Supreme Court ruled that tribes lacked criminal jurisdiction over non-Indians. The existing law was sparse, but the tribe seemed to have the best of it under *Worcester v. Georgia* and other cases upholding tribal sovereignty. Chief Justice Rehnquist, though, would have none of it and, in a charade of an opinion, held against the Suquamish Tribe—and all other tribes as well.

Subsequent opinions extended the *Oliphant* result to civil jurisdiction on a piecemeal basis, with the result that tribes have sharply limited tax and regulatory authority over non-Indian people and businesses within their homelands. The tribes suffer by being prevented from raising needed tax revenues and by being hamstrung in many circumstances from regulating harmful environmental and consumer practices. Good government suffers from a confusing, unwieldy tangle of tribal, federal, state, county, and city jurisdiction in Indian Country when non-Indians are involved.

The dark side court opinions came about because of an unspoken and unwarranted distrust of tribal governments by judges who knew very little about tribal governments. One can hope that the situation will be resolved in the twenty-first century by moving toward a jurisdictional framework based on a more unitary tribal authority as the distrust continues to dissipate and an understanding of, and respect for, tribal governments continues to increase.

As a measure of tribal priorities, it is telling that four of Echo-Hawk's ten cases involve what he calls the Spirit World. For the better part of two centuries, Congress advocated and funded an elaborate Christianization and Americanization program aimed directly at eradicating Indianness, the deeply embedded values and practices that had evolved over thousands of years. Judges ratified the program and issued opinions that failed to give protection to the distinctive aspects of Indian religions and cultures.

Here, too, in recent times Indian people stymied by existing law set out to make new law. The American Indian Religious Freedom Act of 1978 (AIRFA) is an overarching congressional call to protect Indian religion. As Echo-Hawk has recounted, AIRFA has not been given its full force; among other things, the Supreme Court has held that AIRFA does not create enforceable rights against federal agencies. Over time, though, the message that abridgements of Indian religious practices must stop has gotten through, and some federal land agencies acknowledge AIRFA as an important policy directive. The National Park Service, the National Forest Service, the Bureau of Land Management, and the Department of Defense have entered into agreements assuring access to sacred sites, closures of public land areas to assure privacy for cultural gatherings, and collection of medicines and other plants. Congress also has allowed the taking of eagles for religious purposes and prohibited states from prosecuting Indian practitioners using peyote in religious ceremonies. Nevertheless, stronger protections are necessary to preserve worship at holy places. Decisions cannot be left to land managers. Congress needs to take decisive action to provide the full measure of religious liberty to the adherents of the continent's original religions.

Congress, at the behest of Native religious practitioners, has spoken belatedly but strongly and effectively to the protection of Native graves and artifacts. At the heart of the landmark Native American Graves Protection and Repatriation Act of 1990 (NAGPRA) is the requirement that museums return to tribes human remains and certain cultural objects in their collections. It bears noting that Congress used the term *repatriation*. Before NAGPRA, the United States had used *repatriation* to describe returns of prisoners of war and human remains to foreign nations. Indian tribes are sovereigns also, and Congress rightly described returns to them as repatriations.

All of the progress in modern times has required extraordinary commitments of time and energy by Indian people. This has been especially true in these and other initiatives involving culture and religion. Native religious practitioners and members of Congress and other federal officials live in different worlds. After all, the root of the difficulties has been the inability of non-Indians to comprehend the nature—and beauty and dignity—of Indian spirituality. The chances of misunderstandings and breakdowns in the course of creating complex federal legislation ran high. It is only appropriate to mention here that Walter Echo-Hawk served a central, continuing role by bridging the gap: he patiently, over many years, explained the language of Indian spirituality to the non-Indians and the language of the law to religious practitioners.

One of the most heartening aspects of the modern advancements is the Native cultural revival, spurred in part, perhaps, by the more welcoming if still imperfect federal stand on Indian culture wrought by tribal reformers. The sounds of the drums and the flutes, and the rhythms of the old songs, ring out with a vigor not heard for many generations. The reservations, too, are more alive because of the sounds of Native languages, as nearly all contemporary tribes are addressing the daunting task of stemming the loss of indigenous language. Many more Native people, young and old, participate in the precise, artful traditional dances, no longer forced underground, sending out age-old messages of reverence to the Creator and gratitude for the land. The Canoe Journey in the Pacific Northwest and the Zuni Runners in the Southwest embody ancient, exuberant traditions that are returning in all regions. Those numerous, diverse, and colorful sounds and images, those emanations of the Spirit World, are the purest and surest signals that, yes, Indian people have announced their permanence and that they mean to hold it.

For all that Indian people have accomplished, Walter Echo-Hawk is surely correct that the dark side must be finally and fully reformed. Indian Country still suffers from too much poverty and illness and too little education. The current Supreme Court refuses to give tribal sovereignty its full and rightful due.

A central thrust of the modern effort has been to return Indian Country to tribal control so that Native people themselves can finally and completely reestablish sustainable, permanent homelands—and beyond the reservations Indian people have struggled to firm up their rights to fish, hunt, and gather in their traditional areas and to hold ceremonies in their sacred places. As a nation, we all benefit from honoring and learning from the values enshrined in that way of life. Walter Echo-Hawk has identified the problems and solutions as well as anyone ever has. His proposals are sensible and realistic. They can be achieved. Take away the remaining barriers, and tribal societies will once again be stable places of sound governance, workaday skillfulness, and artistry, informed ultimately by the lessons and enrichment of the Spirit World.

—Charles Wilkinson

CHAPTER 1: THE COURTS OF THE CONQUEROR

1. *Johnson v. M'Intosh*, 21 US 543, 588 (1823).

2. Paul Chaat Smith and Robert Allen Warrior, *Like A Hurricane: The Indian Movement From Alcatraz To Wounded Knee* (New York: The New Press, 1996) at 42.

3. This historic social movement is chronicled by the well-known professor of law Charles Wilkinson in *Blood Struggle: The Rise of Modern Indian Nations* (London, New York: W. W. Norton & Co., 2005).

4. Several problems existed in Pawnee country in the late 1960s. Police brutality was commonplace. One of my uncles, a highly decorated war hero, was found dead in the Pawnee City Jail; authorities claimed he hung himself, but few believed them. Pawnee school students were forced by school authorities to cut their braided hair. See *New Rider v. Board of Education*, 480 F. 2d 693 (10th Cir. 1972). The Pawnee tribal government's authority over tribal lands was nascent and uncertain because the reservation status of that land was unresolved, resulting in minimal government operations, without a court system, and exercised under heavy-handed BIA supervision. Since those days, these problems have largely been corrected.

5. See, for example, Wilkinson (2005); and David H. Getches, "Conquering the Cultural Frontier: The New Subjectivism of the Supreme Court in Indian Law," 84 California L. Rev. 1573, 1577-1593 (1996). The authoritative treatise of federal Indian law, *Cohen's Handbook of Federal Indian Law* (2005 ed.), also includes a thorough discussion and analysis of the many significant victories won in the modern era of federal Indian law.

6. See, for example, Robert N. Clinton, "Redressing The Legacy Of Conquest: A Vision Quest For A Decolonized Federal Indian Law," 46 Arkansas L. Rev. 77 (1993); Robert A. Williams, Jr., *The American Indian In Western legal Thought: The Discourses Of Conquest* (New York: Oxford Univ. Press, 1990). Other scholars are concerned about the colonial stigma of the foundational principles in federal Indian law, but remain cautious about departing from them for fear of unraveling the fabric of that body of law. See David H. Getches, "Beyond Indian Law: The Rehnquist Court's Pursuit Of State's Rights, Color-Blind Justice And Mainstream Values," 86 Minn. L. Rev. 267, 352-353 (2001); Getches (1996) at 1579-1582.

7. Robert A. Williams Jr., *Like A Loaded Weapon: The Rehnquist Court, Indian Rights, and the Legal History of Racism in America*, (Minneapolis: Univ. of Minnesota Press, 2005).

8. See Getches (1996).

9. See, for example, Philip P. Frickey, "A Common Law for Our Age of Colonialism: The Judicial Divestiture of Indian Tribal Authority over Nonmembers," 109 Yale L. J. 1 (October, 1999).

10. David Williams, "Legitimation and Statutory Interpretation: Conquest, Consent, and Community in Federal Indian Law," 80 Va. L. Rev. 403, 416 (1994).

11. *Johnson v. M'Intosh*, 21 US at 588.

12. Getches (2001) at 296-297 (footnotes omitted). See also Clinton (1993) at 77.

13. Williams (1994) at 473.

CHAPTER 2: A CONTEXT FOR UNDERSTANDING NATIVE AMERICAN ISSUES

1. Robert N. Clinton, "Redressing the Legacy of Conquest: A Vision Quest for a Decolonized Federal Indian Law," 46 Arkansas L. Rev. 77, 86 (1993).

2. In his groundbreaking treatise, *Indigenous Peoples in International Law* (New York: Oxford Univ. Press, 1996), p. 3, law professor S. James Anaya defines *indigenous peoples* as follows:

> As empire building and colonial settlement proceeded from the sixteenth century onward, those who already inhabited the encroached-upon lands and who were subjected to oppressive forces became known as indigenous, native, or aboriginal. Such designations have continued to apply to people by virtue of their place and condition within the life-altering human encounter set in motion by colonialism.

Today, the term *indigenous* refers broadly to the living descendants of pre-invasion inhabitants of lands now dominated by others. Indigenous peoples, nations, or communities are culturally distinct groups that find themselves engulfed by settler societies born of the forces of empire and conquest. The diverse surviving Indian communities and nations of the Western Hemisphere, the Inuit and Aleut of the Arctic, the Aborigines of Australia, the Maori of New Zealand, the tribal peoples of Asia, and other such groups are among those regarded as indigenous.

While there is no single universal definition of the term *indigenous peoples*, anthropologist Robert Hitchcock at the University of Nebraska applies the term to non-European groups living in lands colonized by Europeans who are the descendants of the original aboriginal populations of those lands. He provides four elements to describe indigenous peoples: (1) *Preexistence*—that is, they were there before the colonists arrived; (2) *Nondominance*—they are often politically powerless within the domestic political system; (3) *Culturally distinct*—the language, religion, traditions, and worldview of indigenous peoples are vastly different from that of the dominant society in a particular nation-state; and (4) *Self-identification*—they have a strong sense of cultural or tribal identity as indigenous people ("I am a Native person"). To that, I would add (5) *Different aspirations*, since the universal indigenous goals of self-determination, autonomy, and cultural integrity differ markedly from the goals of other segments of society. During the civil rights movement, for example, blacks sought equality and integration, while Native Americans sought tribal sovereignty, self-determination, and the protection of their cultural integrity, in addition to equality. Charles Wilkinson compares and contrasts the goals of the civil rights and the tribal sovereignty movements in *Blood Struggle: The Rise of Modern Indian Nations* (New York: W. W. Norton & Co., 2005), pp. 129–149. See also Paul Chaat Smith and Robert Allen Warrior, *Like a Hurricane: The American Indian Movement from Alcatraz to Wounded Knee* (New York: The New York Press, 1996), for an in-depth look at activism in the sovereignty movement.

3.   The incredible diversity of traditional Native American religion is set forth by Arlene Hirschfelder and Paulette Molin (eds.), *Encyclopedia of Native American Religions* (New York: Checkmark Books, 2000); and Suzanne J. Crawford and Dennis F. Kelly (eds.), *American Indian Religious Traditions: An Encyclopedia* (Santa Barbara, CA: ABC-CLIO, 2005), V. I–III. The profound nature of those religions is described by Vine Deloria Jr. in *The World We Used to Live In: Remembering the Powers of the Medicine Men* (Golden, CO: Fulcrum, 2006), published shortly after his death. An example of the rich religious traditions of my own Pawnee Tribe, which are derived exclusively from our Great Plains habitat, is described by James R. Murie in *Ceremonies of the Pawnee* (Lincoln: Univ. of Nebraska Press, 1989). True Pawnee stories from the natural world are compiled by George Dorsey in *The Pawnee Mythology* (Lincoln: Univ. of Nebraska Press, 1997).

4.   See, generally, Eugene Linden, "Lost Tribes, Lost Knowledge," *Time* (Sept. 23, 1991), pp. 46-56. Linden was deeply concerned about the "cultural holocaust" confronting the world's tribes, because when these cultures die, "vast archives of knowledge and expertise are spilling into oblivion, leaving humanity in danger of losing its past" (Id., at 46).

5.   Bartolomé de Las Casas, *The Devastation of the Indies: A Brief Account* (New York: The Seabury Press, 1974 [1542]), translated by Herma Briffault. In this account, Las Casas reported to the king of Spain that mass murder was being committed throughout the Americas, providing horrifying firsthand details. In Hispaniola, almost two million Indians were killed. In Puerto Rico and Jamaica, over 600,000 were killed. Between four and five million people were killed in Guatemala. In Venezuela, the Spanish sold one million Indians into slavery. In Nicaragua, they killed between 500,000 and 600,000 Indians and sold more than 500,000 survivors into slavery. In Honduras and the Yucatán, more than 200,000 were killed. In Peru, more than ten million died by 1542; and at least four million were killed in Mexico, not counting victims who died from mistreatment under servitude. In other places, such as Cuba, the Bahamas, and the islands surrounding Puerto Rico, almost all the Indians were killed, leaving many of these places uninhabited by a single living person. See also Walter R. Echo-Hawk, "Genocide and Ethnocide," in John Hartwell Moore (ed. in chief), *Encyclopedia of Race and Racism, Vol. 2, G–R* (Thompson Gale, 2007), pp. 48–52.

6.   Russell Thornton, *American Indian Holocaust and Survival: A Population History Since 1492* (Norman: Univ. of Oklahoma Press, 1987).

7.   Legal scholars have thoroughly studied the roots of international law as it pertains to the peoples of the New World. My brief overview relies heavily upon the in-depth scholarly examination provided by law professor Robert A. Williams Jr. in "Encounters on the Frontiers of International Human Rights Law: Redefining the Terms of Indigenous Peoples' Survival in the World," 1990 Duke L. J. 660 (September, 1990); *The American Indian in Western Legal Thought: The Discourses of Conquest* (New York: Oxford Univ. Press, 1990); and "The Algebra of Federal Indian Law: The Hard Trial of Decolonizing and Americanizing The Whiteman's Indian Jurisprudence," 1986 Wisconsin L. Rev. 219 (1986). See also Clinton (1993); Tim Allan Garrison, *The Legal Ideology of Removal: The Southern Judiciary and the Sovereignty of Native American Nations* (Athens: Univ. of Georgia Press, 2002), pp. 60–71.

8.   It is entirely fitting that this particular pope issued a bull dispossessing Indians of the Western Hemisphere. Alexander VI (1431–1503), who headed the church from 1492 to 1503, was a distinctively secular and unsavory man who lived a debased, sleazy lifestyle. A man of many mistresses, his papal reign unquestionably epitomizes the dark side of the papacy. There is currently a movement among indigenous peoples calling upon the Vatican to overturn and repudiate the destructive and illegitimate bulls issued by this immoral antipope. The church continues to stand by its preposterous edict, which places its supposed concern for the souls of indigenous peoples (and their gold) over the property, human, cultural, and religious rights of the living Native peoples of the hemisphere. It may be those bulls were at least partially repealed in 1537 by the bull *Sublimis Deus* issued by Pope Paul III. That bull proclaims that "notwithstanding whatever may have been or may be said to the contrary, the said Indians and all other people who may later be discovered by Christians are by no means to be deprived of their liberty or the possession of property, even though they be outside the faith of Jesus Christ" (Felix S. Cohen, "Original Indian Title," 32 Minn. L. Rev. 28, 45 [1947] [quoting the bull *Sublimis Deus*]).

9.   The bull *Inter Caetera*, issued by Pope Alexander VI (May 3, 1493), is contained in Frances G. Davenport, ed., *European Treaties Bearing on the History of the United States and Its Dependencies to 1648* (Washington DC: Carnegie Institute, 1917) at 56–63.

10.   This bull issued by Pope Alexander VI on May 4, 1493, is reproduced in Davenport (1917) at 64–73.

11.   Charles C. Royce, *Indian Land Cessions in the United States*, US Bureau of American Ethnology 18, Part 2 (Washington, DC: Government Printing Office, 1899) at 540.

12.   Franciscus de Victoria, *De Indis et de Belli Reflectiones* (Washington, DC: The Carnegie Institute of Washington, 1917) (J. B., Scott and E, Nys, eds., J. Bate, trans., 1917) at 155.

13.   Id., at 161.

14.   *Calvin's Case*, 77 Eng. Rep. 377 (1608).

15.   The royal charter of April 10, 1606, is reproduced in Henry S. Commager, ed., *Documents of American History, 9th Ed.* (New York: Appleton-Century-Crofts, 1973) at 8–10.

16.   Id.

17.   See, for example, Gesina H. J. Van Der Molen, *Alberico Gentili and the Development of International Law, 2nd Ed.* (A. W. Sijthoff-Leyden, 1968) at 113–54.

18.   Williams, *The American Indian in Western Legal Thought: The Discourses of Conquest*, supra at 196–197 (citing Gentili).

19.   *Johnson v. M'Intosh*, 21 US 543, 573 (1823).

20.   *Cherokee Nation v. Georgia*, 30 US 1, 17 (1831).

21.   *United States v. Kagama*, 118 US 375, 384 (1886).

22.   *Lone Wolf v. Hitchcock*, 187 US 553, 565 (1903).

23.   *Oliphant v. Suquamish Indian Tribe*, 435 US 191 (1978).

24.   Id., at 209.

25.   Theodore Roosevelt, *The Winning of the West, Vol. I* (New York: G. P. Putnam's Sons, 1895) at 90.

26.   Luther Standing Bear, *Land of the Spotted Eagle* (Lincoln: Univ. of Nebraska Press, 1970) at 248.

27.   Reprinted in F. Cohen, *Handbook of Federal Indian Law* (1982 ed.) at v.

28.   United Nations Declaration on the Rights of Indigenous Peoples, UN G.A. Res. 61/295, UN H.R.C., 61st Sess., Annex, Agenda Item 68, UN Doc. A/RES/61/295 (2007). The declaration can be located at: www.narf.org/events/07/declaration.pdf. The contents and background of

the declaration are discussed in "United Nations Adopts Historic Declaration on the Rights of Indigenous Peoples," NARF L. Rev., V. 32, No. 2 (Summer/Fall 2007), pp. 1–17. Originally prepared by indigenous peoples for consideration by the UN, the standards in the draft declaration were written *in their own words* and express the aspirations of the world's indigenous peoples. As approved by the UN, the declaration was modified by member-states in a highly political process. Though the approved document differs from the draft prepared by indigenous peoples, it still embodies most of their standards. It was approved by an overwhelming majority in the UN General Assembly in a 143-4 vote, with 11 abstaining. The four countries who voted against it were the United States, Canada, New Zealand, and Australia—a block of hard-core settler states. The US argued the declaration is not customary international law. Despite this attempt to prevent the development of customary international law by an old-school colonizer nation, the high courts in other nations are citing the declaration as reflecting general principles of international law. See NARF L. Rev. N. 32, No. 2, supra, p. 2 n. 3 (citing a Belize decision). Despite the protestations of the US, Article 43 of the declaration provides: "The rights recognized herein constitute the minimum standards for the survival, dignity, and well-being of the indigenous peoples of the world." In the spring of 2008, Canada bolted from the settler-state block when its national legislative body passed a resolution approving the declaration and directing the Canadian government to implement its provisions. Even merry old England and all the colonizing powers of Europe have approved the declaration, leaving only three hard-core settler states to resist the international obligations established by the United Nations.

CHAPTER 3: JUSTICE, INJUSTICE, AND THE DARK SIDE OF FEDERAL INDIAN LAW

1. *Brown v. Board of Education*, 347 US 483 (1954).
2. Id., at 494.
3. *Wisconsin v. Yoder*, 406 US 205 (1972).
4. *United States of America v. Alstoetter et al.*, 3 T.W.C. 1 (1948), 6 L.R.T.W.C. 1 91948), 14 Ann. Dig. 278 (1948).
5. Ingo Muller, a German law professor, examined the German legal system under Hitler's rule in *Hitler's Justice: The Courts of the Third Reich* (Cambridge, MA: Harvard Univ. Press, 1991) (translated by Deborah L. Schneider). This absorbing ethical subject is also examined in a collection of essays by another German lawyer, Michael Stolleis, in *The Law under the Swastika: Studies on Legal History in Nazi Germany* (Chicago: Univ. of Chicago Press, 1998).
6. See Muller (1991) at 270–283 for a discussion of the trial in *Alstoetter* of sixteen jurists. The evidence exposed a sample of the horrific work done by the Nazi judicial system. The judges were charged by the Americans with "judicial murder and other atrocities which they committed by destroying law and justice in Germany, and by then utilizing the empty forms of legal process for persecution, enslavement, and extermination on a vast scale" (Id., at 271 [quoting from *Trials of War Criminals before the Nuremberg Military Tribunals* (Washington, DC: Government Printing Office, 1951), III at 32–33]). Following an extensive trial, the military court found that the jurists assumed the tasks of destroying the Jewish and Polish populations, terrorizing people in the occupied territories and eliminating domestic political opposition at home. The military court was stunned that these evils were committed in the name of the law and concluded:

> Defendants are charged with crimes of such immensity that mere specific instances of criminality appear insignificant by comparison. The charge, in brief, is that of conscious participation in a nationwide government-organized system of cruelty and injustice, in violation of the laws of war and of humanity, and perpetrated in the name of law by the authority of the Ministry of Justice, and through the instrumentality of the courts. The dagger of the assassin was concealed beneath the robe of the jurist. (Id., at 272 [quoting from *Trials of War Criminals*, supra at 984–985])

The judiciary allowed 350,000 people to be sterilized under Nazi law, handed down an estimated 80,000 death sentences for various, including petty, offenses, and sentenced untold thousands to prison as political prisoners(Id., 121, 196, 227). Judicial cooperation and participation was so widespread, that Muller concluded, at 196:

> No matter how hard one searches for stout-hearted men among the judges of the Third Reich, for judges who refused to serve the regime from the bench, there remains a grand total of one: Dr. Lothar Kreyssig, judge of the Court of Guardianship in Brandenberg on the Havel. Other, less striking cases of judicial resistance to Nazi terror must surely have occurred now and then, and remain to be discovered. Yet they are far from representative of German judges, the over-whelming majority of whom shared responsibility for the terror.

7. The Nuremberg Laws, which may have been patterned on America's Jim Crow laws, limited citizenship in the Third Reich to Aryans and severely restricted the human rights of Jews in German society. See, Noakes, Jeremy, and Geoffrey Pridham, *Documents on Nazism 1919–1945* (New York: Viking Press, 1974) at 463–467. Implementation of the Nuremberg Laws is discussed by Muller (1991) at 96–119.

8. Canon 1A of the American Bar Association's Annotated Model Code of Judicial Ethics (2004 ed.) states: "An independent and honorable judiciary is indispensable *to justice in our* society…The provisions of this Code are to be construed and applied to further that objective" (emphasis added).

9. *United States v. Sioux Nation of Indians*, 448 US 371 (1980).

10. Manifest Destiny is an American concept coined in 1845 by journalist John L. O'Sullivan. It expresses the popular idea that the United States has a divinely sanctioned mission to expand the American frontiers and spread its superior civilization over territory inhabited by uncivilized American Indians and Mexicans. Under this notion, the Indians are supposed to vanish before the oncoming whites. This notion was also used to justify American colonization of the Philippines, Hawaii, Puerto Rico, and Guam because the uncivilized inhabitants would "benefit" from an American presence that would Christianize, civilize, and otherwise uplift them. Similar English ideas are expressed in Rudyard Kipling's poem "The White Man's Burden" (1899), which urged colonization of the Philippines: "Take up the White Man's Burden— / Send forth the best ye breed / …To serve your captives' need; / to wait in heavy harness, / On fluttered folk and wild—/ Your new-caught, sullen peoples, / Half-devil and half-child."

11. *Sioux Nation*, 448 US at 435.

12. Id., at 435, 437.

13. Id., at 437. The majority was puzzled by these remarks since Rehnquist failed to identify any evidence fitting his "revisionist" label, nor did he "identify a single author, revisionist or otherwise, who takes the view of the cession of the Black Hills that [Rehnquist] prefers to adopt, largely, one assumes, as an article of faith" (Id., at 422 n. 32). History is *always* a matter of perspective. It is often said that the "conquerors get to write the history." That history is one-sided when cultures collide and the loser is obliterated, leaving only the victor to write the history books glorifying his cause and often disparaging, belittling, or demeaning the vanquished. As Winston Churchill once said, "history will be kind to us because I intend to write it." Myriad factors compound the well-rounded recording of the past, such as censorship and the suppression of unflattering facts and records. Acknowledging these fundamental problems, historian Patricia Nelson Limerick suggests that "Indian people can and should write their own histories according to their traditions, just as pioneers and their descendants have every right to publish books enshrining their own version of history" (Patricia N. Limerick, *The Legacy of Conquest: The Unbroken Past of the American West* [New York: W. W. Norton & Co., 1987], p. 321). If historians read and pay attention to all these versions of history, "a neutral, omnisciently objective history" will not emerge, but at least more voices will be heard (Id.). As pointed out in *Cohen's Handbook on Federal Indian Law* (2005 ed.) (LexisNexis/Matthew Bender, 2005), Nell Jessup Newton, et al., eds., at pp. 6–10, history matters a great deal in the field of federal Indian law—it is of central importance in analyzing the statutes, treaties, and cases pertaining to Native Americans.

14. *Dred Scott v. John F. A. Sanford*, 60 US 393 (1856).

15. *Elk v. Wilkins*, 112 US 94, 106 (1884).

16. *Cherokee Nation v. Georgia*, 30 US 1 (1831).

17. *United States ex rel. Standing Bear v. Crook*, 27 F. Cas. 695 (C.C.D. Neb. 1879).

18. *Boyce v. Anderson*, 27 US 150 (1829); *The Antelope*, 23 US 66 (1825). Fraught with contradictions, Marshall owned slaves, but is reputed to oppose slavery. In *Boyce*, he admitted to their

humanity, but still considered them property. In *The Antelope*, he upheld the institution of slavery under international law even though he determined slavery violated natural law.

19.   *The Antelope*, 23 US at 66.

20.   Id., at 25.

21.   Id., at 26.

22.   *Dred Scott v. John F. A. Sanford*, 60 US 393 (1856). Lawyer Peter Irons chronicled the history of the Supreme Court in *A People's History of the Supreme Court: The Men and Women Whose Cases and Decisions Have Shaped Our Constitution* (New York: Penguin Books, 2000). He provides an excellent discussion of this infamous case and the context in which it was decided at 147–85.

23.   *Dred Scott*, 60 US at 403.

24.   Id., at 404–405. Taney was a slave owner and chief justice of the Supreme Court from 1836 to 1864, when slavery was a divisive and controversial political, social, economic, and legal question. He is described by Irons (2000), supra note 22, at 147, as "a racist who looked at blacks as items of 'property' and not as 'persons.'" Unlike many other slaveholders, "Taney was infected with racism, unwilling to look at men like Dred Scott as fellow human beings, let alone as fellow citizens" (Id., 183). According to Irons, the racist Taney prejudged the case:

> Seated at the center of the Court's mahogany bench, Chief Justice Taney listened to the arguments with his mind already made up. As the nation's attorney general, he had earlier stated his opinion that blacks, "even if free," had not been "looked upon as citizens by the contracting parties who formed the Constitution." The question that remained, as the lawyers left the podium and the justices trooped out behind Taney, was not how the Court would rule on Dred Scott's suit for freedom, but whether its decision would further inflame the slavery dispute that divided the nation. (Id., 169)

Taney adopted an extremist proslavery position, causing subsequent debates to erupt "into the gunfire and bloodshed of the Civil War" (Id., 176).

25.   *Dred Scott*, 60 US at 405.

26.   Id., at 426.

27.   *Plessy v. Ferguson*, 163 US 537 (1896).

28.   Id., at 543–544. On this point, Martin Luther King Jr. disagreed most strongly. His letter from the Birmingham jail stated: "Any law that degrades human personality is unjust. All segregation statutes are unjust because segregation distorts the soul and damages the personality. It gives the segregator a false sense of superiority, and the segregated a false sense of inferiority" (*A Testament of Hope: The Essential Writings and Speeches Of Martin Luther King Jr.* [San Francisco: Harper, 1991], James M. Washington [ed.] at 293.)

29.   *Plessy*, 163 US at 548.

30.   Id., at 550.

31.   Id., at 551.

32.   Id., at 552.

33.   Id., at 559.

34.   *Gong Lum v. Rice*, 275 US 78 (1927).

35.   *Korematsu v. United States*, 323 US 214 (1945).

36.   Id., at 224.

37.   Id., at 233.

38.   Id., at 240.

39.   Id., at 246.

40.   *Hirabayashi v. United States*, 320 US 81 (1943).

41.   *Korematsu*, 323 US at 247.

42.   Civil Liberties Act of 1988, 50 App. U.S.C.A. §1989. Each reparation check was accompanied by a letter of apology from President Clinton, which states:

> Over fifty years ago, the United States Government unjustly interned, evacuated, or relocated you and many other Japanese Americans. Today, on behalf of your fellow Americans, I offer a sincere apology to you for the actions that unfairly denied Japanese Americans and their families fundamental liberties during World War II.

> In passing the Civil Liberties Act of 1988, we acknowledged the wrongs of the past and offered redress to those who endured such grave injustice. In retrospect, we understand that the nation's actions were rooted deeply in racial prejudice, wartime hysteria, and a lack of political leadership. We must learn from the past and dedicate ourselves as a nation to renewing the spirit of equality and our love of freedom. Together, we can guarantee a future with liberty and justice for all. You and your family have my best wishes for the future.

See www.pbs.org/childofcamp/history/clinton.html.

43. Martin Luther King Jr., *Stride toward Freedom: The Montgomery Story,* reprinted in Washington (1991) at 482.

44. Alexis de Tocqueville, *Democracy In America* (New York: Bantam Dell, [1835], 2004), p. 111.

45. *Lone Wolf v. Hitchcock,* 187 US 553, 564–565 (1903).

46. *Montoya v. United States,* 180 US 261, 265–266 (1901).

47. *Johnson v. M'Intosh,* 21 US 543, 572, 577, 590 (1823).

48. *Webster's New Collegiate Dictionary* (1961) at 696. See also Juan F. Perea, et al., *Race and Races: Cases and Resources for a Diverse America, 2nd Ed.* (Thompson/West, 2007), pp. 5–72, for an in depth definition and discussion of racism. Racism is marked by the inferiorization of certain groups and antipathy towards them. That is, certain groups are seen as inferior by reason of their biological nature and there is race-based antipathy toward them manifested by racial bigotry, hostility, and hatred (Id., at 35). Racism is prejudice manifested by individuals in racist acts, attitudes, and behavior. On a larger social level, racism is manifested in racist beliefs, attitudes, and stereotypes that are widely shared by a population and expressed in many forms and institutions throughout the society (Id., 37).

49. Law professor Robert A. Williams Jr. takes a hard look at the background, roots, and history of racially discriminatory attitudes and stereotypes employed against American Indians in the United States. His comprehensive and scholarly work, *Like a Loaded Gun: The Rehnquist Court, Indian Rights, and the Legal History of Racism in America* (Minneapolis: Univ. of Minnesota Press, 2005), will undoubtedly become a standard text for students of race and racism for years to come.

50. *Tee-Hit-Ton v. United States,* 348 US 272, 289 (1955).

51. Limerick (1987) at 17–18.

52. See Robert N. Clinton, "Redressing the Legacy of Conquest: A Vision Quest for a Decolonized Federal Indian Law," 46 Ark. L. Rev. 77, 78–86 (1993), for a more detailed discussions of these reasons.

53. Limerick (1987) at 338.

54. Martin Luther King Jr.'s "Letter from Birmingham Jail" (1963), reprinted in Washington (1991) at 292.

55. *Black's Law Dictionary,* 6th Ed. (1990) at 894.

56. *Johnson v. M'Intosh,* 21 US at 595. This assumption is made by the British imperial law establishing the colony of South Australia. See South Australia Act of 1834, Act 4 & 5 William IV, Cap 95, 1834, which assumes that not one single Aborigine occupied this entire portion of that continent by declaring all of the land to be "waste and unoccupied lands which are supposed to be fit for the purposes of colonization."). See also Lisa Strelein, "From Mabo to Yorta: Native Title Law in Australia," 19 Wash. U. J. L. & Pol'y 225, 235 (2005) ("Colonization [in Australia] proceeded on the false assumption that the continent was sparsely populated.").

57. See discussion of the enlarged doctrine of *terra nullius* by the Australian High Court in *Mabo v. Queensland,* 174 CLR 1, 32–33 (1992).

58. *Mabo* at 33 recognizes that the enlarged doctrine of *terra nullius* stretches the imagination and creates injustice. The court cited Blackstone's 1830 observation that founding colonies is okay under natural law when it is confined to "desert uninhabited countries," but when inhabited land is seized, serious misgivings arise:

> But how far the seising of countries already peopled, and driving out or massacring the innocent and defenceless natives, merely because they differed from their invaders in language, in religion, in government, or in colour; how far such a conduct was consonant to nature, to reason, or to christianity, deserved to be considered by those, who have rendered their names immortal by thus civilizing mankind.

59. Bartolomé de Las Casas, *The Devastation of the Indies: A Brief Account* (New York: Seabury Press, [542], 1974). See also Walter Echo-Hawk, "Genocide and Ethnocide," in John Hartwell Moore (ed. in chief), *Encyclopedia of Race and Racism, Vol. 2, G-R* (Thompson Gale, 2007) at 48–52; *Cohen's Handbook on Federal Indian Law* (LexisNexis, Mathew Bender, 2005 ed.) (Nell Jessup Newton, ed. in chief) § 1.02, at 13 n. 42.

60. See Stuart Banner, *How the Indians Lost Their Land: Law and Power on the American Frontier* (Cambridge: Belknap Press of Harvard University, 2005) at 18–19. In *Worcester v. Georgia,* 31 US 515, 543–545 (1832), the court rejected this legal fiction. It held that royal charters do not transfer Indian land title to anyone. Rather, the charters and the doctrine of discovery simply granted England and its successor, the United States, an exclusive right to purchase so much Indian land as the Natives were willing to sell, and nothing more, much less empower states to govern Indian tribes or intrude into their self-government.

61. *Worcester,* at 546. See the Royal Charter for the Georgia Colony, issued by King George III in 1732 (http://avalon.law.yale.edu/18th_century/ga01.asp) (the colony was created to resettle "the meanest and most unfortunate of our people" in a colony to be administered by James Oglethorpe and other trustees.).

62. *Johnson v. M'Intosh,* supra.

63. *Worcester v. Georgia,* 31 US at 544. Unfortunately, Marshall's retreat from the discovery doctrine in *Worcester* was not long lived. He died shortly after the decision and President Andrew Jackson's Supreme Court quickly restored the doctrine in a series of five cases decided between 1836 and 1842: *Mitchel v. United States,* 34 US 711 (1835) (*Mitchel I*); *United States v. Fernandez,* 35 US 303 (1836); *Clark v. Smith,* 38 US 195 (1839); *Mitchell v. United States,* 40 US 52 (1842); and *Martin v. Lessee of Waddell,* 41 US 367 (1842). See Lindsay G. Robertson, *Conquest by Law: How the Discovery of America Dispossessed Indigenous Peoples of their Lands* (Oxford: Oxford Univ. Press, 2005) at 135–142. Nor did the belated *Worcester* decision do the Cherokee Nation any good, for it came too late in the day to deter the Indian removal movement. By 1832, federal removal policies were entrenched. Upon learning of the *Worcester* decision, President Jackson reputedly said, "John Marshall has made his decision, now let him enforce it" and did nothing to enforce the judgment (*Cohen's* [2005] at 50). Georgia, of course, ignored the ruling and defiantly refused to comply; and the rest of the South had already lined up under the green light provided by *Cherokee Nation* the year before. See, generally, Tim Alan Garrison, *The Legal Ideology of Removal: The Southern Judiciary and the Sovereignty of Native American Nations* (Athens: Univ. of Georgia Press, 2002).

64. *Johnson v. M'Intosh,* 21 US at 591 ("However extravagant the pretension of converting the discovery of an inhabited country into conquest may appear; if the principle has been asserted in the first instance, and afterwards sustained; if a country has been acquired and held under it; if the property of the great mass of the community originates in it, it becomes the law of the land and cannot be questioned."). See also Strelein (2005) for a discussion of the doctrine of discovery in other British colonies.

65. *Worcester v. Georgia,* 31 US at 544–545.

66. *Tee-Hit-Ton v. United States,* 348 US 272, 322 (1955). The vast majority of Indian land was acquired with tribal assent in treaty purchase agreements, not military conquest. See Robert J. Miller, *Native America, Discovered and Conquered: Thomas Jefferson, Lewis & Clark, and Manifest Destiny* (London: Praeger Publishers, 2006) at 57; Banner (2005); *Cohen's* (2005 ed.) at 8, 16–17, 45, 44, 72, 79; Felix S. Cohen, "Original Law Title," 32 Minn. L. Rev. 28, 34-44 (1947).

67. Williams (1994) 80 Va. L. Rev. 403, 416 (1994) (American courts should find some theory other than conquest, colonization, and racial superiority to justify their decisions.).

68. *Johnson v. M'Intosh,* 21 US at 588–592.

69. As I will discuss in chapter six, the United States is the most warlike nation on earth, with an unrivaled record of almost continual warfare since 1775.

70. *Mabo,* 174 CLR at 27.

71. Banner (2005) at 18-19.

72. *Mabo,* at 21 (citing an 1882 report concerning the Murray Islands).

73. Id., at 18, 20.

74. Banner (2005) at 16–17.

75. Id., at 16–17.

76. *Cherokee Nation v. Georgia*, 30 US 1, 17 (1831) (Indian tribes are "domestic dependant nations" that are "in a state of pupilage" with a relationship to the United States that "resembles that of a ward to his guardian."). *Cherokee Nation* incorporated the guardianship principle from the law of nations as a cornerstone for federal Indian law. Guardianship was also assumed early on by British colonizers around the world on the notion that Natives are backward. Australian courts, for example, denied that Aborigines had laws at all and that they were simply wandering aimlessly without homes, laws, and social organization sufficient to own property. See Strelein (2005) at 238.

77. Franciscus de Victoria, *De Indis et de Belli Reflectiones* (Washington: Carnegie Institute of Washington, 1917) (J.B. Scott and E. Nys, eds. J. Bate, trans., 1917) at 161.

78. See, for example, Las Casas ([1542], 1974).

79. As Lord Gladstone explained in 1837, it was far better for colonists to deal "with civilized men rather than barbarians," because "[s]avages are dangerous neighbors and unprofitable customers, and if they remain as degraded denizens of our colonies they become a burden upon the State" (Alpheus H. Snow, *The Question of Aborigines in the Law and Practice of Nations* [Washington: Government Printing Office, 1919], reprinted in *The Inquiry Handbooks, V. 20* [Wilmington, DE: Scholarly Resources, Inc., 1974] at 12 [quoting an 1837 British House of Commons report made by the Select Committee on Aboriginal Tribes]).

80. *Lone Wolf v. Hitchcock,* 187 US 553, 565 (1903) (The unchecked plenary power of Congress over Indian tribes is derived from Congress' "exercise of guardianship over their interests.").

81. See, for example, *United States v. Clapox,* 35 F. 575 (D. Or. 1888) (Upholding the infamous "Code of Indian Offenses" promulgated by the Bureau of Indian Affairs in 1883 that banned the practice of traditional religion and other attributes of traditional Native American ways of life); *In re Can-Ah-Couqua,* 29 F. 687 (D. Alaska, 1887) (Upholding the power of government-sponsored religious schools to keep Native children against the wishes of their parents).

82. See, for example, *Sandoval v. United States*, 231 US 28, 39, 41–45 (1913); *Tee-Hit-Ton v. United States*, 348 US at 289; *Lone Wolf v. Hitchcock*, 187 US at 564–565; *Montoya v. United States*, 180 US 261, 265-266 (1901); *Johnson v. M'Intosh*, 21 US at 572–73, 590.

83. *Webster's New Collegiate Dictionary* (1961) at 696.

84. Williams (2005).

85. Robert Hughes, *The Fatal Shore: The Epic of Australia's Founding* (New York: Alfred A. Knopf, 1987) at 48.

86. See First Annual Report of the Colonization Commissioners for South Australia (June 24, 1836) at 8. Racism against the Aborigines abounded in the penal colonies (Hughes, 1987).

87. See discussion in *Mabo,* 175 CLR at 32–33, for this fascinating concept.

88. *Cohen's* (2005 ed.), § 1.02, p. 11. The vague and misleading notion of "conquest" in federal Indian law is explored in chapter six.

89. *Brown v. Board of Education*, 347 US at 494–95.

90. *Mabo,* 175 CLR at 23–39 (refusing to follow certain legal fictions underpinning the enlarged concept of *terra nullius*).

91. Id., at 40.

92. Id., at 58. *Mabo* proceeded to reject several legal fictions in Australian law which served as barriers to the recognition of native title: (1) "that there was no law before the arrival of the British colonists"; (2) there was no government before sovereignty was acquired by the Crown; and (3) the land was not vacant, rather it was "an inhabited territory which became a settled colony [and] was no more a legal desert than it was 'desert uninhabited'" (Id.).

93. Id., at 29.

94. Id., at 42.

95. Id.

CHAPTER 4: *JOHNSON V. M'INTOSH*: HOW THE INDIANS LOST LEGAL TITLE TO AMERICA

1. *Johnson v. M'Intosh*, 21 US 543 (1823).

2. *Tee-Hit-Ton v. United States*, 348 US 272, 285 (1955) (citing *Carino v. Insular Government of the Philippine Islands*, 212 US 449, 458 [1908]).

3. Lindsay G. Robertson, *Conquest By Law: How the Discovery of America Dispossessed Indigenous Peoples of Their Lands* (Oxford: Oxford Univ. Press, 2005). In my view, no legal scholar or court should cite *Johnson* without first consulting this important scholarly work.

4. Stuart Banner, *How the Indians Lost Their Land: Law and Power on the Frontier* (Cambridge: The Belknap Press of Harvard Univ. Press, 2005) at 15. Professor Banner carefully traces the manner in which Indian lands were acquired by non-Indians from the colonial period throughout American history, and he examines the legal doctrines and other means by which those transactions occurred.

5. Id., at 18–19.

6. Id., at 18, 20.

7. Id., at 16–17.

8. Charles C. Mann, *1491: New Revelations of the Americas before Columbus* (New York: Alfred E. Knopf, 2005) at 93.

9. Mann describes at 87 the horrific impacts of the Old World diseases to which Native peoples had no immunity: "Smallpox radiated throughout the empire like ink spreading through tissue paper. Millions of people simultaneously experienced its symptoms: high fever, vomiting, severe pain, oozing blisters everywhere on the body. Unable to number the losses, the Jesuit Martin de Murua said only that the toll was 'infinite thousands.'"

10. Id., at 97–99.

11. Banner (2005) at 26–29. See also Neil Jessup Newton, et al. (eds.), *Cohen's Handbook of Federal Indian Law* (2005 ed.) (LexisNexis/Mathew Bender, 2005) at 14–17.

12. Banner (2005) at 100 (quoting from John C. Fritpatrick, ed., *The Writings of George Washington* (Washington: Government Printing Office, 1931–1944), 2:468–70).

13. Id., at 105–107.

14. R. Kent Newmyer, *John Marshall and the Heroic Age of the Supreme Court* (Baton Rouge: Louisiana State Univ. Press, 2001) at 36.

15. Banner (2005) at 125.

16. William Strickland, *Journal of a Tour in the United States of America, 1794–1795.* (The New York Historical Society, 1971), Rev. J. E. Strickland (ed.) at 167–68. Speculators had a "strong inducement" to "extirpate the much injured owners of the soil and in too many instances their destruction is persued with remorseless perseverance and their annihilation spoken of with atrocious pleasure" (Id., at 168).

17. Alexis de Tocqueville, *Democracy in America* (New York: Bantam Dell, 1835, 2000) (translated by Henry Reese) V. I–II, at 341–42.

18. Charles F. Hobson, ed., *The Papers of John Marshall, Vol. IX* (Chapel Hill: Univ. of North Carolina Press, 1998) at 301 n. 12 and accompanying text; Banner (2005) at 102–03. The *Johnson* opinion refers to the forged document at 21 US at 599–600, finding it wholly inapplicable to purchases of Indian land in America.

19. Robertson (2005) at 185 n. 11 (citing business records of the Illinois Land and Wabash Land companies). The laughably low price paid for an area about the size of New Jersey, which is disclosed by the land companies' business records discovered by Robertson, is at odds with the recitation of facts in the *Johnson* opinion, 21 US at 553, 557, which suggests more was paid to the Indians. However, to the extent the two sources conflict, the business records are more reliable, since the facts recited in *Johnson*, as we shall see, were a contrived statement of agreed facts crafted by collusive parties. See note 28, infra, and accompanying text.

20. See US House of Representatives Committee on Ways and Means website, http://waysandmeans.house.gov/Legacy/portraits/1789-1898/harper.htm. Among his many accomplishments as a lawyer, congressman, senator, and general in the War of 1812, Harper (1765–1825) was also a failed land speculator. He was an officer and shareholder in the South Carolina Yazoo Company, formed to develop land in western Georgia, whose unsuccessful claims failed to comply with Georgia law; several associates in that ill-fated venture fell into disrepute for forgery and embezzlement. See Harper Papers website, 1997–98: www.sc.edu/library/socar/uses/1998/harper98.html. Harper's losses, however, were compensated by his marriage to the daughter of one of America's wealthiest men. Robertson (2005) at 32.

21. *Fletcher v. Peck,* 10 US 87 (1810).

22. Robertson (2005) at 31. See also *Cohen's* (2005) at 971 n. 45 (acknowledging that *Fletcher*

"was reportedly collusive") (citing, Lindsay G. Robertson, "*A Mere Feigned Case*": *Rethinking the Fletcher v. Peck Conspiracy and Early Republican Legal Culture,*" 2000 Utah L. Rev. 249, 252.) *Fletcher* was a precursor to *Johnson v. M'Intosh*, in which the Court recognized that the original thirteen states had the preemptive right to purchase Indian land and extinguish Indian title during the days before the US Constitution was adopted; however, the Constitution vests the federal government with exclusive power over Indian affairs. In the Nonintercourse Act of 1790, Congress prohibited the sale of Indian lands to any person or state regardless of the preexisting state right of preemption to Indian lands (*Cohen's* [2005] at 972).

23.   Robertson (2005) at 31. John Marshall "shared land madness with others of his time and place" and was heavily involved in land speculation, along with his father, in Virginia; they were among the biggest and most aggressive land speculators and investors of the day (Newmyer [2001] at 37); see also pp. 9, 17, 36–39. His father, Thomas Marshall, was an ambitious work-ing-class Scott who "moved west to exploit the opportunities the frontier provided" and specu-lated heavily in land as a surveyor and land agent (Jean Edward Smith, *John Marshall: Definer of a Nation* [New York: Henry Holt & Co., 1996] at 26–28). Thomas was a plaintiff in *Marshall v. Clark*, 8 Va. 268, 1791 WL 325 (Va. 1791), which was a lawsuit filed to protect the legality of Virginia's granting of preemptive rights in Cherokee land to veterans. Attorney John Marshall was versed in Virginia land title disputes. In *Hite v. Fairfax* 4 Call 42, 1786 WL 84 (Va. 1786), he defended claims to land in northern Virginia that had been opened to speculators. Through these and other activities, it was well-known that the chief justice's passion for land speculation, including his enormous land holdings obtained through speculation, were "inextricably con-nected" to his dedication to public service (Newmyer [2001] at 37–39).

24.   Robertson (2005) at 35.

25.   *Fletcher,* 10 US at 147–48.

26.   Robertson (2005) at 47–53, 62–64, 66–67. How shall we judge the ethical conduct at play here, where the plaintiff's legal team, according to Robertson, identified and played a role in obtaining their adversary's attorneys and paid their fees and likely told them what arguments to present to the Supreme Court? These acts surely robbed M'Intosh's attorneys of their duty of undivided loyalty to their client and their ability to exercise independent professional judgment in representing M'Intosh. Under today's rules, those ethical duties were apparently breached. Rule 2.1 of the American Bar Association's Model Rules of Professional Conduct (1995 ed.) requires lawyers to exercise independent professional judgment when representing a client.

27.   M'Intosh is described by Robertson as an especially unsavory character with several axes to grind, who was all too willing to accommodate the two land companies. A local malcontent, he had previously been denounced in the press as "an arrant knave, a profligate villain, a dastardly cheat, a perfidious rascal, an impertinent puppy, an absolute liar and a mean cowardly person" (Id., at 52 [quoting the *Indiana Gazette*, August 27, 1804, and September 11, 1804]). By losing the case, M'Intosh could discredit enemies in his various running feuds with prominent locals and undercut the land title of all his neighbors.

28.   Judge Pope's brother, John Pope, was married to plaintiff Thomas Johnson's niece (Robertson [2005] at 51 [citing Johnson family genealogy records]). Today, judicial ethics prevent judges from hearing cases involving relatives in order to protect against bias and conflicts of interest and to safeguard the integrity of the system. For example, Canon 3 E (1)(d)(i) of the American Bar Association's Model Code of Judicial Conduct (2004) requires judges to disqualify them-selves in proceedings where a party is "within the third degree of relationship" to the judge. This includes brothers and nieces. Is it unfair to judge Pope's ethics by a 2004 judicial code? Some ethical benchmark must be employed to assess the shenanigans in *Johnson*. Contemporary eth-ics provide a reasonable benchmark since *Johnson* is still used today and courts should at least know the ethics that produced *Johnson*.

29.   Robertson (2005) at 56–58. If these tactics were used to avoid disclosing material facts or controlling legal authorities to the courts, Harper may have violated the ethical duty of candor owed by attorneys toward the tribunal. That duty is imposed upon modern litigators by Rule 3.3 of the ABA's Model Rules of Professional Conduct (1995 ed.). Is it unfair to measure the "pompous dandy's" tactics by today's standards? Unless we know the ethical means by which court decisions are produced, it is difficult to accord them proper effect. By 1810, the Supreme Court in *Fletcher* had admonished counsel against bringing feigned cases at least in part to

ensure the full and complete disclosure of all pertinent facts and law through a bona fide adversarial process. So while an ethical code may not have been in effect in 1823, the courts and legal counsel were surely aware of the need to be forthcoming with the court.

30.   Robertson (2005) at 62–64, 66.

31.   *Johnson,* 21 US at 563 (describing Harper's position).

32.   Id., at 569–70 (describing M'Intosh's position).

33.   Id., at 590 (Marshall's description).

34.   An ethical observation about these uses of racial invectives against Indians by the Court and the parties in *Johnson* helps us understand the outcome of this case. Public confidence in the courts is eroded when judges engage in or allow conduct that raises questions about the court's ability to carry out judicial responsibilities with integrity and impartiality. For these reasons, judicial ethics forbid the use of racial stereotypes, slurs, or invectives against parties—even ones not before the court—by judges or by attorneys in the courtroom. Under Canon 2 of American Bar Association's Code of Judicial Conduct (1999), the courts discipline judges who use racial slurs or otherwise indicate prejudice against particular groups, whether inside or outside the courtroom. See, for example, *In re Petition for Removal of a Chief Judge,* 592 So.2d 671 (Fal. 1992) (public use of discriminatory stereotypes); *In re Inquiry Concerning Carr,* 593 So.2d 1044 (Fla. 1992) (racial invective against Italians in the courtroom); *In re Mulroy,* 731 N.E.2d 120 (N.Y. 2000) (offensive racial slurs in the courtroom); *Mississippi Judicial Performance Comm'n v. Walker,* 565 So.2d 1117 (Miss. 1990) (racial slurs against blacks used in a contempt proceeding); *Matter of Schiff,* 635 N.E.2d 286 (N.Y. 1994) (disparaging racial remarks about blacks and Puerto Ricans in front of a Hispanic attorney); *In re Moroney,* 914 P.2d 570 (Kan. 1996) (ridiculing a defendant for his inability to speak English). This conduct, according to the courts, casts doubt upon the ability of judges to fairly judge cases that come before them and violates the rules that require judges to uphold the integrity and impartiality of the judiciary. In *Johnson,* the courtroom was apparently filled with discriminatory stereotypes and offensive racial slurs against Indians. This is evident throughout the *Johnson* Court's opinion.

Given the above, do reasonable minds believe that the *Johnson* Court was able to render an impartial decision concerning Indian land and sovereignty rights? It matters not that the Indians were not present before the Court. The use of ethnic slurs or racially charged language directed at someone who is not before the court still violates Canon 3B(4) (requiring judges to perform their duties impartially and requiring attorneys who appear before the court to do the same), because such language casts doubt on the court's ability to render impartial decisions. See *In re Buchanan,* 669 P.2d 1248 (Wash. 1983) (derogatory ethnic comments about a Jewish attorney not before the court); *In re Velie,* 1992 WL 778716 (Wash. Comm'n Jud. Cond. 1992) (slurs against Middle Easterners in the courthouse coffee room). To implement these judicial ethics, federal law currently requires a judge to disqualify himself in any proceeding where his impartiality might reasonably be questioned; and this includes cases where the judge is prejudiced or biased against a party or has an economic interest that could be affected by the outcome of the proceeding. 28 U.S.C.A. § 455.

35.   It was a miscarriage of justice, in my opinion, that the task of advocating and representing the legal interests of the Indian nations in *Johnson* fell to Harper. It is evident from language in the opinion attributed to Harper that he could care less about their well-being. Modern rules governing litigation in federal court require that "[e]very action shall be prosecuted in the name of the real party in interest" (Rule 17, Federal Rules of Civil Procedure). The Indian Nations were surely the real parties in interest insofar as their rights to own and sell land were concerned. The complete absence of the Indian parties should be deeply troubling to any judge who is tempted to rely upon *Johnson* as legal precedent.

36.   Rule 19, Federal Rules of Civil Procedure.

37.   Robertson (2005) at 74 (citing company records).

38.   *Johnson,* 21 US at 594–99, 603.

39.   Id., at 585.

40.   Id., at 585–86.

41.   The procedure for obtaining treasury warrants involved six steps: (1) a treasury warrant is purchased entitling the buyer to acquire land from Virginia at forty pounds per hundred acres; (2) the Land Office issues the warrant authorizing a county surveyor to survey the number of acres

purchased and specified in the warrant; (3) the purchaser identifies the land wanted and enters its general location in county land entry books; (4) the survey is conducted and a plat provided to the owner; (5) the plat and accompanying treasury warrant are presented to the Land Office and, finally, (6) the governor issues the land grant. See Herbert A. Johnson, ed., *The Papers of John Marshall, Vol. I* (Chapel Hill: Univ. of North Carolina Press, 1974) at 103.

42. Id., at 91–92, 164–168. Marshall was a combat-tested Revolutionary War veteran who served with distinction at Valley Forge (Newmyer [2001] at 1–68). Accordingly, he was eligible for land in the military district under Virginia law (Id., at 37). The district consisted of land set aside for veterans in western Kentucky within the Ohio, Green, and Tennessee rivers (Robertson [2005] at 86). This area lies south of the Wabash purchase in *Johnson*.

43. Johnson (1974) at 100–102, 248. One land grant for forty thousand acres of treasury warrant land was issued to Marshall in 1785 (Id. 248).

44. Id., at 102 n. 1.

45. *Johnson* was not the first time that a case involving Marshall's land interests came before the Supreme Court. The first two occasions arose in *Fairfax's Devisee v. Hunter's Lessee,* 11 US 603 (1812) and *Martin v. Hunter's Lessee,* 14 US 304 (1816). Both involved a dispute over more than 300,000 acres of land to which John Marshall and his brother, James, had purchased. The story of this lengthy and costly litigation and Marshall's enormous stake in the outcome is discussed by Peter Irons, a professor and lawyer, in *A People's History of the Supreme Court* (New York: Penguin, 1999), pp. 115–20; by Jean Howard Smith, *John Marshall: Definer of a Nation* (New York: Henry Holt, 1996) at 164–68; and by Newmyer (2001) at 38–39. It involved a lengthy dispute over the immense estate of Lord Fairfax in Northern Virginia, which had been granted to him by the Crown. Lord Fairfax, a Tory loyalist, fled to England during the Revolution, and Virginia subsequently confiscated his plantation. This prompted lengthy lawsuits among persons claiming portions of the land under Virginia land grants and those claiming under grants from Lord Fairfax. The Marshall family was closely connected to the Fairfax plantation, first, because Thomas Marshall was the superintendent of the plantation and, second, John Marshall, the son, had unsuccessfully defended the validity of Lord Fairfax's title in *Hite v. Fairfax,* 4 Call 42, 1786 WL 84 (Va. 1786). Later, brothers John and James Marshall purchased a claim under Fairfax's title to about 300,000 acres of the property from Martin Denny, who was a party seeking to confirm ownership of that tract in *Fairfax's Devisee v. Hunter's Lessee* and *Martin v. Hunter's Lessee.* The brothers could make a fortune if Martin's claim in these cases was upheld, as eventually done by the Marshall Court (See Irons [1999] at 117; Smith [1996] at 164–68). Because of his conflict, Marshall stood aside as these appeals came before his court and allowed Justice Joseph Story, his right-hand man, to uphold what was in effect Marshall's claim (Irons, supra at 116). Justice Story's opinions in both cases ruled in Marshall's favor, but conveniently fail to mention that the chief justice and his brother had bought a large portion of the subject property (Id., at 117). Thus, Marshall's investment was realized through the decisions of his court.

46. *Marshall v. Clark,* 8 Va. (4 Call.) 268, 1791 WL 325 (Va. 1791).

47. Newmyer (2001) at 39.

48. It also favorably solved other nagging problems confronting the Marshall Court in 1823. Many people were squabbling over land in western Virginia—Harper's clients (including M'Intosh), the Marshalls, Virginia and its veterans, the United States, and Kentuckians.

49. *Johnson,* 21 US at 572, 588–89.

50. Id.

51. Id., at 585.

52. Id., at 583, 587–88.

53. Id., at 573.

54. Id., at 574. Marshall's erroneous notion is a key predicate to the *Johnson* holding. Banner (2005) provides compelling evidence that Marshall was flat wrong about British practices. Banner firmly establishes that the British clearly considered the Indians as landowners and purchased their lands for more than 150 years (Accord, *Cohen's* (2005 ed.) at 14–17). Furthermore, Spanish secular law held that the pope's grant of title to Spain was "baseless" (Robert A. Williams, *The Medieval and Renaissance Origins of the Status of the American Indian In Western Legal Thought,* 57 Southern California L. Rev. 1, 70 [1983] [citing Franciscus de Victoria, *On the Indians Lately*

Discovered]). Importantly, almost a decade after *Johnson* was decided, Marshall himself backed off his holding that discovery grants title to Indian land. In *Cherokee Nation v. Georgia*, 31 US 515, 516–17 (1832), Marshall admitted that the British Crown did *not* claim outright ownership of Indian land under the discovery doctrine, but merely a preemptive right to purchase "such land as the natives were willing to convey." This observation is in accord with that of Banner and *Cohen's*. Marshall also conceded that the king neither conquered the American Indian tribes, interfered with their internal affairs, nor sought to govern them; rather, the king simply "purchased their lands when they were willing to sell, at a price they were willing to take; but never coerced a surrender of them" (Id.). Since the premise of *Johnson* is indisputably wrong, we are confronted with unsound legal reasoning. So why is *Johnson* still given effect by the courts?

55.   Id., at 585–86. This reference conclusively solidified Marshall land holdings obtained under Virginia's preemptory rights scheme. At the same time, it also resolved several other problems of interest to Marshall as the chief justice of an embattled Supreme Court. First, approval of Virginia's system in *Johnson* bolstered Virginia's position in its interstate squabble with Kentucky over Virginia's military warrants. Both states were squabbling over the power to acquire the same lands occupied by Indian tribes; and Kentucky sought to invalidate Virginia's warrants in *Green v. Biddle*, 21 US (8 Wheat.) 1 (1823), an important companion case to *Johnson*. Decided just one day after *Johnson*, the *Green* decision invalidated Kentucky's adverse claims to the Virginia warrant land. Second, the Marshall Court was also facing a potential constitutional crisis that had been brewing since *Marbury v. Madison* (1803) and *Fletcher v. Peck* (1810), because the states were angry over the Court's assertion of power to strike down state laws; and both Virginia and Kentucky had made dark threats foreshadowing a constitutional crisis in 1823, according to Robertson. In deciding *Green* in favor of Virginia, Marshall was able, at least, to drive a wedge between these potential allies and hopefully defuse the crisis (Robertson [2005] at 80–92). These factors, combined with the Marshall family land interests, may have preordained the outcome of *Johnson*.

56.   *Johnson*, 21 US at 579–80.

57.   Id., at 588–89.

58.   Id., at 573. This passage contains what can only be described as an example of racism as that term is defined in dictionaries. We have already considered how the use of racial invectives and stereotypes by the Court and the parties likely impugned the Court's ability to render an impartial judgment concerning American Indian interests. Thus, it was only a matter of time for racism to surface in the opinion. Incredibly, the supposed racial superiority of non-Indians is used at page 573 as the predicate for the holding. *We own legal title to all Indian land in North America, because Indians are racially inferior.* Since we are now forced to enter the dark realm of judicial racism that is evident in *Johnson*, it is appropriate to underscore the racist underpinnings of the discovery doctrine. James Scott observed in *The Spanish Origin of International Law: Francisco de Victoria and His Law of Nations* (Oxford, 1934) at p. 106–07, that the initial justification for the doctrine was that Indians are naturally suited for slavery and slaves can not own property. It is a rule based upon the supposed racial superiority of the Spanish over the inhabitants of the New World. To be blunt, the doctrine is founded solely on racism. To what extent should this doctrine be used by courts today, long after such notions have been discarded by other government institutions? At what point must the doctrine of stare decisis (which requires courts to follow judicial precedent) give way to social change?

59.   *Johnson*, 21 US at 589–90.

60.   Id., at 590.

61.   Id.

62.   Id., at 591.

63.   Id., at 591–92. Marshall later admitted that the doctrines of discovery and conquest were absurd in *Worcester v. Georgia*, 31 US 515, 543–44 (1832). In describing the charters of the king of England that purported to convey the soil in North America inhabited by "numerous and warlike nations" who were "willing and able to defend their possessions," Marshall aptly stated, "The extravagant and absurd idea, that the feeble settlements made on the sea coast, or the companies under whom they were made, acquired legitimate power by [the charters] to govern the [Indian tribes], or occupy the lands from sea to sea, did not enter the mind of any man" (Id., at 544–45).

64. *Cohen's* (2005) at 970–74, 986, 998–1005 contains further discussion and analysis of the holdings in *Johnson*.

65. *Georgia v. Tassels* 1 Ga. Ann. 478 (Dud. 229) (Ga. Super. 1830). In *Tassels*, the Georgia court relied heavily on *Johnson* and quoted extensively from Marshall's opinion to support Georgia's ownership of all Cherokee Nation land located within Georgia in fee simple absolute and the exercise of state criminal jurisdiction over the Cherokee Nation and its members. According to *Tassels*, the Cherokee were "a savage race and of imbecile intellect," their discovery by Europeans was equivalent to conquest, and fee title to Cherokee land was vested in the state of Georgia (Id., at 235). So why shouldn't Georgia have jurisdiction over the land? The court stated, "it seems strange that an objection should now be made to that jurisdiction. That a government should be seized in fee of a territory, and yet have no jurisdiction over that country is an anomaly in the science of jurisprudence" (Id., at 236).

66. In *Worcester v. Georgia* (1832), Marshall retreated from the fee title component of the discovery doctrine, which he had added in *Johnson* in his expanded version of the doctrine. In *Worcester,* Marshall now held that the doctrine simply granted to the discoverers a right of preemption, and nothing more. Noting the absurdity of the doctrine, *Worcester* determined that neither the charters, the king, nor the discovery doctrine operated to transfer legal title of Indian lands to any non-Indian government. Rather this body of law operated only to grant the exclusive right of preemption to England and its successor, the United States (Id. 31 US at 543–45).

67. See Robertson (2005) at 138–42 for a discussion of *Martin v. Lessee of Waddell,* 41 US (16 Peters) 367 (1842); *Mitchell v. United States,* 40 US (15 Peters) 52 (1841) (*Mitchell II*); *Clark v. Smith,* 38 US (13 Peters) 195 (1839); *United States v. Fernandez,* 34 US (9 Peters) 303 (1836); *Mitchell v. United States,* 34 US (9 Peters) 711 (1835) (*Mitchell I*).

68. In *City of Sherrill v. Oneida Indian Nation,* 544 US 197 (2005), the court denied tribal sovereignty over aboriginal lands that were reacquired by the Oneida Indian Nation. The court noted "[u]nder the doctrine of discovery…fee title to the lands occupied by Indians when the colonists arrived became vested in the sovereign—first discovering European nation and later the original states and the United States" (Id., at 203 n. 1). According to the court, "[i]n the original 13 States, 'fee title to Indian lands,' or 'the pre-emptive right to purchase from the Indians, was in the State'" (citing *Oneida Indian Nation of NY v. County of Oneida,* 414 US 661, 670 [1974]). The court also observed that upon the 1790 Nonintercourse Act, 1 Stat. 138, and adoption of the Constitution, the United States obtained exclusive power over Indian affairs and ended the states' power to acquire lands directly from the Indians.

69. *Johnson* is fervently relied upon by many settler state courts in Australia, New Zealand, Canada, and other former British colonies to limit Native rights. See, for example, *Wewaykum Indian Band v. Canada,* 4 S.C.R. 245 (2002); Gary D. Meyers and Sally Raine, "Australian Aboriginal Land Rights In Transition (Part II): The Legislative Response to the High Court's Native Title Decision in *Mabo v. Queensland* and *Wik v. Queensland,*" 9 Tulsa L. Comp. & Int'l. 95–96 (2001).

70. Larry McMurtry, *Oh What a Slaughter: Massacres In the American West 1846–1890* (New York: Simon & Schuster, 2005) at 13 (quoting Red Cloud, the patriot Sioux chief).

71. Charles Wilkinson, *Blood Struggle: The Rise of Modern Indian Nations* (New York: W. W. Norton, 2005) at 43; Rennard Strickland, et al., eds., *Cohen's Handbook of Federal Indian Law* (Michie Bobbs-Merrill, 1982 ed.) at 138.

72. *Cohen's* (2005 ed.) at 97.

73. *Cohen's Handbook of Federal Indian Law* (1982 ed.) at 173–75.

74. Wilkinson (2005) at 207.

75. *Tee-Hit-Ton v. United States,* 348 US 272 (1955). Because this case is one of the ten worst cases ever decided, it will receive its own discussion, in chapter thirteen.

76. Id., at 279.

77. Id., at 281.

78. Id., at 289–90.

79. John Treat Irvin, *Indian Sketches Taken During an Expedition to the Pawnee Tribes in 1833* (Santa Barbara, CA: Narrative Press, (1858) 2001) at 117.

80. Id., at 117–118.

81. Bob Blaisdell (ed.), *Great Speeches by Native Americans* (Minola, NY: Dover Publications, 2000) at 76.

82. Martha Royce Blaine, *Pawnee Passage (1870–1875)* (Norman: Univ. of Oklahoma Press, 1990), p. 202. This excellent book chronicles the historical pressures that led to the removal of the Pawnee Nation from its homeland. See also James T. Riding In, *Pawnee Removal: A Study of Pawnee-White Relations in Nebraska* (Master's Thesis, Univ. of California, Los Angeles, 1985).

83. Blaine (1990) at 202.

84. Wilkinson (2005) at 207.

85. *Cohen's* (2005) at 965.

86. The Native American Rights Fund (NARF) (www.narf.org) was founded in 1970 to assert and defend the rights of indigenous peoples in the United States. Since then, NARF has been involved in over seventy Supreme Court cases affecting the treaty, property, cultural, human, and political rights of American Indians, Alaska Natives, and Native Hawaiians. NARF brought historic land claim litigation in *Joint Tribal Council of the Passamaquoddy Tribe v. Morton,* 338 F. Supp. 649 (D. Maine, 1975), *aff'd,* 528 F.2d 370 (1st Cir. 1975), which resulted in the largest return of land to Indian people in US history; over 300,000 acres were reacquired by the Passamaquoddy, Penobscot, and Maliseet Indian tribes under the Maine Indian Claims Settlement Act of 1980, 25 USCA §§ 1721–1735, which was guided through Congress by NARF lobbyist Suzan S. Harjo. Other NARF land claim litigation and legislation includes the Catawba Indian Tribe of South Carolina Land Claims Settlement Act of 1993, 25 USCA §§ 941 et seq. (providing a $50 million land reacquisition fund); *County of Oneida v. Oneida Indian Nation,* 470 US 226 (1985) (confirming the right of Indian tribes to maintain an action for unlawfully taking their possessory rights to land in 1795); *Alabama-Coushatta Tribe of Texas v. United States,* 28 Fed. Cl. 95 (1993) (a congressional reference decision upholding aboriginal title to more than 5 million acres in Texas and finding that the federal government is responsible for the loss of 2.85 million of those acres, which resulted in $270.6 million in damages to the tribe). These victories helped stem the tide of American Indian land loss and address hardships created by *Johnson.* They illustrate the effective use of the law as a shield to protect Native American rights during the modern era of federal Indian law.

87. *Dred Scott,* 60 US at 405; *Johnson,* 21 US at 577, 690–70.

88. United Nations Declaration on the Rights of Indigenous Peoples, UN G.A. Res. 61/295, UN H.R.C., 61st Sess., Annex, Agenda Item 68, UN Doc. A/RES/61/295 (2007). See www.narf.org/events/07/declaration.pdf.

CHAPTER 5: *CHEROKEE NATION V. GEORGIA*: SHUTTING THE COURTHOUSE DOORS

1. Yep, that's right. Many dictionaries peg Georgia as the Cracker State. See *Oxford English Dictionary* (online), 2nd ed. (Oxford, UK: Oxford Univ. Press, 1989); definition of *cracker, Merriam-Webster's Collegiate Dictionary* (11th ed.) (A *cracker* is a "native resident of Florida or Georgia" or "southern white.")

2. House of Representatives Resolution (Dec. 22, 1830), Acts of the General Assembly of the State of Georgia, Annual Sess. in Nov. and Dec. 1830 (Milledgeville: Camak & Ragland, 1831) at 282–283.

3. Forced resettlement of indigenous peoples is considered a genocidal act. *Genocide* is defined in the *United Nation's Convention on the Prevention of and Punishment of the Crime of Genocide* (1948) as "the deliberate destruction of members of a racial, ethnic, or cultural group." Genocidal acts include: (1) killing members of the group; (2) causing serious bodily harm to them; (3) inflicting conditions of life calculated to bring about a group's destruction in whole or part; (4) imposing measures intended to prevent births within the group; and (5) forcibly transferring children of one group to another. Anthropologists familiar with indigenous peoples explain that genocidal acts do not usually succeed in killing all members of the targeted group; however, survivors are sometimes "raped, enslaved, deprived of their property, and forcibly moved to new places" (Robert Hitchcock and Tara Twedt, "Physical and Cultural Genocide of Various Indigenous Peoples," *Century of Genocide: Eyewitness Accounts and Critical Views* [New York: Garland Publishing, 1997] [Samuel Totten, et al., eds] at 379).

4. *Cherokee Nation v. Georgia,* 30 US 1 (1831).

5. Stuart Banner, *How the Indians Lost Their Lands: Law and Power on the American Frontier*

(Cambridge: Belknap Press of Harvard Univ. Press, 2005) at 191.

6.   I have known, represented, and worked with many Cherokee during my days as a Native American Rights Fund attorney. This chapter is respectfully dedicated to my former clients in *Sequoyah v. Tennessee Valley Authority*, 620 F. 2d. 1159 (Cir. 1979), which was a litigation effort to protect sacred ground in Tennessee.

7.   See, generally, James Mooney, *History, Myths, and Sacred Formulas of the Cherokee* (Ashville, NC: Bright Mountain Books, 1992).

8.   Treaty with the Cherokees, 1785, 7 Stat. 18 (Treaty of Hopewell).

9.   Printed in Cherokee and English from the capital of the Cherokee Nation at New Echota, Georgia, the voice of the Cherokee Nation railed against Georgia's anti-Indian statutes and the federal and state Indian removal policies. The *Phoenix* became a tool for enlisting widespread support for the Cherokee efforts to remain in their homeland and keeping the nation united and informed during its struggle with Georgia. The newspaper was effective, attracting subscribers across the nation and in Europe. It was silenced in 1835 when the State of Georgia halted its operations and the Georgia militia destroyed the printing press.

10.   The Charter of Georgia was issued by King George II in 1732. It explains that the colony was created for "the meanest and most unfortunate of our people"—those poor unable to support themselves in England (www.yale.edu/lawweb/avalon/states/ga01.htm). To resettle these unde-sirables, the king created a colony to be administered by James Oglethorpe and other trustees. The charter intended that the convicts would be trained as a military force to protect the fron-tiers of South Carolina.

11.   After American independence was achieved, Australia replaced Georgia as a home for Brit-ish penal colonization. See, generally, Robert Hughes, *The Fatal Shores: The Epic of Australia's Founding* (New York: Alfred E. Knopf, 1987).

12.   See *Oxford English Dictionary*, supra, definition of *cracker*.

13.   Tim Alan Garrison, *The Legal Ideology of Removal: The Southern Judiciary and the Sovereignty of Native American Nations* (Athens: Univ. of Georgia Press, 2002), at 7. This excellent treatment of the Cherokee cases should be required reading in every course on Indian law and history. The author gratefully acknowledges this important source, which is consulted frequently in this chapter.

14.   Stephen Jay Gould, *The Mismeasure of Man* (New York: W. W. Norton, 1981) at 51; Roger C. Echo-Hawk and Walter R. Echo-Hawk, *Battlefields and Burial Grounds* (Minneapolis: Lerner Publications, 1994) at 23–25.

15.   Samuel George Morton, MD, *Crania Americana* (Philadelphia: J. Dobson, Chestnut Street, 1839) at 5, 7.

16.   Id., at 6, 64, 81. Sound familiar? These innate racial traits, supposedly derived from empiri-cal skull measurements and other immutable scientific methods, closely resemble the familiar "trailer trash" characteristics of today. Morton thus placed Indians somewhere near the level of the brawling guests on the *Jerry Springer* show, except Indians do not traditionally live in trailer parks or come from north Georgia these days, and they have not appeared on the show.

17.   Id., at 7.

18.   Charles Caldwell, MD, *Thoughts on the Original Unity of the Human Race* (Cincinnati, OH: J. A. & U. P. James, 1852). Contemporary scientific findings on the earliest hominid species found in the dust of the Ethiopian badlands in Africa's Great Riff Valley suggest that all races originated from a common African source. Imagine Caldwell's disgust at learning that whites are really the stepchildren of the black race.

19.   Id. at 79–80, 83. Caldwell's argument in these pages goes as follows:

> As relates to mental cultivation and improvement, the Indian and African races resemble the inferior animals. They do not profit by experience—Let tribes of Africans or Indians be instructed, during a lifetime, in science and the arts, by Caucasian teachers and then be abandoned to themselves; from that period, instead of advancing in knowledge, or even retaining what they have received, their course will be retrograde, until they shall have returned to their original ignorance. All experience with them, as far as it has extended, tends to the proof of this assertion. In truth, as races, they are not made for science and learning.

The native bent of Caucasians is to civilization. Of the North American Indians, the reverse is true. Savagism, a roaming life, and a home in the forest, are as natural to them, and as essential to their existence, as to the buffalo, or the bear. Civilization is destined to exterminate them, in common with the wild animals among which they have lived, and on which they have subsisted. All experience admonishes this. In numbers the Indians and buffaloes of our western wilds diminish alike, and from similar causes. And they retreat alike from civilization. Neither of them can flourish in a domesticated state…Every effort hitherto made to civilize and educate the Indians has but deteriorated them, and tended to annihilate them as a people. And such, from their moral constitution, must continue to be the case, until the race shall become extinct…[A]s readily shall the wolf and fox become faithful house-dogs, as the entire Indian a civilized and cultivated man.

The truth is, that the Indians were formed, fitted, and intended to inhabit uncultivated forests, and wild prairies. To rove through them, frequent the banks of rivers and lakes, and subsist on game and fish, their aptitude is complete. But as soon as civilization shall have converted those places into fruitful fields, meadows, and gardens, their primitive inhabitants will be no longer wanted. On the contrary, they will be out of place, and without a home adapted to their nature. The issue is plain. They will cease to exist, on the same principle of adaptation that called them into being. In the scheme of creation, and of populating the earth, they have been useful and necessary; but the time is approaching, when they will be so no longer…To cultivated Caucasians, the extinction of their race would be preferable to a compulsory conversion to savagism. Nor to beings constitutionally savage, as the Indians are, is civilization less abhorrent. The wilderness, then, having been deprived of its savage character, and requiring no longer savage inhabitants, the Indians will have finished their work, and been rendered useless…On this ground, we repeat, the destiny of the Indian is fixed…The years of his race are not only numbered; they are comparatively few.

20. Id., at 83.
21. Garrison (2002) at 24.
22. Mooney (1992) at 98–99.
23. Garrison (2002) at 32.
24. See the Compact of April 24, 1802, American State Papers, Public Lands 1:125 (1802).
25. The Cherokee Constitution of 1827 defiantly proclaims the "boundaries of this nation…shall forever remain unalterably the same" (Constitution of the Cherokee Nation, Art. I, reprinted in the Cherokee Nation Memorial to Congress [November, 28, 1834], H. Doc. 91 [January 19, 1835], 23d Cong., 2d Sess., p, 2).
26. Letter from commissioners Campbell and Meriwether to Cherokee Nation (October 21, 1823), reprinted in Message from the President of the United States Transmitting Certain Papers to relating to the Compact between the United States and Georgia of 1802 (April 2, 1824), 18th Cong., 1st Sess. 63 at 28.
27. Id., at 36 (Letter from Path Killer, Major Ridge, and John Ross to commissioners Campbell and Meriwether, October 27, 1823).
28. Id., at 37–38 (Extract of a letter from the Cherokee delegation to the president of the United States, January 19, 1824). In particular, they recommended that Georgia be granted lands in Florida if her boundaries were considered too small, but in any event the "Cherokee Nation have never promised to surrender, at any future period, to the United States, or Georgia, their title to lands" (Id., at 40 [Letter from Cherokee delegation to Secretary of War J. C. Calhoun, February 11, 1824]).
29. Id., at 4–5 (Message from James Monroe, March 30, 1824). Unlike other Indian tribes in the South who resorted to war to defend their lands and protect themselves against removal, the Cherokee Nation elected to defend itself through a sophisticated political campaign of

nonviolence that is documented by Walter H. Conser Jr. in "John Ross and the Cherokee Resistance Campaign, 1833–1838," *The Journal of Southern History,* Vol. XLIV, No. 2 (May 1978) at 191–212. The methods employed by the Cherokee Nation are a precursor to those used by Indian tribes in the modern era and include the employment of legal counsel, pacifism, adroit use of the press, petitioning and lobbying the government, and the enlistment of political support among religious groups and Americans of good conscience.

30. The repeated legislative appeals, resolutions, memorials, and petitions to the federal government between 1821–1826 were unavailing. See, for example, House of Representatives Resolution (May 11, 1821), Acts of the General Assembly of the State of Georgia, Annual Sess. April and May 1821 (Milledgeville: Grantland & Orme 1821) at 37–38 Senate Memorial of December 20, 1823, Acts of the General Assembly of the State of Georgia, Annual Sess. in November and December 1823 (Milledgeville: Camak & Ragland, 1824) at 217–224 (calling upon the president to extinguish Indian title to lands situated in the limits of Georgia under the Compact of 1802, asserting Georgia is vested with legal title to those lands and the Indians own a "mere temporary usufructuary right."); House Resolution of November 27, 1824, Acts of the General Assembly of the State of Georgia, Annual Sess., in November and December 1824 (Milledgeville: Camak & Ragland, 1825) at 190–191 (directing the Georgia delegation in Congress to present a report on the extinguishment of Indian title to territory within the limits of Georgia); Senate Resolution of December 4, 1826, Acts of the General Assembly of the State of Georgia, Annual Sess., Nov. and Dec. 1826 (Milledgeville: Camak & Ragland) at 206–208 (reporting on efforts to extinguish Cherokee title and requesting the president to hold a treaty for the purpose of extinguishing Cherokee title "to all or any part of the lands now in their possession within the limits of Georgia."); Senate Resolution and Report on Indian Affairs of Dec. 22, 1826, Acts of the General Assembly of the State of Georgia, Annual Sess., Nov. and Dec. 1826 (Milledgeville: Camak & Ragland) at 227–235 (asserting that Georgia owns all Indian land within the state and has jurisdiction over the Indians and protesting the assertion of the president that the state has no jurisdiction over Indians or right to enter into Indian Country within its limits).

31. Resolutions of the Legislature of Georgia requesting Congress to Extinguish Indian Title in Georgia (Dec. 19, 1827), reprinted in S. Doc. 80 (Feb. 4, 1828), 20th Cong., 1st Sess. at p. 12. This resolution states that America was inhabited by "wandering tribes of savages," and asserts that as the heir to the sovereigns of Spain, France, England, Holland, and Portugal, the State of Georgia obtained title to Indian land under the doctrines of discovery, domain, and empire. Since the state owns "absolute title to the soil," the legislature proclaimed that "Indians were under *her protection,*" and the Indians' possession of land "was by *her permission*" (Id., at 7). These claims are very pompous given the humble origins of the penal colony. The convict-colonists did not discover or conquer anyone. Nor would their claims to "domain" and "empire" be taken seriously in Europe.

32. Memorial of the Georgia Legislature (Dec. 18, 1823), 18th Cong., 1st Sess., House Doc. 125, Vol. 6, p. 4.

33. Resolution (Dec. 19, 1827), supra, note 31 at 10, 12.

34. Senate Resolution (Dec. 27, 1827), Acts of the General Assembly of the State of Georgia, Annual Sess. in Nov. and Dec. 1827 (Milledgeville: Camak & Ragland, 1827) at 236–250.

35. Id., at 241.

36. Id., at 237–249.

37. Id., at 250.

38. In the "Report concerning the policy of the general government towards the Indians," (Dec. 12, 1829), Acts of the General Assembly of the State of Georgia, Annual Sess., Nov. & Dec. 1829 (Milledgesville: Camak & Ragland 1830) at 267–270, the Georgia legislature intoned at 270 that it approves "the policy of the General Government towards the Indians, so far as it is calculated to induce them to remove beyond the operation of those causes which evidently tend to retard their improvement, and to extend to them, in a favorable position, the fostering protection and assistance of the country."

39. The reprehensible state actions sanctioned by this policy are described in more detail in this chapter. They were in mind when the US Supreme Court observed many years later that Indian tribes receive no protection from the states. "Because of local ill will, the people of the states

are often...the deadliest enemies" of Indian tribes, who must look to the United States for protection (*United States v. Kagama,* 118 US 375, 384 [1886] [discussing the Cherokee cases]).

40.   An Act to prevent the testimony of Indians being received in Courts of Justice, December 26, 1826, Acts of the General Assembly of the State of Georgia, Annual Sess. in Nov. and Dec. 1826 (Milledgeville: Camak & Ragland, 1826) at 62–63.

41.   Section 9, "An Act to add the Territory lying within the limits of this State, and occupied by the Cherokee Indians, to the Counties of Carroll, Dekalb, Hall and Habersham; and to extend the laws of this State over the same, and for other purposes," (Dec. 20, 1828), Acts of the General Assembly of the State of Georgia, Annual Sess. in Nov. and Dec. 1828 (Milledgeville: Camak & Ragland, 1829) at 88–89. See also Section 15, "An Act to add the Territory lying with the chartered limits of Georgia, and now in the occupancy of the Cherokee Indians, etc." (Dec. 19, 1829), Acts of the General Assembly of the State of Georgia, Annual Sess. in Nov. and Dec. 1829 (Milledgeville: Camak & Ragland, 1830) at 98–191 (Indians can testify against whites that reside within the Cherokee Nation).

42.   See Section, 7, "An Act to add the Territory lying with the chartered limits of Georgia, and now in the occupancy of the Cherokee Indians, etc." (Dec. 19, 1829), Acts of the General Assembly of the State of Georgia, Annual Sess. in Nov. and Dec. 1829 (Milledgeville: Camak & Ragland, 1830) at 98–191; Sections 3–4, "An Act to prevent the exercise of assumed and arbitrary power, by all persons under pretext of authority from the Cherokee Indians, and their laws, and to prevent white persons from residing within that part of the chartered limits of Georgia, occupied by the Cherokee Indians, and to provide a guard for the protection of the gold mines, and to enforce the laws of the State within the aforesaid territory," (Dec. 22, 1830), Acts of the General Assembly of the State of Georgia, Annual Sess. in Nov. and Dec. 1830 (Milledgeville: Camak & Ragland, 1831) at 114–117.

43.   "An Act to protect the Frontier Settlements of this State from the intrusion of the Indians of the Creek Nation," (Dec. 20, 1828), Acts of the General Assembly of the State of Georgia, Annual Sess. in Nov. and Dec. 1828 (Milledgeville: Camak & Ragland, 1829) at 87–88.

44.   Sections 7–9, "An Act to prevent the exercise of assumed and arbitrary power, by all persons under pretext of authority from the Cherokee Indians, and their laws, and to prevent white persons from residing within that part of the chartered limits of Georgia, occupied by the Cherokee Indians, and to provide a guard for the protection of the gold mines, and to enforce the laws of the State within the aforesaid territory," (Dec. 22, 1830), Acts of the General Assembly of the State of Georgia, Annual Sess. in Nov. and Dec. 1830 (Milledgeville: Camak & Ragland, 1831) at 114–117.

45.   "An Act to declare void all contracts hereafter made with the Cherokee Indians, so far as the Indians are concerned" (Dec. 23, 1830), Acts of the General Assembly of the State of Georgia, Annual Sess. in Nov. and Dec. 1830 (Milledgeville: Camak & Ragland, 1831) at 118.

46.   "An Act to divide certain counties and add part of the Cherokee Nation to the counties of Carroll and Dekalb, for the purposes of giving criminal jurisdiction to the same," (Dec. 26, 1827), Acts of the General Assembly of the State of Georgia, Annual Sess. in Nov. and Dec. 1827 (Milledgeville: Camak & Ragland, 1828) at 99–101.

47.   "An Act to add the Territory lying within the limits of this State, and occupied by the Cherokee Indians, to the Counties of Carroll, Dekalb, Hall and Habersham; and to extend the laws of this State over the same, and for other purposes," (Dec. 20, 1828), Acts of the General Assembly of the State of Georgia, Annual Sess. in Nov. and Dec. 1828 (Milledgeville: Camak & Ragland, 1829) at 88–89; "An Act to add the Territory lying with the chartered limits of Georgia, and now in the occupancy of the Cherokee Indians, etc." (Dec. 19, 1829), Acts of the General Assembly of the State of Georgia, Annual Sess. in Nov. and Dec. 1829 (Milledgeville: Camak & Ragland, 1830) at 98–191.

48.   Id., Section 14.

49.   Resolution of the House of Representatives (Dec. 15, 1828), Acts of the General Assembly of the State of Georgia, Annual Sess. in Nov. and Dec. 1828 (Milledgeville: Camak & Ragland, 1829) at 208–210.

50.   Sections 8–14, "An Act to add the Territory lying with the chartered limits of Georgia, and now in the occupancy of the Cherokee Indians, etc." (Dec. 19, 1829), Acts of the General Assembly of the State of Georgia, Annual Sess. in Nov. and Dec. 1829 (Milledgeville: Camak & Ragland,

1830) at 98–191; Section 5, "An Act to prevent the exercise of assumed and arbitrary power, by all persons under pretext of authority from the Cherokee Indians, and their laws, and to prevent white persons from residing within that part of the chartered limits of Georgia, occupied by the Cherokee Indians, and to provide a guard for the protection of the gold mines, and to enforce the laws of the State within the aforesaid territory," (Dec. 22, 1830), Acts of the General Assembly of the State of Georgia, Annual Sess. in Nov. and Dec. 1830 (Milledgeville: Camak & Ragland, 1831) at 114–117.

51.   Garrison (2002) at 25.

52.   "Plan for Extinguishing the Cherokee Claim To Land In Georgia, Tennessee, And Alabama," (Doc. No. 215, Jan. 12, 1825), 18th Cong., 2d. Sess.; "Plan For Removing The Several Indian Tribes West Of The Mississippi River (Doc. No. 218, Jan. 27, 1825), printed in *American State Papers: Documents, Legislative and Executive: Indian Affairs* (Washington, DC: Gales and Seaton, 1834), Vol. 2 at pp. 526–29 and 541–47, respectively.

53.   4 Stat. 411.

54.   Rennard Strickland, et al., eds., *Cohen's Handbook of Federal Indian Law* (Michie Bobbs-Merrill, 1982 ed.) at 81.

55.   Sections 1–2, "An Act to prevent the exercise of assumed and arbitrary power, by all persons under pretext of authority from the Cherokee Indians, and their laws, and to prevent white persons from residing within that part of the chartered limits of Georgia, occupied by the Cherokee Indians, and to provide a guard for the protection of the gold mines, and to enforce the laws of the State within the aforesaid territory," (Dec. 22, 1830), Acts of the General Assembly of the State of Georgia, Annual Sess. in Nov. and Dec. 1830 (Milledgeville: Camak & Ragland, 1831) at 114–117.

56.   Id.

57.   "An Act to authorize the survey and disposition of lands within the limits of Georgia, in the occupancy of the Cherokee tribe of Indians, etc." (Dec. 21, 1830), Acts of the General Assembly of the State of Georgia, Annual Sess. in Nov. and Dec. 1830 (Milledgeville: Camak & Ragland, 1831) at 127–143.

58.   Id., Section 31.

59.   Conser (1978) at 205.

60.   "An Act to authorize the Governor to take possession of the Gold, Silver and other Mines, lying and being in that section of the chartered limits of Georgia, commonly called the Cherokee country, etc." (Dec. 2, 1830), Acts of the General Assembly of the State of Georgia, Annual Sess. in Nov. and Dec. 1830 (Milledgeville: Camak & Ragland, 1831) at 154–156.

61.   "Memorial of John Ross and Others, Representatives of the Cherokee Nation of Indians," *New American State Papers: Indian Affairs* IA, Vol. 9 at 136–141.

62.   Id., at 107.

63.   *Georgia v. Tassels,* 1 Georgia Reports, Annotated 478 (Hall Superior Court, 1830) (Charlottesville, VA: The Michie Co., 1903).

64.   Id., at 478.

65.   Id.

66.   Id.

67.   Id., at 479–480.

68.   Id., at 479–481. The *Tassels* court pointed to the historical use of the Constitution's war power provisions in Indian affairs to support its conclusions. It noted that while Congress is empowered to declare war, none of the Indian wars are supported by "a single declaration of war" (Id., at 480). Since tribes are apparently not the proper objects of a declaration of war, the court could not "conceive how any person…can come to the conclusion that the Cherokee Nation is a sovereign and independent State" (Id.). This reasoning assumes, of course, that the Indian wars were legal wars. The legal basis for those wars and the use of force against Native Americans is considered in the next chapter.

69.   Id., at 481.

70.   Id. The court never defined what it meant by the "state of pupilage" relationship. Just when or how Georgia assumed that role is unclear, since it never undertook to educate the Cherokee, instruct them in the finer arts of civilized life, or provide for their well-being. Nor did the Cherokee Nation request tutelage from Georgia. What a cruel joke for the court to rely on that

pretext. Hostile Georgia was bent on destroying and removing the Cherokee; and the Indians were trying to escape Georgia rule. Guardianship under those circumstances would *really* short-change the Indians, since pupilage is no substitute for independent nationhood status, free from state interference, or for enforceable legal protections, which the Cherokee Nation sought from the federal courts.

71. Id.
72. Id., at 480.
73. Id., at 481.
74. House of Representatives Resolution (Dec. 22, 1830), supra, note 2 at 282–283.
75. Id., at 283.
76. *Cherokee Nation v. Georgia,* 30 US 1 (1831).
77. Id., at 3. The complaint added that "from time immemorial the Cherokee nation have composed a sovereign and independent state, and in this character have been repeatedly recognized, and still stand recognized by the United States, in the various treaties subsisting between their nation and the United States" (Id.).
78. Id.
79. Id., at 4.
80. Id.
81. Id., at 7.
82. Id.
83. Id.
84. Id., at 8.
85. Id., at 10.
86. Id., at 12–13.
87. Id., at 12.
88. Id., at 16.
89. Id., at 12.
90. Id., at 14, 52.
91. As noted above, Georgia mooted out the *Tassels* appeal, thus ending the Cherokee Nation's opportunity to obtain direct Supreme Court review of a state court decision upholding the extension laws. Furthermore, Georgia rebuffed Wirt's proposal to litigate their differences in federal court so as to obtain an authoritative declaration of the parties' respective legal rights (Garrison [2002], supra, note 13 at 110–111). Since a suit against state officials was likely barred by Eleventh Amendment sovereign immunity, an original action in the US Supreme Court under Article III, Section 2, of the US Constitution was the only avenue left to obtain judicial review of the extension statutes by the high court.
92. *Cherokee Nation v. Georgia,* 30 US at 15.
93. Id., at 16 (Marshall, C. J., majority opinion).
94. Id., at 18.
95. Id., at 20–21 (Johnson, J., concurring opinion.)
96. Id.
97. Id., at 23.
98. Id., at 24.
99. Id., at 27–28.
100. Id., at 29.
101. Id., at 32 (Baldwin, J., concurring opinion).
102. Id., at 17 (Marshall, C. J., majority opinion).
103. Id.
104. The dissenting opinion of justices Story and Thompson not only considered the Cherokee Nation to be a "foreign" state, it would have granted jurisdiction and entered judgment in favor of the Cherokee. They felt the Nation was a "foreign" state under international law, because "[i]t is governed by its own laws, usages and customs: it has no connection with any other government or jurisdiction, except by way of treaties"; and even though it might be under the protection of the more powerful United States, that fact does not rob a weaker nation of its right of self-government and sovereignty (Id., at 53–57). Their dissent held that Georgia's actions impermissibly violated Cherokee treaty, sovereignty, and property rights, and would

have enjoined the state from enforcing its laws (Id., at 80).

105. Id., at 20 (Marshall, C. J., majority opinion).

106. Id., at 21.

107. Id.

108. Id., at 20, emphasis added.

109. After obtaining legal title to tribal property in the clothing of the Indians' trustee, the United States commonly shrinks from carrying out the fiduciary obligations normally imposed upon trustees—unless some act of Congress unambiguously requires the government to behave like a trustee. See, for example, *United States v. Mitchell,* 445 US 535 (1980). As you might imagine, this arrangement is convenient for the government, but has not worked out well for Indian tribes. In 2001, a federal appeals court found that the United States has mismanaged Indian trust property for "over one hundred years" (*Cobell v. United States,* 240 F.3d 1081, 1086 [D.C. Cir. 2001]). We shall explore the dark side of the federal Indian wardship system in chapter eight.

110. The powers of tribal courts afford one example. Beginning with the decision in *Oliphant v. Suquamish Indian Tribe,* 435 US 191 (1978), the Supreme Court began to trim the judicial attributes of tribal sovereignty. *Oliphant* held that tribal courts have no jurisdiction over white criminal offenders on Indian reservations. Then, in *Duro v. Reina,* 495 US 676 (1990), it ruled that tribal courts have no jurisdiction over Indians of other tribes. But for Congress's intervention to halt the lawlessness on Indian reservations arising from the loophole in law enforcement created by *Duro,* it is conceivable that the Court's next step would be to strip tribal court jurisdiction over tribal members, leaving them without any function at all.

111. *Caldwell v. State,* 1 Stew. & P. 327 (Ala. 1832), 1832 WL 545 (Ala.).

112. Id. 1832 WL 545, at page *3. (Justice Lipscomb's Opinion).

113. Id., page *3.

114. Id., page *22 (Justice Saffold's Opinion). Allowing the fox to guard the henhouse, the court held that guardianship over Indians is vested in the state and local governments (Id., page *26).

115. Id., page *40 (Justice Taylor's Opinion).

116. Id., page *48.

117. Id., page *53.

118. Id., page *57.

119. Id., page *58.

120. Garrison (2002) at 167.

121. *Worcester v. Georgia,* 31 US 515 (1832).

122. Garrison (2002) at 177.

123. *Worcester,* at 542–43.

124. Id., at 544.

125. Id., at 543–45.

126. Id., at 546.

127. Id., at 557.

128. Id., at 559.

129. Id., at 562.

130. Garrison (2002) at 192 (quoting correspondence from Justice Story to his wife).

131. Nell Jessup Newton, editor-in-chief, *Cohen's Handbook on Federal Indian Law* (LexisNexis, 2005 ed.) at 50.

132. *State v. Foreman,* 16 Tenn. 256, 1835 WL 945 (Tenn.).

133. Id., 1835 WL 945, page *4.

134. Id., at *5–6.

135. Id.

136. Id., at *6.

137. Id., at *8.

138. Id., at *12.

139. Id., at *31–32.

140. Article 9, Treaty with the Cherokees, 1835, 7 Stat. 478. T

141. Mooney (2002) at 126.

142. Id., at 130.

143. Id.

144. Id., at 133.
145. Eyewitness accounts of the forced emigration are compiled in Vicki Rozema (ed.), *Voices from The Trail of Tears* (Winston-Salem, NC: John F. Blair, 2003).
146. Joy Harjo, *A Map to the Next World: Poems and Tales* (New York: W. W. Norton, 2000) at 27.
147. The laws, decrees, and regulations comprising Germany's legal framework for removal are found in Joseph Walk, ed., *Das Sonderrecht fur die juden im NS-Staat: Eine Sammlung der gesetzlichen MaBnahmen und Richtlinen—Inhalt und Bedeutung* (Heidelberg, Germany: C.F. Muller Juristischer Verlag, 1981) at 3, 12, 17–18, 36, 53, 55, 86, 98, 104, 115–17, 122, 127, 139–41, 157–58, 161, 164, 173–74, 183, 187–88,191–92, 200, 223, 233–34, 237, 242, 244, 254–55, 276, 317, 347. Translations of this German text were provided to the author by Joanne Hayes.
148. *United States ex rel. Standing Bear v. Crook,* 25 Fed. Cas. No. 14891 (C.C. Neb. 1879). The story of this gripping case is told by Stephen Dando-Collins in *Standing Bear is s Person: The True Story of a Native American's Quest for Justice* (De Capo Press, 2004).
149. Act of August 13, 1946, ch. 959, 60 Stat. 1049. Prior to this act, no tribe could sue the United States without special permission by Congress. The act was passed to begin cleaning up the nation's ethical mess by opening the doors of the federal courts to hear tribal damages claims against the United States arising under the Constitution, laws, treaties, and executive orders for the taking of tribal property without just compensation, for claims stemming from fraud, duress, and unconscionable consideration, and for unfair and dishonorable dealings. About 370 lawsuits were filed by tribes under this law.
150. 28 U.S.C. 1362.
151. For example, in *Pro-Football, Inc. v. Harjo,* 415 F.3d 44 (D.C. Cir. 2005), seven Native Americans brought an action seeking to cancel federally protected Redskin trademarks belonging to the Washington Redskin football team on the grounds that they are impermissible, racially disparaging trademarks. The Trademark Trial and Appeals Board agreed and canceled the offensive trademark registrations. Despite the team's appeal, the case remains pending in the federal courts.
152. Mooney (2002) at 157–181.
153. The legal history of the Eastern Band is chronicled by their longtime tribal attorney, Ben Oshell Bridgers, in "An Historical Analysis of the Legal Status of the North Carolina Cherokees," 58 N.C. Law Rev. 1075 (1980). Eastern Cherokee Band websites are www.nc-cherokee.com and www.cherokee-nc.com.
154. The Cherokee Nation website is www.cherokee.org.
155. Personal Communication from Taylor Keene (January 3, 2008).
156. Many thanks to Myrtle Driver for the Cherokee script and translation.

CHAPTER 6: *CONNORS V. UNITED STATES & CHEYENNE INDIANS*: WERE THE INDIAN WARS LEGAL?

1. Among those wonderful people are my relatives RayLene Echo Hawk, Lance All Runner, and Frank Reynolds. Valued friends include Abraham Spotted Elk, Bernard Red Cherries, Cleo Heap of Birds, Frieda (Roman Nose) Primeaux, Henrietta and Montoya Whiteman, and my longtime sister, Suzan Harjo. I must also mention the late elders Ted Rising Sun, Bill Tall Bull, and Richard Tall Bull; my departed Cheyenne brother, Raymond Spang; and, of course, my former and current clients, the Northern Cheyenne Tribe and Cheyenne-Arapaho Tribes of Oklahoma, respectively. Finally, I am proud to know two especially prominent Cheyenne men, Rick West, attorney and founding director of the National Museum of the American Indian, and Ben Nighthorse Campbell, formerly a US Senator from Colorado. This chapter is respectfully dedicated to these friends and relatives.
2. It may be that our respective fates are also intertwined. During the intertribal wars, the Cheyenne and their allies carried their revered Sacred Arrows and Medicine Hat against the Pawnee Nation on two occasions. These sacred war medicines were gifts to the Cheyenne people from Sweet Medicine and when carried to war must be accompanied by the entire tribe. On the first occasion, in 1830, the Cheyenne located the *Skidi*, or Wolf, Band of the Pawnee Nation on the banks of their Loup River (called *Itskari* by the Pawnee, meaning the "River of Many Potatoes") and attacked while the *Skidi* were engaged in their Morning Star Ceremony. However, protected by the Morning Star—the mighty Pawnee warrior star—the *Skidi* captured the Sacred

Arrows. George Bird Grinnell recounted that fight from eyewitness reports in *The Fighting Cheyennes* (Charles Scribner's Sons, 1915) at 70:

> At the beginning of the fight, when the two tribes were drawn up in line of battle, a Pawnee, who had long been ill and was discouraged and no longer cared to live, went out in front of the Pawnee line and sat down on the ground so that he might be killed at once. He was touched but not killed in the first charge the Cheyennes made. After that, Bull, the Cheyenne who was carrying into the fight the medicine arrows, tied as usual near the head of a lance, rode up to the Pawnee and thrust at him with the lance. The Pawnee avoided the stroke, grasped the lance, and pulled it out of the hands of Bull, who rode away lamenting. The Pawnee, discovering the bundle tied to the lance, called to his tribesmen, who rushed up and took the arrows, though the Cheyennes made a brave charge to try to recover them. The Cheyennes gave up and rode away.

Ah, perhaps the decline and troubles endured by both tribes in the ensuing years can be traced to this incident, when the Cheyenne lost their arrows.

3.   The Iron Shirt song, which is still sung among the Pawnee, illustrates the courage and daring of the Cheyenne warriors. In 1852, the Pawnee were skinning buffalo along the Republican River when they were suddenly set upon by a large war party of five tribes, the Cheyenne, Arapaho, Sioux, Kiowa, and Kiowa-Apache. It had been an especially difficult summer buffalo hunt, because the Pawnee hunters were under constant assault, fending off a different enemy tribe almost every day. However, the Pawnee were large in number, with many warriors able to defend the people. As the battle began, one fearsome Cheyenne warrior kept riding through the Pawnee line, striking the warriors. This terrible warrior could not be killed, no matter how many arrows struck his body and fell harmlessly away. His wonderful power caused terror among the Pawnee ranks. Eagle Chief, a Pawnee chief and participant in the battle, observed:

> [The Pawnee] line of battle must have been a mile and a half long. They fought all through the forenoon and at noon stopped fighting for a time, but began again in the afternoon and presently someone came down the line who was a stranger of some sort. It was Iron Shirt.
>
> He rode one of the largest horses they had ever seen, a roan horse, and in his hand he held a saber. I myself, was standing near the west end of the line and looking over saw the man coming from the east end, holding up the saber in his hand, riding down the front of the line going toward the west. He rode close to where the Pawnees were, and as he passed them they gave back a little. When he reached the end of the Pawnee line this man did not go back the way he had come, but went around on the other side, where his own people were and went along in front of that line very slowly, and when he came to the other end of it he turned and made another charge in front of the Pawnee line, just as he had done before. He had nothing wrapped about him. He could not bend over, but sat straight up on his horse. His head was round and partly covered up by this iron, so that his hair could not be seen. (Grinnell [1915] at 78)

One Pawnee named Carrying the Shield in Front possessed sacred arrows of his own. Ready to die, he awaited the terrible warrior. As the Powers would have it, Carrying the Shield in Front shot the Cheyenne warrior in the eye as he raised his saber, and he fell from his horse. After the battle, the Pawnee discovered that the Cheyenne warrior wore a Spanish shirt of metal under his buckskin war shirt. Consequently, he was called "Iron Shirt" (*Paapicisu' Kasii'u'*) by the Pawnee, who made a song saying: "Iron Shirt, laying there, your power has been set aside." His name was Alights on the Cloud among the Cheyenne, "as handsome a man as you would ever see—a good man, kind-hearted, and very brave" (Id. 77). The Iron Shirt song pays tribute to Alights on the Cloud and to Carrying the Shield in Front, who is the ancestor of some in my own family. Ironically, my cousin, a descendent of Carrying the Shield in Front, married a descendent of Alights on the Cloud!

4.   Here is one such story. The death of Alights on the Cloud and other leading warriors in 1852, mentioned in the previous note, prompted the *Sahi* to bring another great war expedition against

the Pawnee the very next year. On that occasion, Tall Bull assembled Sioux, Arapaho, Kiowa, Apache, and Crow allies. Long Chin carried the Medicine Hat. Black Kettle, who would later survive Sand Creek but die in the attack upon the Cheyenne village at the Washita River in 1868, carried the Sacred Arrows, which had by that year been replaced. This enormous war party confronted my *Kitkahaki* Band of Pawnees during our summer buffalo hunt in the Republican River valley under the leadership of Sky Chief. The *Kitkahakis* had been hunting and camping that summer with Pottawatomie friends, parting company that very morning. When the enemy charged the Pawnee camp with overwhelming force, Sky Chief asked for help from the Pottawatomie chief who immediately sent twenty mounted warriors armed with long rifles. Recent eastern immigrants to the pains, the Pottawatomie were well-trained in the white man's military style of disciplined firing from alternating lines at an oncoming enemy. Their precision gunfire routed the attackers and saved my people from almost certain destruction. Lucky for me—perhaps that is how my family survived to this day! We are indebted to the Pottawatomie.

5.   Many Cheyenne ledger book drawings captured at the Battle of Summits Springs depict exploits between Cheyenne Dog Soldiers and Pawnee warriors, called "Wolf People" by the Cheyenne and other Plains Indians after their tribal custom of imitating the wolf during scouting and war expeditions. Those drawings are reproduced in Jean Afton, et al., *Cheyenne Dog Soldiers: A Ledgerbook History of Coups and Combat* (Boulder: Colorado Historical Society and Univ. of Colorado Press, 1997).

6.   Gregory F. Michno, *Encyclopedia of Indian Wars: Western Battles and Skirmishes, 1850–1890* (Missoula, MT: Mountain Press, 2003) at 364.

7.   Larry McMurtry, *Oh What a Slaughter: Massacres in the American West: 1846–1890* (New York: Simon & Schuster, 2005) at 102.

8.   *Connors v. US and Cheyenne Indians,* 33 C. Cl. 317 (1898), 1800 WL 2047 (Ct. Cl.), aff'd, 180 US 271 (1901).

9.   *Johnson v. M'Intosh,* 21 US 543, 588–592 (1823).

10.   Stuart Banner, *How the Indians Lost Their Land: Law and Power on the Frontier* (Cambridge: Belknap Press of Harvard Univ., 2005). Law professor Robert J. Miller correctly found in his comprehensive examination of the doctrine of discovery in *Native America, Discovered and Conquered: Thomas Jefferson, Lewis & Clark, and Manifest Destiny* (Westport: Praeger Publishers, 2006) at 57 that it "is a proven fact that the vast majority of Indian lands in America were purchased with tribal assent at treaty sessions and were not taken by military conquests."

11.   *Johnson v. M'Intosh,* supra, at 589.

12.   Id., at 591.

13.   Id., at 588.

14.   Philip J. Prygoski, "War As the Prevailing Metaphor in Federal Indian Law Jurisprudence: An Exercise in Judicial Activism," 14 T. M. Cooley L. Rev. 491 (1997).

15.   *Cherokee Nation v. Georgia,* 30 US 1, 22– 23, 29 (1831) (Johnson, J., concurring). Justice Johnson's opinion is jingoistic. It reflects the military mind-set of a nation poised for war against Native Americans. He wrote, "the right of discovery gave the right of dominion over the country discovered" and, finding the continent already inhabited by Indian tribes, "the right was extended to the absolute appropriation of the territory, the annexation of it to the domain of the discoverer…the preemptive right, and exclusive right of conquest in case of war was never questioned—[Indian tribes merely] receive the territory allotted to them as a boon, from a master or conqueror," and, finally, he characterized Georgia's claims of ownership and sovereignty as a "war in disguise" that cannot be resolved by "any arbiter but the sword." To him, the Indian nations were proper subjects for conquest, and the courts should not interfere.

16.   See, for example, Tim Alan Garrison, *The Legal Ideology of Removal: The Southern Judiciary and the Sovereignty of Native American Nations* (Athens: Univ. of Georgia Press, 2002) at 117. The Southern judiciary made much of the fact that the United States fought many wars against Indian nations yet never issued a declaration of war against them, suggesting that savage Indian tribes do not merit declarations of war like other sovereign nations. Some of these judges fought against Indians in the Creek War of 1813–14, and their opinions exhibit marked antipathy toward them (Id., at 156).

17.   *Tee-Hit-Ton v. United States,* 348 US 272, 322 (1955). Recent legal research on the comprehensive history of Indian land acquisition in the United States demonstrates that Justice Reed's

statement is erroneous. See Miller (2006) and Banner (2005).

18. *Worcester v. Georgia,* 31 US 515, 544–45 (1832). Justice Marshall continued: "They were well understood to convey the title which, according to the common law of European sovereigns respecting America, they might rightfully convey, and nothing more. This was the exclusive right of purchasing such lands as the natives were willing to sell. "

19. *Brown v. Board of Education,* 347 US 483 (1954); *Plessy v. Ferguson,* 163 US 537 (1896).

20. *Worcester v. Georgia,* 31 US at 552.

21. Id., at 555.

22. Id., at 561.

23. Id., at 556.

24. Id., at 582 (M'Lean, J., concurring).

25. Id., at 583 (M'Lean, J., concurring).

26. *Merriam-Webster's Collegiate Dictionary* (Springfield: Merriam-Webster, 11th ed., 2005) at 264.

27. Miller (2006) and Banner (2005). There are isolated instances of Indian land appropriated by war. For examples, the Creek Nation lost about one-half of its aboriginal land as a result of the Creek War of 1813; some of the other five Civilized Tribes lost land in treaties following the Civil War as a result of their affiliation with the Confederacy; and a few eastern tribes lost land in treaties following the Revolutionary War due to their alliance with Britain (*Cohen's Handbook of Federal Indian Law,* [LexisNexis, Mathew Bender, 2005 ed.] [Nell Jessup Newton, editor-in-chief] at 44, 72). However, appropriation of Indian land by war was not the general policy. Far more acres were obtained by treaty cessions, which account for two billion acres, the Indian Removal policy, and the allotment of Indian lands, which account for more than fifty million acres (Id., at 8, 16–17, 45, 79). See also Felix S. Cohen, "Original Land Title," 32 Minn. L. Rev. 28, 34–43 (1947) (discourse on "How we bought the United States").

28. *Montoya v. United States,* 180 US 261, 267 (1901). By 1973, the courts seem to have accepted that the law of war applies to the Indian wars but still continued to suggest that different standards might apply (*Fort Sill Apache Tribe v. United States,* 477 F.2d 1310, 1370 [Ct. Cl., 1973] [wondering, but not deciding, whether standards applicable to "warfare between civilized nations generally, or special ones developed for frontier conflicts with savage tribes" applied to the Indian wars]).

29. *Cohen's* (2005 ed.) at 79.

30. The United States' war record began in the eighteenth century, with armed conflict in the Revolutionary War (1775–1783) and the numerous Indian wars (1790–1890), which were waged almost continuously for a hundred years. That conflict was punctuated throughout the nineteenth century by naval operations against France (1798–1801), the War of 1812 (1812–15), the Mexican-American War (1846–58), the American Civil War (1861–65), the overthrow of the Kingdom of Hawaii (1887), and the Spanish-American War (1898–1902). The twentieth century began with quelling rebels in lands occupied by the United States, such as in the Boxer Rebellion (1900–01) and the Philippine-American War (1899–1913), immediately followed by the occupation of Vera Cruz, Mexico (1914), the Pershing Expedition into Mexico (1916), and an all-out war in World War I (1917–19). The remainder the twentieth century and up to the present is marked by total war during World War II (1941–45), a constant state of alert during the cold war (mid-1940s to early 1990s)—including extensive conflict in Korea (1950–53) and Vietnam (1963–1974)—followed by the invasions of Lebanon (1982), Grenada (1983), Libya (1986), Panama (1989), Iraq (1990–91), Somalia (1991), Afghanistan (2001–present), and Iraq (2003–present). War, it seems, is our way of life. Aside from the conquest of outer space and the conquest of nature, we also have the drug war, the war on crime, and the war on terror, which have preoccupied the government for many years. I do not count them as "real" wars in the eyes of the law, because they are not waged against any particular nation and may be unknown to the law of war. They are waged by the government to punish legal wrongs committed against the United States, to be sure. However, the enemies are merely individuals or groups of criminals, drug dealers, and Islamic terrorists, wherever located.

31. Prygoski (1997) at 496–97.

32. Felix S. Cohen, *Cohen's Handbook of Federal Indian Law* (Albuquerque: Univ. of New Mexico Press, reprint of 1942 ed.) at 28 (quoting a 1938 Bureau of Indian Affairs Report), 93.

33. Some have argued in recent times that courts are incapable of defining war or when or whether

a formal declaration of war is required under the US Constitution before the country can legally go to war, because these are "political questions" which can only be answered by the executive or legislative branches of government. This argument was advanced by President George W. Bush in *Dellums v. Bush,* 752 F. Supp. 1141 (D.D.C. 1990), when fifty-four members of Congress sued the president, asserting that only Congress may authorize war in Iraq. The president's argument was rejected. The court stated, "courts have historically made determinations about whether this country was at war for many other purposes—the construction of treaties, statutes, and even insurance contracts" (Id., at 1146). Courts are competent to construe the Constitution, including the War Powers Clause. Though the court dismissed the action as being premature, it stated that it would not hesitate to hold that "an offensive entry into Iraq by several hundred thousand United States servicemen" is "a 'war' within the meaning of Article I, Section 8, Clause 11, of the Constitution" (Id.).

34. *Tingy v. Bas,* 4 US 37, 40–41 (1800).

35. Id.

36. The Supreme Court reaffirmed *Tingy's* distinction between perfect and imperfect war in *Talbot v. Seeman,* 5 US (1 Cranch) 1 (1801), and the courts were still relying upon that dichotomy as late as 1886, in *Gray v. United States,* 21 Ct Cl. 340, 375 (1886). More recently, commentators have advanced the state-of-war doctrine as a subjective test for determining whether a state of war exists based upon the following criteria: (1) There is a declaration of war; (2) In the absence of a declaration of war, one nation commits hostilities against another and requests others to observe rules of neutrality; or (3) An act of aggression is committed against a nation who regards it as creating a state of war (Jeffrey C. Tuomala, "Just Cause: The Thread That Runs So True," 13 Dick. J. Int'l L. 1, 253–60 [1994]).

37. *Montoya v. United States,* supra, 180 US at 267. By contrast, the arrest of a small group of Indians by the military sent to an Indian reservation to quell unrest does not amount to a war, even though shots may be exchanged (*Ex parte Bi-A-Lil-Le,* 100 P. 450 [S. Ct. Az. Terr., 1909]).

38. US Bureau of the Census (1894), cited in Russell Thornton, *American Indian Holocaust and Survival: A Population History Since 1492* (Norman: Univ. of Oklahoma Press, 1987) at 48.

39. Id., at 49.

40. Michno (2003) at 3.

41. Id., at 360.

42. Id.

43. Recalling this campaign and other Indian wars, one Pawnee Scout veteran named Arrives First made these observations in 1900, while making cylinder recordings at the Smithsonian Institution:

> I think back over my long life with its many experiences; of the great number of Pawnees who have been with me in war, nearly all of whom have been killed in battle. I have been severely wounded many times—see this scar over my eye. I was with those who went to the Rocky Mountains to the Cheyennes, when so many soldiers were slain that their dead bodies lying there looked like a great blue blanket spread over the ground. When I think of all the people of my own tribe who have died during my lifetime and then of those in other tribes that have fallen by our hands, they are so many they make a vast cover over Mother Earth. I once walked with these prostrate forms. I did not fall but I passed on, wounded sometimes, but not to death, until I am here today doing this thing, singing these sacred songs into that great pipe [the graphophone] and am telling you of these ancient rites of my people. It must be that I have been preserved for this purpose, otherwise I should be lying back there among the dead. (Alice C. Fletcher, *The Hako: A Pawnee Ceremony,* [Washington: Government Printing Office, 1904] at 278)

This difficult winter campaign is chronicled in Jerome A. Greene's excellent account, *Morning Star Dawn: The Powder River Expedition and the Northern Cheyenne, 1876* (Norman: Univ. of Oklahoma Press, 2003). The colorful history of the Pawnee Scouts is recounted by Martinus J. M. van de Logt, "War Party in Blue: Pawnee Indian Scouts in the United States Army, 1864–1877," (PhD Dissertation, Oklahoma State University, Oklahoma, 2002).

44. Act of March 3, 1891, c. 538, sec. 1, 26 Stat. 851.
45. *Connors,* 1800 WL 2047 at *3.
46. Id., at *6.
47. Id., at *2.
48. Id., at *3.
49. Id., at *3–4.
50. Id., at *2.
51. Id., at *4.
52. Id. By October 3, when Morning Star's band surrendered, thirty-one soldiers and settlers had been killed.
53. Thomas R. Buecker, *Fort Robinson and the American West, 1874–1899* (Norman: Univ. of Oklahoma Press, 1999) at 125–148.
54. *Connors,* at *4.
55. Captain Henry W. Wessells Jr., the post commander, acted on his own in cutting off the food, fuel, and water in an effort to persuade the Cheyenne to return to Indian Territory. He reported his actions to his superiors and received no objection from them (Mari Sandoz, *Cheyenne Autumn* [New York: Hastings House Publishers, 1953] at 240; Buecker [1991], supra, note 53 at 139 [citing military records]).
56. The Cheyenne account of the tragic breakout is reported by Grinnell (1915), supra, note 2 at 399–411; and Sandoz (1953), supra, note 55 at 194–237. The same account based upon military records is presented in Buecker (1999), supra, note 53 at 125–48.
57. *Connors,* at *4–5. This does not account for Little Wolf's Band, who successfully made their way to Montana and eventually settled on the Tongue River Reservation, Montana, which is the present homeland of the Northern Cheyenne Tribe. Nor does it account for small groups of Indians who escaped from Fort Robinson into the snowy night, including Morning Dtar, who found refuge among the Sioux and ultimately resettled on the Tongue River Reservation.
58. Bueker (1999) at 146–47.
59. Sandoz (1953) at 270.
60. *Connors,* at *5.
61. Id.
62. Id.
63. Id.
64. Id.
65. *United State ex rel. Standing Bear v. Crook,* 25 Fed. Cas. No. 14891 (C.C. Neb. 1879).
66. Rejecting the government's contention that Indians cannot sue in the courts of the United States since they are not citizens, the court observed "it would be a sad commentary on the justice and impartiality of our laws to hold that Indians, though natives of, our own country, cannot test the validity of an alleged illegal imprisonment in this manner, as well as a subject of a foreign government who may happen to be sojourning in this country, but owing it no sort of allegiance" (Id.).
67. The court stated:

> I have searched in vain for the semblance of any authority justifying the commissioner in attempting to remove by force any Indians, whether belonging to a tribe or not, to any place, or for any other purpose than [being on an Indian reservation other than their own in violation of federal law]. Certainly without some specific authority found in an act of congress, or in a treaty with the Ponca tribe of Indians, he could not lawfully force the [Poncas] back to the Indian Territory, to remain and die in that country, against their will. In the absence of all treaty stipulations or laws of the United States authorizing such removal, I must conclude that no such authority exists. It is true, if the…government might, in time of war, remove them to any place of safety so long as the war should last, but perhaps no longer, unless they were charged with the commission of some crime. This is a war power merely, and exists in time of war only. Every nation exercises the right to arrest and detain an alien enemy during the existence of a war, and all subjects or citizens of the hostile nations are subject to be dealt with under this rule.

The Northern Cheyenne situation seems similar. They were friendly Indians not at war with the United States at the time they were ordered back to the reservation and fired upon, as found in the *Connors* case. As such, they might have successfully tested the legality of their purported confinement in civilian courts and established that they were not hostile Indians detained as prisoners of war under the war powers of the United States or any other legal authority. See, for example, *Fort Sill Apache Tribe v. United States*, 477 F.2d at 1371–72 (Nichols, J., dissenting) (noting in dicta that the Apaches might not have successfully obtained a writ of habeas corpus in civilian courts under *Standing Bear's* rule, since they had specifically surrendered as "prisoners of war to an army in the field" and were detained under the government's war powers.)

68.   Id. Likewise, Felix S. Cohen found no legal authority to force Indians to stay on reservations: "Although there never was any legal authority for confining Indians on reservations, administrators relied upon the magic solving word "wardship" to justify the assertion of such authority" (*Felix S. Cohen's Handbook of Federal Indian Law* [1942 ed.] at 177). Military authorities cannot simply arrest and confine Indians without some legal source of authority, even though they are wards of the government (*Ex Parte Bi-A-Lil-Le*, 100 P. 450 [S. Ct. Az. Terr. 1909]).

69.   Sandoz (1953), supra, note 55 at 96.

70.   The Prize Cases, 67 US (2 Black) 635, 670 (1862).

71.   See, generally, Tuomala (1994) at 2.

72.   In The Prize Cases, supra, the Supreme Court held that a legal public war existed between the United States and its southern states, even though the South was not an independent nation in the ordinary sense of the word, and, as such, the customary international law of war governed the conflict. The Court observed that normally "[t]he parties belligerent in a public war are independent nations," but ruled that under international law "it is not necessary to constitute war, that both parties should be acknowledged as independent nations or sovereign States" since "[a] war may exist where one of the belligerents, claims sovereign rights as against the other" (67 US at 666). See also *Mathews v. McStea*, 91 US 7 (1875) (holding that civil war brings with it all the legal consequences that attend a war between independent foreign nations). The Revolutionary War was a public war, even though one of the belligerents, the United States, may not technically have been considered an independent nation at that time (*Ware v. Hylton*, 3 US 199, 210–11 [1796]). Thus, under US law, the law of nations pertaining to war clearly applies to an internal war waged by an independent nation against inhabitants organized for rebellion.

73.   In *Montoya v. United States*, supra, the Supreme Court held that the United States may engage in public war against Indian nations, even though they are not independent nations in the ordinary sense contemplated by international law. It observed that Indian wars are public wars that can be commenced without a declaration of war. Since war can exist when one belligerent is an Indian nation, the law of nations pertaining to war comes into play.

74.   *Cherokee Nation v. Georgia*, 30 US at 16, describes Indian tribes as "domestic dependent nations," with sufficient sovereignty to be "capable of maintaining the relations of peace and war" and "of being responsible in their political character...for any aggression committed on the citizens of the United States, by any individual of their community." Thus, even though Indian nations were placed under the protection of the United States, they still retained control over relations of war and peace with the United States. *Worcester v. Georgia*, 31 US at 548, reiterated that both England and the United States regarded Indian nations "as nations capable of maintaining the relations of peace and war." The Court stated:

> We have recognized in them the right to make war. No one has ever supposed that the Indians could commit treason against the United States. We have punished them for their violation of treaties; but we have inflicted the punishment on them as a nation, and not on individual offenders among them as traitors. (Id., M'Lean, J., concurring)

Further, in *Marks v. United States*, 161 US 297 (1896), the Supreme Court rejected a contention that Indian tribes, as dependent people, "are not capable of making war with the United States" for purposes of applying the Indian Depredation Act. See also Carol Chomsky, "The United States-Dakota War Trials: A Study in Military Justice," 43 Stan. L. Rev. 13, 74–81 (1990) (pointing out that the treatment of Indian tribes in wartime over the course of US history shows consistent recognition of their right to wage war.)

75. *Tingy v. Bas*, supra. By contrast, ants draw no distinction between general and limited war. They stick to general warfare, leaving us to wonder whether our concept of limited war is too nebulous to be of much use in the natural world.

76. Tuomala (1994) at 3.

77. The Prize Cases, supra, at 690 (Nelson, J., dissenting).

78. See, for example, Gesina H. J. Van Der Molen, *Alberico Gentili and the Development of International Law* (A. W. Sijthoff—Leyden, 1968) (2nd ed.); at 80–86; James Brown Scott, *The Spanish Origins of International Law: Francisco de Victoria and His Law of Nations* (Oxford: Clarendon Press, 1934) (Part 1) at 9a. Emmerich de Vattel's *Law of Nations* has also exercised immense influence on the American legal tradition, as pointed out by Tuomala (1994) at n.1. Vattel is frequently cited in nineteenth-century Indian cases, such as *Johnson v. M'Intosh*, supra, 21 US at 571 (1823), *Cherokee Nation v. Georgia*, supra, 30 US at 53 (Thompson, J., dissenting), *Worcester v. Georgia*, supra, 31 US at 520, 561, and war cases, such as *Ware v. Hylton*, supra, (*in passim*), the Prize Cases, supra, 67 US at 645, 667, *Tingy v. Bas*, supra, 4 US at 37, and *Marks v. United States*, supra, 161 US at 301. See also *Cohen's Handbook of Federal Indian Law* (2005 ed.) at 10–14.

79. The Prize Cases, supra.

80. Tuomala (1994) at 20–34.

81. For example, in 1690, Victoria arbitrarily articulated four flimsy legal wrongs, supposedly derived from immutable principles of natural law, which if violated by Indians furnish Spain with just cause for an offensive war of conquest. See Franciscus de Victoria, *De Indis Et De Ivre Belli Relectiones* (Carnegie Institute of Washington, 1917) (James B. Scott and Ernest Nys, eds.) at 151–57. According to Victoria, Indians must allow Spanish colonists the rights to:

    1. travel and sojourn in Indian lands under Victoria's "be-kind-to-tourists" rule
    2. commercially exploit the New World whether Indians like it or not
    3. partake in communally-owned property under Victoria's "me-too" rule
    4. convert Indians to Christianity

    Victoria concluded: "If the Indians wish to prevent the Spaniards from enjoying any of their above-named rights under the law of nations…they deny the Spaniards their rights under the law of nations [and] do them a wrong. Therefore, if it be necessary, in order to preserve their right, that they should go to war, they may lawfully do so" (Id., at 154). These innocuous-sounding rights rest on flaky ground today, just as they did in 1690. The Spanish have no inherent right to do any of these things in the United States. Victoria's self-serving grounds for war are exceedingly transparent. They were espoused solely to allow Spain to wage offensive war in the New World for illegitimate purposes—conquest and religious conversion, and nothing more. Manufactured by a Spanish partisan, Victoria's incorporation of these so-called legal wrongs into his law of war illustrates the evil of judging conquest by the law of the would-be conqueror. Those irregularities impugn the integrity of Victoria's law and rightfully arouse cynicism and suspicion about the law of the conqueror.

82. Scott (1934) at 181 (citing St. Augustine).

83. Id., at 208. For example, in discussing the Mexican-American War, the Supreme Court in *Fleming v. Page*, 50 US 603, 614–15 (1850), noted that the president as commander-in-chief does not have the power to conduct war simply for conquest or to acquire territory, since Congress cannot be presumed to issue a declaration of war for those purposes.

84. John Alan Cohan, "Legal War: When Does It Exist, and When Does It End?," 27 Hastings Int'l & Comp. L. Rev. 221, 225 (2004). For example, in the Prize Cases (1862), the Supreme Court stated, "War has been well defined to be, 'That state in which a nation prosecutes its right by force'" (67 US at 666).

85. The Supreme Court correctly identified the sweeping legal consequences of war in the Prize Cases, 67 US at 687–88 (dissenting opinion). The people of the warring nations immediately become enemies. Intercourse between them is illegal. Treaties, contracts, and debts among belligerents are suspended. The property of each enemy is subject to capture and confiscation, ports blockaded, and land invaded. International relations with neutral nations are affected. Together, these factors work tremendous psychological, legal, and social changes that profoundly affect every nation and its citizens.

86. Tuomala (1994) at 10–11 (citing Vattel).
87. Id., at 11.
88. Id. (citing Vattel).
89. Similarly, when the issuance of a declaration of war becomes a hollow formality, its important purposes are disserved. This is the case with Spain's rote declaration of war against indigenous peoples in the New World. The *Requeremiento* was a nonsensical ultimatum read to uncomprehending Indians, and sometimes whispered out of earshot, before an attack upon them could legally begin under Spanish law. The silly procedure accomplished none of the objectives sought by international law and was invoked purely as a pretext for war. The *Requeremiento* is also flawed because its contents do not disclose a just cause for offensive war. Only religious conversion and a bare desire for domain and empire were asserted as grounds for war, which are inherently unjust causes of war. The demented declaration of war reads more like a TV sermon delivered by a barefooted preacher urgently demanding a love offering from late-night viewers:

> In the name of King Ferdinand and Juana, his daughter, Queen of Castile and Leon, etc., conquerors of barbarian nations, we notify you as best we can that our Lord God Eternal created Heaven and earth and a man and woman from whom we all descend for all times and all over the world. In the 5,000 years since creation the multitude of these generations caused men to divide and establish kingdoms in various parts of the world, among whom God chose St. Peter as leader of mankind, regardless of their law, sect or belief. He seated St. Peter in Rome as the best place from which to rule the world but he allowed him to establish his seat in all parts of the world and rule all people, whether Christians, Moors, Jews, Gentiles or any other sect. He was named Pope, which means admirable and greatest father, governor of all men. Those who lived at that time obeyed St. Peter as Lord and superior King of the Universe, and so did their descendants obey his successors and so on to the end of time.
>
> The late Pope gave these islands and mainland of the ocean and the contents thereof to the above-mentioned King and Queen, as is certified in writing and you may see the documents if you should so desire. Therefore, Their Highnesses are lords and masters of this land; they were acknowledged as such when this notice was posted, and were and are being served willingly and without resistance; then, their religious envoys were acknowledged and obeyed without delay, and all subjects unconditionally and of their own free will became Christians and thus they remain. Their Highnesses received their allegiance with joy and benignity and decreed that they be treated in this spirit like good and loyal vassals and you are under the obligation to do the same.
>
> Therefore, we request that you understand this text, deliberate on its contents within a reasonable time, and recognize the Church and its highest priest, the Pope, as rulers of the universe, and in their name the King and Queen of Spain as rulers of this land, allowing the religious fathers to preach our holy Faith to you. You owe compliance as a duty to the King and we in his name will receive you with love and charity, respecting your freedom and that of your wives and sons and your rights of possession, and we shall not compel you to baptism unless you, informed of the Truth, wish to convert to our holy Catholic Faith as almost all your neighbors have done in other islands, in exchange for which Their Highnesses bestow many privileges and exemptions upon you. *Should you fail to comply, or delay maliciously in so doing, we assure you that with the help of God we shall use force against you, declaring war upon you from all sides and with all possible means, and we shall bind you to the yoke of the Church and of Their Highnesses; we shall enslave your persons, wives, sons, sell you or dispose of you as the Kings sees fit; we shall seize your possessions and harm you as much as we can as disobedient and resisting vassals. And we declare you guilty of resulting deaths and injuries, exempting Their Highnesses of such guilt as well as ourselves and the gentlemen who accompany us.* We hereby request that legal signatures be affixed to this text and pray those present to bear witness for us, etc. (Reprinted in Bartolomé de Las Casas, *History*

of the Indies [New York: Harper & Row, 1971] [Andree Collard, tr.] at 192–93 [emphasis added])

90.   Tuomala (1994) at 54–57.

91.   Id., at 57–58.

92.   Id., at 58–59.

93.   Id. 59 (citing St. Augustine).

94.   See notes 71–74 and accompanying text.

95.   *Montoya v. United States,* supra, 180 US at 267.

96.   Id. See also note 74 (citing *Cherokee Nation, Worcester,* and *Marks*); *Cohen's Handbook of Federal Indian Law* (2005 ed.), supra note 27 at 27 (noting that the capacity of Indian nations to make war was frequently recognized in treaties.)

97.   *Cohen's Handbook of Federal Indian Law* (1942 ed.) at 274.

98.   *Montoya v. United States,* 180 US at 267. A fact-based test was used by the courts under the Indian Depredation Act to determine whether an Indian nation was at peace or war. The Indian Depredation Act test asked only whether a state of war *in fact* existed by looking at the following factors, leaving aside the legal aspects of war: "the fact that Indians are engaged in acts of general hostility to settlers, especially if the government has deemed it necessary to dispatch a military force for their subjugation, is sufficient to constitute a state of war" (Id., citing *United States v. Marks,* supra). *Connors* itself used this test to determine the rancher's damages claim. The definition of a *state of war* in the above context was espoused simply to assist the Court in construing Congress's intended meaning of the statutory phrase *in amity.* It does not necessarily articulate a state of war in the *legal* sense nor purport to apply the law of nations. See *Marks v. United States,* supra, 161 US at 301. Thus, the *Montoya* and *Marks* definitions were not intended to be declarations of international law.

99.   *Dobbs v. United States and Apache Indians,* 33 Ct. Cl. 308, 1800 WL 2046 (Ct. Cl.), p. *4. Judge Nott noted that principles of international law applicable to the determination of peace and war are comparatively easy to apply to well-defined Indian tribes with whom the United States has entered into distinct treaties and with whom the United States has specifically made peace or engaged in war, however, it becomes much harder to apply those principles to indistinct bands having no semblance of tribal government (Id., at *5).

100. *Tingy v. Bas,* supra; *Ware v. Hylton,* supra.

101. *Matthews v. McStea,* supra; the Prize Cases, supra; *Dole v. Merchants' Mutual Marine Insurance Co.,* 51 Me. 465 (Me. 1863), 1863 WL 1315 (Me) .

102. Article I, Sec. 8, Cl. 10–11 authorize Congress to declare war, grant letters of marquee and reprisal, and define and punish offenses against the law of nations. Under Article II, Sec. 2, Cl. 1, the president is commander-in-chief of the US armed forces and the state militia.

103. Northwest Ordinance of 1781, reenacted by the Act of August 7, 1879, ch. 8, 1 Stat. 50.

104. In the Prize Cases, 67 US at 668, the Supreme Court recognized that Congress alone can declare war, but noted that if war begins by the invasion of a foreign nation or an internal attack by rebels, "the President is not only authorized but bound to resist force by force."

105. During the nineteenth century, nations increasingly failed to commence war through formal declarations of war (Tuomala [1994] at 31–33). Precisely when a formal declaration of war was needed under American law is confusing. Congress has only issued five declarations of war, usually after hostilities have commenced: in the War of 1812, the Mexican War of 1846, the Spanish-American War of 1898, World War I, and World War II; and no declaration of war was issued in any of the Indian wars (*Cohen's Handbook of Federal Indian Law* [2005 ed.], at 243–45, 264–66).

American law distinguished between (1) offensive and defensive war and (2) wars of the general and limited kind. The courts affirmed that only Congress has the authority to initiate all offense wars. A declaration of war was clearly required for a general offensive war between independent nations, but not to repel attack in a defensive war that could be waged by the president without a declaration of war. Nor was a declaration of war required to wage an internal civil war or a limited war authorized by Congress by statute. See the Prize Cases, 67 US at 667–70; *Tingy v. Bas,* 4 US at 43; Tuomala (1994) at 33. The rule that the president "has no power to initiate or declare a war either against a foreign nation or a domestic State," espoused in the Prize Cases at 668, clearly applies to an offensive general war. Furthermore, limited war could be waged only within parameters set by Congress despite the absence of a formal declaration of war; however this requirement was honored more in the breach since many statutes authorizing limited war were enacted after hostilities had already commenced. As late as 1896, some litigants still argued that war between nations cannot exist without a formal declaration of war by Congress. See *Montoya v. United States,* supra, 180 US at 267; *Marks v. United States,* supra, 161 US at 300–01. The Supreme Court in *Montoya* stated in dicta that "as between the United States and other civilized nations, an act of Congress is necessary to a formal declaration war, no such act is necessary to constitute a state of war with an Indian tribe" (180 US at 267). Like other types of limited war, then, Indian wars are internal domestic wars that can be waged pursuant to statutory authorization in the absence of a formal declaration of war.

106. *Tingy v. Bas,* 4 US at 43 (Chase, J., concurring) ("If a general war is declared, its extent and operations are only restricted and regulated by the *jus belli,* forming a part of the law of nations; but if a partial war is waged, its extent and operation depend on our municipal laws"; but even then the rules of war apply to limited partial wars.).

107. In the naval operations against France, for example, which constituted a limited war, Congress "authorized hostilities on the high seas by certain persons in certain cases," but there was "no authority to commit hostilities on land...and the authority [was] not given, indiscriminately, to every citizen of *America,* against every citizen of *France*; but only to citizens appointed by commissions, or exposed to immediate outrage" (Id.). It was an imperfect war "as to certain objects, and to a certain extent" (Id., at 45 [Paterson, J., concurring]). Thus, it is necessary to make a particularized inquiry into the law authorizing each limited war, such as an Indian war, to determine the extent and limits of the hostilities authorized by Congress.

108. The Civil War is a case in point. See the Prize Cases, 67 US at 667 ("it is evident that the common laws of war—those maxims of humanity, moderation, and honor—ought to be observed by both parties in every civil war.") In *Mathews v. McStea,* supra, 91 US at 10, the Supreme Court explained that "civil war brings with it all the consequences...which attend upon and follow a state of foreign war." In short, no distinction is made between foreign and domestic war—the rules of war apply with equal force in both instances. See, for example, the Prize Cases, supra (right of prize and capture of enemy ships); *Ware v. Hylton,* supra (treatment of debts between enemies during the Revolutionary War); *Mathews v. McStea,* supra (commercial intercourse during the Civil War); *Dole v. Merchants' Mutual Marine Insurance Co.,* supra (rebels were lawful belligerents during the Civil War).

109. Chomsky (1990) at 66. The Lieber Code, "Instructions for the Government of Armies of the United States in the Field," US Army, General Orders No. 100 (April 24, 1863), can be found on the Internet at www.civilwarhome.com/liebercode.htm.

110. Section I, Paragraph 22 of the code states: "the unarmed citizen is to be spared in person, property, and honor as much as the exigencies of war will admit."

111. § III, ¶ 57. When the Apaches under Geronimo surrendered in 1886, one hundred years of battles with the Apache Indians ended. They surrendered "as prisoners of war to an army in the field," which removed them beyond the jurisdiction of civilian authority and placed them into military custody where they were confined for twenty-seven years as prisoners of war (*Fort Still Apache Tribe v. United States,* 477 F.2d at 1367).

112. § III, ¶ 56.

113. § III, ¶¶ 75–76.

114. § III, ¶ 77.

115. § III, ¶ 71.

116. See, for example, Art. I, Fort Laramie Treaty with the Northern Cheyenne and Northern Arapaho of May 10, 1868, 15 Stat. 655 (establishing peace between the Northern Cheyenne and the United States) signed by Morning Star and Little Wolf and other Northern Cheyenne leaders.

117. *Dobbs v. United States and Apache Indians,* 1800 WL 2046 (Ct. Cl. 1898), p. *4.

118. Bueker (1999) at 128 (citing Phillip H. Sheridan, *Record of Engagements with Hostile Indians within the Military Division of the Missouri* ([Washington: Government Printing Office, 1882. Reprint. The Old Army Press, 1969] at 79).

119. Id., at 136 (citing "Briefs of Dispatches," received at division headquarters and found in "Papers Relating to Military Operations," telegrams of Oct. 28, Nov. 1, 19, 1878).

120. In 1872, the commissioner of Indian Affairs wanted Indians on reservations to be placed under strict reformatory control, stating: "[T]hat Indians should be made as comfortable on, and as uncomfortable off, their reservations as it was in the power of the Government to make them; that such of them as went right should be protected and fed, and such as went wrong should be harassed and scourged without intermission…Such a use of the strong arm of the Government is not war, but discipline" (*Cohen's Handbook of Federal Indian Law* [2005 ed.] at 65 n. 416).

121. Lieber Code, § III, ¶¶ 57, 75–75.

122. Id. § I, ¶ 22.

123. Id. §. III, ¶ 57.

124. The War Department took extensive testimony from the participants, including Chivington, to determine whether the attack was conducted according to the recognized rules of civilized warfare, which is complied in Senate Report No. 26, 39th Cong., 2d Sess. (Washington: Government Printing Office, 1867) (Military Report). The House of Representatives conducted its own investigation, which is compiled in the Report of the Joint Committee on the Conduct of the War, Senate Document 142, Vol. 3, 38th Cong., 2d Sess. (Washington: Government Printing Office, 1865) (House Report). The House Report found that the Indians were friendly and had been induced to camp at the site under the protection of the government, when they were attacked on November 29 while camping under the American flag and a white flag of truce (Id., at I–III). The report found that "men, women, and children were indiscriminately slaughtered…surrounded and shot down in cold blood, offering but feeble resistance. From the suckling babe to the old warrior, all who were overtaken were deliberately murdered" (Id., at III).

125. House Report, at III–IV.

126. Id., at V–VI. Despite these stern words, no one was ever punished. Civilian courts had no jurisdiction over the soldiers at the time the acts were committed, and they mustered out of the service before the military tribunals began to investigate the matter.

127. Sandoz (1953), at 270; Chomsky (1990). There is a long list of Dakota Sioux, Cheyenne, Kiowa, and Modoc Indians tried in the courts of the conqueror for acts of war, many of whom were hanged or incarcerated. The list of prisoners of war from many Indian tribes incarcerated in places like Fort Marion, Florida, Fort Robinson, Nebraska, and Fort Sill, Oklahoma, is even longer.

128. Personal interview with Richard B. Williams, director of the American Indian College Fund and a member of the Oglala Sioux Tribe with mixed Northern Cheyenne heritage, August 13, 2007. His great-grandmother Ida White Eyes was an eight- or nine-year-old Cheyenne child during the 1878–79 period of the Cheyenne breakouts, old enough to remember those events that she experienced and recount them to family members until her death at age ninety-one, in 1961.

129. Personal interview with John E. Echohawk, who is currently the executive director of the Native American Rights Fund, January 24, 2007.

130. See note 17 and accompanying text.

131. The United Nations Declaration on the Rights of Indigenous Peoples, UN G.A. Res. 61/295, UN H.R.C., 61st Sess., Annex, Agenda Item 68, UN Doc. A/RES/61/295 (2007) can be found at www.narf.org/events/07/declaration.pdf.

132. As I will discuss in chapter fifteen, interracial civilian violence remains a serious problem on Indian reservations in 2009. This is due to jurisdictional loopholes in law enforcement created by the Rehnquist Court.

133. Vernon R. Maddux and Albert Glenn Maddux, *In Dull Knife's Wake: The True Story of the Northern Cheyenne Exodus of 1878*(Norman, OK: Horse Creek Publications, 2003), pp. 192–193. Today, the Northern Cheyenne sometimes retravel Morning Star's trail, as seen in the moving journey described by Alan Boye, *Holding Stone Hands: On the Trail of the Cheyenne Exodus* (Lincoln: Univ. of Nebraska Press, 1990).

134. A precedent for Senator Brownback's measure is Congress's apology to Native Hawaiians for the overthrow of the Kingdom of Hawaii made in Senate Joint Resolution 19, PL 103–150 (Nov. 23, 1993). It states that Congress "apologizes to Native Hawaiians on behalf of the people of the United States for the overthrow of the Kingdom of Hawaii on January 17, 1893, with the participation of agents and citizens of the United States, and the deprivation of the rights of Native Hawaiians to self-determination." Warlike nations, it seems, have much to regret and apologize for.

CHAPTER 7: *LONE WOLF V. HITCHCOCK*: BREAKING THE TREATIES

1.   Some greedy participants in the Oklahoma land rushes illegally entered the area early and hid out until the run started. They wanted to be there first to claim the choicest homesteads. The cheaters were called "Sooners." This nickname became such a badge of honor that Oklahoma is proudly known as the Sooner State.

2.   Medicine Lodge Treaty, 15 Stat. 581 (1867).

3.   Article 2, Medicine Lodge Treaty, supra.

4.   Article 12 reads: "No treaty for the cession of any portion or part of the reservation herein established...shall be of any validity or force as against the said Indians, unless executed and signed by at least three-fourths of all the adult male Indians occupying the same."

5.   Section 6 of the Act of June 6, 1900, 31 Stat. 672.

6.   Bryan H. Wildenthal, "Fighting the Lone Wolf Mentality: Twenty-First-Century Reflections on the Paradoxical State of American Indian Laws," in *Symposium: Lone Wolf v. Hitchcock: One Hundred Years Later*, 38 Tulsa L. Rev. 113, 118 (2002).

7.   General Allotment Act of 1887, 24 Stat. 388, commonly known as the Dawes Act.

8.   Theodore Roosevelt, *Addresses and Presidential Messages of Theodore Roosevelt, 1902–1904* (New York: Knickerbocker Press, 1904) at 336.

9.   Rennard Strickland (editor-in-chief), *Cohen's Handbook of Federal Indian Law* (Charlottesville, VA: Michie Bobbs-Merril Law Publishers) (1982 ed.) at 614.

10.   *Lone Wolf v. Hitchcock*, 187 US 553 (1903).

11.   Id., at 568.

12.   See, for example, Blue Clark, *Lone Wolf v. Hitchcock: Treaty Rights & Indian Law at the End of the Nineteenth Century* (Lincoln: Univ. of Nebraska Press, 1999); and the collection of law review articles compiled in *Symposium: Lone Wolf v. Hitchcock: One Hundred Years Later*, 38 Tulsa L. Rev. 1 (2002), analyzing the many disturbing ramifications of this landmark case.

13.   *Sioux Nation v. United States*, 601 F.2d 1157, 1173 (Ct. Cl. 1979), aff'd, 448 US 371 (1980).

14.   *Dred Scott v. John F. A. Sanford*, 60 US 393 (1856). See also Peter Irons, *A People's History of the Supreme Court: The Men and Women Whose Cases and Decisions Have Shaped Our Constitution* (New York: Penguin, 2000) at 147–85; Stacy L. Leeds, "The More Things Stay the Same: Waiting on Indian Law's *Brown v. Board of Education*" in *Symposium: Lone Wolf v. Hitchcock: One Hundred Years Later*, 38 Tulsa L. Rev. 73 (2002).

15.   *Federal Power Com'n v. Tuscarora Indian Nation*, 362 US 99, 142 (1960) (Black, J., dissenting).

16.   US Const. art. II, § 2, cl. 2. Treaties with Indian nations are given the same dignity, force, and legal status as that accorded to United States treaties with foreign nations. *Worcester v. Georgia*, 31 US 515 (1832); *United States v. 43 Gallons of Whiskey*, 93 US 188, 197 (1876) ("the power to make treaties with Indian tribes is, as we have seen, coextensive with that to make treaties with foreign nations."). See also *Cohen's Handbook of Federal Indian Law* (1982 ed.) at 62–63. Unfortunately, the legal force of the Indian treaties has not always assured their enforcement, and the United States failed to fulfill many treaty promises (Id., at 63–64). About 369 Indian treaties were made and ratified by the United States (Vine Deloria Jr. and Raymond J. DeMallie, *Documents of American Indian Diplomacy: Treaties, Agreements, and Conventions, 1775–1979*, Vol. I [Norman: Univ. of Oklahoma Press, 1999] at 181–82).

17.   US Const. art. VI, cl. 2.

18.   Foreword by Senator Daniel K. Inouye in Deloria and DeMallie (1999) at ix.

19.   As Felix S. Cohen, the father of federal Indian law, observed in 1947:

> Every American schoolboy is taught to believe that the lands of the United States were acquired by purchase or treaty from Britain, Spain, France, Mexico, and Russia, and that for all the continental lands so purchased we paid about 50 million dollars out of the Federal Treasury. Most of us believe this story as unquestionably as we believe in electricity or corporations. We have seen little maps of the United States in our history books and big maps in our geography books showing the vast area that Napoleon sold us in 1803 for 15 million dollars and the various other cessions that make up the story of our national expansion. As for the original Indian owners of the continent, the common impression is that we took the land from them by force and proceeded to lock them up in concentration

camps called "reservations." Notwithstanding this prevailing mythology, the historic fact is that practically every acre of the real estate acquired by the United States since 1776 was purchased not from Napoleon or any other emperor or czar but from its original Indian owners. (Felix S. Cohen, "Original Indian Title," 32 Minn. L. Rev. 28, 34–35 [1947])

20. Act of Mar. 3, 1871, ch. 120, §1, 16 Stat. 544 (codified as 25 U.S.C. § 71).
21. Many facts in this section are taken from eyewitness press accounts of the treaty negotiations and research compiled by Douglas C. Jones, *The Treaty of Medicine Lodge: The Story of the Great Treaty Council As Told by Eyewitnesses* (Norman: Univ. of Oklahoma Press, 1966).
22. Act to establish Peace with certain Hostile Indian Tribes of July 20, 1867, 15 Stat. 17 (July 20, 1867). Specifically, the Indian Peace Commission's statutory instructions were:

> to call together the chiefs and headmen of such bands or tribes of Indians as are now waging war against the United States or committing depredations upon the people thereof, to ascertain the alleged reasons for their acts of hostility, and in their discretion, under the direction of the President, to make and conclude with said bands or tribes such treaty stipulations, subject to the action of the Senate, as may remove all just causes of complaint on their part, and at the same time establish security for person and property along the lines of railroad now being constructed to the Pacific and other thoroughfares of travel to the western Territories, and such as will most likely insure civilization of the Indians and peace and safety for the whites.

23. Treaty of Fort Laramie of 1868, 15 Stat. 635.
24. Jones (1966) at 65.
25. Id., at 84–85. Jones captures the moment:

> In the twilight after the October 15 meeting, the correspondents saw a group of Indians of about eighty mounted Indians on the far side of Medicine Lodge Creek, directly opposite the Peace Commission camp. When they heard chanting—which served to excite everyone in the camp—they moved to the edge of the ambulance compound to watch and listen. General Harney and a few other commissioners were already there, looking across the stream. The tribesmen pushed into the water, still chanting, and rode directly toward the Commission camp. An armed sentry, his carbine on the ready, moved out and stood near General Harney. The Indians crossed the stream at a trot and rode to within a few yards of the sentry and General Harney, drawing rein and quitting their singing. The Indians' faces were painted, and feathers hung from their ponies' tails. The heavily armed warriors were all Cheyenne who had ridden in from the Cimarron... Ominously, only a few of the Indians dismounted. Friendly talk and laughter notwithstanding, a false move could cause the war to start again right on the banks of the Medicine Lodge. The tension eased, however, when Harney invited Tall Bull and Gray Head to his tent and the soldier and two chieftains faded back into the shadows...Late that night, some of the newsmen heard the Cheyenne party leaving Black Kettle's camp, the sound of their horses fading slowly as the warrior band returned to their own camp on the Cimarron...The first contingent from the Cimarron camp had come and gone without incident. Even so, nerves remained taut...the sudden and unexpected appearance of the plains warriors had certainly done nothing to quiet Commission nerves.

26. Id. 105–106.
27. Id., at 111.
28. Id.
29. Id.
30. Chief Ten Bears is the great-great-grandfather of Wallace Coffey, chairman of the Comanche Tribe in 2009. Like Ten Bears, Wallace is known as a great orator. High oratory must run in the family on the southern plains.

31. The Institute for the Development of Indian Law, *United States Indian Peace Commission (1867–1868): Proceedings Of The Great Peace Commission of 1867–1868* (Washington, DC: Institute for the Development of Indian Law, 1975) at 68.

32. Id., at 69.

33. Id.

34. Id.

35. Id., at 71.

36. Id., at 72–73.

37. Jones (1966) at 123–129.

38. *United States Indian Peace Commission (1867–1868): Proceedings Of The Great Peace Commission of 1867–1868* (1975), supra, note 29 at 74.

39. Id., at 74.

40. Jones (1966) at 114. One reporter observed: "Satanta is a powerful speaker...Even the commissioners could not help expressing their admiration at his magnificent figure...Savage-like as he is, there is a specimen of nobleness in him which two or three of the Commission might do well to imitate" (Id.).

41. The Kiowa chief stated:

> The white man once came to trade; he now comes as a soldier. He once put his trust in our friendship and wanted no shield but our fidelity. But now he builds forts and plants big guns on the walls. He once gave us arms and powder and bade us hunt the game. We then loved him for his confidence...He now covers his face with the cloud of jealousy and anger and tells us to be gone, as an offended master speaks to his dog. Look at this medal I wear. By wearing this, I have been made poor. Before, I was rich in horses and lodges. Today I am the poorest of all. When you gave me this silver medal on my neck, you made me poor. We thank the Great Spirit that all these wrongs are now to cease. You have not tried, as many have done, to make a new bargain merely to get the advantage. Do for us what is best. Teach us the road to travel. We know you will not forsake us; and tell your people also to act as you have done, to be as you have been. I am old...I shall soon have to go the way of my fathers. But those who come after me will remember this day...And now the time has come that I must go. You may never see me more, but remember Satank as the white man's friend. (Jones [1966] at 157)

42. Id.

43. Art. 3, Treaty of Medicine Lodge, supra.

44. Brad D. Lookingbill, *War Dance at Fort Marion: Plains Indian War Prisoners* (Norman: Univ. of Oklahoma Press, 2006).

45. Id., at 39. No military trial was afforded because the Justice Department advised that "a state of war could not exist between a nation and its wards," and it was unlikely that a fair trial could be held for the Indians in Texas and Kansas (Id.). To avoid this conundrum, the government simply arrested and incarcerated them without any trial whatsoever, avoiding in the courts of the conqueror altogether. Legal niceties aside, the incarceration of the prisoners of war for three years following the conclusion of the Buffalo War seems anomalous since the common practice is to *release* prisoners of war at the conclusion of hostilities and send them home, as done in most wars, such as in the Civil War. See chapter six for a discussion of the law of war pertaining to the Indian wars.

46. See, generally, Clark (1999) at 27–37.

47. Id., at 30–32.

48. Id., at 31.

49. Id., at 33–34. See also *Cohen's Handbook of Federal Indian Law* (2005 ed.), § 1.04 at 80–81.

50. Clark (1999) at 35–37.

51. Id., at 47.

52. Id., at 38–49.

53. Id., at 43.

54. Id., at 46–47.

55. Id., at 48.

56. Id., at 50–56. See the Act of June 6, 1900, 31 Stat. 672, as § 6 of the Fort Hall Agreement.
57. Clark (1999) at 36.
58. *Plessy v. Ferguson,* 163 US 537 (1896). Justice Steven J. Field had left the court by the time of *Lone Wolf* in 1903 and Justice Steven Mckenna was added in 1898. Otherwise, the composition of the *Plessy* and *Lone Wolf* courts was the same.
59. *Lone Wolf,* 187 US at 565.
60. Id., at 565.
61. Id., at 565–66.
62. Id., at 568. The political-question doctrine is a judge-made doctrine that this judicial power to review political issues uniquely committed to the discretion of other branches of government. It was frequently used in the nineteenth and twentieth centuries to avoid ruling on controversial questions pertaining to Indian affairs and slavery issues, as well. However, today it is settled that courts may review acts by Congress and federal actions affecting Indians under ordinary constitutional and administrative law principles. See, generally, *Cohen's Handbook of Federal Indian Law* (2005 ed.), § 5.04[2][a] at 413–414.
63. *Lone Wolf,* at 567–68.
64. Id., at 568.
65. Id. ("relief must be sought by an appeal to that body for redress, and not to the courts").
66. The primary *Insular Cases* decided during the *Lone Wolf* era are: *Downes v. Bidwell,* 182 US 244 (1901); *Dooley v. United States,* 182 US 222 (1901); *Hawaii v. Mankichi,* 190 US 197 (1903); *Dorr v. United States,* 195 US 138 (1904); and *Rassmussen v. United States,* 197 US 516 (1905). Also decided in this era was *Cherokee Nation v. Hitchcock,* 187 US 294 (1902), which held that Congress's plenary control over Indian tribes includes the power to authorize the secretary of the interior to lease minerals underlying tribal land against the wishes of the Cherokee Nation, which had a treaty-protected right of self-government over its own lands. While *Cherokee Nation* might be said to be the precursor to *Lone Wolf*'s plenary-power doctrine, the plenary power of Congress recognized in that case uniquely derived from language in Cherokee treaties placing the Cherokee Nation under the protection of the United States subject to the paramount authority of the United States. 187 US at 305–307. *Lone Wolf,* decided one year later, expanded that doctrine to all Indian tribes regardless of their particular legal histories based upon rationales similar to those employed in the *Insular Cases.*
67. *Downes v. Bidwell,* 182 US at 300–304 (White, J., concurring).
68. *Johnson v. M'Intosh,* 21 US 543 (1823); *Kagama v. United States,* 118 US 375 (1886).
69. *Downes v. Bidwell,* 182 US at 303–304.
70. Id., at 300.
71. *Hawaii v. Mankichi,* 190 US at 236–237 (Harlan, J., dissenting).
72. Id., at 239.
73. Id., at 239–240.
74. *Downes v. Bidwell,* 182 US at 306 (White, J., concurring).
75. Id., at 313.
76. Id., at 268 (Brown, J., majority).
77. *Hawaii v. Mankichi,* 190 US at 240.
78. Id., at 241.
79. *Worcester v. Georgia,* 31 US 515 (1832).
80. The takings implications of *Lone Wolf* are discussed by Joseph William Singer, "Lone Wolf, Or How To Take Property by Calling It A 'Mere Change in the Form of Investment," in *Symposium: Lone Wolf v. Hitchcock: One Hundred Years Later,* 38 Tulsa L. Rev. 37 (Fall 2002).
81. Judith V. Royster, "Foreword: Look Back in Anger," in *Symposium: Lone Wolf v. Hitchcock: One Hundred Years Later,* 38 Tulsa L. Rev. 1, 3 (Fall 2002).
82. The Sooner State's Indian landgrabs rival Georgia's frenzy for Indian land. With the possible exception of Georgia's conduct in *Cherokee Nation v. Georgia* (1832), no state seems more blemished by avarice and the incessant demand for Indian land than Oklahoma. It's origins and legal history epitomize human greed and dispossession.
83. See foreword by Senator Daniel K. Inouye in Deloria and DeMallie (1999); note 18, supra, and accompanying text. Normally, nations cannot abrogate treaties with impunity, because there are international consequences that must be faced. Furthermore, the signatories return to the

status quo ante as separate nations and the repudiating nation does not control their internal affairs. None of these consequences pertain to the United States' abrogation of Indian treaties. See Singer (2002) at 43.

84. J. L. Brierly, *The Law of Nations: An Introduction to the International Law of Peace* (New York: Oxford Univ. Press, 1963) at 15.

85. Numerous laws extend federal hegemony over Indian tribes, dismantle their land base, terminate the United States' treaty relationship with many tribes, and extend state jurisdiction over reservations—all done free from judicial review. See, for example, Major Crimes Act, 23 Stat. 385 (1885) (extending federal criminal jurisdiction over Indian reservations); General Allotment Act, 24 Stat. 388 (1887) (allotting tribal land). For a summary of the termination legislation, see *Cohen's Handbook of Federal Indian Law* (1982 ed.) at 170–177. Comparable laws affecting states and non-Indian citizens would likely be unconstitutional, or at least subject to judicial review.

86. John Stuart Mill, *On Liberty* (New York: Barnes & Noble Publishing, (1859) 2004) at 10.

87. Id.

88. Id., at 5. His "harm principle" states:

> The object of this Essay is to assert one very simple principle, as entitled to govern absolutely the dealings of society with the individual in the way of compulsion and control, whether the means used be physical force in the form of legal penalties, or the moral coercion of public opinion. That principle is, that the sole end for which mankind are warranted, individually or collectively in interfering with the liberty of action of any of their number, is self-protection. That the only purpose for which power can rightfully be exercised over any member of a civilized community, against his will, is to prevent harm to others. His own good, either physical or moral, is not a sufficient warrant. He cannot rightfully be compelled to do or forebear because it will be better for him to do so, to do so would be wise, or even right. These are good reasons for remonstrating with him, or reasoning with him, or persuading him, or entreating him, but not for compelling him, or visiting him with any evil, in case he do otherwise…The only part of the conduct of any one, for which he is amenable to society, is that which concerns others. In the part which merely concerns himself, his independence is, of right, absolute. Over himself, over his own body and mind, the individual is sovereign. (Id.)

89. Id.

90. Alexis de Tocqueville, *Democracy in America* (New York: Bantam Dell, (1835) 2004) at 295.

91. Id., at 302–03.

92. Id., at 304.

93. *The Kiowa, Comanche, and Apache Tribes of Indians v. United States,* 4 Ind. Cl. Comm. 111 (Docket No. 32, Dec. 15, 1955).

94. *Kiowa Tribe of Oklahoma v. Manufacturing Technologies, Inc.,* 523 US 751 (1998) upheld the Kiowa Tribe's sovereign immunity from suit, just like other governments in the American political system.

95. *Delaware Tribal Business Committee v. Weeks,* 430 US 73 (1977).

96. *Sioux Nation v. United States,* 448 US 371 (1980). See also *Shoshone Tribe v. United States,* 299 US 476, 497 (1937) (holding that Congress' paramount power over Indian property does not enable the government to give Indian land to others or appropriate it to itself without rendering the government liable for just compensation.)

97. Id., at 414–415.

98. *Santa Clara Pueblo v. Martinez,* 436 US 49, 57 (1978).

99. See, generally, Singer (2002).

100. Judge Boldt's historic decision in *United States v. Washington,* 384 F. Supp. 312 (W.D. Wa. 1974) inaugurated the era of treaty enforcement by the federal courts. Other NARF cases filed to interpret and enforce Indian treaties during this period included *Kimball v. Callahan,* 493 F.2d 564 (9th Cir. 1974, *cert. denied,* 419 US 1019 (1974) (*Kimball I*); *Kimball v. Callahan,* 590 F.2d 768 (9th Cir. 1979), *cert. denied,* 444 US 826 (1979); (*Kimball II*); *United States v. Adair,* 723 F.2d 1392 (9th Cir. 1984), *cert. denied,* 467 US 1394 (1984); *Muckleshoot Tribe v. Puget*

Sound Power & Light Co., 875 F.2d 695 (9th Cir. 1989).

101.   *United States v. Washington*, 384 F. Supp. at 330.

102.   *Washington v. Fishing Vessel Association*, 443 US 658 (1979).

103.   Id., at 667, 675. *Minnesota v. Mille Lacs Band of Chippewa Indians*, 526 US 172 (1999) made it clear that Indian treaty rights survive statehood and are compatible with state sovereignty.

104.   *United States v. Braren*, 338 F.3d 971 (9th Cir. 2003).

105.   See N. Scott Momaday, *The Names: A Memoir* (Tuscon: Univ. of Arizona Press, 1999) at. 26–27, 169. Other books by Momady include *The Way to Rainy Mountain* (1969) and the Pulitzer Prize novel, *House Made of Dawn* (1969).

106.   *The Way to Rainy Mountain* (Albuquerque: Univ. of New Mexico Press, 1969) at 33.

CHAPTER 8: *UNITED STATES V. SANDOVAL*: RULE BY GUARDIANSHIP

1.   *Felix S. Cohen's Handbook of Federal Indian Law* (Albuquerque: Univ. of New Mexico Press, 1948) at 175. is An appropriate period for examining the growth of guardianship is 1886 through 1934. It begins with the Supreme Court's approval of the Major Crimes Act in *Kagama v. United States*, 118 US 375 (1886), extending federal police power over Indian tribes, and spans the years when the General Allotment Act of 1887 (GAA) was enacted and implemented, including passage of the Indian Citizenship Act of 1924, up until 1934, when the Indian Reorganization Act repealed the GAA and established the process for restoring control over the internal affairs and social relations of Indian tribes to tribal governments.

2.   *United States v. Sandoval*, 231 US 28 (1913).

3.   *Worcester v. Georgia*, 31 US 515 (1832), discussed in chapter five, laid down the origins and purposes of the United States' protectorate relationship with Indian nations; and the American Indian protectorates envisioned in *Worcester* should be strengthened and maintained, as shall be discussed in chapter fifteen. While *Sandoval* chose to emphasize the supposed inferiority of the Pueblo Indian race, culture, religion, and governance, there were several more principled bases for the *Sandoval* Court to uphold federal jurisdiction over the Pueblo people. As explained in *Alaska v. Native Village of Veneite Tribal Government*, 522 US 520, 528 (1998), the recognition and treatment of Pueblo land title by the executive and legislative branches and the exercise of guardianship over them by the political branches as dependent Indian communities are the bases for the United States' jurisdiction over Pueblo lands. See also *Tee-Hit-Ton Indians v. United States*, 348 US 272, 288 n. 20(1955).

4.   *In re Can-ah-couqua*, 26 F. 687 (D.D. Alaska, 1887); *United States v. Clapox*, 35 F. 575 (D. Or. 1888).

5.   *Cohen's Handbook of Federal Indian Law* (2005 ed.) at 82. Many Indians were renamed by Indian agents when they signed up for allotments during the 1890s. For example, the Pawnee agent asked my great-grandfather for his name. "Kutawikusu Towakua," he replied. "That is too difficult to pronounce or write. What does it mean," the agent asked. "Echo Hawk," he responded. "It is a warrior's name." "Why not use your neighbor's name who lives across the river? He is a good man whose name is Price," suggested the agent. After thinking it over for a while, my great-grandfather answered, "No, thanks. I'll use the name Echo Hawk." Otherwise, our last name today would be Price, and I would be called Walter Price.

6.   Acts of ethnocide include denying a group its right to speak its language, practice its religion, teach its traditions and customs, create art, maintain social institutions, or preserve its memories. As stated in Robert Hitchcock and Tara Twedt, "Physical and Cultural Genocide of Various Indigenous Peoples," in *Century of Genocide: Eyewitness Accounts and Critical Views* (New York: Garland, 1997) at 373: "Indigenous populations frequently have been denied the right to practice their own religions and customs and to speak their own languages by nation-states, a process described as cultural genocide or ethnocide."

7.   Franciscus de Victoria, *De Indis et de Belli Reflections* (Washington: The Carnegie Institutions of Washington, 1917) (J. B., Scott and E., Nys, eds., J. Bate, trans., 1917) at 161.

8.   S. James Anaya, *Indigenous Peoples in International Law* (New York: Oxford Univ. Press, 1996) at 23–24.

9.   Alpheus H. Snow, *The Question of Aborigines in the Law and Practice of Nations* (Washington: Government Printing Office, 1919), reprinted in *The Inquiry Handbooks*, V. 20 (London:

Scholarly Resources, Inc., 1974) at 12 (quoting an 1837 British House of Commons report made by the Select Committee on Aboriginal Tribes).

10. Id., at 108.

11. Id.

12. Id., at 42.

13. Desmond M. Tutu, preface in John Witte Jr. and Johan D. van der Vyver (eds.), *Religious Human Rights in Global Perspective* (Boston: Martinus Nuhoff Publishers, 1996), p. ix.

14. Allison M. Dussias, "Ghost Dance and Holy Ghost: The Echoes of Nineteenth-Century Christianization Policy in Twentieth-Century Native American Free Exercise Cases" in *First Amendment Law Handbook* (St. Paul, MN: West Group, 1998–99 ed.), James L. Swanson (ed.), pp. 553–659, provides an excellent historical and legal analysis of Native American Free Exercise and Establishment Clause problems.

15. Id., at 568. In 1890 the Rules for Indian Schools required students to observe the Christian Sabbath, and attend services and Sunday school (Id., at 571).

16. Id., at 573, 596–597.

17. Id., at 555, 581.

18. *Cohen's Handbook of Federal Indian Law* (2005 ed.) at 936–937. The First Amendment provides: "Congress shall make no law respecting an establishment of religion or prohibiting the free exercise thereof."

19. Snow (1919) at 22.

20. Id., at 23.

21. *United States v. Rickert*, 188 US 432, 437 (1903) (holding state taxations of Indian trust land and cattle furnished to Indians by the government might defeat federal guardianship and trust obligations.)

22. Snow (1919) at 37.

23. *Cherokee Nation v. Georgia*, 30 US 1, (1831)

24. *Worcester v. Georgia*, 31 US 515, 552–560 (1832).

25. 31 US at 555, 560. This resembles the suzerainty relation, where a dominant state controls the foreign relations of a vassal or weaker state but allows it sovereign authority over its internal affairs. Domestically, this relationship may be resemble Congress's relationship to Washington, DC, which is granted a limited form of home rule subject to the control and authority of Congress. Similarly, many tribes can be said to have voluntarily entered American suzerainty through treaty agreements that established a protectorate relation with the United States. Many treaties commonly acknowledge and bring signatory tribes under US protection. They granted the United States power to control trade and the signatory tribes agreed to bow to no other sovereign. Guardianship under those circumstance arises with the assent of Indian tribes as domestic dependent nations. Consent of the governed is a key element to governance in a democracy.

26. 31 US at 560.

27. 31 US at 581–582 (M'Lean, J., concurring).

28. *Cherokee Nation* merely said the relationship between Indian tribes and the United States "resembles" that of a ward to his guardian. Guardianship was used in a descriptive sense to describe the relationship, and the court did not intend to apply the private law of guardianship in whole cloth to that relationship. Indeed, there are distinct differences between guardianship and trusteeship in private law. Further, though many important similarities do exist, the meaning of key legal terms—such as *guardian, ward, trustee,* and *beneficiary*—and legal principles for defining the rights, roles, and responsibilities between fiduciaries and beneficiaries that are found in private law are not always applied in federal Indian law, causing some confusion (*Felix S. Cohen's Handbook of Federal Indian Law* [Albuquerque: Univ. of New Mexico Press, 1948] at 169–173; Nancy Carol Carter, "Race and Power Politics as Aspects of Federal Guardianship over American Indians: Land-Related Cases, 1887–1924," 4 Am. Indian L. Rev. 197, 199–206 [1976]). At common law, guardianship normally arises when a person labors under a disability needing special care or protection. In that instance, courts appoint a guardian and create the guardianship, which is conducted under court supervision. A guardian has legal custody of the ward and is given parental control with authority to decide what is best and manage the ward's affairs and property for his benefit. The guardian has a duty to maintain and educate the ward and is responsible to the court and the ward for an accounting for the property under

the guardian's care as well as the overall conduct of the guardianship. Under the common law, a guardian does not own legal title to the ward's property. By contrast, during the 1886–1934 period, guardianship arose as a result of treaty agreements or in later years as a result of the raw power of the United States over the tribes. Courts had little to do with supervising federal guardianship, as it was done under the plenary power of Congress. Further, the courts did not always enforce the fiduciary obligations of guardianship or trusteeship found in private law in cases pertaining to the United States' administration of Indian affairs.

29. *Johnson v. M'Intosh,* 21 US 543 (1823).

30. See discussion in chapters five and fifteen.

31. *Ex Parte Crow Dog,* 109 US 556, 568–570 (1883) (Indian tribes are exempt from federal or state criminal laws and are ruled by the tribal laws and traditions of their domestic governments, even though they may be dependent communities subject to the guardianship of the United States, unless and until Congress directs otherwise.).

32. *Kagama v. United States,* 118 US 375, 383–384 (1886).

33. Id., at 384–385.

34. *Elk v. Wilkins,* 112 US 94, 106–107 (1884) held that Indians are noncitizen wards of the government until emancipated by Congress:

> The national legislation has tended more and more towards the education and civilization of the Indians, fitting them to be citizens. But the question whether any Indian tribes, or any members thereof, have become so far advanced in civilization that they should be let out of the state of pupilage, and admitted to the privileges and responsibilities of citizenship, is a question to be decided by the nation whose wards they are and whose citizens they seek to become, and not by each Indian for himself.

35. *Lone Wolf v. Hitchcock,* 187 US 553, 565 (1903).

36. See, generally, cases such as *Williams v. Lee,* 358 US 217 (1959) (protection from state taxation); *Chase v. Masters,* 573 F.2d 1011 (8th Cir. 1978), *cert. denied,* 439 US 965 (1978) (allottees can enjoy the beneficial use of their property free from impairment or interference by local regulation or taxation).

37. *Morton v. Mancari,* 417 US 535 (1974) (upholding Indian hiring preferences for qualified Indians in the Bureau of Indian Affairs when done to further Congress's trust obligations toward Indian tribes.)

38. In *Peyote Way Church of God v. Thornburgh,* 922 F.2d 1210, 1216 (5th Cir. 1991), the court upheld an exemption from the Controlled Substances Act for the religious use of peyote by Indians, stating it is a legitimate government objective to preserve Native American culture that "is fundamental to the federal government's trust relationship with tribal Native Americans." See also *People of Togiak v. United States,* 470 F. Supp. 423, 428 (D.D.C. 1979) (there is a federal trust duty to protect the subsistence way of life and distinct culture of Alaska Native communities).

39. Act of January 30, 1897, 29 Stat. 506.

40. *United States v. Joseph,* 94 US 614 (1876); *United States v. Lucero,* 1 N.M. 422 (N.M. Terr. 1869).

41. *United States v. Joseph,* supra, 94 US at 616.

42. Id.

43. 94 US at 618.

44. *Lucero* suggested that federal guardianship and acts of Congress pertaining to Indians apply only to "wild, half-naked, thieving, plundering, murdering savages"—folks who are "wandering savages, given to murder, robbery, and theft, living on the game of the mountains, the forest, and the plains, unaccustomed to the cultivation of the soil, and unwilling to follow the pursuits of civilized man" (1 N.M. 522 at page *2).

45. *United States v. Sandoval,* 198 F. 539 (D.C.N.M. 1912).

46. 198 F. at 551.

47. Id.

48. 321 US 28, 39.

49. Id., at 41.

50. Id., at 41–45.
51. Id., at 47.
52. Id., at 48 ("citizenship is not an obstacle to the exercise by Congress of its power to enact laws for the benefit and protection of tribal Indians as a dependent people" and though they own land in fee simple title it is "communal land" subject to congressional legislation enacted in the exercise of government guardianship over them and their affairs).
53. See note 3, supra. As noted in *Alaska v. Native Village of Veneite Tribal Government*, 522 US at, 528, the recognition and treatment of Pueblo land title by the executive and legislative branches and the exercise of guardianship over these Indian tribes as dependent Indian communities by the political branches are the proper bases for the United States' jurisdiction over Pueblo lands. See also *Tee-Hit-Ton Indians v. United States*, 348 US 272, 288 n. 20(1955).
54. *Clapox v. United States*, 35 F. 575, 578 (D.D. Or., 1888). Luckily, my great-grandfather Kutawi-kusu Towakua (see note 4) was never prosecuted on the Pawnee Reservation for his plural marriage to two sisters during this same time period, otherwise I might not have been born. My other Pawnee great-grandfather, Arusa Todahe (meaning "Good Horse") a.k.a. Robert Taylor, was not so lucky. He was married to three sisters, and the agent said he must pick one to be his wife, under the agency rules, and let the other two go. What a dilemma!
55. Id., at 575. The federal criminal law stated: "Every person…who by force of arms sets at liberty or rescues any person committed for or convicted of any offense other than capital, shall be fined not more than $500, and imprisoned not more than one year."
56. Dussias (1998–99) at 574.
57. *Cohen's Handbook of Federal Indian Law* (2005 ed.) at 80–81.
58. *Clapox*, 35 F. at 578–579. Judge Deady, the presiding judge, lightly poo-pooed the need for written court documents and procedures for reservation Indians with this merry ditty, the meaning of which is obscured by the mists of time: "The Old Knickerbocker, Wouter van Twiller, when exercising the office of magistrate, paid no heed to parchment, but delivered to the constable, as the symbol of his authority, his well-known jack-knife and tobacco box, armed with which the Dogberry of New Amsterdam might safely 'comprehend all vagrom men'" (Id., at 579). Though it must have amused Judge Deady, the quip was no doubt confusing to Minnie's rescuers, just as it is to this writer today.
59. Teller's 1883 "Rules for Indian Courts" are contained in the Regulations of the Indian Office, April 1, 1904 (Washington: Government Printing Office, 1904), Sec. 584 (Courts of Indian Offenses) at 101–105.
60. Id., at 102.
61. Id., at 102–103.
62. Id., at 103.
63. Id., at 105. Felix S. Cohen points out there was never any legal authority to confine Indians on the reservation. It was an abuse of administrative power done under the name of guardianship: "Although there was never any statutory authority for confining Indians on reservations, administrators relied upon the magic solving word 'wardship' to justify the assertion of such authority…It is now recognized that there is no legal authority for confining any Indian within a reservation" (*Felix S. Cohen's Handbook of Federal Indian Law* (1948) at 177).
64. *Clapox*, 35 F. at 576.
65. Id., at 577.
66. Id., at 577, 578.
67. Id., at 579.
68. *In re Can-ah-couqua*, 29 F. 687 (D.D. Alaska, 1887).
69. Id., at 688.
70. Id., at 689.
71. Id., at 690.
72. Id.
73. Dussias (1998–99) at 589–597.
74. Id., at 596–597, and 597 note 235 (citing the Orders of January 3, 1934, entitled "Indian Religious Freedom and Indian Culture," and Order of January 15, 1934).
75. *Cohen's Handbook of Federal Indian Law* (2005 ed.) at 111.
76. I shall return to this recommendation in chapter fifteen.

77. See Senator Daniel K. Inouye, "Discrimination and Native American Religious Rights," 23 UWLA L. Rev. (1992) 319; Dussias (1998–99); Walter R. Echo-Hawk, "Native American Religious Liberty: Five Hundred Years after Columbus," *American Indian Culture and Research Journal* 17:3 (1993), 33–51.

78. 42 U.S.C. § 1996.

79. As discussed in later chapters, the AIRFA policy provides the policy backdrop and legislative agenda for several landmark human-rights laws, such as the American Indian Religious Freedom Act Amendment of 1994, 42 U.S.C. § 1996a (protecting the religious use of peyote by Indians); the Native American Graves Protection and Repatriation Act, 25 U.S.C. § 3001 et seq. (protecting Indian graves and requiring the repatriation of certain religious and cultural objects, and dead bodies held by museums and federal agencies to their tribes of origin); the National Museum of the American Indian Act of 1989, 20 U.S.C. § 80q et seq. (establishing an Indian museum as part of the Smithsonian Institution and requiring the Smithsonian to repatriate Native American human remains to culturally affiliated tribes); and other federal laws. See, generally, Walter R. Echo-Hawk, "Law, Legislation and Native Religion," in Suzanne J. Crawford and Dennis F. Kelley, eds., *American Indian Religious Traditions: An Encyclopedia,* Vol. 2, J-P (Santa Barbara, California: ABC-CLIO, 2005), pp. 455–473.

80. See, generally, Dussias (1998–99) at 597–657; Inouye (1992); *Cohen's Handbook of Federal Indian Law* (2005 ed.) at 936–949.

81. *Brown v. Board of Education,* 347 US 483 (1954).

82. *Santa Clara Pueblo v. Martinez,* 436 US 49 (1978).

83. Id., at 55.

84. Id., at 73.

85. 25 U.S.C. § 461 et seq. See *Cohen's Handbook of Federal Indian Law* (2005 ed.) at 84–89 for a discussion of the new policy direction represented by the IRA.

86. See *Oliphant v. Suquamish Indian Tribe,* 435 US 191 (1978) (no tribal sovereignty over non-Indian crimes); *Duro v. Reina,* 495 US 676 (1990) (no tribal sovereignty over nonmember Indians); *Nevada v. Hicks,* 533 US 353 (2001) (intrusion by state agents on Indian reservation is allowed).

87. *Cohen's Handbook of Federal Indian Law* (2005 ed.) at 111–112, 407–410; *Cobell v. Norton,* 240 F.3d. 1081, 1089 (D.C. Cir. 2001)

88. 25 U.S.C. §§ 4001–4061, 151–162a.

89. *Cobell v. Kempthorne,* 569 F. Supp.2d. 224 (D.D.C., 2008). The judgment was on appeal in 2009.

90. "Leave No Tribe Behind: NARF Takes on a Class Action for Billions of Dollars of Government Mismanagement of Tribal Trust Funds," 32 NARF Legal Rev. No. 1 (Winter/Spring 2007) (Boulder: Native American Rights Fund). The named tribal plaintiffs in the case are the Nez Perce Tribe (Idaho), the Mescalero Apache Tribe (New Mexico), the Tule River Indian Tribe (California), the Hualapai Tribe (Arizona), the Klamath Tribes (Oregon), the Yurok Tribe (California), the Cheyenne-Arapaho Tribe (Oklahoma), the Pawnee Nation (Oklahoma), the Sac and Fox Nation (Oklahoma), the Santee-Sioux Tribe (Nebraska), and the Tlingit & Haida Tribes (Alaska). NARF attorneys of record on this massive case are Melody McCoy, Donald Wharton, David Gover, Dawn Baum, Mark Tilden, John Echohawk, and Walter Echo-Hawk.

91. Id., at 8 (reprinting testimony of NARF executive director John Echohawk before the United States Senate Committee on Indian Affairs on March 29, 2007).

92. *Cobell,* 240 F.3d 1081.

93. Id., at 1086.

94. Id., at 1089.

95. Personal interview with the author on January 1, 2008.

96. The covenant of the Cayuse, Umatilla, and Walla Walla people was mentioned by Young Chief in the 1855 Treaty Council:

> I wonder if the ground has anything to say: I wonder if the ground is listening to what is said. I wonder if the ground would come alive and what is on it; though I hear what this earth says, the earth says, God placed me here. The earth says, that God tells me to take care of the Indians on this earth; the Earth says to the

Indians that stop on the Earth feed them right. God names the roots that he should feed the Indians on: The water speaks the same way: God says feed the Indians upon the Earth: the grass says the same thing: feed the horses and cattle. The Earth and water and grass says God has given our names and we are told those names; neither the Indians or the Whites have a right to change those names: The Earth says, God has placed me here to produce all that grows upon me, the trees, fruit, etc. The same way the Earth says, it was from her man was made. God on placing them on the Earth desired them to take good care of the earth and do each other no harm (Clifford E. Trafzer and Richard D. Scheuerman, *Renegade Tribe: The Palouse Indians and the Invasion of the Inland Pacific Northwest* [Pullman: Washington State Univ. Press, 1986], p. 54)

See also "Our History and Culture (Part III)," p. 8 at the Confederated Tribes of the Umatilla Reservation website, www.umatilla.nsn.us.

97. The Confederated Tribes' website (note 96) contains tribal history and much contemporary information.

98. See note 54, supra. Echo Hawk and Good Horse enjoyed plural marriages to sisters. The institution worked well in the busy traditional Pawnee lifestyle. Extended family made large earth lodge households easier to manage and maintain. The many tasks imposed by child rearing and the ceremonial and subsistence cycles of agriculture and communal buffalo hunting required many people working together to discharge obligations to the family, various tribal religious, medicine, and military societies, and to the tribe. See Gene Weltfish, *The Lost Universe: Pawnee Life and Culture* (Lincoln: Univ. of Nebraska Press, 1977). By comparison, the instability and loneliness of small nuclear families adrift in the urban setting, with which most westerners with marital difficulties are most familiar, seems inadequate and unsatisfying.

CHAPTER 9: *IN RE ADOPTION OF JOHN DOE V. HEIM:* TAKING THE KIDS

1. Personal Interview with Bertram E. Hirsch (Feb. 22, 2007).

2. Manuel P. Guerrero, "Indian Child Welfare Act of 1978: A Response to the Threat to Indian Culture Caused by Foster and Adoptive Placements of Indian Children," 7 Am. Ind. L. Rev. No. 1 (1979) 51, 52 (citing state survey data collected by the Association on Indian Affairs in 1969 and 1974).

3. The names of parties and minors in adoption and related proceedings are normally withheld by the courts to protect their identity and privacy. That protocol will be respected here.

4. *In the Matter of the Adoption of John Doe; Grandfather Doe, on behalf of John Doe, a child, v. Heim,* 89 N.M. 606, 555 P.2d 906 (Ct. App., 1976).

5. House Report No. 1386 on H.R. 12533, 95th Cong., 2d Sess. (July 24, 1978), p. 9.

6. For example, in 1968 the Spirit Lake Sioux Tribe had little idea of the magnitude of the child-removal problem in its communities on or near the Fort Totten Reservation, North Dakota. After the Association on American Indian Affairs (AAIA) got involved in a local child-custody case in 1968–69, the executive director, Bill Byler, thought, "this cannot be an isolated incident." Upon investigation, AAIA and the tribe discovered that fully one-third of the children had been removed from their families by the state system and placed into non-Indian homes or institutions. No one realized the enormity of the problem, and the community was shocked at what appeared to be a clear-cut case of genocide in rural North Dakota (Personal interview with Bertram E. Hirsch [Feb. 22, 2007]). This shocking discovery galvanized AAIA into action in the coming years to help reform abusive state child-welfare systems though a robust program of litigation, legislation, and public education that will be discussed later in this chapter. AAIA thus joined the ranks of others in Indian Country who were mobilizing in the 1960s to address this national tribal concern.

7. Indian Child Welfare Act of 1978, Pub. L. 95–608 (Nov. 8, 1978), 92 Stat. 3069, 25 U.S.C. §§ 1901–1963.

8. "Full faith and credit" is the practice of the courts to apply the law or judicial decisions of other jurisdictions in appropriate instances as a matter of comity between the courts.

9. In the winter of 2007, we sat in a Manhattan restaurant near Grand Central Station, recalling the old days as warhorses often do. I contacted Bert after many years, because I wanted to hear

firsthand the story of his work during the ten-year period leading up to the passage of ICWA during 1968–78. My focus throughout the 1970s as a NARF attorney was on prison litigation on behalf of Indian inmates, when Bert was crisscrossing the country as an AAIA attorney involved in Indian child-welfare litigation. Our paths rarely crossed during that period, and I was only vaguely familiar with what AAIA and Indian Country were doing in that area of federal Indian law. He stands out in my memory of that time as a fearless and highly intelligent litigator, a man passionately devoted to rectifying the abuses seen in the state child-welfare systems. I wanted to hear the events that led to the enactment of ICWA from a Native rights litigator who was directly involved.

10.   25 U.S.C. § 1901 (3).

11.   The Committee on Interior and Insular Affairs observed in 1978: "In addition to the trauma of separation from their families, most Indian children in placement or in institutions have to cope with the problems of adjusting to a social and cultural environment much different than their own (House Report No. 1386 on H.R. 12533, 95th Cong., 2d Sess. [July 24, 1978], p. 9).

12.   In a 1978 congressional hearing, one tribal leader, Calvin Isaac, the Tribal Chief of the Mississippi Band of Choctaw Indians, pointed these fears out to Congress:

> Culturally, the chances of Indian survival are significantly reduced if our children, the only real means for the transmission of the tribal heritage are to be raised in non-Indian homes and denied exposure to the ways of their People. Furthermore, these practices seriously undercut the tribes' ability to continue as self-governing communities. Probably in no area is it more important that tribal sovereignty be respected than in an area as socially and culturally determinative as family relationships. (*Mississippi Band of Choctaw Indians v. Holyfield*, 490 US 1597, 1600–1601 [1989] [quoting testimony from Hearings on S. 1214 before the Subcommittee on Indian Affairs and Public Lands of the House Committee on Interior and Insular Affairs, 95th Cong., 2d Sess. (1978) at 183])

13.   Art. 2 (e), Convention on the Prevention of and Punishment of the Crime of Genocide, UN Gen. Assembly Res. 260 (III) (approved Dec. 9, 1948) (www.hrweb.org/legal/genocide.html).

14.   Art. 7, § 2, Declaration of the Rights of Indigenous Peoples, UN Gen. Assembly Res. 217A (III) (approved, Sept. 13, 2007).

15.   Historian Kirkpatrick Sale documents that Columbus brought Native American captives to Spain as living proof of his discovery of the New World, but it is unclear in his book, *The Conquest of Paradise* (New York: Alfred E. Knopf, 1990), if any were children, and if so how many.

16.   See discussion in chapters eight and eleven.

17.   *Cohen's Handbook of Federal Indian Law* (2005 ed.), § 1.04, p. 81 (quoting Richard Henry Pratt, founder of the Carlisle School and earlier experimenter in assimilating Indian prisoners of war and boarding school students). See also Jon Allan Reyhner, *Education and Language Restoration: Assimilation versus Cultural Survival* (New York: Chelsea House, 2005) for a discussion of the dark side of Indian education.

18.   Every Indian family has boarding-school stories. Two from my own family are shared here. Some children escaped, such as my wife's great-grandmother Annie (Long Hair) Johnson from the Umatilla Reservation, Oregon. As a young child, around the year 1900, she lived in the village of Wallula on the Columbia River. Adults would hide the kids when the steamboats appeared bearing soldiers to take the kids. Annie ran with all her might toward her father's hiding place and lay quiet under a thicket, hoping she might turn invisible. She was so quiet, she fell asleep. When she awoke, three white men in military uniforms on horseback were looking at her and talking in a foreign language she did not understand. She closed her eyes again and tried to become invisible, since the thought of being separated from her remaining family members terrified the child. At last, she heard the men leave and she was safe. In later years, this elder wondered whether she really turned invisible, or not! Others were not so fortunate. Several children from the Pawnee Indian Reservation, Oklahoma, were sent to the Carlisle Indian Boarding School, Pennsylvania, in the early 1900s, including Elmer Echo Hawk (1892–1942). He ran away, going on a remarkable, cross-country journey to find his way home, but to no avail, for he was sent back to Carlisle shortly after his return.

19.   See *In re Can-ah-couqua*, 26 F. 687 (D.D. Alaska, 1887) and discussion in chapter six.

20.   *In re Lelah-Puc-Ka-Chee,* 98 F. 429 (N.D. Iowa, 1899).

21.   98 F. at 434 (citing the Act of Mar. 3, 1893, 27 Stat. 612).

22.   98 F. at 434 (citing the Act of Mar. 2, 1895, 28 Stat. 906, 25 U.S.C. § 286).

23.   There were no secondary public schools (grades 9–12) in rural Alaska, so the state made funds available for transportation, room, and board for Native students to attend school away from home, rather than furnish schools in their home communities (*Hootch v. Alaska State-Operated School System,* 536 P.2d 793 [Alaska 1975]).

24.   See Testimony of Harold C. Brown, Hearing on S. 1214, Senate Select Committee on Indian Affairs, 95th Cong., 1st Sess., (Aug. 4, 1977), pp. 204–216.

25.   House Report No. 1386 on H.R. 12533, 95th Cong., 2d Sess. (July 24, 1978), p. 9.

26.   Id. See also Guerrero (1979) at 52 n. 7.

27.   See, generally, the following website: Indian Adoption Project Evaluation, 1958 through 1967, www.uoregon.edu/~adoption/archive/LysolAP.htm. This federally funded project of the Child Welfare League of America, a federation of approximately seventy organizations, was brought to Congress's attention and was one of the factors animating the passage of ICWA. See Hearing on S. 1214, Senate Select Committee on Indian Affairs, 95th Cong., 1st Sess. (August 4, 1977): Testimony of Adoption Resource Exchange of North America, Mary Jane Fales pp. 389 et seq.; Testimony of Jewish Family and Children's Service of Phoenix (pp. 414 et seq.). The project ended through the efforts of AAIA in 1967 (Personal Communication from Bertram E. Hirsch [January 16, 2008]).

28.   House Report on No. 1386 (1978), supra, note 24 (In sixteen states with large Indian populations surveyed in 1969, 85 percent of all Indian children in foster care were placed in non-Indian homes; and in some states the figure was higher.)

29.   Id.

30.   Id.

31.   Id., at 10. The extended family is the backbone of Native American society and family structures in tribal communities. It is a traditional child-welfare system. The concept is not well understood by non-Indian society, which is based upon the nuclear-family concept. In this kinship system, grandparents play an honored role, brothers and sisters of the parents have parental relationships to a child with distinct responsibilities for its care and upbringing, and its cousins are considered brothers and sisters. Each member bears a close relationship with these relatives within the structure that defines their roles, duties, and relationships. Those family relationships and duties are placed above all else. The close-knit kinship system ensures that there are no orphans, everyone's needs are met, and traditions are carried on. The system is well suited for survival. It ensures that many hands are available to provide subsistence, shelter, and clothing, as well as emotional and spiritual support. For example, when my father died at an early age, six uncles stepped in to fill his place. They took me under their wings as if I were their own son. I also enjoyed a special relationship with not just four grandparents, but many more, who deeply enriched my life. Under that family support system, there are no orphans in the Echo Hawk family. See, generally, Guerrero (1979), supra, note 1, at 53 note 9, 57–60.

32.   Personal interview with Bertram E. Hirsch (Feb. 22, 2007).

33.   House Report on No. 1386 (1978) at 11.

34.   Id.

35.   Congress found that Indian kids were removed at rates varying from five to twenty-five times higher than non-Indians (Statement of Senator James Abourezk, Oversight Hearing on Indian Child Welfare Problems, Senate Subcommittee on Indian Affairs of the Committee on Interior and Insular Affairs, 93rd Cong. 2nd Sess. [Ap. 8–9, 1974] at 1).

36.   Institutional racism refers to a form of systematic racism that occurs in institutions, rather than in individuals, that maintain policies, practices, beliefs, or other built-in racial or cultural biases that result in the failure to provide appropriate service or treatment for classes of people due to their race, religion, or culture. Institutional racism usually results in disparate treatment that can be measured statistically. The term is defined in Juan F. Perea, et al., *Race and Races: Cases and Resources for a Diverse America* (Thompson West, 2000) at 37 as "racial inferiorizing or antipathy perpetrated by specific social institutions such as schools, corporations, hospitals, or the criminal justice system totally," and it is said that institutional racism "encourages personal belief in, or suspicion of, racial inferiority." The textbook explains that institutional racism

can be overtly racist or commit discrimination in the absence of official policies of racism (Id. 37–38).

37. See note 30, supra.

38. The Association on American Indian Affairs (AAIA) is a private, nonprofit citizen group founded in 1922 to assist American Indian and Alaska Native communities in their efforts to achieve full economic, social, and civil equality, and to defend their rights (www.indian-affairs. org). AAIA is a leading Native rights organization that has been deeply involved throughout the Native American sovereignty movement. It has made lasting contributions to that movement in the courts, Congress, and the executive branch of the federal government during the modern era of federal Indian law. It has been and continues to be involved in legislative advocacy of important federal Indian statutes, such as ICWA and many more. The current executive director is Jack F. Trope, who is, among other things, a leading legal expert on Native American religious freedom and cultural rights.

39. Personal Interview with Bertram E. Hirsch (Feb. 22, 2007).

40. *Heim,* 555 P. 2d at 913.

41. Id.

42. Id., at 912–13.

43. Id., at 914.

44. Id.

45. Id.

46. Id., at 911.

47. Id., at 914.

48. Id., at 915. Native artists commonly travel to attend area events in Indian Country to vend their wares.

49. Id., at 916–17. A *parens patriae* relation is the parental-type relationship between a government and its citizenry that permits the government to represent citizens in matters affecting their well-being. States rely on that principle in litigation, as seen in interstate disputes over water.

50. Id., at 914.

51. Id.

52. Id., at 915–17, 921–22.

53. Personal Interview with Bertram E. Hirsch (Feb. 22, 2007).

54. *Decoteau v. District Court,* 420 US 425 (1975). The issue in this child-welfare case was whether the South Dakota Welfare Department had jurisdiction over Indian children living on non-Indian land within the boundaries of the Lake Traverse Indian Reservation. The court held South Dakota had jurisdiction based upon the legal history of that reservation and the particular jurisdictional facts in that case, laying out guidelines for determining when a reservation has been diminished or terminated.

55. Senate Oversight Hearings Before The Subcommittee On Indian Affairs On Problems That American Indian Families Face In Raising Their Children and How These Problems Are Affected By Federal Action or Inaction, 93rd Cong., 2d Sess. (April 8–9, 1974), pp. 1–2 (Opening Statement of Senator James Abourezk).

56. President Carter's campaign pledge is contained in the Testimony of Bertram E. Hirsch, Association of American Indian Affairs, Hearing on S. 1214, Senate Select Committee on Indian Affairs, 95th Cong., 1st Sess. (Aug. 4, 1977) at 151:

> Indian families and children, like all American families, deserve to be protected and supported by government rather than ignored and destroyed. The rights of Indian families to raise their children as they wish have not always been respected by government. Today, up to 25 percent of all Indian children are raised in foster homes or adoptive institutions. Some of these placements are unwarranted, and many could be prevented if proper social services as well as sufficient educational, economic, and housing resources were available to Indians. If I am elected president, I intend to insure that Indian families are assisted and bolstered by government policies.

57. Work on S. 3777 actually began when Abourezk was a congressman in the House of Representatives (1971–1973). On the AAIA drafting team, Arthur Lazarus did most of the drafting and

relied upon Hirsch's Indian child-welfare legal expertise for the substance, as well as information provided by Bill Byler (Personal Communication from Bertram E. Hirsch [Jan. 10, 2008]).

58. Senate Report on S. 1214 (H.R. No. 95–597), The Indian Child Welfare Act of 1977, 95th Cong., 1st Sess. (Nov. 3, 1977) at 13. No action was taken on the AAIA bill that year (Id.). Senator Abourezk felt it was critical to introduce a bill then focus attention on the subject and set the stage for possible enactment in the next year (Personal Communication to the Author from Bertram E. Hirsch [Jan. 10, 2008]). Indeed, a similar bill, S. 1214, was introduced the next year, which became the vehicle for the final law.

59. Telephone interview with Tony Strong (January 15, 2008).

60. The American Indian Policy Review Commission was a body created by a 1975 act of Congress (88 Stat. 1910) to review federal Indian policies, identify problems, and make recommendations to Congress.

61. Task Force Four: Federal, State, and Tribal Jurisdiction, "Report on Federal, State, and Tribal Jurisdiction," of the "Final Report To the American Indian Policy Review Commission" (Washington: Government Printing Office, 1976) at 78–88, 176–241. The findings are contained at page 87:

   1. The removal of Indian children from their natural homes and tribal setting has been and continues to be a national crisis.
   2. Removal of Indian children from their cultural setting seriously impacts a long-term tribal survival and has damaging social and psychological impact on many individual Indian children.
   3. Non-Indian public and private agencies, with some exceptions, show almost no sensitivity to Indian culture and society.
   4. Recent litigation in attempting to cure the problem of the removal of Indian children, although valuable, cannot affect a total solution.
   5. The current systems of data collection, concerning the removal and placement of Indian children are woefully inadequate and "hide" the full dimension of the problems.
   6. The US Government, pursuant to its trust responsibility to Indian tribes, has failed to protect the most valuable resource of any tribes—
      its children.
   7. The policy of the United States should be to do all within its power to insure that Indian children remain in Indian homes.

62. Id., at 79–80. For a discussion the role of the Final Report in the passage of ICWA, see H.R. No. 1386, 95th Cong., 2d Sess. (July 24, 1978) at 27.

63. Hirsch labored in the bill-drafting process as a resource relied upon by Senate and House committee staff legal counsel, Pete Taylor and Franklin Ducheneaux, for providing legal substance from the cases. The three collaborated closely throughout 1977 and 1978 in drafting and refining bill language that ultimately became ICWA. Though Hirsch had significant involvement, he will be the first to say that literally dozens of people and members of Congress had important input—as is the case in any legislative measure of any consequence—so that no one person can take exclusive credit (Personal Communication from Bertram E. Hirsch [Jan. 10, 2008]).

64. H.R. 1386, 95th Cong., 2d Sess. (July 24, 1978) at 12–19.

65. *Cherokee Nation v. Georgia,* 30 US 1 (1831). See also discussion in chapter five.

66. *Kamaga v. United States,* 118 US 375, 384 (1886).

67. See, generally, Native American Rights Fund, *A Practical Guide to the Indian Child Welfare Act* (Native American Rights Fund, 2007) and www.narf.org/icwa for detailed information and documents on the implementation of ICWA by practitioners of federal Indian law and tribal administrators.

68. Here I pay tribute to the dedicated attorneys I have worked with over the years in the field of federal Indian law, including the present and former Native American Rights Fund staff attorneys. They are too many to name. Only rarely does the opportunity to make social change come along into the lives of most people, but these attorneys made social change every day during the Native American sovereignty movement.

CHAPTER 10: *WANA THE BEAR V. COMMUNITY CONSTRUCTION*: TAKING THE DEAD

1. *Wana the Bear v. Community Construction, Inc.,* 128 Cal. App. 3d 536, 538 (Cal. App. 1982).
2. Russell Thornton, *American Indian Holocaust and Survival: A Population History Since 1492* (Norman: Univ. of Oklahoma Press, 1987) at 109.
3. *Wana the Bear,* 128 Cal. App. 3d at 538.
4. 128 Cal. App. 3d at 539.
5. 128 Cal. App. 3d at 541.
6. Robert M. Peregoy, "Nebraska's Landmark Repatriation Law: A Study of Cross-Cultural Conflict and Resolution," Vol. 16 No. 2 (1992), 139–195; Robert M. Peregoy, "The Legal Basis, Legislative History, and Implementation of Nebraska's Landmark Reburial Legislation," 24 Az. St. L. J. No. 1 (Spring 1992) pp. 329–389; Roger C. Echo-Hawk and Walter R. Echo-Hawk, *Battlefields and Burial Grounds* (Minneapolis: Lerner, 1994).
7. H. Marcus Price III, *Disputing the Dead: US Law on Aboriginal Remains and Grave Goods* (Columbia: Univ. of Missouri Press, 1991) at 22–23.
8. Id., at 116.
9. Historians have thoroughly documented what can only be described as a gruesome history of taking Indian dead. See, for example, the writings of historians Douglas Cole in *Captured Heritage: The Scramble for Northwest Coast Artifacts* (Seattle: Univ. of Washington Press, 1985), and Robert E. Beider, PhD, "A Brief Historical Survey of the Expropriation of American Indian Remains," (Boulder, CO: Native American Rights Fund, 1990) (reprinted in Hearing on S. 1021 and S. 1980, Senate Select Committee on Indian Affairs, 101st Cong., 2d Sess. (May 14, 1990), pp. 278–364, and "The Collecting of Bones for Anthropological Narratives" *Am. Ind. Culture & Research J.* 16:2 (1992), pp. 21–36; Orlan J. Svingen, "The Pawnees of Nebraska: Twice Removed," *Am. Ind. Culture & Research J.* 16:2 (1992), pp. 121–138. Facets of this historical problem are documented and examined in a series of articles by history, religion, and legal scholars in *Am. Indian Culture and Research Journal* 16:2 (1992), including Vine Deloria Jr., historians Robert E. Beider, Roger C. Echo-Hawk, and James Riding In, archaeologist Larry Zimmerman, NARF attorney Robert Peregoy, and other contributors. See also the excellent compilation of writings by authors, some of whom participated in the development and passage of the Native American Graves Protection and Repatriation Act of 1990 in *Symposium: The Native American Graves Protection and Repatriation Act of 1990 and State Repatriation-Related Legislation,* 24 Az. Stat. L. J. No. 1 (Spring 1992). Much has been written on this subject in recent years.
10. Native American Graves Protection and Repatriation Act of 1990, 25 U.S.C. §§ 3001, *et seq.*
11. Personal Communication (Jan. 31, 2008). Wallace H. Johnson is a former assistant attorney general, Land and Natural Resources Division of the United States Department of Justice, chancellor for the Episcopal Diocese in Wyoming, and a trustee for the Buffalo Bill Historical Center in Cody, Wyoming. A student of ancient law, I have valued his thoughtful contributions to the issues that are discussed in this book.
12. In his last book, the late Vine Deloria Jr. compiles and recounts the mystical powers seen in Native American spiritual life in *The World We Used to Live In: Remembering the Powers of the Medicine Men* (Golden, CO: Fulcrum, 2006).
13. Jack F. Trope and Walter R. Echo-Hawk, "The Native American Graves Protection and Repatriation Act: Background and Legislative History," 24 Az. State L. J. No. 1 (Spring 1992) 35, 38 (quoting R. F. Martin, Annotation, *Corpse Removal and Reinterment,* 21 A.L.R.2d 472, 475–76 [1950] [citations omitted]).
14. A family story told to the author by his uncle, the late Bruce Echo Hawk.
15. See, generally, Arlene Hirschfelder and Paulette Molin, *Encyclopedia of Native American Religion* (Updated ed.) (New York: Checkmark Books, 2001); Roger C. Echo-Hawk, "Pawnee Mortuary Traditions," *Am. Indian Culture & Research Journal* 16:2 (1992) at 77–99. Accounts by early explorers and ethnographers are filled with their observations of the reverence held by the tribes for their dead and places of sepulture, including their religious ceremonies, rites, and practices pertaining to the treatment of the dead.
16. Id. Another family story helps illustrate these points. When my uncle Brummett Echo Hawk

was a boy, there was once a wild boy from a neighboring family who rummaged through an old Indian grave and brought home a pipe taken from the grave. Brummett was sternly told to stay away from him by his father, Elmer Echo Hawk, because the neighbor boy violated a taboo against disturbing the dead. The family of the young grave robber told him to return the pipe to the grave, but the youth was too afraid, since the sun was falling down. That night, in the home of the grave robber, moccasin steps were heard in the kitchen, drawers and doors opened and closed, as the spirit (*rarukuata*) came looking for his stolen property. The next day, the boy became ill and later died. Do souls actually use burial offerings in the next life? If Indians believe that they do, that is all the more reason why their graves should be protected. Vine Deloria Jr. notes that this belief is comparable to the situation in the non-Indian world where folks place rosaries, prayer books, medals, good luck charms, wedding rings, spurs and chaps, and other items in the grave. He asks,

> Does anyone seriously support the right of a museum or historical society to dig up graves and take possession of these things for their own enrichment? All burial offerings and personal goods of non-Indians are protected by law. Non-Indians are not required to cite scholarly articles which suggest that the deepest beliefs of Catholics hold that the spirit of the dead will need the beads and prayer books in the afterlife, that the buried war hero will need his medals for a parade in Valhala, or that the dead rodeo rider will need his equipment in that heavenly roundup. Yet museum people and state historical societies argue that Indians must justify the protection of burial offerings with some scholarly evidence as to the utility of the object in the afterlife. (Deloria, "A Simple Question of Humanity: The Moral Dimensions of the Reburial Issue," NARF L. Rev., Vol. 14, No. 4 [Fall 1989] at 10)

17. Martin (1950) (quoted in Trope and Echo-Hawk (1992).

18. A summary of those statutes was provided to Congress in exhibit 5 to Statement of Walter R. Echo-Hawk, Hearings on S. 1021 and S. 1980, Senate Select Committee on Indian Affairs, 101st Cong., 2d Sess. (May 14, 1990), pp. 248–266 (Memorandum from Jo Wilkerson to Walter Echo-Hawk, March 26, 1990). See, generally, Percival E. Jackson, *The Law of Cadavers and of Burials and Burial Places* (2d. ed., 1950).

19. See, for example, Jackson (1950).

20. See note 9, supra.

21. See note 9, supra; and Rayna Green and Nancy Marie Mitchell, eds., *American Indian Sacred Object, Skeletal Remains, Repatriation, and Reburial: A Resource Guide* (1990) for a bibliography of almost 200 articles.

22. Jeanette Greenfield, *The Return of Cultural Treasures* (Cambridge: Cambridge Univ. Press, 1989), documents the extensive collection of cultural patrimony by European colonial powers from colonized lands and the repatriation issues now faced by the museums in those nations that have inherited that legacy.

23. Cole (1985) at 214 (citing a letter from Boas to the editor, *New York Times,* January 7, 1916).

24. See, generally, Elizabeth Simpson, ed., *The Spoils of War (World War II and Its Aftermath: The Loss, Reappearance, and Recovery of Cultural Property)* (New York: Harry N. Abrams, 1997).

25. See discussion in chapters six and eight.

26. Section 2, Articles 31–47, Instructions For The Government Of Armies Of The United States In The Field, General Orders No. 100 (April 24, 1863) (reprinted in Simpson [1997] at 272–273). See also discussion of the Lieber Code in chapter six.

27. Jean Afton, et al., *Cheyenne Dog Soldiers: A Ledgerbook History of Coups and Combat* (Boulder: Colorado Historical Society and Univ. of Colorado Press, 1997). Normally, captured works of art, such as these drawings, belonging to a hostile nation can be removed, but that is done by the victorious nation for the benefit of the conquered nation under the rules of war, and the art is held for it until the issue of ultimate ownership is settled by the ensuing treaty of peace. (Sec. 2, Art. 36, Lieber Code).

28. Cole (1985) and Beider (1990, 1992).

29. Beider (1990 & 1992).

30. Trope and Echo-Hawk (1992) at 40–41. James Riding In documents one case study in the decapitation of dead Indians under the surgeon general's order in "Six Pawnee Crania:

Historical and Contemporary Issues Associated with the Massacre and Decapitation of Pawnee Indians in 1869," *Am. Ind. Culture and Research J.* 16:2 (1992) at 101–119.

31.   Trope and Echo-Hawk (1992) at 41. See also Vernon R. Maddox and Albert Glenn Maddox, *In Dull Knife's Wake: The True Story of the Northern Cheyenne Exodus of 1878* (Norman, OK: Horse Creek Publications, 2003) at 106–07.

32.   Cole (1985) at 119.

33.   Bieder (1990) at 45–46.

34.   Tamara L. Bray and Thomas Killion, *Reckoning with the Dead: The Larsen Bay Repatriation and the Smithsonian Institution* (Washington, DC: Smithsonian Institution Press, 1994); Henry Sockbeson, "Repatriation Act Protects Native Burial Remains and Artifacts," NARF Legal Rev. (Winter 1990), p. 2; Bieder (1992) at 31.

35.   Cole (1985) at 286. See also Bieder (1992) at 29–31.

36.   Phyllis Mauch Messenger, ed., *The Ethics of Collecting Cultural Property* (Albuquerque: Univ. of New Mexico Press, 1989); Jeanette Greenfeld, *The Return of Cultural Treasures* (Cambridge: Cambridge Univ. Press, 1989) at 187.

37.   See, for example, Stephen Jay Gould, *The Mismeasure of Man* (New York: W. W. Norton., 1981); Samuel George Morton, MD, *Crania Americana* (Philadelphia: J. Dobson, Chestnut Street, 1839); Charles Caldwell, MD, *Thoughts on the Original Unity of the Human Race* (Cincinnati, OH: J. A. & U. P. James, 1852); Tim Allan Garrison, *The Legal Ideology of Removal: The Southern Judiciary and the Sovereignty of Native American Nations* (Athens: Univ. of Georgia Press, 2002).

38.   See note 9, supra.

39.   See Messenger (1989); Greenfeld (1989) at 6, 8, 106.

40.   Vine Deloria Jr., "Secularism, Civil Religion, and the Religious Freedom of American Indians," *Am. Ind. Culture and Research J.* 16:2 (1992) 9, 17.

41.   Trope and Echo-Hawk (1992) at 53; Echo-Hawk and Echo-Hawk (1994).

42.   See, for example, Deloria (1992), supra note 40; Deloria (1989), supra note 16.

43.   Deloria (1992) at 10.

44.   Id., at 15.

45.   Id., at 16.

46.   Id., at 16–17.

47.   Antiquities Act of 1906, 16 U.S.C. § 432; Archeological Resources Protection Act of 1978, 16 U.S.C. § 470bb(1), 470(b)(3).

48.   Bieder (1992) at 22–23.

49.   Deloria (1992) at 17.

50.   Peregoy (1992), supra note 6, 24 Az. St. L. J. No. 1 at 357.

51.   Id., at 366 (quoting a Lincoln Journal newspaper article, Dec. 18, 1988).

52.   Price (1991) at 50. See Cal. Public Code, §§ 5097.9, *et seq.* The legislature found that state laws did not protect Native American burial grounds and there was no means available for Native American descendants to control the disposition of their dead. The constitutionality of the statute was upheld against a challenge by an archaeologist who dug Indian graves in violation of the statute and sought to retain the burial goods in *People v. Van Horn,* 218 Cal. App. 3d 1378 (Cal. App., 1990).

53.   See Price (1991) at 43–115.

54.   Trope and Echo-Hawk (1992) at 52–53.

55.   The heart-wrenching story about the Cheyenne delegation's discovery of the Smithsonian's enormous collection is reported in Sockbeson (1990) at 1 (citing "Skeletons in our Museums' Closets," *Harper's* [Feb. 1989] at 68); Trope and Echo-Hawk (1992) at 54–55. Footage of that storage room was captured in a film sponsored by the National Congress of American Indians, which was deeply involved in negotiations over the treatment, care, display, and repatriation of those dead, and others entitled "A Museum to the American Indian."

56.   See Trope and Echo-Hawk (1992) at 53–54.

57.   NARF litigators Arlinda Locklear and Rick Dauphinais represented the Tunica and Biloxi Indian Tribe in *Charrier v. Bell,* 496 So.2d 601 (La. App. 1986), to defeat an amateur archaeologist's ownership claim to one and a half tons of funerary objects taken by him from 150 Indian graves located on private land. NARF attorney Robert Peregoy represented the Pawnee Tribe in *Nebraska State Historical Society v. Pawnee Tribe,* (Neb. D.C. No. 448) (Order of May

31, 1991), filed by the society in an unsuccessful attempt to prevent the tribe from researching public records to obtain facts surrounding the expropriation of Pawnee dead from tribal cemeteries in Nebraska. See Peregoy (1992), supra note 6, 24 Az. Stat. L. J. No. 1 at 376–378. NARF lobbyists during this period included Walter Echo-Hawk in Kansas; a team led by Peregoy in Nebraska, consisting of NARF co-counsel Steven C. Moore and Echo-Hawk, along with James Botsford of Nebraska Legal Aid. On the federal level, a former NARF lobbyist, Suzan S. Harjo, who was then the Executive Director of NCAI, worked closely with Echo-Hawk in legislative advocacy, negotiations, testimony, bill drafting, and other work that contributed to the passage of NMAI and NAGPRA. NARF attorneys also represented clients in various administrative appeals, disputes, and claims implementing the new federal and state repatriation laws and wrote legal articles to educate the public about these issues. That extensive work was supported by many NARF staff members, including law clerks, such as Edward Ayau, a Native Hawaiian law student who went on to become a prominent attorney and repatriation advocate for Native Hawaiian dead in museums in the United States and around the world.

58.   American Indian Religious Freedom Act of 1978, 42 U.S.C. §1996.

59.   Today, Harjo is the president of the Morning Star Institute, a cultural-rights policy and advocacy organization in Washington, DC. As a poet, columnist, writer, lecturer, curator, and policy advocate, Harjo is one of the icons and elder statesmen in the modern era of federal Indian law.

60.   National Museum of the American Indian Act of 1989, 20 U.S.C. §§ 80q-80q-15.

61.   See Report of the Panel for a National Dialogue on Museum/Native American Relations (Feb. 28, 1990), reprinted in 24 Az. Stat. L. J. No. 1(Spring 1992) at 487–500.

62.   The legal standards, burden of proof, and procedures specified for the repatriation process in NAGPRA are described in Trope and Echo-Hawk (1992) at 61–76.

63.   The proposed rule is published in the Federal Register, Vol. 72, No. 199 (October 16, 2007) at 58582–90.

64.   See, for example, a summary of the laws in all fifty states and the District of Columbia that guarantee the burial of every person, presented in the letter from Walter R. Echo-Hawk and Rebecca Tsosie to Dr. Sherry Hutt, National NAGPRA Program, Jan. 11, 2008, available in NARF files and on the NARF website at www.narf.org.

65.   See, for example, Robert J. Lifton, *The Nazi Doctors: Medical Killing and the Psychology of Genocide* (New York: Basic Books, 1986).

66.   Peregoy (1992), supra note 6, 24 Az. St. L. J. No. 1 at 388 (quoting, Vicki Quade, *Who Owns the Past?* Barrister, Spring 1990 at 30).

67.   See Jackson (1950).

68.   Messenger (1989) at 5–6.

69.   Declaration on the Rights of Indigenous Peoples, U.N.G.A. Res. 61/295, U.N. H.R.C., 61st Sess., Annex. Agenda Item 68, U.N. Doc. A/Res/61/295 (2007), www.narf.org/events/07/declaration.pdf.

70.   Greenfeld (1989) at 296–297.

71.   See Larry J. Zimmerman. "Archeology, Reburial, and the Tactics of a Discipline's Self-Delusion," *Am. Indian Culture and Research J.* 16:2 (1992) 37, 43.

72.   Deloria (1989) at 5.

73.   National Congress of American Indians Resolution No. ABQ-03-068 (Nov. 21, 2003).

74.   Greenfeld (1989) at 6.

75.   Peregoy (1992), *Am. Ind. Culture and Research J.* 16 at 169; Peregoy (1992), 24 Az. St. L. J. No. 1 at 380–381.

CHAPTER 11: *EMPLOYMENT DIVISION V. SMITH:* TAKING THE RELIGION

1.   Personal communication, March 15, 2008.

2.   *Employment Division, State of Oregon v. Smith,* 494 US 872 (1990). This case will be called *Smith II*, because it actually went to the Supreme Court twice. The first occasion was in *Employment Division, State of Oregon v. Smith,* 485 US 660 (1988) in *Smith I.* I appeared before the Supreme Court as one of the attorneys of record in *Smith I* and *Smith II* and later represented the Native American Church of North America (NACNA) as one of its attorneys in the legislative movement led by Reuben Snake to overturn *Smith II.*

3. American Indian Religious Freedom Act Amendments of 1994, 42 U.S.C. §1996a. In Congress, I worked closely on this legislation as legal counsel along with two colleagues, attorneys Robert M. Peregoy and James Botsford. This chapter is respectfully dedicated to them, because they guided the strategy that secured passage of the law that overturned *Smith II.*

4. *Smith II* (1990) (peyote religion); *Lyng v. Northwest Indian Cemetery Association,* 485 US 439 (1989) (worship at a tribal holy place located on federal land); *Smith I* (1988) (peyote religion); *Bowen v. Roy,* 476 US 693 (1986) (religious belief). *Bowen* will not be analyzed much in this chapter, because it does not involve recognizable tribal religious beliefs. It involved an offbeat, idiosyncratic religious belief against obtaining a social security number that was only incidentally described as Native American. The *Bowen* ruling was nonetheless given talismanic effect and cited by the Reagan Court in all subsequent Indian religion cases.

5. Laurent B. Frantz, "The First Amendment in the Balance," 71 YALE L. J. 1424, 1448, n. 100 (1962) (quoting 1 Annals of Congress 139 [1789]).

6. *Gonzales v. O Centro Espirita Beneficente,* 546 US 418 (2006); *Church of the Lukumi Babalu Aye v. Hialeah,* 508 US 520 (1993).

7. Patricia Nelson Limerick, "The Repression of Indian Religious Freedom," NARF Legal Rev. Vol. 18, No. 2 (Summer 1993) (Boulder, CO: Native American Rights Fund), p. 12.

8. See chapter eight.

9. *Lyng v. Northwest Indian Cemetery Association,* supra. This case is one of the ten worst Indian cases ever decided and it will be discussed in chapter twelve.

10. Religious, tribal, legal, medical, law enforcement, and regulatory issues regarding the religious use of peyote by Indians are thoroughly documented in two congressional hearings and legislative history behind the American Indian Religious Freedom Act Amendments of 1994. See American Indian Religious Freedom Act—Part II, Oversight Hearing Before the Subcommittee on Native Affairs of the Committee on Natural Resources, House of Representatives, 103rd Cong., 1st Sess., March 16, 1993; American Indian Religious Freedom Act Amendments of 1994, Hearing before Subcommittee on Native American Affairs of the Committee on Natural Resources, House of Representative, 103rd Cong., 2nd Sess., on H.R. 4155 and H.R. 4230, June 30, 1994; and American Indian Religious Freedom Act Amendments of 1994 Report, H.R. Rep. No. 103–675, 103rd Cong., 2nd Sess. (Aug. 4, 1994). A battery of medical research in a long line of studies has uniformly found no medical problems associated with the religious use of peyote by Indians. See, most recently, John H. Hapern, Andrea R. Sherwood, James L. Hudson, Deborah Yurgelun-Todd and Harrison G. Pope Jr., "Psychological and Cognitive Effects of Long-Term Peyote Use Among Native Americans," *Bio Psychiatry* 58, 624–631 (2005).

11. Jay C. Fikes, "A Brief History of the Native American Church," in Huston Smith and Rueben Snake, eds., *One Nation under God: The Triumph of the Native American Church* (Santa Fe, NM: Clear Light Publishers, 1996), p. 167; Omer C. Stewart, *Peyote Religion: A History* (Norman: Univ. of Oklahoma Press, 1987), p. 17.

12. Fikes (1996) at 167.

13. Huston Smith, *The World's Religions: Our Great Wisdom Traditions* (San Francisco: Harper, 1991), pp. 365–382.

14. *Smith II,* 494 US at 888.

15. *Smith II,* 494 US at 890. ("It may fairly be said that leaving accommodation to the political process will place at a relative disadvantage those religious practices that are not widely engaged in; but that unavoidable consequence of democratic government must be preferred to a system in which each conscience is a law unto itself or in which judges weigh the social importance of all laws against the centrality of all religious beliefs.")

16. A small sampling of pertinent law review articles includes: Allison M. Dussias, "Ghost Dance and Holy Ghost: The Echoes of Nineteenth-Century Christianization Policy in Twentieth-Century Native American Free Exercise Cases," 49 Stan. L. Rev. 773, 851 (1997) (*Smith II*'s "willingness to accept the denial of Native American religious rights as an acceptable sacrifice to democracy suggests continuing hostility toward Native American religious traditions…[This] seems even more unjust when compared to the Court's stronger defense of other minority interests from the adverse effects of majoritarian politics."); Walter R. Echo-Hawk, "Native American Religious Liberty: Five Hundred Years After Columbus," *Am. Ind. Culture & Research*

Journal 17:33, 46 (1993) (*Smith II* "departs dramatically from First Amendment law, weakens the Free Exercise Clause and religious liberty and makes it easier for government to intrude upon freedom of worship."); Senator Daniel K. Inouye, "Discrimination and Native American Religious Rights," 23 UWLA L. Rev. 3, 16–17 (1992) (*Smith II* "broke with precedent and rejected the traditional balancing test" and "creates a frightening return to the era when tribal people could be imprisoned for practicing their religion."); John Delaney, "Police Power Absolutism and Nullifying the Free Exercise Clause: A Critique of *Oregon v. Smith*," 25 Indiana L. Rev. 71 (1991) (*Smith II* fashioned an inappropriate, one-sided test that gives talismanic effect to criminal statutes.); Danielle A. Hess, "The Undoing of Mandatory Free Exercise Accommodation—*Employment Division Department of Human Resources v. Smith*," 66 Wash. L. Rev. 586, 596 (1991) (*Smith II* is inconsistent with the Bill of Rights, because it "underprotects" religious conduct and the Court "severely diminished religion's preferred constitutional status."); note, "*Employment Division, Department of Human Resources v. Smith*: Religious Peyotism and the "Purposeful" Erosion of Free Exercise Protections," 36 S. Dak. L. Rev. 358, 373 (1991) (*Smith II* "represented a radical departure from Free Exercise doctrine."); Michael McConnell, "Free Exercise Revisionism and the Smith Decision," 57 U. Chi. L. Rev. 1109, 1111, 1116, 1120, 1129 (1990) (*Smith II* ignores the text and history of the Free Exercise Clause, took liberties with case precedent, and abandoned the traditional role of the Court as the protector of minority rights against majority oppression.).

17.   The tug-of-war commenced when Congress condemned *Smith* and enacted the Religious Freedom Restoration Act of 1993, 42 U.S.C. § 2000bb *et seq.* (RFRA). One year later, Congress passed the American Indian Religious Freedom Act Amendments of 1994. Both laws overturned *Smith* and restored stringent legal standards for protecting religious liberty. The Supreme Court retaliated by striking down RFRA as an unconstitutional law as applied to the states in *Boerne v. City of Flores,* 521 US 507 (1997). Congress countered by enacting the Religious Land Use and Institutionalized Persons Act of 2000, 42 U.S.C. § 2000cc *et seq.* (RILUPA).

18.   See *Church of the Lukumi Bablu Aye v. City of Hialeah,* 508 US 520, 559 (1993) (J. Souter, concurring) ("I have doubts about whether the *Smith* rule merits adherence...the Court should reexamine the rule *Smith* declared.") (J. Blackmun, concurring) ("I continue to believe that *Smith* was wrongly decided, because it ignored the value of religious freedom as an affirmative individual liberty and treated the Free Exercise Clause as no more than an antidiscrimination principle."); *Boerne v. Flores,* 521 US at 544–565 (J. O'Connor, dissenting) ("I remain of the view that *Smith* was wrongly decided, and I would...reexamine the Court's holding there."), 565–566 (J. Souter, dissenting) ("I have serious doubts about the precedential value of the *Smith* rule."), 566 (J. Breyer, dissenting); *Smith II,* 494 US at 891–907, 907–921 (J. O'Connor, concurring) (J. Blackmun, dissenting). Despite these attacks, Justice Scalia has persistently defended his narrow view of the First Amendment in *Hialeah, Boerne,* and *Smith II.*

19.   Quoted in Kirkpatrick Sale, *Conquest of Paradise* (New York: Alfred A. Knopf, 1990), 96–97.

20.   Dussias (1997) at 14–26 discusses the inability of the courts to recognize Indian religious beliefs and practices as real religion using Anglo American perspectives. The results can be quite amusing.

21.   *New Rider v. Board of Education,* 480 F.2d 693, 700–701 (10th Cir. 1973) (wearing long, traditional hairstyles is a personal preference and not religiously motivated conduct); *Diaz v. Collins,* 872 F. Supp. 353, 263 (E.D. Tex. 1994) (wearing a headband is more cultural than religious conduct). Indian claimants must spend inordinate time convincing courts, who are unfamiliar with tribal religious beliefs and practices, that their practices do constitute a religion. Sometimes this is successful. See *Teterud v. Gillman,* 385 F. Supp. 153 (S.D. Iowa, 1974), *aff'd sub nom, Teterud v. Burns,* 522 F.2d 357 (8th Cir. 1974) (wearing long traditional hairstyle is religiously motivated conduct). But the risk remains in far too many cases that not all courts will reach the same conclusion, because after all these years, the religion of the red man still remains a mystery to most uniformed Americans, including judges.

22.   In contrast, the courts are quick to grasp and protect non-Indian religions that are holistic in nature and pervade community life. See *Wisconsin v. Yoder,* 406 US 205 (1972).

23.   *Badoni v. Higginson,* 455 F. Supp. 641 (D. Utah 1977), *aff'd,* 638 F.2d 172 (10th Cir. 1980).

24.   *Sequoyah v. Tennessee Valley Authority,* 620 F.2d 1159, 1163 (6th Cir. 1979)

25.   *Lyng,* supra, 485 US, at 452 (Indians' attempt to protect holy place located on federal land from

destruction was really an attempt to impose a "religious servitude" on federal property); *Wilson v. Block,* 708 F.2d 735 (D.C. Cir. 1983); *Crow v. Gullet,* 541 F. Supp. 785 (D.S.D. 1982), *aff'd,* 706 F.2d 856 (8th Cir. 1983)(per curium); *Sequoyah v. Tennessee Valley Authority,* supra; *Badoni v. Higginson,* supra. In characterizing Indian religious claims as attempts to establish de facto beneficial property rights on land owned by others, it is easy to elevate property rights over Native American religious beliefs and reject those claims under basic property law principles (especially since private property rises to a religion in the eyes of many).

26. The limitations of science in providing answers about reality and the big questions in life are thoughtfully discussed by Huston Smith in *Why Religion Matters: The Fate of the Human Spirit in an Age of Disbelief* (San Francisco: Harper, 2001).

27. Smith (1991).

28. Huston Smith and Phil Cousineau (eds.), *A Seat at the Table: Huston Smith in Conversation with Native Americans on Religious Freedom* (Berkeley: Univ. of California Press, 2006) at 3–4.

29. Smith (1991) at 366.

30. John C. Fremont, *Memoirs of My Life, 1842–1854, Vol. 1* (Chicago: Belford Clarke & Co., 1897), p. 297.

31. Quoted in Paul Goble, *All Our Relatives: Traditional Native American Thoughts about Nature* (Bloomington, IN: World Wisdom, 2005) (citing Joseph Epps Brown, *The Sacred Pipe* (Norman: Univ. of Oklahoma Press, 1953).

32. Smith (1991) st 378–379.

33. Id. 379.

34. Id. (quoting Francois Petitpierre, "The Symbolic Landscape of the Musicas," *Studies in Comparative Religion* [Winter 1975]: 48).

35. Id., at 384.

36. Id., at 386.

37. See, for example, Suzanne J. Crawford and Dennis F. Kelley (eds.), *American Indian Religious Traditions: An Encyclopedia, Vol. 1–3* (Santa Barbara, CA: ABC-CLIO, 2005); Arlene Hirschfelder and Paulette Molin, (eds.), *Encyclopedia of Native American Religions* (New York: Checkmark Books, 2001).

38. Melvin R. Gilmore, *Uses of Plants by the Indians of the Missouri River Region* (Lincoln: Univ. of Nebraska Press, (1914) 1977) at 1–2.

39. Vine Deloria Jr., *The World We Used to Live In: Remembering the Powers of the Medicine Men* (Golden, CO: Fulcrum, 2006), p. 125.

40. Smith (1991) at 372–272.

41. Quoted in Frances Densmore, *Teton Sioux Music* (Washington, DC: Smithsonian Institution, Bureau of American Ethnology, Bulletin 16, 1918), p. 184.

42. Luther Standing Bear, *My Indian Boyhood* (Boston: Houghton Mifflin, 1931), p. 13.

43. Richard Erdoes, *Lame Deer* (London: Davis Poynter, 1973), p. 136.

44. John G. Neihart, *Black Elk Speaks* (New York: William Morrow, 1932), p. 58.

45. James Dorsey, *A Study of Siouan Cults* (Smithsonian Institution BAE 11th Report, 1894), p. 435.

46. Dorsey ((1906) 1997) at 426.

47. Jay C. Fikes (ed.), *Reuben Snake: Your Humble Serpent—Indian Visionary and Activist* (Santa Fe, NM: Clear Light, 1996) at 8.

48. Walter R. Echo-Hawk, "Law, Legislation, and Native Religion," in *American Indian Religious Traditions: An Encyclopedia, Vol. 2 J-P* (Santa Barbara, CA: ABC-CLIO, 2005) (Suzanne J. Crawford and Dennis F. Kelley, eds.) p. 465.

49. See, for example, Melvin R. Gilmore, *Uses of Plants by the Indians of the Missouri River Region* (Lincoln: Univ. of Nebraska Press, 1977 [1914]).

50. See, generally, James R. Murie, *Ceremonies of the Pawnee* (Lincoln: Univ. of Nebraska Press, 1989) (Douglas R. Parks, ed.); George A. Dorsey, *The Pawnee Mythology* (Lincoln: Univ. of Nebraska Press, (1906) 1997); Paul Goble, *Mystic Horse* (New York: Harper Collins, 2003).

51. Gilmore ((1914) 1977) at 15–16; George F. Will and George E. Hyde, *Corn among the Indians of the Upper Missouri* (Lincoln: Univ. of Nebraska Press, (1917) 1964); Murie (1989), supra.

52. See, generally, Von Del Chamberlain, *When Stars Came Down to Earth: Cosmology of the Skidi Pawnee Indians of North America* (Los Altos, CA: Ballena Press, 1982).

53. George A. Dorsey, *The Pawnee Mythology* (Lincoln: Univ. of Nebraska Press, (1906) 1997).

54. Id., at 50–52.

55. Id., at 58–61.

56. Id. 295–300.

57. Virginia Morell, "Minds of Their Own: Animals are Smarter than you Think," *National Geographic* (March, 2008), pp. 36–61.

58. The leading historical and anthropological text is Stewart (1987), supra. Testimonial information about the meaning and importance of the religion to the practitioners themselves is found in Smith and Snake (1996), supra. The legal history of the Native American Church can be found in James Botsford and Walter Echo-Hawk, "The Legal Tango: *The Native American Church v. the United States of America*," in Smith and Snake (1996), pp. 123–142 and Robert M. Peregoy, Walter R. Echo-Hawk, and James Botsford, "Congress Overturns Supreme Court's Peyote Ruling," 20:1 NARF Legal Rev. (Winter/Spring 1995) (Boulder, CO: Native American Rights Fund). For related religious, legal, medical, law enforcement, and regulatory issues, see American Indian Religious Freedom Act—Part II, Oversight Hearing Before the Subcommittee on Native Affairs of the Committee on Natural Resources, House of Representatives, 103rd Cong., 1st Sess., March 16, 1993, supra; American Indian Religious Freedom Act Amendments of 1994, Hearing before Subcommittee on Native American Affairs of the Committee on Natural Resources, House of Representative, 103rd Cong., 2nd Sess., on H.R. 4155 and H.R. 4230, June 30, 1994, supra; and H.R. Rep. No. 103–675 (Aug. 4, 1994), supra.

59. Stewart (1987) at 17. ("For perhaps ten thousand years before the discovery of America, the aborigines living in the area of peyote growth, along the lower Rio Grande and south into Mexico as far as Queretaro, were undoubtedly familiar with peyote and its psychedelic properties.")

60. Id.

61. David Watchel, "Peyotism: Ritual, History, Legality," *The Indian Historian* 13:4, 39, 41 (Fourth Quarter, 1980).

62. Story told by my uncle, the late Owen Echo Hawk, Sr. (*Kaa ka' raarihuu*). His father, Elmer Echo Hawk (*Sire ritawe*), was a prominent NAC roadman in the 1930s.

63. American Indian Religious Freedom Act Amendments of 1994, Hearing before Subcommittee on Native American Affairs of the Committee on Natural Resources, House of Representative, 103rd Cong., 2nd Sess., on H.R. 4155 and H.R. 4230, June 30, 1994, page 119 (Testimony of Walter Echo-Hawk on behalf of the Native American Church of North America).

64. Smith and Snake (1996), supra.

65. *Cantwell v. Connecticut,* 310 US 296, 310 (1940).

66. Michael McConnell, "The Origins and Historical Development of Free Exercise of Religion," 103 Harv. L. Rev. 1410, 1419–1420 (1990).

67. *People v. Woody,* 394 P.2d 813 (1964).

68. Id., at 821.

69. Id., at 821–822.

70. *State of Arizona v. Whittingham,* 504 P.2d 950 (Az. Ct. App. 1973); *Whitehorn v. State of Oklahoma,* 561 P.2d 539 (Okla. Cr. 1977). *Compare, State of Oregon v. Soto,* 537 P.2d 142 (Or. App. 1975) (First Amendment does not protect possession of peyote by an NAC member in Oregon). The *Soto* case was later overturned by the Oregon Supreme Court in the *Smith* cases, only to eventually be reversed by the United States Supreme Court in *Smith II.*

71. This religious exemption was formalized as 21 CFR § 1307.31, which provides: "The listing of peyote as a controlled substance in Schedule I does not apply to the nondrug use of peyote in bona fide religious ceremonies of the Native American Church."

72. *Peyote Way Church of God v. Thornburgh,* 922 F. 2d 1210 (5th Cir. 1991).

73. Id., at 1216.

74. Id., at 1217.

75. Congress enacted the American Indian Religious Freedom Act Amendments of 1994 pursuant to the federal guardianship powers described in *Peyote Way.* See H.R. Rep. No. 103–675, supra, at 8–9. The constitutionality of the federal government's exemption for the religious use by Indians was not disturbed by the Supreme Court when it reviewed that system in *Gonzales,* supra, 546 US 418, 432–436.

76. *Prince v. Commonwealth of Massachusetts,* 321 US 158, 175 (1944) (Murphy, J., dissenting).

77. Daniel K. Inouye, "Discrimination and Native American Religious Rights," 23 UWLA L. Rev. 3, 12 (1992).

78. Luke Timothy Johnson, "Religious Rights Christian Texts" in John Witte Jr. and Johan D. van der Vyver, *Religious Human Rights in Global Perspectives* (The Hague: Martinus Nijhoff Publishers, 1996) at 65–95.

79. Id., at 76–80.

80. Id., at 81.

81. James E. Wood Jr., "An Apologia For Religious Human Rights," in Witte and van der Vyver (1996) at 462.

82. See discussion in chapters two and eight.

83. Quoted in Brian Tierney, "Religious Rights: An Historical Perspective," in Witte and van der Vyver (1996) at 23.

84. Inouye (1992) at 12–13 (citations omitted).

85. The bulls *Inter Caetera* (Alexander VI) (May 3 and 4, 1493) are reproduced in Frances G. Davenport, ed., *European Treaties Bearing on the History of the United States and Its Dependencies to 1648* (Washington, DC: Carnegie Institution, 1917) at 56–63, 64–73.

86. Royal Charter for the Virginia Company (April 16, 1606), reproduced in Henry S. Commager, ed., *Documents of American History,* 9th ed. (New York: Appleton-Century-Crofts, 1973) at 8–10.

87. Alpheus H. Snow, *The Question of Aborigines in the Law and Practice of Nations* (Washington: Government Printing Office, 1919), reprinted edition (Wilmington, DE: Scholarly Resources, 1974).

88. James E. Wood Jr., "An Apologia For Religious Human Rights," in Witte and van der Vyver (1996) at 462 (quoting Hubert Miller, *Religious Freedom in the Modern World* (Chicago, 1963), p. 52).

89. Limerick (1993); Dussias (1997); Robert M. Keller Jr., *American Protestantism and United States Indian Policy, 1869–82* (Lincoln: Univ. of Nebraska Press, 1983) at 207 (quoting 1887 Superintendent of Indian Education Ann. Rep. 131); Francis Paul Prucha, *American Indian Policy in Crisis: Christian Reformers and the Indian, 1865–1900* (Norman: Univ. of Oklahoma Press, 1976).

90. Dussias (1997) at 776–787; Prucha (1976) at 30–33, 46–71.

91. Prucha (1976) at 30 (quoting Secretary of the Interior Delano).

92. Dussias at 773 (quoting 1869 Board of Indian Commissioners Annual Report at 10).

93. Keller (1983) at 207 (quoting 1887 Superintendent of Indian Education Ann. Rep. 131).

94. Limerick (1993) at 10.

95. Id.

96. See chapter eight for a discussion of *In re Can-ah-couqua,* 26 F.687 (D.D. Alaska, 1887).

97. Dussias (1997) at 787–794; *Cohen's Handbook of Federal Indian Law* (2005 ed.) at 80–81. See chapter eight for a more detailed discussion of the Code of Indian Offenses.

98. "Rules for Indian Courts" (1883) printed in Regulations of the Indian Office, April 1, 1904 (Washington: Government Printing Office, 1904), § 584 (Courts of Indian Offenses) at 102.

99. *United States v. Clapox,* 35 F. 575 (D. Or. 1888).

100. Dussias (1997) at 787–805.

101. Id., at 794–800.

102. Id. at 798 [citations omitted] (quoting James Mooney, an anthropologist who investigated the incident, in *The Ghost-Dance Religion and the Sioux Outbreak of 1890* [Lincoln: Univ. of Nebraska Press (1896) 1991] at 869).

103. Inouye (1992) at 13.

104. Secretary of the Interior, Federal Agencies Task Force Report. "American Indian Religious Freedom Act Report, P.L. 95–341," (Department of the Interior, August, 1979), p. 4. This report was submitted to Congress as required by Section 2 of the American Indian Religious Freedom Act, 42 U.S.C. §1996.

105. *Tee-Hit-Ton v. United States,* 348 US 272, 322 (1955).

106. Inouye (1992) at 14.

107. 42 U.S.C. §1996.

108. H.R. Rep. No. 1308, 95th Cong., 2d. Sess. (1978) at 3; S. Rep. No. 709, 95th Cong., 2d. Sess. (1978) at 3.

109. Inouye (1992) at 15 (citations omitted).

110. Smith (1991) at 381.

111. Id. at 382 (footnotes omitted) (quoting John Collier, *Indians of the Americas* [New York: New American Library, 1947]).

112. *Scopes v. State*, 278 S.W. 57 (Tenn. 1925). Though any case arising out of Tennessee might be taken with a grain of salt, many believe the "Monkey Trial" is a watershed case that checked the influence of religious fundamentalism in public education and marked the displacement of religious faith by science and modernity as the predominate modes of American thought.

113. Quoted in Huston Smith, *Why Religion Matters: The Fate of the Human Spirit in an Age of Disbelief* (San Francisco: Harper, 2001) at 72.

114. See, generally, Smith (2001).

115. Id., at 121–134.

116. Douglas Laycock, "Essay: Free Exercise and the Religious Freedom Restoration Act," 62 Fordham L. Rev. 883, 884 (1994).

117. *Wisconsin v. Yoder*, 406 US 205, 217 (1972).

118. *Turner v. Safely*, 482 US 78, 89 (1987).

119. *O'Lone v. Estate of Shabazz*, 482 US 342, 349 (1987). ("To ensure that courts afford appropriate deference to prisons officials, we determined that prison regulations alleged to infringe upon constitutional rights are judged under a 'reasonableness' test less restrictive than that ordinarily applied to alleged infringements of fundamental rights…When a prison regulation impinges on inmates' constitutional rights, the regulation is valid if it is reasonably related to legitimate penological interests" [quoting *Turner*, 482 US at 89]).

120. *Turner*, 482 US at 100–101 (Stevens, J., dissenting).

121. The late Justice Brennan pointed out (482 US at 355) that inmates are still part of our society:

> Prisoners are persons whom most of us would not rather think about. Banished from everyday sight, they exist in a shadow world that only dimly enters our awareness. They are members of a "total institution" that controls their daily existence in a way that few of us can imagine…It is thus easy to think of prisoners as members of a separate netherworld, driven by its own demands, ordered by its own customs, ruled by those whose claim to power rests on raw necessity. Nothing can change the fact, however, that the society that these prisoners inhabit is our own. Prisons may exist on the margins of that society, but no act of will can sever them from the body politic. When prisoners emerge from the shadows to press a constitutional claim, they invoke no alien set of principles drawn from a distant culture. Rather, they speak the language of the charter upon which all of us rely to hold official power accountable. They ask us to acknowledge that power exercised in the shadows must be restrained at least as diligently as power that acts in the sunlight.

122. Id. 482 US at 357 (Brennan, J., dissenting) (quoting *Korematsu v. United States*, 323 US 214, 246 [1944] [Jackson, J., dissenting]).

123. See Stewart (1987).

124. *Hobbie v. Unemployment Security Div.*, 480 US 136 (1987); *Thomas v. Review Board*, 450 US 707 (1981); *Sherbert v. Verner*, 374 US 398 (1963). These cases hold that the denial of unemployment benefits solely from the practice of religion places pressure upon citizens to forego their religious practices—by forcing them to choose between following the dictates of their religion and forfeiting benefits, on the one hand, or abandoning their religious precepts in order to accept work, on the other hand.

125. *Smith v. Employment Division*, 721 P.2d 445 (Or., 1986); *Black v. Employment Division*, 721 P.2d 451 (Or., 1986).

126. *Whitehorn v. State of Oklahoma*, supra; *State v. Whittingham*, supra; *People v. Woody*, supra. Interestingly, the peyote meetings at issue in *Smith* were not conducted by an incorporated NAC chapter and neither Smith nor Black was an NAC member. See Carolyn Long, *Religious Freedom and Indian Rights: The Case of Oregon v. Smith* (Lawrence: Univ. of Kansas Press, 2000) at 1, 92–93.

127. As the attorney general of Oregon from 1981 to 1991, Frohnmayer filed briefs in the United

States Supreme Court to limit the right of worship by Islamic prison inmates in the *O'Lone* case and to ban the Native American Church in Oregon in the *Smith* cases; and he spent most of one term in office combating an East Indian religious sect that took up residence in Antelope, Oregon. See Garrett Epps, *To An Unknown God: Religious Freedom on Trial* (New York: St. Martin's Press, 2001) at 66–89; Long (2000) at 92–93.

128. At the Supreme Court level, I joined the legal team for the oral argument in *Smith I*. Our team was led by the late Suanne Lovendahl, who argued the case, and it included my longtime friend, the late Sandy Schmidt, both of whom were Oregon Legal Aid attorneys.

129. *Employment Division v. Smith*, 485 US 660 (1988) (*Smith I*).

130. Epps (2001) at 184–204; Long (2000) at 164–178.

131. Epps (2001) reports at 99, 108–09, 135–36 that Galen Black was a white man who knew very little about traditional Native American ways and used peyote just once (Id. 108.) Smith was an Indian, but reportedly had no long involvement with the Peyote Religion and was not a member of the Native American Church (Id. at 65, 109, 183, 197). Their litigation implicated the religious rights of 250,000 NAC members.

132. Dorsay replaced Lovendahl as lead attorney in 1988. See Long (2000) at 155. He requested NARF's assistance in preparing for oral argument in *Smith II*. The legal team at the argument consisted of Dorsay, who argued the case, and two NARF attorneys, Steven C. Moore and myself.

133. Official Transcript, Proceedings before the Supreme Court of the United States, Employment Division, Department of Human Resources of Oregon, et al., Petitioners v. Alfred L. Smith, et al. (Case No. 1213) (Nov. 6, 1989) at 45.

134. Id., at 43.

135. *Employment Division v. Smith*, 494 US 872 (1990) (*Smith II*).

136. *Smith II,* at 894 (O'Connor, J., concurring).

137. The premise of the compelling-state-interest test is that religious liberty is so important that no mere colorable state interest can be used by the government to restrict and override that freedom, rather, "only the gravest abuses endangering paramount [state interests] give occasion for permissible limitation" of religious freedom (*Sherbert v. Verner,* supra, 374 US at 406–07). Thus, the state may abridge religious practices only upon an empirical demonstration that some narrowly drawn compelling state interest outweighs a citizen's interest in religious freedom (Id.). See also *Wisconsin v. Yoder,* 406 US 205, 213–215 (1972); *Braunfeld v. Brown,* 366 US 599, 613–614 (1960); *West Virginia State Board of Education v. Barnette,* 319 US 624, 643–644 (1942); *Cantwell v. Connecticut,* 310 US 296, 311 (1940); *People v. Woody,* supra, 394 P.2d at 815–816.

138. *Smith II,* 494 US at 888.

139. Id.

140. *Lone Wolf v. Hitchcock,* 187 US 553 (1903). See chapter seven.

141. *Smith II,* 494 US at 890.

142. See *Smith II,* 494 US at 920 (Brennan, J., dissenting).

143. Id., at 921.

144. *Smith II,* 494 US at 891 (O'Connor, J., concurring).

145. Id., at 901.

146. Id., at 902–903 (O'Connor, J., concurring) (quoting *West Virginia Bd. Educ. v. Barnette,* 319 US 624, 638 [1943]).

147. Id., at 903 (O'Connor, J., concurring), 908–909 (Blackmun, J., dissenting).

148. Id. 909–910 (Blackmun, J., dissenting).

149. Id., at 908–909, 911–921 (Blackmun, J., dissenting).

150. Id. 920.

151. See *Church of the Lukumi Babalu Aye v. City of Hialeah,* 508 US 520, 561–577, 577–580 (1993) (Souter, J., concurring) (Blackmun, J., concurring); *City of Boerne v. Flores,* 521 US 506, 544–566 (1997) (O'Connor, J., dissenting) (Souter, J., dissenting) (Breyer, J., dissenting).

152. Garrett Epps, "To An Unknown God: The Hidden History of *Employment Division v. Smith*," 30 Az. St. L. J. 953, 956 (Winter, 1998).

153. Douglas Laycock, "The Supreme Court's Assault on Free Exercise, and the Amicus Brief that Was Never Filed," 9 J. L. & Religion 99, 102 (1990).

154. John Delaney, "Police Power Absolutism and Nullifying the Free Exercise Clause: A Critque of *Oregon v. Smith*," 25 Ind. L. Rev. 71 (1991).

155. Michael W. McConnell, "Free Exercise Revisionism and the Smith Decision," 57 U. Chi. L. Rev. 1109, 1120 (1990).

156. Harry F. Tepker Jr., "Hallucinations of Neutrality in the Oregon Peyote Case," 16 Am. Ind. L. Rev. 1, (1991).

157. See, for example, law review articles cited by Epps (1998) at 956, n.11.

158. *Yang v. Sturner,* 750 F. Supp. 558 (D. R.I., 1990).

159. *Salaam v. Lockhart,* 905 F.2d 1168, 1171 n.7 (8th Cir. 1990).

160. The two laws are: Religious Freedom Restoration Act of 1993, 42 U.S.C.§§ 2000bb *et seq* (RFRA); American Indian Religious Freedom Act of 1978, 42 U.S.C. §1996a (AIRFA Amendments). Both laws expressly condemn and overturn the *Smith* decision. RFRA, 42 U.S.C. §§ 2000bb(a)(4) and (b)(1); AIRFA Amendment, 42 U.S.C. § 1996a(a)(4). RFRA goes on to restore the compelling-state-interest test, which the AIRFA Amendment simply declares that (1) the use, possession, and transportation of peyote by an Indian religious purposes is legal notwithstanding any other law and (2) no Indian shall be discriminated against or penalized for the religious use of peyote or denied otherwise applicable public benefits.

161. Quoted in Testimony of Walter Echo-Hawk, American Indian Religious Freedom Act Amendments of 1994, Hearing Before the Subcommittee on Native American Affairs of the Committee on Natural Resources, House of Representatives on H.R. 4155 and H.R. 4230, 103rd Cong., 2nd Sess. (June 10, 1994) (Washington: Government Printing Office, 1994) (hereinafter, "Hearing on H.R. 4155 and H.R. 4230") at 121 (hereinafter, "Echo-Hawk Testimony").

162. *Boerne v. Flores,* 521 US 507 (1997). The Court held that Congress did not have the constitutional power to make the law applicable to the states.

163. Echo-Hawk Testimony at 122.

164. Smith and Snake (1996) at 70 (quoting Robert Billie White Horse, president of the Native American Church of Navajoland).

165. Id., at 70 (quoting Loretta Afraid-of-Bear Cook.)

166. Id., at 69 (quoting John Emhoola, Kiowa Tribe).

167. Id. (quoting Troy Nakai, Dine').

168. Id., at 15.

169. Id., at 16, 19.

170. The inspirational life story of this compassionate man is told in his posthumous biography in Jay C. Fikes (ed.), *Reuben Snake: Your Humble Serpent—Indian Visionary and Activist* (Santa Fe, NM: Clear Light, 1996).

171. Id., at 8.

172. See, for example, James Botsford and Walter R. Echo-Hawk, "The Legal Tango: *The Native American Church v. the United States of America,*" in Smith and Snake (1996) at 123–143; Smith and Snake (2001), generally; Walter R. Echo-Hawk, Afterword in Fikes (1996) at 243–250. The most detailed account of the lobby effort in Congress can be found in an article authored by the three attorneys who guided that effort: Robert M. Peregoy, Walter R. Echo-Hawk, and James Botsford, "Congress Overturns Supreme Court's Peyote Ruling," NARF L. REV., Vol. 20, No. 1 (Winter/Spring, 1995) (Boulder, CO: Native American Rights Fund). See also Report on H.R. 4230, supra.

173. Report on H.R. 4230, supra, at 8–9. *Worcester* clothes Congress with the power to do good in American Indian affairs, as discussed in previous chapters.

174. Quoted in Peregoy, Echo-Hawk, and Botsford (1995) at 23.

175. Id.

176. Smith and Snake (1996) at 71.

177. Echo-Hawk Testimony at 115–16.

178. Quoted in Fikes (1996) at 250 (emphasis added).

CHAPTER 12: *LYNG V. NORTHWEST INDIAN CEMETERY ASSOCIATION:* TAKING THE HOLY PLACES

1. Exodus, 3:1–6.

2. See "Draft Environmental Impact Statement, Gasquet-Orleans Road, Chimney Rock Section," included in the Joint Appendix filed in the United States Supreme Court in *Lyng v. Northwest*

Indian Cemetery Association, No. 86–1013 (August, 1987) at 209.

3. *Lyng v. Northwest Indian Cemetery Association,* 485 US 439 (1988).

4. *Lyng,* 485 US at 451 (O'Connor, J., majority).

5. Id., at 477.

6. Id., at 451–452.

7. Id., at 472 (Brennan, J., dissenting) (emphasis added).

8. The most recent example of the shameful conduct of this insensitive agency is seen in *Navajo Nation et al. v. US Forest Service,* 535 F.3d 1058 (9th Cir., 2008) (rehearing en banc), *cert. den.,* 174 L.Ed.2d 270 (2009) (hereinafter, *"Navajo Nation"*).

9. Aldo Leopold, *A Sand County Almanac* (New York: Oxford Univ. Press, [1949] 1989) at 203.

10. Id., at 204.

11. *Lyng,* 485 US at 473 (Brennan, J., dissenting).

12. 124 Cong. Rec. H6842 (July 17, 1978) (Statement of Congressman Udall).

13. See Religious Land Use and Institutionalized Persons Act of 2000, 42 U.S.C. §§ 2000cc *et seq.* (imposing the compelling-government-interest test on land use regulations that restricts the religious use of land owned by the claimants) (RLUIPA). This law does not protect Indian holy places located on federal land, because Indians no longer own a property interest in them as required by the law. See *Navajo Nation* (Sl. Op. at 10066–67, n. 22); Walter Echo-Hawk, "Law, Legislation, and Native Religion," in Susanne J. Crawford and Dennis F. Kelley (eds.), *American Indian Religious Traditions: An Encyclopedia, Vol. 2, J-P* (Santa Barbara, CA: ABC-CLIO, 2005) at 469.

14. Israel's Protection of Holy Places Law of (1967) (Sefer ha-Chukin, 1967) reads as follows:

    1. The Holy Places shall be protected from desecration and any other violation from anything likely to violate the freedom of access of members of the different religions to the places sacred to them or their feelings with regard to those places.

    2. (a) Whosoever desecrates or otherwise violates a Holy Place shall be liable to imprisonment for a term of seven years.
        (b) Whosoever does anything likely to violate the freedom of access of the members of the different religions to the places sacred to them or their feelings with regard to those places shall be liable to imprisonment for a term of five years.

    3. This law shall add to and not derogate from any other law.

    4. The Minister of Religious Affairs is charged with the implementation of this law...

15. Mircea Eliade, *The Myth of the Eternal Return* (Princeton, NJ: Princeton Univ. Press, 1971) (trans. by Willard R. Trask) at 14–15.

16. Huston Smith, *The World's Religions: Our Great Wisdom Traditions* (San Franscico: Harper, 1991) at 371.

17. Mircea Eliade, *Patterns in Comparative Religions* (Meridian Books, 1974) (trans. by Rosemary Sheed), pp. xiv–xv, 7–37 (*hierophanies* in its widest sense is "anything that manifests the sacred."), 367–285; Eliade (1971) at 3–4.

18. See, for example, Arlene Hirschfelder and Paulette Molin, *Encyclopedia of Native American Religions* (New York: Checkmark Books, 2001); Andrew Gulliford, *Sacred Objects and Sacred Places: Preserving Tribal Traditions* (Boulder: Univ. of Colorado Press, 2000).

19. In the northwest, the Creator placed a sacred Black Star and gave it certain powers. In the east rises the Morning Star, the great warrior, and his brothers. In the southeast stands the Male Red Star (*Upirit Pahat*); and the southern sky is ruled by a mysterious Spirit Star, who oversees the Land of the Dead. To the southwest stands the White Female Star (*Upirit taka*); and in the west resides the great Evening Star, a woman deity who gifted Mother Corn to the people and presides over the life-making forces of the heavens, such as thunder, lightning, rain, and clouds. In the northwest is the female Yellow Star, who has appeared in visions to the people in times past; and the North Star is the chief of the northern sky. The Milky Way divides the firmament—with male stars on the east and females in the western skies—and it forms the Spirit Trail, which takes Pawnee souls to the Spirit World far beyond the southern horizon. Pawnee star knowledge and associated religious traditions are compiled by archaeoastronomer Von Del

Chamberlain in *When Stars Came down to Earth: Cosmology of the Skidi Pawnee Indians of North America* (Los Altos, CA: A Ballena Press/Center for Archeoastromony Cooperative Publication, 1982). The Pawnee star deities' role in creation are portrayed in a forty-minute film, "Spirits from the Sky: Thunder on the Land," available at some planetariums, such as the Fiske Planetarium in Boulder, Colorado.

20.   Eliade (1974) at 40.

21.   Gulliford (2000).

22.   Cecile Andrus, secretary of the interior, "American Indian Religious Freedom Act Report, P.L. 95–341," (US Dept. Interior, 1979), p. 52. Section 2 of the American Indian Religious Freedom Act of 1979, 42 U.S.C. § 1996, directed the president to conduct a one-year study of federal regulations and practices that adversely affect the practice of traditional Native American religion and report the findings to Congress.

23.   Archaeological evidence establishes human occupation of the upper Klamath River basin since at least 5000 BC with cultural links to its historical tribal inhabitants (Theodore Stern, "Klamath and Modoc," in *Handbook of North American Indians, Vol. 12*, "Plateau," Deward E. Walker Jr., ed., [Washington: Smithsonian Institution, 1998] at 446).

24.   Arlinda Locklear (Lumbee), a former NARF attorney, was the first. She successfully argued the case in *County of Oneida v. Oneida Indian Nation,* 470 US 226 (1985).

25.   Mircea Eliade, *The Sacred and the Profane,* (New York: Harcourt Brace Jovanovich, 1959) at 74, quoted in Smith (1991) at 372.

26.   Smith (1991) at 376.

27.   Eliade (1971).

28.   According to Eliade (Id., at 157–158), the profound world renewal feature found in primal religion is hard for many in the modern world to imagine:

> Every year...archaic man takes part in the repetition of the cosmology, the creative act *par excellence.* We may even add that, for a certain time, man was creative on the cosmic plane, imitating this periodic cosmogony...and participating in it. [I]t does not accept the destiny of the human being as final and irreducible. [The] techniques attempt above all to annul or transcend the human condition. In this respect, it is justifiable to speak not only of freedom (in the positive sense) or deliverance (in the negative sense) but actually of creation; for what is involved is creating a new man and creating him on a suprahuman plane, a man-god, such as the imagination of historical man has never dreamed it possible to create.

29.   Blue Creek is rich in chinook, coho, and steelhead trout. It accounts for about 5 percent of the total anadromous fish production for the entire Klamath River system. See *Lyng,* 565 F. Supp. 586, 590 n. 2.

30.   The description of Yurok religion provided in this section comes from the evidence offered in an eleven-day trial in the *Lyng* case. That evidence came from the religious practitioners themselves and was corroborated by an independent expert report commissioned by the Forest Service based upon interviews with 166 tribal informants. That report was written by Dorthea Theodoratus, PhD, entitled "Cultural Resources of the Chimney Rock Section, Gasquet-Orleans Road, Six Rivers National Forest" (hereafter, "Theodratus report"); and it was heavily relied upon by the district court and court of appeals to protect the Indians' worship in the High Country under the First Amendment.

31.   Theodoratus report at 132–133 (pages are cited from the parties' Joint Appendix filed in the Supreme Court).

32.   Id., at 134.

33.   Id., at 172–173.

34.   Id., at 168.

35.   Id.

36.   Complaint, ¶ 44 (Joint Appendix at 24).

37.   *Lyng,* 485 US at 442.

38.   Id.

39.   Id.

40.   Brief for the Petitioners filed in the Supreme Court in *Lyng,* 1987 WL 880342, at page *6.

41. Id., ¶ 53 (Joint Appendix at 27). See also Brief for the Petitioners filed in the Supreme Court in *Lyng*, 1987 WL 880342, at page *8.

42. Letter of Decision, July 26, 1982 (Joint Appendix at 96–97).

43. Wolfgang Saxon, "Judge Stanley Weigel, 93, dies; Acted to Improve Prisons," *The New York Times*, Sept. 4, 1999.

44. "CILS History: G-O Road Case," *CILS News* 10, Fall 2002, www.calindian.org/nl_fall2002.5.htm. My rendition of the *Lyng* trial in the federal district court is based on this article posted on the California Indian Legal Services (CILS) website and upon transcript excerpts of the hearing that are contained in the Joint Appendix filed in the United States Supreme Court. CILS is the forerunner and incubator of the Native American Rights Fund (NARF), which began its existence in the late 1960s as a CILS project and then spun off as a national legal organization headquartered in Boulder, Colorado.

45. Id.

46. Since the *Lyng* case, Chris Peters has served many years as the director of the Seventh Generation Fund and has been a leading grassroots activist on Native American cultural issues during the modern era of federal Indian law.

47. Trial Transcript (Joint Appendix at 258).

48. Id., at 259.

49. Id., at 262.

50. Id., at 275.

51. "CILS History: G-O Road Case," supra, at 3.

52. Id.

53. Id.

54. Id.

55. Id.

56. Some of the great trials where this tactic was successfully used to protect Native American religious freedom were: the trial in *People v. Woody*, 394 P.2d 813 (Calif., 1964) (Peyote Religion protected following an extensive trial); and the hearings in the NARF cases of *Northern Lights, Inc.* (FERC Project No. 2752–000), 39 FERC 61,352 (June 25, 1987) (Protecting a tribal vision questing site following extensive hearings) and *Teterud v. Burns*, 385 F. Supp. 153 (S.D. Iowa, 1974), *aff'd*, 522 F.2d 357 (1975) (Protecting an Indian inmate's right to wear traditional hairstyle for religious purposes following an extensive trial on the merits) fall in this category, where the winning formula was used. In these cases, medicine people provided very powerful testimony, bringing the spirits right into the courtroom and often spellbinding the presiding judge. Outside the religion context, the formula was followed in other important federal Indian law trials. See, for example, *United States v. Washington*, 384 F. Supp. 312 (W.D. Wa., 1975), *aff'd*, 520 F.2d 676 (9th Cir. 1975) (Treaty fishing rights protected by Judge Boldt in a landmark decision following an extensive trial).

57. *Northwest Indian Cemetery Protective Association v. Peterson*, 565 F. Supp. 585, 591 (N.D. Cal., 1983).

58. Id.

59. Id., at 592 (citations to the record omitted).

60. Id., at 594.

61. Id. (citations to the record and legal authority omitted).

62. Id., at 595–596 (citing with approval the Forest Services' own expert study, the Theodoratus report).

63. Id., at 594–597.

64. Id., at 597. Judge Weigel cited a long line of authority holding that government actions that are necessary to accommodate religious practices to the extent required by the Free Exercise Clause do not result in excessive government entanglement with religious nor amount to the fostering of religion or favoring one particular religion over another religion in contravention of the Establishment Clause of the First Amendment.

65. *Northwest Indian Cemetery Protective Association v. Peterson*, 795 F.2d 688 (9th Cir. 1986) (on rehearing). Appointed to the bench in 1980 by President Carter, Judge Canby is a scholar and expert on federal Indian law, having written extensive law reviews and books on the subject. See William C. Canby Jr., *American Indian Law in a Nutshell*, 4th Ed. (Thompson West, 2004).

66. *Lyng,* 794 F.2 at 691.

67. Id., at 691, 693.

68. Id., at 692.

69. Id.

70. Id., at 693.

71. *Bowen v. Roy,* 476 US 693 (1980) is discussed in the *Lyng* opinion at page 693.

72. Id., at 693.

73. *Lyng v. Northwest Indian Cemetery Protective Association,* 485 US 439, 448–449 (1988).

74. Id.

75. Id., at 449.

76. Id., at 470 (Brennan, J., dissenting).

77. Id., at 470–471.

78. Id., at 472.

79. Id., at 465–466.

80. Id., at 452–453.

81. Id.

82. Id., at 450–451 ("The crucial word in the constitutional text is 'prohibit'"), 456 (The Constitution does not protect against *any* form of government action that inhibits religious practices: "Rather, it states: 'Congress shall make no law...*prohibiting* the free exercise [of religion]"). Justice Brennan took issue with the majority's narrow definition of *prohibit* in his dissenting opinion, saying it turns on a distinction without any constitutional significance and incorrectly places the form of the restraint over its effect (Id., at 466–467). Regardless of this judicial debate over the meaning of that word, the narrow reading of the scope of religious liberty by the majority is impossible to reconcile with the long line of leading Supreme Court decisions that do protect religious practices from indirect government burdens, penalties, and coercion, such as *Frazee v. Illinois Dept. of Employment Sec.,* 489 US 829 (1089); *Hobbie v. Unemployment Appeals Comm'n of Fla.,* 480 US 136 (1987); *Thomas v. Review Board, Indiana Employment Security Div.,* 450 US 707 (1981); *Wisconsin v. Yoder,* 406 US 205 (1972); *Sherbert v. Verner,* 374 US 398 (1963). These prominent cases contain well-reasoned First Amendment jurisprudence with far more constitutional stature than the obscure *Roy* case, which was accorded talismanic effect in *Lyng.* The sad irony here is that the restraint upon Indian religious exercise in *Lyng* was "to a far greater degree" than in *any* of those cases (*Lyng,* supra, at 467 [Brennan J., dissenting]).

83. Id., at 451.

84. Id., at 453.

85. This is evident in a long line of adverse cases that uniformly deny constitutional protection of Indian worship at holy places for almost any reason imaginable. See, for example, *Lyng,* supra (the High Country); *Navajo Nation v. US Forest Service,* supra (San Francisco Peaks); *United States v. Means,* 858 F.2d 404 (8th Cir. 1988) (Black Hills); *Wilson v. Block,* 708 F.2d 735 (D.C. Cir. 1983), cert. den., 464 US 956 (1983) (San Francisco Peaks); *Inupiat Community of the Arctic Slope v. United States,* 746 F.2d 570 (9th Cir. 1984) (Artcic seas); *Badoni v. Higginson,* 638 F.2d 172 (10th Cir. 1980), cert. den., 452 US 954 (1981) (Rainbow Bridge); *Sequoyah v. TVA,* 620 F.2d 1159 (6th Cir. 1980), cert. den., 449 US 953 (1980) (Cherokee homeland and burial grounds); *Crow v. Gullet,* 706 F.2d 856 (8th Cir.1983), cert. den., 464 US 977 (1983) (Bear Butte).

86. RLUIPA, 42 U.S.C. §§2000cc *et seq.* As discussed in note 13, supra, RLUIPA does not protect Indian holy places located on federal land, because Indians no longer own a property interest in them, as required by the law.

87. Echo-Hawk (2005) at 469.

88. Executive Order 13007 (Indian Sacred Sites), 61 *Federal Register* 26771 (May 24, 1996). Section 4 states that the executive order does not create any right enforceable at law.

89. See note 8, supra.

90. *Cohen's Handbook of Federal Indian Law* (2005 ed.), §8.01[2], p. 672.

91. *Lyng* and *Smith* both direct Indians to Congress to accommodate their religious practices. Other cases instruct that it is permissible for federal agencies to voluntarily accommodate tribal worship at holy places located on federal land. See *The Access Fund v. US Dept. of Agriculture,* 499 F.3d 1036 (9th Cir. 2007); *Wyoming Sawmills Inc. v. US Forest Service,* 383 F.3d 1241 (10th

Cir. 2004); *Bear Lodge Multiple Use Association v. Babbitt,* 2 F. Supp.2d 1448 (D. Wyo. 1988), *aff'd,* 175 F.3d 814 (10th Cir. 1999); *National Arch and Bridge Society v. Alston,* 209 F. Supp. 2d 1207 (D. Utah, 2002).

92. The power and duty of the United States to protect the cultural and religious integrity of domestic dependant nations arises under the protectorate relationship first recognized in *Worcester v. Georgia,* 31 US 515 (1832), as discussed in earlier chapters of this book.

93. See discussion in chapter eleven.

94. *City of Boerne v. Flores,* 521 US 507, 554 (1997) (O'Connor, J., dissenting).

95. Id., at 555.

96. Id., at 556 (quoting G. Hunt, "James Madison and Religious Liberty," in 1 Annual Report of the American Historical Association, H.R. Doc. No. 702, 57th Cong., 1st Sess., 163, 166–167 [1901]) (emphasis added).

97. Id., at 560–564.

98. Id., at 564.

99. James E. Wood Jr., "An Apologia for Religious Human Rights," in John Witte Jr. and Johan D. van der Vyver, eds., *Religious Human Rights in Global Perspective* (The Hague: Martinus Nijhoff Publishers, 1996) at 456–463.

100. See, generally, Witte and van der Vyver (1996).

101. Brian Tierney, "Religious Rights: An Historical Perspective," in Witte and van der Vyver (1996) at 31–32; Luke Timothy Johnson, "Religious Rights and Christian Texts," in Witte and van der Vyver (1996) at 73–80; Wood (1996) at 456–57, 462–63.

102. Tierney (1996) at 35.

103. Id., at 43.

104. Art. 2, ¶1, United Nations Declaration on the Rights of Indigenous Peoples (Sept. 13, 2007).

105. Quoted in Huston Smith and Phil Cousineau, eds., *A Seat at the Table: Huston Smith in Conversation with Native Americans on Religious Freedom* (Berkeley: Univ. of California Press, 2006) at XIII.

106. Sec. 5 (H), Smith River National Recreational Area, PL. 101–612 (Nov. 16, 1990).

CHAPTER 13: *TEE-HIT-TON INDIANS V. UNITED STATES*: CONFISCATING INDIGENOUS HABITAT

1. This migration story was told to me in 2006 by my friend Walter A. Soboleff, a venerated Tlingit elder who turned 100 years old on November 14, 2008. This chapter is respectfully dedicated to this tribal leader.

2. See chapters two through four for a discussion of the doctrine of discovery. The application of that doctrine in Alaska will be discussed in this chapter.

3. Art. III, Treaty with Russia of 1867, 15 Stat. 539.

4. The Tlingit Indians were classified as an "uncivilized tribe" within the meaning of *treaty* in *United States v. Lynch,* 7 Alaska 568, 572 (D. Territory of Alaska, 1927).

5. Kirkpatrick Sale, *The Conquest of Paradise: Christopher Columbus and the Columbian Legacy* (New York: Alfred A. Knopf, 1990).

6. *Johnson v. M'Intosh,* 21 US 543, 590–591 (1823).

7. Walter Echo-Hawk, "Genocide and Ethnocide in Native North America," in John Hartwell Moore (editor-in-chief), *Encyclopedia of Race and Racism, Vol. 2, G–R* (New York: Thompson Gale, 2007), p. 48; Russell Thornton, *American Indian Holocaust and Survival: A Population History Since 1493* (Norman: Univ. of Oklahoma Press, 1987).

8. In this chapter, I adopt the Tee-Hit-Ton spelling utilized by the courts, even though the correct spelling is Teey Hít Taan.

9. *Tee-Hit-Ton v. United States,* 348 US 272 (1955).

10. Id., at 289–90.

11. Id., at 279.

12. *Johnson v. M'Intosh,* supra; *Lone Wolf v. Hitchcock,* 187 US 553 (1903).

13. *Tee-Hit-Ton,* 348 US at 279.

14. US Const., Fifth Amendment.

15. Id.

16. See, generally, Lawrence Rakestraw, *A History of the United States Forest Service in Alaska: Tongass Centennial Special Edition* (USDA Forest Service, June 2002).

17. Nell Jessup Newton, "At the Whim of the Sovereign: Aboriginal Title Reconsidered," *The Hastings Law Journal* 31:1215, 1243 (July 1980). Chapter six discusses the law of war in more detail. It is clear that no legally recognized war of conquest was waged in southeast Alaska under the domestic or international law of war discussed therein.

18. Id., at 1244.

19. See, generally, Charles Wilkinson, *Blood Struggle: The Rise of Modern Indian Nations* (London: W. W. Norton, 2005).

20. *Brown v. Board of Education,* 347 US 483 (1954).

21. It was most recently cited with approval by the Supreme Court in *Idaho v. United States,* 533 US 262, 277 (2001).

22. Alaska Native Claims Settlement Act, 43 U.S.C. §§ 1603 *et seq.* (ANCSA) (extinguishing all aboriginal land claims in Alaska in exchange for various forms of compensation); Indian Claims Commission Act of 1946, 62 Stat. 683 (ICCA) (creating a special commission to hear native claims against the United States).

23. Huston Smith, *The World's Religions: Our Great Wisdom Traditions* (San Franscico: Harper, 1991) at 376. See chapters eleven through twelve for a more thorough discussion of the nature of primal religion.

24. Mircea Eliade, *The Myth of the Eternal Return* (Princeton, NJ: Princeton Univ. Press, 1971) (trans. by Willard R. Trask). See chapters eleven through twelve for a more thorough discussion of the nature of primal religion.

25. Gregory Cajete, *Native Science: Natural Laws of Interdependence* (Santa Fe, NM: Clear Light, 2000).

26. Id., at 94.

27. Id., at 188 (citations omitted).

28. See Articles 18–20, 24–29, 31–32, 38–40, United Nations Declaration on the Rights of Indigenous Peoples (approved by General Assembly Resolution 61/295, September 13, 2007).

29. See United Nations Convention on the Prevention of and Punishment of the Crime of Genocide (1948).

30. Robert Hitchcock and Tara Tweed, "Physical and Cultural Genocide of Various Indigenous Peoples," in Samuel Totten, *et al.*, eds., *Century of Genocide: Eyewitness Accounts and Critical Views* (New York: Garland, 1997), p. 378.

31. *Tee-Hit-Ton,* 348 US at 287.

32. Id., at 286.

33. Letter from Claude R. Wichard, secretary of agriculture to secretary of the interior (February, 5, 1944), p. 2 (author's files).

34. Richard B. Lee and Irven DeVore, eds., *Man The Hunter* (Chicago: Aldine Atherton, 1966).

35. See, for example, William S. Laughlin, "Hunting: An Integrating Biobehavior System and Its Evolutionary Importance," in Lee and DeVore (1966) at 305; Barry Lopez, *Of Wolves and Men* (New York: Scribner, 1978) at 90–97; Smith (1991) at 372–377; Eliade (1971); Cajete (2000) at 156–165.

36. Lee and Devor (1966).

37. See note 20, supra.

38. *Toharu* possess supernatural power in the Pawnee belief system. They play several ceremonial roles in Pawnee ceremonies, such as the Pipe Dance, Kitkahaki Dance, and Young Dog Dance. The Plant World is one of the powers who make life possible, and plants helped early humans understand the meaning of sacred things. See, for example, Alice C. Fletcher, *The Hako: Song, Pipe, and Unity in a Pawnee Calumet Ceremony* (Lincoln: Univ. of Nebraska Press, [1904] 1996), p. 31.

39. Lopez (1978) at 90–95.

40. Quoted in Paul Goble, *All Our Relatives: Traditional Native American Thoughts about Nature* (Bloomington, IN: World Wisdom, 2005).

41. See George A. Dorsey, *The Pawnee Mythology* (Lincoln: Bison Books, [1906] 1997) (based on turn-of-the century interviews with Pawnee elders); James R. Murie, *Ceremonies of the Pawnee* (Lincoln: Univ. of Nebraska Press, 1981), Douglas Parks, ed.; George Bird Grinnell, *Pawnee*

Hero Stories and Folk Tales (Lincoln: Univ. of Nebraska Press, [1889] 1961).

42. Quoted in Goble (2005).

43. "The Wolf and the Warpath," told by the late Owen Echo Hawk Sr. (*Kaaka' raariihuu,* meaning "Big Crow") on January 2, 1982, recorded and edited by Roger Echo-Hawk. It was handed down by his father, Elmer Echo Hawk (*Siire riitawe,* meaning "Well-Known"). The wolf power given to that warrior is said to explain our family's ability to travel as warriors to distant places without fear and to be successful on those journeys.

44. "Death of the Flint-Monster: Origin of Birds," told by Curly-Head between 1899–1902 in George A. Dorsey, ed., *Traditions of the Skidi Pawnee* (Boston: American Folklore Society, 1904), pp. 24–30.

45. "Seventh Son," told by Myron Echo Hawk in the fall of 1970, edited by Roger Echo-Hawk.

46. Jim Mason, *An Unnatural Order: Uncovering the Roots of Our Domination of Nature and Each Other* (New York: Simon & Schuster, 1993), 21–22.

47. Quoted in Goble (2005).

48. Mason (1993) at 21–22.

49. Id., at 25.

50. Cited by Charles Patterson, *Eternal Treblinka: Our Treatment of Animals and the Holocaust* (New York: Lantern Books, 2002), p. 3 (quoting Sigmund Freud, "A Difficulty in the Path of Psycho-Analysis," [1979] in *The Standard Edition of the Complete Psychological Works of Sigmund Freud* [London: Hogarth Press, 1955], Vol. XVII, 130, James Strachey, trans.).

51. Id. (quoting Sigmund Freud, "Fixation to Traumas—The Unconscious" in Introductory Lectures on Psychoanalysis—Part III [1916–1917], Lecture XVIII, *Complete Works*, Vol. XVI, 285).

52. Genesis 1:26.

53. Genesis 1:28.

54. Genesis 9:2.

55. Mason (1993) at 28.

56. Id., at 33–49; Lopez (1978) at 147.

57. North America hunters believe animals have souls. In 1918, Bear-With-Paws (Lakota) stated: "The bear has a soul like ours, and his soul talks to mine in my sleep and tells me what to do." Pete Catches (Lakota) explained: "All animals have power, because the Great Spirit dwells in all of them, even a tiny ant, a butterfly, a tree, a flower, a rock." Thus, the Sioux say, "Do not harm your weaker brothers, for even a little squirrel may be the bearer of good fortune." See quotes in Goble (2005).

58. Mason (1993) at 38.

59. Cajete (2000) at 211.

60. Patterson (2002).

61. For the strong at heart, see Jim Mason and Peter Singer, *Animal Factories: The Mass Production of Animals for Food and How it Affects the Lives of Consumers, Farmers, and the Animals Themselves* (New York: Crown, 1980)

62. Scott Sonner (Associated Press writer), "Palin Appeals to Nevadans to Help Swing Election," San Jose Mercury News (Nov. 4, 2008), www.mercurynews.com/news/ci_10893972.

63. Patterson (2002).

64. Id., at 25–50.

65. Interview with the author (October, 2006).

66. Stephen Haycox, "*Tee-Hit-Ton* and Alaska Native Rights," in *Law for the Elephant, Law for the Beaver: Essays in the Legal History of the North American West* (Regina, SK: Canadian Plains Research Center, Univ. of Regina and Ninth Judicial Circuit Historical Society, 1992), p. 128–143. Paul's bibliography is published in Nora Marks Dauenhauer and Richard Dauenhauer, eds., *Haa Kusteeyi, Our Culture: Tlingit Life Stories* (Seattle: Univ. of Washington Press and Sealaska Heritage Foundation, 1994), pp. 503–524.

67. Soboleff's remarkable biography is published in Dauenhauer and Dauenhauer (1994) at 565–582.

68. Interview with the author (October, 2006).

69. Personal communication from Rosita Worl (2009).

70. See *Miller v. United States,* 159 F.2d 997 (9th Cir. 1947) and discussion *infra.*

71. The proclamation establishing the TNF provided that nothing shall be construed "to deprive any person of any valid right" secured by the Treaty with Russia or any federal law pertaining to Alaska.

72. Rakestraw (2002) at 70, 77.

73. Id., at 74.

74. Id. 83.

75. Id., at 112.

76. The agency asserted the authority of the regional forester to do all these things. See, for example, Regional Forester Memorandum, C. M. Archbold, October 9, 1953 (Author's files). See also Rakestraw (2002).

77. Walter R. Goldschmidt and Theodore H. Haas, *Haa Aani: Tlingit and Haida Land Rights and Use* (Seattle: Univ. of Washington Press and Sealaska Heritage Foundation [1946] 1998), pp. xvii–xviii.

78. Id.

79. Id.

80. Interview with the Author (October, 2006).

81. "Claims of the Natives of Hydaburg, Klawock, and Kake, Alaska," (Department of the Interior, July 27, 1945) (author's files).

82. See, for example, Letter from Secretary of Agriculture Claude R. Wickard to Secretary of the Interior Harold L. Ickes (Feb. 5, 1945) (author's files); Memorandum from Lyle F. Watts, Chief, Forest Service to Secretary of Agriculture (Dec. 11, 1944) (author's files), p. 2.

83. See, for example, Memorandum from B. Frank Heintzleman, Regional Forester, to Chief, Forest Service (June 11, 1946) (relaying territorial opposition to aboriginal rights in the TNF and legislative efforts to extinguish those rights); Memorandum from B. Frank Heintzleman, Regional Forester, to Chief, Forest Service (Oct. 30, 1946) (author's files) (passing along helpful political information about local opposition to aboriginal rights in the TNF); Letter from B. Frank Heintzleman to Region 10 (May 27, 1947) (author's files) (Complaining about Tlingit opposition at a congressional hearing to H.R. 204, which would authorize timber sales in the TNF regardless of any aboriginal property right claims).

84. Memorandum from Regional Forester B. Frank Heintzleman to Chief, Forest Service (Nov. 5, 1945) (author's files); Memorandum from Regional Forester B. Frank Heintzleman to Chief, Forest Service (Oct. 17, 1947) (author's files) (aboriginal land is located in "the most commercially useful zone of the forest").

85. Letter from Secretary of Agriculture Claude R. Wickard to Secretary of the Interior Harold L. Ickes (Feb. 5, 1945) (author's files), p. 3.

86. Id.

87. Memorandum from B. Frank Hentzleman, Regional Forester, to Chief, Forest Service (June 25, 1946) (author's files) (calling attention to Indian protects to a timber sale in aboriginal land recognized by the Interior Department: "We can expect frequent protests...until the whole question is finally settled by Congressional action," but in the meantime "it would be inadvisable to try to compromise with the Interior Department in any of these cases at this time."); Memorandum from B. Frank Hentzleman, Regional Forester, to Division Supervisors, Southern and Petersburg (June 12, 1946) (author's files) ("I cannot see that we are justified in suspending any form of Forest Service administration while awaiting a higher decision in the matter."); Confidential Memorandum of C. M. Archbold, Division Supervisor (July 1, 1946) and attachments (passing along confidential orders from Hentzleman to be more careful when awarding special-use permits that affect Indian structures, but continue making timber sales in designated areas); Letter from Don C. Foster, General Superintendent, to William A. Brophy, Commissioner of Indian Affairs (June 21, 1946) (author's files) (complaining that the Forest Service sold 1,300,000 feet of timber in an area set aside by the secretary of the interior for the aboriginal uses of the Kake community).

88. Memorandum from B. Frank Hentzleman, Regional Forester, to Division Supervisors (Oct. 20, 1947) (author's files) (ordering the supervisors to investigate any Indian timber sale as a high priority for possible trespass actions); Confidential and Personal Letter from "Arch" (presumably C. M. Archbold, Division Supervisor) to "Frank" (presumably Hentlzeman) (Oct. 17, 1947) (author's files) ("We will try to stop such cutting [at Kake and Klawock] by trespass

proceedings"); Memorandum from C. M. Archbold, Division Supervisor, to Regional Forester (Dec. 9, 1947) (author's files) (reporting on timber-cutting contract between the Kaasan community and the Timber Development Corp.); Memorandum from A. W. Hodgman, Forest Manager, to C. M. Archbold, Division Supervisor (Dec. 8, 1947) (author's files) (reporting investigation on a possible Tlingit sale of timber on aboriginal land claimed by the Kaasan Village); Letter from Lyle F. Watts, Chief, to Georgia Hardwood Timber Company (Dec. 10, 1947) (author's files) (asserting "the Indians have no authority to sell the timber on the national forest land").

89.   Statement of Thomas L. Jackson, Timber Committeeman of the Kake Indian Village (undated) (author's files).

90.   *Miller v. United States,* 159 F.2d 997 (9th Cir. 1947).

91.   *Miller* held the government is liable for taking Tlingit tidelands. It reached this result in a roundabout way. The court first recognized aboriginal title, then ruled that the Russia Treaty extinguished it. Nonetheless, the court still awarded damages, because it determined that Congress has repeatedly recognized and protected a Tlingit right to possess traditional lands. For example, the Alaska Organic Act of 1884 provides that Indians "shall not be disturbed in the possession of any lands actually in their use or occupancy." *Miller* sent shockwaves through the Forest Service, because the disturbance of Tlingit land use and possession was at the core of its administration of the TNF.

92.   Joint Resolution, 61 Stat. 920 (August 8, 1947).

93.   Heintzleman's letter to Region 10 (May 27, 1947) (author's files) (Reporting on the congressional hearing on the bill and complaining about Tlingit opposition) suggests that he went to Washington, DC, to lobby for the measure.

94.   *Tee-Hit-Ton,* 348 US at 275.

95.   Rakestraw (2002) at 127.

96.   Id.

97.   Timber-hungry Japanese would establish a second pulp mill at Sitka in 1959 (Id., at 128).

98.   Wilkinson (2005).

99.   See chapter three.

100. *Lone Wolf v. Hitchcock,* 187 US 553 (1903); *United States v. Sandoval,* 231 US 28 (1913). See discussion in chapters seven and eight.

101. John D. Fassett, *New Deal Justice: The Life of Stanley Reed of Kentucky* (New York: Vantage Press, 1994) at 19.

102. See, for example, Kenneth Jost, ed., *The Supreme Court A–Z* (Washington, DC: CQ Press, 2003) at 357; Thomas T. Lewis, Richard L. Wilson, eds., *Encyclopedia of the US Supreme Court, Vol. II* (Pasadena, CA: Salem Press, 2001) at 774; Richard Kluger, *Simple Justice: The History of Brown v. Board of Education and Black America's Struggle for Equality* (New York: Alfred A. Knopf, 2004) at 598–599, 615, 617, 658–659, 683–684, 686, 698, 701–702, 711–712.

103. Stanley Forman Reed, http://en.wikipedia.org/wiki/Stanley_Reed.

104. *United States v. Alcea Band of Tillamooks et al.,* 329 US 40, 58 (1946) (Reed, J., dissenting).

105. The Tlingit brief in the Supreme Court is reproduced at 1954 WL 72830.

106. Sec. 8, Organic Act for Alaska of May 17, 1884, 23 Stat. 24.

107. Sec. 27, Act of June 6, 1900, 31 Stat. 321, 330.

108. *Tee-Hit-Ton,* 348 US at 280.

109. Id., at 281 (quoting *Beecher v. Wetherby,* 95 US 517, 525).

110. Id. (quoting *Beecher*).

111. Id.

112. Id., at 282.

113. Id., at 290–291.

114. Id., at 279.

115. Newton (1980) at 1241–1242.

116. *Tee-Hit-Ton,* 348 US at 289–90.

117. Id., at 288–289.

118. Id., at 278. The Court took the all-Indians-are-alike approach, even though the Tlingit lived in major permanent communities and enforced sanctions for violating their property rights and extended them to the early settlers.

119. Id., at 288.

120. Id., at 289.

121. Id., at 290.

122. Id., at 285, n. 18 (quoting from *Carino v. Insular Government of the Philippine Islands,* 212 US 449, 458 [1908] and 32 Stat. 695).

123. Id. (quoting from *Carino*).

124. Rakestraw (2002), pp. 139–145, 155–176.

125. *Tlingit and Haida Indians v. United States,* 389 F.2d 778, 791 (Court of Claims, 1968).

126. 49 Stat. 388.

127. 43 U.S.C. §§ 1601 *et seq.* The complex statutory settlement scheme is described in *Cohen's Handbook of Federal Indian Law* (Lexis Nexis, 2005 ed.), § 4.07[3].

128. Rakestraw (2002), pp. 159–160.

129. For example, the Tlingits are still implementing their land entitlements under ANCSA, nearly thirty years later. In addition, they must now contend with some environmentalists who consider *Haa Aaní* their new fiefdom, as well as Forest Service holdouts who harbor old notions of conquest and dominionism. However, the days of absolute rule of *Haa Aní* by the Forest Service as a de facto colony are gone.

130. *Cohen's* (2005 ed.), § 4.07[3][a]. The extinguishment of aboriginal hunting, fishing, and gathering rights by ANCSA was preceded by the Supreme Court decision in *Organized Village of Kake v. Egan,* 369 US 60 (1962), which subjected Tlingit trap fishing to state regulation.

131. 16 U.S.C. §§ 3101 *et seq.* That complex scheme and the enormous ongoing efforts to implement it are described in *Cohen's,* supra, § 4.07[3][c].

132. Record of Decision entered by Regional Forester Dennis E. Bschor (Feb. 24, 2003), pp. 19, 26.

133. See *United States v. Washington,* 384 F. Supp. 312 (W.D. Wash., 1974), *aff'd,* 520 F.2d 676 (9th Cir. 1975); and *United States v. Adair,* 478 F. Supp. 336 (D. Or., 1979), *aff'd,* 723 F.2d. 1394 (9th Cir. 1983). Both cases have long litigation histories entailing many reported decisions. See, for example, *Washington v. Fishing Vessel Ass'n,* 443 US 658 (1979); *Adair v. United States,* 187 F. Supp. 1273 (D. Or. 2002), *vacated and remanded on other grds. sub nom, Braren v. United States,* 338 F.3rd 971 (9th Cir. 2003).

134. *United States v. Washington,* No. CV 9213RSM (W.D. Wash.), Order on Cross-Motions for Summary Judgment (August 22, 2007), p. 5.

135. Id., at 12.

136. *The Nature Conservancy et al. vs. United States and Klamath Tribes,* Case 277 (Klamath Basin Adjudication, Water Resources Department, State of Oregon), Amended Order on Motions for Ruling on Legal Issues (Feb. 12, 2007), p. 11.

137. See, for example, *United States v. Washington,* No. CV 9213RSM (W.D. Wash.), Order on Cross-Motions for Summary Judgment (August 22, 2007) (treaty imposes duty on the state to provide salmon access to habitat); *Adair v. United States,* supra (there is a federally reserved water right to support habitat needed for hunting, fishing, and gathering). See also *Klamath Water Users Protective Ass'n v. Patterson,* 204 F. 3rd 1206 (9th Cir. 2000) (irrigation water diversions can affect critical habitat); *Pyramid Lake Paiute Tribe v. Navy,* 898 F.2d 1410 (9th Cir. 1990) (certain water levels are needed to protect fish population); *Joint Board of Control v. United States,* 832 F.2d 1127 (9th Cir. 1985) (stream depletion by irrigators can affect fish habitat); *Kittias Reclamation District v. Sunnyside Irrigation District,* 763 F.2d 1032 (9th Cir., 1985) (salmon redds need sufficient water flows to survive); *Coleville Confederated Tribes v. Walton,* 752 F.2d 397 (9th Cir. 1985) (sufficient water is needed to permit spawning); *Kandra v. United States,* 145 F. Supp.2d 1192 (D. Or. 2001) (irrigation diversions can harm critical fish habitat); *Pacific Coast Federation of Fishermen's Ass'n. v. US Bur. Reclamation,* 138 F.Supp. 2d 1128 (N.D. Ca., 2001) (water diversions can harm critical fish habitat); *Klamath Tribes v. United States,* 1996 WL 924509 (D. Or., 1996) (Logging can impair treaty hunting and fishing rights); *Carson-Truckee Water Cons. Dist. v. Clark,* 741 F.2d 257 (9th Cir. 1984) (fish cannot reproduce when water temperature is too warm); *Pyramid Lake Paiute Tribe v. Morton,* 354 F. Supp. 252 (D. D.C., 1973) (water availability can affect fish habitat).

138. See, for example, *Klamath Water Users Protective Ass'n v. Patterson,* supra; *Kandra v. United States,* supra; *Pacific Coast Federation of Fishermen's Ass'n. v. US Bur. Reclamation,* supra.

139. See *Tennessee Valley Authority v. Hill,* 437 US 154, 180 (1978).

140.   *Palila v. Hawaii Dept. of Land and Natural Resources,* 471 F. Supp. 985, 994995 (D. Haw. 1979). See *Tennessee Valley Authority v. Hill,* 437 US at 168–169 (the social and scientific costs attributable to the disappearance of a species cannot be calculated); *Kandra v. United States,* supra (extinction is the *ultimate harm*); *State of Ohio v. US Dept. of the Interior,* 880 F.2d 432 (D.C. Cir. 1989) (animals have value that cannot be captured by their monetary worth); *Palila v. Hawaii Dept. of Land and Natural Resources,* supra (endangered species are of the utmost importance to mankind); *Rio Grande Silvery Minnow v. Keys,* 333 F.3d 1109 (10th Cir. 2003) (Endangered species take precedence over the "primary mission" of federal agencies).

141.   *Mayagna (Sumo) Awas Tingni Community v. Nicaragua,* [2001] IACHR Petition No. 11 577.

142.   Id.

143.   *Maya Indigenous Community of the Toledo District v. Belize,* Case No. 12.053, Report No. 40/04, Inter-Am. C.H.R. OEA/Ser.L/V/II.122 Doc. 5 rev, 1 at 727 (2004), ¶ 1, www1.umnn .edu/humanrts/cases/40-04.html.

144.   The Brown Bear Clan is part of the *Tantakwaan* (People of the Sea Lion), which is also known as the Tongass Tribe. Ester's mother, like William Paul, was born at Tongass Village in 1879.

CHAPTER 14: WAS GENOCIDE LEGAL?

1.   David E. Stannard, *American Holocaust: The Conquest of the New World* (Oxford: Oxford Univ. Press, 1992), p. xiii.

2.   Id., at xiii–xv.

3.   *Johnson v. M'Intosh,* 21 US 543, 573, 590 (1823).

4.   *Cherokee Nation v. Georgia,* 30 US 1, 18, 20–21 (1931).

5.   *United States v. Sandoval,* 231 US 28, 39 (1913); *Clapox v. United States,* 35 F. 575, 578 (D.D. Or., 1888); *In re Can-ah-couqua,* 29 F. 687, 690 (D.D. Alaska, 1887).

6.   *Tee-Hit-Ton Indians v. United States,* 348 US 272, 281, 289–90 (1955).

7.   Stannard (1992) at 247, 268–281.

8.   Samuel Totten, William S. Parsons, Robert K. Hitchcock, "Confronting Genocide and Ethnocide of Indigenous Peoples: An Interdisciplinary Approach to Definition, Intervention, and Advocacy," in Alexander Laban Hinton, ed., *Annihilating Difference: The Anthropology of Genocide* (Berkeley: Univ. of California Press, 2002) at 57; Stannard (1992) at 243–244.

9.   Convention on the Prevention and Punishment of the Crime of Genocide (approved by UN General Assembly, Dec. 11, 1946), Art. 2.

10.   Robert K. Hitchcock and Tara M. Twedt, "Physical and Cultural Genocide of Various Indigenous Peoples," in Samuel Totten, Israel W. Charney, and William S. Parsons, eds., *Century of Genocide: Eyewitness Accounts and Critical Views* (New York: Garland, 1997) at 373.

11.   Totten, Parsons, and Hitchcock (2002) at 61.

12.   Id.

13.   Id.

14.   Id., at 54, 66–66.

15.   Stannard (1992) at 256 (quoting from Leo Kuper, "The United States Ratifies the Genocide Convention," *Internet on the Holocaust and Genocide,* 19 [February, 1989], reprinted in Frank Chalk and Kurt Jonassohn, *The History and Sociology of Genocide: Analyses and Case Studies* [New Haven, CT: Yale Univ. Press, 1990] at 422–425).

16.   Quoted in Totten, Parsons, and Hitchcock (2002) at 59.

17.   Hitchcock and Twedt (1997) at 379.

18.   Walter R. Echo-Hawk, "Genocide and Ethnocide" in John Hartwell (editor-in-chief), *Encyclopedia of Race and Racism, Vol. 2, G–R* (New York: Thompson Gale, 2007) at 48.

19.   Hitchcock and Twedt (1997) at 373.

20.   Totten, Pasons, and Hitchcock (2002) at 66.

21.   Robert K. Hitchcock, "Genocide of Indigenous Populations," in Israel W. Charny (editor-in-chief), *Encyclopedia of Genocide, Vol. II, I–Y* (Santa Barbara, CA: ABC-CLIO, 1999) at 349.

22.   Id., at 349–350.

23.   Id., at 351.

24.   Totten, Pasons, and Hitchcock (2002) at 54–55.

25.   Id., at 64 (citing Helen Fein, "Genocide: A Sociological Perspective," *Current Sociology* 38:79

[1990]).

26. Id., at 67 (citing Leo Kuper, *The Prevention of Genocide* [New Haven, CT: Yale Univ. Press, 1985] at 151).

27. Hitchcock and Twedt (1997) at 382.

28. Echo-Hawk (2007) (citing Hitchcock and Twedt [1997] at 382).

29. Totten, Pasons, and Hitchcock (2002) at 67 (citing Kuper [1985:151] and Leo Kuper, "Other Selected Cases of Genocide," in Israel W. Charny, ed., *Genocide: A Bibliographical Review* [New York: Facts on File, 1988] at 156).

30. Bartolomé de Las Casas, *The Devastation of the Indies: A Brief Account* (New York: Seabury Press, [1542] 1974).

31. Las Casas's appalling data is summarized in Echo-Hawk (2007) at 49.

32. Stannard (1992) at x.

33. Id. (the words of Gonzalo Ferníndez de Oviedo y Valdís, from his *Historia Natural y General de las Indias,* quoted in Carl Ortwin Sauer, *The Early Spanish Main* [Berkeley: Univ. of California Press, 1966] at 252–253).

34. See, generally, Stannard (1992).

35. Hitchcock and Twedt (1997) at 384; Stannard (1992) at xiii–xiv, 258.

36. Russell Thornton, *American Indian Holocaust and Survival: A Population History Since 1492* (Norman: Univ. of Oklahoma Press, 1987) at 43–44.

37. Quoted in Thornton (1987) at 131–132.

38. Id., at 43.

39. Many of these arguments are advanced by Guenter Lewy, a political scientist, in a 2004 essay entitled, "Were American Indians the Victims of Genocide?" (http://hnn.us/articles/7302.html).

40. See discussion in chapter two.

41. Thornton (1987) at 48–49.

42. Id., at 107. See also discussion of the Wounded Knee Massacre in chapter eleven.

43. Stannard (1992) at 126–134, 243–245.

44. Quoted in Id., at 129.

45. Thornton (1987) at 109.

46. Id., at 107–113.

47. Hitchcock and Twedt (1997) at 388.

48. Thornton (1987) at 47.

49. Totten, Parsons, and Hitchcock (2002) at 61.

50. See discussion in chapter eight.

51. *In re Can-ah-couqua,* 29 F. 687, 688 (D.D. Alaska, 1887).

52. Thornton (1987) at 50, 113–123 (removal and relocation), 50–51 (land loss), 122–123 (land allotment). See also Echo-Hawk (2007) at 50–51.

53. *Cherokee Nation v. Georgia,* supra; *Caldwell v. State,* 1 Stew. & P. 327 (Ala. 1832), 1832 WL 545 (Ala.); *State v. Foreman,* 16 Tenn. 256, 1835 WL 945 (Tenn.); *State of Georgia v. Tassels,* 1 Georgia Reports, Annotated 478 (Hall Superior Court, 1830) (Charlottesville, VA: The Michie Co., 1903).

54. Thornton (1987) at 50–51.

55. Martha Royce Blaine, *Some Things Are Not Forgotten: A Pawnee Family Remembers* (Lincoln: Univ. of Nebraska Press, 1997) at 18.

56. Gregory Cajete, *Native Science: Natural Laws of Interdependence* (Santa Fe, NM: Clear Light, 2000) at 188.

57. *Tee-Hit-Ton v. United States,* 348 US 272, 289–290 (1955).

58. Hitchcock (1999) at 353.

59. Id.

60. Id.

61. Thornton (1987) at 51–53, 123–131.

62. Id., at 51–52.

63. See Martha Royce Blaine, *Pawnee Passage, 1870–1875* (Norman: Univ. of Oklahoma Press, 1990).

64. Totten, Parsons, and Hitchcock (2002) at 61.

65. Thornton (1987) at 51–53, 123–131.

66. See discussion in chapters eight, eleven, and twelve.

67. Wallace Coffey and Rebecca Tsosie, "Rethinking the Tribal Sovereignty Doctrine: Cultural Sovereignty and the Collective Future of Indian Nations," *Stanford Law & Policy Rev.* 12: 2 (Spring 2001) 191, 207.

68. See, for example, Allison M. Dussias, "Ghost Dance and Holy Ghost: The Echoes of Nineteenth-Century Christianization Policy in Twentieth-Century Native American Free Exercise Cases," in James L. Swanson, ed., *First Amendment Law Handbook* (St. Paul, MN: West Group, 1998–99 ed.), pp. 553–659.

69. Hitchcock and Twedt (1997) at 379–380.

70. Stannard (1992) at 281.

71. Rennard Strickland, "Genocide-At-Law: An Historic and Contemporary View of the Native American Experience," 34 Kans. L. Rev. 713, 714 (1986).

72. Id., at 715.

CHAPTER 15: REFORMING THE DARK SIDE OF FEDERAL INDIAN LAW

1. Quoted in W. C. Vanderwerth, ed., *Indian Oratory: Famous Speeches by Noted Indian Chieftains* (Norman: Univ. of Oklahoma Press, 1971) at 230.

2. Sun Tzu, *The Art of War* (New York: Barnes & Nobles Books, 2003) (Dallas Galvin, ed., transl. by Lionel Giles) at 39.

3. See Robert A. Williams Jr., *Like a Loaded Weapon: The Rehnquist Court, Indian Rights, and the Legal History of Racism in America* (Minneapolis: Univ. of Minnesota Press, 2005).

4. Id.

5. Id. The cited phrase is from *Korematsu v. United States,* 323 US 214, 246 (1945) (Murphy, J., dissenting).

6. Wallace Coffey and Rebecca Tsosie, "Rethinking the Tribal Sovereignty Doctrine: Cultural Sovereignty and the Collective Future of Indian Nations," *Stanford Law & Policy Review* 12:2 (2001) 191, 194.

7. *Oliphant v. Suquamish Indian Tribe,* 435 US 181 (1978) (tribes have no power to prosecute crimes committed by non-Indians on the reservation). See also, for example, *Nevada v. Hicks,* 533 US 353 (2001) (tribes have no power to adjudicate torts committed by state police against tribal members in their reservation homes); *Strate v. A-1 Contractors,* 520 US 438 (1997) (tribes have no jurisdiction over accidents caused by non-Indian motorists on reservation roads); *Duro v. Reina,* 495 US 676 (1990) (tribes have no power to prosecute crimes committed by nonmember Indians on the reservation); *Montana v. United States,* 450 US 544 (1981) (tribes have no civil jurisdiction over non-Indian activities on fee lands within the reservation except in limited instances).

8. Jacob T. Levy, "Three Perversities of Indian Law," *Texas Rev. of Law & Politics* 12:2 (2008), 329.

9. Charles Wilkinson, *Blood Struggle: The Rise of Modern Indian Nations* (New York: W. W. Norton, 2005).

10. Red Lake Net News, www.rlnn.com/ArtJune06/HUMGeorgeCarlinOnIndians.html.

11. See *Cohen's Handbook of Federal Indian Law* (2005 ed.) § 5.07[3].

12. Id., § 5.07 [4]–[5].

13. *Washington v. Confederated Bands and Tribes of the Yakima Indian Nation,* 439 US 463, 500–501(1979) (The tribes' interest in self-government is not a "fundamental right"); *Santa Clara Pueblo v. Martinez,* 49, 57 (1978) ("Congress has plenary power to limit, modify, or eliminate the powers of local self-government which the Tribes otherwise possess").

14. Peter F. Lau (ed.), *From the Grassroots to the Supreme Court* (Durham, NC: Duke Univ. Press, 2004) at 2.

15. See, for example, Richard Kluger, *Simple Justice: The History of* Brown v. Board of Education *and Black America's Struggle for Equity* (New York: Alfred A. Knopf, [1975] 2004); Robert J. Cottrol, Raymond T. Diamond, and Leland B. Ware, *Brown v. Board of Education: Caste, Culture, and the Constitution* (Lawrence: Univ. of Kansas Press, 2003); Waldo E. Martin, Jr., *Brown v. Board of Education: A Brief History with Documents* (Boston: Bedford St. Martin's, 1998); James T. Patterson, *Brown v. Board of Education: A Civil Rights Milestone and Its Troubled Legacy* (Oxford: Oxford Univ. Press, 2001); Paul E. Wilson, *A Time to Lose: Representing Kansas*

in Brown v. Board of Education (Lawrence: Univ. of Kansas Press, 1995);

16. See Rennard Strickland (editor-in-chief), *Felix S. Cohen's Handbook of Federal Indian Law* (1982 ed.) at 144–145, 205.

17. Many of these legislative movements are discussed in chapters nine through eleven. The "Duro Fix," 42 U.S.C. § 1301 (2), was passed to overturn the Supreme Court decision in *Duro v. Reina,* 495 US 676 (1990). *Duro* created an intolerable law enforcement loophole on Indian reservations by holding that Indian tribes lack the power to try members of other tribes for committing crimes on their reservations.

18. An excellent, authoritative overview of international law developments pertaining to indigenous peoples and federal Indian law, leading up to the UN approval of the UNDRIP in 2007 is analyzed and provided in *Cohen's Handbook of Federal Indian Law* (2005 ed.) § 5.07.

19. *Worcester v. Georgia,* 31 US 515, 552 (1832).

20. Id., at 555.

21. Id., at 552, 561–561 (relying upon Vattel).

22. Id., at 556.

23. Id.

24. Id., at 583 (M'Lean, J., concurring).

25. See discussion in chapters five and six about the *Worcester* decision.

26. See, for example, *Morton v. Mancari,* 417 US 535 (1974) (power to provide Indian employment preference necessary to discharge the government's special relationship and obligations with Indian tribes); *United States v. Lara,* 541 US 193 (2005) (power to adjust and expand tribal sovereignty); *Washington v. Fishing Vessel Association,* 443 US 658 (1979) (power to enforce Indian treaty rights); *Peyote Way Church of God v. Thornburgh,* 922 F.2d 1210 (5th Cir. 1991) (power to protect Native American religion and culture).

27. *United States v. Lara,* 541 US at 203–204.

28. *Lone Wolf v. Hitchcock,* 187 US 553, 565 (1903).

29. *Worcester,* 31 US at 543–545.

30. Id., at 544–545.

31. Nell Jessup Newton (editor-in-chief), *Cohen's Handbook of Federal Indian Law* (2005 ed.), § 5.07 (Role of International Law).

32. *Nevada v. Hicks,* 533 US 353, 361 (2001) (citing *White Mountain Apache Tribe v. Bracker,* 448 US 136, 141 [1980]).

33. See chapter five for a discussion of Indian law in the antebellum South.

34. The *Johnson* doctrine of discovery was cited with approval most recently in *City of Sherrill v. Oneida Indian Nation,* 544 US 197, 203 n.1 (2005).

35. See amicus brief filed by eighteen states in the *Hicks* case, 2000 WL 1784130 (US) at *23–24.

36. Lindsay C. Robertson, *Conquest by Law: How the Discovery of America Dispossessed Indigenous Peoples of Their Lands* (Oxford: Oxford Univ. Press, 2005).

37. See chapter four; Robertson (2005) at 138–142 for a discussion of the five cases decided between 1835 and 1842 that reinstated the discovery doctrine.

38. *Mabo v. Queensland (No. 2),* 175 C.L.R. 1, 107 A.R.L. 1 (Austl., 1992). See discussion of *Mabo* in chapter three.

39. Id. 175 C.L.R. at 23.

40. Id., at 28.

41. Id., at 39. Whether *Mabo* will ultimately result in a retreat from injustice in Australia remains to be seen. The watershed decision prompted litigation and legislation to further define, refine, and apply *Mabo.* Aboriginal land rights are in a state of flux as the settler-state legal system in Australia continues to develop indigenous land rights law. See, for example, Lisa Strelein, "From Mabo to Yorta: Native Title Law in Australia," *Wash. U. J. L. & Policy* 19:225 (2005); Gary D. Meyers and Sally Reine, "Australian Aboriginal Land Rights in Transition (Part II): The Legislative Response to the High Court's Native Title Decision in Mabo v. Queensland and Wik v. Queensland," *Tulsa L. Comp. & Int'l.* 9:95 (2001).

42. *Brown v. Board of Education,* 347 US 483, 492 (1954).

43. Id., at 494.

44. Id., at 494–495.

45. *United States v. Lara,* 541 US 193, 200–207 (2004).

46. *United States v. Adair,* 723 F.2d 1394, 1401 n. 3 (9th Cir. 1984).
47. Lawrence A. Greenfield and Steven K. Smith, "American Indians and Crime," (Washington, DC: US Dept. of Justice, Bureau of Justice Statistics, February 1999).
48. Id., at iii.
49. Id.
50. *Oliphant v. Suquamish Indian Tribe,* supra; *Strate v. A-1 Contractors,* 520 US 438 (1997).
51. Levy (2008) at 345.
52. Quoted in Levy (2008) at 344–345 (citing Janet Reno, *US Department of Justice Commitment to American Indian Tribal Justice Systems,* JUDICATURE, Nov.–Dec. 1995, at 133, 113–17).
53. Id.
54. See *United States v. Lara,* supra.
55. Echohawk's Senate testimony is reprinted in "Leave No Tribe Behind: NARF Takes on a Class Action for Billions of Dollars of Government Mismanagement of Tribal Trust Funds," 32 NARF Legal Rev. No. 1 (Winter/Spring 2007) (Boulder: Native American Rights Fund).
56. Indeed, in December 2009, the parties to the Cobell litigation announced and filed a settlement agreement to end that litigation over the mismanagement of individual Indian trust funds. Among other things, the settlement provides a $3.4 billion award to some 300,000 individual Indians, including $1.4 billion to compensate them for lost accounting funds and a $2 billion fund to buy back fractionalized interests in allotted trust land. The agreement will become final when endorsed by the court and implementing legislation is enacted by Congress.
57. *United States v. Lara,* 541 US 193, 201 (2004) (quoting *Missouri v. Holland,* 252 US 416, 433 [1920]).
58. See discussion in chapter seven.
59. *Tee-Hit-Ton,* 348 US at 285 n.1 (quoting *Carino,* 212 US at 458).
60. *Lone Wolf v. Hitchcock,* 187 US at 565.
61. *United States v. Lara,* 541 US at 201 (quoting *United States v. Curtiss-Wright Export Corp.,* 299 US 304, 315–322 [1936]).
62. *Carino v. Insular Government of the Philippine Islands,* 212 US 449, 458 (1909) (quoting the Organic Act of July 1, 1902, 32 Stat. 695). The *Carino* case is mentioned in *Tee-Hit-Ton,* 348 US at 285 n.18. *Tee-Hit-Ton* hastened to distinguish the charitable purpose in colonizing the Philippines from the United States' darker purposes in colonizing Indian land: the settlement of the white race and to occupy the land.
63. Id., at 458.
64. Id. ("The acquisition of the Philippines was not like the settlement of the white race in the United States. Whatever consideration may have been shown to the North American Indians, the dominant purpose of the whites in America was to occupy the land. It is obvious that, however stated, the reason for our taking over the Philippines was different.")
65. Alexis de Tocqueville, *Democracy in America* (New York: Bantam Dell, [1835] 2004) at 295.
66. *Employment Division, State of Oregon v. Smith,* 494 US 872, 902–903 (1990) (O'Connor, J., concurring) (quoting *West Virginia Bd. Educ. v. Barnette,* 319 US 624, 638 [1943]).
67. President-elect Obama's announcement of Ken Salazar as nominee for secretary of the Department of the Interior (December 17, 2008).
68. Tsosie and Coffey (2001).
69. Quoted in Tsosie and Coffey (2001) at 202 (citing Michelle Hibbert, *Galileos or Grave Robbers? Science, the NAGPRA, and the First Amendment, Am. Indian L. Rev.* 23:425, 434 n. 66 [1998–1999]).
70. Robert J. Miller, "Exercising Cultural Self-Determination: The Makah Indian Tribe Goes Whaling," *Am. Indian L. Rev.* 25:165, 206 (2000–2001).
71. Id., at 233.
72. *Lyng v. Northwest Indian Cemetery Association,* 485 US 439 (1988).
73. *Navajo Nation et al. v. United States Forest Service,* 535 F.3d 1058 (9th Cir. 2008) (*en banc*).
74. See discussion in chapter twelve.
75. Id.
76. Id.
77. *Lyng,* 485 US at 472 (Brennan, J., dissenting) (emphasis added).
78. For example, in *Macedonia Baptist Church v. Christian Knights of the KKK,* No. 96-CP-14-217

(3rd Cir., S.C., Verdict entered July 24, 1998), the KKK was ordered to pay $21.5 million damages for its conspiracy to burn a black church. Other verdicts in this hate crime litigation campaign are listed at the Southern Poverty Law Center's website, www.splcenter.org.

79.　*Apache Tribe v. United States,* 477 F.2d 1310 (Ct. Cl., 1978).

80.　The fish kill is documented in the documentary film *River of Renewal* (Pinkiawish Partners Productions, in association with Lobitos Creek Ranch, 2008). See also the Yurok Tribe website for more information, www.yuroktribe.org.

81.　In *Exxon Valdez v. Alaska Native Class,* 104 F.3d 1196 (9th Cir. 1997), Native Alaskans asserted a claim for cultural damage caused by the oil spill, relying upon traditional public nuisance principles, but the claim was denied for failure to state a special injury required for such claims. The court did not recognize harm to an indigenous way of life. Reformers must develop an appropriate definition of cultural harm recognizable in tort law that includes economic, emotional, and physical interests in the land, habitat, and natural resources necessary to protect the tribal hunting, fishing, and gathering way of life in the United States.

82.　Jennifer B. Wriggins, "Torts, Race, and the Value of Injury," *How. L. J.* 49:99 (2005). See also *Restatement of Torts (Second)* (1978), § 822, comment g.

83.　This chapter is respectfully dedicated to NARF staff attorney Amy Bowers and the new generation. Amy assisted me in pulling together the thoughts and research for this final chapter. The new generation is too numerous to name. But talented lawyers like Amy Bowers (Yurok) and David Gover (Pawnee/Choctaw) of the Native American Rights Fund will make history reforming the law, along with colleagues like Wilson K. Pipestem (Oto-Missouri/Osage) and Lael Echo-Hawk (Pawnee). They personify the new warriors.

INDEX